I0299335

Paul F. Mottelay, T. Campbell-Copeland, Robert B. Beath

The Soldier in our Civil War

A pictorial History of the Conflict - Vol. II

Paul F. Mottelay, T. Campbell-Copeland, Robert B. Beath

The Soldier in our Civil War
A pictorial History of the Conflict - Vol. II

ISBN/EAN: 9783337135584

Printed in Europe, USA, Canada, Australia, Japan

Cover: Foto ©ninafisch / pixelio.de

Frank Leslie's

ILLUSTRATIONS.

THE SOLDIER IN OUR CIVIL WAR:

COLUMBIAN MEMORIAL EDITION.

A PICTORIAL HISTORY OF THE CONFLICT. 1861–1865,

ILLUSTRATING THE VALOR OF THE SOLDIER AS DISPLAYED ON THE BATTLE FIELD.

FROM SKETCHES DRAWN BY

FORBES. WAUD, TAYLOR, HILLEN, BECKER, LOVIE, SCHELL, CRANE, DAVIS,

And numerous other Eye-witnesses to the Strife.

EDITED BY

PAUL F. MOTTELAY and T. CAMPBELL-COPELAND.

ASSISTED BY THE MOST NOTABLE GENERALS AND COMMANDERS OF BOTH SIDES.

WITH AN INTRODUCTION BY

ROBERT B. BEATH,

PAST COMMANDER-IN-CHIEF GRAND ARMY OF THE REPUBLIC.

HISTORY OF THE GRAND ARMY OF THE REPUBLIC, BY PAUL VANDERVOORT, PAST COMMANDER-IN CHIEF.

HISTORY OF THE CONFEDERATE VETERANS' ASSOCIATION, BY COL. I. W. AVERY, ATLANTA, GEORGIA.

HISTORY OF THE SONS OF VETERANS, BY A. P. DAVIS, ORIGINATOR, AND BY FRANK P. MERRILL, COMMANDER-IN CHIEF.

Valuable information has been contributed and courtesies extended by Generals GRANT, HANCOCK, LOGAN, Brevet Maj.-Gen. (S. N. Y.), J. WATTS DE PEYSTER, Generals BEAUREGARD, FITZHUGH LEE, LONGSTREET, EARLY, Captain WADDELL, late of the C. S. Navy, War and Navy Departments, etc.

VOL. II.

NEW YORK AND ATLANTA, GA.:

STANLEY BRADLEY PUBLISHING COMPANY,

1893.

SOLD ONLY BY SUBSCRIPTION.

INDEXED LIST

OF

DOUBLE-PAGE ILLUSTRATIONS.

VOL. II.

INDEX TO ILLUSTRATIONS AND GENERAL INDEX AT THE END OF THE VOLUME.

THE SOLDIER IN OUR CIVIL WAR.

VOLUME II.

THE ARMY OF THE POTOMAC.

BURNSIDE'S CAMPAIGN — BATTLE OF FREDERICKSBURG.

ON the evening of the 7th of November, General Catharinus P. Buckingham arrived at headquarters, with orders from the Secretary of War and General Halleck directing McClellan to immediately turn over his command to General Burnside and repair to Trenton, N.J., for further orders.*

NOVEMBER, 1862.

Immediately upon assuming command of the Army of the Potomac, as the successor of General McClellan, Burnside reorganized his forces with the view of insuring the early capture of Richmond.

The army was at that time distributed as follows: The First, Second and Fifth Corps and the Reserve Artillery were at Warrenton; the Sixth Corps, at New Baltimore; the Ninth Corps, in the vicinity of Waterloo; the Eleventh Corps at New Baltimore, Gainesville and Thoroughfare Gap; Sickles's division of the Third Corps, along the Orange and Alexandria Railroad, from Manassas Junction to Warrenton Junction; Pleasanton, across the Rappahannock, at Amissville, Jefferson, etc., with his pickets on Hazel River, facing Longstreet's, six miles from Culpepper Court House; Bayard, near Rappahannock Station.

At the end of about ten days, Burnside had formed the army into three Grand Divisions. The Right Grand Division, composed of General D. N. Couch's (formerly Sumner's) Second Corps and General O. B. Wilcox's (formerly Burnside's) Ninth Corps, was given to General Edwin V. Sumner; while the Left Grand Division, composed of General John F. Reynolds's (formerly Hooker's) First Corps and General W. F. Smith's (formerly Franklin's) Sixth Corps, was placed in charge of General William B. Franklin; and the Centre Grand Division, composed of General George Stoneman's Third Corps (taken from the Washington garrison) and General Daniel Butterfield's (formerly Fitz John Porter's) Fifth Corps, was given to General Joseph Hooker. The Eleventh Corps constituted a reserve force under the command of General Franz Sigel.

These divisions began to move from Warrenton late on the 15th of November, in the direction of Fredericksburg, the advance of Sumner's grand division reaching Falmouth, opposite the former city, on the 17th. Three days later, Sumner demanded the surrender of Fredericksburg, under threat of a bombardment in case of refusal. The surrender was refused, and the Federals remained on the north bank of the Rappahannock pending the arrival of means of transportation and of supplies from Aquia Creek.

In the meantime, the Confederate troops occupying the southern bank of the river were being very materially strengthened, and, by the end of November, Lee had an army of fully 80,000 men, forming nearly a semi-circle around Fredericksburg.

The Confederate forces were organized into two Corps, under command of Generals "Stonewall" Jackson and James Longstreet. Jackson's corps embraced the divisions of Generals A. P. Hill, D. H. Hill, R. S. Ewell and Benjamin Taliaferro; and Longstreet's corps consisted of the divisions of Generals Lafayette McLaws, M. W. Ransom, R. H. Anderson, George E. Pickett, and S. A. M. Wood.

D. H. Hill's force, forming the extreme Confederate right, lay at Port Royal, in order to prevent the Federal gunboats from ascending the river beyond that point, whilst the extreme left was also on the Rappahannock, nearly six miles above Fredericksburg. Stuart's cavalry guarded all the intervening fords.

The Federals had apparently, for the time, the advantage of position, as they occupied Stafford Heights, which lay close to the river and completely commanded the plain and valley of Fredericksburg, while the Confederate earthworks stood about a mile from the banks.

Burnside's plans for a forward movement were finally completed on the evening of the 10th of December. His chief of artillery, General Henry J. Hunt, had placed in position, upon the crest of the Heights, twenty-nine batteries comprising 147 guns, which were to cover the building of five ponton-bridges, and the subsequent passage of the troops. The grand divisions of Sumner and Franklin were to cross respectively by the upper and lower bridges, and Hooker's grand division was to be held in reserve to support the other two.

DECEMBER, 1862.

At about one o'clock on the morning of the 11th, the pontons were brought down to the river-bank, and the building of the bridges was begun in the midst of a very heavy fog and under protection of the Fifty-sixth and Fifty-seventh New York Regiments, belonging to Hancock's division. The work had progressed but little when the Confederates opened a heavy fire at short range, which proved very destructive.

The Federals were driven back, but made repeated attempts. In each of them they were, however, subjected to such renewed attacks that no effective work could be done. Seeing this, Burnside ordered the batteries to open upon the city. The latter was set afire in several places during the two hours' cannonading that followed, and, under cover of the artillery, fresh attempts were made to complete the bridges, but to no avail. When the fog lifted at noon, the Confederates were seen still lining the opposite banks, from which they could not be dislodged by the Stafford Heights batteries, in consequence of the high elevation of the guns, but few of which could be depressed enough to bear effectively upon the immediate river-front.

It was evident that the bridges could not, under the circumstances, be completed, and that a crossing must be effected in open boats. The Seventh Michigan, the Nineteenth and Twentieth Massachusetts and the Forty-second New York Regiments, belonging to General O. O. Howard's division, promptly responded to the call for volunteers needed to make the perilous attempt.

In a short time they had crossed the river, effected the desired landing, dislodging the Mississippi troops from their shelter, and had taken possession of the river-front after capturing many prisoners.

Half an hour later the lower bridges were completed, the others being finished shortly after, though at a sacrifice of nearly three hundred men, who were picked off by the sharpshooters from the Seventeenth Mississippi Regiment, occupying rifle-pits near the mouth of Deep Run.

Howard's division crossed late in the afternoon, and, after a spirited but short engagement, drove away the Eighth Florida as well as the Eighteenth and Nineteenth Mississippi Regiments, and occupied the town. They were joined during the following day by all but Hooker's grand division of Burnside's army, which crossed under cover of guns firing wildly from the heights through a very thick fog, and at night preparations were completed for an assault early the next morning.

It was decided, at a council held late on Friday, the 12th, that there should be a simultaneous attack at dawn along the entire line, for the purpose of carrying the heights occupied by the Confederates, and, the better to effect this, two of Hooker's divisions were brought over and added to Franklin's force. The latter was relied upon for the main attack on the extreme Federal left, which was to be followed by an advance of the Federal right and centre.

Lee's army was also made ready for the encounter that could not but immediately follow the Federal advance. Anderson's division occupied the extreme left of Longstreet's force, resting upon the river; next came, along Marye's and Lee's Hills, the divisions of McLaws, Picket and Hood, the latter holding the first range of heights to the left of Deep Run. Jackson's corps extended thence to the Hamilton Railroad Crossing. Three brigades from the division of A. P. Hill occupied the edge of a wood in the immediate front, a second line being formed by the other brigades and by the divisions of Early and Taliaferro, while D. H. Hill's division, composed of part of Fields's brigade and of Gregg's and Thomas's full brigades, made up the reserve. Stuart's two brigades of cavalry and horse-artillery were in position between the Hamilton Crossing and the Massaponax Run.

Colonel Walton's New Orleans batteries were posted on the crest of Marye's Hill, the heights on either side of the latter being held by Colonel E. Porter Alexander's Reserve Artillery and by the batteries belonging to the divisions of Generals Anderson, McLaws and Ransom. In addition to the above were fourteen pieces of artillery, under Lieutenant Walker, posted on the right of the woods, and supported by two Virginia regiments under Colonel Brockenborough.

Owing to a heavy fog and to delays attending the transmission of orders, Franklin's force could not effectively be brought forward until after nine o'clock on the morning of the 13th. General Reynolds's entire corps was sent ahead, Gibbon's division occupying the extreme right in immediate support of Meade's, which was in the centre, while Doubleday's division was on the latter's left, somewhat in the rear.

Meade's advance force soon came upon a battery

---

* *General Orders No. 182*: "By direction of the President of the United States, it is ordered that Major-general McClellan be relieved from the command of the Army of the Potomac, and that Major-general Burnside take command of the army. By order of the Secretary of War."

General Halleck to General McClellan: "General, on the receipt of the order of the President, sent herewith, you will immediately turn over your command to Major-general Burnside, and repair to Trenton, N. J., reporting on your arrival at that place by telegraph, for further orders."

MAJOR-GENERAL AMBROSE E. BURNSIDE ISSUING ORDERS TO HIS

MAJOR-GENERAL AMBROSE E. BURNSIDE ISSUING ORDERS TO HIS STAFF UPON TAKING COMMAND OF THE ARMY OF THE POTOMAC

BURNSIDE'S ARMY CROSSING THE RAPPAHANNOCK FROM FALMOUTH TO FREDERICKSBURG, AT MIDNIGHT, WEDNESDAY, DECEMBER 10TH, 1862.

From a Sketch by H. Lovie.

of Stuart's horse-artillery, and bore the brunt of a rapid enfilading fire, directed by Major Pelham, which for a while arrested Meade's progress. The battery being at last silenced, he advanced his guns down the Port Royal Road, and began shelling the woods in his immediate front. As this elicited no response, he moved ahead unchecked until, after crossing the railroad, he had reached a point about eight hundred yards distant from the position held by Lieutenant-colonel Walker. The reserved fire of fourteen pieces of artillery was then suddenly opened upon his force, and he found that he had unwittingly entered a wide gap temporarily existing

As Meade's force gradually fell back toward the railroad, it was met by Gibbon's division, which for awhile checked the Confederate advance. The Federals were successively joined during the afternoon by the forces under Generals Birney and Sickles, but these were in turn subjected to repeated attacks by the fresh brigades of Generals Lawton, Field, Walker, Trimble, and Hayes, which finally compelled them to fall back, and would no doubt have succeeded in overpowering them but for the opportune arrival of additional reinforcements from Hooker's grand division. Such an imposing front was then presented, and such a

that led to a succession of hills and abrupt declivities, and finally to a deep ravine fronting the City of Fredericksburg. All of these were of course invisible from below. At the foot of the hill, and behind a stone wall, stood part of Longstreet's force, with heavy reserves.

The Federals advanced under cover of the Stafford Heights batteries, which, however, seemed to fail of their object in silencing the Confederate guns. Wilcox's Ninth Corps occupied the left of the line toward Franklin's position, and Couch's Second Corps stood on the right at Fredericksburg. General William H. French's division was to com-

PONTON-WAGONS ON THEIR WAY FROM AQUIA CREEK TO THE RAPPAHANNOCK.
FROM A SKETCH BY H. LOVIE.

in the first Confederate line. In face of the murderous fire of shell and canister which was directed upon their front as well as upon both their flanks by Archer's and Lane's brigades, the Federals not only stood their ground well, but succeeded, after a fierce and prolonged encounter, in turning both brigades, and in fully repulsing Lane's before Thomas's force could come to the latter's support.

Meade pressed on until the second Confederate line was reached. There he was met by Gregg's South Carolina Brigade, and subjected to another fierce attack, which his troops also withstood bravely, until Early's division had made a rapid circuit, enabling it to attack Meade's flanks, and compelling him to retire with heavy loss.

heavy artillery fire opened upon the Confederates, that the latter abandoned all further pursuit, and were made to retire to their old position, upon which the Federal batteries kept a steady fire until dark.

While Franklin had thus been operating upon the extreme left, the Federal right held by Sumner had met with still greater opposition at the foot of Marye's Hill, toward which it had begun moving as soon as the fog lifted, at about noon.

The Confederate position on the heights was a very strong one. Guns from the Washington Artillery lined the crest, and about fifty heavy guns were stationed so as to enfilade the columns which could not but approach through the narrow road

mence the attack with the brigades of Kimball, Palmer and Anderson, and was to be closely followed by Hancock's division, comprising the brigades led by Meagher, Caldwell and Zook.

With Kimball in front, each successive brigade made its way along the narrow road until it reached the foot of Marye's Hill. There it came within range of the Confederate guns, which opened upon the Federals with terrible effect, mowing down column after column, and creating huge gaps in every direction.

In face of this deadly fire, the ranks were nevertheless steadily closed up, and the troops moved onward; but, as they neared the foot of the hill, they were unexpectedly met by murderous volleys

VOLUNTEER STORMING PARTIES, TAKEN FROM THE SEVENTH MICHIGAN AND THE NI
IN ADVANCE OF THE GRAND ARMY, TO DRIVE OFF THE CONFEDER
FROM A SK

VOLUNTEER STORMING PARTIES, TAKEN FROM THE SEVENTH MICHIGAN AND THE NINETEENTH AND TWENTIETH MASSACHUSETTS REGIMENTS CROSSING THE RAPPAHANNOCK, IN ADVANCE OF THE GRAND ARMY, TO DRIVE OFF THE CONFEDERATE SHARPSHOOTERS ANNOYING THE PONTONIERS, DECEMBER 11th, 1862.

directed from the sunken road, and with which it was found impossible to cope. French's entire division was forced back with the loss of nearly half its numbers.

The remnants of French's command then joined Hancock's division, which followed closely; and in face of a scathing artillery fire all advanced once more toward the point which French had reached, but only to meet with the same result.

The divisions led by Howard, Getty, and Sturgis, came to the support of the others, but unavailingly. The front was so narrow that it could be occupied but by one brigade at a time, and each advanced toward the wall only to meet a scathing musketry fire, poured at short range from Longstreet's lines, in addition to the well-directed artillery fire from the hills.

After dispatching part of Hooker's corps to Sumner's aid, and seeing, from his station at Stafford Heights, that brigade after brigade had been almost swept away, Burnside concluded to send Hooker's remaining divisions across the river. Hooker rode forward to consult with the other generals, and immediately thereafter sent a message to Burnside in order to dissuade him from attempting to carry out what Couch, Wilcox, Hancock, French, and himself, justly thought a useless undertaking. Burnside was immovable, and Hooker lost no time executing his orders.

After successfully posting his guns so as to make a breach in the wall, and finding that the latter was too far in the sunken road to be reached from the plain, Hooker ordered the firing stopped, and directed Humphreys's 4,000 men to advance for a bayonet-charge. As soon as they reached the stone wall, however, another storm of iron was poured into them, with such deadly effect that in about fifteen minutes over seventeen hundred of their number lay *hors de combat*. The last of this series of fruitless assaults was made just before dark.

Hooker had intended sending Sykes's division to support Humphreys, but when he saw the latter driven back he concluded to abandon all further attempts to carry a position which he had already deemed impregnable. "Finding," he says, "that I had lost as many as my orders required me to lose, I suspended the attack, and directed that the men should hold, for an advanced line, a ditch (ravine), which would afford them shelter."

Both the Confederates and Federals lay on their arms in the expectation that the conflict would be renewed the following day. While the Confederates naturally knew they had inflicted severe losses upon all of the attacking columns, they as yet little realized the frightful extent to which the Federal ranks had been decimated, else they would, doubtless, have instituted an aggressive movement, which, in the then practically disorganized state of the Federal forces, could not but have proven successful. As it was, the Confederates only strengthened their lines by the construction of earthworks at all exposed points.

Burnside was naturally anxious to retrieve his losses, and at the council held the same evening laid his plans for a renewal of the attack on the following morning, which, contrary to the opinion of the majority of his officers, he thought could be easily carried out. All preparations were accordingly made for assaulting the stone wall by another but more powerful direct movement, which he thought would enable the Federals to reach the second Confederate line and readily capture the heights.

December, 1862.

When, on the morning of Sunday, the 14th, all was in readiness for the desperate movement, Sumner was once more induced to remonstrate with Burnside. He asked him to reconsider his decision, which, said he, had not met the approval of any of the officers, and could not, they all thought, but prove disastrous to the army. Burnside finally yielded, and after duly weighing the doubtful possibility of holding Fredericksburg, it was determined to withdraw the army to the north bank of the Rappahannock River, and to abandon the enterprise as a failure.

The two armies maintained their respective positions until the night of the 15th, when the Federals availed themselves of the prevalence of a violent rainstorm to cross the river. After all the artillery had been safely carried over, the pontoon-bridges were taken up, and by the morning of the 16th Burnside's army had reoccupied Stafford Heights. The Confederates immediately took possession of the town, and resumed their former positions.

The losses sustained by the Federals in the short but unusually sanguinary engagements w[illegible]

Pleasanton. Bayard. Wyndham.

GENERALS PLEASANTON AND BAYARD, AND COLONEL PERCY WYNDHAM, MAKING A CAVALRY RECONNOISSANCE NEAR FREDERICKSBURG, VA.

much more than twice as large as those experienced by the Confederates.*

In officers, the losses were especially severe, the killed and mortally wounded including Generals George D. Bayard and Conrad F. Jackson, on the Federal side; and Generals Maxey Gregg and Thomas R. R. Cobb, on the side of the Confederates; whilst amongst those less severely injured were Generals John Gibbon, Nathan Kimball, Francis L. Vinton, Thomas Francis Meagher and James Caldwell.

Burnside soon made preparations for another advance upon Richmond, and had about completed his arrangements for the passage of Kelley's Ford, with the view of cutting off Lee's communications and engaging upon extensive and important raids, when he received a dispatch from President Lincoln directing him not to enter upon any general movement without his (the President's) knowledge.

This was a great disappointment to Burnside, and, although he felt no doubt as to the success- a feint below the city. Sigel's reserves were to remain between the two wings.

Late in the afternoon, however, an extraordinarily fierce storm of wind, rain, and sleet, suddenly broke upon them, and transformed the ground into a succession of quagmires that absolutely prevented the moving of ponton-wagons or of artillery. The troops remained under arms in the expectation that the storm would subside, but nothing could be done that night, nor was any progress made, while the rain continued pouring, the following day.

Lee had in the meantime discovered the Federal movement, and naturally prepared to meet it. It was, therefore, wisely determined to return the troops to their former positions.

Burnside soon after went again to Washington, and finding that he was not receiving the cordial support of the Administration, tendered his resignation, which was accepted on the 26th of January, Major-general Joseph Hooker being appointed his successor in command of the Army of the Potomac.

Burnside's expedition to North Carolina. In July, 1862, he was promoted to be a major-general of Volunteers, and during the following month was assigned to the command of the Ninth Army Corps, which he led both at the second battle of Bull Run and at Chantilly. Was killed at South Mountain, while at the head of his command, on the 14th of September, 1862.

THOMAS R. R. COBB.

Born in the County of Jefferson, Ga., in the year 1820; studied law and became a very prominent member of his profession, being, for culture and intellect, recognized by many as the leading lawyer of his native State. Became reporter of the Georgia Supreme Court, and a professor of the Lumpkin Law School at Athens, Ga. He was the author of a "Digest of Georgia Laws," of an erudite work on the "Law of Slavery," and of other legal works, which, aside from the marked success he attained in the practice of law, would have gained for him very great distinction. He was appointed by Governor Brown to assist in the codification of Georgia laws, his collaborators being David Irwin and Richard H. Clark, both on the Supreme Court Bench. On the 16th of January, 1861, he was chosen a member of the Georgia Convention that carried the State out of the Union. With Judge Eugenius A. Nisbet, the author of the Ordinance of Secession, he joined in a vigorous advocacy of the immediate withdrawal of the State, and was a central figure in the Convention. When Georgia was called upon to subscribe to the $50,000,000 Loan of Bonds for war purposes, he and his brother Howell issued an address to the planters, urging them to invest on patriotic grounds, appealing to their State pride, and reminding them that, besides being the only State that had unanimously adopted the Confederate Constitution, Georgia had offered the largest number of volunteers to support it. He became a prominent member of the Provisional Congress of the Confederate States, in which body he served as chairman of the Committee on Military Affairs, and subsequently entered the army as brigadier-general in command of the "Georgia Legion." He was killed at Fredericksburg, December 13th, 1862.

EFFECT OF THE BOMBARDMENT OF FREDERICKSBURG.—FEDERAL SOLDIERS ON GUARD.
FROM A SKETCH BY HENRY LOVIE.

ful carrying out of his new plans, he recalled the cavalry detachments already sent ahead, and hastened to Washington. There he saw the President and General Halleck, but could get no encouragement, no one being apparently willing to assume the responsibility for such a demonstration as he proposed making. Burnside, therefore, returned to the army, and after again uselessly communicating with Halleck, decided to move as he had at first intended.

By the 20th of the following month all was ready. The two Grand Divisions under Franklin and Hooker had quietly advanced up the river by parallel roads, and were encamped close by Banks's and the United States Fords, which were to be crossed that night above Fredericksburg, while Couch's corps made

JANUARY, 1863.

* Federals.	Killed.	Wounded.	Missing.	Total.
Sumner's Division	490	4,130	555	5,124
Hooker's Division	327	2,400	748	3,548
Franklin's Division	339	2,470	1,571	4,679
Engineer Corps	7	43	100	50
Total				13,771

Confederates.	Killed.	Wounded.	Missing.	Total.
Jackson's Corps	344	2,545	526	3,415
Longstreet's Corps	250	1,516	127	1,894
Total				5,309

GEORGE D. BAYARD.

Born in New York in 1835; entered the United States Military Academy at West Point when seventeen years of age, and graduated therefrom in 1856, being afterward appointed a second lieutenant in the First United States Cavalry. In August, 1861, he was promoted to a captaincy, and soon became colonel of the First Pennsylvania Cavalry, attached to General McCall's Reserves. He took part in all the battles wherein they served, from the Peninsular to the Maryland campaign, and in June, 1862, was made a brigadier-general of Volunteers. He served with very great distinction in the Army of the Potomac, and became known as one of the most daring cavalry officers in the service. While fighting with Franklin's left wing at the battle of Fredericksburg, December 13th, 1862, he was struck on the hip by a cannon-ball, which threw him off his saddle, wounding him so severely that he died shortly after.

JESSE L. RENO.

Born in Virginia in 1823; admitted to the United States Military Academy at West Point at an early age; and in July, 1846, entered the army as brevet second lieutenant of Ordnance, receiving shortly after the commission of brevet first lieutenant for distinguished services at the siege of Vera Cruz and at the battles of Cerro Gordo, Contreras, Churubusco and Chapultepec. He was in command of the Mount Vernon (Alabama) Arsenal, at the time of its capture, in January, 1861; was appointed a brigadier-general of Volunteers the following November, and as such accompanied

CAMP NEAR FREDERICKSBURG,
December, 16th, 1862.

GENERAL HOWELL COBB: General, I beg leave to express my deep sympathy in your great sorrow. Your noble and gallant brother has met a soldier's death, and God grant that this army and our country may never again be called upon to mourn so great a sacrifice.

Of his merits, his lofty intellect, his accomplishments, his professional fame, and above all, his Christian character, I need not speak to you, who knew him so intimately and well. But as a patriot and soldier, death has left a deep gap in the army, which his military aptitude and skill render it hard to fill. In the battle of Fredericksburg he won an immortal fame for himself and his brigade. Hour after hour he held his position in front of our batteries, while division after division of the enemy was hurled against him. He announced the determination of himself and his men never to leave their post until the enemy was beaten; and with unshaken courage and fortitude he kept his promise. . . . .

With great esteem your obedient servant, R. E. LEE.

BOMBARDMENT OF FREDERICKSBURG, VA., BY THE ARMY OF THE POTC

BOMBARDMENT OF FREDERICKSBURG, VA., BY THE ARMY OF THE POTOMAC COMMANDED BY GENERAL BURNSIDE TUESDAY, DECEMBER 11th, 1862

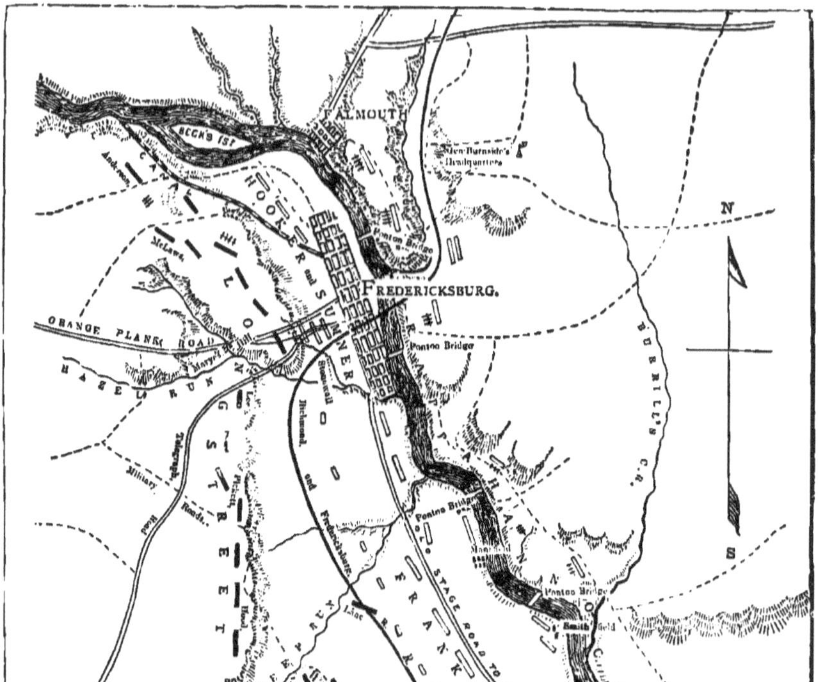
MAP OF THE
BATTLE of FREDERICKSBURG
DECEMBER 13TH 1862.
SCALE OF MILES
Confederate Troops,
Federal Troops
"THE SOLDIER IN OUR CIVIL WAR."
Walter A Lane, C.E.
FALMOUTH
FREDERICKSBURG.
BECK'S ISL
CANAL
HOOKER
SUMNER
FRANKLIN
LONGSTREET
JACKSON
RAPPAHANNOCK RIVER
STAGE ROAD TO RICHMOND
ORANGE PLANK ROAD
HAZEL RUN
DEEP RUN
MINE ROAD
MASSAPONAX CR.
BURRILL'S CR.
Pontoon Bridge
Gen. Burnside's Headquarters
General Lee's Headquarters
D.H. Hill
Hamilton
Stuart's Cavalry
N
S

JOHN MILTON BRANNAN.

Born in the District of Columbia in 1810, and graduated from the United States Academy at West Point in 1841; was engaged at seaboard posts until the war with Mexico, when he took part in the battles of Vera Cruz, Cerro Gordo, La Hoya, Contreras, Churubusco, and the City of Mexico. He was given the commission of brevet-captain for gallantry at Churubusco, and received very severe wounds at the assault of the Belen Gate. Upon his recovery, he was engaged in the suppression of the Florida hostilities, and afterward placed in command of the Department of Key West, Fla. While subsequently at the head of the Department of the South, 1862-63, he conducted the expedition to Pocotaligo, S. C. Took part in the Tennessee campaigns, and in the battle of Chickamauga, where he gained the promotion of brevet-colonel; and, as Chief of Artillery, Department of the Cumberland, 1863-65, was engaged at Missionary Ridge and in the operations of the Atlanta campaign. Was made a brevet brigadier-general, and placed in command of the District of Savannah, and subsequently in charge of the Department of Georgia, having received, March 13th, 1865, the commission of brevet-major-general.

OFFICIAL ROSTERS
OF THE
FEDERAL AND CONFEDERATE TROOPS
ENGAGED AT
ANTIETAM AND AT FREDERICKSBURG.

ANTIETAM.

Major-general George B. McClellan commanding Federal Forces known as the Army of the Potomac.

CENTRE.

SECOND ARMY CORPS.

Major-general Edwin V. Sumner commanding.

First Division: Brigadier-general Israel B. Richardson.
First Brigade—Brigadier-general Thomas F. Meagher.
Second Brigade—Brigadier-general John C. Caldwell.
Third Brigade—Colonel John R. Brooke.

Second Division: Major-general John Sedgwick.
First Brigade—Brigadier-general W. A. Gorman.
Second Brigade—Brigadier-general O. O. Howard.
Third Brigade—Brigadier-general N. J. T. Dana.

Third Division: Brigadier-general W. H. French.
First Brigade—Brigadier-general Nathan Kimball.
Second Brigade—Colonel Dwight Morris.
Third Brigade—Brigadier-general Max Weber.

TWELFTH ARMY CORPS.

(1) Major-general Joseph K. F. Mansfield commanding.
(2) Brigadier-general Alpheus S. Williams commanding.

First Division: Brigadier-general S. W. Crawford.
First Brigade—Colonel J. F. Knipe.
Third Brigade—Brigadier-general George H. Gordon.

JESSE L. RENO.

Second Division: Brigadier-general George S. Greene.
First Brigade—Lieutenant-colonel Hector Tyndale.
Second Brigade—Colonel Henry J. Stainrook.
Third Brigade—Colonel William B. Goodrich.

RIGHT WING.

FIRST ARMY CORPS.

Major-general Ambrose E. Burnside commanding
Major-general Joseph Hooker.

First Division: (1) Brigadier-general Rufus King; (2) Brigadier-general John P. Hatch; (3) Brigadier-general Abner Doubleday.
First Brigade—(1) Brigadier-general John P. Hatch; (2) Colonel Walter Phelps, Jr.
Second Brigade—(1) Brigadier-general Abner Doubleday; (2) Colonel William P. Wainwright; (3) Lieutenant-colonel J. W. Hoffman.
Third Brigade—Brigadier-general M. R. Patrick.
Fourth Brigade—Brigadier-general John Gibbon.

Second Division: Brigadier-general James B. Ricketts.
First Brigade—Brigadier-general A. Duryee.
Second Brigade—Colonel William H. Christian.
Third Brigade—Brigadier-general Geo. L. Hartsuff.

Third Division: Brigadier-general George G. Meade.
First Brigade—Brigadier-general Geo. T. Seymour.
Second Brigade—Colonel A. L. Magilton.
Third Brigade—(1) Colonel Thomas F. Gallagher; (2) Lieutenant-colonel Robert Anderson.

NINTH ARMY CORPS.

(1) Major-general Jesse L. Reno
(2) Brigadier-general Jacob D. Cox.

First Division: Brigadier-general O. B. Willcox.
First Brigade—Colonel B. C. Christ.
Second Brigade—Colonel Thomas Welsh.

Second Division: Brigadier-general S. D. Sturgis.
First Brigade—Colonel James Nagle.
Second Brigade—Colonel Edward Ferrero.

Third Division: Brigadier-general Isaac P. Rodman.
First Brigade—Colonel H. S. Fairchild.
Second Brigade—Colonel Edward Harland.

LEFT WING.

SIXTH ARMY CORPS.

Major-general William B. Franklin.

First Division: Major-general Henry W. Slocum.
First Brigade—Colonel A. T. A. Torbert.
Second Brigade—Colonel J. J. Bartlett.
Third Brigade—Brigadier-general John Newton.

Second Division: Major-general William F. Smith.
First Brigade—Brigadier-general W. S. Hancock.
Second Brigade—Brigadier-general W. T. H. Brooks.
Third Brigade—Colonel W. H. Irwin.

Couch's Division (Fourth Corps): Major-general D. N. Couch.
First Brigade—Brigadier-general Charles Devens.
Second Brigade—Brigadier-general A. P. Howe.
Third Brigade—Brigadier-general John Cochrane.

FIFTH ARMY CORPS.

Major-general Fitz John Porter.

First Division: Brigadier-general George Morell.
First Brigade—Colonel James Barnes.
Second Brigade—Brigadier-general Charles Griffin.
Third Brigade—Colonel T. B. W. Stockton.

Second Division: Brigadier-general George Sykes.
First Brigade—Lieutenant-colonel R. C. Buchanan.
Second Brigade—Lieutenant-colonel William Chapman.
Third Brigade—Colonel G. K. Warren.

FREDERICKSBURG.

Major-general Ambrose E. Burnside commanding Federal Forces known as the Army of the Potomac.

CENTRE GRAND DIVISION.

Major-general Joseph Hooker commanding.

THIRD CORPS.

Brigadier-general Geo. Stoneman commanding.

FIRST DIVISION—Brigadier-general D. B. Birney.

Infantry.

First Brigade—Brigadier-general John C. Robinson.
Twentieth Indiana Regiment—Colonel John Van Valkenburg.
Sixty-third Pennsylvania Regiment—Major J. A. Danks.
Sixty-eighth Pennsylvania Regiment—Colonel A. H. Tippen.
One Hundred and Fifth Pennsylvania Regiment—Colonel A. A. McKnight.
One Hundred and Fourteenth Pennsylvania Regiment—Colonel C. H. T. Collis.
One Hundred and Forty-first Pennsylvania Regiment—Colonel H. J. Madill.

Second Brigade—Brigadier-general J. H. Hobart Ward commanding.
Fifty-seventh Pennsylvania Regiment—Colonel C. T. Campbell.
Ninety-ninth Pennsylvania Regiment—Colonel A. S. Leidy.

JOHN MILTON BRANNAN.

Second Brigade (continued)—Fifty-fifth New York Regiment—Colonel R. de Trobriand.
Thirty-eighth New York Regiment—Lieutenant-colonel William Birney.
Fortieth New York Regiment—Lieutenant-colonel N. A. Gesner.
Third Maine Regiment—Colonel M. B. Lakeman.
Fourth Maine Regiment—Colonel E. Walker.

Third Brigade—Brigadier-general H. G. Berry commanding.
First New York Regiment—Colonel J. Frederick Pierson.
Thirty-seventh New York Regiment—Colonel S. B. Hayman.
One Hundred and First New York Regiment—Colonel G. F. Chester.
Seventeenth Maine Regiment—Colonel T. A. Roberts.
Third Michigan Regiment—Lieutenant-colonel Byron R. Pierce.
Fifth Michigan Regiment—Lieutenant-colonel John Gilluly.

Artillery.

Captain J. E. Randolph commanding.

Battery E, First Rhode Island—Lieutenant P. S. Jastram.
Batteries F and K, Third United States—Captain L. L. Livingston.

SECOND DIVISION—Brigadier-general Daniel E. Sickles commanding.

Infantry.

First Brigade—Brigadier-general Joseph B. Carr commanding.
First Massachusetts Regiment—Lieutenant-colonel C. B. Baldwin.
Eleventh New Jersey Regiment—Colonel R. McAllister.
Twenty-sixth Pennsylvania Regiment—Lieutenant-colonel B. C. Tilghman.
Eleventh Massachusetts Regiment—Col. W. B. Blaisdell.
Sixteenth Massachusetts Regiment—Colonel T. R. Tannatt.
Second New Hampshire Regiment—Colonel G. Marston.

Second Brigade—Colonel George B. Hall commanding.
One Hundred and Twentieth New York Regiment—Colonel George H. Sharp.
Seventieth (First Excelsior) New York Regiment—Colonel J. Egbert Farnum.
Seventy-first (Second Excelsior) New York Regiment—Major Thomas Rafferty.
Seventy-second (Third Excelsior) New York Regiment—Colonel William O. Stevens.
Seventy-third (Fourth Excelsior) New York Regiment—Colonel William R. Brewster.
Seventy-fourth (Fifth Excelsior) New York Regiment—Lieutenant-colonel W. H. Lounsbury.

Third Brigade—Brigadier-general J. W. Revere commanding.
Fifth New Jersey Regiment—Colonel William J. Sewell.
Seventh New Jersey Regiment—Colonel Louis R. Francine.

TERRIFIC CHARGE OF THE FEDERAL TROOPS (SUMNER'S DIVISION) UPON THE CONFEDER

TERRIFIC CHARGE OF THE FEDERAL TROOPS (SUMNER'S DIVISION) UPON THE CONFEDERATE FORTIFICATIONS LOCATED ON THE TERRACE BEHIND FREDERICKSBURG, VA, DECEMBER 13th, 1862.

Artillery.

Battery B, First New Jersey—Captain A. J. Clark.
Fourth Battery, New York—Captain James E. Smith.
Battery H, First United States—Lieutenant J. E. Dimick.
Battery K, Fourth United States—Lieutenant F. W. Seeley.

THIRD DIVISION: Brigadier-general A. W. Whipple commanding.

Infantry.

First Brigade—Brigadier-general A. Sanders Piatt commanding.
One Hundred and Twenty-second Pennsylvania Regiment—Colonel Emlen Franklin.
Eighty-sixth New York Regiment—Lieutenant-colonel B. L. Chapin.
One Hundred and Twenty-fourth New York Regiment—Colonel A. V. Ellis.
Second Brigade—Colonel S. S. Carroll commanding.
Eighty-fourth Pennsylvania Regiment—Colonel S. M. Bowman.
One Hundred and Tenth Pennsylvania Regiment—Lieutenant-colonel J. Crowther.
One Hundred and Sixty-third New York Regiment—Major J. J. Byrne.
Independent Command—Colonel J. H. Potter commanding.
Twelfth New Hampshire Regiment.

Second Brigade (*continued*)—Sixty-second Pennsylvania Regiment—Lieutenant-colonel J. C. Hull.
Third Brigade—Colonel T. B. W. Stockton commanding.
Twelfth New York Regiment—Lieutenant-colonel R. M. Richardson.
Seventeenth New York Regiment—Captain John Vickers.
Forty-fourth New York Regiment—Lieutenant-colonel F. Conner.
Sixteenth Michigan Regiment—Lieutenant-colonel N. E. Welch.
Twentieth Maine Regiment—Colonel Adelbert Ames.
Eighty-third Pennsylvania Regiment—Colonel Strong Vincent.

Artillery.

Captain A. P. Martin, Battery C, Massachusetts Artillery, commanding.
Battery C, Third Massachusetts—First-lieutenant V. M. Drum.
Battery E, Fifth Massachusetts—Captain C. A. Phillips.

SECOND DIVISION: Brigadier-general George Sykes commanding.

Infantry.

First Brigade—Lieutenant-colonel R. C. Buchanan, Fourth United States Infantry, commanding.
Third United States Infantry—Captain John D. Wilkins.
Fourth United States Infantry—Captain Hiram Dryer.

THIRD DIVISION: Brigadier-general A. A. Humphreys commanding.

Infantry.

First Brigade—Brigadier-general E. B. Tyler commanding.
Ninety-first Pennsylvania Regiment—Colonel E. M. Gregory.
One Hundred and Twenty-sixth Pennsylvania Regiment—Colonel James G. Elder.
One Hundred and Twenty-ninth Pennsylvania Regiment—Colonel J. G. Frick.
One Hundred and Thirty-fourth Pennsylvania Regiment—Lieutenant-colonel E. O'Brien.
Second Brigade—Colonel P. H. Allabach, One Hundred and Thirty-first Pennsylvania Regiment, commanding.
One Hundred and Twenty-third Pennsylvania Regiment—Colonel J. B. Clark.
One Hundred and Thirty-first Pennsylvania Regiment—Lieutenant-colonel W. B. Shaut.
One Hundred and Thirty-third Pennsylvania Regiment—Colonel B. F. Speakman.
One Hundred and Fifty-fifth Pennsylvania Regiment—Colonel E. J. Allen.

Artillery.

Captain A. M. Randol, First United States Artillery, commanding.
Battery H, First United States—Captain A. M. Randol.

THE GRAND ARMY RECROSSING THE RAPPAHANNOCK FROM FREDERICKSBURG TO FALMOUTH, MONDAY NIGHT, DECEMBER 15TH, 1862.

Artillery.

Battery H, First Ohio—Lieutenant G. W. Norton.
Second Battery (Excelsior), New York—Captain J. T. Brown.
Eleventh Battery, New York—Captain A. A. Von Puttkammer.

FIFTH CORPS.

Brigadier-general Daniel Butterfield commanding.

FIRST DIVISION: Brigadier-general Charles Griffin commanding.

Infantry.

First Brigade—Colonel James Barnes, Eighteenth Massachusetts Regiment, commanding.
Eighteenth Massachusetts Regiment—Lieutenant-colonel J. Hayes.
Twenty-second Massachusetts Regiment—Lieutenant-colonel W. S. Tilton.
Second Maine Regiment—Lieutenant-colonel G. Varney.
One Hundred and Eighteenth Pennsylvania Regiment—Lieutenant-colonel J. Gwyn.
First Michigan Regiment—Lieutenant-colonel I. C. Abbott.
Thirteenth New York Regiment—Colonel E. G. Marshall.
Twenty-fifth New York Regiment—Captain P. Connelly.
Second Brigade—Colonel J. B. Sweitzer commanding.
Fourteenth New York Regiment—Lieutenant-colonel T. M. Davies.
Fourth Michigan Regiment—Lieutenant-colonel G. W. Lombard.
Ninth Massachusetts Regiment—Colonel P. R. Guiney.
Thirty-second Massachusetts Regiment—Lieutenant-colonel G. L. Prescott.

First Brigade (*continued*)—First Battalion, Twelfth United States Infantry—Captain M. M. Blunt.
Second Battalion, Twelfth United States Infantry—Captain T. M. Anderson.
First Battalion, Fourteenth United States Infantry—Captain J. D. O'Connell.
Second Battalion, Fourteenth United States Infantry—Captain G. B. Overton.
Second Brigade—Major George L. Andrews, Seventeenth United States Infantry, commanding.
Eleventh United States Infantry—Captain C. S. Russell.
Battalion of First and Second United States Infantry—Captain Salem S. Marsh.
Battalion of Sixth United States Infantry—Captain Levy C. Bootes.
Battalion of Seventh United States Infantry—Captain D. P. Hancock.
Battalion of Tenth United States Infantry—H. E. Maynadier.
Battalion of Seventeenth and Nineteenth United States Infantry—Captain J. P. Wales.
Third Brigade—Brigadier-general G. K. Warren commanding.
Fifth New York Regiment—Colonel C. Winslow.
One Hundred and Fortieth New York Regiment—Colonel P. H. O'Rorke.
One Hundred and Forty-sixth New York Regiment—Colonel K. Garrard.

Artillery.

First-lieutenant M. F. Watson, Fifth United States Artillery, commanding.
Battery I, Fifth United States—Lieutenant M. F. Watson.
Battery L, First Ohio—First-lieutenant F. Dorries.

Section of Battery C, First New York—Lieutenant W. H. Phillips.
Grand Division of Cavalry: Brigadier-general W. W. Averill commanding.

RIGHT GRAND DIVISION.

Major-general E. V. Sumner, U. S. A., commanding.

SECOND CORPS.

Major-general D. N. Couch commanding.

FIRST DIVISION: Brigadier-general W. S. Hancock commanding.

Infantry.

First Brigade—Brigadier-general J. C. Caldwell commanding.
Sixty-first New York Regiment—Colonel N. A. Miles.
Sixty-fourth New York Regiment—Captain Harvey L. Jones.
One Hundred and Forty-fifth Pennsylvania Regiment—Colonel H. L. Brown.
Eighty-first Pennsylvania Regiment—Lieutenant-colonel H. B. McKeen.
Fifth New Hampshire Regiment—Colonel E. E. Cross.
Seventh New York Regiment—Col. George Von Schack.
Second Brigade—Brigadier-general Thomas Francis Meagher commanding.
Sixty-ninth New York Regiment—Colonel R. Nugent.
Eighty-eighth New York Regiment—Colonel P. Kelly.
Sixty-third New York Regiment—Major J. O'Neil.
Twenty-eighth Massachusetts Regiment—Colonel R. Byrnes.
One Hundred and Sixteenth Pennsylvania Regiment—Colonel D. Heenan.

Third Brigade—Colonel S. K. Zook, Fifty-seventh New York Regiment, commanding.
Fifty-seventh New York Regiment—Major N. G. Throop.
Fifty-third Pennsylvania Regiment—Col. John R. Brooke.
Third Delaware Regiment—Colonel W. P. Bailey.
Fifty-second New York Regiment—Colonel Paul Frank.
Sixty-sixth New York Regiment—Captain Julius Wehle.
Twenty-seventh Connecticut Regiment—Colonel R. S. Bostwick.

Artillery.

Battery G, Fourth United States—Lieutenant Evan Thomas.
Battery B, First New York—Captain R. D. Pettit.

SECOND DIVISION: Brigadier-general O. O. Howard commanding.

Infantry.

First Brigade—Brigadier-general Alfred Sully commanding.
Thirty-fourth New York Regiment—Colonel J. A. Suiter.
Eighty-second New York Regiment—Colonel H. W. Hudson.
Fifteenth Massachusetts Regiment—Major C. Philbrick.
Nineteenth Maine Regiment—Colonel F. D. Sewell.
First Minnesota Regiment—Colonel G. N. Morgan.
Second Brigade—Colonel J. T. Owen, Sixty-ninth Pennsylvania Regiment, commanding.
Sixty-ninth Pennsylvania Regiment—Lieutenant-colonel D. O'Kane.
Seventy-first Pennsylvania Regiment—Lieut.-colonel J. Markoe.
Seventy-second Pennsylvania Regiment—Col. D. W. C. Baxter.
One Hundred and Sixth Pennsylvania Regiment—Colonel T. G. Morehead.
Third Brigade—Colonel Norman J. Hall commanding.
Nineteenth Massachusetts Regiment—Captain J. F. Plimpton.
Twentieth Massachusetts Regiment—Captain George N. Macy.
Forty-second New York Regiment—Lieutenant-colonel G. W. Bomford.
Fifty-ninth New York Regiment—Lieutenant-colonel William Northedge.
Seventh Michigan Regiment—Lieutenant-colonel Henry Baxter.
One Hundred and Twenty-seventh Pennsylvania Regiment—Colonel W. W. Jennings.

Artillery.

Battery A, First Rhode Island—Captain Tompkins.
Battery B, First Rhode Island—Captain J. G. Hazard.

THIRD DIVISION: Brigadier-general W. H. French commanding.

Infantry.

First Brigade—Brigadier-general Nathan Kimball commanding.
Fourth Ohio Regiment—Colonel John S. Mason.
Fourteenth Indiana Regiment—Major E. H. C. Cavins.
Twenty-fourth New Jersey Regiment—Colonel W. B. Robertson.
Twenty-eighth New Jersey Regiment—Colonel M. N. Wisewell.
Seventh Virginia Regiment—Colonel James Snyder.
Eighth Ohio Regiment—Lieutenant-colonel F. Sawyer.
Second Brigade—Colonel O. H. Palmer, One Hundred and Eighth New York Regiment, commanding.
Fourteenth Connecticut Regiment—Lieutenant-colonel S. H. Perkins.
One Hundred and Eighth New York Regiment—Lieutenant-colonel Charles J. Powers.
One Hundred and Thirtieth Pennsylvania Regiment—Colonel H. I. Zinn.
Third Brigade—Lieutenant-colonel John W. Marshall commanding.
Fourth New York Regiment—Colonel John D. McGregor.
Tenth New York Regiment—Colonel John E. Bendix.
First Delaware Regiment—Colonel J. W. Andrews.
One Hundred and Thirty-second Pennsylvania Regiment—Lieutenant-colonel Charles Albright.

Artillery.

Battery G, First New York—Captain John D. Frank.
Battery G, First Rhode Island—Captain C. D. Owen.

Second Corps Reserve Artillery.

Battery I, First United States—Lieutenant E. Kirby.
Battery A, Fourth United States—Lieutenant R. King.

NINTH CORPS.

Brigadier-general O. B. Willcox commanding.

FIRST DIVISION: Brigadier-general W. W. Burns commanding.

Infantry.

First Brigade—
Second Michigan Regiment—Colonel Orlando M. Poe.
Seventeenth Michigan Regiment—Colonel W. H. Withington.
Twentieth Michigan Regiment—Colonel A. W. Williams.
Seventy-ninth New York Regiment—Lieutenant-colonel David Morrison.
Third Brigade—
Forty-fifth Pennsylvania Regiment—Colonel Thomas Welsh.

Artillery.

Battery D, First New York—Captain T. W. Osborn.

SECOND DIVISION: Brigadier-general S. D. Sturgis commanding.

Infantry.

First Brigade—Brigadier-general James Nagle commanding.
Second Maryland Regiment—Major H. Howard.

First Brigade (continued)—Sixth New Hampshire Regiment—Colonel S. G. Griffin.
Seventh Rhode Island Regiment—Colonel Z. R. Bliss.
Twelfth Rhode Island Regiment—Colonel George H. Browne.
Ninth New Hampshire Regiment—Colonel E. Q. Fellows.
Forty-eighth Pennsylvania Regiment—Colonel J. K. Sigfried.
Second Brigade—Brigadier-general Edward Ferrero commanding.
Twenty-first Massachusetts Regiment—Lieut.-colonel W. S. Clark.
Thirty-fifth Massachusetts Regiment—Lieutenant-colonel S. Carruth.
Eleventh New Hampshire Regiment—Colonel W. Harriman.
Fifty-first New York Regiment—Colonel R. B. Potter.
Fifty-first Pennsylvania Regiment—Colonel J. F. Hartranft.

Artillery.

Battery D, First Rhode Island—Captain W. W. Buckley.
Battery E, Fourth United States—Lieutenant Geo. Dickenson.

THIRD DIVISION: Brigadier-general George W. Getty commanding.

Infantry.

First Brigade—Colonel Rush C. Hawkins commanding.
Tenth New Hampshire Regiment—Col. M. T. Donohoe.

ISRAEL B. RICHARDSON.

First Brigade (continued)—Thirteenth New Hampshire Regiment—Colonel A. F. Stevens.
Twenty-fifth New Jersey Regiment—Colonel Andrew Derrom.
Ninth New York Regiment—Major E. A. Kimball.
Eighty-ninth New York Regiment—Colonel H. S. Fairchilds.
One Hundred and Third New York Regiment—Major B. Ringold.
Second Brigade—Colonel Edward Harland commanding.
Eleventh Connecticut Regiment—Colonel Griffin A. Stedman, Jr.
Fifteenth Connecticut Regiment—Lieutenant-colonel Samuel Tolles.
Sixteenth Connecticut Regiment—Colonel Frank Beach (Captain Fourth United States Artillery).
Twenty-first Connecticut Regiment—Colonel Arthur H. Dutton.
Fourth Rhode Island Regiment—Major Martin P. Buffum.

Artillery.

Battery A, Fifth United States—Lieutenant G. P. Muhlenberg.
Battery E, Second United States—Lieutenant S. N. Benjamin.

Cavalry Division: Brigadier-general Alfred Pleasanton commanding.

First Brigade—Brigadier-general J. H. Farnsworth commanding.
Sixth New York Regiment—Colonel T. C. Devin.
Eighth New York Regiment—Colonel B. F. Davis.
Eighth Illinois Regiment—Colonel W. Gamble.
Second Brigade—Colonel D. McM. Gregg, Eighth Pennsylvania Regiment, commanding.
Sixth United States Cavalry—Captain G. C. Cram.
Eighth Pennsylvania Regiment—Colonel D. McM. Gregg.

Artillery.

Battery M, Second United States—Captain A. C. M. Pennington.

LEFT GRAND DIVISION.

Major-general W. B. Franklin commanding.

SIXTH CORPS.

Major-general W. F. Smith commanding.

FIRST DIVISION: Brigadier-general W. T. Brooks commanding.

Infantry.

First Brigade—Colonel A. T. A. Torbert, First New Jersey Regiment, commanding.
First New Jersey Regiment—Lieutenant-colonel M. W. Collet.
Second New Jersey Regiment—Colonel Samuel L. Buck.
Third New Jersey Regiment—Colonel Henry W. Brown.
Fourth New Jersey Regiment—Colonel William B. Hatch.
Fifteenth New Jersey Regiment—Lieutenant-colonel E. L. Campbell.
Twenty-third New Jersey Regiment—Lieutenant-colonel H. O. Ryerson.
Second Brigade—Brigadier-general J. J. Bartlett commanding.
Sixteenth New York Regiment—Lieutenant-colonel J. J. Seaver.
Twenty-seventh New York Regiment—Colonel A. D. Adams.
One Hundred and Twenty-first New York Regiment—Colonel Emory Upton.
Fifth Maine Regiment—Colonel E. A. Scammon.
Ninety-sixth Pennsylvania Regiment—Colonel H. L. Cake.
Third Brigade—Colonel G. W. Town, Ninety-fifth Pennsylvania Regiment, commanding.
Ninety-fifth Pennsylvania Regiment—Lieut.-colonel E. Hall.
Eighteenth New York Regiment—Colonel George R. Myers.
Thirty-first New York Regiment—Lieutenant-colonel L. C. Newman.
Thirty-second New York Regiment—Captain Charles Hubbs.

Artillery.

Battery A, First New Jersey—Captain W. Hexamer.
Battery A, First Massachusetts—Captain W. H. McCartney.
Battery A, First Maryland—Captain J. W. Wolcott.
Battery D, Second United States—First Lieutenant E. B. Williston.

SECOND DIVISION; Brigadier-general A. P. Howe commanding.

Infantry.

First Brigade—Brigadier-general Calvin E. Pratt commanding.
One Hundred and Nineteenth Pennsylvania Regiment—Colonel P. C. Ellmaker.
Sixth Maine Regiment—Colonel Hiram Burnham.
Fifth Wisconsin Regiment—Colonel Amasa Cobb.
Forty-ninth Pennsylvania Regiment—Colonel William H. Irwin.
Forty-third New York Regiment—Colonel B. F. Baker.
Second Brigade—Colonel Henry Whiting, Second Vermont Regiment, commanding.
Second Vermont Regiment—Colonel ——.
Third Vermont Regiment—Colonel B. N. Hyde.
Fourth Vermont Regiment—Colonel C. B. Stoughton.
Fifth Vermont Regiment—Colonel Lewis A. Grant.
Sixth Vermont Regiment—Colonel N. Lord, Jr.
Twenty-sixth New Jersey Regiment—Colonel A. J. Morrison.
Third Brigade—Brigadier-general Francis L. Vinton commanding.
Seventy-seventh New York Regiment—Colonel James B. McKean.
Forty-ninth New York Regiment—Colonel D. D. Bidwell.
Twentieth New York Regiment—Colonel E. Von Vegesack.
Thirty-third New York Regiment—Colonel Robert F. Taylor.
Twenty-first New Jersey Regiment—Colonel Gilliam Van Houten.

Artillery.

Battery F, Fifth United States—Captain R. B. Ayres.
Battery B, First Maryland—Captain Alonzo Snow.
First Battery New York L. A.—Captain Andrew Cowan.
Third Battery New York L. A.—Captain William Stewart.

THIRD DIVISION: Brigadier-general John Newton commanding.

Infantry.

First Brigade—Brigadier-general John Cochrane commanding.
Eighty-second Pennsylvania Regiment—Colonel D. H. Williams.
Twenty-third Pennsylvania Regiment—Colonel T. H. Neill.
Sixty-first Pennsylvania Regiment—Colonel O. C. Spear.
Sixty-fifth New York Regiment (First United States Chasseurs)—Colonel Alexander Shaler.
One Hundred and Twenty-second New York Regiment—Colonel Silas Titus.
Sixty-seventh New York Regiment (First Long Island)—Lieutenant-colonel Nelson Cross.
Second Brigade—Brigadier-general Charles Devens commanding.
Second Rhode Island Regiment—Colonel Frank Wheaton.
Seventh Massachusetts Regiment—Colonel D. A. Russell.
Tenth Massachusetts Regiment—Colonel H. L. Eustis.
Thirty-sixth New York Regiment—Colonel W. H. Browne.
Thirty-seventh Massachusetts Regiment—Colonel O. Edwards.

Third Brigade—Colonel Thomas A. Rowley commanding.

Sixty-second New York Regiment—Colonel David I. Nevin.

Ninety-third Pennsylvania Regiment—Colonel J. M. McCarter.

Ninety-eighth Pennsylvania Regiment—Colonel J. F. Ballier.

One Hundred and Second Pennsylvania Regiment—Lieutenant-colonel J. M. Kinkead.

One Hundred and Thirty-sixth Pennsylvania Regiment—Colonel F. H. Collier.

Artillery.

Battery C, First Pennsylvania Artillery—Captain J. McCarthy.

Battery G, Second United States Artillery—Lieutenant J. H. Butler.

FIRST CORPS.

Brigadier-general J. F. Reynolds commanding.

FIRST DIVISION: Brigadier-general Abner Doubleday commanding.

Infantry.

First Brigade—Colonel Walter Phelps, Jr., commanding.

Second United States Sharpshooters—Major H. B. Stoughton.

Fourteenth New York Militia—Lieutenant-colonel W. H. De Bevoise.

Twenty-second New York Regiment—Lieutenant-colonel J. McKee, Jr.

Twenty-fourth New York Regiment—Major R. Oliver, Jr.

Thirtieth New York Regiment—Lieutenant-colonel M. H. Chrysler.

Second Brigade—Colonel James Gavin commanding.

Fifty-sixth Pennsylvania Regiment—Lieutenant-colonel J. W. Hofmann.

Ninety-fifth New York Regiment—Lieutenant-colonel J. B. Post.

Seventy-sixth New York Regiment—Colonel W. P. Wainwright.

Seventh Indiana Regiment—Lieutenant-colonel J. F. Cheek.

Third Brigade—Brigadier-general G. R. Paul commanding.

Twentieth New York Militia—Lieutenant-colonel J. D. Hardenbergh.

Twenty-first New York Regiment—Captain G. N. Layton.

Twenty-third New York Regiment—Colonel H. C. Hoffman.

Thirty-fifth New York Regiment—Colonel N. B. Lord.

Fourth Brigade—Colonel L. Cutler commanding.

Second Wisconsin Regiment—Colonel L. Fairchild.

Sixth Wisconsin Regiment—Lieutenant-colonel E. S. Bragg.

Seventh Wisconsin Regiment—Lieutenant-colonel C. A. Hamilton.

Nineteenth Indiana Regiment—Lieutenant-colonel A. J. Williams.

Twenty-fourth Michigan Regiment—Col. H. A. Morrow.

Artillery.

Captain G. A. Gerrish commanding.

Battery B, Fourth United States—Lieutenant James Stewart.

Battery D, First Rhode Island—Lieutenant G. C. Harrison.

Battery D, First New Hampshire—Lieutenant F. M. Edgell.

Battery L, First New York—Captain J. A. Reynolds.

SECOND DIVISION: Brigadier-general John Gibbon commanding.

Infantry.

First Brigade—Colonel Adrian R. Root commanding.

Sixteenth Maine Regiment—Lieutenant-colonel C. W. Tilden.

One Hundred and Seventh Pennsylvania Regiment—Colonel T. F. McCoy.

Ninety-fourth New York Regiment—Major John A. Kress.

One Hundred and Fourth New York Regiment—Major G. G. Prey.

One Hundred and Fifth Regiment—Major D. A. Sharp.

Second Brigade—Colonel P. Lyle, Ninetieth Pennsylvania Regiment, commanding.

Ninetieth Pennsylvania Regiment—Lieutenant-colonel W. A. Leech.

One Hundred and Thirty-sixth Pennsylvania Regiment—Colonel Thomas M. Bayne.

Twelfth Massachusetts Regiment—Colonel J. L. Bates.

Twenty-sixth New York Regiment—Colonel R. H. Richardson.

Third Brigade—Brigadier-general Nelson Taylor commanding.

Eighty-third New York Regiment—Colonel John W. Stiles.

Ninety-seventh New York Regiment—Colonel Charles Wheelock.

Thirteenth Massachusetts Regiment—Col. S. H. Leonard.

Eleventh Pennsylvania Regiment—Col. Richard Coulter.

Eighty-eighth Pennsylvania Regiment—Colonel G. P. McLean.

Artillery.

Captain George F. Leppien commanding.

Battery D, Maine—Captain J. A. Hall.

Battery E, Maine—Captain G. F. Leppien.

Battery F, First Pennsylvania—Lieutenant R. B. Ricketts.

Independent Battery, Pennsylvania—Captain J. Thompson.

THIRD DIVISION: Brigadier-general George G. Meade commanding.

Infantry.

First Brigade—Colonel William Sinclair, Sixth Pennsylvania Reserves, commanding.

First Infantry Pennsylvania Reserve Corps—Captain W. C. Talley.

Second Infantry Pennsylvania Reserve Corps—Colonel W. McCandless.

Sixth Infantry Pennsylvania Reserve Corps—Major W. H. Ent.

First Rifles Pennsylvania Reserve Corps—Captain D. McGee.

One Hundred and Twenty-first Pennsylvania Regiment—Colonel C. Biddle.

Second Brigade—Colonel A. L. Magilton, Fourth Pennsylvania Reserves, commanding.

Third Pennsylvania Reserve Corps—Col. H. G. Sickle.

Fourth Pennsylvania Reserve Corps—Lieutenant-colonel R. H. Woolworth.

Seventh Pennsylvania Reserve Corps—Colonel H. C. Bolinger.

Eighth Pennsylvania Reserve Corps—Major S. M. Bailey.

One Hundred and Forty-second Regiment—Colonel R. P. Cummins.

Third Brigade—Brigadier-general C. Feger Jackson commanding.

Fifth Pennsylvania Reserve Corps—Colonel J. W. Fisher.

Ninth Pennsylvania Reserve Corps—Lieutenant-colonel R. Anderson.

Tenth Pennsylvania Reserve Corps—Lieutenant-colonel A. J. Warner.

Eleventh Pennsylvania Reserve Corps—Colonel T. F. Gallagher.

Twelfth Pennsylvania Reserve Corps—Colonel M. D. Hardin.

Artillery.

Battery A, First Pennsylvania—Lieutenant J. G. Simpson.

Battery B, First Pennsylvania—Captain J. H. Cooper.

Battery C, Fifth United States—Captain D. R. Ransom.

Battery G, First Pennsylvania—Captain F. P. Amsden.

Line of Extra Caissons.

Captain J. M. Clark, Company F, Second Pennsylvania Reserve Corps, commanding.

Cavalry Brigade: Brigadier-general George D. Bayard commanding.

First New Jersey Cavalry—Lieutenant-colonel Joseph Karge.

Second New York Cavalry—Major H. E. Davies.

Tenth New York Cavalry—Lieutenant-colonel William Irvine.

First Pennsylvania Cavalry—Colonel Owen Jones.

Artillery.

Battery C, Third United States—Captain H. G. Gibson.

ANTIETAM AND FREDERICKSBURG.

General Robert E. Lee commanding the Confederate Forces known as the Army of Northern Virginia.

FIRST CORPS.

Major-general James Longstreet commanding the right wing at Antietam, and the left wing at Fredericksburg.

Major-general Lafayette McLaws's Division.

Barksdale's Brigade—13th, 17th, 18th and 21st Mississippi Regiments.

Kershaw's Brigade—2d, 3d, 7th, and 8th South Carolina Regiments.

Semmes's Brigade—10th and 53d Georgia, and 15th and 32d Virginia Regiments, and Manly's Battery.

Cobb's Brigade (Colonel Sanders commanding at Sharpsburg)—Cobb's Georgia Legion, 16th and 24th Georgia, and 15th North Carolina Regiments, and Read's Battery.

Major-general Richard H. Anderson's Division.

Brigadier-general Cadmus M. Wilcox commanding.

Wilcox's Brigade—8th, 9th, 10th and 11th Alabama Regiments.

Pryor's Brigade—5th and 8th Florida, 14th Alabama, and 3d Virginia Regiments.

Featherston's Brigade (General Featherston and Colonel Posey commanding)—2d Mississippi Battalion, 12th, 16th and 19th Mississippi Regiments.

Wright's Brigade—3d, 22d, 44th and 48th Georgia, and 44th Alabama Regiments.

Armistead's Brigade—14th, 38th, 53d and 57th Virginia Regiments, and Chapman's Dixie Battery.

Mahone's Brigade (Colonel Parham commanding at Sharpsburg)—6th, 12th, 16th and 41st Virginia Regiments.

Major-general D. R. Jones's Division.

G. T. Anderson's Brigade—General Evans commanding: 1st, 7th, 8th and 9th Georgia Regiments.

Toombs's Brigade (Colonel Benning commanding in Maryland, while Toombs commanded three brigades)—2d, 15th, 17th and 20th Georgia Regiments.

Drayton's Brigade—15th, 50th and 51st South Carolina Regiments.

Kemper's Brigade (Colonel Corse commanding at the battles of Groveton and Second Manassas)—1st, 7th, 11th, 17th and 24th Virginia Regiments.

Pickett's Brigade (General R. B. Garnett commanding in Maryland)—8th, 18th, 19th, 28th and 56th Virginia Regiments.

Jenkins's Brigade (Colonel Walker commanding)—1st, 2d, 5th and 6th South Carolina Regiments, and the Palmetto Sharpshooters.

Major-general R. L. Walker's Division.

Ransom's Brigade—24th, 25th, 35th and 49th North Carolina Regiments, and J. R. Branch's Battery.

Walker's Brigade (Colonel Manning commanding)—30th Virginia, 27th, 46th and 48th North Carolina, and 3d Arkansas Regiments; also French's Battery.

Major-general George E. Pickett's Division.

Kemper's Brigade (General D. R. Jones commanding in Maryland)—1st, 7th, 11th, 17th and 24th Virginia Regiments.

Garnett's Brigade (General Pickett commanding in Maryland)—8th, 18th, 19th, 28th and 56th Virginia Regiments.

Major-general J. B. Hood's Division.

Infantry: Hood's Brigade (Colonel Wofford commanding)—18th Georgia, 1st, 4th and 5th Texas Regiments; also the Hampton Legion.

Whiting's (Law's) Brigade—4th Alabama, 6th North Carolina, and 2d and 11th Mississippi Regiments.

Evans's Brigade (General Evans and Colonel Stevens commanding)—17th, 18th, 22d and 23d South Carolina Regiments; also the Holcombe Legion and Boyce's Battery, Macbeth's Artillery.

Artillery: Lee's Artillery and Walton's Artillery Battalions, and the Bachman, Garden and Reilly Batteries.

SECOND CORPS.

Major-general T. J. (Stonewall) Jackson commanding the left wing at Antietam, and the right wing at Fredericksburg.

Major-general T. J. Jackson's Division.

Generals Taliaferro (1), Starke (2), and J. R. Jones (3) commanding.

Infantry: Winder's Brigade (Baylor and Grigsby commanding)—2d, 4th, 5th, 27th and 33d Virginia Regiments.

Campbell's Brigade (Jones, Johnson and Seddon commanding)—21st, 42d and 48th Virginia Regiments; also the 1st Virginia Battalion.

Taliaferro's Brigade (Taliaferro and Warren commanding)—10th, 23d and 37th Virginia, and the 47th and 48th Alabama Regiments.

Starke's Brigade (Starke, Stafford and Pendleton commanding)—1st, 2d, 9th, 10th and 15th Louisiana Regiments, and Coppen's Battalion.

Artillery: Major L. M. Shumaker commanding—Brockenbrough's, Carpenter's, Caskie's, Poague's, Raine's and Wooding's Batteries.

Major-general Richard S. Ewell's Division.

Generals Ewell (1), Lawton (2) and Early commanding.

Infantry: Early's Brigade—13th, 25th, 31st, 44th, 49th, 52d and 58th Virginia Regiments.

Hays's Brigade (Hays, Forno and Strong commanding)—5th, 6th, 7th and 8th Louisiana Regiments.

Lawton's Brigade (Lawton and Douglas commanding)—13th, 31st, 60th and 61st Georgia Regiments.

Trimble's Brigade (Trimble, Brown and Walker commanding)—12th and 21st Georgia, 15th Alabama, and 20th and 21st North Carolina Regiments.

Artillery: Major W. C. Courtney commanding—Balthis's, Brown's, D'Aquin's, Dement's and Latimer's Batteries.

Major-general Ambrose P. Hill's Division.

Infantry: Archer's Brigade—1st, 7th and 14th Tennessee, and 19th Georgia Regiments; also the 5th Alabama Battalion.

Field's Brigade—40th, 47th and 55th Virginia Regiments; also the 2d Virginia Battalion.

Pender's Brigade—16th, 22d, 34th and 38th North Carolina Regiments.

Thomas's Brigade—14th, 19th, 35th, 45th and 49th Georgia Regiments.

Branch's (or Lane's) Brigade—7th, 18th, 28th, 33d and 37th North Carolina Regiments.

Gregg's (or McGowan's) Brigade—1st South Carolina Rifles, and the 1st, 12th, 13th and 14th South Carolina Infantry Regiments.

Artillery: Major R. L. Walker commanding—Braxton's, Crenshaw's, Davidson's, Latham's, McIntosh's and Pegram's Batteries.

Major-general Daniel H. Hill's Division.

Infantry: Anderson's Brigade—2d, 4th, 13th, 14th, 30th and 30th North Carolina Regiments.

Colquitt's Brigade—19th, 23d, 27th and 28th Georgia and 13th Alabama Regiments.

Garland's Brigade (Garland and McRae commanding)—1st, 3d, 5th and 20th North Carolina Regiments.

Ripley's Brigade—4th, 6th, 21st and 44th Georgia Regiments.

Rodes's Brigade—3d, 5th, 6th, 12th and 26th Alabama Regiments.

Artillery: Bondurant's, Hardaway's, Jones, Lane's and King William Batteries.

Major-general James E. B. Stuart's Cavalry Division.

Hampton's Brigade—Two companies of the Jeff. Davis Legion, nine companies of the Cobb Legion, five companies of the Phillips Legion, the 1st North Carolina and the 2d South Carolina Cavalry.

Robertson's Brigade—The 17th Virginia Battalion, and the 2d, 6th, 7th and 12th Virginia Cavalry.

Fitzhugh Lee's Brigade—The 1st, 3d, 4th and 5th Virginia Cavalry, Stuart's Horse Artillery, and White's Battalion of Virginia Independent Cavalry.

GEORGE D. BAYARD.

GEORGE W. CULLUM.

GEORGE W. CULLUM.

Born in New York City, February 25th, 1809; entered the United States Military Academy at West Point, and graduated from it in 1833; served in the construction and improvement of Fort Adams, Rhode Island, 1833-34, 1836-38, and 1858-61; during the intervening periods was assistant to chief engineer, 1834-36; engaged in the construction of the lighthouse at Goat Island between the years 1836 and 1838, and in the erection of defenses in the harbor of New London, Conn., at different periods between 1838 and 1855. In the meantime, he had aided in the construction of the fortifications of Boston Harbor, Mass.; in organizing engineer troops and preparing engineer and ponton equipage for the Mexican War, in teaching practical military engineering, etc., at the West Point Military Academy, and in building the United States Assay Office in New York City. From 1855 to 1858 he had charge of public works in both North and South Carolina, especially the construction of the defenses, light-houses and channel improvements of Charleston Harbor. Between 1858 and 1861 he was a member of special boards, and was placed in charge of the sea-coast defenses from New Bedford, Mass., to the Sound entrance to New York Harbor. At the time of the breaking out of the Civil War he was aide-de-camp (rank of colonel) to Lieutenant-general Scott, then became chief of staff and of engineers to General Halleck, while the latter was in command of the Departments of Missouri and Mississippi, and also while General-in-chief of the armies of the United States. On the 1st of November, 1861, he was made a brigadier-general of Volunteers. Up to the year 1864 he was engaged in establishing defensive works, directing at Cairo operations auxiliary to the Western armies in the field, fortifying the approaches to Corinth after its evacuation, and organizing the defenses of Nashville, Tenn., the great depot of supplies for the Western armies. From 1864 to 1866 he was superintendent of the United States Military Academy. He was made brevet-colonel, brigadier-general and major-general in the Regular Army, "for faithful, meritorious and distinguished services," and afterward became a member of the Board of Engineers for Fortifications. On the 4th of May, 1867, he was appointed colonel of Engineers, and retired from active service, January 13th, 1874, since which time he has been a resident of New York City. He is the author of several important engineering, military and other works.

FEDERAL TROOPS MARCHING INTO FALMOUTH

OPERATIONS AT THE WEST AND SOUTHWEST.

Battles of Perryville, Iuka, Corinth, and the Hatchie.

We have seen that subsequent to the occupation of Corinth (Vol. I., page 2?9) General Halleck was called to Washington, and was there given the command of all the Federal forces. General Grant was thus left at the head of the Army of the Tennessee; General Buell had command of the Army of the Ohio; and General Pope commanded the Army of the Mississippi.

General Pope had pursued the Confederate army as far as Baldwin, when he was relieved by General Rosecrans and called East to take command of the Army of the Potomac, with which he fought the unsuccessful battles of the Second Bull Run and Chantilly.

Generals Grant, Sherman and Rosecrans remained at Corinth as well as in its immediate vicinity, and did not participate in any engagements worth noting until the middle of September.

General Buell was ordered, early in June, to advance upon Nashville and Chattanooga. He left Corinth on the 10th of the month, and upon reaching Huntsville appointed General Rousseau to take the command of that part of the army previously held by General O. M. Mitchell. His forces were then divided and placed in possession of Huntsville, Battle Creek and McMinnsville.

June, 1862.

General Bragg, who had succeeded Beauregard in command of the Department of the Mississippi, and had taken the greater portion of the Confederate army with him to Tupelo, Miss., immediately hurried his forces from the latter place, so as to menace Buell and invade Kentucky. General E. Kirby Smith's corps marched to and occupied Knoxville, while the corps of General William J. Hardee and Leonidas Polk took possession of Chattanooga.

After a few days' preparations, General Smith's corps moved northward, and succeeded in entering Kentucky without encountering any opposition except at a small town called Tazewell, just southeast of Cumberland Gap, where a skirmish took place on the 6th of August. The two remaining corps of Bragg's army crossed the Tennessee River at Harrison on the 21st of August, and reached Pikeville nine days later. From the last-named place Bragg sent out a heavy cavalry force, under General Forrest, against Buell's left at McMinnsville, as a feint, while the army continued its way northward.

Quite a severe engagement took place at the last-named locality (also called Little Pond), late on Saturday, the 30th of August, between Forrest's men and a portion of General T. J. Wood's division, embracing the Seventeenth and Fifty-eighth Indiana and the Twenty-sixth Ohio Regiments, with the Eighth Indiana Battery. This force, placed in charge of Colonel E. P. Fyffe, of the Twenty-sixth Ohio, succeeded in routing the Confederates, who sustained heavy losses, after quite a protracted fight. Forrest rejoined the main body without delay, and on the 5th of September Bragg's army entered Kentucky, two of General Buckner's brigades reaching Munfordsville eight days later, and compelling the surrender of Colonel J. T. Wilder's forces at that place.

Through the interception of dispatches, Buell had meanwhile learned that Louisville was Bragg's objective point, and not Nashville, as he had supposed. On the 15th of September he left Nashville, and succeeded in reaching Louisville on the 25th, ahead of Bragg's army, which had been detained by the destruction of the Salt River bridge at Bardstown.

General Nelson's force, then holding Louisville, increased Buell's army to about 100,000 men. It remained there until the 1st of the following month, when General Buell (who had meanwhile been temporarily relieved by General George H. Thomas) marched his army in three corps toward Bardstown.

October, 1862.

Bragg fell back to Springfield and directed Kirby Smith to leave Frankfort, so that they could unite their forces at Perryville (Chaplin's Hills), to which place Hardee's corps was also ordered.

Late on the 7th, General R. B. Mitchell, who led General Charles C. Gilbert's centre column, came upon the rear of Bragg's army, without, however, bringing about any engagement. In anticipation of a battle next morning, Buell ordered General Alexander McD. McCook's two divisions, under Lovell H. Rousseau and James S. Jackson (the third, under General J. W. Sill, having been sent to Harrodsburg,) to hasten along the Mackville Road, and to close up on his left, the right column of the Federal advance, under General Thomas L. Crittenden, being expected by way of Bardstown.

General Sheridan's division was posted on the heights near Doctor's Creek.

Early on the morning of the 8th, the Confederates attacked Colonel D. McCook's brigade, belonging to General Philip Sheridan's division, which Gilbert had ordered to advance to a more favorable position from the heights near Doctor's Creek.

The Eighty-fifth Illinois was in the lead, closely followed by the Second Michigan Cavalry, the Fifty-second Ohio, and the Eighty-sixth and One Hundred and Twenty-fifth Illinois Regiments, but the engagement was almost entirely confined to the cavalry until McCook's force reached the field.

The Confederates were then opening a fierce artillery fire, under cover of which they intended effecting the capture of a hill facing the centre of the Federal line, and which Buell had determined upon taking, as it commanded Chaplin's Creek, whence water could be readily obtained for the troops.

CUVIER GROVER.

McCook made a rapid disposition of his forces and, while responding to the Confederate artillery, established his line to the left of Gilbert's; William R. Terrill's brigade, of James S. Jackson's division and Colonels William H. Lytle and L. A. Harris' brigades, of Rousseau's division, opposing respectively the Confederate divisions of Polk's corps, led by Generals Benjamin F. Cheatham, S. B. Buckner and R. Anderson. The Federal brigades under Colonels Starkweather, Hall, and Webster, were held as reserves, the two latter being stationed close by the Russell House.

Shortly after noon Cheatham's division opened fiercely upon Terrill's force of raw troops both with artillery and infantry, and although the latter were repeatedly rallied by General Jackson himself, the Federals were at last driven from the field with the loss of nearly all of Captain Parson's battery. General Jackson was killed while at the head of the troops, and General Terrill received a wound from which he died the same evening.

Having practically disposed of Terrill's force, the Confederates, led by General Bragg in person, fell heavily upon Rousseau's two brigades, directing their attention more especially to Lytle's troops, which occupied the extreme right. The attack of Anderson's division was so fiercely made that the brigade was hurled back with heavy losses, and in such manner as to expose the divisions of Generals Albin Schoepf and Philip Sheridan, belonging to Gilbert's corps. Against these the Confederates charged up the hills, but unavailably. Sheridan had so well trained his guns that after a sharp but short engagement the Confederates were driven back to the bluffs through the Mackville Road by Carlin's brigade, which latter had opportunely taken position on Sheridan's right.

In the meantime, both the divisions of Cheatham and Buckner had been gaining ground toward the extreme Federal left. An attempt to flank Harris had been prevented by Starkweather's force, as well as by portions of Hall's and Webster's brigades, and a fierce conflict had been raging for nearly three hours, when the ammunition for both infantry and artillery had to be replenished.

The Federal line was drawn back a short distance from the Russell House, and the Confederates were pressing closely upon them, when reinforcements arrived under Colonel Gooding, who had been placed in command of one of R. B. Mitchell's brigades.

Gooding quickly formed his men on the extreme left, and with one of Gilbert's brigades upon his right, at once engaged in the fray. The Federals fought with great determination, though with

GEORGE W. DIETZLER.

heavy losses, and after contesting almost every inch of the ground, succeeded before dark in regaining their lost positions, with the additional aid of Wagner's brigade, which had just then reached the field.

In this last engagement the losses were especially severe. Colonel Webster had been killed, and Colonel Gooding had been taken a prisoner, after having a horse shot under him, and of the 1,423 men composing his brigade, 549 were reported killed or wounded, while the casualties in Rousseau's division were over 2,000, and the total losses for the day far exceeded 4,000 men.

The Federals rested on their arms, expecting the arrival of the remainder of Crittenden's corps, which had been delayed by skirmishes along the road, and made preparations for a renewal of the conflict the next morning.

It was then found that Bragg's army had retreated to Harrodsburg, where it was joined by from Topelo, with his army of about 12,000 men, and to offset all possible demonstrations on the part of Rosecrans in aid of Buell. A strong force of about 5,000 cavalry, led by General Armstrong, was detailed to sever the Federal communications along the Mississippi Central Railway, notably at Bolivar, Jackson, and also at Brittar's Lane. Severe engagements followed at these points, that which took place at the last-named locality, on the 1st of September, lasting nearly four hours, and resulting, like the others, in a Federal success.

When Grant realized the threatening attitude about to be assumed by the Confederates upon his several lines of communication, he notified Rosecrans to leave his station at Tuscumbia, Ala., on the Memphis and Charleston Railway, and to proceed, with part of General Daniel S. Stanley's division, toward Corinth.

Rosecrans immediately left Tuscumbia, stopped C. S. Hamilton in order to attack in the rear, while he himself would leave Corinth and accompany General E. O. C. Ord's division in the advance upon the Burnsville Road.

General Rosecrans reached Jacinto late on the 18th, and bivouacked in the midst of a severe rainstorm. The following day, he made a forced march of about twenty miles, through heavy roads, and after an active cavalry skirmish at Barnett's Corners, came, late in the afternoon, upon a strong force of the enemy, posted on a high and thickly-wooded ridge, nearly two miles from Iuka.

As Grant had directed him to make the first attack, Rosecrans arranged his troops so as to partially surround the Confederates. He gave his right wing to General Hamilton, and the left to General Stanley, keeping the centre for himself.

At about half-past four o'clock, General Hamilton formed in line of battle, after sending out his skirmishers, but found that, owing to the nature

BATTLE OF CORINTH, MISS., OCTOBER 4TH, 1862.—SCENE IN THE ROUNDABOUTS OF FORT ROBINETT AFTER THE REPULSE OF THE CONFEDERATES.

Kirby Smith's and by J. M. Wither's forces, and whence they all hurried into East Tennessee by way of Danville, Loudon and Powell's Gap, after leaving their sick and wounded, and abandoning a large quantity of provisions.

With the exception of sending one of Crittenden's divisions as far as London, without, however, bringing on any engagement, no pursuit was made by the Federals, and the Confederate army was thus allowed to carry with it an immense amount of plunder which Bragg exacted along his entire route, and which he finally decided to take to Murfreesboro', where he soon concentrated all his forces.

Buell sent the main army to Nashville, in charge of General Thomas, while he went to Louisville, where, on the 30th of the month,

OCTOBER, 1862.

he was relieved of his command. The Army of the Ohio was given the name of the Army of the Cumberland (the "Fourteenth Army Corps"), and General Rosecrans was placed at its head.

As soon as Bragg had determined upon the invasion of Kentucky, Price was ordered to follow at Iuka, where the Federals had a large amount of medical and commissary stores, and after placing Colonel R. C. Murphy in charge, with a small force taken from the Eighth Wisconsin Regiment, he advanced upon and encamped at Clear Spring (Creek), about six miles east of Corinth.

Price's army moved rapidly northward, and reached Jacinto on the 10th of September. Upon

SEPTEMBER, 1862.

learning that a body of cavalry was approaching Iuka, Murphy abandoned the latter place, and fled to Corinth, without, however, destroying the stores which had been left in his care.

Price's forces, immediately thereafter, occupied Iuka, and took possession of all the Federal property abandoned by Colonel Murphy, whom General Rosecrans ordered to be put under arrest.

Grant determined to attack Price at Iuka before he could be joined by Van Dorn's force, and without endangering the safety of Corinth he ordered Rosecrans to advance from Clear Spring upon Jacinto, with his two divisions of about twenty thousand men, under Generals D. S. Stanley and of the ground, he could bring but a single battery, that of the Eleventh Ohio, to bear effectively upon the Confederate position. The Eleventh and Twenty-sixth Missouri and the Fifth Iowa supported the battery, and stood bravely the perfect storm of shot, shell, and canister, which the Confederates hurled from their more advantageous position, until Price saw the limited support necessarily given the Federal artillery, and ordered a charge to be made upon the guns.

Under the fierce onslaught that followed from much superior numbers, the Eleventh Ohio Battery was captured; but before more than two of its six guns could be spiked, Colonel Eddy had brought up the Forty-eighth Indiana, which was closely followed by the Sixteenth Ohio, Colonel Chambers, and the Fourth Minnesota, under Captain Le Gro, and after a bayonet-charge, the guns were retaken. These were held but for a moment, however, for new troops coming up, under General Price, hurled back the Federals with great loss, and once more seized and carried away the guns, as well as a great many prisoners.

In this struggle, which ended at nightfall, and

RECAPTURE OF BATON ROUGE, LA., DECEMBER 17TH, 1862.—FEDERAL TROOPS, UND

in which Colonel Eddy was killed, and Colonel Boomer severely wounded, the total Federal loss exceeded 700 men. The Confederate loss was not large, but it included Generals Henry Little and Berry among the killed, and General Whitfield amongst those mortally wounded.

Neither Rosecrans nor Stanley could bring any of their troops to bear upon the enemy. Ord had been directed to remain with General Ross's troops, about four miles from Iuka, and to await there the sound of Rosecrans's guns, before taking part in the conflict.

The intervening hills and the direction of the wind, however, prevented the report of Hamilton's artillery from reaching him, and he remained idle until the next morning, when he marched to Iuka. There he found Rosecrans's force about commencing a pursuit of Price's army, which had fled during the night in the direction of Ripley.

Upon entering Iuka, the Federals found the six guns which had been taken from the Eleventh Ohio, as well as a large quantity of all kinds of stores and equipage. A pursuit was kept up all day by three companies of cavalry, which resulted in several light engagements with the Confederate rear-guard, and the capture of a few prisoners.

General Price's army marched twenty-seven miles to Bay Spring, thence to Baldwin, and to Ripley, where he was joined by Van Dorn, who assumed the chief command on September 28th. General Grant proceeded to Jackson, leaving General Ord at Bolivar, while General Rosecrans marched to Corinth, arriving there on the 26th.

In the uncertainty attending the early movements of the united Confederate armies, Rosecrans set about strengthening all the defenses of Corinth, especially to the northwest, under the able direction of Major Prime, General Grant's chief engineer. He likewise sent out cavalry skirmishers at all exposed points, and called in the outposts at Rienzi, Iuka and Burnsville.

It was not until early on the 3d of October that he became satisfied Corinth was the Confederates' objective point. The detachments sent along the Chewalla Road had been driven back by a heavy force, which was reported advancing toward the position held by Colonel Oliver's brigade.

October, 1862.

The troops were immediately formed in battle order, General C. S. Hamilton being given the right wing, General Thomas J. McKean the left, and General T. A. Davies the centre. Of the Confederate forces, General Mansfield Lovell's division held the right, on the northwestern side of the town, with the brigades of Generals Bowen, Rust and Villipigue; and General Price, the left, with the divisions of Generals S. Herbert and Dabney H. Maury.

Shortly before eight o'clock Lovell's force attacked Oliver's, and soon pressed it so fiercely that Generals McArthur and McKean were in turn sent to its assistance. A determined fight was maintained, but after repeated charges, in which part of Davies's force also took part, the Federals were driven from the hill with the loss of two guns, and were only again formed close by the line of inner intrenchments, protected by Forts Robinett, Williams and Phillips.

The new lines had barely been formed when a renewed, and, if possible, more determined, Confederate advance forced back the centre, under Davies, and would probably have overwhelmed it with its superior numbers but for darkness ending the conflict.

During the ensuing night both armies prepared for a renewal of hostilities by the erection of earthworks and batteries, and at daybreak of the 4th the Confederates opened upon the town from a redoubt erected opposite Fort Robinett; but its fire was soon silenced by the heavy guns which had been mounted at Fort Williams.

This was followed by an active interchange of artillery and infantry fire until about half-past nine o'clock, when masses of Confederate troops emerged from the cover of the railway and advanced in wedge-like form along the Bolivar Road toward Fort Powell. They met, close by the earthworks, with a direct as well as an enfilading fire of ball, grape, and canister, that rent hideous gaps in their serried lines; but they advanced, nevertheless, in admirable order.

General Davies's force was the first encountered by the Texan and Mississippi troops. It tried to overcome the overpowering weight directed against it on all sides, but it had to yield the ground; seeing which, General Rosecrans dashed forward, endeavoring vainly to rally the men. The Confederates pressed on the more eagerly, and in a few moments had possession of Fort Powell, the capture of which afforded them entrance to the city.

The most sanguinary and the conclusive encounter of the day, however, took place in the neighborhood of Fort Robinett. As the Confederates approached it they were met by such a terribly destructive fire from the Ohio Brigade, that they had to retire to the neighboring woods. There they were quickly re-formed, and once more advanced, to be met with an equally well-directed fire, which mowed them down by the hundreds.

As they approached the fort for the second time, Colonel William P. Rodgers, leading the Second Texas Sharpshooters, headed the attack, flag in hand, and succeeded, with his immediate followers, in crossing the ditch and in scaling the parapet; but they were met on the opposite side by a perfect storm of shot from Colonel Fuller's Ohio troops, and from Colonel Mower's Eleventh Missouri Regiment, which lay hidden until the enemy got within easy range.

A terrific hand-to-hand fight followed within the battery, during which the Confederates had for a time possession of the guns; but ere those could be trained to advantage a general charge was ordered, and the Confederates, abandoning everything, fled in confusion to the woods beyond.

The battle was now over. Van Dorn realized that, even without the reinforcements which were likely to reach Rosecrans at any moment, he could not easily conquer the Federal position, and he therefore wisely ordered his troops to retire from the field. When Rosecrans became satisfied that no renewal of the attack was contemplated, and that the Confederates were preparing to march southward, he ordered a vigorous pursuit.

At three o'clock on Sunday morning, the 5th of October, General McPherson was ordered to take three of the five regiments which he had brought the night before from Jackson, and, with five days' rations, to follow the retreating army along the Chewalla Road. Rosecrans's characteristic instructions were: "Follow close; force them to pass to the rear; compel them to form often in line of battle, and so harass and discourage them; prevent them from communicating from front to rear; give them no time to distribute subsistence; don't let them sleep."

McPherson followed the Confederates fifteen miles, and found that after crossing the Hatchee River they had burned Crown's Bridge. He rebuilt it, and followed the next day, soon reaching the village of Ripley, where he received orders to return, as Van Dorn's army had in the meantime been intercepted and badly beaten by the force under General E. O. C. Ord.

The latter, in command of his own as well as of General S. A. Hurlbut's troops, which Grant had sent on the 4th to either attack the Confederate rear or to intercept its retreat, met early on the following morning the advance of Van Dorn's force at Pocahontas. A fierce encounter followed, which resulted in the defeat of the Confederates, and compelled them to fall back across the Hatchee River, after sustaining the loss of two batteries of 6 guns each, and of about 500 men.

This engagement, called the battle of the Hatchee, necessitated a change in the plans of General Van Dorn, who had to retrace his steps and to cross at Crown's Bridge, which McPherson afterward found destroyed.

The total losses of the Federals in the engagements at Corinth and at the Hatchee exceeded 2,400 men, embracing General Hackleman among the killed, and Generals Ord and Oglesby among the severely wounded. The Confederates lost fully twice as many, including Colonel Rodgers, who died while bravely leading his troops in the attack on Fort Robinett, and whose body was tenderly cared for by the Federal commander.

On October 16th the Department of the Tennessee was organized by Grant into four districts. The first, or Memphis district, was placed in charge of General W. T. Sherman; the second, at Jackson, in charge of General S. A. Hurlbut; the third, at Corinth, in charge of General C. S. Hamilton; and the fourth, at Columbus, in charge of General T. A. Davies.

Van Dorn's army was given in command of General J. C. Pemberton, and moved to a place close by Holly Springs, Mississippi, whither it was followed by Grant's much-strengthened force, the main portion of which encamped at Lampkin's Mills, just north of Van Dorn's position on the Tallahatchie.

CAMP-LIFE AT CORINTH—ARMY HUTS ERECTED BY FEDERAL SOLDIERS.

OPERATIONS IN THE DEPARTMENTS OF THE SOUTH AND OF NORTH CAROLINA.

We have seen that, by a series of well-organized and brilliantly-executed movements on the part of the combined Federal Army and Navy, the entire Atlantic Coast, with the exception of Charleston, was, early in May, 1862, repossessed by the Union forces.

The capture of Roanoke Island had been rapidly followed by that of the islands of Jekyl, St. Simon, Greene and Skiddaway; of Forts Marion, Clinch, Macon, Jackson and St. Philip; and of the towns of Fernandina, St. Marys, Brunswick, St. Augustine, Jacksonville, Darien, Beaufort and Norfolk.

The withdrawal of the Federal forces from James Island, after the battle of Secessionville, prevented for the time any progress being made toward their effecting the much-coveted capture of Charleston. The Department of the South was, on September 16th, 1862, placed in charge of General O. M. Mitchell, and General Hunter succeeded General Sigel in the command of the Department of West Virginia.

General Mitchell's tenure was destined to be of short duration. He had planned several expeditions for the purpose of weakening, if not altogether destroying, the hold of a number of important points which the Confederates still maintained in South Carolina, and had completed his arrangements for an advance upon the line of the Charleston and Savannah Railroad, when he was attacked by yellow fever, and died from its effects on the 30th of October.

BRIDGE OVER THE TAR RIVER, IN NORTH CAROLINA, BUILT BY THE FEDERAL TROOPS.

FROM A SKETCH BY F. B. SCHELL.

A DETACHMENT OF THE FIRST SOUTH CAROLINA (COLORED) FEDERAL VOLUNTEERS, COLONEL BEARD, REPELLING AN ATTACK OF THE CONFEDERATE TROOPS IN THE VICINITY OF DOBOY RIVER, GA.

FROM A SKETCH BY COLONEL BORWERTON.

CAPTURE OF COLONEL ISAAC W. AVERY, OF SOUTH CAROLINA, BY LIEUTENANT HAMMOND, OF THE U. S. GUNBOAT "HETZEL," WHILE RALLYING HIS PANIC-STRICKEN REGIMENT.

FROM A SKETCH BY F. B. SCHELL.

General Hunter shortly after resumed command of the Department of the South, originally taken by him on the 15th of March; but in the meantime General John M. Brannan had prepared to carry out Mitchell's plans.

On the 21st of October nearly 5,000 men, belonging to the Third Rhode Island, Third and Fourth New Hampshire, Sixth and Seventh Connecticut, Forty-seventh, Fifty-fifth and Seventy-sixth Pennsylvania, Forty-eighth New York Infantry, the First New York Engineers, the First Massachusetts Cavalry, the Batteries D and M, First United States Artillery, and Battery E, Third United States Artillery, embarked on transports and gunboats at Hilton Head, and were landed on the same and the

INTERIOR OF THE UNITED STATES HOSPITAL AT HILTON HEAD, S.C.

From a Sketch by W. T. Crane

following day close by Pocotaligo and at Coosawhatchie.

The main portion of the troops proceeded toward the railway, and soon encountered Confederate pickets, who were driven back toward Pocotaligo after quite a lively skirmish. When in front of the latter place General W. S. Walker opened from the swamps a heavy infantry and artillery fire upon the Federals. It was quickly responded to, and kept up until, ammunition becoming scarce, General Brannan justly deemed it wise to order the re-embarkation of the troops.

When the remainder of Brannan's force, under Colonel Barton, had landed at Coosawhatchie, they were passed by a train of cars filled with troops, under the command of Major Harrison, and which had been sent from Savannah to General Walker's assistance. The Federals fired upon the train, killing a number of the Confederates, as well as their commander, and hurried toward the neighboring woods; but, soon meeting with a larger force well supported by artillery, and fearing, as Brannan had, the reinforcements arriving on the way from Savannah and Charleston, Colonel Barton also re-embarked his troops, and, with the rest of the expedition, returned to Hilton Head.

ARTILLERY PRACTICE.—CARRYING THE SHELL.

Several other minor engagements took place in the department during the remainder of the year, but without leading to important results.

On the 30th of January, Lieutenant Conover was engaged in reconnoitring the Stono River, on board the steamer *Isaac Smith*, and had proceeded beyond Legaréville, when the vessel was suddenly assailed by three masked shore batteries, which opened upon it a concentrated fire from heavy rifled guns. The *Isaac Smith* replied vigorously, but was soon disabled to such an extent that Conover had to surrender.

January, 1863.

ARTILLERY PRACTICE.—FIRING THE MORTAR.

The Confederates followed up their success the next day by attacking the weaker vessels of the blockading fleet off Charleston. Having found that the *Powhatan* and the *Canandaigua* had gone to Port Royal to coal, the ram *Palmetto State* left the harbor before daybreak, and, running into the *Mercedita*, made a large breach in that vessel, which, with the explosions caused by the firing of heavy rifled shells into her boilers, soon disabled her.

The ram next opened upon the *Keystone State*. The latter returned the fire, and even attempted to run down the ram; but her machinery was soon so badly injured that she was almost helpless, and would doubtless have soon been obliged to surrender but for the timely succor afforded by some of the remaining vessels of the squadron. Before the *Memphis*, *Quaker City*, *Augusta* and *Housatonic* came within range, the *Palmetto State* and another vessel, the *Chicora*, which had followed her, returned to Charleston.

It was ascertained on the 27th of February that the Confederate privateer *Nashville* had got aground while lying under the guns of Fort McAllister, on the Ogeechee River, waiting for an opportunity to go to sea. She had been watched for quite a while by Commander J. L. Worden, stationed on board the monitor *Montauk*, at the mouth of the Ogeechee, and he decided to engage her at once.

February, 1863.

He called up the gunboats *Wissahickon*, *Dawn* and *Seneca*, and, leading the way, proceeded up the river early the following morning. When within range of the *Nashville* he opened upon her with the *Montauk's* 12-inch and 15-inch guns, the heavier draft gunboats also firing at a distance. In a short time the privateer was in flames, her magazine exploded and she went to the bottom of the river. The Federal vessels returned to their anchorage, having sustained no loss from the fire of Fort McAllister.

On the 3d of the following month it was determined to attack Fort McAllister with the monitors *Passaic* (flagship), *Nahant* and *Patapsco*, and three mortar-boats. The monitors advanced to Genesis Point, as far as the obstructions would permit, and kept up an incessant fire on the fort until late in the afternoon, when they retired, and the mortar-boats threw shells at regular intervals until the following morning. It was then found that the fort had, like the monitors, suffered but little from the fire to which they had both been subjected, and that the Confederates were not likely thus to be easily driven away. Commander Drayton, therefore, withdrew his vessels, and took the *Passaic* and *Nahant* to Port Royal for repairs.

March, 1863.

While the Department of the South had thus been actively engaged, the Department of North Carolina had not remained idle.

General J. G. Foster, the successor of General Burnside, when the latter was called to McClellan's aid in July, 1862, had then with him scarcely enough men to properly withstand the Confederate attacks likely to be made upon his most exposed points. He, nevertheless, kept the enemy on the *qui vive* whenever opportunities warranted it; laying his plans for more extensive operations whenever the promised reinforcements would reach him. The necessarily small force which he had posted under Colonel Potter for the protection of the village of Washington was, early on the morning of the 6th of September, 1862, surprised by an attack of Confederate cavalry.

The horsemen invaded the place and did some little damage before the troops could be brought effectively against them. A lively and protracted street fight ensued, in which the crews of the gunboats *Pickett* and *Louisiana* proved of great assistance, and the Confederates were repulsed after

THE CONFEDERATE IRONCLAD RAM "GEORGIA."

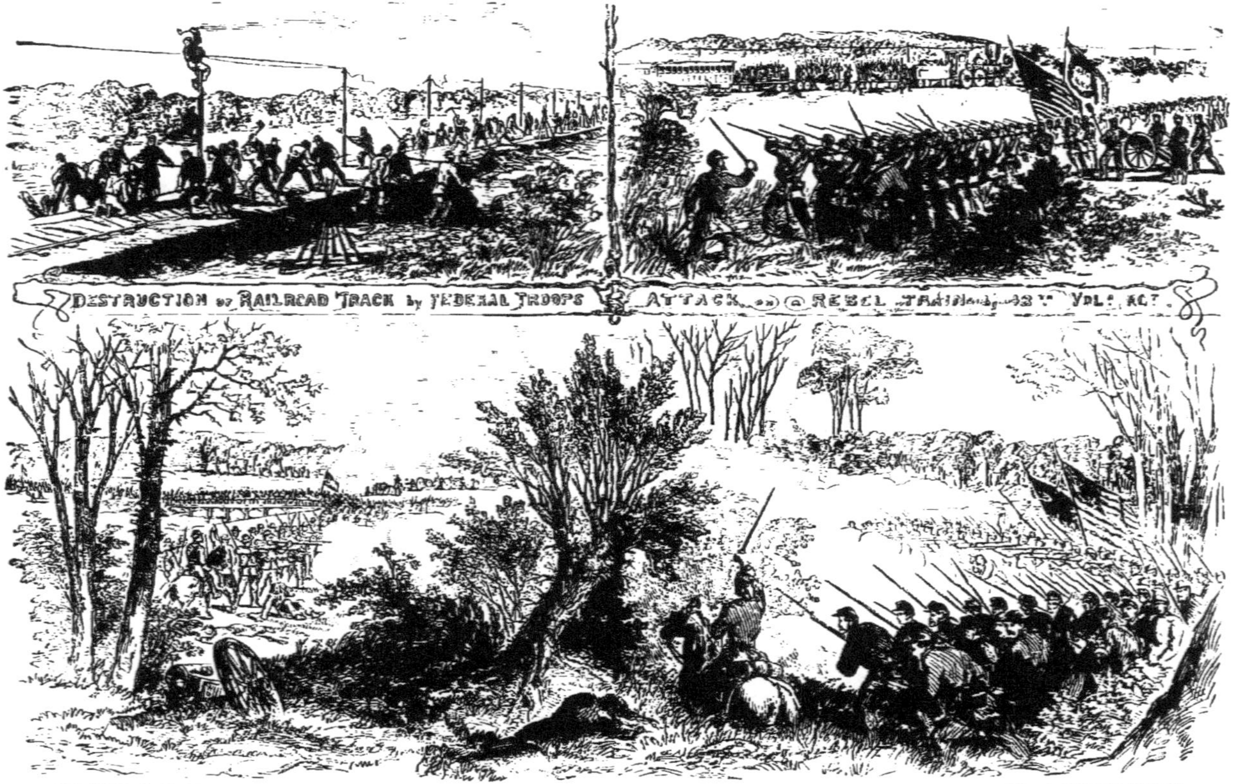

THE FEDERAL TROOPS, UNDER GENERALS BRANNAN AND TERRY, DRIVING THE CONFEDERATES, UNDER GENERAL WALKER, ACROSS THE POCOTALIGO BRIDGE, NEAR THE CHARLESTON AND SAVANNAH RAILROAD, OCTOBER 22D, 1862.—FROM A SKETCH BY W. T. CRANE.

THE CONFEDERATE STEAMER "ANGLIA," CAPTURED OFF BULL'S BAY, TWENTY-FIVE MILES FROM CHARLESTON, S. C., BY THE U. S. GUNBOATS "RESTLESS" AND "FLAG," SUNDAY, OCTOBER 19TH, 1862.

sustaining a loss of over one hundred killed and wounded.

Later on, Foster made several expeditions from New Berne to Williamston, Hamilton and Tarboro; but it was not until December that he felt strong enough for more important operations.

He had planned the destruction of railways centring at Goldsboro, and, taking with him the brigades under General Wessel and Colonels Amory, Lee, and Stevenson, as well as the Third New York Cavalry and several New York and Rhode Island batteries, he set out from New Berne on the 11th of the month.

Two days later his advance was disputed at Southwest Creek by General Evans's force of about 2,000 men, but the resistance was overcome after a charge in which

DECEMBER, 1862.

the Ninth New Jersey and the Eighty-fifth Pennsylvania Regiments took a leading part.

Upon nearing Kinston late on Saturday, the 13th, he learned that 6,000 Confederates held the place, and early the following morning he advanced toward it in two lines, opening fire upon the enemy at about half-past ten o'clock. A very active encounter followed, the Ninth New Jersey again becoming conspicuous in the attack. It fought until its ammunition gave out, and, with the Seventeenth Massachusetts, maintained its stand on a bridge which was the key to the Confederate position, although exposed to a heavy fire from the batteries fronting it.

To capture the latter, a combined flank movement was made on the right by the Twenty-third and the Forty-fifth Massachusetts Regiments, and on the left by the Third New York Cavalry, while Major Garrard advanced a large force of infantry, cavalry and artillery from the centre. This movement proved successful, and, after a three hours' fight, the Confederates were obliged to evacuate the place, having abandoned 11 pieces of artillery, besides small arms and ammunition, and lost about 300 in killed and wounded. The Federal loss was nearly equal.

The Confederates retreated toward Goldsboro, whither, on the 15th, General Foster marched his force. Toward evening a reconnoissance made by Major Garrard in the direction of Whitehall led to a brisk but short skirmish, and on the following day an engagement of nearly three hours' duration was brought about at the last-named place, the Confederates being finally driven back upon Goldsboro.

CAPTURE OF THE U. S. MAIL STEAMER "ARIEL" OFF THE EAST END OF CUBA, BY THE PRIVATEER "ALABAMA," DECEMBER 7TH, 1862.

FROM A SKETCH BY R. G. THOMAS.

Fort Moultrie. Rafts. Fort Sumter. Blockading Fleet. Cummings's Point

THE CONFEDERATES BUILDING FORTIFICATIONS ON JAMES ISLAND, S. C., UNDER DIRECTIO

FROM A SKETCH BY A. P. PALMER, OF THE TWENTY-FIRST

THE CONFEDERATES BUILDING FORTIFICATIONS ON JAMES ISLAND, S. C., UNDER DIRECTION OF GENERAL BEAUREGARD, TO REPEL THE LAND ATTACK OF THE FEDERAL TROOPS

THE CITIZENS OF CHARLESTON, S. C., DESERTING THEIR HOMES ON THE THREATENED ATTACK OF THE CITY BY THE FEDERAL FORCES.

From a Sketch by Lieutenant G. P. Kirw

General Foster still continued his march along the River Neuse, and came upon Goldsboro on the 17th. The place was held by a strong force under General Gustavus W. Smith, in addition to that which had reached it from Kinston, and, when the Federals began shelling it, quite a heavy fire was returned from several points, showing that the Confederates had strongly prepared to defend it.

By judicious and persistent shelling, however, the troops protecting the immediate approaches to the railway bridge were forced to retire. Then followed a series of Federal attacks at different points, some of the troops crossing a stream to enter thick woods which opened on the railway to the left.

The contest around the bridge was a very severe one, and, although the Confederate artillery was chiefly directed on this point, two Federals succeeded in getting close enough to it to set it afire. Lieutenant George W. Graham, belonging to the Twenty-third New York Rocket Battery, and aid to Colonel Hickman, was the first to apply the torch. In face of continued heavy firing the railway-track was then torn up, and, after destroying the rails and ties, as well as several railroad-cars, the depot and a water-station, Foster's expedition was withdrawn and encamped for the night.

The Federals reached New Berne on the 20th, having lost a total of 90 killed and 354 wounded, and captured nearly 500 prisoners.

Several other expeditions and raids followed throughout Jones, Onslow and Trent Counties, as well as in other directions, until early in March, when, after an unsuccessful attack by D. H. Hill upon some of Foster's earthworks at New Berne, the Confederate general made a demonstration against the same village of Washington where an engagement had already taken place on the 6th of September.

JOHN A. DAHLGREN.

CAPTAIN FRAZER, OF THE TWENTY-FIRST MASSACHUSETTS REGIMENT, TURNING UPON AND CAPTURING HIS GUARD WHILE BEING CONVEYED TO THE CONFEDERATE CAMP.

Leaving General Palmer in command of New Berne, Foster hastened by water to Washington, with some of his troops and with some from Suffolk, and prepared to defend the place. On the 30th of March, Hill demanded its surrender.

March, 1863.

It was refused, and from that time all communication was cut off by land as well as by water, the obstructions in the Pamlico River making it unsafe for vessels to approach.

The gunboat *Ceres*, Captain McDermott, succeeded, however, on the night of the 3d of April, in bringing ammunition and in staking the channel, although exposed to a heavy cannonading most of the way, and ten days later the steamer *Escort*, Captain Wall, also took General Palmer, Colonel McChesney and Lieutenant Hoffman, with the Fifth Rhode Island Regiment and large supplies, into the Federal position.

The *Escort* remained but one day at Washington, and during the following night once more ran the gantlet, having on board General Foster, who had decided to return to New Berne for the organization of troops to raise the siege. But before his arrangements were completed Hill had withdrawn his forces and taken them in the direction of Suffolk.

The Confederates were pursued by General Palmer, who had quite a severe engagement with them close by Kinston, near which place also several encounters were brought about, the following month, by the troops under Colonel J. Richter Jones, who died on the 23d of May from the effects of a shot received at Bachelor's Creek.

GEORGE W. DEITZLER.

Born in Pennsylvania, and settled in Kansas in the year 1855. Took an active part in the organization of the Free State Party, and paid the usual penalty for patriotism there, by being arrested for treason, a compliment which his friend, Governor C. Robinson, shared with him. For three months of the Summer of 1856 he was closely guarded by United States troops. In 1857 he was elected to the Legislature, and chosen Speaker of the House, a position which he filled with great honor and ability. When the Civil War broke out, he was very energetic in raising a regiment, and in June, 1861, was appointed by his old friend, Governor Robinson, to the command of the First Kansas Volunteers. At the battle of Wilson's Creek he led his men with distinguished gallantry, being severely wounded. Resigned from the service, August 24th, 1863.

CUVIER GROVER.

Born in Bethel, Me., July 24th, 1829 entered the United States Military Academy at West Point, and graduated therefrom in July, 1850; entered the Army as brevet-second-lieutenant of artillery and in September of the same year was promoted to be a second-lieutenant. From 1850 to 1858 he was engaged on frontier duty, in the Northern Pacific Railway exploration, and in the Utah expedition, receiving, meanwhile, the commission of first-lieutenant and of captain of the Tenth Infantry, respectively, in March, 1855, and in September, 1858. At the time of the breaking out of the Civil War, he was stationed in New Mexico, whence he came to the East in April, 1862. He was then commissioned a brigadier-general of Volunteers, and assigned to duty in the Army of the Potomac, taking an active part in the several battles of McClellan's Peninsular campaign, as well as in the second battle of Bull Run. In December, 1862, he was in command of a division of the Nineteenth Corps, which figured in the battles at Baton Rouge, Port Hudson, and elsewhere in the Department of the Gulf. In August, 1864, he was raised to the command of the Nineteenth Corps, and took part in the Shenandoah campaign, at the battles of Opequan, Fisher's Hill and Cedar Creek, being wounded at the last-named engagement. He subsequently commanded the District of Savannah, Ga., and was mustered out of the Volunteer service in August, 1865. Since the close of the Civil War, he has been engaged on frontier duty, being transferred in 1870 to the Third Cavalry as lieutenant-colonel, and becoming, five years later, the colonel of the First Regular Cavalry. His gallant conduct had meanwhile won for him the brevets of brigadier and of major-general in the Regular Army.

JOHN A. DAHLGREN.

Born in Philadelphia on the 13th of November, 1809, entered the Navy as midshipman, February 1st, 1826; becoming a passed midshipman in 1832, a lieutenant in 1837, and a commander in 1855. On the 22d of April, 1861, he became commandant of the United States Navy Yard at Washington, when Captain Franklin Buchanan resigned the post with the intention of entering the Confederate service, and it was in a great measure due to the energy and sound judgment which he then displayed that the Yard did not fall into the hands of the enemy. He was made a captain in 1862, and appointed chief of the Bureau of Ordnance. In June of the following year he was placed at the head of the South Atlantic Blockading Squadron, relieving Rear-admiral Samuel F. Dupont of that command, in the harbor of Port Royal, S. C., July 6th, 1863. In conjunction with General Gillmore, U.S.A., he at once commenced active operations, which speedily resulted in the possession of the greater part of Morris Island and the silencing of Fort Sumter, besides securing a safe anchorage for the monitors inside the bar of Charleston, and effectually putting a stop to the blockade running at that port

A FLAG OF TRUCE.

THANKSGIVING FESTIVITIES AT FORT PULASKI, GA., NOVEMBER 27TH, 1862.

From a Sketch by W. T. Crane.

He was in the meantime appointed a rear admiral, and after the fall of Charleston, in 1865, resigned his command. From 1866 to 1868 he was at the head of the South Pacific Squadron, resuming in the last-named year his former position as chief of the Bureau of Ordnance. Of this he was relieved at his own request in 1870 to take command once more of the United States Navy Yard at Washington, where he died, on the 12th of July of the same year.

He published in 1852 "System of Boat Armament, United States Navy," and "Exercise and Manœuvre for the Boat Howitzer, United States Navy," following them up with "Ordnance Memoranda" in 1853, and with "Shells and Shell Guns" three years later.

It is mainly to his labors that the Navy is indebted for the great improvement which has taken place in its ordnance since 1840. The 9-inch Dahlgren "smoothbores" are still the favorites of American seamen, and for lightness, range and accuracy combined, the Dahlgren howitzer is unsurpassed by any boat-gun in the world. His guns are of cast-iron, cast solid and cooled from the exterior, with the exception of the 15-inch and 20-inch guns, which are cast hollow and cooled from the inside. The 11-inch gun shares the popularity of the 9-inch, and, like it, is adapted exclusively for hollow projectiles, although a 10-inch naval gun for firing solid shot has also been put into service, and proven itself to be a very effective weapon.

JOHN GRAY FOSTER.

Son of Major Perley Foster, who was in active service during the War of 1812. Born at Whitefield, N. H., May 27th, 1823, whence his family removed when he was eight years of age. Entered West Point in 1842, and graduated thence, July 1st, 1846, as brevet second-lieutenant of Engineers. Was ordered to Mexico as lieutenant in the company of Sappers and Miners, and took part in all the battles fought between Vera Cruz and El Molino del Rey, receiving very severe wounds at the last-named. Was engaged in the construction of fortifications at Fort Carroll and elsewhere, and on coast-survey duty from 1848 to 1854. During the subsequent three years was assistant professor of engineering at West Point; then, until 1861, superintended the construction of engineering works at Sandy Hook, N. J., and in North Carolina, as well as the completion of Forts Sumter and Moultrie, in the harbor of Charleston. When Major Anderson abandoned Fort Moultrie, Captain Foster spiked the guns and destroyed all the Federal property that could not be carried away, and which might prove useful to the Confederates. He was present at Fort Sumter during its bombardment and at the time of its surrender. Was appointed a brigadier-general of Volunteers in October, 1861, and at the head of one of Burnside's brigades, distinguished himself at the capture of Roanoke Island, of New Berne and of Fort Macon. In July, 1862, he received the commission of major-general, and succeeded Burnside in command of the Department of North Carolina (Eighteenth Army Corps), organizing the expeditions made to Washington, Kinston, Whitehall, Goldsboro, etc. Was appointed commander of the Department of Virginia and North Carolina in July, 1863; of the Department of Ohio in December, 1863; of the Department of the South in May, 1864; and of the Department of Florida, early in 1865, being mustered out of service in September, 1866. His great engineering skill was shown subsequently in the construction of defenses for the harbors of Portsmouth, N. H., and Boston, Mass. He also wrote several important works and treatises upon Submarine Blasting. Died at Nashua, N. H., September 2d, 1874.

REMAINS OF THE CONFEDERATE PRIVATEER "NASHVILLE," IN THE OGEECHEE RIVER, NEAR FORT M'ALLISTER, GA.

From a Sketch by W. T. Crane.

NAVAL OPERATIONS IN THE GULF AND ALONG THE MISSISSIPPI.

SHORTLY after the occupation of Baton Rouge (Vol. I., page 383) Farragut continued on his way up the river, and, after temporarily occupying Natchez, on the 12th of May, 1862, and meeting with opposition only at Ellis's Cliffs, June 3d, and at Grand Gulf, June 9th, where small detachments of troops were left, he reached Vicksburg, June 26th.

The advance division of Farragut's fleet, under Commander S. P. Lee, had previously arrived before the place and demanded its surrender, but it had been contemptuously refused, both by the military governor, James L. Autry, and by L. Lindsay, mayor of the city.

Fire was immediately opened upon Vicksburg from the gun and mortar boats of Farragut's fleet, and it was kept up at intervals during the two ensuing nights and days; but it was found ineffectual in either injuring the batteries or developing their strength. It was then decided to attempt the cutting of a canal across the narrow neck of the peninsula opposite Vicksburg, in order that the transports could be taken through to the opposite bend of the Mississippi, and Farragut also determined, meanwhile, to attempt a junction with Commodore Davis's flotilla.

Shortly after three o'clock on the morning of the 28th of June all was in readiness, and the mortar-boats commenced firing upon the batteries as Farragut prepared to run them.

The fleet was composed of the steamships *Hartford*, *Brooklyn* and *Richmond*, and of the gunboats *Sciota*, *Pinola*, *Wissahickon*, *Iroquois*, *Winona*, *Oneida* and *Kennebec*. It was arranged that the vessels were to fire broadsides into the earthworks along the river and on the heights, and that the *Iroquois*, *Oneida*, and *Kennebec*, were to drop down again when they reached the bend in case the batteries were not thoroughly silenced. The batteries were, however, silenced, and all but three of the vessels went by in company with the flagship.

Farragut was met on the other side by Lieutenant-colonel C. R. Ellett, of the ram fleet, and shortly after had an interview with Commodore Davis, with whom he arranged for an expedition to reconnoitre the Yazoo River, pending the arrival of a sufficient force of troops which he had asked Halleck to send him for an immediate attack upon Vicksburg. Upon the return of the *Carondelet* and *Tyler* from their reconnoissance (Vol. I., page 373), Farragut decided to repass the Vicksburg batteries, which he did successfully on the night of the 15th of July, without being able to engage the Confederate ram *Arkansas*, then lying concealed under protection of the batteries.

An attempt to capture or destroy the *Arkansas* was made, July 22d, by the *Essex*, Captain W. D. Porter, and the ram *Queen of the West*, Colonel Alfred Ellett, but it was unsuccessful. At about this time the river commenced falling, and it was deemed best to withdraw the fleet. The bombardment and the construction of the canal were abandoned, and, acting under instructions from Washington, Farragut took his vessels to New Orleans on the 28th of July, having on the way left General Williams and his troops at Baton Rouge.

As soon as the bombardment of Vicksburg was abandoned, General John C. Breckinridge determined upon attacking Baton Rouge, and began his advance on the 26th of July. The troops were taken by the New Orleans and Jackson Railway to Tangipahoa, where the Confederate base of operations was established, and close by which place they remained until advised that the *Arkansas* and two other boats would be sufficiently repaired to co-operate on the river.

General Van Dorn finally notified Breckinridge that the vessels would arrive off Baton Rouge early on the 5th of August, and the troops were accordingly advanced. They arrived within three miles of the city shortly before midnight of the 4th.

In anticipation of an attack, General Williams had called up and posted the gunboats *Essex*,

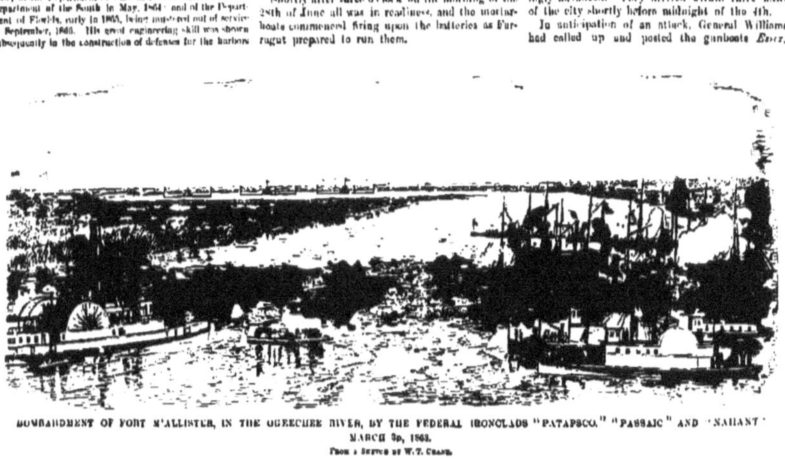

BOMBARDMENT OF FORT M'ALLISTER, IN THE OGEECHEE RIVER, BY THE FEDERAL IRONCLADS "PATAPSCO," "PASSAIC" AND "NAHANT" MARCH 3D, 1863.

From a Sketch by W. T. Crane.

DESTRUCTION OF THE PRIVATEER "NASHVILLE" BY THE MONITOR "MONTAUK," CAPTAIN J. R. WORDEN, IN THE OGEECHEE RIVER, GA., FEBRUARY 28TH, 1863.

From a Sketch by W. T. Crane.

Rinco, Sumter, Katahdin and *Cayuga* close by the river-front, and had distributed his land force as follows: The Sixth Michigan Regiment, with two guns, stood across the Clay Cut and the Cemetery Roads; the Twenty-first Indiana, with four guns, occupied the woods in the rear of Magnolia Cemetery, to the right of the Greenwell Springs Road; while behind these stood the Seventh Vermont and the Thirtieth Massachusetts, with Nim's battery occupying the extreme right. The extreme left, on Bayou Gros, was protected by the Fourth Wisconsin, with two guns of Manning's battery, the remaining four guns of this battery being held by the Ninth Connecticut Regiment in the Government Cemetery. The Fourteenth Maine stood on the left of the Greenwell Springs Road, and in the rear of the Bayou Sara Road.

Early on the morning of the 5th of August, 1862, the Confederate right wing, led by General Breckinridge himself, fell upon the Sixth Michigan, Fourteenth Maine and Twenty-first Indiana Regiments, whom they forced back after a most determined resistance, during which every inch of their respective positions was obstinately contested.

The Fourth Wisconsin and the Thirtieth Massachusetts, and later on the Seventh Vermont, were called up, with their batteries, to support the other three regiments, and for about two more hours the battle raged furiously, but the momentary weakening of the Seventh Vermont after their commanding officer, Colonel Roberts, was killed, as well as the almost entire depletion of officers, especially in the Twenty-first Indiana, which held one of the most exposed positions, enabled the Confederates to force them back once more.

Seeing this, General Williams advanced to the immediate front, and, rallying the Indiana troops, placed himself at their head, shouting, *"Boys, your field-officers are all killed! I will lead you!"* This was met with cheers along the whole line, and the troops were about advancing once more, when Williams fell, mortally wounded by a bullet passing through his heart.

After a renewed hand-to-hand conflict, Colonel F. W. Cahill, of the Ninth Connecticut, who had taken the chief command, ordered the troops to retire from the field, and left the gunboats to fire over the city upon the enemy. The shelling by the Federal vessels proved very destructive, and soon compelled the retreat of the Confederates.

JOHN G. FOSTER.

The Federal loss was 321; that of the Confederates being reported at 427, and including Brigadier-general Clarke, who was left on the field mortally wounded.

The ram *Arkansas*, then in command of Lieutenant Stevens, which was to co-operate with Breckinridge's attack, had, unfortunately for him, become unmanageable, on her way down, by reason of defects in her machinery.

Early on the morning of the 6th, Commodore Wm. D. Porter went in quest of the ram, with the *Essex, Cayuga* and *Sumter*. They found her a short distance up the river, and engaged her so fiercely that her commander finally set fire to her and abandoned her on the river-bank, where her magazine exploded and she was blown to pieces.

Ten days later the Federal land forces left Baton Rouge under the protection of some of the gunboats, and Commodore Porter began a series of reconnoissances up the river. After bombarding Bayou Sara and Natchez, in return for an attempted attack upon his force, he returned to Port Hudson, where, on the 7th of September, he had quite a sharp encounter with the shore and inland batteries.

In the meantime Farragut had ordered the bombardment of the village of Donaldsonville, at Bayou La Fourche, where the Federals had been attacked while descending the river; and he had afterward gone to Ship Island and Pensacola, the last-named place having become the depot of the Western Gulf Squadron.

Apart from the recapture of the La Fourche district (Vol. I., page 305), no engagement of any moment took place in the Department of the Gulf until toward the end of the year.

Galveston had on the 8th of October been surrendered to Commodore W. B. Renshaw, U.S.N., who on the 31st of December was still holding the place with the gunboats *Westfield* (flagship), *Harriet Lane, Owasco, Clifton, Corypheus* and *Sachem*, and the transports *Saxon* and *M. A. Boardman*, besides about 250 land troops, under Colonel Burrill, of the Forty-second Massachusetts Regiment.

JANUARY, 1863.

At about half past one o'clock on the morning of the 1st of January a large force of Confederates attacked Colonel Burrill's troops, while General J. B. Magruder, then in chief command, directed a heavy fire upon the gunboats from a battery, erected during the night, upon Pelican Island.

The small force of Federals succeeded in repulsing the attack of the storming party, and the

FEDERAL TROOPS FORAGING IN GEORGIA.

FROM A SKETCH BY GR. CRAVEN.

SIEGE OF VICKSBURG.—SHERMAN'S ATTACK ON THE CONFEDERATE WORKS MAY [illegible], 1863

BATTLE OF BAKER'S CREEK, MAY 16TH, 1863.—DEFEAT OF THE CONFEDERATE TROOPS UNDER GENERAL PEMBERTON BY THE INDIANA TROOPS UNDER GENERAL McGINNIS.

gunboats *Harriet Lane*, *Clifton*, and *Westfield*, had just silenced the guns on Pelican Island, when four Confederate steamers appeared on the scene.

Two of these vessels, the *Bayou City* and *Neptune*, made a fierce attack upon the *Harriet Lane*, but Commander J. M. Wainwright succeeded in running down the *Neptune* and in engaging the *Bayou City* just as the latter's only gun had burst at the third fire. The commander of the last-named vessel succeeded, however, in running her bow into the wheel of the *Harriet Lane*, thus rendering almost harmless the fire of her guns, and boarded her after an interchange of musketry, which drove the Federals from their guns, killing Commander Wainwright and mortally wounding Lieutenant Lee.

A hand-to-hand combat ensued until resistance seemed useless. The *Harriet Lane* was in possession of the Confederates, and the *Owasco*, which had been protecting the town, came up to engage her; but she had to retire before the heavy musketry and artillery fire directed upon her.

The *Clifton* had meanwhile gone to the assistance of the *Westfield*, which had got aground while attacking the Fort Point batteries, captured by the Confederates, and succeeded in driving back the assailants up the beach.

At about eight o'clock the Confederates raised a flag of truce [illegible] and demanded the unconditional surrender of the Federal vessels, allowing but one hour for deliberation.

FIGHTING WITH HAND-GRENADES AT THE SIEGE OF VICKSBURG

From a Sketch by F. B. Schell

After consultation with Lieutenant Law, of the *Clifton*, Commodore Renshaw decided that, as further resistance was absolutely useless in presence of the superior force arrayed against the only efficient vessel, the *Owasco*, left to them, they had better attempt to escape after destroying the flagship, which could not be got afloat. While thus deliberating, the *Harriet Lane* had been hauled alongside the wharf, and had made prisoners of Colonel Burrill's much-reduced force.

All was made ready aboard the *Westfield*; the vessel was saturated with turpentine, the safety-valve of her engine [illegible] and the powder-magazine thrown open. The crew was then transferred to the *M. A. Boardman*, and the commodore's gig stood ready to take away the officers; but as they were about entering the boat, a premature explosion took place, shattering the *Westfield* into fragments, and instantly killing Commodore Renshaw, Lieutenant Zimmerman, Engineer Green, and several others. The explosion was to be the signal for escaping across the bar, and the gunboats were soon out to sea. The Confederate vessels pursued them for a while, but did not overtake them.

Farragut immediately after sent Commodore Bell with the *Brooklyn* (flagship) and six other vessels to re-establish the blockade of Galveston. They had been there but a few days, when, late on the 11th of January, a strange craft was seen approaching the squadron from the southeast.

The *Hatteras* was ordered to proceed and ascertain her character, but had not gone far when the stranger turned and appeared making efforts to

BOMBARDMENT OF PORT HUDSO

ASSAULT OF THE SECOND LOUISIANA (COLORED) REGIMENT O

FROM A SKETCH

BOMBARDMENT OF PORT HUDSON [illegible]AL FARRAGUT'S FLEET

RETURN OF A FORAGING PARTY OF THE TWENTY-FOURTH REGIMENT, CONNECTICUT VOLUNTEERS, WITH THEIR SPOIL, TO BATON ROUGE, HAVING CAPTURED HORSES, CARTS, WAGONS, MULES, CONTRABANDS, PROVISIONS, ETC.

FROM A SKETCH BY J. H. SCHELL.

W. T. SHERMAN.

A. P. HOVEY.

escape. The *Hatteras* soon overtook and hailed her, receiving the answer: "Her Majesty's ship *Spitfire.*" Captain Blake replied that he would send a boat, but before this was done the stranger moved a little ahead and revealed herself as the privateer *Alabama*.

Her commander, Raphael Semmes, poured a tremendous broadside into the *Hatteras*, and although the latter responded, she was soon in a sinking condition, and all her officers had to surrender.

The Confederates were again successful on the 21st of the same month, when, after a short encounter with the *Uncle Ben* and *John Bell*, they overpowered and captured the two vessels *Morning Light* and *Velocity*, blockading the Sabine Pass.

While all this occurred in the Gulf, General Banks had arranged to stop the depredations which the Confederate steamer *J. A. Cotton* had long been committing along the Bayou Teche. He had advanced from Labadieville (Thibodeauxville) on the 11th of January, with the gunboats *Calhoun*, *Estrella*, *Diana* and *Kinsman*, and with the Sixth Michigan, Eighth Vermont, Twelfth Connecticut, Sixteenth and Seventy-fifth New York, and the Twenty-first Indiana Regiments of Infantry, as well as the First Louisiana Cavalry, and the First Maine, and Fourth and Sixth Massachusetts Artillery, reaching Carney's Bridge, near Pattersonville, early on the 14th.

Their progress here was stopped by several earthworks, under whose guns lay the *J. A. Cotton*. Early on the 15th, Commander McKean Buchanan opened fire from the *Calhoun*, and was joined in it by the other gunboats, while the troops were advancing on shore to engage the Confederate vessels and batteries from the rear.

The troops were not long in subjecting their enemy to a fierce enfilading musketry and artillery fire from the woods, and such was its destructive effect that the *J. A. Cotton* had finally to retire toward an upper battery at Butte La Rose, on the Atchafalaya, with the men hitherto occupying the earthworks.

The Confederates lost in the engagement 15 killed, 50 wounded and 43 prisoners; the entire Federal loss not exceeding 27 wounded and 6 killed. The latter included Commander Buchanan, who received a mortal wound in the thigh while standing on the *Calhoun*, directing the movements of the vessels in avoidance of torpedoes.

Early on the following morning the *J. A. Cotton* was seen floating down the bayou in a sheet of flame, having been set afire and abandoned by the Confederates. The troops, therefore, returned

REINFORCEMENTS FOR GRANT'S ARMY LEAVING MEMPHIS
FROM A SKETCH BY F. B. SCHELL.

BATTLE OF CHAMPION HILLS, MAY 16TH, 1863.—THE POSITION OF GENERAL PE

BATTLE OF CHAMPION HILLS, MAY 16th, [illegible] — THE POSITION OF GENERAL PEMBERTON CARRIED BY [illegible] HOVEY, LOGAN AND CROCKER OF GENERAL GRANT'S ARMY

EXTEMPORE MUSICAL AND TERPSICHOREAN ENTERTAINMENT AT THE UNITED STATES ARSENAL, BATON ROUGE, UNDER THE PATRONAGE OF THE FORTY-FIRST MASSACHUSETTS, ONE HUNDRED AND THIRTY-FIRST NEW YORK, AND THIRTY-FIFTH CONNECTICUT VOLUNTEERS.

From a Sketch by F. B. Schell.

to Brashear City; the Federal wounded having been meanwhile placed upon a raft and towed down the river.

While all this was going on, General Grant had been making rapid headway toward securing the possession of Vicksburg. Upon hearing that Pemberton had fallen back beyond Grenada, he had moved his army to Oxford, after leaving a strong force for the protection of the valuable stores at Holly Springs.

The latter place was in charge of Colonel R. C. Murphy, and, although it was enjoined upon him to make preparations against all expected attacks, he allowed his men to be surprised by a large force of Van Dorn's cavalry, early on the 20th of December. All the stores fell into the hands of the Confederates, who destroyed a great deal of valuable property and captured besides Murphy's entire force with the exception of the Second Illinois Cavalry. This regiment refused to surrender, and cut its way out of the town after a sharp encounter. Murphy accepted a parole for himself and his men, and for "his cowardly and disgraceful conduct" Grant dismissed him from the army.

Van Dorn followed the attack by so many threatening movements against Bolivar and other points of communication with Columbus and Corinth, that Grant had to fall back upon Grand Junction.

General Grant had meanwhile directed General Sherman to take the right wing of the Thirteenth Corps to the north of the Yazoo and there prepare for an attack upon Vicksburg from the north side, while taking the left wing to Jackson to operate in the Confederate rear. In compliance therewith, General Sherman left Memphis for Friar's Point, where he was joined on the 21st of December by Admiral D. D. Porter and the gunboats *Black Hawk* (flagship), *Conestoga* and *Marmora*, as well as the troops brought down from Helena. After destroying Friar's Point, they all moved down on the following day to the mouth of the White River, and on the 23d they were at Gaines's Landing, reaching Milliken's Bend on the 24th, and the mouth of the Yazoo River on the 25th.

With the later accessions from Memphis, Sherman's army comprised fully 42,000 men. These were organized into four divisions, which he placed in charge of Generals Morgan L. Smith, A. J. Smith, G. W. Morgan and Frederick Steele; and on the 26th the entire force ascended the Yazoo, with Porter's fleet in the lead.

By noon of Saturday, the 27th, the troops were landed near the mouth of Chickasaw Bayou, and reconnoissances were instituted in all directions. These led to some very important skirmishes, which served to develop the strength of the Confederates, and in one of which General L. M. Smith was so severely wounded in the hip as to be compelled to yield his command to General David Stuart.

All was made ready for a general assault on the 29th. General A. J. Smith was ordered to take his own division and part of General Stuart's, and engage the first line of rifle-pits, thus preventing a concentration upon Morgan's division, which, with the support of Steele's division, along the county road, was to carry the position on the top of the hill.

Early on the 29th the Confederate batteries opened upon General Morgan's position on the south side of the Chickasaw, and continued firing until about noon. By that time the Federals had succeeded in completing a bridge just above the Lake House, and General Frank P. Blair, Jr., was ordered by General Morgan to advance across the bayou for the purpose of assaulting the bluffs.

He crossed with great difficulty while exposed to a raking fire from the hills, and likewise succeeded in driving the Confederates from the first and second lines of rifle-pits, but failing to receive the support needed to maintain his position, exposed as it was to a destructive cross-fire of grape and canister from the upper batteries, he reluctantly ordered the troops to fall back. In this they were followed by Colonel Williamson's Fourth Iowa, the only regiment which had also crossed the bridge with General Thayer, and had likewise maintained its position on the plateau at Morgan's right against much superior numbers.

It was then found that Thayer's other regiment had been ordered to support General Morgan on the right, whither they had been followed by the other troops destined to support the left, and that the remaining divisions had not succeeded in constructing the necessary bridges, under the scathing fire to which they were exposed.

The assault on the left had been made with about 3,000 men, of which the loss was nearly 800, including Colonel J. B. Wyman, who was killed while at the head of the Thirteenth Illinois Regiment.

General Sherman soon realized that he could make no successful movement toward the enemy's position until a lodgment could be effected upon Haine's Bluff, and this was not practicable without the aid of the navy.

In the uncertainty of Grant's early co-operation Sherman arranged a plan with Admiral Porter for a combined land and naval movement on the Confederate right that would insure the substantial possession of the Yazoo River, while a strong force

SKIRMISHING IN THE WOODS ON THE ADVANCE TO VICKSBURG.

HEAD OF THE CANAL OPPOSITE VICKSB

HEAD OF THE CANAL OPPOSITE VICKSBURG, MISS., CUT BY ORDER OF GENERAL GRANT

[illegible]

THE CONFEDERATE PRIVATEER STEAMER "ALABAMA" ("290"), CAPTAIN RAPHAEL SEMMES.—From a Photograph Taken at Liverpool when she was Built.

MOUTH OF THE YAZOO RIVER, MISS., WITH THE FEDERAL FLOTILLA.
From a Sketch by Henry Lovie.

was operating directly from the bayou and holding the enemy in check until the Federals had established a firm footing.

The assault was to take place at four o'clock on the morning of the 1st, but when the expedition was about proceeding, the fog had become so thick that the vessels could not safely advance, and the expedition had necessarily to be deferred.

January, 1863.

Pemberton, meanwhile, discovered the Federal plans; and as Grant's retreat to Grand Junction became known, and would naturally prevent his early coöperation, Sherman decided to fall back to Milliken's Bend.

General John A. McClernand arrived from Cairo the next day, and took the chief command on January 4th. The army was thereafter divided into two corps; one, the Fifteenth, under the command of General Sherman; and the other, the Thirteenth, under General George W. Morgan. The latter comprised Morgan's late division, now in charge of General P. J. Osterhaus, and General A. J. Smith's division, while the Fifteenth Corps embraced the divisions led by Generals Frederick Steele and David Stuart.

Prior to the arrival of General McClernand, Sherman and Porter had matured a plan for the capture of Fort Hindman, commonly known as Arkansas Post, and located on the north bank of the Arkansas River, about 170 miles below and to the southeast of Little Rock. McClernand approved of it, and on the afternoon of the 10th a force of about 25,000 men had landed at a point about three miles below the fort.

January, 1863.

Without loss of time the gunboats opened upon the fort, and continued a fierce bombardment until dark, while the Fifteenth Corps took the advance toward the rear of the Confederate works, and was followed by the Thirteenth Corps, which took position on the extreme left. By afterward extending their lines, the Federals at nightfall completely invested Fort Hindman, both their wings resting on the river.

At one o'clock on the 11th, all was ready for the assault. The gunboats and the field-batteries opened fire upon the Confederate earthworks, and the Federals advanced at the double-quick until they had reached a thick belt of woods. There they were subjected to a severe fire, and made a temporary rest, but shortly after two o'clock Sherman's force had passed the open space in front of the fort, and was engaging the Confederates within 100 yards of their trenches.

By this time most of the Confederate guns had

GENERAL BANKS ADDRESSING THE LOUISIANA PLANTERS AT THE ST. CHARLES HOTEL, NEW ORLEANS, LA.
From a Sketch by F. H. Schell.

SURPRISE AND CAPTURE OF THE UNITED STATES STEAMER "HARRIET LANE." BY THE CO

SURPRISE AND CAPTURE OF THE UNITED STATES STEAMER "HARRIET LANE," BY THE CONFEDERATES, UNDER GENERAL MAGRUDER, AND THE DESTRUCTION OF THE FLAGSHIP "WESTFIELD," IN GALVESTON HARBOR, TEXAS, JANUARY 1st, 1863.

OFFICER PARKER, OF THE UNITED STATES GUNBOAT "ESSEX," HOISTING THE FEDERAL ENSIGN ON THE STATE CAPITOL, BATON ROUGE, ON ITS OCCUPATION BY GENERAL GROVER'S TROOPS

SCENE ON THE LEVEE, BATON ROUGE, LA.—UNLOADING MILITARY STORES FOR THE FEDERAL FORCES, FROM THE TRANSPORT "NORTH STAR," OVER THE MISSISSIPPI STEAMER "IBERVILLE."

been silenced by Porter's vessels, as well as by Captain Hoffman's Fourth Ohio Artillery, and by Barrett's and Wood's batteries, but a brisk fire of musketry was kept up along the entire fort until shortly after three o'clock, when, the troops on the Federal left having carried the rifle-pits close by the eastern side of the fort, another assault was ordered.

In a short time the deep ravine and the ditch surrounding the fort were passed, and the parapet was scaled under a murderous fire; the troops belonging to Sherman's corps taking possession of the works on the north side, while General Morgan's force was occupying those on the east. Seeing this, the Confederates displayed the white flag, and the land and naval forces soon had possession of the entire fort and all of its approaches.

The honor of planting the first flag upon the ramparts seems due to Lieutenant Philip Jenkins, of Company C, Seventy-seventh Illinois Regiment, though it was strongly denied by R. P. Wallace, of the One Hundred and Twentieth Ohio Regiment, which was the first to make the attempt upon the eastern bastions, and also led the advance of Burbridge's brigade when the latter entered the works.

The surrender was complete. It embraced 5,000 prisoners, including General T. J. Churchill, the commander of the post, Colonels Deshler, Dunnington and Garland, as well as many other officers; also 17 pieces of cannon and a very large quantity of small-arms and ammunition.

The total losses in killed and wounded were reported at 977 on the Federal side, and about 650 on the part of the Confederates.

The prisoners were sent to St. Louis, and Fort Hindman was then entirely destroyed, with all its contents, preparatory to its abandonment.

On the 13th of January an expedition of light-draft steamers, under General Gorman and Lieutenant-commanding Walker, proceeded up the White River, and, after destroying the towns of Des Arc and Duvall's Bluff, joined McClernand's force, then at Napoleon, whence all departed on the 17th for Milliken's Bend, in accordance with orders received from General Grant.

After encountering severe weather on the way, the fleet reached Young's Point on the 21st of January, and the troops were landed there the following day. General Grant himself reached the Point on the 2d of February, having been preceded there by all the divisions of the Army of the Tennessee, with the exception of the troops under General Logan, and of such as were detailed at different posts in Tennessee.

In order to successfully accomplish the capture of Vicksburg, Grant set about establishing different means of readily transporting his land and naval force below Vicksburg, so as to attack it from the south.

Not only was work resumed on the canal across the peninsula, but he also commenced the cutting of two channels from Milliken's Bend through the bayous to the Mississippi, near New Carthage, as well as through Moon Lake and the Cold Water and Tallahatchie Rivers to the Yazoo, and a third channel from a point on the Mississippi about forty-five miles above Vicksburg to Lake Providence. Work progressed actively on all until the 8th of March, when, owing to the great pressure of water, the dam across the mouth of the canal gave way, and all the works were submerged. The canal project was then abandoned.

Special attention was given to the construction of the channel leading to Lake Providence, to establish communication with General Banks's forces through both the Tensas and Black into the Red River, and thence through the Atchafalaya River, thus avoiding the Vicksburg and Port Hudson batteries. Meanwhile, important reconnoissances in force were made in different directions.

BENJAMIN H. GRIERSON.

BURNING OF THE STATE CAPITOL, BATON ROUGE, SHORTLY AFTER ITS OCCUPATION BY THE FEDERAL TROOPS.

ADMIRAL PORTER'S FLOTILLA RUNNING PAST THE BATTERIES OF VICKSBURG ON THE BLUFF

ADMIRAL PORTER'S FLOTILLA RUNNING PAST THE BATTERIES OF VICKSBURG, MISS., ON THE NIGHT OF THE 16th APRIL, 1863—CONFEDERATES BURNING BEACONS ON THE [illegible] THEIR FIRE.

CONVEYING WOUNDED SOLDIERS OF A [illegible] DOWN THE RIVER, AFTER THE BATTLE OF BAYOU TECHE.

GENERAL S. G. BURBRIDGE, ACCOMPANIED BY HIS STAFF, PLANTING THE STARS AND STRIPES ON THE CONFEDERATE FORT HINDMAN, ARKANSAS POST, ARK., JANUARY 11TH, 1863.

FROM A SKETCH BY W. R. McCOMAS.

SCENE ON THE HURRICANE-DECK OF THE "NORTH STAR"—SOLDIERS OF THE FORTY-FIRST MASSACHUSETTS WRITING HOME ON THEIR ARRIVAL OFF SHIP ISLAND.

From a Sketch by F. H. Schell.

On the day of Grant's arrival at Young's Point, the ram *Queen of the West*, Colonel C. L. Ellett, was ordered to run the Vicksburg batteries before dawn, in order to attack the steamer *City of Vicksburg* and several transports known to be supplying the Confederates both at Vicksburg and at Port Hudson.

She passed the batteries successfully, and attacked the *City of Vicksburg* by ramming her and subjecting her to the fire of her 30, 20 and 12-pounders, but she had to retire before completing her work, as the cotton bales surrounding her machinery had been set afire by the shells directed upon her from the batteries, as well as from the *City of Vicksburg*. As soon as the fire was extinguished, Colonel Ellett proceeded toward Natchez and captured three steamers—the *A. W. Baker*, *Moro* and *Berwick Bay*—loaded with provisions, after which she ran back past Vicksburg.

A few days later the *Queen of the West*, accompanied by the small steamboat *De Soto*, once more ran the batteries, with the ultimate intention of likewise passing the Port Hudson batteries and joining the fleet below under Farragut.

ADVANCE UPON PORT HUDSON.—BAGGAGE-TRAIN OF GENERAL AUGUR'S DIVISION CROSSING BAYOU MONTECINO, MARCH 13th, 1863.

From a Sketch by W. F. Schell.

ATTACK OF THE FEDERAL FORCES ON THE CONFE

ATTACK OF THE FEDERAL FORCES ON THE CONFEDERATE WORKS DURING THE SIEGE OF VICKSBURG, MAY 22, 1863

SIEGE OF VICKSBURG.—LIFE IN THE TRENCHES DURING THE INVESTMENT OF VICKSBURG BY THE ARMY UNDER GENERAL GRANT.

They anchored on the night of the 12th at the mouth of the Old River, and, leaving the *De Soto* there as a guard, the *Queen of the West* entered the Atchafalaya the following morning. After capturing a train of eleven army-wagons, as well as a large quantity of provisions, and destroying a great many dwellings on six sugar plantations, she entered the Red River, and, when just above the mouth of the Black River, captured the Confederate steamer *Era*, heavily laden with provisions.

This was followed the next day by an advance of about twenty miles, as far as Fort Taylor, in engaging which the *Queen of the West* got aground and had to be abandoned. Colonel Ellett and his crew escaped by floating down the river upon cotton bales until picked up by the *De Soto*. The latter, however, soon becoming unmanageable by reason of the unshipping of her rudder, ran into the river-bank, and had also to be abandoned for the *Era*.

By this time several steamers were in pursuit. The cargo of the *Era* was thrown overboard, to lighten her, and she was hurried to the Mississippi, which she reached the following morning. As she passed Ellis's Cliffs she came upon the United States steamer *Indianola*, which had come down from the mouth of the Yazoo and successfully run the batteries. The pursuing Confederate vessels, led by the ironclad ram *Webb*, soon appeared, but upon being pursued by the *Indianola* and *Era*, they turned back and fled.

On Tuesday, the 24th of February, the *Indianola* was attacked, when close by the mouth of the Big Black River, by the ram *Webb* and the ram *Queen of the West*, which latter had been repaired by the Confederates. The *Indianola* was soon overpowered, and, when in a sinking condition, her commander, Lieutenant Brown, was compelled to surrender.

By the 1st of the following month, another expedition was arranged, to proceed up the Yazoo for the purpose of destroying gunboats and other vessels which the Confederates were reported to be building. The land force, numbering about 5,000 men, under General L. F. Ross, and the naval force, consisting of seven gunboats, two mortar-boats, and about twenty transports, under Lieutenant-commanding Watson Smith, proceeded down the Cold Water and the Tallahatchie until it reached a point four miles north of Greenwood.

Here stood a line of cotton-bale breastworks mounting several heavy guns, which completely commanded the approach from the Tallahatchie. In front of it lay a sunken steamboat and rafts of logs to obstruct the channel.

Several attempts were made to overcome the obstructions on the 11th of March, but without success. The following day was devoted to reconnoissances and to the construction of land batteries, which, on the 13th, opened fire simultaneously with the gun and mortar-boats. It was found impracticable to land troops owing to the sloughy nature of the ground, and fire was continued all of the 13th and 14th, in order to silence the Confederate guns and enable the transports to carry up the troops, so as to land them directly on the fort itself. But whatever damage was done during the day was repaired at night by the Confederates, who, under the able management of General Tilghman, succeeded in holding the Federals at bay to such an extent as to force the abandonment of the expedition.

While on his way back, General Ross was met by General I. F. Quinby, whom Grant had sent with a detachment of General McPherson's corps, and who was to be followed by McPherson himself; but when, upon returning to Fort Pemberton, it was found that a sufficient number of troops could not be made to work effectively, the expedition was ordered to return to the Mississippi.

Another expedition, consisting of five gunboats and a number of transports, under Admiral Porter and accompanied by General Grant, entered Steele's Bayou, on the 15th of March, and turned into Black's Bayou, for an extended reconnoissance, but the passage was found to be so much obstructed by fallen and overhanging trees that the vessels made very slow progress. When near Rolling Fork, the Confederates were seen advancing, and soon opened upon the Federals, who would have been easily overcome but for the opportune sending of one of Sherman's divisions. As it was, the Federal troops had to battle their way back, and it was not until the 25th that they reached Hill's Plantation and felt they were in complete security. On the 28th, the troops were again at Young's Point.

On the 29th of March, Grant sent McClernand's Thirteenth Corps, to be followed by the Fifteenth and Seventeenth Corps, to New Carthage, by way of land on the west side of the Mississippi, and also arranged to run all of Porter's fleet by the Vicksburg batteries.

All was ready, late on the 16th of April. At ten o'clock the *Benton* took the lead, closely followed by the *Lafayette*, towing the gunboat *Price*, and the *Carondelet*, *Pittsburg*, *Louisville*, *Mound City* and *Tuscumbia*, as well as the steam-transports *Henry Clay*, *Forest Queen* and *Silver Wave*. They all passed successfully except the *Henry Clay*, which was set afire by the Confederate shells and burned to the water's edge, and the *Forest Queen*, which received so many shots that she had to be towed down the river.

The transports *Anglo-Saxon*, *Cheeseman*, *Empire City*, *Arizona*, *Moderator*, and *Tigress*, likewise ran past the batteries, six days later, with the loss only of the last named; and on the 29th of April an advance was made toward Grand Gulf. Nearly all of the batteries there were silenced, after a contest of about five hours; and the next morning the troops were landed at Bruinsburg, after all the vessels had got by Grand Gulf.

From Bruinsburg the Federals advanced in the direction of Port Gibson, very early on the morning of the 1st of May, but, when about eight miles out, the advance met a Confederate force, with which it had quite a lively skirmish. As soon as the main body came up an engagement followed, and the Confederates were gradually pressed back to Port Gibson until dark, when the troops lay on their arms for the night.

It was found on the following day that Port Gibson (Thompson's Hill) had been abandoned, and that the Confederates had retreated across the Bayou Pierre toward Vicksburg, after destroying the bridges over both forks of the bayou. They were pursued as far as Hawkinson's Ferry, where the Federals remained, awaiting the arrival of supplies, as well as of General Sherman's corps. The latter reached the Ferry on the 8th, having during the previous two days made a menacing demonstration against the Haine's Bluff batteries, in the expectation that Grant would make a simultaneous movement upon Grand Gulf. Grant had, however, in the meantime, abandoned his original plan for the more important attack upon the railway connecting Vicksburg with Jackson.

As the Federals approached, early on the 12th, they met the enemy, and had an engagement of three hours' duration, within two or three miles of Raymond. The Confederate force, which was under General Gregg consisted of about 6,000 men, and was strongly posted in the woods and

SIEGE OF VICKSBURG. — SCENE AT GENERAL LOGAN'S HEADQUARTERS, JUNE 25TH, 1863.
FROM A SKETCH BY F. B. SCHELL.

LOADING A 15-INCH GUN.

FEDERAL TROOPS IN THE [

INVESTMENT OF FORT HINDMAN, ARKANSAS POST, BY THE FEDERAL TROOPS, [
COMMANDED BY REAR-ADMIRAL PO[

LOADING A [illegible]-INCH GUN

FEDERAL TROOPS IN THE INTRENCHMENTS BEFORE VICKSBURG

NAVAL HOSPITAL, VICKSBURG

INVESTMENT OF FORT HINDMAN, ARKANSAS POST, BY THE FEDERAL TROOPS UNDER MAJOR-GENERAL M'CLERNAND, AND ITS BOMBARDMENT BY THE FEDERAL GUNBOATS COMMANDED BY REAR-ADMIRAL PORTER, JANUARY 11th, 1863.—[illegible]

SIEGE OF VICKSBURG.—CANNON DISMOUNTED INSIDE THE CONFEDERATE WORKS.
SKETCHED, WITH A GLASS, FROM THE RIFLE PITS, BY F. B. SCHELL.

along the hills near Farnden's Creek, but after repeated assaults, in which Logan's division took a leading part and suffered greatly, the Confederates were driven at the point of the bayonet from the Creek, and retreated toward Jackson.

General McPherson's force entered Clinton late on the 13th, and, after destroying part of the railway, was joined by Sherman, and pushed on toward Jackson with Crocker's division in the advance. The latter encountered the Confederate pickets when about five miles from Jackson, and were soon confronted by a strong body of the enemy under General W. H. T. Walker, but after a prolonged and fierce engagement, ending in an assault along the crest of the hill, whence the Confederate batteries had been doing much damage, the position was abandoned and General McPherson's force entered Jackson.

The Fifty-ninth Indiana at once raised the flag upon the State House; and General Grant arrived in the evening. Learning, however, that General J. E. Johnston had, on the 9th of May, taken supreme command, and that Pemberton had been ordered to leave Vicksburg and advance toward the rear of the Federals, Grant directed McPherson to fall back to Clinton while the others would march by roads converging near Bolton to Edwards's Station, after completing the destruction of the railways and all valuable property in Jackson.

On the morning of the 16th, General A. P. Hovey's division, occupying the right of McClernand's corps, encountered the Confederate pickets, but no engagement took place until about eleven o'clock, when the Indiana troops, led by General McGinnis, made a deliberate attack upon the rapidly increasing force which Pemberton had brought together at Champion Hills, or Baker's Creek.

Two batteries, which had been planted along a high ridge, were doing considerable damage, and it was finally determined to assault them. They were both taken by the Eleventh and Forty-sixth Indiana and the Twenty-ninth Wisconsin, after a fierce hand-to-hand fight, but the arrival of fresh Confederate troops and the want of reinforcements prevented their being held for any length of time. The Federals withdrew, and remained under cover of their artillery till joined by part of Quinby's late division, commanded by General M. M. Crocker.

Another advance was then ordered, and while Pemberton's right was thus engaged, Logan's division attacked his left, and succeeded in flanking and in forcing it back in such manner as to completely isolate for a while the whole of General Loring's brigade, which occupied the extreme Confederate right. The attack was so fierce that Stevenson's line became completely demoralized, yielded in turn, and by four o'clock the Confederates were in full retreat toward the Big Black River.

Just then the other divisions of McClernand's corps came upon the scene, and a pursuit was ordered by Generals Carr and Osterhaus. This lasted until dark, and resulted in the capture of many prisoners, and arms of all descriptions. The total loss in killed and wounded on both sides approximated to 4,000, including that of the Confederate general, Lloyd Tighlman, who died from the effects of a shell fired from the Chicago Mercantile Battery.

The pursuit was continued on the next day—Sunday—as far as the Big Black River Bridge, which was found well defended on both sides. Active skirmishing ensued until the Federals could be formed into line, when General Lawler, on the extreme right, discovered that, by moving a portion of his brigade under cover of the river-bank, he could get a position from which the Confederates could be successfully assaulted.

A charge was ordered, and, notwithstanding the fact that the troops had to wade through a wide ditch in front of the Confederate earthwork, the position was carried, with its seventeen guns and such of the garrison as could not get across the river. The latter, upon escaping, destroyed the bridges, and thus prevented the retreat of their comrades to the west bank.

By this time General Sherman had reached Bridgeport, and on the 18th had laid his pontoon bridge and crossed the river. The Confederates, who were thus in danger of being flanked, had meanwhile fled toward Vicksburg, and Generals McClernand and McPherson were enabled to build floating bridges, by which all their troops reached the opposite banks.

McClernand's force followed the direct road to Vicksburg, and encamped at a point slightly to the

SIEGE OF VICKSBURG.—THE TWENTY-THIRD INDIANA AND THE FORTY-FIFTH ILLINOIS REGIMENTS STORMING FORT HILL AFTER THE EXPLOSION OF THE MINE, JUNE 25TH, 1863.
FROM A SKETCH BY F. B. SCHELL.

left of Mount Albans, on the Baldwin's Ferry Road. Sherman took possession of Walnut Hills, close by the Chickasaw Bayou, and McPherson followed him as far as the fork of the Bridgeport Road, a little to the left of which his troops were halted.

Vicksburg was thus completely invested from the land side, while Porter's fleet commanded it from the river.

On the 19th, McClernand's corps occupied the hills across Two Mile Creek, and, later on, the Fourth Ohio Cavalry took possession of Haine's Bluff, which the rapid advance of Grant's army had compelled the Confederates to abandon.

Orders were given that all the corps commanders gain as close a position as possible to the Vicksburg approaches, preparatory to a general assault, which should take place at two o'clock in the afternoon. At that hour all was ready. The extreme left, resting upon the Mississippi, in immediate communication with Porter's fleet, was held by Sherman's force; the centre, by McPherson; and the extreme left by McClernand.

During the engagement that followed the two last-named only succeeded in gaining very advantageous advanced positions, but Sherman's corps, with Blair's division in the lead, actually reached the Confederate intrenchments.

The assault was made upon the work known as the Graveyard Bastion, and the forces under McPherson and under McClernand operated toward the centre and the extreme left.

With Ewing's brigade in the lead, Blair's force advanced unexposed along the crown of an interior ridge, and finally reached the crest of the hill, when they came in full sight of the Confederates. The storming party then dashed up the road at a double-quick, immediately followed by the Thirtieth Ohio Regiment, of Ewing's brigade, under cover of the concentrated fire of Barrott's, Hart's, Waterhouse's, Wood's and Spoor's batteries. This was chiefly directed upon a bastion which the Confederates had put up to command this approach.

The salient of the bastion was reached, and the storming party was about passing to the sallyport, when a perfect mass of heads suddenly arose from behind the walls, and such a destructive volley was poured into the advanced Federal lines that they necessarily recoiled. The rear pressed on, but unavailingly. The fire was so hot and so well directed that no progress was made until part of Ewing's force was shifted toward the left face of the bastion, and succeeded in crossing the ditch, that enabled it to reach, and to plant its colors upon, the exterior slope, although exposed the while to a terrible flank fire.

Giles Smith's force was then moved toward a point about three hundred yards to the left, and Kilby Smith's deployed on the off slope of one of the spurs of a neighboring hill, whence it directed a continued fire from both its infantry and artillery.

This was kept up until half-past two o'clock, when Grant received a message from McClernand, telling him that he held two of the Confederate forts, and that he desired to have Sherman and McPherson make a diversion in his favor. The fact is, that, after a fiercely contested encounter, Landram's and Lawler's brigades had first carried a redoubt in their immediate front, and that a second earthwork had shortly after been likewise taken by the brigades of Benton and Burbridge, though at a great sacrifice of life.

As soon as Grant received the message he directed Sherman to renew the assault with Tuttle's reserve division. Mower's brigade charged furiously, under cover of the artillery, and, after many a recoil, the Eleventh Missouri succeeded in planting its colors alongside those previously there; but it could make no satisfactory advance against the storm of shot and shell directed against it, and, after holding their ground till late in the afternoon, Sherman ordered the troops to fall back.

General Steele's division had made a fierce attack upon the Graveyard Bastion. He had reached it after pushing across deep ravines, and along ground still more exposed than almost any other position to the flank fire of well-posted batteries; but he found it impossible to carry the works; and retired to the cover of the hillside, where he remained until recalled at dark.

McPherson's force had been equally unfortunate in its assault upon the main fort, located near the Vicksburg and Jackson Railway. He had gained some ground after battling against great difficulties, but he had been forced back, and all progress made had to be abandoned before dark set in.

As it afterwards turned out, it would have been better had Grant and Sherman not been able to act so promptly upon McClernand's message, for it was soon followed by others informing Grant that, although the two forts were occupied, the troops had been brought to a stand by a fire from earthworks commanding his rear. McClernand's force battled as well as it could against these disadvantages, but to no avail, and, like the rest of the army, it had finally to yield all the ground it had gained.

The total loss of the Federals was put at 3,000 in killed, wounded and missing, or two-thirds more than that sustained by the Confederates.

General Grant now determined upon a regular siege of Vicksburg, and commenced from the following day steadily throwing up earthworks, erecting forts and mining his way closer and closer to the Confederate lines, under cover of his artillery, and with the steady co-operation of Porter's fleet. The latter kept up an incessant bombardment from the gun and the mortar boats, as well as from the opposite peninsula, which bombardment, as it was afterward shown, did a large amount of damage in the city.

SIEGE OF VICKSBURG.—WATERHOUSE'S BATTERY, SHERMAN'S CORPS, BEFORE THE CITY.
From a Sketch by F. B. Schell.

Port Hill and facing the northeastern section of the city held by General Shoup's Louisiana Brigade. Blair's force advanced upon it in a solid column, but was not molested until it came within thirty yards of the lines, when the reserved fire of the Confederates was opened upon them, and caused them to waver. But this was only momentarily. Rallying quickly, the ditch was crossed, though at a frightful loss of officers and men, and the outer slope was gained by the Thirteenth United States Regulars, as well as by the Eighty-third Indiana and the One Hundred and Twenty-seventh Illinois Infantry Regiments. The fire which there met the Federals was, however, so destructive, that no satisfactory progress could be made, and the troops were recalled to a position behind the hills.

The 20th and 21st of May was spent in perfecting communications, bringing up supplies and posting artillery under cover of a continued bombardment, arrangements being completed for a second assault upon Vicksburg, which Grant had ordered to take place on the 22d, with Porter's co-operation.

At ten o'clock on the morning of the last-named date all the Federal columns advanced simultaneously, and the fleet opened a furious fire of shot and shell upon the city. As at the time of the previous assault, on the 19th, Blair's second division of Sherman's corps led the attack upon Fort Hill, while Steele's division advanced to the right upon

The complete investment of Vicksburg was the better facilitated by the arrival, on the 11th of June, of General F. J. Herron's division from the Department of the Missouri, followed three days later by General J. G. Parke's two divisions of the Ninth Army Corps. These, with General C. C. Washburne's force, increased Grant's forces to about 70,000 men.

The army was thereafter subdivided as follows. General William T. Sherman's corps embraced the brigades of Frank Blair, Jr., Fred Steele, J. M. Tuttle and J. McArthur; General James B. McPherson's corps (taken by General E. O. C. Ord, June 28th), the brigades of John A. Logan and M. M. Crocker; General John A. McClernand's corps, the brigades of Eugene A. Carr, P. J. Osterhaus, A. J. Smith and A. P. Hovey; General C. C. Washburne's force, the brigades of N. Kimball, F. J. Herron, W. S. Smith and E. G. Lanman; General John G. Parke's force, the brigades of J. Walsh and R. B. Potter.

During the progress of the siege no serious engagements took place between the contending forces, with the exception of an attack on Milliken's Bend, made on the 7th of June, and in which the Confederates were repulsed after a total loss of about 600 men on both sides.

NEW YEAR'S CONTRABAND BALL AT VICKSBURG, MISS., DURING THE SIEGE. From a Sketch by F. B. Schell.

PLANTATION POLICE, OR HOME-GUARD, EXAMINING PASSES ON THE ROAD LEADING TO THE LEVEE OF THE MISSISSIPPI RIVER.

From a Sketch by F. B. Schell.

SIEGE OF VICKSBURG.—THE FIGHT IN THE CRATER OF FORT HILL, AFTER THE EXPLOSION, JUNE 27TH, 1863.

The gunboat *Cincinnati*, Lieutenant-commanding George M. Bache, while making an attempt to silence a water-battery, early on the 27th of May, received a shot in her magazine, which caused its explosion, with the loss of forty in killed, drowned and wounded. Apart from this, no casualties of any account occurred in the fleet.

The most important of Grant's mines were completed under the Fort Hill bastion, and fired on the 25th and 28th of June. As this had been somewhat anticipated, there were but few Confederates injured. On each occasion a face of the bastion was destroyed, and an unsuccessful attempt made afterward by the Federals to reach the inner works.

A prolonged hand-to-hand fight, led by the Twenty-third Indiana and the Forty-fifth Illinois Regiments, and in which the free use of hand-grenades was made, followed the explosion of the 25th, but the Confederates brought up their artillery and their lines of sharpshooters to bear so destructively upon the Federals, that the latter were compelled to abandon the attack and retire, after experiencing a heavy loss in men and officers.

As soon as Grant deemed his line of intrenchments strong enough to guard against all possibility of a sortie, he assigned to General Sherman the duty of watching the movements of General Joseph E. Johnston, who was reported to have collected a large army at Jackson for the purpose of attacking the Federal rear and of raising the siege of Vicksburg.

Preparations were subsequently made for another and more extended assault, to take place on the 6th of July, but at about half-past seven o'clock, on the morning of the 3d, a flag of truce was seen approaching the position held by General Burbridge. This was accompanied by General Bowen and Colonel Montgomery, of Pemberton's staff, who were the bearers of the following letter to General Grant:

HEADQUARTERS, VICKSBURG, July 3d, 1863.

Major-general U. S. Grant, Commanding United States Forces.

GENERAL: I have the honor to propose to you an armistice for — hours, with a view of arranging terms for the capitulation of Vicksburg. To this end, if agreeable to you, I will appoint three commissioners to meet a like number to be named by yourself, at such place and hour to-day as you may find convenient. I make this proposition to save the further effusion of blood, which must otherwise be shed to a frightful extent, feeling myself able to maintain my position for a yet indefinite period.

This communication will be handed you, under a flag of truce, by Major-general Bowen.

Very respectfully, your obedient servant,

JOHN C. PEMBERTON.

General Grant's reply was as follows:

HEADQUARTERS, DEPARTMENT OF TENNESSEE,
In the Field, near Vicksburg, July 3d, 1863.

Lieutenant-general J. C. Pemberton, Commanding Confederate Forces, etc.

GENERAL: Your note of this date, just received, proposes an armistice for several hours for the purpose of arranging terms of capitulation, through commissioners to be appointed, etc. The effusion of blood you propose stopping by this course can be ended at any time you may choose, by an unconditional surrender of the city and garrison. Men who have shown so much endurance and courage as those now in Vicksburg will always challenge the respect of an adversary, and, I can assure you, will be treated with all the respect due them as prisoners of war.

I do not favor the proposition of appointing commissioners to arrange terms of capitulation, because I have no other terms than those indicated above.

I am, general, very respectfully, your obedient servant,

U. S. GRANT,
Major-general.

At General Bowen's request, Grant appointed three o'clock as the hour for meeting General Pemberton, and, at the designated time, the latter appeared in company with General Bowen and Colonel Montgomery. General Grant stood at the meeting-place, under an oak close by a fruit orchard, about half-way between the front of the two contending forces, attended by his staff and Generals McPherson, Logan, Ord and A. J. Smith. The two commanders shook hands, and after a few moments held a private conference, whereat Grant promised to send his propositions in writing the same day.

During the afternoon the following letter was transmitted by General Logan and Colonel Wilson:

HEADQUARTERS DEPARTMENT OF THE TENNESSEE,
Near Vicksburg, July 3d, 1863.

Lieutenant-general J. C. Pemberton, Commanding Confederate Forces, Vicksburg, Miss.

GENERAL: In conformity with agreement of this afternoon, I will submit the following proposition for the surrender of the City of Vicksburg, public stores, etc. On your accepting the terms proposed, I will march in one division as a guard, and take possession at 8 P. M. to-morrow. As soon as paroles can be made out, and signed by officers and men, you will be allowed to march out of our lines—the officers taking with them their regimental clothing; and staff, field, and cavalry officers, one horse each.

The rank and file will be allowed all their clothing, but no other property. If these conditions are accepted, any amount of rations you may deem necessary can be taken from the stores you now have, and also the necessary cooking-utensils for preparing them.

Thirty wagons also, counting two two-horse or mule teams as one, will be allowed you to transport such articles as cannot be carried along. The same conditions will be allowed to all sick and wounded officers and privates as fast as they become able to travel.

SIEGE OF VICKSBURG.—GENERAL GRANT MEETS GENERAL PEMBERTON AT THE STONE HOUSE, INSIDE OF THE CONFEDERATE WORKS ON THE MORNING OF JULY 4TH, 1863.

From a Sketch by F. B. Schell.

THE FEDERAL ARMY, UNDER GENERAL GRANT

THE FEDERAL ARMY, UNDER GENERAL GRANT, TAKING FORMAL POSSESSION OF VICKSBURG, JULY 4th, 1863 AFTER THE SURRENDER

From a Sketch by [illegible]

HEADQUARTERS OF THE FEDERAL ARMY, UNDER GENERAL GRANT, ON THE BANKS OF THE MISSISSIPPI, NEAR VICKSBURG.—From a Sketch by H. Lovie.

The paroles for these latter must be signed, however, whilst officers are present authorized to sign the roll of prisoners.

I am, general, very respectfully, your obedient servant,

U. S. GRANT,
Major-general.

The following correspondence was then exchanged:

HEADQUARTERS, VICKSBURG, July 3d, 1863.

Major-general U. S. Grant, Commanding United States Forces.

GENERAL: I have the honor to acknowledge the receipt of your communication of this date, proposing terms for the surrender of this garrison and post. In the main, your terms are accepted, but in justice both to the honor and spirit of my troops, manifested in the defense of Vicksburg, I have the honor to submit the following amendments which, if acceded to by you, will perfect the agreement between us. At ten o'clock to-morrow, I propose to evacuate the works in and around Vicksburg, and to surrender the city and garrison under my command, by marching out with my colors and arms, and stacking them in front of my present lines, after which you will take possession. Officers to retain their side-arms and personal property, and the rights and property of citizens to be respected.

I am, general, yours, respectfully,

J. C. PEMBERTON,
Lieutenant-general.

HEADQUARTERS DEPARTMENT OF THE TENNESSEE,
Before Vicksburg, July 4th, 1863.

Lieutenant-general J. C. Pemberton, Commanding Forces in Vicksburg.

GENERAL: I have the honor to acknowledge your communication of 3d July. The amendments proposed by you cannot be acceded to in full. It will be necessary to furnish every officer and man with a parole, signed by himself, which, with the completion of the rolls of prisoners, will necessarily take some time. Again, I can make no stipulation in regard to the treatment of citizens and their private property.

While I do not propose to cause any of them any undue annoyance or loss, I cannot consent to leave myself under restraint by stipulations. The property which officers can be allowed to take with them will be as stated in proposition of last evening: that is, officers will be allowed their private baggage and side-arms, and mounted officers one horse each. If you mean by your proposition for each brigade to march to the front of the lines now occupied by it, and stack their arms at 10 o'clock A.M., and then return to the inside, and remain as prisoners until properly paroled, I will make no objection to it.

Should no modification be made of your acceptance of my terms by 9 o'clock A.M., I shall regard them as having been rejected, and act accordingly. White flags will be displayed along your lines, to prevent such of my troops as may not have been notified from firing upon your men.

I am, general, very respectfully, your obedient servant,

U. S. GRANT,
Major-general.

Major-general U. S. Grant, Commanding United States Forces.

GENERAL: I have the honor to acknowledge the receipt of your communication of this date, and, in reply, to say that the terms proposed by you are accepted.

Very respectfully, your obedient servant,

J. C. PEMBERTON,
Lieutenant-general.

JULY, 1863.

At ten o'clock on the morning of the 4th, the brigades began marching out of the city, and in three hours Pemberton's entire force had stacked arms in front of the works, and under guard of McPherson's corps. Vicksburg was afterwards occupied by the divisions of Generals Logan, Herron and Smith.

The surrender of Vicksburg included 27,000 officers and men, as prisoners; 128 pieces of artillery; 80 siege-guns; arms and ammunition for fully 60,000 men: besides an immense quantity of property, such as cars, railroad equipments, steamboats, cotton, etc., etc.

The total Federal losses in the engagements fought at Port Gibson, Fourteen Mile Creek, Raymond, Jackson, Champion Hills, at the Big Black River Railroad Bridge, and around Vicksburg, proved to be 9,855 in killed and wounded; the Confederates losing about the same number.

Immediately after the surrender of Vicksburg, Sherman's five divisions were strengthened by the remainder of the Thirteenth and Fifteenth Corps, and ordered in pursuit of Johnston, who, upon hearing of Pemberton's capitulation, had withdrawn his force from the Black River back to Jackson.

Johnston's four divisions, commanded by Generals Loring, Breckinridge, French and Walker, were strongly intrenched around

STEPHEN GANO BURBRIDGE.

Jackson, but Sherman did not press an attack. His artillery was brought up to the front, and several cavalry expeditions succeeded in destroying much of the neighboring railways, without bringing about anything more than active skirmishing. By the 13th of the month he had completely invested the town, both of his flanks resting on Pearl River, and late on the 16th he received a much-delayed ammunition-train, which would enable him to commence active operations.

In the meantime Johnston had removed his stores, and began evacuating Jackson, the remaining troops leaving the town during the night of the 16th, after burning the floating bridges across the Pearl River.

The city was occupied the following day; and a pursuit of Johnston's army was made as far as Brandon. Sherman caused the destruction of such valuable property as remained at Jackson, and sent expeditions everywhere to destroy all bridges, culverts, tanks, as well as all the rolling-stock that could be found on the railways. He then left a force at Jackson, and returned to the line of the Big Black River.

As a result of the fall of Vicksburg, Port Hudson was surrendered to General Banks on the 9th of July, the day Sherman's army appeared before the town of Jackson.

CHRISTOPHER COLON AUGUR.

Banks's troops had remained but a short time at Brashear City after their original expedition along the Bayou Teche. They had failed in several attempts to capture Butte La Rose, and were finally concentrated at Baton Rouge, whence reconnoissances and expeditions were made in different directions.

Shortly after the loss of the *Queen of the West*, it was arranged that Farragut's fleet should endeavor to join Porter's, and on the 13th of March the vessels were gathered at Prophet's Island, and made ready to run the Port Hudson batteries. In order to divert the attention of the Confederates, Banks sent about 12,000 men in the rear of Port Hudson, and, while a demonstration was thus being made against it, accompanied by a bombardment of the works from the gunboats *Essex* and *Sachem*, Farragut advanced toward the batteries.

The *Hartford* (flagship) took the lead, with the *Albatross* lashed to her side, and was followed by the *Richmond* with the *Genesee*, by the *Monongahela* with the *Kineo*, and by the *Mississippi* with the *Essex* and *Sachem*. Their approach was discovered by the Confederates, who, by the aid of an immense bonfire, that had long been prepared to meet just such an attempt, and which suddenly blazed up in front of the batteries, were enabled to direct a scathing fire upon the vessels.

The firing continued nearly an hour and a half. It was then found that the *Hartford*, with the *Albatross*, had alone passed the batteries. The *Richmond* had received a shot through her steam-drum, and had fallen back toward Prophet's Island, whither she was soon followed by all the other vessels, except the *Mississippi*. The whole fleet suffered terribly from the severe fire concentrated upon it, and the last-named vessel had besides run aground while abreast of the heaviest battery. Her commander, Melancthon Smith, continued firing until it was no longer possible to withstand the storm being centred upon her, when he spiked the guns, set her on fire, and escaped with the crew to the opposite shore.

As the land force was not sufficiently large to attempt the capture of Port Hudson, it was ordered back to Baton Rouge, and, on the 10th of April, it was again sent to Brashear City, and to Berwick, for renewed operations along the Atchafalaya.

Two days later, General Emory's division took the lead toward Franklin, forcing General Richard Taylor's force to fall back on Fort Bisland, near Pattersonville; the gunboats *Calhoun*, *Clifton*, *Arizona* and *Estrella*, and the transports with General Grover's division, entering Grand Lake with the view of gaining the Confederate rear.

Grover landed his force the next day about three miles west of Franklin, upon seeing which the Confederates blew up the *Queen of the West*, which had been newly refitted and strengthened. He marched along the Teche, but met no opposition until at Irish Bend. There Taylor made a vigorous stand, but had finally to abandon the position, after burning five loaded transports and a gunboat. He then fell back to New Iberia, and thence to Vermillionville, destroying the bridges after him, and closely pursued by the Federals, with whom he had a brief engagement at Bayou Vermillion.

Taylor continued his retreat toward Alexandria, on the Red River, and General Banks's force entered Opelousas, April 20th, the same day that the gunboats, under Lieutenant A. R. Cooke, succeeded, after a brief contest, in capturing Butte La Rose with all its garrison, and a large quantity of arms and ammunition.

The Federal army moved from Opelousas to Alexandria, which latter place Admiral Porter had seized, May 6th, and thence to Shreveport, close on to the Texas border, where the main pursuit was discontinued.

Through the occupation of Butte La Rose

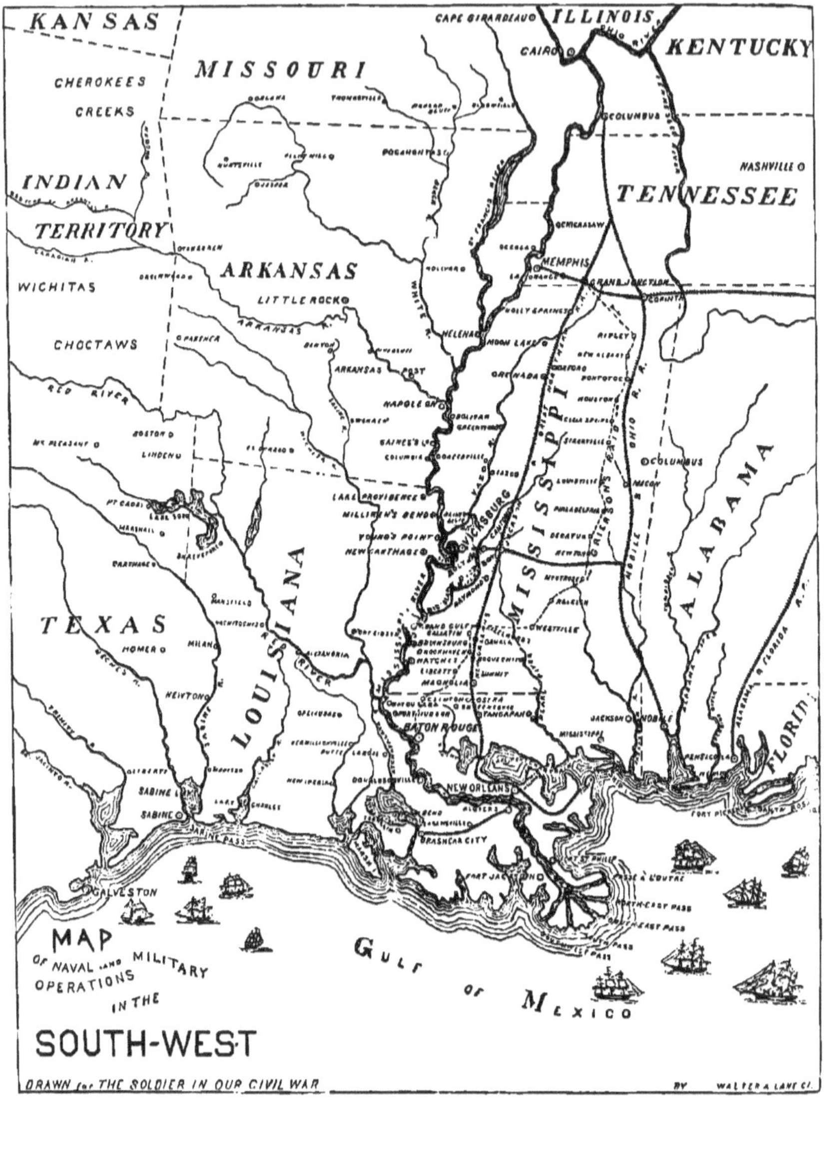

MAP
OF NAVAL AND MILITARY OPERATIONS IN THE
SOUTH-WEST

DRAWN for THE SOLDIER IN OUR CIVIL WAR BY WALTER A LANE CI.

the free navigation of the Atchafalaya was opened to the Red River, and the *Arizona* passed through it, establishing communication with Farragut's fleet, above Port Hudson, on the Mississippi, early on the 2d of May.

On that same day Colonel Benjamin H. Grierson completed one of the most important raids known in the history of the Civil War. His force, consisting of his own regiment, the Sixth Illinois Cavalry, and of the Seventh Illinois and Second Iowa Cavalry, under Colonels Loomis, Prince and Hatch, was sent from Northern Tennessee to destroy the Confederate lines of communication, and thereby assist Grant's operations against Vicksburg.

With the Sixth Illinois Cavalry in the advance, Grierson set out from the town of La Grange, Tennessee, on the 17th of April, and passed through Ripley the day following. While the main body continued on its way to the eastward of New Albany, the Second Iowa took a southeasterly direction, and crossed the Tallahatchie, on the left flank of the column, a battalion of the Seventh Illinois marching on the right flank, and crossing the river near Albany.

These different detachments succeeded in destroying a large amount of property, and encountered many bodies of Confederates, but without bringing about any engagement of moment.

Grierson's command rested for the night in the vicinity of New Albany, whence, after repelling a Confederate attack upon the Second Iowa, and making a demonstration toward King's Bridge, it proceeded to Pontotoc. A small force, occupying the latter place, was driven through the town, with the loss of all their camp equipage and of most of their provisions, and the Federals encamped on Mr. Wetherall's plantation, located about eight miles south of Pontotoc.

A feint was made in a northwardly direction, leading the enemy to believe that the expedition was upon its return, after which the Federals proceeded through the town of Houston, and reached Clear Spring on the 21st. Quite a lively engagement was brought about meanwhile at Columbus, whither Colonel Hatch was sent to destroy the line of the Mobile and Ohio Railroad. A much superior force was encountered there, and, although the Federals succeeded in accomplishing their intended work, they could not attack the town itself, as had likewise been designed, and were obliged to retire toward the main column, which was joined the following day, close by Louisville, Miss.

Other detachments had, in the interval, operated successfully at Starkville and at Macon, though exposed to considerable dangers, especially while traversing the swamps of the Okanoxubee River.

The main column passed successfully through Philadelphia, Decatur, Newton, Montrose and Raleigh, and reached Westville after destroying the bridge over the Leaf River. It then crossed the Pearl River, halting at Hazlehurst, on the line of the New Orleans, Jackson and Great Northern Railway, and proceeded thence to Gallatin, where they captured a rifled 32-pounder Parrott gun with 1,400 pounds of gunpowder, and from which place demonstrations were made against Port Gibson and Grand Gulf.

Bahala and Union Church were reached on the 28th, and at Brookhaven, on the main line of railway, the depots, cars, bridges, track, and stores, were destroyed the following day. This had likewise been done at Bahala, and was afterward repeated at Bogue Chitto and at Summit.

From the last-named place Grierson advanced upon Liberty, and made a demonstration upon the Osyka and Clinton Road. He found one regiment of Confederates posted at Wall's Bridge, and another at Edwards's Bridge. He engaged both successfully, and then pushed on the main body toward Greensburg, while a detachment was sent in the direction of Osyka.

Preparations had been made at the latter place to stop his progress, and as he approached it, Grierson unexpectedly found that a body of cavalry was so posted as to flank him, while a force of infantry should operate in his front. Realizing his danger, he ordered a charge through the infantry, which was successfully executed before the Confederate cavalry could attack him, though at the loss of a number of wounded, which included Lieutenant-colonel Blackburn, of the Seventh Illinois.

Greensburg, La., was reached, May the 1st. Thence Grierson proceeded to Clinton, crossing the Amite River during the ensuing night, and followed the Greenville Spring Road until he reached a point on the Big Sandy Creek about ten miles distant from Baton Rouge. At the Big Sandy Bridge he encountered a Confederate force, which he dispersed after destroying the camp and capturing forty-two cavalry, as well as their commander, Colonel Stewart. He then pushed on rapidly, and reached Baton Rouge, entering the city at about four o'clock, on the afternoon of the 2d of May, amid the plaudits of the people and of Banks's army.

In sixteen days Grierson's force had marched over 800 miles, captured nearly 1,000 prisoners, and destroyed property valued at over $5,000,000; sustaining a total loss of but twenty-seven men and twenty-five horses.

Shortly after the occupation of Butte La Rose,

GEORGE W. MORGAN.

THOMAS W. SHERMAN.

GODFREY WEITZEL.

Banks placed himself in communication with General Grant, and upon the latter's promise to aid him, later on, to the extent of 5,000 men, he prepared to invest Port Hudson. He placed all the troops he could on board of the transports, and sent them to Port Hudson (Hickey's Landing), while the remainder of his force was marched to Simm's Point, and across the Atchafalaya to a place opposite Bayou Sara.

On the night of the 23d of May, this force crossed the Mississippi, and on the 24th, it was closely investing Port Hudson from the north, while a body of about 3,500 men, which had advanced from Baton Rouge under Generals C. C. Augur and Thomas W. Sherman, invested it completely from the east and south.

General Godfrey Weitzel's troops occupied the extreme right, resting upon Thompson's Creek and across Foster's Creek, back of and up to the Big Sandy. Next came the forces under Generals Cuvier Grover, Halbert E. Paine, Chris. C. Augur and Thomas W. Sherman, in the order named; the extreme Federal left extending just above Prophet's Island, where stood the gunboats *Monongahela*, *Essex*, *Genesee* and *Richmond*, and several mortar boats, under Commander C. H. B. Caldwell. Farragut was stationed above Port Hudson, with the *Hartford*, *Albatross*, and a few smaller vessels.

The gun and mortar boats kept up such a steady bombardment of the works at Port Hudson that the first Confederate line had to be abandoned on the 25th. It was reported soon after that the Confederates were evacuating the place, and, as no reconnoissances had succeeded in developing the truth of the report, or even in determining the strength of the inner line of defenses, it was decided to ascertain the same by a general assault.

On the 27th of May, all the gun and mortar boats opened upon Port Hudson, and at about ten o'clock the troops, under Generals Weitzel, Grover and Paine, made a determined attack upon the Confederate left. They succeeded, after a bitter contest and three repeated charges—the last of which was not over until about four o'clock—in driving the enemy through the woods to the fortifications, and in maintaining their ground.

The Federal left was not so successful. It was nearly noon before Augur's and Sherman's troops could be got ready. They then likewise made a fierce attack upon the Confederate batteries, and drove the enemy to the interior, but had to withdraw toward night before a concentrated fire, which was ably directed against their flank.

The day closed with a decided advantage gained on the Confederate left, where Banks's batteries could be moved to a more effective position, but at a frightful loss of life. While the Confederates suffered to the extent of only 300 in killed and wounded, the Federals, through their more exposed position, experienced a total loss of fully 1,800. Among the Federal killed were Colonels Payne, Clark, Chapin and Cowles, commanding respectively the Second Louisiana, Sixth Michigan, Thirtieth Massachusetts, and One Hundred and Twenty-eighth New York Regiments. General Neal Dow was slightly wounded, but General T. W. Sherman was injured so severely that one of his legs had to be amputated.

The first assault was followed by a second one, on the 11th of June, the Federals having, in the meantime, advanced their lines through a steady bombarding, active skirmishing, and the construction of mines in different directions. At three o'clock on the morning of the last-named date, the troops moved upon the works, and succeeded in cutting through the abatis and in reaching the parapets; but, in attempting to scale the latter, they were repulsed by the terrible fire directed against them, and had to fall back after losing a great many in killed, wounded and prisoners.

A third assault was made at dawn of the 14th of June, after the refusal of General Frank K. Gardner to accept Banks's demand for an unconditional surrender.

It was originally intended to make a simultaneous attack by Weitzel's, Grover's and Paine's divisions, but the obstructions to be overcome were such that the plan was abandoned, and the troops were finally so disposed as to enable Grover and Weitzel to attack on the extreme Confederate left, while Augur's and Dwight's forces would operate on their extreme right.

In the Federal advance was placed a strong force of sharpshooters, fully supplied with five-pound hand-grenades, which it was intended to throw over the parapets, and the Twenty-fourth Connecticut was, besides, detailed to carry bags filled with cotton, which were to be thrown into the ditch to insure the more ready passage of the storming party.

The troops advanced in the face of a scathing fire of shot and shell, and reached the ditch, but they could go no further, as the Confederates were then enabled to enfilade their ranks to such a frightful extent, that, after repeated charges, they had to fall back along the entire line. Nor did the hand-grenades serve their purpose. In many instances they were caught up by the Confederates, and by them hurled back upon the assailants, thus, as it was afterward shown, actually doing most damage to the Federals.

At eleven o'clock the firing had ceased, except on the part of the gunboats, which continued their steady bombardment of the most important works.

The troops, under Generals Grover, Weitzel, Paine, and Dwight, had succeeded in improving their respective positions in closer proximity to the Confederate breastworks, but this had been once more achieved at the expense of about 700 men, mostly taken from the division of General P[illegible], who himself lost a leg in the engagement.

The siege went on, and, by means of mining, the Federal lines were brought so close as to pr[illegible] an early surrender, when, on the 7th of July, [illegible] of Vicksburg's surrender reached the contending armies.

At midnight General Gardner sent, by flag of truce, a note to General Banks, asking if the report was correct, and received the following in return:

HEADQUARTERS, DEPARTMENT OF THE GULF,
Before Port Hudson, July 8th, 1863.

To Major-general Frank Gardner, Commanding C. S. Forces, Port Hudson.

GENERAL: In reply to your communication, dated the 7th instant, by flag of truce, received a few moments since, I have the honor to inform you that I received yesterday morning, July 7th, at 10:45, by the gunboat *General Price*, an official despatch from Major-general Ulysses S. Grant, United States Army, whereof the following is a true extract:

"HEADQUARTERS, DEPARTMENT OF THE TENNESSEE,
"Near Vicksburg, July 4th, 1863.

"*Major-general N. P. Banks, Commanding Department of the Gulf.*

"GENERAL: The garrison of Vicksburg surrendered this morning. The number of prisoners, as given by the officer, is [illegible] field artillery, [illegible] pieces; and a large number of siege-guns, probably not less than eighty. Your obedient servant,
"U. S. GRANT, Major-general."

LAKE PROVIDENCE, LA., HEADQUARTERS OF GENERAL McPHERSON.
FROM A SKETCH BY F. B. SCHELL.

I regret to say that, under present circumstances, I cannot consistently with my duty consent to a cessation of hostilities for the purpose you indicate.

Very respectfully, your obedient servant,

N. P. BANKS.

General Gardner thereupon called a council, at which were present General Beale, Colonels Lyle, Miles, Shelby and Steedman, and Lieutenant-colonel M. J. Smith. It was agreed to appoint joint commissioners to arrange terms for the surrender, and, after consultation with General Charles P. Stone, Colonel H. W. Birge and Lieutenant-colonel R. B. Irwin, the capitulation was completed early on the 9th of July.

JULY, 1863.

General George L. Andrews received the unconditional surrender of General Gardner, with his 445 officers and 6,408 men. Port Hudson was immediately occupied by the land forces, and the fleet anchored off the city. With it, the Federals became possessed of 51 pieces of artillery, about 5,000 stand of arms, 150,000 rounds of ammunition, 1,800 pounds of cannon-powder, besides two steamers, and much other valuable property.

The total loss of the Federals during the forty-five days' siege was about 2,500; the Confederates losing, during the same period, not more than 800 in killed and wounded.

ISRAEL B. RICHARDSON.

BORN at Burlington, Vt., in 1815; entered the United States Military Academy at West Point, whence he graduated in 1841, and was appointed a second-lieutenant in the Third Infantry; served in Florida and on frontier duty until the breaking out of the Mexican War. He took part in the battles of Palo Alto, Resaca de la Palma, Monterey, and in nearly all the engagements led by General Scott from the siege of Vera Cruz to the fall of the City of Mexico, receiving the brevets of captain and of major for gallant and meritorious conduct at Contreras, Churubusco and Chapultepec. In March, 1851, he was promoted to a captaincy, and remained on frontier duty until 1855, when he resigned from the army and retired to private life in Michigan. Upon the breaking out of the Civil War he offered his services to the Government, and was made colonel of the Second Michigan Volunteer Regiment, which he had helped to organize, and which he accompanied to Washington. On the 17th of May, 1861, he was appointed a brigadier-general of Volunteers, and given a brigade at the first Bull Run. At the battle of the Chickahominy he commanded one of Sumner's divisions, and greatly distinguished himself, receiving the commission of major-general, July 4th, 1862. He subsequently took part in the battles fought at South Mountain and at Antietam (Sharpsburg), receiving at the last-named the wounds which caused his death on the 3d of November, 1862.

BENJAMIN H. GRIERSON.

BORN in July, 1827, at Pittsburg, Pa., whence he removed at an early age to Ohio, and subsequently to Illinois. Upon the breaking out of the Civil War he tendered his services to the United States Government, and was given a position on the staff of General B. M. Prentiss, being afterward commissioned major and colonel of the Sixth Illinois Cavalry. With the latter he was, on the 16th day of April, 1863, given the Seventh Illinois and the Second Iowa Cavalry, and ordered to sever all possible communications of the Confederates, in order to facilitate Grant's operations against Vicksburg. He left La Grange, Tenn., on the last-named date, and entered Baton Rouge, La., on the 2d of May, having meanwhile with but small loss defeated the Confederates in several engagements, destroying much valuable railway and other property, and raided more than eight hundred miles of country. This expedition was followed by others throughout the Western section, until 1865, when, having been commissioned a major-general of Volunteers, in recognition of his valuable services, he was given an important command against Mobile, Ala. In June, 1866, he received the colonelcy of the Tenth United States Cavalry, which position he still holds at the time of writing.

THOMAS LEONIDAS CRITTENDEN.

GEORGE W. MORGAN.

BORN in Washington County, Pa., September 20th, 1820; at the age of sixteen joined the Texan Army for Independence, wherein he was given the commission of captain; entered the United States Military Academy at West Point in 1841, but retired therefrom without graduating, and settled at Mount Vernon, O., where he commenced the practice of law in 1843. He tendered his services to the Government upon the breaking out of the Mexican War, and served throughout the latter successively as colonel of the Second Ohio Volunteers and of the Fifteenth United States Infantry, being severely wounded at Churubusco, and receiving the brevet of brigadier-general for "gallant and meritorious services both at the last-named battle and at Contreras." Was appointed United States Consul to Marseilles in 1855, and continued as such until 1858, when he was made United States Minister to Portugal. He renewed his offer of service to the Government at the time of the Civil War, and commanded divisions in the Army of the Ohio and in the Army of the Tennessee, taking an active part in the assaults along Chickasaw Bayou, Vicksburg, Miss., and upon Fort Hindman, Arkansas Post, Ark. In June, 1863, he was compelled to relinquish his command by reason of ill health. He has since given much of his attention to politics, being in 1865 the unsuccessful Democratic candidate for Governor of Ohio, and serving two successive terms as a member of the United States House of Representatives at Washington.

THOMAS LEONIDAS CRITTENDEN.

SON of the well-known United States Senator, John Gordon Crittenden; born at Russellville, Ky., in 1819; served with distinction in the Mexican War, being especially commended for his services while acting as volunteer aid to General Taylor at the battle of Buena Vista, and as a lieutenant-colonel of the Third Kentucky Infantry in the latter part of the year 1847. He afterward received the appointment of United States Consul at Liverpool, England; and upon the breaking out of the Civil War tendered his services to the Federal Government. He received the commission of brigadier-general of Volunteers on the 27th of September, 1861, and took part in several engagements at the West and Southwest, being given command of Buell's Fifth Division at the battle of Shiloh, or Pittsburg Landing, and the command of Buell's Second Corps in October, 1862. He served with distinction at the battles of Stone River, Chattanooga and Chickamauga, and by Court of Inquiry was found innocent of the charges of negligence, which some fellow-officers had raised against him after the retreat of the Federals from the last-named place. He retired from the Army on the 10th of May, 1881, after having been appointed colonel of the Thirty-second Regiment of Infantry on the 28th of July, 1866, and being transferred to the Seventeenth Regular Infantry on March 15th, 1869.

DAVID DIXON PORTER.

BORN in Pennsylvania, June 8th, 1813; entered the Navy as midshipman aboard the *Constellation* in 1829, and passed his examination in 1835, after which he served six years in the Coast Survey. He was commissioned a lieutenant in 1841, and served four years, with that rank, on board the frigate *Congress*. Was afterward placed on duty under Commodore Tatnall in the Mexican Gulf, and took an active part in the naval operations connected with the War with Mexico. Upon the breaking out of the Civil War, he was given the command of the *Powhatan*, and sent to the relief of Fort Pickens, Florida. This duty accomplished, he set about fitting out a mortar flotilla for the reduction of Forts Jackson and St. Philip, guarding the approaches to New Orleans; and, after the fall of the latter city, proceeded up the Mississippi and took part in a number of engagements. Late in 1862, he was placed in command of all the naval forces on the Western rivers above New Orleans, with the rank of rear-admiral, his squadron being held distinct from the Western Gulf Blockading Squadron under Admiral Farragut. In 1864 he was transferred to the Atlantic coast, to command the naval forces destined to operate against the defenses of Wilmington, N. C., and effected the capture of Fort Fisher on the 15th of January, 1865. In 1866 he was made vice-admiral, and appointed superintendent of the Naval Academy at Annapolis; and four years later, upon the death of Admiral Farragut, he succeeded that illustrious man as the Admiral of the United States Navy.

DAVID DIXON PORTER.

WILLIAM STARKE ROSECRANS.

BORN in Berkshire, Delaware County, O., September 6th, 1819; entered the United States Military Academy at West Point in July, 1838; graduated therefrom, four years later, as third and fifth in a list of fifty-six, including such men as John Pope, James Longstreet, Earl Van Dorn, Abner Doubleday, Lafayette McLaws, George Sykes, Daniel H. Hill, and others, who afterward became generals in the Federal and in the Confederate service. On the 1st of July 1842, he received the commission of brevet-second-lieutenant in the Corps of Engineers, and was sent on duty at Fortress Monroe, after which he became in turn an assistant professor of the science of engineering, of natural and experimental philosophy, and of practical engineering, at West Point. Leaving the Academy in 1847, he went successively to Newport, R. I., New Bedford, Mass., and Providence, R. I., where he was mainly engaged in the construction of fortifications and of the surveys of harbors until 1853, when he was ordered to the Washington Navy Yard. He remained one year at the latter post, and then resigned from the Army with the intention of establishing himself at Cincinnati, O., as a civil engineer and architect. From 1855 to 1857 he was president of a coal company in Virginia, and likewise engaged in the manufacture of oils at the West. When the Civil War broke out, he abandoned his business and tendered his services to the United States Government. He became a volunteer aid to General McClellan, when the latter was at the head of the Department of the Ohio, and was greatly instrumental in the organization of the troops sent from that State. He was appointed Chief Engineer of Ohio, June 9th, and on the 10th was made colonel of the Twenty-third Regiment of Ohio Volunteers. Four days later he was commissioned a brigadier-general, and placed at the head of a force embracing the Eighth and Tenth Indiana and the Seventeenth and Nineteenth Ohio Regiments. With these he fought the battle of Rich Mountain, on the 11th of July, 1861. Ten days later he succeeded to the command of the Department of the Ohio, and in the ensuing September became commander of the Department of West Virginia. In March, 1862, he was appointed a major-general, and during the following month of May was relieved by General Fremont. He was then assigned to the command of a division of the Army of the Mississippi at the siege of Corinth, and he succeeded to the command of that army when Pope was transferred to Virginia. He fought the battle of Iuka, September 19th, and the battle of Corinth, October 4th, 1862, and on the 27th of the last-named month assumed command of the "Fourteenth Army Corps," otherwise known as the Army of the Cumberland. From the 31st of December, 1862, to the 3d of January, 1863, occurred the battle of Murfreesboro', or Stone River, Tenn., wherein Rosecrans forced the retirement of Bragg's army to Shelbyville and Tullahoma. He subsequently advanced upon the latter place, then occupied Bridgeport and Stevenson, in July, and, after crossing the Cumberland Mountains, fought unsuccessfully against Bragg at Chickamauga, on Septembe-

FEDERAL GUNBOATS AND IRONCLADS, UNDER ADMIRAL PORTER, S

FEDERAL GUNBOATS AND IRONCLADS UNDER ADMIRAL [illegible] SILENCING THE CONFEDERATE WORKS AT GRAND [illegible], MISS. [illegible], 1863

[illegible]

ARRIVAL AT CHICKASAW BAYOU OF THE SLAVES OF PRESIDENT DAVIS FROM HIS MISSISSIPPI PLANTATION.

FROM A SKETCH BY F. B. SCHELL

19th-20th, 1863. He was relieved from command by General Thomas, October 30th, 1863; but, on the 24th of January, 1864, he was restored to duty, and ordered to relieve General Schofield, at the head of the Department of the Missouri. He succeeded in repelling Price's contemplated invasion of the State, and in practically destroying the treasonable organizations known as the Order of the American Knights, of the Knights of the Golden Circle, and of the Sons of Liberty, all of which intended co-operating with the Confederates. In 1866 Rosecrans was mustered from the Volunteer service, and in 1867 he resigned a second time from the Army. President Johnson appointed him Minister to Mexico, 1868-69, and he afterward became a resident of San Rafael, Cal., where, with the exception of occasional trips to Mexico, 1871-73, he remained up to the time of his election to Congress in 1880. He was re-elected a Representative of the State of California in 1882, and has succeeded, at the head of several important committees, notably that on Military Affairs, in materially advancing the interests of the Volunteer forces, and in achieving a large share of well-deserved popularity.

THOMAS W. SHERMAN.

Born at Newport, March 26th, 1813; entered the United States Military Academy at West Point in 1832, and graduated therefrom in July, 1836, being commissioned a second-lieutenant in the Third Artillery; appointed assistant commissary of subsistence in 1837; on frontier duty, and employed in recruiting as well as in garrison, until 1846. Served during the Mexican War, and especially distinguished himself at Buena Vista, receiving afterward the brevet of major. From 1848 until the breaking out of the Civil War he was again engaged in garrison and on the frontier. In April, 1861, he was assigned to the duty of guarding the lines of railway communication with Washington, being made a lieutenant-colonel on the 14th of May, and a brigadier-general of Volunteers on the 17th of the same month. He was placed at the head of the land forces of the Port Royal Expedition in October, 1861, and remained in South Carolina until the end of March, 1862, when he was assigned to the Army of the Tennessee, in which he commanded a division during the Corinth campaign. He was then transferred to the Department of the Gulf, and again commanded a division in the vicinity of New Orleans until May, 1863, when he joined the expedition against Port Hudson. During the investment and attacks upon the latter place he was at the head of the Second Division of the Nineteenth Corps, which formed the left wing of the Federal army, and in the attack of the 27th of May he lost a leg while leading the assaulting column. He was commissioned colonel of artillery, June 1st, 1863, and after his return to duty in February, 1864, held various commands in Louisiana until April 30th, 1866, when he was mustered out of the Volunteer service. He retired from active duty with the rank of major-general on the 31st of December, 1870, and died at Newport, R. I., on the 16th of March, 1879.

CHRISTOPHER COLON AUGUR.

Born in New York, 1821; entered the United States Military Academy at West Point in 1839, and graduated in 1843; breveted second-lieutenant of Infantry, July 1st of the last-named year. He served mainly at frontier posts; took part in the military occupation of Texas, 1845–46; in the War with Mexico, 1846–48; and the scouting expeditions against the Northern Pacific Indians, 1855–56. In February, 1847, he was made a first-lieutenant, and in August, 1852, was promoted to a captaincy for distinguished and meritorious services. He was commandant of Cadets at West Point in 1861, and on the 14th of May of that year was given the commission of major, which was followed by that of brigadier-general on the 12th of the coming November, and by that of major-general of Volunteers on the 9th of August, 1862. He took part in the operations along the Rappahannock and in the Shenandoah, was placed in command of a division in the Fifth Corps, and especially distinguished himself at the battle of Cedar Run, or Cedar Mountain, where he was severely wounded. He was soon after given the rank of colonel in the Regular Army, in addition to the promotion in the Volunteer service already referred to, and joined the expedition of General Banks to New Orleans, being afterward placed in command of the district of Baton Rouge, and taking part in the expedition to Port Hudson. He commanded the Department of Washington, 1863-66, and the Department of the Platte, 1867-71, having in the meantime received the brevets of brigadier-general and of major-general in the Regular Army. He has since the last-named year been at the head of the Departments of Texas and of the Missouri, and at the time of writing (1884) holds the latter appointment, with headquarters at Fort Leavenworth, Kan.

GODFREY WEITZEL.

Born in Cincinnati, O., November 1st, 1835, and when sixteen years of age was transferred from the High School of Ohio to the United States Military Academy at West Point. In June, 1855, he graduated second in his Class of thirty-four members, and entered the Regular Army, joining the Engineer Corps as a brevet-second-lieutenant. Shortly after he was engaged in the completion of Fort St. Philip, New Orleans. He subsequently became assistant professor of civil and military engineering at West Point, and on the 1st of July, 1860, was promoted to first-lieutenant.

When the "Butler Expedition" to New Orleans was organized, the commander applied for the services of Lieutenant Weitzel as chief engineer on his staff, and the application was immediately complied with by the appointment of that officer to the specified position. He sailed with General Butler to Ship Island, the rendezvous of the expedition, and after the defenses of New Orleans had been reduced—the land forces operating in the rear of Fort St. Philip being led by Lieutenant Godfrey Weitzel—that officer advanced with the army for the occupation of the city, which was immediately placed under martial law, with Lieutenant Weitzel as assistant military commander. When the office of Mayor was suspended, he was appointed to act in that capacity. On the 29th of August, 1862, he was commissioned a brigadier-general of Volunteers, and when apprised of this appointment requested to be relieved as soon as possible from the duties appertaining to the offices of acting Mayor and assistant military commandant. His request was complied with during the following October, when he took the field at the head of the "Reserve Brigade," which consisted of a force numbering about five thousand men, organized under his personal supervision in a camp north of the city.

With these troops General Weitzel started for Donaldsonville, La., and soon took military possession of the place. He then moved on to Napoleonville, and cleared the enemy from the La Fourche district, which he remained in possession of until April, 1863. He then joined his force to that besieging Port Hudson, and was placed in command of the right wing up to the time of the surrender on July 8th, 1863.

The Port Hudson campaign ended, General Weitzel was next placed in command on the western shore of the Mississippi River, for the purpose of clearing the enemy from the plantations within that part of the Department of the Gulf, and took part in the Sabine Pass expedition during September, 1863. He was then transferred to the Atchafalaya region, and succeeded in restoring Brashear City to Federal rule, it having been retaken by the enemy during the interval when the troops were fully employed in the vicinity of Port Hudson. After having performed other duties of merit in the Department of the Gulf, General Weitzel was recalled to the North and assigned to the command of a division of the Eighteenth Corps, with which he participated in the strategic operations by which a lodging was effected on the south side of the James River. He also led the advance of the troops engaged in the destruction of the railroad connections with Richmond, and participated in the contest near Swift Creek, May 9th, 1864, and in the subsequent attack upon Fort Darling. He was afterward relieved of his infantry command and assigned to duty as chief engineer on the staff of General Butler, the commander of the Department of Virginia. He continued to employ himself with this duty until about the beginning of August, 1864, when, in consequence of ill health, he had to be temporarily relieved in order to regain his strength. He, however, soon returned to his post, and in September was breveted major-general of Volunteers for distinguished services in the Department of Virginia. He was shortly after appointed as chief of staff to General Butler, but continued to act as chief engineer of the united Departments of Virginia and North Carolina, as also of the Army of the James.

During September, 1864, General Weitzel was temporarily placed in command of the Eighteenth Corps, but being relieved by General Ord, resumed his position on the staff. During November he was regularly appointed to that command, with the full rank of major-general of Volunteers, to date from November 17th, 1864. Upon the consolidation of the Tenth and Eighteenth Corps as the Twenty-fourth, General Weitzel was detached to conduct the expedition against Fort Fisher during December, 1864; but in this instance his knowledge of the science of engineering led him astray, and he gave it as his opinion that the works were unassailable. He was afterward in command of the Twenty-fifth Army Corps, which was composed entirely of the colored troops of the old Tenth and Eighteenth Corps, known for a time as the Army of the James. General Weitzel earned particular distinction as an officer of the Union Army as the leader of the Union troops into Richmond at the seizure of that city on the 3d of April, 1865. His valor as a soldier earned him quick promotion.

His line of advancement in the Volunteer service, in chronological order, was: Brigadier-general, August 29th, 1862; brevet-major-general, August 26th, 1864; major-general, November 17th, 1864. In the Regular Army he was breveted second-lieutenant of engineers, July 1st, 1855; made second-lieutenant, July 27th, 1856; first-lieutenant, July 1st, 1860; captain, March 3d, 1863; major, August 7th, 1866; and lieutenant-colonel, June 23d, 1882. He returned to duty with the United States Engineer Corps in April, 1866, and became engaged in some of the most important engineering works of the Government, notably the Louisville and Portland Canal, St. Mary's Falls Canal, and the improvement of the Falls of Ohio, and on lighthouse construction. He was a member of the board of engineering officers appointed in January, 1874, to examine into and report upon the James River and Kanawha Canal project. One of his greatest feats of engineering was the construction of the largest lift-lock on the globe at Sault Sainte-Marie, Mich. This monstrous structure is 515 feet in length and 80 feet in width, with a lift of 18 feet, and has gates of sufficient width to admit a vessel of 60-feet beam. General Weitzel so managed the details of this marvelous affair as to require only eleven minutes to pass a vessel through, including the time necessary to pass in and out of the lock. General Weitzel took charge of the river and harbor improvements of Philadelphia in the Summer of 1882, and continued in charge of the Philadelphia station up to the time of his death, which occurred there on the 19th of March, 1884.

GENERAL RANSOM TAKING POSSESSION OF THE COURT HOUSE AT NATCHEZ, TENN.

STEPHEN GANO BURBRIDGE.

Born in Scott County, Ky., August 19th, 1831; educated at Georgetown College and at the Kentucky Military Institute at Frankfort, and studied law in the office of the late Senator Garrett Davis, at Paris, Ky. From 1849 to 1859 he engaged in mercantile pursuits, and then gave his attention to farming, which he was carrying on at the time of the breaking out of the Civil War. His services were then tendered to and accepted by the Federal Government, and he was placed at the head of the Twenty-sixth Regiment of Kentucky Volunteers, which he was instrumental in raising, and which he led at the battle of Shiloh. For his distinguished services in the last-named engagement he was promoted to be a brigadier-general of United States Volunteers. He was ordered to Kentucky at the time of Bragg's invasion, and remained there until the latter was driven from the State, when he was ordered to join the expedition against Vicksburg. He led the charge at Arkansas Post and at Port Gibson, being conspicuous for his bravery at both places, as well as in the various actions about and at the siege of Vicksburg. He afterward commanded the Military District of Kentucky, and it was during this time that he defeated John Morgan in his raid and drove him into Tennessee. For this service he received the thanks of President Lincoln, and was breveted major-general. He resigned from the Volunteer service in 1865.

ALVIN P. HOVEY.

Born at Mount Vernon, Ind., May 6th, 1821. On coming of age he studied law, and successfully practiced his profession, attaining great eminence by the time of the breaking out of the Civil War, when he tendered his services to the Federal Government, and received the appointment of major of the Twenty-fourth Regiment of Indiana Volunteers. He served under General Pope in the Army of the Mississippi, soon becoming a colonel, and served in the Southwest under Grant, notably at the battle of Shiloh, where he fought at the head of his regiment in Smith's brigade, of Lewis Wallace's division. He commanded a division at the battle of Champion Hills, contributing largely to the success of that day, and subsequently took part in the Vicksburg campaign. He was made a brigadier-general on the 28th of April, 1862, breveted major-general of Volunteers in July, 1864, and resigned from the service in October of the year following. In 1866 he was appointed United States Minister to Peru.

MAXEY GREGG.

Born at Columbia, S. C., in 1814; studied law and was admitted to the Bar in 1839, attaining great prominence in his profession, which he practiced with much success for many years in his native city; served in Mexico as major of the Twelfth Infantry; was a member of the South Carolina State Convention of 1860 and of the committee to prepare the Ordinance of Secession. When the Civil War broke out he was placed in command of the First Regiment of South Carolina Volunteers, which was the first force from that State which arrived in Virginia, and it was accordingly received

DECISIVE CHARGE UPON BYRNE'S CONFEDERATE BATTERY, BY THE SEVENTY-EIGHTH PENNSYLVANIA AND TWENTY-FIRST OHIO VOLUNTEERS, AT THE BATTLE OF MURFREESBORO', JANUARY 2D, 1863.

with extraordinary demonstrations of joy and welcome. When its term of enlistment expired, it returned to South Carolina; but Colonel Gregg remained in Virginia, and subsequently reorganized the regiment, which was afterward constantly and conspicuously in the service. Colonel Gregg was made a brigadier-general prior to the battle of Fredericksburg, where he lost his life, on the 13th of December, 1862. As a military man, he had a wide reputation for coolness and self-possession in danger, and became very popular with all the men that ever came under his command.

THE BATTLE OF MURFREESBORO', OR STONE RIVER.

As soon as General Rosecrans was placed in chief command of the Army of the Cumberland ("Fourteenth Army Corps"), he set about organizing his forces into a more effective body, so as to be in position to operate against the increased army which Bragg was assembling at Murfreesboro', and with which he was threatening Nashville.

The "Fourteenth Army Corps" was then distributed between Bowling Green, Glasgow and Nashville. It was at once arranged into three corps.

The work of repairing the destroyed sections of the line of the Louisville and Nashville Railway was prosecuted with the utmost vigor; but it was not until the 26th of November, 1862, that the cars could be run to Nashville. In the meantime, Rosecrans had ordered McCook's corps to advance upon the last-named city, and, after two days' steady marching, its vanguard reached Edgefield on the afternoon of November 6th.

The Confederates had already made several unavailing efforts to capture the capital before Rosecrans's army could reach it. Generals Forrest and Morgan, at the head of large bodies of cavalry, reported to consist of 3,250 men respectively, had, on November 5th, inaugurated a series of almost simultaneous attacks upon the Federal lines south and north of the city; but when General Sill's division entered Nashville early on the 7th, the Confederates had ceased all demonstrations and retired southward.

General Rosecrans reached Nashville on the 10th, and from that time until the 25th of the following month he was engaged in accumulating supplies and in disciplining and organizing his forces, so as to assume the offensive against Bragg.

This could not, however, be done peacefully, for Confederate detachments were constantly harassing and threatening the Federal lines of communication. The cavalry forces, led by Forrest and Morgan, and which covered respectively Bragg's left and right wings, under Generals William J. Hardee and E. Kirby Smith, were especially active, and succeeded in doing much damage to the supply-trains before the completion of the railway.

On the 27th of November General Kirk's force drove out General Wheeler from Lavergne, and Sheridan compelled Wharton's troops to leave Nolensville; but ten days later a large part of Dumont's division was surprised and captured, after a brief contest, in the vicinity of Hartsville. Apart from these engagements, no conflicts of any importance took place between the contending forces until Rosecrans moved against Bragg's position across the Stone River.

Early on the 26th of December the Federal army broke up camp, and commenced its march in the midst of a cold and drizzling rain. General McCook's right wing proceeded along the Nolensville Turnpike in the direction of Triune, where Hardee was posted, while Crittenden's left took the Murfreesboro' Pike toward Lavergne, and Thomas advanced with two of his divisions along the Franklin and Wilkinson Pikes, his other two divisions being at Nolensville, where they could best support McCook.

DECEMBER, 1862.

After considerable skirmishing, which did not, however, at any point, develop into anything of moment, McCook and Crittenden reached Nolensville and Lavergne the same evening, and twenty-four hours later they were respectively at Triune and Stewart's Creek, on the Jefferson Pike, from both of which places the enemy was compelled to fall back.

Thomas's force joined the left, across Stewart's Creek, on Sunday, the 28th. Riggs's Cross Roads was reached by McCook's corps the following morning, while Crittenden's and Thomas's forces were advancing along the Murfreesboro' Turnpike. When about three miles from Murfreesboro', it was erroneously reported that the Confederates had evacuated it, and one of Crittenden's divisions was in consequence ordered across the river, to occupy the town. The advance, under General C. G. Harker, reached the opposite side, and drove in the Confederate pickets; but on finding that Breckinridge's force was strongly posted on his front, the troops were recalled before night to their former position.

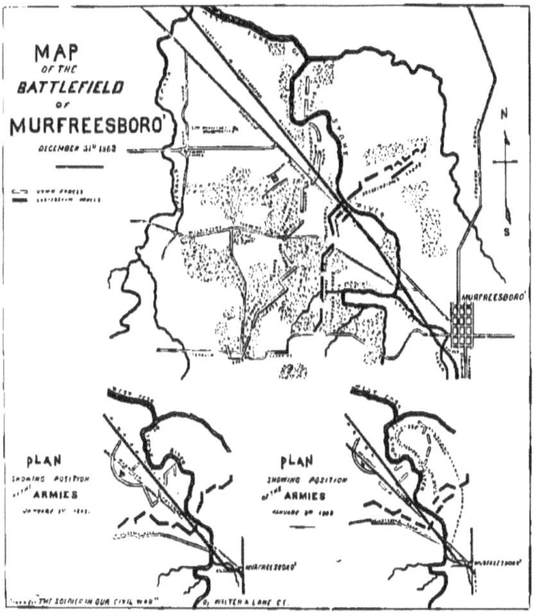

Rosecrans made his headquarters the same afternoon just ahead of Stewart's Creek, and by evening of the 30th of December the Federals had, after considerable skirmishing, established their lines on the western side of Stone River.

The extreme left, under Crittenden, stretched from the river-bank across both the Nashville and Chattanooga Railway and the Nashville Turnpike, until it joined Thomas's centre, extending across the Wilkinson Turnpike. The extreme Federal right wing extended as far as the Franklin Road, McCook's three divisions being given to General Sheridan, Davis and Johnson, in the order named. Part of Johnson's division was ranged parallel with the Franklin Road, whence it was made to turn inwardly and in a northerly direction.

The Confederate army was formed in line about two miles from Murfreesboro', with Breckinridge's force on the extreme right, across the northeastern bank of Stone River, Polk's corps in the centre, and Hardee's force on the extreme left, across the Franklin Road, and opposite the position held by Johnson's and Davis's divisions.

At a Federal council of war, held on the evening of the 30th, it was decided that Crittenden should move early the next day against Breckinridge, with the view of finally turning his right, and gaining Murfreesboro' in the rear, while Thomas and McCook would engage and hold in check the Confederate left and centre. With the large force under Crittenden, this plan would doubtless have proved successful, had it not happened that, while Rosecrans was preparing for battle, Bragg had arranged to use his army, massed on the southwestern side of the river, against the Federal left, hoping to sever its line of communication with Nashville.

In obedience to Rosecrans's orders, Van Cleve's division of Crittenden's corps crossed the river before sunrise, followed by Wood's division, when news came that the Federal right had been surprised and driven back.

Bragg had made a furious onslaught upon McCook's extreme right before Van Cleve had even moved. By advancing his troops until the line could overlap Johnson's force beyond the Franklin Road, and suddenly deploying them from the woods, McCown had fallen upon Johnson so heavily as to sweep the latter's men completely from the field. Cleburne's force moved upon Davis's division, which held its own against great odds until Polk lent his aid, and the Confederate cavalry gained the Federal rear, capturing the ammunition trains, and inflicting great damage.

Sheridan's division met the enemy bravely. Posting its three batteries upon a height, it poured into the assailants' ranks a most destructive fire; but after three furious charges the heavily reinforced divisions of Polk and Hardee had advanced more impetuously than before, and gained the ground. The latter was not, however, given up until, the ammunition having become exhausted, with no possibility of its then being replenished, and several of his best officers gone, Sheridan had made a most audacious bayonet-charge. What remained of his division had then been taken near the Nashville Pike.

After thus having thoroughly broken up the right wing, the Confederates directed all their attention to Thomas's centre, which had been reformed at right angles to the original line, and which had bravely held its own against an apparently ever-increasing force, until its ammunition was well-nigh exhausted. Assistance was then called for, and Rosecrans ordered forward Rousseau's reserves through the cedars, Major Ring's Regular troops being sent to take the place of Negley's fast-recoiling force.

By Negley's retirement the Confederates were enabled to reach the rear, which they subjected to a terrific cross-fire, finally compelling Thomas to

BATTLE OF STONE RIVER, TENN.—THE DECISIVE CHARGE OF GENERAL N

BATTLE OF STONE RIVER, TENN.—THE DECISIVE CHARGE OF GENERAL NEGLEY'S DIVISION ACROSS THE RIVER—THE CONFEDERATES FLYING IN CONFUSION.

[illegible]

NIGHT BURIAL OF COLONEL GARESCHE, ON THE BATTLEFIELD OF STONE RIVER, TENN.

withdraw from the cedars, and to form into the open space crossed by the Nashville Pike.

Nearly all of Crittenden's force had long before been withdrawn from the river-front and placed along an eminence overlooking the plain which the Confederates would have to cross upon debouching from the cedar brakes. Palmer's division, which had already been under fire, alone remained in the original front. Its left wing, now in fact the extreme Federal left, under command of Colonel W. B. Hazen (Nineteenth Brigade), occupied the ground between the Nashville Pike and the railway, while the right and centre, under Lieutenant-colonel Charles F. Cross, U. S. A., and Colonel Charles Craft, U. S. V., extended westward toward the woods.

The fierceness with which Palmer's right and centre were attacked soon overcame them. They had to fall back with heavy losses, and it was quite a while before their much-demoralized ranks could be once more re-formed. In the meantime Hazen's small force was violently attacked at different points, but, with his left flank well protected by the river, he managed to screen his men from absolute capture, besides covering the formation of a new line, until some reserves and the reorganized forces of Cross and Craft could be added to his own.

With but a little over twelve hundred men at the outset, Hazen kept his assailants at bay, his force being so skilfully handled as to be able, like Sheridan's, to repel assault upon assault, and thus, for the second time in the history of the day, absolutely arrest the progress of the enemy.

This was done, however, at a frightful loss of life, as attest the records of Colonel W. H. Blake's Ninth Indiana, Colonel W. C. Whittaker's Sixth Kentucky, Colonel A. Wiley's Forty-first Ohio, Colonel T. S. Casey's One Hundred and Tenth Illinois, and Cockerill's First Ohio Battery. All of these organizations fought with the most heroic bravery, and by their behavior maintained what proved to be in fact the key to the Federal position.

Through the success attending Hazen's extraordinary defense, Rosecrans was enabled to complete his preparations for covering the Federal right, of which the extreme was now held by Van Cleve; and when, at about three o'clock, the Confederates emerged from the cedars, they were met by a concentrated fire from the massed lines of infantry, and from the artillery occupying most of the hilly position commanding both the Nashville Pike and line of railway. The effect of this fire was as destructive as it was unexpected. The fierceness with which it was delivered caused the assailants to fall back in utter dismay. The Confederate line was re-formed close by the woods, and another advance attempted, but when it had reached the fields the right flank became exposed to the batteries stationed close by the railway, and which from their elevation inflicted upon Polk's force a greater loss than it had previously experienced.

Bragg having become satisfied that it was well-nigh impossible to move the Federals from the strong position in which they had been formed, withdrew his troops again to the woods, and determined upon making a renewed attack upon the as yet undaunted Federal left. Some of Breckinridge's fresh troops was brought across Stone River upon Polk's right, and at about four o'clock the first line advanced furiously against Hazen's force.

The latter, which had been very materially strengthened, met the advance bravely, and after a bitter contest brought to bear their batteries so successfully upon the Confederates that the latter fell back in confusion. The second line then entered the fray, but it withstood its ground less determinedly than the first, and at dark the day's engagements ended with its retirement from the field.

Both contestants lay on their arms during the whole of the ensuing chilly and rainy night. Hazen withdrew his force slightly to the rear of the position he had so long and so obstinately defended, and the Confederates maintained the ground they had succeeded in wresting from the extreme Federal right.

Rosecrans's total losses were nearly seven thousand in killed, wounded and missing. His chief of staff, Colonel J. P. Garesché, was killed late in the afternoon, while at his side examining the advance of Hazen's force, which was then being subjected to such a trying ordeal as to cause extreme solicitude throughout the army. The shell which carried off Garesché's head grazed the person of his commander, whose brave officers were then again fast falling around him.

Earlier in the day, Brigadier-general J. W. Sill, acting Brigadier-generals George W. Roberts and J. W. Schaeffer, had been killed; Generals T. J. Wood, H. P. Van Cleve, and acting Brigadier-general E. W. Kirk, were severely wounded; and acting General August Willich had been made prisoner while on the way to rejoin his command from Johnson's headquarters. Sheridan's division had alone subsequently lost nearly eighteen hundred men, including as many as seventy-two officers; some five hundred men and twenty-two officers being likewise placed *hors de combat* in Lieutenant-colonel Shepherd's brigade of Regulars.

The Confederates lost about four thousand men in killed and wounded. They captured some three thousand prisoners, two hundred wagons and teams, and as many as thirty-one guns, the latter representing fully one-fifth of Rosecrans's artillery, and embracing the whole of Edgarton's and Houghtaling's, as well as part of Brush's and of Goodspeed's, batteries.

At a council of war held during the night at Rosecrans's headquarters, close by the Nashville Pike, it was decided to continue the fight the next morning, but the whole of that New Year's Day passed by unmarked by anything of moment save the skirmishes naturally attending two confronting armies.

JANUARY 1ST, 1863.

Late in the afternoon Rosecrans was reinforced by Walker's and Starkweather's brigades, and somewhat changed the disposition of his troops. The division of Van Cleve, which, owing to his being wounded, had been placed in charge of Colonel Beatty, of the Nineteenth Ohio Regiment, was sent across the river, and with one of Palmer's brigades was afterward made to occupy a strong position upon an eminence near the upper ford. Palmer's remaining brigades were placed east of the Nashville Railway, close to Rousseau's, with Negley's force as a reserve in the rear; and McCook's corps occupied the extreme right.

At about eight o'clock on the morning of Friday, the 2d of January, a heavy fire was opened upon the position held by Colonel Loomis, of Rousseau's division, from four strong batteries which Bragg had erected during the previous night. A furious artillery duel followed, but with a concentration of fire from additional guns the batteries were silenced, and the Confederates abandoned the contest.

The ensuing lull was occupied by the Confederates in reconnoitring and in massing their troops for a final assault upon the Federal left. Shortly after three o'clock in the afternoon, Beatty's division (late Van Cleve's) was attacked by Breckinridge's entire force, which was strongly supported by artillery under Captain Robertson, as well as by Pegram's and Wharton's cavalry. The assault was so formidable that the first Federal line gave way. Its place was taken by the reserve, composed of Ohio and Kentucky regiments, but after battling a while, Beatty was obliged to withdraw his troops across the river under cover of nearly sixty guns judiciously posted along the opposite bank.

From there such a destructive fire was opened upon the advancing Confederates, that in less than an hour Breckinridge had lost nearly one-third of his entire force.

Three fresh brigades and St. Clair Morton's Corps of Engineers were sent to the front, where for a while occurred the most obstinate and sanguinary battle of the campaign. The artillery on both sides was brought to bear with destructive effect, until a charge was ordered along the whole Federal line.

GORDON GRANGER.

The Seventy-eighth Pennsylvania, Colonel Stillwell, took the lead, and was closely followed by the Eighteenth, Twenty-first, and Seventy-fourth Ohio, the Eleventh Michigan, Nineteenth Illinois, and Thirty-seventh Indiana Regiments. Charge after charge was made, and gallantly repulsed by the Confederates, but the assistance given by Stanley's cavalry, in conjunction with Hazen's force and Negley's reserves, proved at last insurmountable.

Bragg's right wing was first to yield, and in its retreat toward Lytle's Creek was not long after followed by the Confederate centre, whose flank had become exposed to a terrible fire from the fast-advancing Federals. At nightfall the entire Confederate line lay in front of Murfreesboro', where Rosecrans concluded not to follow it, owing to the darkness and to a heavy rainstorm.

During the ensuing night Crittenden's entire corps was sent across Stone River, and notwithstanding the storm, which continued all the following day, the Federals constructed everywhere additional lines of intrenchments, and prepared for a renewal of the struggle. No movement was, however, made on either side, and on Sunday morning, the 4th of January, it was found that the Confederates had passed through Murfreesboro' during the preceding night, on their way to Tullahoma and Shelbyville.

Bragg's army had so much the advance, and the roads were in such a deplorable condition through the protracted rain, that an effective pursuit could not be made. The Confederate rear-guard was, however, forced back toward Manchester by Thomas's force, which was first to occupy Murfreesboro', and Rosecrans established his headquarters in the town during the afternoon of the 5th.

The additional casualties sustained on both sides made the total losses, in killed, wounded and missing, to foot up nearly twelve thousand on the part of the Federals, those of the Confederates being reported at only ten thousand, although more than two thousand wounded were left in the Murfreesboro' hospitals when Bragg abandoned the place. His killed included Generals James E. Rains and Roger M. Hanson, among the wounded being Generals Adams and Chalmers. The Federal General Alexander McD. McCook was likewise disabled during the last day's engagement.

JANUARY, 1863.

Rosecrans established himself strongly at Murfreesboro' on the 6th, and reorganized his army into three corps, as follows: The Fourteenth Army Corps, under General George H. Thomas, comprised the divisions of Generals J. C. Starkweather, J. S. Negley, J. M. Brannan, and J. J. Reynolds; the Twentieth Corps, under General A. McDowell McCook, included the divisions of Generals J. C. Davis, R. W. Johnson, and P. H. Sheridan; and the Twenty-first Army Corps, under General Thomas L. Crittenden, embraced the divisions of Generals T. J. Wood, Charles Craft and H. P. Van Cleve.

General D. S. Stanley remained in chief command of the cavalry, with Generals J. B. Turchin and R. B. Mitchell at the head of the First and Second Divisions, and the reserves were given to General Gordon Granger, who had under him Generals W. C. Whittaker, G. W. Morgan, and R. S. Granger.

Bragg's two principal bases of supplies were established at Chattanooga and at Tullahoma. He also reorganized his army, and subdivided it into three corps. One corps was given to Lieutenant-general Leonidas Polk, who had under him the divisions of Generals Simon B. Buckner, B. F. Cheatham, and J. M. Withers, located at Shelbyville; another corps was placed in charge of Lieutenant-general W. J. Hardee, with Generals P. R. Cleburne and A. P. Stewart in command of his two divisions, then posted at the Liberty, Hoover and Bellbuckle Gaps; while the Third or Cavalry Corps was given to General J. H. Wheeler, who had his force well deployed from Columbia to and somewhat beyond McMinnville. These dispositions were maintained by both armies for several months, during which were undertaken on both sides a number of armed expeditions. The latter did not, however, lead to any change of moment until toward the latter part of June, when Rosecrans once more assumed the offensive against Bragg, which led to a series of important engagements in Southern Tennessee.

ROSTER OF THE FEDERAL ARMY

ENGAGED AT

THE BATTLE OF MURFREESBORO' (STONE RIVER),

AND BELONGING TO

THE FOURTEENTH ARMY CORPS, DEPARTMENT OF THE CUMBERLAND.

MAJOR-GENERAL W. S. ROSECRANS COMMANDING.

CENTRE.

Major-general George H. Thomas.

FIRST DIVISION.

Brigadier-general S. S. Fry.

First Brigade: Colonel M. B. Walker—Eighty-second Indiana, Twelfth Kentucky, Seventeenth Ohio, Thirty-first Ohio, Thirty-eighth Ohio.

Second Brigade: Colonel J. M. Harlan—Tenth Indiana, Seventy-fourth Indiana, Fourth Kentucky, Tenth Kentucky, Fourteenth Ohio.

Third Brigade: Brigadier-general J. B. Steedman—Eighty-seventh Indiana, Second Minnesota, Ninth Ohio, Thirty-fifth Ohio, Eighteenth United States.

THE SWEEPSTAKES.—JUMPING THE DITCH.

JUMPING THE HURDLE

THE RACECOURSE.—THE RACE FOR ALL COMERS.

THE MULE RACE.—JUMPING THE DITCH.

THE GRAND STAND.—THE FINISH.

THE IRISH BRIGADE, GENERAL T. F. MEAGHER, CELEBRATING ST. PATRICK'S DAY IN THE CAMP AT FALMOUTH, VA

Artillery: Fourth Michigan Battery, First Ohio Battery "C," Fourth United States Battery "I."

THIRD DIVISION.

Brigadier-general L. H. Rousseau.

Ninth Brigade: Colonel B. F. Scribner—Thirty-eighth Indiana, Second Ohio, Thirty-third Ohio, Ninety-fourth Ohio, Tenth Wisconsin.

Seventeenth Brigade: Colonel J. G. Jones—Forty-second Indiana, Eighty-eighth Indiana, Fifteenth Kentucky, Third Ohio, Tenth Ohio.

Twenty-eighth Brigade: Colonel H. A. Hambright—Twenty-fourth Illinois, Seventy-ninth Pennsylvania, First Wisconsin, Twenty-first Wisconsin.

Artillery: Fourth Indiana Battery, Fifth Indiana Battery, First Kentucky, First Michigan Battery "A."

Cavalry: Second Kentucky (Battalion), Eleventh Kentucky (Detachment), Fourth Indiana (Detachment).

EIGHTH DIVISION.

Brigadier-general J. S. Negley.

Seventh Brigade: Colonel John F. Miller—Thirty-seventh Indiana, Seventy-eighth Pennsylvania, Twenty-first Ohio, Seventy-fourth Ohio, Independent Battalion—Captain Casey.

Twenty-ninth Brigade: Colonel T. R. Stanley—Nineteenth Illinois, Eleventh Michigan, Eighteenth Ohio, Sixty-ninth Ohio.

Fifth Brigade: Colonel E. N. Kirk—Thirty-fourth Illinois, Seventy-ninth Illinois, Twenty-ninth Indiana, Thirtieth Indiana, Seventy-seventh Pennsylvania.

Sixth Brigade: Brigadier-general Willich—Eighty-ninth Illinois, Thirty-second Indiana, Thirty-ninth Indiana, Fifteenth Ohio, Forty-ninth Ohio.

Artillery: First Ohio Battery "A," First Ohio Battery "E," Fifth United States Battery "I."

Cavalry: Second Kentucky (two Companies).

NINTH DIVISION.

Brigadier-general J. C. Davis.

Thirtieth Brigade: Fifty-ninth Illinois, Seventy-fourth Illinois, Seventy-fifth Illinois, Twenty-second Indiana.

Thirty-first Brigade: Twenty-first Illinois, Thirty-eighth Illinois, One Hundred and First Ohio, Fifteenth Wisconsin.

Thirty-second Brigade: Twenty-fifth Illinois, Thirty-fifth Illinois, Eighty-first Indiana, Eighth Kansas.

Artillery: Second Minnesota Battery, Fifth Wisconsin Battery, Eighth Wisconsin Battery.

ELEVENTH DIVISION.

Brigadier-general P. H. Sheridan.

Thirty-fifth Brigade: Colonel F. Schaefer—Forty-fourth and Seventy-third Illinois, Second and Fifteenth Missouri.

Thirty-sixth Brigade: Colonel Moore—Eighty-fifth Illinois, Eighty-sixth Illinois, One Hundred and Twenty-fifth Illinois, Fifty-second Ohio.

SIXTH DIVISION.

Brigadier-general M. S. Hascall.

Fifteenth Brigade: Colonel G. P. Buell—One Hundredth Illinois, Seventeenth Indiana, Fifty-eighth Indiana, Third Kentucky, Twenty-sixth Ohio.

Twentieth Brigade: Colonel G. C. Harker—Fifty-first Indiana, Seventy-third Indiana, Thirteenth Michigan, Sixty-fourth Ohio, Sixty-fifth Ohio.

Twenty-first Brigade: Colonel G. D. Wagner—Fifteenth Indiana, Fortieth Indiana, Fifty-seventh Indiana, Ninety-seventh Ohio.

Artillery: Major S. Race.

CAVALRY.

Brigadier-general David Stone Stanley.

FIRST DIVISION.

Colonel Kennett.

First Brigade: Colonel E. H. Murray—Second Indiana, First Kentucky, Third Kentucky, Fourth Kentucky, Fourth Michigan, Seventh Pennsylvania.

Second Brigade: Colonel L. Zahm—Fifth Kentucky, First Ohio, Third Ohio, Fourth Ohio, First Ohio Artillery Battery "D."

UNATTACHED FORCES.

First Michigan Engineers, Ninth Michigan (Detached), Third Eastern Tennessee, Sixth Eastern Tennessee, Fifteenth Pennsylvania.

BUTCHERING AND DRESSING CATTLE IN THE ARMY.

FROM A SKETCH BY F. B. SCHELL.

Artillery: First Kentucky Battery "B," First Ohio Battery "G," First Ohio Battery "M."

Cavalry: Seventh Pennsylvania, First Tennessee.

SEVENTH DIVISION.

Brigadier-general J. M. Palmer.

First Brigade: Colonel G. W. Roberts—Twenty-second Illinois, Twenty-seventh Illinois, Forty-second Illinois, Fifty-first Illinois.

Second Brigade: Brigadier-general J. D. Morgan—Tenth Illinois, Sixteenth Illinois, Sixtieth Illinois, Tenth Michigan, Fourteenth Michigan.

Artillery: First Illinois Battery "C," Tenth Wisconsin Battery.

Cavalry: Seventh Illinois Company "G."

TWELFTH DIVISION.

Brigadier-general E. Dumont.

Fortieth Brigade: Colonel A. O. Miller—Ninety-eighth Illinois, Seventy-second Indiana, Seventy-fifth Indiana.

—— Brigade: Colonel W. T. Ward—One Hundred and Second Illinois, One Hundred and Fifth Illinois, Seventieth Indiana, Seventy-ninth Ohio.

Artillery: Eighteenth Indiana Battery.

Cavalry: Fourth Indiana (Detachment), Seventh Kentucky, Eleventh Kentucky (Detachment).

RIGHT WING.

Major-general A. McD. McCook.

SECOND DIVISION.

Brigadier-general J. W. Sill.

Fourth Brigade: Colonel Buckley—Sixth Indiana, Fifth Kentucky, First Ohio, Ninety-third Ohio, Sixteenth United States, Nineteenth United States.

Thirty-seventh Brigade: Colonel N. Greusel—Thirty-sixth Illinois, Eighty-eighth Illinois, Twenty-first Michigan, Twenty-fourth Wisconsin.

Artillery: Second Illinois Battery "I," First Missouri Battery "G."

Cavalry: Second Kentucky Company "L."

LEFT WING.

Major-general T. L. Crittenden.

FOURTH DIVISION.

Brigadier-general W. S. Smith.

Tenth Brigade: Colonel W. Grose—Eighty-fourth Illinois, Thirty-sixth Indiana, Twenty-third Kentucky, Sixth Ohio, Twenty-fourth Ohio.

Nineteenth Brigade: Colonel W. B. Hazen—One Hundred and Tenth Illinois, Ninth Indiana, Sixth Kentucky, Forty-first Ohio.

Twenty-second Brigade: Colonel Enyart—Thirty-first Indiana, First, Second and Twentieth Ky., and Ninetieth Ohio.

Artillery: Captain Standart.

FIFTH DIVISION.

Brigadier-general H. P. Van Cleve.

Eleventh Brigade: Col. Samuel Beatty—Seventy-ninth Indiana, Ninth Kentucky, Nineteenth and Fifty-ninth Ohio.

Fourteenth Brigade: Colonel J. P. Fyffe—Forty-fourth Indiana, Eighty-sixth Indiana, Eleventh Kentucky, Thirteenth Ohio.

Twenty-third Brigade: Colonel S. Matthews—Thirty-fifth Indiana, Eighth Kentucky, Twenty-first Kentucky, Fifty-first Ohio, Ninety-ninth Ohio.

Artillery: Captain G. R. Swallow.

Cavalry: Fourth United States Cavalry (Detached), Signal Corps, Stokes's (Illinois) Battery.

GARRISONS.

Bowling Green, Ky.: Brigadier-general Granger—One Hundred and Twenty-ninth Illinois, Twenty-sixth Kentucky, Twenty-third Michigan, One Hundred and Second Ohio, One Hundred and Eleventh Ohio, Fourth Kentucky, Cavalry.

Nashville, Tenn.: Brigadier-general R. B. Mitchell—First Middle Tennessee, Eleventh Indiana Battery, Twelfth Indiana Battery, First Michigan Artillery (Fifth Battery), Third Indiana Cavalry (one Company).

GORDON GRANGER.

Born in New York city in 1821; entered the United States Military Academy at West Point, and upon graduating therefrom in July, 1845, was commissioned brevet-second lieutenant of Infantry, being transferred to the Mounted Rifles within the ensuing year. He took part in the War with Mexico, especially distinguishing himself at the siege of Vera Cruz; also at the battles of Cerro Gordo, Contreras, Churubusco, and Chapultepec, as well as in the engagements around the City of Mexico, receiving for his gallantry the promotion to a full second-lieutenancy. Up to the time of the breaking out of the Civil War he was mostly engaged on frontier duty against the Indians. In 1852 he was made a first lieutenant; advanced to a captaincy in May, 1861; and in June of the same year was assigned to duty on the staff of General Sturgis, participating in the

BATTLE OF CHANCELLORSVILLE, VA., MAY 1-3, 1863.—From a Sketch by Edwin Forbes.

battles of Dug Spring and Wilson's Creek. He was transferred to the Third Cavalry in August, 1861; made colonel of the Second Michigan Cavalry in September, 1861; and appointed a brigadier-general of Volunteers in March, 1862. He commanded a brigade in the operations against New Madrid and Island No. 10, and led the cavalry under General Pope at Corinth, as well as during the subsequent pursuit of Beauregard's army as far as Baldwin. Promoted to a major-generalship in September, 1862, he commanded various districts in Tennessee and Kentucky, and successfully repulsed the attacks of General Van Dorn. At the battle of Chickamauga he reached the field in time to drive back Longstreet's columns. At the battle of Missionary Ridge he commanded the Fourth Army Corps, and with the Fourteenth Corps afterward engaged in the siege of Fort Morgan and Spanish Fort, as well as in the storming of Battery Blakely and the occupation of Mobile. He afterward commanded the District of Texas and the Department of Kentucky, and before the close of the Civil War was made a major-general. In July, 1866, he received the appointment of colonel of the Twenty-fifth Regular Infantry, whence he was transferred in 1870 to the Fifteenth Infantry, holding command in the latter until his death, January 10th, 1876.

ard (Sigel's Eleventh Corps), and Henry W. Slocum, the last-named taking with his Twelfth Corps the place of Burnside's Ninth Corps, which latter was originally assigned to the Department of the Ohio, with General W. F. Smith, but was finally taken to its destination by General J. G. Parke.

The infantry divisions were given to Generals J. S. Wadsworth, J. C. Robinson, A. Doubleday, W. S. Hancock, J. Gibbon, W. H. French, D. D. Birney, H. G. Berry, A. W. Whipple, W. T. H. Brooks, A. P. Howe, J. Newton, C. Griffin, George Sykes, A. A. Humphreys, C. Devens, A. Von Steinwehr, Carl Schurz, S. Williams, and J. W. Geary. The three divisions of cavalry—"the eyes of the army"—were placed in charge of Generals A. Pleasanton, J. Buford and W. W. Averill, with General George Stoneman in chief command.

General Lee's Army of Northern Virginia remained throughout the ensuing campaign subdivided into two corps. These were commanded, as

Four days later, March 17th, General Averill had crossed the Rappahannock at Kelley's Ford, twenty-seven miles above Fredericksburg, for the purpose of raiding the country in the direction of Calpepper Court House. His force consisted of two brigades of artillery, commanded by Colonels McIntosh and Duffie. These embraced respectively two squadrons of the Fourth Pennsylvania, besides the Third and Sixteenth Pennsylvania, and the Sixth New York Mounted Battery, as well as detachments from the First and Fifth United States, in addition to the First Rhode Island, Fourth New York and Sixth Ohio Regiments.

The Federals had proceeded about a mile from the ford when they encountered General Fitzhugh Lee's brigade of cavalry, consisting of the First, Second, Third, Fourth and Fifth Virginia Regiments. These were in line of battle, and first made an effort to turn the Federal right, but the Sixth New York there subjected them to such a scathing

GENERAL REYNOLDS ON THE MARCH TO THE BATTLEFIELD OF CHANCELLORSVILLE.
From a Sketch by Edwin Forbes.

THE ARMY OF THE POTOMAC.
HOOKER'S CAMPAIGN
THE BATTLE OF CHANCELLORSVILLE.

The retirement of General Burnside from the command of the Army of the Potomac in January, 1863, was followed by the withdrawal of Generals Sumner and Franklin, who were respectively assigned to duty in the Departments of Missouri and of the Gulf. We have already seen, however (Vol. I., page 317), that General Sumner died at Syracuse, N. Y., before reaching his post.

Upon relieving Burnside, General Hooker had lost no time in reorganizing the Army of the Potomac upon an entirely new basis. The heavy reinforcements which were being continually sent forward enabled him to subdivide his forces into as many as seven distinct corps, embracing in all twenty divisions of infantry and three divisions of cavalry.

The different corps were placed in command of Generals J. F. Reynolds, D. N. Couch, Daniel E. Sickles, G. G. Meade, John Sedgwick, O. O. How-

at Fredericksburg, by General James Longstreet and "Stonewall" Jackson, and with the exception of the temporary withdrawal during February of part of Longstreet's Corps to the James River, were posted along the north side of the Rappahannock until Hooker resumed the offensive, toward the end of April.

During the previous two months there had been a number of skirmishes between the opposing armies, the most important being confined to the cavalry.

Early in February one of Stuart's brigades, under General W. H. F. Lee, made a bold though unsuccessful attempt to capture the Federal post at Gloucester Point, whence the Confederates were driven back with great loss. The latter were more fortunate, however, on the 12th of the following month, when Colonel John S. Mosby led a small body of horse as far into the Federal lines as Fairfax Court House, retiring thence only after he had effected the capture of Colonel Stoughton and a large part of his brigade, besides destroying and carrying away much valuable property.

March, 1863.

fire as to promptly cause their retirement from the road. An attempt was then made upon Averill's left, but without any greater success, for Duffie's brigade boldly attacked the Confederate troops, and by its superiority in number was enabled to drive back the assailants with great loss.

Charges and counter-charges followed rapidly until darkness set in, when General Averill withdrew across the river, having lost in all about seventy men, while the loss sustained by his antagonist was nearly twice as great in killed and wounded alone.

In anticipation of a general movement, Stoneman was ordered on the 13th of April to take detachments of cavalry, infantry and artillery upon reconnoissance to Bealton, Warrenton, Liberty, and at Rappahannock Bridge; and, after meeting with but little opposition, and destroying a large amount of property, he took possession of the fords of the Rapidan.

The heavy rains prevented a more extended expedition, and also delayed Hooker's advance upon Lee's rear until the 27th. The next day the right

BATTLE OF CHANCELLORSVILLE, SUNDAY, MAY 3D, 1863.—GE

FROM A SK

BATTLE OF CHANCELLORSVILLE, SUNDAY, MAY 3d, 1863—GENERAL HOOKER REPULSING THE ATTACK OF THE CONFEDERATES.

From a Sketch by [illegible]

ATTACK ON GENERAL SEDGWICK'S CORPS, ON MONDAY, MAY 4TH, 1863, AS SEEN FROM FALMOUTH HEIGHTS.—From a Sketch by Edwin Forbes.

Federal turning column, composed of the Fifth, Eleventh, and Twelfth corps, under Meade, Howard and Slocum, each with three batteries, and all commanded by the last-named, passed the Rappahannock on pontons at Kelley's Ford, and then waded across the Rapidan at the Elley (Ely) and Germania Fords, reaching the Wilderness around Chancellorsville on the evening of the 30th.

April, 1863.

General Hooker at once established his headquarters at the last-named place, and sent out cavalry expeditions to cut Lee's railway communications with Richmond.

The divisions of French and Hancock, belonging to Couch's Second Corps, had meanwhile crossed on pontons at the Banks and United States Fords, marching thence directly upon Chancellorsville. They were rapidly followed thither in turn by Sickles's Third Corps and two of Reynolds's divisions under Doubleday and Robinson. Brooks's division dale's brigade, to guard against any possible attack on the part of Sedgwick.

Of the two armies now confronting each other, the Federal was by far the stronger. In round numbers, the First Corps, under Reynolds (Wadsworth, Doubleday and Robinson); the Second Corps, under Couch (French, Hancock and Gibbon); the Fifth Corps, under Meade (Humphreys, Griffin and Sykes); and the Twelfth Corps, under Slocum (Geary and Williams), had each about seventeen thousand men; while Sickles's Third Corps (Berry, Birney and Whipple) had 18,000; Howard's Eleventh Corps (Devens, Schurz and Steinwehr), 11,000; and Sedgwick's Sixth Corps (Howe, Newton and Brooks), 22,000—a total, with the cavalry, of 120,000 men.

On the Confederate side the number was as follows: Jackson's corps (embracing the divisions of A. P. Hill, 11,800; Robert E. Rodes, 9,000; Jubal A. Early, 7,800; and R. E. Colston, 6,400)—a total of 35,000 men; Longstreet's corps (including the what beyond Aldrich. Pleasanton's cavalry, leading the central column, had, however, become engaged in the meantime with the Eleventh Virginia Regiment, which was in McLaws's advance, when not much more than about a mile out from Chancellorsville.

The Confederates were driven back by Sykes's division, after a spirited contest; but when Anderson's division and part of Rodes's force had come up to McLaws's assistance, Sykes was compelled to fall back on Hancock's division, by which it was replaced in the immediate front. The fresh troops soon regained the ground Sykes had held, and the Federals were enabled to occupy a most advantageous position upon a ridge commanding Chancellorsville, as well as its immediate vicinity.

Slocum had meanwhile been fighting gallantly the advance of Jackson's force, and was forging ahead, in the belief that the distance between his column and Sykes's would soon enable him to make

CONFEDERATE PRISONERS BROUGHT IN AFTER THE BATTLE OF CHANCELLORSVILLE.
From a Sketch by Edwin Forbes.

of Sedgwick's Sixth Corps had crossed the river about two miles below Fredericksburg, and Wadsworth's division of Reynolds's First Corps also afterward crossed the Rappahannock about a mile further down. Gibbon's division, of Couch's corps, was left openly in position at Falmouth, opposite Fredericksburg, while Howe and Newton's divisions of Sedgwick's corps were made to march across the hills in such way as to impress Lee with the belief that Hooker had a large force there still confronting him.

As soon as Lee realized Hooker's true purpose, he called up Jackson from Moss Neck, and ordered him to join his force to that of Anderson's, which had fallen back when the Federals approached Chancellorsville. The two were united early on Friday, the 1st of May, close by the Tabernacle Church, at a point located about half way between Chancellorsville and Fredericksburg, where Anderson was then strongly intrenched. McLaws was brought to the front from Fredericksburg, where Jackson's remaining division, under General Early, was left, with Barks-

May, 1863.

divisions of R. H. Anderson, 9,500, and of Lafayette McLaws, 8,500), in all 18,000 men; all of which, with the artillery and cavalry, represented a grand total of 62,000 men.

Lee had determined to take the initiative, and at about eleven o'clock on the 1st of May, Jackson led his own column to the left, along the Plank Road, while McLaws took the right column, along the Turnpike, likewise leading to Chancellorsville.

It was also on both sides of these roads, as well as along the one leading to Banks's Ford, that Hooker had, later the same morning, decided to march against the Confederates. Shortly after eleven o'clock, Slocum's corps, followed by Howard's, had taken the Plank Road, on the extreme right, and Sykes's and Hancock's divisions, in the centre, were advancing along the Turnpike, while the divisions of Griffin and Humphreys successively occupied the extreme left, and moved on the military road leading to Banks's Ford.

The latter point was reached by the left column without any opposition, nor did the extreme right encounter the enemy until it had advanced some- the desired junction with the latter, when Jackson made a flank movement endangering both columns. These were now so vigorously attacked by the Confederates as to render possible their destruction before proper reinforcements could be sent them. Hooker, therefore, ordered the whole line to fall back under cover of the intrenchments at Chancellorsville, which was done in good order and without very serious loss, although the Confederates were pressing hard upon the retreating forces. At nightfall Hooker's army occupied the same positions it had held early in the day.

Yielding to Hooker's preference for a defensive attitude, as expressed at a council held the same evening, preparations were made for the protection of all roads leading through Chancellorsville. On the following morning the extreme left, under Meade, stretched from near Scott's Dam, on the Rappahannock, to the Elley Ford Road. Hancock's division rested *en échelon* eastwardly along the Turnpike, with French and Berry, in reserve, at and close by the intersection of the Chancellorsville Roads. Slocum's corps and Sickles's Third Division held the

THE ARMY OF GENERAL HOOKER ON THE MARCH TO THE

Ruined Depot of Shreveport and Texas Railroad.

VIEW OF THE CITY OF VICKSBURG, MISS., BEFORE ITS INVESTMENT.

THE ARMY OF GENERAL HOOKER ON THE MARCH TO THE BATTLEFIELD OF CHANCELLORSVILLE [illegible]

VIEW OF THE CITY OF VICKSBURG, MISS., BEFORE ITS INVESTMENT BY GENERAL GRANT AND ADMIRAL PORTER.—From a Sketch by [illegible]

RECRUITING IN THE NEW YORK CITY HALL PARK

centre, just south of Fairview; whilst to the rear, along the Orange Plank Road, Howard's corps protected the extreme right. Reynolds's corps and Humphreys's division rested upon the two roads leading from the United States Ford to the Old Mine and to the Elley Ford Roads.

The Confederate line extended from the Old Mine Road, where Wickham's and Owens's Virginia Cavalry protected Lee's extreme right, to the Catharine Furnace, which was guarded by part of Stuart's and by Fitzhugh Lee's cavalry, the intervening space being occupied by the forces of Anderson and of McLaws, extending from the Chancellorsville Plank Road to and across the Old Turnpike. Wilcox's brigade alone protected Banks's Ford. It had been determined thus to hold Hooker in check, as he could not well be attacked in his immediate front, and then to make an attempt to gain the Federal rear by turning its right flank.

Jackson started early on Saturday, the 2d of May, called for reinforcements, and a detachment of Pleasanton's cavalry was accordingly sent him, together with Barlow's brigade, of Howard's corps, and Williamson's brigade, of Slocum's corps.

With these additional troops Sickles attacked the Confederates so fiercely as to for a while throw them into great confusion. During the excitement that followed he was able to cut off and capture nearly the whole of the Twenty-third Georgia Regiment; but a force of infantry and artillery, taken from Anderson's force, coming up to the support of the Confederates, Sickles withdrew his troops to their former position.

Jackson's force continued its march, his leading column under Rodes having by that time already crossed the Orange Plank Road, and being on its way northward across the Culpepper Plank Road toward the Old Turnpike.

Under cover of the intervening thick Wilderness jungle, the Pike was reached at five o'clock, and improvised earthworks near Dowdall's Tavern until both its flanks had been almost completely turned by Colston's additional forces.

It was now nearly seven o'clock. The Eleventh Corps was completely demoralized and in retreat past Hooker's late headquarters. Lee had ordered a general advance to be made as soon as Hill's force could be brought up to the front to replace Rodes's and Colston's troops, which had become disordered after battling through the woods. In a short time the Confederates were assailing not only Slocum's corps to the south of Fairview, but also the centre under Couch, and the extreme of Meade's line to the northeast, which McLaws and Anderson were attacking so as to prevent reinforcements coming from what was originally the extreme Federal left.

Hooker had, however, meanwhile posted most of the Eleventh Corps artillery across the Plank Road, and he had also lined Fairview with additional guns, mainly taken from the Third Corps batteries. With

HAND-TO-HAND COMBAT BETWEEN FEDERAL CAVALRY, COMMANDED BY GENERAL AVERILL, AND STUART'S CONFEDERATE TROOPS, AT KELLEY'S FORD, ON THE RAPPAHANNOCK, VA., MARCH 17TH, 1863.

with his three divisions, under Generals Hill, Colston, and Rodes, and proceeded by the Furnace and Brock Roads, his advance being protected by a large detachment of Fitzhugh Lee's cavalry, commanded by General Stuart in person. The Confederates met with no opposition until the right of the advancing column had reached an elevation close by Catharine Furnace, which was about the only point along the intended route that was not completely hidden by intervening forests. Jackson's force then came in full view of Birney's division, which had been located to the northeast, between the Furnace and Chancellor's (Dowdall's) Tavern, close by Barlow's brigade, as well as Williams's and Whipple's divisions.

As the road there turns almost directly southward, the Federals were naturally led to the belief that Jackson was directing a retreat toward Richmond. Sickles was therefore ordered to attack, and at about three o'clock in the afternoon he crossed the Wilderness and reached the road, striking the rear of Jackson's column, and taking many prisoners. He soon became so much elated at his success that he one hour later Rodes, Colston, and Hill, were posted in successive lines of battle across the Pike and in readiness to move. When the advance was sounded they rushed forward simultaneously against both the flank and rear of Howard's forces.

The onslaught was so furiously made that Devens's division, occupying the extreme right, near the Tally House, was completely swept away before it could be brought effectively into position to meet this unexpected attack. McLean's brigade followed Van Gilsa's, which was the first to bear the brunt of Jackson's advance. The whole division was driven upon that of Schurz, occupying the centre, thus embarrassing the successful formation of the latter, which broke in turn, although Schimmelfennig's brigade, by a rapid and well-executed change of front, bitterly contested for a while the Confederate advance.

By this time all had the appearance of a perfect rout, and the disorder would have been also shared by Steinwehr's division but for the stand bravely taken by Buschbeck's brigade, which was located on the extreme left, and which did not leave its rapidly these a scathing fire was poured into the advancing right columns of the enemy, while Meade's line bravely withstood its attack, and while Colonel N. A. Miles's force of Hancock's division was heroically sustaining the more important assault upon the Federal centre.

With the additional artillery, General Hooker had called up both Berry's and French's divisions, which had come accompanied by Pleasanton's cavalry from Hazel Grove. These hurried forward, and by the time Jackson had nearly reached Fairview they were in position to open a most destructive fire upon the Confederates. The latter's progress was, however, so steadily made that it was found necessary to stem the advance effectually lest the neighboring batteries fall into the hands of the superior numbers now concentrating before them.

Pleasanton had then with him only two regiments of cavalry, the Eighth and Seventeenth Pennsylvania, besides his battery of horse-artillery, and if the intended check be attempted with that small force, it must needs apparently be at the risk of certain death. But brave men were there equal to the occasion, and as soon as Major Peter Keenan, commanding the Eighth Pennsylvania, realized the situation, he asked leave to lead in the attack.

Cheers followed the order then given, and with an enthusiasm scarcely paralleled throughout the Civil War the cavalry burst from the woods upon the Confederate flanks. The charge was brilliantly made and sustained in face of the great disparity of numbers, but in ten minutes nearly one-half the cavalry were disabled, the leader of the troop having been killed at the first volley directed upon them.

Short as was the delay occasioned by this attack, it proved sufficient for the more effective posting of the horse-artillery, and also enabled the placing into position of the remnants of the Eleventh Corps, as well as of the additional troops under Warren, Birney, Barlow, and Whipple, which had since likewise reached this part of the field.

The contest soon became general, and upon Jackson's right, as well as in his centre, the battle raged furiously, with immense losses on both sides, especially from the Federal artillery, which had been judiciously posted in advance of and close by the intersection of the Chancellorsville roads. The united fire of some forty guns directed along the Plank Road held at bay the entire Confederate force, and compelled it to halt in the woods until reinforcements could be brought up.

A greater loss than any yet sustained by the Confederates was now in store for them. During the interval that followed the last attack, Jackson set out on the Plank Road with his staff to reconnoitre the position. He had left orders to his troops not to fire unless approached by Federal cavalry, and he was about re-entering the lines, after completing an examination which carried him much further than he had anticipated, when he was fired upon by his own soldiers, who mistook the horsemen for some of Pleasanton's cavalry. The party scattered, and Jackson rapidly entered the forest, but he was there again fired upon by some of his infantry and fatally injured. He had received a mortal wound just below the shoulder-joint, and was besides badly wounded in the right hand and left arm. Nearly all of his escort had been killed and wounded.

General A. P. Hill took Jackson's place, but being shortly after wounded by the fragments of a shell, the chief command was given temporarily to General Rodes, and afterward to General J. E. B. Stuart. Further reconnoissances were made, but owing mainly to the increased darkness, the Confederates decided to abandon for the time all further movements. Nor did the Federals thereafter make any more demonstrations, except in Birney's front, whence Ward's brigade, toward midnight, charged upon the Confederates along the Plank Road, taking some prisoners, and bringing in a few abandoned guns and caissons.

Sunday, the 3d of May, found the opposing armies upon entirely new lines. The divisions of Hill, Colston and Rodes were successively ranged across the Plank Road, Hill's extreme left and centre respectively facing Berry and Williams, who occupied the extreme Federal right and centre, while his own extreme right lay upon Hazel Grove, behind which Geary's force curved toward the Chancellorsville Cross Roads. Anderson's and McLaws's divisions completed a line extending from the Furnace to a point very near the Old Mine Road.

The division of Hancock formed a curve almost at right angles with Geary's left, resting upon the Cross Roads, and traversed both the Mott Run and the River Road, while Birney's, French's and Whipple's divisions were stationed at Fairview and along the Elley's Ford Road. The troops of Meade and Howard were deployed along the road leading to Scott's Dam. Sykes had the artillery posted close by, where the last-named road intersects the Elley's Ford Road, and Reynolds's corps was posted further up the latter, a little beyond the United States Ford Road.

Early on the 3d, Stuart renewed the attack upon Hooker's force, with the battle-cry, "*Charge, and remember Jackson!*" and the advance was made with such impetuosity that in a short time he was in possession of the crest from which the Eleventh Corps had been driven the preceding day. No time was lost in crowning that eminence with all the heavy artillery obtainable, and as soon as this could be made to play upon the Federal lines a charge was successively ordered upon the positions held by Generals Berry and French, both of whom were supported by the divisions of Williams and Whipple.

After a severe struggle the Confederates succeeded in capturing the high ground where the Federals had posted some more heavy artillery, and in turning the latter upon the Federals, who soon had to fall back to their second and third line of intrenchments. The Confederates followed close upon them, and made charge after charge in order to capture the new positions, but unavailingly, and when reinforcements arrived from Meade's corps, they were forced to abandon the attack.

While this had been going on, Slocum and Hancock were assailed by Anderson and McLaws. The contest between these forces was no less bitter, and for a brief time neither side appeared to have the advantage; but the arrival of additional troops upon Anderson's left enabled the Carter and Jones batteries to be put into a position from which they could do a great deal of damage. Renewed charges were made by the Confederates under cover of the additional guns brought up, and it was not long before the Federals were compelled, after heavy losses, to yield enough ground to admit Anderson's junction with Stuart's extreme right.

When this was effected, the whole Confederate line eagerly pressed forward, and with the exception of Geary's and Hancock's divisions, all of the centre was forced back, as the right had already been, toward Chancellorsville and Fairview. Reinforcements and additional ammunition had long before this been asked for, but Hooker had in the meantime become disabled by the falling of one of the pillars of the Chancellorsville House, which had been struck by a cannon-ball near where he was standing, and he had been taken away from the field. The chief command had devolved upon General Couch, but all was then in such turmoil consequent upon the retirement of the Federals, that no substantial aid could at the moment be obtained

KELLEY'S FORD, THE SCENE OF THE COMBAT OF MARCH 17TH, AND OF GENERAL STONEMAN'S RECONNOISSANCE OF APRIL 21ST, 1863

FROM A SKETCH BY EDWIN FORBES.

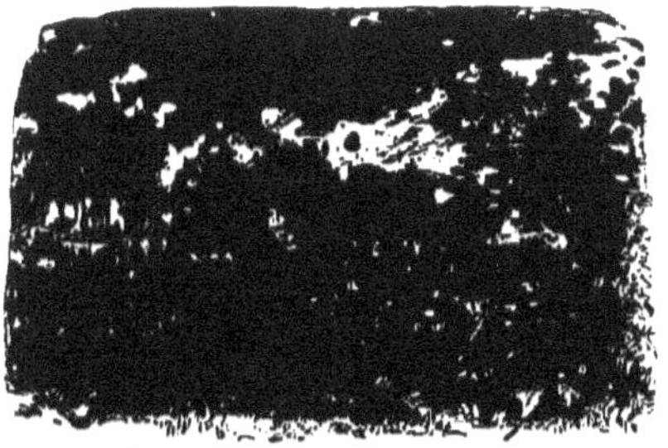

STONEMAN'S EXPEDITION.—BIVOUAC AT LOUISA COURT HOUSE.

BURNING CONFEDERATE STOREHOUSES.

Hancock and Geary had to fall back finally toward the Chancellorsville Cross Roads, where a stand was attempted. Rank after rank of the Federal army was mowed down by the successful Confederates, whose artillery was brought up, together with the guns previously abandoned by the Federals, and was made to bear with destructive effect, until at last an overwhelming charge gave them possession of Chancellorsville. It was then ten o'clock. Couch quickly formed a new line, somewhat in a V-shape, with its extreme right resting on the Rapidan, and the left on the Rappahannock, the apex being at Bullock's.

Lee's victorious forces hesitated pressing their advantages by attacking this new Federal position, not only because it was naturally one of great strength, and was admirably protected by the fresh troops of Meade and Reynolds, but because news then reached him that Sedgwick had succeeded in driving back Early's force at Fredericksburg, and was then advancing to Hooker's aid.

Immediately after Saturday night's battle, Sedgwick had been ordered to advance through Fredericksburg and unite with the main body, then at and near Chancellorsville. He had at once abandoned the position which he had been holding on the southern bank of the Rappahannock, and had advanced toward Fredericksburg, which he occupied early on Sunday morning.

An unsuccessful attempt had then been made by him to enter the Confederate works back of the town, after which Gibbon's division was called up from Falmouth. With the latter he had afterward made another ineffectual effort to pass around Early's extreme left, then held by Barksdale, who was later on joined by a brigade under Hayes. Up to eleven o'clock several other equally unsuccessful attacks had been made upon the Confederate centre, and at the extreme right, held by Early's own division.

It was then decided to move strong storming parties against the rifle-pits at Marye's Hill, and upon the works near Hazel Run (See Map, page 16). These parties were led by Generals Howe and Neil, and by Colonels Burnham, Grant and Seaver, and their first attack was admirably resisted; but the renewed assaults which followed soon after almost simultaneously along the whole line proved too much for the Confederates. The rifle-pits and earthworks at Marye's Hill and along Hazel Run were captured, and Early's force was driven back southwardly along the Telegraph Road. Immediately thereafter Sedgwick had moved out of the town along the Plank Road, leaving Gibbon in charge of Fredericksburg, and Howe in position to check Early.

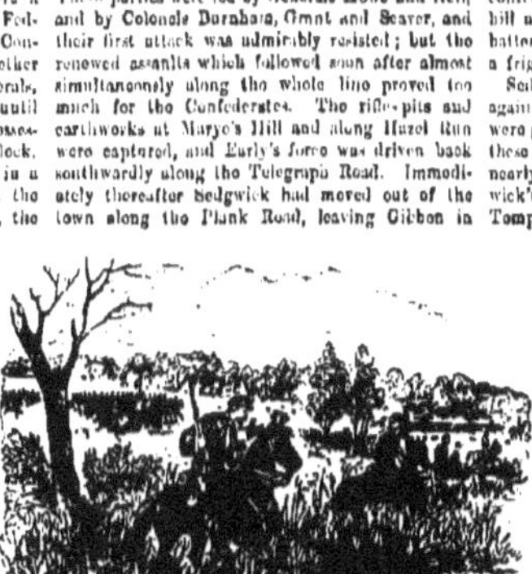

CROSSING THE RAPIDAN RIVER.

Upon learning this, Lee had detached McLaws and accompanied him with four brigades to meet Sedgwick; and before the latter had reached Salem Church he had formed in line of battle, ready to dispute the passage, nearly the whole of this force, as well as Wilcox's brigade, which had come up too late from Banks's Ford to assist Early, and had gradually fallen back before Sedgwick's advance.

Brooks's division was in the lead, closely followed by Newton's force, which likewise took part in the sanguinary battle that followed. After a prolonged contest, Bartlett's brigade seized the crest of the hill upon which the Confederates had posted their batteries, taking a great many prisoners, though at a frightful loss of life.

Sedgwick successfully maintained this position against repeated attacks, until heavy reinforcements were given to Generals Wilcox and Semmes. With these they were enabled to drive back the Federals nearly up to their line of reserves, where Sedgwick's admirably served batteries, under Colonel Tompkins, arrested their further progress. By this time darkness had come upon the scene, and both contestants lay on their arms during the ensuing night.

Before morning of the 4th, General J. T. Owens's brigade left Scott's Dam, which it had been guarding, and crossed a bridge constructed by General H. W. Benham, in order to come to Sedgwick's assistance.

May, 1863.

Lee had in the meantime ordered forward the remainder of Anderson's division to McLaws's aid, leaving only what remained of Jackson's original force to oppose Hooker, who had then resumed command, but who had apparently abandoned all idea of an offensive movement. Anderson's three brigades arrived shortly before noon and took place around Sedgwick's left, just beyond Salem Heights. Preparations were then made to act in concert with Early's force, which had late on Sunday night succeeded in retaking the Fredericksburg Heights, and compelled Gibbon's return on ponton-bridges across the river; but it was not till about six o'clock that the new lines were formed for a renewal of the conflict.

Of Sedgwick's Sixth Corps, Howe's division still held the position which had been given it just beyond Marye's Hill, and which stretched out as far as Taylor's Hill, on the River Road. Early had engaged in lively skirmishing with the Federals throughout most of the day, and had even made an attempt to turn the extreme Federal left, but to no purpose, for the artillery at that point was in the

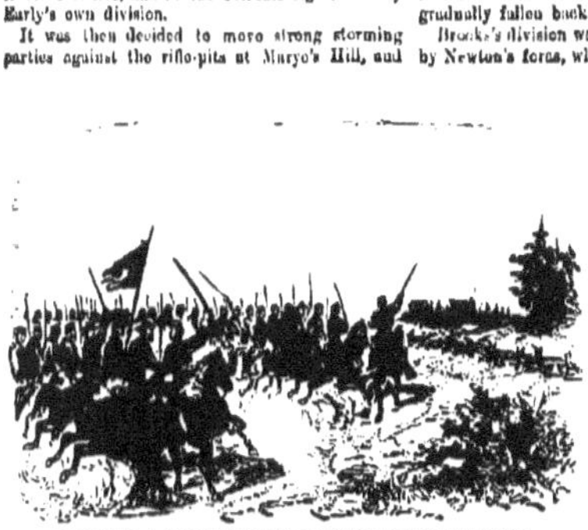

CHARGING A CONFEDERATE BATTERY NEAR RICHMOND.

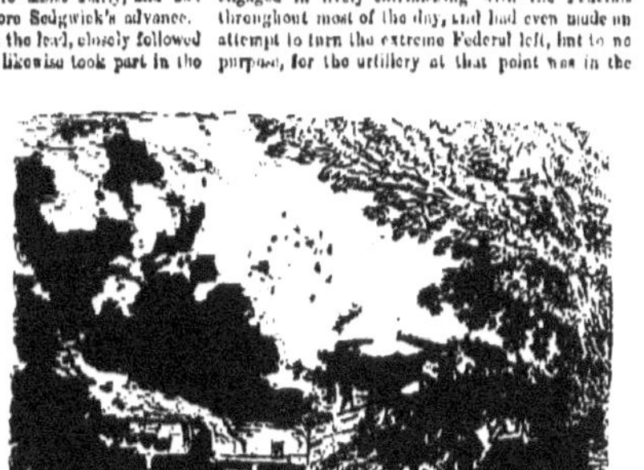

DESTROYING CANAL LOCKS AND BOATS.

nands of Major J. W. de Peyster, Jr., who had posted and served it so ably as to force the retirement of the Confederates after sustaining a heavy loss.

The other two divisions of Sedgwick's corps—Newton's and Brooks's—were posted respectively opposite McLaws's force, stretching on either side of the Plank Road, just in the rear of Salem Church, and opposite Anderson's line, which extended westward of the Telegraph Road, about on a parallel with the Chancellorsville and Fredericksburg Plank Road.

When the signal was given at six o'clock, McLaws advanced against the left of Newton's and the right of Brooks's divisions, and an obstinate conflict followed. Sedgwick's force tried to overcome the attacks which were repeatedly directed mainly against his left, but his efforts proved futile, and he had finally to abandon the ground in a retreat toward Banks's Ford. The darkness by this time had become so thick that the Confederates could not institute a pursuit, and Sedgwick was therefore enabled to take his force across the Rappahannock before the following morning.

At about the time McLaws made the above-named attack, Early renewed his attempt to turn Howe's left, his efforts being mainly directed against a battery which Major de Peyster, Jr., had established in an effective position somewhat in advance of the main line. But in this Early's troops failed signally, as they likewise did a little later when attempting to turn Howe's extreme right. Each assault was bravely repulsed by the Federals, until a large body having been suddenly brought to bear against General Neil's brigade, it was forced to yield the ground just as darkness was setting in. The engagement then ceased, and during the ensuing night Howe was ordered to join Sedgwick's other two divisions across Banks's Ford, the passage of all being successfully made under cover of thirty-two pieces of artillery, posted on the northern side of the river.

At a council of war held the same evening, Hooker asked the opinion of his general officers regarding the continuation of the struggle, and, yielding to the majority, he ordered a retreat across the Rappahannock. This was made in good order, under cover of Meade's corps, during the ensuing very dark and stormy night, and without attracting the attention of the opposing forces, although Hooker was compelled to leave behind all his dead and wounded, as well as fourteen pieces of artillery, much ammunition, and a large number of small arms.

Three days later Hooker's army was joined at its old headquarters by the detachments of Stoneman's cavalry, which had been scouring the neighboring country while the Federals were operating around Chancellorsville, the separate bodies under Davis and Kilpatrick being then at Gloucester Point.

In addition to making numerous reconnoissances, more particularly toward Rapidan Station, Louisa Court House, White House, Gordonsville and Hanover Junction, Stoneman's force had destroyed much of the line of the Virginia Central Railway, as well as the canal-bridges and part of the stone aqueduct spanning the Rivanna at Columbia. The most important demonstrations were, however, made by a detachment of the Twelfth Illinois, under Colonel Hasbrook Davis, and by a detachment from the Sixth New York Cavalry, led by Judson Kilpatrick.

Davis's force captured and paroled a train-full of Confederates, and destroyed much of the railway at Ashland, just north of Richmond, besides burning the Virginia Central depots at, and damaging the lines leading to, Hanover Court House. Kilpatrick's force advanced up to within about two miles of Richmond, and created great consternation in the Confederate capital, especially while part of his command was for a while engaged in destroying a large amount of property inside the fortifications, as well as much of the line of the Richmond and Fredericksburg Railway. After burning the depots and other buildings at Hungary Station, the Federals crossed the Virginia Central, destroying the Meadow Bridge and all neighboring structures, and did not join the garrison still holding Gloucester Point, on the York River, until the 7th of May.

Kilpatrick's force subsequently operated around

RETURN TO NEW YORK, APRIL 28TH, 1863, OF THE SEVENTH AND EIGHTH NEW YORK VOLUNTEER REGIMENTS, AFTER A SERVICE OF TWO YEARS IN THE FIELD.

Urbanna, and after successfully engaging several bodies of Confederates, capturing many prisoners and destroying many thousand dollars worth of additional property, it rejoined General Hooker's army at Falmouth, on the 3d of the following month.

June, 1863.

The total number killed, wounded and missing, in the operations above described, were reported at 17,197 on the Federal side, and 13,020 on part of the Confederates, the greatest losses being sustained by General Hill's and General Rodes's divisions, and by Sickles's Third and Sedgwick's Sixth Corps.

In addition to the loss of General Jackson, already alluded to, the Confederate list included General Hill among the wounded, while the Federals had among their killed Generals Berry, Devens and Whipple, and Generals Sickles and Mott among the wounded.

The contending armies maintained comparative quiet until the commencement of June, when it was learned that Lee contemplated making a second invasion of the North, and that he was already concentrating some of his forces at Culpepper Court House for that purpose.

Strong reconnoissances made along the southern bank of the Rappahannock, notably by Howe's division, which had quite a heavy skirmish with Hill's corps, developed the fact that many of the Confederates had already moved in the direction named. Hooker determined to arrest, if possible, all further progress on their part, and for that purpose the Fifth Corps was so posted as to check all attempted movements by way of either the Banks or the United States Ford.

In addition to this, a reconnoissance in force toward Culpepper Court House was ordered to be made by General Pleasanton, who had meanwhile been promoted to command the Federal cavalry, by reason of Stoneman having incurred Hooker's displeasure. The reconnoissance was made on the 9th of June, and resulted in quite a severe battle at Brandy Station (Fleetwood Hill), as well as in an engagement at Beverly Ford, between two divisions of Federal cavalry under Generals Gregg and Buford, supported by light artillery as well as by Ames's and Russell's infantry brigades, and the remainder of Stuart's forces, the greater part of which were supposed then to be already at Culpepper Court House. The infantry, cavalry and artillery forces opposed to Pleasanton's detachment proved much more important than had been anticipated, and after a series of engagements in which he lost about 800 men, including Colonel B. F. Davis, of the Eighth New York, he had to retreat in the afternoon, lest his passage to the Rappahannock be seriously impeded, if not entirely cut off, by the superior numbers everywhere opposing him.

On the same day, two new Departments were created by the Government, and placed in charge of Generals D. N. Couch and W. T. H. Brooks, thus making in all nineteen Military Departments, as follows:

Department of New England—Major-general John A. Dix.
Department of New Mexico—Brigadier-general James H. Carlton.
Departments of North Carolina and of Virginia—Major-general J. G. Foster.
Department of Kansas—Major-general James G. Blunt.
Department of Key West—Brigadier-general J. M. Brannan.
Department of Missouri—Major-general John M. Schofield.
Department of Washington—Major-general S. P. Heintzelman.
Department of Western Virginia—Brigadier-general B. F. Kelley.
Department of the Cumberland—Major-general W. S. Rosecrans.
Department of the Gulf—Major-general N. P. Banks.
Department of the Monongahela—Major-general W. T. H. Brooks.
Department of the Northwest—Major-general John Pope.
Department of the Ohio—Major-general A. E. Burnside.
Department of the Pacific—Brigadier-general G. Wright.
Department of the South—Brigadier-general Q. A. Gillmore.
Department of the Susquehanna—Major-general Darius N. Couch.
Department of the Tennessee—Major-general U. S. Grant.
Middle Department—Major-general Robert C. Schenck.

On the 10th, Ewell began his march northward from Culpepper, which he and Longstreet reached two days before, and, passing the Blue Ridge Mountains at Chester Gap, entered the Shenandoah Valley by way of Front Royal, detaching Rodes at the latter place, in order to cut off Federal communication with Berryville. Three days later, he had, by a forced march of seventy miles, reached Winchester with the divisions of Jubal Early and Edward Johnston. He had thus actually extended the Confederate lines over one hundred miles of country, for the main body of Lee's army at this moment still lay in its former position, the extreme right under Hill being at Fredericksburg, and the centre under Longstreet occupying Culpepper Court House.

By the 13th, Hooker became satisfied that Lee's early invasion had been fully determined upon, especially on learning of Ewell's entrance into the Shenandoah Valley, and he accordingly prepared to immediately move northward for the protection of Washington. The Third and Fifth Corps were temporarily left to guard the fords, and the rest of the army was taken through Bealton, Catlett's Station and Warrenton, and afterward to Fairfax Court House and Manassas, the latter place being reached on the 15th and 16th of June, with the First, Sixth and Eleventh Corps. The Third Corps soon joined him at Manassas, and the Second, Fifth and Twelfth Corps were brought up in reserve at Fairfax Court House, while Pleasanton's cavalry guarded the extreme left of the army at Warrenton.

Hill abandoned his position on the Rappahannock as soon as Hooker had gone, and joined Longstreet at Culpepper. He remained there but a short time, and then moving into Ewell's track, entered the Shenandoah Valley, finally taking position at Winchester, while Longstreet pushed on at once toward the Ashby and Snicker Gaps, in the Blue Ridge.

SHOOTING CATTLE FOR THE SUPPLY OF THE FEDERAL ARMY.
From a Sketch by Edwin Forbes.

While Hooker and Hill were departing from their respective positions at Fredericksburg, Ewell was preparing to invest Winchester, then held by General Robert H. Milroy, whose actual force did not at the time exceed seven thousand men. Imboden had been sent out in the direction of Romney to cover the movement on Winchester, and to cut off Milroy's communication by way of the Baltimore and Ohio Railroad, and it was not until the 14th that Milroy heard through scouts and from Colonel McReynolds, who had withdrawn his brigade from Berryville, that the Confederates were with a much superior force about surrounding him.

At a council of officers held late the same evening, it was decided to retreat from Winchester toward the Potomac, as the position seemed untenable. The guns were spiked, and the garrison marched out before daylight of the 15th in the direction of Harper's Ferry; but it had not proceeded more than about four miles when Johnston fell heavily upon Milroy's force, which he had headed off, and succeeded in completely dispersing the entire body. Some Confederates had likewise

VIEW FROM LOUDON HEIGHTS, VA., SHOWING HARPER'S FERRY, MARYLAND HEIGHTS, BOLIVAR, ETC.

ARMY OF THE POTOMAC.—SCENE AT THE CROSSING OF A STREAM ON AN IMPROVISED BRIDGE.

ALDIE, THE SCENE OF GENERAL PLEASANTON'S VICTORIOUS CAVALRY ENGAGEMENT.

FROM SKETCHES BY EDWIN FORBES.

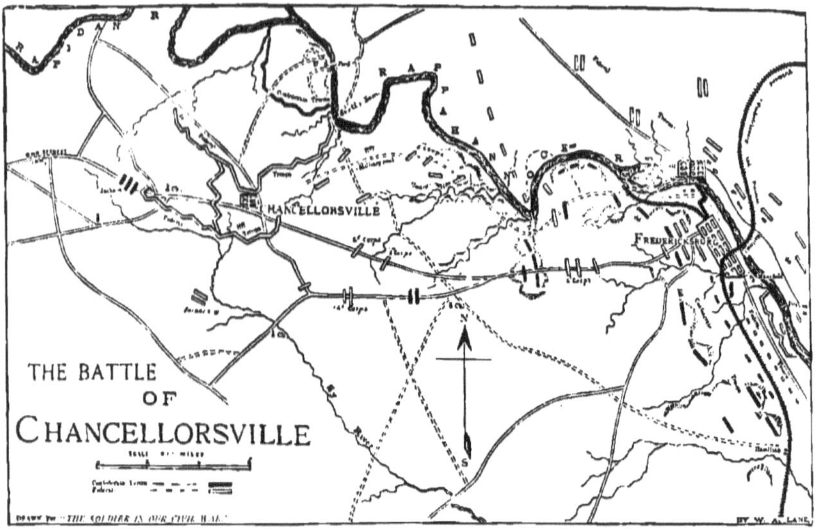

followed and attacked the Federal rear, and Milroy barely succeeded in saving himself and a small troop from capture by hastening to the river. His total loss was about four thousand killed, wounded and made prisoners, besides twenty-nine guns, many wagons and horses, and a large quantity of stores and ammunition.

While Longstreet was occupying the Gaps, the cavalry of both armies had several encounters. The most important of these took place at Aldie, where, on the 17th of June, the First Massachusetts, the First Maine, and part of the Second and Fourth New York, as well as the Sixth Ohio and First Rhode Island Regiments, under Judson Kilpatrick, drove back Stuart's force to Ashby Gap, and followed it beyond Upperville, while Longstreet and Hill were proceeding in the direction of Winchester. Two days later, June 19th, part of the same force, with the addition of the Tenth New York and of the Fourth and Sixteenth Pennsylvania Cavalry, again successfully engaged Stuart at Middleburg, and forced him to retire after a running fight of nearly eight miles, during which there were heavy losses on both sides.

After Milroy's flight, Ewell had in succession gone to Williamsport, Shepherdstown, Hagerstown and Chambersburg, arriving before the latter place

ARMY BLACKSMITH SHOEING A REFRACTORY MULE.
From a Sketch by Edwin Forbes.

late on the 22d. The small force of Federal troops stationed at these points fell back before Ewell, and he was enabled a few days later to proceed with Rode's division as far north as Kingston, thirteen miles from Harrisburg, while Early's force was raiding Emmittsburg, Gettysburg and York, going as far as Wrightsville.

Rodes found it advisable not to proceed beyond Kingston, as the people had by this time risen *en masse*, and joined the militia and volunteers called out by the President* and by the Governors of the States for the protection of the North from the threatened invasion. Nor could Early advance beyond Wrightsville, as, before the Confederates reached the town, the Federal troops guarding Columbia, on the opposite side of the river, had

SOLDIERS' GRAVES AT FALMOUTH, VA.

by Colonel Frick's orders set fire to the large bridge (of twenty-eight arches, and one and a quarter miles in length) there spanning the Susquehanna.

In the meantime Hill and Longstreet had continued in Ewell's track, and after fording the Potomac at Williamsport and Shepherdstown on the 24th and 25th, had united at Hagerstown, whence they advanced together until they reached Chambersburg on the 27th.

Hooker had followed close upon the Confederates, and with the reinforcements that had been sent him, crossed the Potomac at Edward's Ferry on the 26th, and advanced toward Frederick City. His intention was to await there the passage of French's corps, then garrisoning Harper's Ferry, whither he had already ordered Slocum's force. This he did in the expectation that Halleck would allow him to withdraw the former, and that the two could then advance together along the western side of the South Mountain range and attack Lee's rear at Chambersburg, while Hooker would move his own force northward from Frederick.

General Halleck's opinion relative to the value of Harper's Ferry as a permanent post being then entirely opposite of that entertained by General Hooker, the latter's request as to the removal of French's corps could not be entertained. Hooker reiterated his request, and meeting with another refusal, advised Halleck that he deemed it impossible to carry out the original plan with the forces then at his disposal, and desired therefore to be relieved of his command. His resignation was at once accepted, and General George G. Meade, then at the head of the Fifth Corps, was, late on the 27th of June, appointed to command the Army of the Potomac in his stead.

HIRAM GEORGE BERRY.

Born in Thomaston (now Rockland), Me., August 27th, 1824. Represented his native town several times in the State Legislature, and became Mayor of Rockland, as well as President of the Lime Rock Bank. Organized and for many years commanded the Rockland Guard, which attained a high reputation for the excellency of its drill and discipline. Entered the Volunteer service, at the time of the breaking out of the Civil War, as colonel of the Fourth Maine Volunteers, after having raised four of its companies, and with it took part in the first battle of Bull Run, and in the siege of Yorktown. Having received the appointment of brigadier general of Volunteers, he was given the Third Brigade of the Third Division of Heintzelman's Third Army Corps. Participated in the engagements of Williamsburg, Fair Oaks, and in nearly all of the Seven (Six) Days' battles, as well as in those fought at Manassas, the second Bull Run, Chantilly and Fredericksburg. In January, 1863, he was given the commission of major-general of Volunteers, to date from November 29th, 1862, and placed at the head of the Second Division of the Third Army Corps, which greatly distinguished itself at the battle of Chancellorsville, where he was killed, on the 2d of May, 1863, while leading a desperate bayonet charge against the Confederates.

ROBERT H. MILROY.

Born in Indiana about 1811; became a lawyer; served in the Mexican War as captain of Indiana Volunteers; tendered his services to the United States Government on the breaking out of the Civil War; was given the commission of brigadier general in 1861, and figured in many of the engagements fought under Generals McClellan and Rosecrans throughout Western Virginia. He afterward served under Fremont in the Shenandoah Valley, taking command of his central column at the battle of Cross Keys. He was appointed a major-general of Volunteers on the 29th of November, 1862, and

---

* The following is the text of the President's proclamation:

"Whereas, The armed insurrectionary combinations now existing in several of the States are threatening to make inroads into the States of Maryland, West Virginia, Pennsylvania and Ohio, requiring immediately an additional military force for the service of the United States.

"Now, therefore, I, Abraham Lincoln, President of the United States, and Commander-in-Chief of the Army and Navy thereof, and of the Militia of the several States when called into actual service, do hereby call into the service of the United States one hundred thousand Militia from the States following, namely:

"From the State of Maryland, ten thousand.

"From the State of Pennsylvania, fifty thousand.

"From the State of Ohio, thirty thousand.

"From the State of West Virginia, ten thousand.

"To be mustered into the service of the United States forthwith, and to serve for the period of six months from the date of such muster into said service, unless sooner discharged; to be mustered in as infantry, artillery and cavalry, in proportions which will be made known through the War Department, which Department will also designate the several places of rendezvous.

"These Militia are to be organized according to the rules and regulations of the Volunteer service and such orders as may hereafter be issued. The States aforesaid will be respectively credited, under the Enrollment Act for the Militia, services rendered under this proclamation.

"In testimony whereof I have hereunto set my hand and caused the seal of the United States to be affixed.

"Done at the City of Washington this 15th day of June, in the year of our Lord 1863 and of the Independence of the United States the eighty-seventh.

"By the President. ABRAHAM LINCOLN."

"WILLIAM H. SEWARD, *Secretary of State*."

CONSECRATION OF THE NATIONAL CEMETERY AT GETTYSBURG, PA., NOVEMBER

CONSECRATION OF THE NATIONAL CEMETERY AT GETTYSBURG, PA., NOVEMBER 19th, 1863, BY ABRAHAM LINCOLN, PRESIDENT OF THE UNITED STATES AND HIS CABINET

HIRAM G. BERRY.

WILLIAM H. FRENCH.

held Winchester, Va., when it was invested by Ewell's forces, which compelled him to retreat toward the Potomac with the loss of about one-half of his force. He proceeded to Harper's Ferry, and was subsequently called before a court of inquiry touching his conduct at Winchester, but escaped a threatened court martial, as the President could find no cause for "serious blame" regarding his conduct on the occasion referred to. He was assigned to different commands up to the close of the Civil War, the last finding him at Tullahoma, Tenn., in charge of the defenses of the Nashville and Chattanooga Railway.

WILLIAM HENRY FRENCH.

Born at Baltimore, Md., on January 13th, 1815; graduated at the United States Military Academy at West Point, July 1st, 1837; entered the army as second-lieutenant of the First Artillery. In December of that year he was made assistant commissary of subsistence. He took part in many of the troubles occurring along the Florida and Canadian borders. During the War with Mexico he served on the staff of General Patterson as assistant acting adjutant-general, and as aid to General Franklin Pierce. He was brevetted captain at Cerro Gordo; distinguishing himself particularly at the battles of Contreras and Churubusco—where he was brevetted major—and in the engagements before the City of Mexico. He was then assigned to garrison and frontier duty up to the time of the breaking out of the Civil War, when he was transferred from his station at Fort Duncan, Tex., to Key West, Fla. In September, 1861, he was appointed a brigadier-general, serving in the Army of the Potomac during the Virginia Peninsular, as well as in the Maryland and Rappahannock campaigns, and taking part more especially in the battles of Fair Oaks, Gaines's Mills, Peach Orchard, Savage's Station, Malvern Hill, Antietam, Fredericksburg and Chancellorsville. He was made a major-general of Volunteers in November, 1862, and placed in command of the Third Army Corps from July, 1863, to March 1864, when was he ordered to report at Philadelphia, and shortly afterward mustered out of the Volunteer service. From 1865 to 1872 he served on the Pacific Coast in the Second United States Artillery, having been promoted through the successive grades up to lieutenant-colonel. From 1872 to 1875, he was in command of the Second United States Artillery, at Fort McHenry, Maryland.

EARL VAN DORN.

Born in Mississippi in 1821; graduated from the United States Military Academy at West Point in 1842, and entered the army as brevet second-lieutenant in the Ninth Infantry; became a second-lieutenant in 1844, and a first-lieutenant in 1847; received the brevets of captain for gallantry at Cerro Gordo, and of major for gallantry at Contreras and Churubusco; distinguished himself at Chapultepec, and was wounded at the final assault upon the City of Mexico. From January, 1852, to June, 1855, he was secretary and treasurer of the Military Asylum at Pascagoula, Miss. He afterward took part in three different expeditions against the Comanches in Texas, and was very severely wounded at Washita Village, Indian Territory, October 1st, 1858. Upon the breaking out of the Civil War, he resigned his commission of major of the Second U. S. Regular Cavalry, to accept a position of colonel of a regiment of Confederate Texas Volunteers. In the Spring of 1861, he captured the U. S. steamer *Star of the West* at Indianola, and, a few days later, received at Saluria the surrender of Major Sibley, with seven companies of U. S. Infantry, following it up shortly after by the capture of Lieutenant-colonel Reeve, with eight companies of the Eighth Infantry. He received not long after the grades of brigadier-general and of major-general, and on the 10th of January, 1862, was placed in command of the Trans-Mississippi District; defeated at the battle of Pea Ridge, superseded by General T. N. Holmes, and transferred to the Army of the Mississippi. He commanded at the battle of Corinth, where he was again unsuccessful, and was superseded by General John C. Pemberton. He subsequently made his headquarters in Maury County, Tenn., where he was shot on the 8th of May, 1863, by a Dr. Peters, on account of a private grievance.

EARL VAN DORN.

ROBERT H. MILROY.

THE BATTLE OF GETTYSBURG.

LEE'S SECOND INVASION.

WITH the command of the Army of the Potomac, Meade obtained permission to make such use of French's force as he might think proper, and he immediately ordered the latter to abandon Harper's Ferry and to occupy Frederick City, as well as the line of the Baltimore and Ohio Railway.

On the 30th of June, Meade issued a stirring address to his troops,* and by evening of the same day he had selected the course of the Big Pipe Creek, just beyond the Westminster Hills, for his battle line, and given directions for the movements of the army on the following morning. Sedgwick's Sixth Corps, occupying the extreme right, was ordered to move to Manchester, in the rear of the Big Pipe Creek, and the First, Third and Eleventh Corps, forming the extreme left, were to be taken by General Reynolds from Marsh Creek, along the Emmettsburg Turnpike, to Gettysburg, where Buford had just preceded him from Middleburg; while the centre, consisting of Sykes's Fifth and Slocum's Twelfth Corps, would advance upon Two Taverns and Hanover. Hancock was ordered to move with the Second Corps to Taneytown, where the commanding general established his headquarters.

As soon as Lee perceived Meade's first operations, he ordered Ewell to recall his forces from Carlisle toward Gettysburg, and instructed Hill and Longstreet to advance in the same direction from Fayetteville and Chambersburg. Stuart had in the meantime brought up his cavalry through Westminster as far as Carlisle, after once more encountering and being again defeated by Kilpatrick's force while passing through Hanover.

At about nine o'clock on Wednesday, the 1st of July, Buford, who was in position on the Chambersburg Road, just beyond Seminary Ridge, and close by Willoughby's Run, was attacked by Hill's leading division, under General Henry Heth, then on its way to Gettysburg. Believing that Reynolds's force would hasten toward him on hearing the noise of the conflict, Buford disputed the advance, and handled his force so ably during the ensuing hour, that his lines were found to have been forced back but a short distance toward the Ridge by the time Wadsworth's leading division of the First Corps approached the scene.

JULY, 1863.

Reynolds, who had accompanied Wadsworth, immediately posted Cutler's brigade upon each side of the Chambersburg Road, as well as along the unfinished railroad cut; but before the line could be properly deployed, Davis's Mississippi and North Carolina regiments fell upon its right and forced it back, so that finally one of the guns belonging to Hall's battery had to be abandoned.

At the same time a small force of skirmishers, previously taken from Cutler's brigade, was disputing Archer's advance toward the woods across Willoughby's Run. The skirmishers would soon have been compelled to retire before the large numbers centring at this point but for the opportune arrival of General Meredith's ("Iron") brigade, the remainder of Wadsworth's division. The latter succeeded in flanking the enemy, and was reformed upon the heights fronting the western side of Willoughby's Run, after capturing Archer himself, with nearly eight hundred of his men.

The latter movement was personally directed by General Reynolds, who then deemed the possession of the line of woods along Willoughby's Run the real key to the whole position. While Meredith's charge was in progress, Reynolds naturally felt much solicitude as to its result. He approached the borders of a grove close by the Run, whence he could best observe the advance of the troops, and there remained until he saw the movement well under way; but he had gone too far, and when he turned to rejoin his staff, a bullet fired by a Confederate sharpshooter struck him in the neck, and passing through the head, caused his instant death.

General Doubleday, who had been already given charge of the First Corps, and who had in turn placed his own division with General Rowley, assumed command in Reynolds's stead. He withdrew Meredith's brigade across Willoughby's Run, and sent a force to aid Cutler's men, who were still battling with Davis. As the reinforcements came up, three of Cutler's remaining regiments rapidly changed front, and not only were then enabled to gain possession of the gun previously abandoned, but to likewise surround and finally capture two of Davis's Mississippi regiments who had sought shelter in a deep cut of the old railway grading. Immediately after this the whole of Cutler's force was re-formed, and was once more brought into position on the extreme right.

At about eleven o'clock the other two divisions of the First Corps, under Generals Rowley and Robinson, reached Gettysburg, with Stewart's, Cooper's Reynolds's and Stevens's batteries. Rowley's three brigades were at once advanced in support of the extreme left, and Robinson's force was held in reserve along Seminary Ridge, between the Chambersburg and the Fairfield Pikes, until it was found that Ewell's advance, under General Rodes, had come up from Heidlersburg and connected with Hill's left. This was close by and along an eminence called Oak Hill, situated near the northern extremity of Seminary ridge, between the Carlisle and Mummasburg Pikes.

Rodes's division in fact already occupied quite a commanding position on the ridge north of Gettysburg, thus threatening the extreme Federal right. Baxter's Second Brigade was then posted on Cutler's right, and rested upon the Mummasburg Road, whither General Paul's First Brigade followed it as soon as the Federals become engaged with Rodes's division.

O'Neal's brigade, belonging to the latter, had first attacked the Federal right so fiercely on all sides as to compel Baxter to repeatedly change front. When it was finally learned that Iverson's brigade was coming up to O'Neal's support, Baxter deployed his force behind an angular stone wall or fence along the Mummasburg Road in such way as to thoroughly conceal for the time both his front and right flank from observation.

CITIZENS OF PENNSYLVANIA WORKING IN THE FORTIFICATIONS TO REPEL THE INVASION OF LEE'S ARMY.

FROM A SKETCH BY GEORGE LAW.

Iverson brought up his men unsuspectingly, until the Twelfth Massachusetts, the Eighty-eighth and Ninetieth Pennsylvania, and the Eighty-third and Ninety-seventh New York Regiments, rose almost simultaneously from their hiding-place, and delivered so destructive a volley along the whole line as to disable nearly one-third of Iverson's entire force. The firing was so sudden that Iverson's men were thrown into great confusion, and through the aid Cutler gave Baxter, after he himself had repulsed O'Neal, nearly all that remained of Iverson's four North Carolina regiments were soon after compelled to surrender.

While O'Neal and Iverson were thus engaged, Daniel's brigade joined Davis's force, of Hill's corps, and the two afterward attacked Stone's brigade, of Rowley's division, which had been posted to the left of the Chambersburg Road, in the rear of quite an elevated ridge, which proved afterward to be the real key to the Federal position.

Upon Stone's left stood Meredith's brigade, then commanded by Colonel Morrow. The latter occupied the woods along Willoughby's Run, and a little behind Morrow stood Rowley's late brigade, in charge of Colonel Biddle. The latter was posted to the right of the Fairfield Road, in a line almost parallel with Cutler's.

Pender's division, of Hill's corps, had likewise reached the field, and been placed in position to support Heth. Scales's brigade extended its line southward from the Chambersburg Road, directly in the rear of Pettigrew and Brockenborough.

* "HEADQUARTERS ARMY OF THE POTOMAC, June 30th, 1863.

"The Commanding General requests that, previous to the engagement soon expected with the enemy, corps and all other commanding officers address their troops, explaining to them the immense issues involved in the struggle. The enemy is now on our soil. The whole country looks anxiously to this army to deliver it from the presence of the foe. Our failure to do so will leave us no such welcome as the swelling of millions of hearts with pride and joy at our success would give to every soldier of the Army. Homes, firesides and domestic altars are involved. The army has fought well heretofore. It is believed that it will fight more desperately and bravely than ever if it is addressed in fitting terms.

"Corps and other commanders are authorized to order the instant death of any soldier who fails to do his duty at this hour.

"By command of "GEORGE G. MEADE, Major-general.

S. WILLIAMS, Assistant Adjutant-general."

CONFEDERATE CAVALRY [illegible] OF LEE'S ARMY INVADING THE NORTHERN STATES.

Barracks. General Smith's Headquarters.

CARLISLE, PA., SHOWING GENERAL SMITH'S HEADQUARTERS, AND THE BARRACKS DESTROYED BY GENERAL FITZ HUGH LEE.

FROM A SKETCH BY GEORGE LAW.

whose brigades formed Hill's centre, while Thomas's brigade stood behind Davis's, northward from the Chambersburg Road to and across the unfinished railway grading. Lane's brigade was posted behind that of Thomas, and Perrin's (McGowan's) followed Scales's line, while the artillery battalions of Major D. G. McIntosh and of Major W. P. Pegram occupied the crest of a hill running westward from Willoughby's Run.

Just before one o'clock the advance of the Eleventh Corps, under Schimmelpfennig, reached Gettysburg. General Howard had preceded it by nearly an hour, and had assumed command of the left wing after turning over his own (the Eleventh) corps to General Carl Schurz. Schimmelpfennig was closely followed into Gettysburg by General Barlow's (late Schurz's) force, and both divisions were posted along Seminary Ridge to the right of the First Corps. The last division of the Eleventh Corps, under Steinwehr, was placed as a reserve upon Cemetery Hill with Major Osborn's artillery.

Upon hearing that Early's division, of Ewell's force, was fast approaching, the two divisions of the Eleventh Corps were directed to move from Seminary Ridge to the north of Gettysburg. Barlow's force crossed the Mummasburg and the Carlisle Roads, and the brigades led by General Ames and by Colonel Von Gilsa took position upon a ridge west of the Harrisburg Road, just in the rear of Rock Creek, while both of Schimmelpfennig's brigades were ranged across the Carlisle Road. Coster's brigade, of Steinwehr's division, was brought up across the Harrisburg Road, a short distance out of Gettysburg.

The attack upon Stone's brigade began at about half-past one, and was bravely sustained at the outset, mainly by Colonel Dwight's One Hundred and Forty-ninth Pennsylvania Regiment, which stood in position at the railway cut. With the aid of the One Hundred and Forty-third and of the One Hundred and Fiftieth Pennsylvania Regiments, it succeeded after a bitter contest in driving away Daniel's force at the point of the bayonet. In this engagement Stone was wounded, and Colonel Wister took his place, giving the command of his own (the One Hundred and Fifteenth Pennsylvania) regiment to Lieutenant-colonel Huidekoper.

The Confederates soon renewed the assault, Davis's force engaging the One Hundred and Fifteenth Pennsylvania, and Daniel's opposing the other two regiments more to the westward, while Pettigrew and Brockenborough were advancing against Morrow; but they were all repulsed with severe losses. Wister was shot in the face, and Huidekoper received a severe wound in the arm, both being replaced respectively by Colonel E. L. Dana and Major Thomas Chamberlain.

By this time more than half of Stone's force was disabled, and Morrow, who had borne the flag after several color-bearers had fallen, was twice wounded, the second time fatally, while in advance of the Twenty-fourth Michigan Regiment, whose colonel, W. W. Robinson, replaced him in command of the brigade.

The repulse of the Confederates was but temporary, however, as their strong reserve divisions were brought up against Robinson, while Pender's and Heth's leading brigades were operating against the extreme Federal left, along Willoughby's Run. A terrible fight ensued, for the determination of the Federals to hold more particularly the line of woods, and likewise the position then occupied by

CITIZENS OF BALTIMORE BARRICADING THE STREETS, MONDAY EVENING, JUNE 29TH, 1863.

FROM A SKETCH BY EDWIN FORBES.

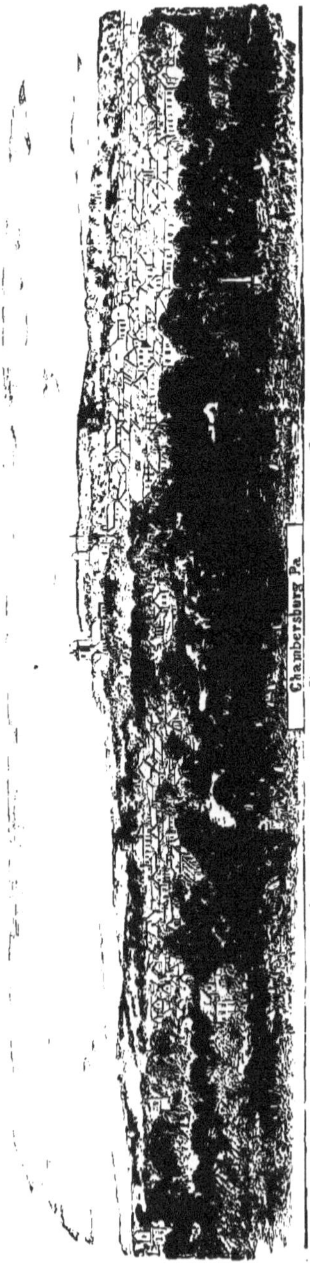

THE CONFEDERATE CAVALRY CHARGING THROUGH THE STREETS OF CHAMBERSBURG PA., JUNE 16th, 1863.

GENERAL LEE'S ARMY CROSSING THE POTOMAC AT WILLIAMSPORT, IN SCOWS GUIDED BY WIRES.

FROM A SKETCH BY C. E. H. BONWILL.

Stone's force, seemed desperate. The losses were frightful, especially from the well-served artillery of the Confederates, which succeeded in gaining a position from which they could pour such a destructive cross-fire as to prevent the maintenance of opposing batteries at every important point.

The Federals were driven back on all sides. The line along Willoughby's Run was first abandoned, and the retirement of Hall's battery was rapidly followed by the withdrawal of the batteries of Captain Reynolds and Cooper and of Lieutenant J. H. Calef.

After one of the most sanguinary encounters of the war, the First Corps formed a new line along Seminary Ridge, and what remained of the artillery was posted to the south and north of the railway cut, as well as to the rear of the Seminary building. Buford's cavalry was ordered along to protect the possible line of retreat by way of the Fairfield Road to Cemetery Hill.

The extreme left of the Eleventh Corps was thus left uncovered, and when, at about half-past three o'clock, a general advance was ordered by the Confederates, Rodes broke through the Federal centre with comparatively little difficulty, and by turning the right of the First Corps and the left of the Eleventh Corps, occupied the intervening space, throwing the entire line into disorder.

Both corps fell back upon Gettysburg, the First Corps reaching the town after the Eleventh, and bringing along all the artillery with which the left had attempted a final though unsuccessful stand upon Seminary Ridge, and in which Generals Pender and Scales were severely wounded. When the Federals passed through the Gettysburg streets, they became so utterly confused that Early succeeded, after a series of rapid dashes, in capturing about 5,000 prisoners.

The Confederates pressed on and occupied Gettysburg. The Eleventh Corps took position on Cemetery Hill, in front and to the right of Steinwehr's reserves, while the Second and Third Divisions of the First Corps were deployed upon Steinwehr's left and rear, Wadsworth's division being made to occupy Culp's Hill, which commanded the approaches to the town by the Baltimore Road.

Just then Hancock arrived. Upon learning of Reynolds's death, Meade ordered Hancock to leave his (Second) corps with General Gibbon, and to proceed to Gettysburg, there to assume the chief command. Hancock accordingly took Howard's place, and, with the aid of the latter, completed the formation of the new line, by placing upon the heights, to the extreme left, Geary's division of Slocum's Twelfth Corps, as soon as it reached the field.

By six o'clock, Ruger's division also arrived from Littlestown, and before morning Stannard's fine Vermont brigade, as well as all of Sickles's Third Corps, had come up from Emmettsburg, and likewise taken position on the left as a reserve, and in continuation of the line of the First Corps.

Upon Ruger's arrival, Hancock turned the command over to General Slocum, and transferred the First Corps to General Newton, Doubleday resuming command of his division, after which he returned to Meade's headquarters at Taneytown, where he arrived at nine o'clock in the evening.

Lee, who had reached Gettysburg just before Hancock's arrival, did not order a general pursuit, not knowing then the reinforcements that might have been received by the Federals, and he decided to wait especially the arrival of Johnson's strong division of Ewell's corps before proceeding.

Meade determined to make a stand at Gettysburg, and at about one o'clock on the morning of Wednesday, the 2d, Hancock and himself had reached the house of Mrs. Leister, on the Taneytown Road, where headquarters were established. Lee made his headquarters that night at the Marshall House, on Seminary Ridge, and before morning he had formed a new line, which extended five miles in length from Rock Creek along the southern border of Gettysburg, and down the continuation of Seminary Ridge to a point a little beyond the Round Top.

JULY, 1863.

Upon the extreme Confederate right stood two of Longstreet's divisions under Hood and McLaws, facing the corps of Sickles and Hancock, which latter were in position along the Cemetery Ridge, extending from the Little Round Top to Zeigler's Grove, while Ewell's division formed the extreme Confederate left from Gettysburg to Rock Creek, and Hill's corps occupied the centre around Seminary Ridge, facing Howard's corps and Stannard's brigade upon the ridge to the northeast of Culp's Hill. The latter were supported by the divisions of Generals Doubleday, Wadsworth and Robinson.

Slocum's corps joined Wadsworth's division, already upon Culp's Hill, opposite to which stood Ewell; and Sykes's Fifth Corps, when it arrived from Union Mills, stood in reserve south of the Twelfth Corps. Sedgwick's Sixth Corps was the last to come upon the ground, which it reached late Wednesday afternoon, after a forced march of nearly thirty-six miles from Manchester. It then took

BATTLE OF GETTYSBURG, FRIDAY, JULY 3D, 1863.

FROM A SKETCH BY EDWIN FORBES.

GENERAL BUFORD'S ENGAGEMENT WITH STUART'S

GENERAL BUFORD'S ENGAGEMENT WITH STUART'S CONFEDERATE CAVALRY AT BOONSBORO, MD., JULY 8TH, 1863

OCCUPATION OF WRIGHTSVILLE, PA., BY LEE'S ARMY, AND DESTRUCTION OF THE COLUMBIA RAILROAD BRIDGE BY THE FEDERAL FORCE, JUNE 28TH, 1863.

FROM A SKETCH BY A. BERGHAUS.

position along the Taneytown Road, a little to the northeast of the Little Round Top.

Neither of the two armies, then only about a mile apart, appeared willing to take the initiative, and, aside from quite a lively skirmish which took place shortly after nine o'clock in the morning between the forces near the Peach Orchard, no attack was made until about half-past three o'clock, when Lee ordered a simultaneous advance against each flank of the Federal army, while demonstrations were being kept up against the centre.

The attacks were not, however, made simultaneously, as Lee had intended. Longstreet began by sending Hood's force against Sickles's extreme left, then held by General J. H. H. Ward, of Birney's division, whose three brigades extended their line from the Round Top across the Devil's Den, to and beyond the Peach Orchard, along the Emmettsburg Road.

Ward's force was driven back after a bitter contest, and before De Trobriand, who stood next in line, could give him any assistance. Upon turning Ward's left, Hood fell upon De Trobriand's flank and rear, leading part of his force between that portion of the field and the Round Top, while the battery was dragged and with great difficulty got into position upon the summit of the Little Round Top. Thence it immediately began pouring most destructive volleys into the ranks of the assailants below. A terrible struggle followed, and the ground was contested bitterly at all points.

The odds against the Federals were great, but in face of heavy losses they fought with a bravery rarely equaled. The Confederates were at last beaten back from the face of the hill, but passing along the ravine, they penetrated between both the Round Tops, thus flanking the Federals. The conflict was renewed more bitterly than before. The Federal ammunition again gave out, but the bayonet was once more made to play such an effective part, that at nightfall the Confederates had entirely withdrawn from the Little Round Top. They had suffered most from the last attack, which was sustained chiefly by the Twentieth Maine regiment, under Colonel Chamberlain, who captured a great many prisoners.

What Warren justly deemed to be, and what really was at that juncture, the most important position in the field, had thus been successfully maintained, though at a frightful cost of life. The the two brigades were soon so much cut up that Caldwell's second line, under General Zook and Colonel J. R. Brooke, had to be called to their relief.

General Zook was killed while leading his men into the severe action that followed. The fight was stubborn on both sides, and Brooke was enabled to drive back the Confederates up to their second line of batteries, with the aid of the remainder of General Ayres's force on the left, but to no lasting purpose. Promptly forming a new line, the Confederates drove back Caldwell's men, notwithstanding their obstinate resistance, causing them to rapidly lose all the advantage they had previously gained at the cost of nearly half the division.

Caldwell's division fell back under cover of part of the artillery stationed upon the Little Round Top, and McLaws's brigade, under Kershaw and Wofford, with Anderson's brigade, of Hood's division, then rushed in front of the main Federal line, extending from the wheat-field to the Little Round Top. General Crawford, commanding the Third Division of Sykes's corps, was ordered to drive them away, and taking with him the remaining brigade of his division, led by Colonel McCandless, he made a

GENERAL KILPATRICK REPULSING GENERAL J. E. B. STUART AT BOONSBORO', JULY 8TH, 1863.

FROM A SKETCH BY C. E. H. BONWILL.

McLaws, with Anderson's support, was assaulting De Trobriand's centre. The attack was made with such vigor that Sickles called for reinforcements, and Burling's brigade, of Humphreys's division, as well as the two brigades of Barnes's division, under Tilton and Sweitzer, were therefore sent him.

Barnes's remaining brigade, under Colonel Strong Vincent, had just then, at the request of General Warren, Meade's chief-engineer, been sent to occupy and hold the Little Round Top. Warren happened to be at the latter point just as Hood commenced his attack, and foreseeing the danger of such an important position falling into the hands of the Confederates in the event of Birney's defeat, he took upon himself to order forward Vincent's brigade, as stated.

Vincent reached the spot just before Hood's men came in sight and attempted its capture. The Federals met them bravely. A prolonged hand-to-hand fight followed the exhaustion of ammunition consequent upon the repeated attempts which Hood's men for a long time made to turn Vincent's position, and for a while the entire crest was alive with combatants.

Reinforcements were called up, and Weed's brigade, of Ayres's division, belonging to the Fifth Corps, was sent, with Hazlett's battery, the four regiments taking place upon Vincent's right, while losses were especially great in the last charges made by and against Hood's Texans, wherein Chamberlain lost nearly one-third of his command. The deaths included General Weed, Colonels Vincent and O'Rorke, and Lieutenant Charles E. Hazlett. After Chamberlain's last charge, Vincent's brigade, then led by Colonel J. C. Rice, had been reinforced by Fisher's brigade, of Crawford's division.

McLaws's assault was especially directed upon the angle formed by the Peach Orchard and the Emmettsburg Road, and the reinforcements reaching Sickles enabled him for a while only to stem the tide which had apparently set against him. The opposing force was too strong, and after a stubborn resistance on the part of the Federals, they were obliged to abandon the position. The line of Graham's brigade and of Humphreys's division, which stretched along the Emmettsburg Road, was under protection of McGilvery's artillery, then drawn around eastwardly, with the extreme right still resting upon the road.

Caldwell's division of the Second Corps was ordered ahead, and, with Cross and Kelly in the front, the conflict was renewed. This first line engaged the enemy with great vigor, but almost at the outset Colonel and Acting Brigadier-general Cross was mortally wounded while bravely leading the "Fighting Fifth" New Hampshire Regiment, and charge that threw dismay into the Confederate ranks, and compelled the enemy to fall back some distance beyond the wheat-field, where the conflict was brought to an end, as night was setting in.

The demonstrations which had been kept up against Humphreys's division meanwhile developed into a real attack by Hill's force, which had advanced from Seminary Ridge.

Hancock had strengthened Humphreys's flank with two regiments from Harrow's brigade, of Gibbon's division, which were shortly followed by the Nineteenth Massachusetts and the Forty-second New York Regiments, taken from Hall's brigade, and he had likewise detached Willard's brigade from General Alexander Hays's division of the Second Corps in order to fill up a gap existing upon Humphreys's left. Hill, however, outnumbered the Federals to such an extent, and his attack was so furiously made, both in Humphreys's front as well as upon his flanks, that the Federal line had to fall back to the crest of Cemetery Hill, after a most obstinate and sanguinary encounter.

In this Humphreys lost nearly one-half of his five thousand men, besides three guns from one of his batteries. Colonel George L. Willard was killed, Sickles had one of his legs so badly shattered that it had to be amputated, and General Graham was likewise severely wounded and taken prisoner.

BATTLE OF GETTYSBURG, THURSDAY EVENING, JULY [illegible] HILL ON MEADE'S LEFT.—[illegible] BY EDWIN FORBES.

Hill's force dashed up to the base of the crest, where it met the line which Hancock had caused to be rapidly formed of the previously disordered brigades, and which, with a new line of artillery, made a most spirited stand under Hancock's leadership. In this Hancock was ably seconded by General Birney, who had meanwhile taken Sickles's place at the head of the Third Corps. Meade had also come upon the field, leading two regiments of Lockwood's brigade, of the Twelfth Corps, which he posted toward the left at about the same time that Stannard's brigade, of Doubleday's division, and the First Minnesota Regiment, had got into position more toward the centre of the enemy's advance.

The fire that met the Confederates at the foot of the ridge was so hot that the entire line of the now fairly exhausted Confederates for a moment wavered and then recoiled. Seeing this, Meade ordered a general advance, in which the remainder of Doubleday's force participated. After another spirited contest, it succeeded just before sunset in driving back the Confederates nearly up to their line of reserves, and in taking some of the guns that had been previously captured.

Thus ended the engagement on the left centre. A new line was then formed with the divisions of Doubleday and Robinson, and by part of the Twelfth Corps, then under General A. S. Williams, who had taken Slocum's place when the latter assumed command of the entire right wing.

men also played an important part. Only two of the latter's guns could be spiked, as all further progress on the part of the Confederates was arrested by a well-directed flank and cross fire from the batteries of Stevens, Reynolds and Stewart, which had been promptly brought to the front.

Fortunately for Ames and Von Gilsa, Hancock detached Carroll's brigade from General Alexander Hays's division and sent it also to the front, where the One Hundred and Sixth Pennsylvania, of Webb's brigade, and part of Schurz's force, soon joined it. With these heavy reinforcements the Federals became in turn the aggressors, and were enabled to beat back Early's force, which was at last compelled to seek its original position before darkness had fully set in.

During the ensuing night Johnson's division was reinforced by Daniel's and O'Neal's brigades, from Rodes's division, and Geary's two brigades rejoined Greene's at Culp's Hill, where additional batteries had been erected at all exposed points.

July, 1863.

At break of day on Friday, the 3d of July, the Federal guns opened a heavy fire upon Johnson's position, where, from the nature of the ground, it had not been possible to bring up any artillery. The fire was so destructive that Johnson was compelled to charge up-hill in order to seek, if possible, a more favorable position. General Walker's "Stonewall" Brigade took the lead, and soon encountered Kane's (late Cobham's)

their preparations for the attack, and the fire from one hundred and fifteen guns was directed against Hancock's command, then embracing Newton's First, Gibbon's Second, Birney's Third and Howard's Eleventh Corps, for the purpose of opening a passage for Pickett's division. General H. J. Hunt, Meade's chief of artillery, promptly brought up all the guns that could be spared—about eighty in number—and an artillery duel was kept up incessantly for two hours, during which both sides experienced very heavy losses. Shortly after three o'clock General Hunt ordered the fire to cease, in order to cool the guns, replenish ammunition, and prepare for the contest at close quarters which, he justly thought, could not but soon follow.

The cessation of the Federal fire led Pickett to believe that he had silenced Hancock's artillery, and he therefore ordered an advance to be made over the one and a quarter miles then separating the contending armies.

As they proceeded, with Garnett's and Kemper's brigades in the immediate front, the Confederates were at first subjected to a withering fire of solid shot, which was followed by shell and canister as they approached nearer the Federal lines. They advanced bravely, notwithstanding the sad havoc already made in their immediate front as well as upon their flank, the latter suffering greatly from the simultaneous and well-directed shelling of batteries located upon the Little Round Top.

GALLANT CHARGE OF THE SIXTH MICHIGAN CAVALRY OVER THE CONFEDERATE BREASTWORKS, NEAR FALLING WATERS, JULY 14TH, 1863.

Contrary to Lee's expectation, Ewell, on the extreme left, did not advance until quite a while after Longstreet had attacked Birney's division. Johnson's force crossed Rock Creek, and with its extreme right moved against Wadsworth and Greene, the latter being the only brigade of Geary's division left at Culp's Hill. Geary's other brigades, under Colonels Charles Candy and George Cobham, had previously been ordered away by Meade toward the Little Round Top.

A brisk though short engagement took place, and resulted before dark in the repulse of Johnson's force, which suffered heavy losses, mainly from the artillery fronting the entire crest of the hill. Johnson then took possession of the works on the extreme Federal right which had been abandoned by Geary's men early in the day.

While Johnson was operating against Culp's Hill, Early made an attempt to carry Cemetery Hill after opening upon it with his artillery from Benner's Hill. His fire was quickly responded to and his batteries promptly silenced. He then advanced with General H. S. Hays's brigade on the right, and Colonel J. E. Avery's (late Hoke's) brigade upon the left, with Gordon's force in reserve, and fell first upon Von Gilsa's brigade, and then upon Ames's brigade, of Barlow's division, both of which protected Ricketts's and Wiedrick's batteries.

Von Gilsa's force was driven back by the assailants, and Ames's brigade was so covered as to expose the batteries. One of these, Wiedrick's, was captured after a bitter resistance, in which Ricketts's

brigade, of Geary's division, with which it had a fierce engagement, while the remainder of Johnson's force was battling furiously throughout other parts of the hill.

While they were thus engaged Ruger's division of the Twelfth Corps came up on the left, where the Confederates were taken in flank, and Shaler's brigade, from Wheaton's division, formed, with others, in the immediate front, where a bitter contest was kept up until nearly eleven o'clock.

At that time Meade sent an additional force toward Rock Creek, in order to check the Confederate advance. Upon learning this, Johnson slowly fell back, and, abandoning the hill, resumed his former position upon the extreme left of Ewell's army, whence he was not allowed again to advance.

Lee and Longstreet had in the meantime made an examination of the extreme Federal left, in hopes that another assault in that direction might prove successful; but, it being found that the Round Top had been strongly fortified during the previous night, the idea was abandoned, and Lee determined to make a supreme effort to crush the Federal centre, which had not yet been assailed.

Pickett's fresh division of Longstreet's corps was to make the chief attack, with the support of Pettigrew's (late Heth's) division on the left, where likewise stood Trimble's (late Pender's) division, and by Wilcox's and Perry's brigades, under Colonel Long, on the right, with Wright's brigade, of the same (Third) corps, as a reserve.

By one o'clock the Confederates had completed

By reason of Pickett having swerved from a direct course when about five hundred yards distant from the Federal lines, the first attack fell upon the Second Corps. Gibbon's skirmishers drove back the Confederate advance from the line of the Emmettsburg Road, and the main body reserved its fire until Pickett and Pettigrew had reached close quarters. The Confederates were then met with most destructive volleys of musketry, mainly from Hays's and Gibbon's men in front, and from Stannard's Vermont troops on Pickett's flank, as well as by a perfect storm of shot and shell continuously kept up along the whole line of batteries extending from the Round Top to Cemetery Hill.

The ranks which had already bravely withstood the frightful ordeal to which they had been subjected while crossing the intervening space from the Emmettsburg Road now wavered, and when the fire from some of the Federal batteries was turned obliquely upon their flank, the entire left gave way and broke in disorder, leaving about two thousand prisoners and fifteen standards in the hands of the Federals. The wounded included General Pettigrew and all but one of the officers of his brigade.

As Wilcox had not advanced on the right, Pickett was left alone by the retreat of Pettigrew's force; but notwithstanding the great odds against him he advanced boldly toward Gibbon's front line, occupied by Webb's brigade, part of which lay in the rear of a stone wall, and the remainder behind a crest a short distance beyond. As the Confederates rushed upon them, the two regiments behind the

BATTLE OF GETTYSBURG—CHARGE OF THE LOUISIANA TIGERS ON CEMETERY HILL THURSDAY NIGHT, JULY 2d, 1863.

stone wall abandoned their position, seeing which, Pickett, Kemper and Armistead scaled the wall, upon which they planted their standard, and then charged among the batteries. Here a fierce hand-to-hand fight at once took place with the force which General Webb had rapidly formed in front of Hancock's other troops.

The advance of the Confederates was made with great impetuosity, and Armistead succeeded in capturing one of the Federal batteries; but this he was able to hold only a few moments, for Hancock ordered forward the two brigades of N. J. Hall and William Harrow, which engaged the assailants so fiercely as to arrest their further progress along the hill. The Nineteenth Massachusetts and the Forty-second New York Regiments, which had so greatly distinguished themselves the previous day at the time Humphreys's division was attacked, had asked to be placed in the front, and greatly contributed to checking the Confederate advance; but the final blow was given when Stannard's force, having rapidly changed front, advanced against Pickett's right flank.

There was then but little chance for retreat, owing to the narrow space necessarily occupied by the troops, and after renewed but more desperate struggles, in which Garnett was killed and both Kemper and Armistead were very severely wounded, the Confederates were forced to surrender, thus swelling Hancock's captures for the day to about forty-five hundred prisoners. Among the Federal wounded were Generals Hancock and Gibbon, the former, though suffering greatly, refusing to allow the ambulance in which he lay to leave the field until the success of the Federals was assured. General J. C. Caldwell succeeded Gibbon in command of the Second Corps.

Wilcox advanced his force to the attack as soon as he learned of Pickett's repulse, but he also was subjected to such a heavy direct and cross artillery fire, that his lines were thrown back in disorder. Just then the Fourteenth and the Sixteenth Vermont regiments, which Stannard had detached from his command, came upon the Confederate flank and rear. These were attacked so vigorously that Wilcox had to order a retreat, during which several hundred more prisoners fell into the hands of the Federals.

After the decisive repulse of the Confederate attack against the Federal centre, Meade ordered forward Crawford's division to make a demonstration against the extreme Confederate right. Hood's advance was attacked, and after a sharp though brief encounter the Confederates fled, leaving about two hundred of their number prisoners. Sykes, having found the remainder of Longstreet's corps in position and well fortified, did not attempt any further assault with the limited force then at his disposal.

While all these operations were going on around Gettysburg, the cavalry had not been idle. Kilpatrick engaged in a severe fight late on the 2d of July with General J. E. B. Stuart's force, which he had tried to intercept at Hunterstown, and after defeating it returned to Two Taverns, getting close upon the extreme right and rear of the Confederates along the Emmettsburg Road early on the morning of the 3d.

There he remained until he saw, late in the afternoon, the brigades led by Benning, Laws and Robertson advancing toward both the Round Tops, in order to prevent reinforcements being sent Hancock. Kilpatrick then stationed himself upon the extreme Federal left, and with one of his own brigades, under General E. J. Farnsworth, and a brigade of Regulars, under General Wesley Merritt, so harassed the Confederates that they could neither make an effective demonstration against the Round Tops nor detach reinforcements in aid of General Pickett.

Kilpatrick's other brigade, under General George A. Custer, had been detained to aid Gregg's three cavalry brigades in protecting Slocum's right and rear from the threatened attacks of General Stuart. Lee had sent the latter in the vicinity of White's Creek to make a demonstration against the extreme Federal right.

A very lively engagement was commenced at about the time Kilpatrick was attacking Longstreet, and charge after charge was made during the afternoon, without any noticeable progress on either side, until part of the Third Pennsylvania Cavalry made a flank movement, which so checked the Confederates as to enable Custer to bring up the First Michigan Regiment. With the latter Custer led a charge, in which McIntosh and all of his officers took part, and with the aid of the horse-artillery succeeded in driving off from the field the Confederate cavalry, led by Generals Wade Hampton and Fitz Hugh Lee.

The day's engagements thus came to an end. On the 4th Lee abandoned all idea of renewing the conflict, sent away his sick and wounded, as well as his wagon-trains and stores, by way of the Chambersburg and Hagerstown Roads, and made preparations to retreat across the Potomac. Nothing of moment occurred, aside from a reconnoissance in force, made in the evening and during the prevalence of a heavy rainstorm, by the cavalry and by part of Birney's force, in the direction of Fairfield, where a short engagement took place with one of Lee's retreating columns. Sedgwick's troops, whose position had been taken by General Couch's body of about eleven thousand men, under General W. F. (Baldy) Smith, followed the Confederates on the 5th as far as the Fairfield Pass of South Mountain, and, with the aid of Kilpatrick's cavalry, harassed Early's rear guard, without, however, bringing on an engagement.

The Confederates had so much the lead of the Federals, by reason of the delay which had forcibly taken place in reorganizing the latter after the three days' battle, that it was not deemed possible to make an advantageous pursuit. Lee was therefore enabled to cross into Virginia between the 13th and 14th, Hill and Longstreet crossing or

MEADE'S ARMY CROSSING THE ANTIETAM IN PURSUIT OF GENERAL LEE, JULY 12TH, 1863.
From a Sketch by Edwin Forbes.

A CHARACTERISTIC SOUTHERN SCENE—STREET OF AN INTERIOR TOWN.
From Sketch by C. E. H. Bonwill.

THE ARMY OF THE POTOMAC INTERRUPTED IN IT

THE ARMY OF THE POTOMAC INTERRUPTED IN ITS PROGRESS BY ITS OLD ENEMY, VIRGINIA MUD.

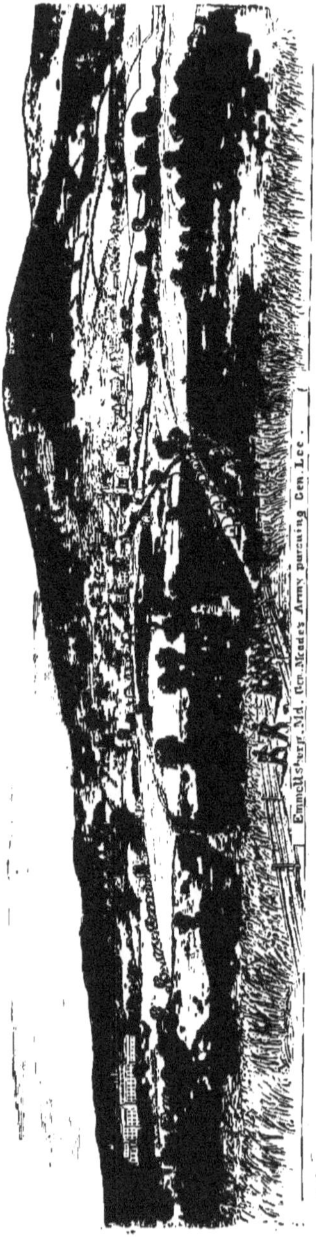

DESPERATE ATTACK OF THE CONFEDERATE FORCES AFTER GAINING THE HILL AND PASSING THE CEMETERY GATE.

From a Sketch by Edwin Forbes.

improvised bridges at Falling Waters, and Ewell fording the river at Williamsport.

Before crossing the river, Hill's rear guard was attacked by a small troop under Kilpatrick, who retired after capturing about fifteen hundred prisoners, and killing nearly as many as he lost himself, about one hundred and twenty-five men. Major Webb, who led the body taken from the Sixth Michigan Cavalry, was killed; and Pettigrew, who commanded the rear guard and was wounded on the 3d, received additional wounds, from which he died shortly after the engagement.

The total Federal casualties in this campaign were put at 23,186, and the Confederate lost estimated at 22,728, killed, wounded and missing.

The following is the complete roster of both armies, showing additional names of the most prominent sufferers on either side:

ROSTER OF THE FEDERAL ARMY

ENGAGED IN THE

BATTLE OF GETTYSBURG.

MAJOR-GENERAL GEORGE GORDON MEADE COMMANDING.

STAFF.

Major-general Daniel Butterfield, Chief of Staff (wounded).
Brigadier-general M. R. Patrick, Provost-Marshal-general.

GEORGE GORDON MEADE.

JOHN F. REYNOLDS.

Brigadier-general Seth Williams, Adjutant-general.
Brigadier-general Edmund Schriver, Inspector-general.
Brigadier-general Rufus Ingalls, Quartermaster-general.
Colonel Henry F. Clarke, Chief Commissary of Subsistence.
Major Jonathan Letterman, Surgeon, Chief of Medical Department.
Brigadier-general G. K. Warren, Chief Engineer (wounded).
Major D. W. Flagler, Chief Ordnance Officer.
Major-general Alfred Pleasonton, Chief of Cavalry.
Brigadier-general Henry J. Hunt, Chief of Artillery.
Captain L. B. Norton, Chief Signal Officer.

---

(1) Major-general John F. Reynolds; (2) Major-general O. O. Howard, commanding the First, Third, and Eleventh Corps, July 1st.
Major-general Henry W. Slocum, commanding the Right Wing, July 2d and 3d.
Major-general W. S. Hancock, commanding the Left Centre, July 2d and 3d.

FIRST CORPS.

(1) Major-general John F. Reynolds (killed, July 1st).
(2) Major-general Abner Doubleday, commanding, July 1st.
(3) Major-general John Newton, commanding, July 2d and 3d.

FIRST DIVISION.

Brigadier-general James S. Wadsworth commanding.

First Brigade: (1) Brigadier-general Solomon Meredith (wounded); (2) Colonel Henry A. Morrow (wounded); (3) Colonel W. W. Robinson—Second Wisconsin, Colonel Lucius Fairchild (wounded), Lieutenant-colonel George H. Stevens (wounded), Major John Mansfield (wounded), Captain George H. Otis; Sixth Wisconsin, Lieutenant-colonel R. R. Dawes; Seventh Wisconsin, Colonel W. W. Robinson; Twenty-fourth Michigan, Colonel Henry A. Morrow (wounded), Lieutenant-colonel Mark Flanigan (wounded), Major Edwin B. Wright (wounded), Captain Albert M. Edwards; Nineteenth Indiana, Colonel Samuel Williams.

Second Brigade: Brigadier-general Lysander Cutler commanding—Seventh Indiana, Major Ira G. Grover; Fifty-sixth Pennsylvania, Colonel J. W. Hoffman; Seventy-sixth New York, Major Andrew J. Grover (killed), Captain John E. Cook; Ninety-fifth New York, Colonel George B. Biddle (wounded), Major Edward Pye; One Hundred and Forty-seventh New York, Lieutenant-colonel F. C. Miller (wounded), Major George Harney; Fourteenth Brooklyn, Colonel E. B. Fowler.

SECOND DIVISION.

Brigadier-general John C. Robinson commanding.

First Brigade: Brigadier-general Gabriel R. Paul commanding (wounded), Colonel S. H. Leonard, Colonel Richard Coulter—Sixteenth Maine, Colonel Charles W. Tilden (captured), Lieutenant-colonel N. E. Welch, Major Archibald D. Leavitt; Thirteenth Massachusetts, Colonel S. H. Leonard (wounded); Ninety-fourth New York, Colonel A. R. Root (wounded), Major S. H. Moffat; One Hundred and Fourth New York, Colonel Gilbert G. Prey; One Hundred and Seventh Pennsylvania, Colonel T. F. McCoy (wounded), Lieutenant-colonel James McThompson (wounded), Captain E. D. Roath; Eleventh Pennsylvania, Colonel Richard S. Coulter, Captain J. J. Bierer.

Second Brigade: Brigadier-general Henry Baxter commanding—Twelfth Massachusetts, Colonel James L. Bates; Eighty-third New York, Lieutenant-colonel Joseph R. Moesch; Ninety-seventh New York, Colonel Charles Wheelock; Eighty-eighth Pennsylvania, Major Benezet F. Faust, Captain E. Y. Patterson; Ninetieth Pennsylvania, Colonel Peter Lyle.

THIRD DIVISION.

(1) Major-general Abner Doubleday, commanding, July 2d and 3d (wounded).
(2) Brigadier-general Thomas A. Rowley, commanding, July 1st.

First Brigade: Brigadier-general Thomas A. Rowley, July 2d and 3d; Colonel Chapman Biddle, July 1st—One Hundred and Twenty-first Pennsylvania, Colonel Chapman Biddle, Major Alexander Biddle; One Hundred and Forty-second Pennsylvania, Colonel Robert P. Cummings (killed), Lieutenant-colonel A. B. McCalmont; One Hundred and Fifty-first Pennsylvania, Lieutenant-colonel George F. McFarland (lost a leg), Captain Walter L. Owens; Twentieth New York State Militia, Colonel Theodore B. Gates.

Second Brigade: (1) Colonel Roy Stone commanding (wounded); (2) Colonel Langhorne Wister (wounded); (3) Colonel Edmund L. Dana—One Hundred and Forty-third Pennsylvania, Colonel Edmund L. Dana, Major John D. Musser; One Hundred and Forty-ninth Pennsylvania, Lieutenant-colonel Walton Dwight (wounded), Captain A. J. Sofield (killed), Captain John Irvin; One Hundred and Fiftieth Pennsylvania, Colonel Langhorne Wister (wounded), Lieutenant-colonel H. S. Huidekoper (wounded), Major Thomas Chamberlain (wounded), Captain C. C. Widdis (wounded), Captain G. W. Jones.

Third Brigade: Brigadier-general George J. Stannard commanding (wounded)—Twelfth Vermont, Colonel Asa P. Blunt; Thirteenth Vermont, Colonel Francis V. Randall; Fourteenth Vermont, Colonel William T. Nichols; Fifteenth Vermont, Colonel Redfield Proctor; Sixteenth Vermont, Colonel Wheelock G. Veazey.

Artillery Brigade: Colonel Charles S. Wainwright commanding—Second Maine, Captain James A. Hall; Fifth Maine, G. T. Stevens; Battery B, First Pennsylvania, Captain J. H. Cooper; Battery B, Fourth United States, Lieutenant James Stewart; Battery L, First New York, Captain J. A. Reynolds.

SECOND CORPS.

(1) Major-general Winfield S. Hancock (wounded).
(2) Major-general John Gibbon (wounded).
(3) Brigadier-general John C. Caldwell.

FIRST DIVISION.

(1) Brigadier-general John C. Caldwell.
(2) Colonel John R. Brooke (wounded).

First Brigade: Colonel Edward E. Cross (killed); Colonel H. B. McKeen—Fifth New Hampshire, Colonel E. E. Cross, Lieutenant-colonel C. E. Hapgood; Sixty-first New York, Lieutenant-colonel Oscar K. Broady; Eighty-first Pennsylvania, Colonel H. Boyd McKeen, Lieutenant-colonel Amos Stroho; One Hundred and Forty-eighth Pennsylvania, Lieutenant-colonel Robert McFarland.

Second Brigade: Colonel Patrick Kelly commanding—Twenty-eighth Massachusetts, Colonel Richard Byrnes; Sixty-third New York, Lieutenant-colonel R. C. Bentley (wounded), Captain Thomas Touhy; Sixty-ninth New York, Captain Richard Maroney (wounded), Lieutenant James J. Smith; Eighty-eighth New York, Colonel Patrick Kelly, Captain Dennis F. Burke; One Hundred and Sixteenth Pa., Major St. Clair A. Mulholland.

Third Brigade: Brigadier-general S. K. Zook commanding (killed); Lieutenant-colonel John Fraser—Fifty-second New York, Lieutenant-colonel Charles G. Freudenberg (wounded), Captain William Scherrer; Fifty-seventh New York, Lieutenant-colonel Alford B. Chapman; Sixty-sixth New York, Colonel Orlando W. Morris (wounded), Lieutenant-colonel John S. Hammell (wounded), Major Peter Nelson; One Hundred and Fortieth Pennsylvania, Colonel Richard P. Roberts (killed), Lieutenant-colonel John Fraser.

Fourth Brigade: Colonel John R. Brooke commanding (wounded)—Twenty-seventh Connecticut, Lieutenant-colonel Henry C. Merwin (killed), Major James H. Coburn; Sixty-fourth New York, Colonel Daniel G. Bingham; Fifty-third Pennsylvania, Colonel J. R. Brooke, Lieutenant-colonel Richard McMichael; One Hundred and Forty-fifth Pennsylvania, Colonel Hiram L. Brown (wounded), Captain John W. Reynolds (wounded), Captain Moses W. Oliver; Second Delaware, Colonel William P. Bailey.

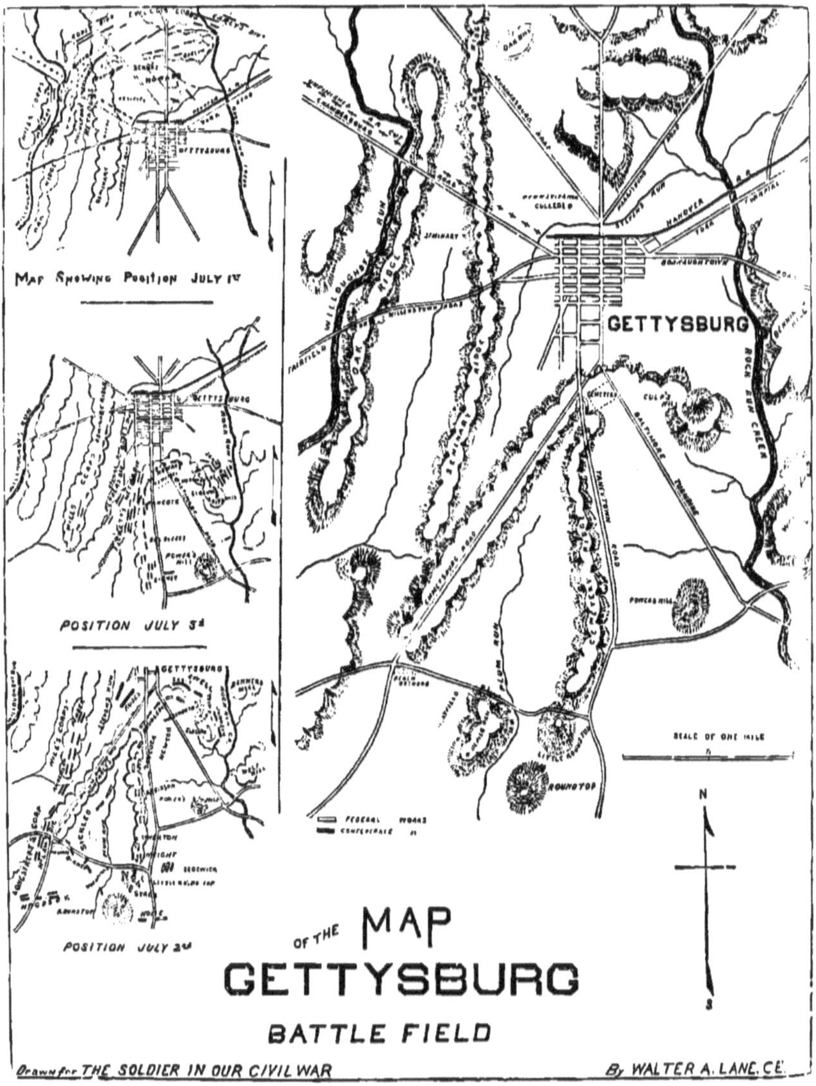

SECOND DIVISION.

(1) Brigadier-general John Gibbon (wounded).
(2) Brigadier-general William Harrow.

First Brigade: Brigadier-general William Harrow commanding; Colonel Francis E. Heath—Nineteenth Maine, Colonel F. E. Heath, Lieutenant-colonel Henry W. Cunningham; Fifteenth Massachusetts, Colonel George H. Ward (killed), Lieutenant-colonel George C. Joslin; Eighty-second New York, Colonel Henry W. Huston (killed), Captain John Darrow: First Minnesota, Colonel William Colville (wounded), Captain N. S. Messick (killed), Captain Wilson B. Farrell, Captain Louis Muller, Captain Joseph Periam, Captain Henry C. Coates.

Second Brigade: Brigadier-general Alex. S. Webb commanding (wounded)—Sixty-ninth Pennsylvania, Colonel Dennis O. Kane (killed), Lieutenant-colonel M. Tschudy (killed), Major James Duffy (wounded), Captain William Davis; Seventy-first Pennsylvania, Lieutenant-colonel Richard Penn Smyth, Seventy-second Pennsylvania, Colonel De Witt C. Baxter; One Hundred and Sixth Pennsylvania, Lieutenant-colonel Theodore Hesser.

Third Brigade: Colonel Norman J. Hall commanding—Nineteenth Massachusetts, Colonel Arthur F. Devereux; Twentieth Massachusetts, Colonel Paul J. Revere (killed), Captain H. L. Abbott (wounded); Forty-second New York, Colonel James E. Mallon; Fifty-ninth New York, Lieutenant-colonel Max A. Thoman (killed); Seventh Michigan, Colonel N. J. Hall, Lieutenant-colonel Amos E. Steele (killed), Major S. W. Curtis.—*Unattached:* Andrew Sharpshooters.

THIRD DIVISION.

Brigadier-general Alexander Hays commanding.

First Brigade: Colonel Samuel S. Carroll commanding—Fourth Ohio, Lieutenant-colonel James H. Godman, Lieutenant-colonel L. W. Carpenter; Eighth Ohio, Colonel S. S. Carroll, Lieutenant-colonel Franklin Sawyer; Fourteenth Indiana, Colonel John Coons; Seventh West Virginia, Colonel Joseph Snyder.

Second Brigade: Colonel Thomas A. Smyth, commanding (wounded); Lieutenant-colonel F. E. Pierce—Fourteenth Connecticut, Major John T. Ellis; Tenth New

York (battalion), Major George F. Hopper; One Hundred and Eighth New York, Colonel Charles J. Powers; Twelfth New Jersey, Major John T. Hill; First Delaware, Colonel Thomas A. Smyth, Lieutenant-colonel Edward P. Harris, Captain M. B. Ellgood (killed), Lieutenant William Smith (killed).

Third Brigade: Colonel George L. Willard commanding (killed); Colonel Eliakim Sherrill (killed); Lieutenant-Colonel James M. Bull—Thirty-ninth New York, Lieutenant-colonel James G. Hughes; One Hundred and Eleventh New York, Colonel Clinton D. McDougall (wounded), Lieutenant-colonel Isaac M. Lusk, Captain A. P. Seeley; One Hundred and Twenty-fifth New York, Colonel G. L. Willard (killed), Lieutenant-colonel Levi Crandall; One Hundred and Twenty-sixth New York, Colonel E. Sherrill (killed), Lieutenant-colonel J. M. Bull.

Artillery Brigade: Captain J. G. Hazard commanding—Battery B, First New York, Captain James McK. Rorty (killed); Battery A, First Rhode Island, Lieutenant William A. Arnold; Battery B, First Rhode Island, Lieutenant T. Frederick Brown (wounded); Battery I, First United States, Lieutenant G. A. Woodruff (killed); Battery A, Fourth United States, Lieutenant A. H. Cushing (killed).

Cavalry Squadron: Captain Riley Johnson commanding—D and K, Sixth New York.

THIRD CORPS.

(1) Major-general Daniel E. Sickles (wounded).
(2) Major-general David B. Birney (wounded).

Lieutenant-colonel E. S. Pierce; Fifth Michigan, Lieutenant-colonel John Pulford (wounded), Major S. S. Matthews; Fortieth New York, Colonel Thomas W. Egan; Seventeenth Maine, Lieutenant-colonel Charles B. Merrill; One Hundred and Tenth Pennsylvania, Lieutenant-colonel David M. Jones (wounded), Major Isaac Rogers.

SECOND DIVISION.

Brigadier-general Andrew A. Humphreys commanding.

First Brigade: Brigadier-general Joseph B. Carr commanding—First Massachusetts, Colonel N. B. McLaughlen; Eleventh Massachusetts, Lieutenant-colonel Porter D. Tripp; Sixteenth Massachusetts, Lieutenant-colonel Waldo Merriam; Twenty-sixth Pennsylvania, Captain George W. Tomlinson (wounded), Captain Henry Goodfellow; Eleventh New Jersey, Colonel Robert McAllister (wounded), Major Philip J. Kearny (killed), Captain William B. Dunning; Eighty-fourth Pennsylvania (not engaged), Lieutenant-colonel Milton Opp; Twelfth New Hampshire, Captain J. F. Langley.

Second Brigade: Colonel William R. Brewster commanding—Seventieth New York (First Excelsior), Major Daniel Mahen; Seventy-first New York (Second Excelsior), Colonel Henry L. Potter; Seventy-second New York (Third Excelsior), Colonel William O. Stevens (killed), Lieutenant-colonel John S. Austin; Seventy-third New York (Fourth Excelsior), Colonel William R. Brewster, Major M. W. Burns; Seventy-fourth New York (Fifth Excelsior), Lieutenant-colonel Thomas Holt; One Hundred and Twentieth N. Y., Lieutenant-colonel C. D. Westbrook (wounded), Major J. R. Tappen, Captain A. L. Lockwood.

Provost; First Michigan, Colonel Ira C. Abbot (wounded), Lieutenant-colonel W. A. Throop.

Second Brigade: Colonel J. B. Sweitzer commanding—Ninth Massachusetts, Colonel Patrick R. Guiney; Thirty-second Massachusetts, Colonel George L. Prescott (wounded), Lieutenant-colonel Luther Stephenson (wounded), Major J. Cushing Edmunds; Fourth Michigan, Colonel Harrison H. Jeffords (killed), Lieutenant-colonel George W. Lumbard; Sixty-second Pennsylvania, Colonel J. B. Sweitzer, Lieutenant-colonel James C. Hull.

Third Brigade: Colonel Strong Vincent (killed); Colonel James C. Rice—Twentieth Maine, Colonel Joshua L. Chamberlain; Forty-fourth New York, Colonel James C. Rice, Lieutenant-colonel Freeman Conner; Eighty-third Pennsylvania, Major William H. Lamont, Captain O. E. Woodward; Sixteenth Michigan, Lieutenant-colonel N. E. Welch.

SECOND DIVISION.

Brigadier-general Romayn B. Ayres commanding.

First Brigade: Colonel Hannibal Day, Sixth United States Infantry, commanding—Third United States Infantry, Captain H. W. Freedley (wounded), Captain Richard G. Lay; Fourth United States Infantry, Captain J. W. Adams; Sixth United States Infantry, Captain Levi C. Bootes; Twelfth United States Infantry, Captain Thomas S. Dunn; Fourteenth United States Infantry, Major G. R. Giddings.

Second Brigade: Colonel Sidney Burbank, Second United States Infantry, commanding—Second United States Infantry, Major A. T. Lee (wounded), Captain S. A. McKee; Seventh United States Infantry, Captain D. P.

J. H. HOBART WARD.

JOHN SEDGWICK.

FIRST DIVISION.

(1) Major-general David B. Birney.
(2) Brigadier-general J. H. H. Ward.

First Brigade: Brigadier-general C. K. Graham commanding (wounded and captured); Colonel Andrew H. Tippin—Fifty-seventh Pennsylvania, Colonel Peter Sides, Lieutenant-colonel William P. Neeper (wounded), Captain A. H. Nelson; Sixty-third Pennsylvania, Lieutenant-colonel John A. Danks; Sixty-eighth Pennsylvania, Colonel A. H. Tippin (all the field officers wounded); One Hundred and Fifth Pennsylvania, Colonel Calvin A. Craig; One Hundred and Fourteenth Pennsylvania, Lieutenant-colonel Frederick K. Cavada (captured); One Hundred and Forty-first Pennsylvania, Colonel Henry J. Madill, Captain E. R. Brown.

Second Brigade: (1) Brigadier-general J. H. H. Ward commanding; (2) Colonel H. Berdan—First United States Sharpshooters, Col. H. Berdan, Lieutenant-colonel C. Tripp; Second U. S. Sharpshooters, Major H. H. Stoughton; Third Maine, Colonel M. B. Lakeman, Captain William C. Morgan; Fourth Maine, Colonel Elijah Walker (wounded), Major Ebenezer Whitcomb (wounded), Captain Edwin Libby; Twentieth Indiana, Colonel John Wheeler (killed), Lieutenant-colonel William C. L. Taylor; Ninety-ninth Pennsylvania, Major John W. Moore; Eighty-sixth New York, Lieutenant-colonel Benjamin Higgins (wounded); One Hundred and Twenty-fourth New York ("Orange Blossoms"), Colonel A. Van Horn Ellis (killed), Lieutenant-colonel Francis M. Cummings (wounded), Major James Cromwell (killed).

Third Brigade: Colonel Philip R. de Trobriand commanding—Third Michigan, Colonel Byron R. Pierce (wounded),

Third Brigade: Colonel George C. Burling commanding—Fifth New Jersey, Colonel William J. Sewall (wounded), Captain Virgil M. Healey (wounded), Captain T. C. Godfrey, Captain H. H. Woolsey; Sixth New Jersey, Colonel George C. Burling, Lieutenant-colonel S. R. Gilkyson; Seventh New Jersey, Colonel L. R. Francine (killed), Lieutenant-colonel Francis Price; Eighth New Jersey, Colonel John Ramsey (wounded), Captain John G. Langston; One Hundred and Fifteenth Pennsylvania, Lieutenant-colonel John P. Dunne; Second New Hampshire, Colonel Edward L. Bailey (wounded), Major Samuel P. Sayles (wounded).

Artillery Brigade: Captain George E. Randolph commanding—Battery E, First Rhode Island, Lieutenant John K. Bucklyn (wounded), Lieutenant Benjamin Freeborn; Battery B, First New Jersey, Captain A. J. Clark; Battery D, First New Jersey, Captain George T. Woodbury; Battery K, Fourth United States, Lieutenant F. W. Seeley (wounded), Lieutenant Robert James; Battery D, First New York, Captain George B. Winslow; Fourth New York, Captain James E. Smith.

FIFTH CORPS.

Major-general George Sykes commanding.

FIRST DIVISION.

Brigadier-general James Barnes (wounded).

First Brigade: Colonel William S. Tilton commanding—Eighteenth Massachusetts, Colonel Joseph Hayes; Twenty-second Massachusetts, Colonel William S. Tilton, Lieutenant-colonel Thomas Sherman, Jr.; One Hundred and Eighteenth Pennsylvania, Colonel Charles M.

Hancock; Tenth United States Infantry, Captain William Clinton; Eleventh United States Infantry, Major De L. Floyd Jones; Seventeenth United States Infantry, Lieutenant-colonel Durrell Green.

Third Brigade: Brigadier-general S. H. Weed (killed); Colonel Kenner Garrard—One Hundred and Fortieth New York, Colonel Patrick H. O'Rorke (killed), Lieutenant-colonel Louis Ernst; One Hundred and Forty-sixth New York, Colonel K. Garrard, Lieutenant-colonel David T. Jenkins; Ninety-first Pennsylvania, Lieutenant-colonel Joseph H. Sinex; One Hundred and Fifty-fifth Pennsylvania, Lieutenant-colonel John H. Cain.

THIRD DIVISION.

Brigadier-general S. Wiley Crawford commanding.

First Brigade: Colonel William McCandless commanding—First Pennsylvania Reserves, Colonel William Cooper Talley; Second Pennsylvania Reserves, Colonel William McCandless, Lieutenant-colonel George A. Woodward; Sixth Pennsylvania Reserves, Colonel Wellington H. Ent; Eleventh Pennsylvania Reserves, Colonel S. M. Jackson; First Rifles (Bucktails), Colonel Charles J. Taylor (killed), Lieutenant-Colonel A. E. Niles (wounded), Major William R. Hartshorn.

Second Brigade: Colonel Joseph W. Fisher commanding—Fifth Pennsylvania Reserves, Colonel J. W. Fisher, Lieutenant-colonel George Dare; Ninth Pennsylvania Reserves, Lieutenant-colonel James McK. Snodgrass; Tenth Pennsylvania Reserves, Colonel A. J. Warner; Twelfth Pennsylvania Reserves, Colonel M. D. Hardin.

Artillery Brigade: Captain A. P. Martin commanding—Battery D, Fifth United States, Lieutenant Charles E. Hazlett (killed), Lieutenant B. F. Rittenhouse; Battery I,

VIEW OF THE BATTLEFIELD [illegible] BY EDWIN FORBES.

Fifth United States, Lieutenant Leonard Martin; Battery C, First New York, Captain Albert Barnes; Battery L, First Ohio, Captain N. C. Gibbs; Battery C, Massachusetts, Captain A. P. Martin.

Provost Guard: Captain H. W. Ryder—Companies E and D, Twelfth New York.

Sixth Corps.

Major-general John Sedgwick.

FIRST DIVISION.

Brigadier-general H. G. Wright commanding.

First Brigade: Brigadier-general A. T. A. Torbert commanding—First New Jersey, Lieutenant-colonel William Henry, Junior; Second New Jersey, Colonel Samuel L. Buck; Third New Jersey, Colonel Henry W. Brown; Fifteenth New Jersey, Colonel William H. Penrose.

Second Brigade: Brigadier-general J. J. Bartlett commanding—Fifth Maine, Colonel Clark S. Edwards; One Hundred and Twenty-first New York, Colonel Emory Upton; Ninety-fifth Pennsylvania, Lieutenant colonel Edward Carroll; Ninety-sixth Pennsylvania, Lieutenant-colonel William H. Lessig.

Third Brigade: Brigadier-general D. A. Russell commanding—Sixth Maine, Colonel Hiram Burnham; Forty-ninth Pennsylvania, Colonel William H. Irvin; One Hundred and Nineteenth Pennsylvania, Colonel P. C. Ellmaker; Fifth Wisconsin, Colonel Thomas S. Allen.

SECOND DIVISION.

Brigadier-general A. P. Howe commanding.

Second Brigade: Colonel L. A. Grant commanding—Second Vermont, Colonel J. H. Walbridge; Third Vermont, Colonel T. O. Seaver; Fourth Vermont, Colonel E. H. Stoughton; Fifth Vermont, Lieutenant-colonel John R. Lewis; Sixth Vermont, Lieutenant-colonel Elisha L. Barney.

Third Brigade: Brigadier-general T. A. Neill commanding—Seventh Maine, Lieutenant-colonel Seldon Connor; Forty-ninth New York, Colonel D. D. Bidwell; Seventy-seventh New York, Colonel J. B. McKean; Forty-third New York, Colonel B. F. Baker; Sixty-first Pennsylvania, Major George W. Dawson.

THIRD DIVISION.

Brigadier-general Frank Wheaton commanding.

First Brigade: Brigadier-general Alexander Shaler commanding—Sixty-fifth New York, Colonel J. E. Hamblin; Sixty-seventh New York, Colonel Nelson Cross; One Hundred and Twenty-second New York, Lieutenant-colonel A. W. Dwight; Twenty-third Pennsylvania, Lieutenant-colonel John F. Glenn; Eighty-second Pennsylvania, Colonel Isaac Bassett.

Second Brigade: Colonel H. L. Eustis commanding—Seventh Massachusetts, Lieutenant-colonel Franklin P. Harlow; Tenth Massachusetts, Lieutenant-colonel Joseph B. Parsons; Thirty-seventh Massachusetts, Colonel Oliver Edwards; Second Rhode Island, Colonel Horatio Rogers.

Third Brigade: Colonel David I. Nevin commanding—Sixty-second New York, Colonel D. I. Nevin, Lieutenant-colonel Theodore B. Hamilton; One Hundred and Second Pennsylvania, Colonel John W. Patterson; Ninety-third Pennsylvania, Colonel James M. McCarter; Ninety-eighth Pennsylvania, Major John B. Kohler; One Hundred and Thirty-ninth Pa., Lieutenant-colonel William H. Moody.

Artillery Brigade: Colonel C. H. Tompkins commanding—Battery A, First Massachusetts, Captain W. H. McCartney; Battery D, Second United States, Lieutenant E. B. Williston; Battery F, Fifth United States, Lieutenant Leonard Martin; Battery G, Second United States, Lieutenant John H. Butler; Battery C, First Rhode Island, Captain Richard Waterman; Battery G, First Rhode Island, Captain G. W. Adams; First New York, Captain Andrew Cowan; Third New York, Captain William A. Harn.

Cavalry Detachment: Captain William L. Craft commanding—H, First Pennsylvania; L, First New Jersey.

Eleventh Corps.

(1) Major-general O. O. Howard.
(2) Major-general Carl Schurz.

FIRST DIVISION.

(1) Brigadier-general Francis C. Barlow (wounded).
(2) Brigadier-general Adelbert Ames.

First Brigade: Colonel Leopold Von Gilsa commanding—Forty-first New York, Colonel L. Von Gilsa, Lieutenant-colonel D. Von Einsiedel; Fifty-fourth New York, Colonel Eugene A. Kozlay; Sixty-eighth New York, Colonel Gotthilf Bourry de Ivernois; One Hundred and Fifty-third Pennsylvania, Colonel Charles Glanz.

Second Brigade: Brigadier-general Adelbert Ames commanding; Colonel Andrew L. Harris—Seventeenth Connecticut, Lieutenant-colonel Douglass Fowler (killed), Major A. G. Brady (wounded); Twenty-fifth Ohio, Lieutenant-colonel Jeremiah Williams (captured), Lieutenant William Maloney (wounded), Lieutenant Israel White; Seventy-fifth Ohio, Colonel Andrew L. Harris (wounded), Lieutenant-colonel Ben Morgan (wounded), Major Charles W. Friend; One Hundred and Seventh Ohio, Captain John M. Lutz.

SECOND DIVISION.

Brigadier-general A. Von Steinwehr commanding.

First Brigade: Colonel Charles R. Coster commanding—Twenty-seventh Pennsylvania, Lieutenant-colonel Lorenz Cantador; Seventy-third Pennsylvania, Captain Daniel F. Kelly; One Hundred and Thirty-fourth New York, Colonel Charles R. Coster, Lieutenant-colonel Allan H. Jackson; One Hundred and Fifty-fourth New York, Colonel Patrick H. Jones.

Second Brigade: Colonel Orlando Smith commanding—Thirty-third Massachusetts, Lieutenant-colonel Adin B. Underwood; One Hundred and Thirty-sixth New York, Colonel James Wood, Jr.; Fifty-fifth Ohio, Colonel Charles B. Gambee; Seventy-third Ohio, Colonel Orlando Smith, Lieutenant-colonel Richard Long.

THIRD DIVISION.

(1) Major-general Carl Schurz.
(2) Brigadier-general Alex. Schimmelpfennig.

First Brigade: Brigadier-general A. Von Schimmelpfennig commanding (captured); Colonel George Von Amsberg—Forty-fifth New York, Colonel G. Von Amsberg, Lieutenant-colonel Adolphus Dobke; One Hundred and Fifty-seventh New York, Colonel Philip P. Brown, Jr.; Seventy-fourth Pennsylvania, Colonel Adolph Von Hartung (wounded), Lieutenant-colonel [illegible] Mitzel (captured), Major [illegible] Schleiter; Sixty-first Ohio, Colonel S. J. McGroarty; Eighty-second Illinois, Colonel J. Hecker.

Second Brigade: Colonel Waldimir Kryzanowski commanding—Fifty-eighth New York, Colonel W. Kryzanowski, Lieutenant-colonel Albert Otto, Captain Emil Koenig, Lieutenant-colonel Frederick Gellman; One Hundred and Nineteenth New York, Colonel J. T. Lockman, Lieutenant-colonel James C. Rogers; Seventy-fifth Pennsylvania, Colonel Francis Mahler (wounded), Major August Ledig; Eighty-second Ohio, Colonel James S. Robinson (wounded), Lieutenant-colonel D. Thomson; Twenty-sixth Wisconsin, Colonel William H. Jacobs.

Artillery Brigade: Major Thomas W. Osborn commanding—Battery I, First New York, Captain Michael Wiedrick; Battery I, First Ohio, Captain Hubert Dilger; Battery K, First Ohio, Captain Lewis Heckman; Battery G, Fourth United States, Lieutenant Bayard Wilkeson (killed), Lieutenant E. A. Bancroft; Thirteenth New York, Lieutenant William Wheeler.

Twelfth Corps.

(1) Major-general Henry W. Slocum.
(2) Brigadier-general Alpheus S. Williams.

FIRST DIVISION.

Brigadier-general Thomas H. Ruger commanding.

First Brigade: Colonel Archibald L. McDougall commanding—Fifth Connecticut, Colonel Warren W. Packer; Twentieth Connecticut, Lieutenant-colonel William B. Wooster; One Hundred and Twenty-third New York, Colonel A. L. McDougall, Lieutenant-colonel James C. Rogers; One Hundred and Forty-fifth New York, Colonel E. L. Price; Forty-sixth Pennsylvania, Colonel James L. Selfridge; Third Maryland, Colonel J. M. Sudsburg.

Second Brigade: Brigadier-general Henry H. Lockwood commanding—One Hundred and Fiftieth New York, Colonel John H. Ketcham; First Maryland (P. H. B.) Colonel William P. Maulsby; First Maryland (E. S.), Colonel James Wallace.

Third Brigade: Colonel Silas Colgrove commanding—Second Massachusetts, Colonel Charles R. Mudge (killed), Lieutenant-colonel Charles F. Morse; One Hundred and Seventh New York, Colonel Miron M. Crane; Thirteenth New Jersey, Colonel Ezra A. Carman (wounded), Lieutenant-colonel John R. Fesler; Twenty-seventh Indiana, Colonel Silas Colgrove, Lieutenant-colonel John R. Fesler; Third Wisconsin, Lieutenant-colonel Martin Flood.

SECOND DIVISION.

Brigadier-general John W. Geary commanding.

First Brigade: Colonel Charles Candy commanding—Twenty-eighth Pennsylvania, Captain John Flynn; One Hundred and Forty-seventh Pennsylvania, Lieutenant-colonel Ario Pardee, Jr.; Fifth Ohio, Colonel John H. Patrick; Seventh Ohio, Colonel William R. Creighton; Twenty-ninth Ohio, Captain W. F. Stevens (wounded), Captain Edward Hayes; Sixty-sixth Ohio, Colonel C. Candy, Lieutenant-colonel Eugene Powell.

Second Brigade: (1) Colonel George A. Cobham, Jr.; (2) Brigadier-general Thomas L. Kane—Twenty-ninth Pennsylvania, Colonel William Rickards; One Hundred and Ninth Pennsylvania, Captain Fred L. Gimber; One Hundred and Eleventh Pennsylvania, Lieutenant-colonel Thomas M. Walker, Lieutenant-colonel Frank J. Osgood.

Third Brigade: Brigadier-general George S. Greene commanding—Sixtieth New York, Colonel Abel Godard; Seventy-eighth New York, Lieutenant-colonel Herbert Von Hammerstein; One Hundred and Second New York, Lieutenant-colonel James C. Lane (wounded); One Hundred and Thirty-seventh New Yor[illegible] J[illegible] David Ireland; One Hundred and Forty-ninth [illegible] W[illegible]

JUDSON KILPATRICK.

EDWARD E. CROSS.

CAVALRY SKIRMISHERS ADVANCING ON THE PASSES OF THE BLUE RIDGE MOUNTAINS.
FROM A SKETCH BY F. B. SCHELL.

York, Colonel Henry A. Barnum, Lieutenant-colonel Charles B. Randall.

Artillery Brigade: Lieutenant Edward D. Muhlenberg commanding—Battery F, Fourth United States, Lieutenant E. D. Muhlenberg, Lieutenant S. T. Rugg; Battery K, Fifth United States, Lieutenant D. H. Kinzie; Battery M, First New York, Lieutenant Charles E. Winegar; Knap's Pennsylvania Battery, Lieutenant Charles Atwell.

Headquarter Guard: Battalion Tenth Maine.

CAVALRY CORPS.

Major-general Alfred Pleasanton commanding.

FIRST DIVISION.

Brigadier-general John Buford commanding

First Brigade: Colonel William Gamble commanding—Eighth New York, Colonel Benjamin F. Davis; Eighth Illinois, Colonel William Gamble, Lieutenant-colonel D. R. Clendenin; Two Squadrons Twelfth Illinois, Colonel Amos Voss; Three Squadrons Third Indiana, Colonel George H. Chapman.

Second Brigade: Colonel Thomas C. Devin commanding—Sixth New York, Colonel Thomas C. Devin, Lieutenant-colonel William H. Crocker; Ninth New York, Colonel William Sackett; Seventeenth Pennsylvania, Colonel J. H. Kellogg; Third Virginia (Detachment).

Reserve Brigade: Brigadier-general Wesley Merritt commanding—First United States, Captain R. S. C. Lord; Second United States, Captain T. F. Rodenbough; Fifth United States, Captain J. W. Mason; Sixth United States, Major S. H. Starr (wounded), Captain G. C. Cram; Sixth Pennsylvania, Major James H. Haseltine.

SECOND DIVISION.

Brigadier-general D. McM. Gregg commanding.
(Headquarter Guard—Company A, First Ohio.)

First Brigade: Colonel J. B. McIntosh commanding—First New Jersey, Major M. H. Beaumont; First Pennsylvania, Colonel John P. Taylor; Third Pennsylvania, Lieutenant-colonel Edward S. Jones; First Maryland, Lieutenant-colonel James M. Deems; First Massachusetts at Headquarters Sixth Corps.

Second Brigade: Colonel Pennock Huey commanding—Second New York, Fourth New York, Eighth Pennsylvania, Sixth Ohio.

Third Brigade: Colonel J. I. Gregg commanding—First Maine, Colonel Charles H. Smith; Tenth New York, Major W. A. Avery; Fourth Pennsylvania, Lieutenant-colonel W. E. Doster; Sixteenth Pennsylvania, Lieutenant-colonel John K. Robison.

THIRD DIVISION.

Brigadier-general Judson Kilpatrick commanding.
(Headquarter Guard—Company C, First Ohio.)

First Brigade: (1) Brigadier-general E. J. Farnsworth (killed); (2) Colonel N. P. Richmond—Fifth New York, Major John Hammond; Eighteenth Pennsylvania, Lieutenant-colonel William P. Brinton; First Vermont, Colonel Edward B. Sawyer; First West Virginia, Colonel N. P. Richmond.

Second Brigade: Brigadier-general George A. Custer commanding—First Michigan, Colonel Charles H. Town; Fifth Michigan, Colonel Russell A. Alger; Sixth Michigan, Colonel George Gray; Seventh Michigan, Colonel William D. Mann.

HORSE ARTILLERY.

First Brigade: Captain John M. Robertson commanding—Batteries B and L, Second United States, Lieutenant Edward Heaton; Battery M, Second United States, Lieutenant A. C. M. Pennington; Battery E, Fourth United States, Lieutenant S. S. Elder; Sixth New York, Lieutenant Joseph W. Martin; Ninth Michigan, Captain J. J. Daniels; Battery C, Third United States, Lieutenant William D. Fuller.

Second Brigade: Captain John C. Tidball commanding—Batteries G and E, First United States, Captain A. M. Randol; Battery K, First United States, Captain William M. Graham; Battery A, Second United States, Lieutenant John H. Calef; Battery C, Third United States.

ARTILLERY RESERVE.

(1) Brigadier-general R. O. Tyler (wounded).
(2) Captain John M. Robertson.

First Regular Brigade: Captain D. R. Ransom commanding (wounded)—Battery H, First United States, Lieutenant C. P. Eakin (wounded); Batteries F and K, Third United States, Lieutenant J. C. Turnbull; Battery C, Fourth United States, Lieutenant Evan Thomas; Battery C, Fifth United States, Lieutenant G. V. Weir.

First Volunteer Brigade: Lieutenant-colonel F. McGilvery commanding—Fifteenth New York, Captain Patrick Hart; Independent Battery Pennsylvania, Captain R. B. Ricketts; Fifth Massachusetts, Captain C. A. Phillips; Ninth Massachusetts, Captain John Bigelow.

Second Volunteer Brigade: Captain E. D. Taft commanding—Battery B, First Connecticut; Battery M, First Connecticut; Fifth New York, Captain Elijah D. Taft; Second Connecticut, Lieutenant John W. Sterling.

Third Volunteer Brigade: Captain James F. Huntington commanding—Batteries F and G, First Pennsylvania, Captain R. B. Ricketts; Battery H, First Ohio, Captain James F. Huntington; Battery A, First New Hampshire, Captain F. M. Edgell; Battery C, First West Virginia, Captain Wallace Hill.

Fourth Volunteer Brigade: Captain R. H. Fitzhugh commanding—Battery B, First New York, Captain James McRorty (killed); Battery G, First New York, Captain Albert N. Ames; Battery K, First New York (Eleventh Battery attached), Captain Robert H. Fitzhugh; Battery A, First Maryland, Captain James H. Rigby; Battery A, First New Jersey, Lieutenant Augustin N. Parsons; Sixth Maine, Lieutenant Edwin P. Dow.

Train Guard: Major Charles Ewing commanding—Fourth New Jersey Infantry.

Headquarter Guard: Captain J. C. Fuller commanding—Battery C, Thirty-second Massachusetts.

DETACHMENTS AT HEADQUARTERS ARMY OF THE POTOMAC.

Command of the Provost-marshal-general: Brigadier-general M. R. Patrick commanding—Ninety-third New York, Eighth United States; First Massachusetts Cavalry; Second Pennsylvania Cavalry; Batteries E and I; Sixth Pennsylvania Cavalry; Detachment Regular Cavalry, United States Engineer Battalion, Captain George H. Mendell, United States Engineers.

Guards and Orderlies: Captain D. P. Mann commanding—Independent Company Oneida Cavalry.

ROSTER OF THE CONFEDERATE ARMY

ENGAGED AT THE

BATTLE OF GETTYSBURG.

GENERAL ROBERT E. LEE COMMANDING.

STAFF.

Colonel W. H. Taylor, Adjutant-general.
Colonel C. S. Venable, A.D.C.
Colonel Charles Marshall, A.D.C.
Colonel James L. Corley, Chief Quartermaster.
Colonel R. G. Cole, Chief Commissary.
Colonel B. G. Baldwin, Chief of Ordnance.
Colonel H. L. Peyton, Assistant Inspector-general.
General W. N. Pendleton, Chief of Artillery
Doctor L. Guild, Medical Director.
Colonel W. Proctor Smith, Chief Engineer.
Major H. E. Young, Assistant Adjutant-general.
Major G. B. Cook, Assistant Inspector-general.

FIRST CORPS.

Lieutenant-general James Longstreet commanding.

MAJOR-GENERAL M'LAWS'S DIVISION.

Kershaw's Brigade: Brigadier-general J. B. Kershaw commanding—Fifteenth South Carolina Regiment, Colonel W. D. De Saussure; Eighth South Carolina Regiment, Colonel J. W. Henagan; Second South Carolina Regiment, Colonel John D. Kennedy; Third South Carolina Regiment, Colonel James D. Nance; Seventh South Carolina Regiment, Colonel D. Wyatt Aiken; Third (James's) Battalion South Carolina Infantry, Lieutenant-colonel R. C. Rice.

Benning's Brigade: Brigadier-general H. L. Benning commanding—Fiftieth Georgia Regiment, Colonel W. R. Manning; Fifty-first Georgia Regiment, Colonel W. M. Slaughter; Fifty-third Georgia Regiment, Colonel James P. Simms; Tenth Georgia Regiment, Lieutenant-colonel John B. Weems.

Barksdale's Brigade: Brigadier-general William Barksdale (killed)—Thirteenth Mississippi Regiment, Colonel J. W. Carter; Seventeenth Mississippi Regiment, Colonel W. D. Holder; Eighteenth Mississippi Regiment, Colonel Thomas M. Griffin; Twenty-first Mississippi Regiment, Colonel B. G. Humphreys.

Wofford's Brigade: Brigadier-general W. T. Wofford commanding—Eighteenth Georgia Regiment, Major E. Griffs; Phillips's Georgia Legion, Colonel W. M. Phillips; Twenty-fourth Georgia Regiment, Colonel Robert McMillan; Sixteenth Georgia Regiment, Colonel Goode Bryan; Cobb's Georgia Legion, Lieutenant-colonel L. D. Glewn.

MAJOR-GENERAL GEORGE E. PICKETT'S DIVISION.

Garnett's Brigade: Brigadier-general R. B. Garnett (killed)—Eighth Virginia Regiment, Colonel Eppa Hunton; Eighteenth Virginia Regiment, Colonel R. E. Withers; Nineteenth Virginia Regiment, Colonel Henry Gantt; Twenty-eighth Virginia Regiment, Colonel R. C. Allen; Fifty-sixth Virginia Regiment, Colonel W. D. Stuart.

CHIMNEY OF A VIRGINIA MANSION IMPROVISED AS A COOK-HOUSE.
FROM A SKETCH BY EDWIN FORBES.

Armistead's Brigade: Brigadier-general L. A. Armistead (killed)—Ninth Virginia Regiment, Lieutenant-colonel J. M. Gilliam; Fourteenth Virginia Regiment, Colonel J. G. Hodges; Thirty-eighth Virginia Regiment, Colonel E. C. Edmonds; Fifty-third Virginia Regiment, Colonel John Grammer; Fifty-seventh Virginia Regiment, Colonel J. B. Magruder.

Kemper's Brigade: Brigadier-general J. L. Kemper (wounded)—First Virginia Regiment, Colonel Lewis B. Williams, Jr.; Third Virginia Regiment, Colonel Joseph Mayo, Jr.; Seventh Virginia Regiment, Colonel W. T. Patton; Eleventh Virginia Regiment, Colonel David Funsten; Twenty-fourth Virginia Regiment, Colonel W. R. Terry.

Toombs's Brigade: Brigadier-general R. Toombs commanding—Second Georgia Regiment, Colonel E. M. Butt; Fifteenth Georgia Regiment, Colonel E. M. DuBose; Seventeenth Georgia Regiment, Colonel W. C. Hodges; Twentieth Georgia Regiment, Colonel J. B. Cummings.

Corse's Brigade: Brigadier-general M. D. Corse commanding—Fifteenth Virginia Regiment, Colonel T. P. August; Seventeenth Virginia Regiment, Colonel Morton Marye; Thirtieth Virginia Regiment, Colonel A. T. Harrison; Thirty-second Virginia Regiment, Col. E. B. Montague.

MAJOR-GENERAL J. B. HOOD'S DIVISION.

Robertson's Brigade: Brigadier-general J. B. Robertson commanding—First Texas Regiment, Colonel A. T. Rainey; Fourth Texas Regiment, Colonel J. C. G. Key; Fifth Texas Regiment, Colonel R. M. Powell; Third Arkansas Regiment, Colonel Van H. Manning.

Law's Brigade: Brigadier-general E. M. Law commanding—Fourth Alabama Regiment, Colonel P. A. Bowls; Forty-fourth Alabama Regiment, Colonel W. H. Perry; Fifteenth Alabama Regiment, Col. James Canty; Forty-seventh Alabama Regiment, Col. J. W. Jackson; Forty-eighth Alabama Regiment, Col. J. F. Shepherd.

Anderson's Brigade: Brigadier-general G. T. Anderson (wounded)—Tenth Georgia Battalion, Major J. E. Rylander; Seventh Georgia Regiment, Colonel W. M. White; Eighth Georgia Regiment, Lieutenant-colonel J. R. Towers; Ninth Georgia Regiment, Colonel B. F. Beck; Eleventh Georgia Regiment, Colonel F. H. Little.

Jenkins's Brigade: Brigadier-general M. Jenkins commanding—Second South Carolina Rifles, Colonel Thomas Thompson; First South Carolina Regiment, Lieutenant-colonel David Livingstone; Fifth South Carolina Regiment, Col. A. Coward; Sixth South Carolina Regiment, Col. John Bratton; Hampton's Legion, Col. M. W. Gary.

ARTILLERY OF THE FIRST CORPS.

Colonel J. B. Walton commanding.

Battalion: Colonel H. C. Cabell; Major Hamilton. Batteries—McCarty's, Manly's, Carlton's, Fraser's.

Battalion: Major Dearing; Major Reed. Batteries—Macon's, Blount's, Stribling's, Caskie's.

Battalion: Major Henry. Batteries—Bachman's, Reilly's, Latham's, Gordon's.

Battalion: Colonel E. P. Alexander; Major Huger. Batteries—Jordan's, Rhett's, Moody's, Parker's, Taylor's.

Battalion: Major Eshleman. Batteries—Squires's, Miller's, Richardson's, Norman's.

Total number of guns, Artillery of the First Corps, 83.

SECOND CORPS.

Lieutenant-general R. S. Ewell.

MAJOR-GENERAL J. A. EARLY'S DIVISION.

Hays's Brigade: Brigadier-general H. S. Hays commanding—Fifth Louisiana Regiment, Colonel Henry Forno; Sixth Louisiana Regiment, Colonel William Monaghan; Seventh Louisiana Regiment, Colonel D. B. Penn; Eighth Louisiana Regiment, Colonel Henry B. Kelley; Ninth Louisiana Regiment, Colonel A. L. Stafford.

Gordon's Brigade: Brigadier-general J. B. Gordon commanding—Thirteenth Georgia Regiment, Colonel J. M. Smith; Twenty-sixth Georgia Regiment, Colonel E. N. Atkinson; Thirty-first Georgia Regiment, Colonel C. A. Evans; Thirty-eighth Georgia Regiment, Major J. D. Matthews; Sixtieth Georgia Regiment, Colonel W. H. Stiles; Sixty-first Georgia Regiment, Colonel J. H. Lamar.

Smith's Brigade: Brigadier-general William Smith commanding—Thirteenth Virginia Regiment, Colonel J. E. B. Terrill; Thirty-first Virginia Regiment, Colonel John S. Hoffman; Forty-ninth Virginia Regiment, Colonel Gibson; Fifty-second Virginia Regiment, Colonel Skinner; Fifty-eighth Virginia Regiment, Colonel F. H. Board.

Hoke's Brigade: Colonel J. E. Avery commanding (General R. F. Hoke being absent, wounded)—Fifth North Carolina Regiment, Colonel J. E. Avery; Twenty-first North Carolina Regiment, Colonel W. W. Kirkland; Fifty-fourth North Carolina Regiment, Colonel J. C. T. McDowell; Fifty-seventh North Carolina Regiment, Colonel A. C. Godwin; First North Carolina Battalion, Major R. H. Wharton.

MAJOR-GENERAL R. E. RODE'S DIVISION.

Daniel's Brigade: Brigadier-general Junius Daniel commanding—Thirty-second North Carolina Regiment, Colonel E. C. Brabble; Forty-third North Carolina Regiment, Colonel Thomas S. Kenan; Forty-fifth North Carolina Regiment, Lieutenant-colonel Samuel H. Boyd; Fifty-third North Carolina Regiment, Colonel W. A. Owens; Second North Carolina Battalion, Lieutenant-colonel H. S. Andrews.

Doles's Brigade: Brigadier-general George Doles commanding—Fourth Georgia Regiment, Lieut.-colonel D. R. E. Winn; Twelfth Georgia Regiment, Colonel Edward Willis; Twenty-first Georgia Regiment, Colonel John T. Mercer; Forty-fourth Georgia Regiment, Colonel S. P. Lumpkin.

Iverson's Brigade: Brigadier-general Alfred Iverson commanding—Fifth North Carolina Regiment, Captain S. B. West; Twelfth North Carolina Regiment, Lieutenant-colonel W. S. Davis; Twentieth North Carolina Regiment, Lieutenant-colonel N. Slough; Twenty-third North Carolina Regiment, Colonel D. H. Christie.

Ramseur's Brigade: Brigadier-general S. D. Ramseur commanding—Second North Carolina Regiment, Major E. W. Hurt; Fourth North Carolina Regiment, Colonel Bryan Grimes; Fourteenth North Carolina Regiment, Colonel R. T. Bennett; Thirtieth North Carolina Regiment, Colonel F. M. Parker.

Rodes's Brigade: Colonel E. A. O'Neal commanding—Third Alabama Regiment, Colonel C. A. Battle; Fifth Alabama Regiment, Colonel J. M. Hall; Sixth Alabama Regiment, Colonel J. N. Lightfoot; Twelfth Alabama Regiment, Colonel S. B. Pickens; Twenty-sixth Alabama Regiment, Lieutenant-colonel J. C. Goodgame.

MAJOR-GENERAL ED. JOHNSON'S DIVISION.

Steuart's Brigade: Brigadier-general George H. Steuart commanding—Tenth Virginia Regiment, Colonel E. T. H. Warren; Twenty-third Virginia Regiment, Colonel A. G. Taliaferro; Twenty-seventh Virginia Regiment, Colonel T. V. Williams; First North Carolina Regiment, Colonel J. A. McDowell; Third North Carolina Regiment, Lieutenant-colonel Thurston.

"Stonewall" Brigade: Brigadier-general James A. Walker commanding—Second Virginia Regiment, Colonel J. Q. A. Nadenbousch; Fourth Virginia Regiment, Colonel Charles A. Ronald; Fifth Virginia Regiment, Colonel J. H. S. Funk; Twenty-seventh Virginia Regiment, Colonel J. K. Edmondson; Thirty-third Virginia Regiment, Colonel F. M. Holladay.

Jones's Brigade: Brigadier-general John M. Jones (wounded)—Twenty-first Virginia Regiment, Captain Moseley; Forty-second Virginia Regiment, Lieutenant-colonel Withers; Forty-fourth Virginia Regiment, Captain Buckner; Forty-eighth Virginia Regiment, Colonel T. S. Garnett; Fiftieth Virginia Regiment, Colonel Vandeventer.

Nicholls's Brigade: Colonel J. M. Williams commanding (General F. T. Nicholls being absent, wounded)—First Louisiana Regiment, Colonel William R. Shivers; Second Louisiana Regiment, Colonel J. M. Williams; Tenth Louisiana Regiment, Colonel E. Waggaman; Fourteenth Louisiana Regiment, Colonel Z. York; Fifteenth Louisiana Regiment, Colonel Edward Pendleton.

ARTILLERY OF THE SECOND CORPS.

Colonel S. Crutchfield commanding.

Battalion: Lieutenant-colonel Thomas H. Carter; Major Carter M. Braxton. Batteries—Page's, Fry's, Carter's, and Reese's.

THE ARMY OF THE POTOMAC PASSING OVER THEIR OLD BATTLE-GROUND AT MANASSAS, VA.

FROM A SKETCH BY EDWIN FORBES.

Battalion: Lieutenant-colonel R. P. Jones; Major Brockenborough. Batteries—Carrington's, Garber's, Thompson's, Tanner's.

Battalion: Lieutenant-colonel S. Andrews; Major Latimer. Batteries—Brown's, Dement's, Carpenter's, Raine's.

Battalion: Lieutenant-colonel Nelson; Major Page. Batteries—Kirkpatrick's, Massie's, Milledge's.

Battalion: Colonel J. T. Brown; Major Hardaway. Batteries—Dance's, Watson's, Smith's, Huff's, Graham's.

Total number of guns, Artillery of the Second Corps, 82.

THIRD CORPS.

Lieutenant-general Ambrose P. Hill commanding.

MAJOR-GENERAL R. H. ANDERSON'S DIVISION.

Wilcox's Brigade: Brigadier-general C. M. Wilcox commanding—Eighth Alabama Regiment, Colonel T. L. Royster; Ninth Alabama Regiment, Colonel S. Henry; Tenth Alabama Regiment, Colonel W. H. Forney; Eleventh Alabama Regiment, Colonel J. C. C. Saunders; Fourteenth Alabama Regiment, Colonel L. P. Pinkard.

Mahone's Brigade: Brigadier-general William Mahone commanding—Sixth Virginia Regiment, Colonel G. T. Rogers; Twelfth Virginia Regiment, Colonel D. A. Weisiger; Sixteenth Virginia Regiment, Lieutenant-colonel Joseph H. Ham; Forty-first Virginia Regiment, Colonel W. A. Parham; Sixty-first Virginia Regiment, Colonel V. D. Groner.

Posey's Brigade: Brigadier-general Carnot Posey commanding—Forty-sixth Mississippi Regiment, Colonel Joseph Jayne; Sixteenth Mississippi Regiment, Colonel Samuel E. Baker; Nineteenth Mississippi Regiment, Colonel John Mullins; Twelfth Mississippi Regiment, Colonel W. H. Taylor.

Wright's Brigade: Brigadier-general A. R. Wright commanding—Second Georgia Battalion, Major G. W. Ross; Third Georgia Regiment, Colonel E. J. Walker; Twenty-second Georgia Regiment, Colonel R. H. Jones; Forty-eighth Georgia Regiment, Colonel William Gibson.

Perry's Brigade: Brigadier-general E. A. Perry commanding—Second Florida Regiment, Lieutenant-colonel S. G. Pyles; Fifth Florida Regiment, Colonel J. C. Hately; Eighth Florida Regiment, Colonel David Lang.

MAJOR-GENERAL HENRY HETH'S DIVISION.

First, Pettigrew's Brigade: Forty-second, Eleventh, Twenty-sixth, Forty-fourth, Forty-seventh, Fifty-second and Seventeenth North Carolina Regiments.

Second, Field's Brigade: Fortieth, Fifty-fifth and Forty-seventh Virginia Regiments.

Third, Archer's Brigade: First, Seventh and Fourteenth Tennessee, and Thirteenth Alabama Regiments.

Fourth, Cook's Brigade: Fifteenth, Twenty-seventh, Forty-sixth and Forty-eighth North Carolina Regiments.

Fifth, Davis's Brigade: Second, Eleventh, Forty-second Mississippi and Fifty-fifth North Carolina Regiments.

MAJOR-GENERAL WILLIAM D. PENDER'S DIVISION.

First, McGowan's Brigade: First, Twelfth, Thirteenth and Fourteenth North Carolina Regiments.

Second, Lane's Brigade: Seventh, Eighteenth, Twenty-eighth, Thirty-third and Thirty-seventh Georgia Regiments.

Third, Thomas's Brigade: Fourteenth, Thirty-fifth, Forty-fifth and Forty-ninth Georgia Regiments.

Fourth, Pender's Old Brigade: Thirteenth, Sixteenth, Twenty-second, Thirty-fourth and Thirty-eighth North Carolina Regiments.

CONFEDERATE SIGNAL STATION, NEAR BEVERLEY FORD, VA.

FROM A SKETCH BY EDWIN FORBES.

ARTILLERY OF THE THIRD CORPS.

Colonel R. Lindsay Walker commanding.

Battalion: Major D. G. McIntosh; Major W. T. Poague. Batteries—Hurt's, Rice's, Luck's, Johnson's.

Battalion: Lieutenant-colonel Garnett; Major Richardson. Batteries—Lewis's, Maurin's, Moore's, Grandy's.

Battalion: Major Cutshaw. Batteries—Wyatt's, Woolfolk's, Brooke's.

Battalion: Major Willie P. Pegram. Batteries—Brunson's, Davidson's, Crenshaw's, McGraw's, Marye's.

Battalion: Lieutenant-colonel Cutts; Major Lane. Batteries—Wingfield's, Ross's, Patterson's.

Total number of guns, Artillery of the Third Corps, 83.

Total number of guns, Army of Northern Virginia, 248.

LIEUTENANT-GENERAL J. E. B. STUART'S CAVALRY CORPS.

Brigadier-general Wade Hampton's Brigade—Brigadier-general Fitz Hugh Lee's Brigade—Brigadier-general W. H. F. Lee's Brigade, under Colonel Chambliss—Brigadier-general B. H. Robertson's Brigade—Brigadier-general William E. Jones's Brigade—Brigadier-general J. D. Imboden's Brigade—Brigadier-general A. G. Jenkins's Brigade—Colonel White's Battalion—Baker's Brigade.

GEORGE GORDON MEADE.

BORN December 31st, 1815, at Cadiz, Spain, where his father was at that time United States Consul; entered, in 1831, the United States Military Academy at West Point, from which he graduated, June 30th, 1835; was appointed a brevet-second-lieutenant of the Third United States Artillery, July 1st, 1835; receiving his full commission in December of the same year. He took part in the Florida campaign against the Seminole Indians, and resigned from the Army on the 26th of October, 1836, to enter the profession of civil engineer. During the ensuing six years he was employed by the Government to assist in an elaborate survey of the mouths of the Mississippi River. There he made some original experiments which elicited facts leading to important advantages in the improvement of that river. He was next engaged in the survey of the boundary-line of Texas, and subsequently in the survey of the northeastern boundary-line between the United States and Great Britain. In May, 1842, he returned to the Army as second-lieutenant of topographical engineers, serving in that capacity throughout the Mexican War. He was made a staff officer under Generals Taylor and Scott, and greatly distinguished himself in the battles of Palo Alto, Resaca de la Palma, and Monterey, receiving the brevet of first-lieutenant for gallantry at the last-named engagement. In August, 1851, he was promoted to be first-lieutenant in the topographical corps, and attained a captaincy in 1856. During the four years preceding the Civil War he had charge of the geodetic survey of the great lakes, and in that period added largely to his scientific and engineering reputation. On the 31st of August, 1861, he was appointed a brigadier-general of Volunteers, and was placed in command of the Second Brigade of the Pennsylvania Reserve Corps. The latter afterward constituted a division of the Army of the Potomac, with which Meade remained prominently identified until the close of the war. In the Virginia Peninsula campaign of 1862, he took an active part in the battles of Mechanicsville, Gaines's Mills and Glendale, being severely wounded in the latter, and receiving for bravery the brevet of lieutenant-colonel of engineers in the Regular Army. Returning to the field as soon as his wounds would permit, he was assigned to the command of a division, and distinguished himself in the battles of South Mountain and Antietam, being placed in command of the First Corps when General Hooker was wounded at the last-named battle. Although he had likewise received wounds, and nearly all of his officers were disabled, he remained on the field and stood at the head of his troops throughout the engagement. For these services he was promoted to be major-general of Volunteers on the 29th of November, 1862.

Upon the recovery of General Hooker, Meade returned to the command of the Second Division of the First Army Corps, and at Fredericksburg, in December, 1862, he led the attack which broke through the right of Lee's line, and penetrated far to the rear of the Confederates, where he maintained his ground until greatly outnumbered and driven back with heavy loss. In the latter part of December he was promoted to the command of the Fifth Corps, which figured at Chancellorsville in May, 1863. He had become so popular, and was so admired for his soldier-like qualities, that when General Hooker requested to be relieved of the command of the Army of the Potomac, the corps commanders requested that General Meade be appointed in his stead, which was done by President Lincoln on the 28th of June, 1863. With his new command the great battle of Gettysburg was won, in the subsequent month of July, and he not only earned therefor the thanks of Congress, but was promoted to the rank of brigadier-general in the Regular Army. But little was done during the Winter of 1863-64. By the time the season for active operations had fairly reopened, General Grant was placed in command of all the armies, with the rank of lieutenant-general, and had taken up his headquarters with the Army of the Potomac. During the extraordinary campaign which opened in May, 1864, with the battle of the Wilderness, and only terminated with the surrender of the Army of Northern Virginia, Meade's ability as a commander was conspicuous. He discharged his duties in such a manner as to command the respect and esteem of the lieutenant-general, and his services were recognized in August, 1864, by his promotion to the rank of major-general in the Regular Army.

After the close of hostilities, Meade was, on the 1st of July, 1865, assigned to the command of the Military Division of the Atlantic, with his headquarters at Philadelphia. This post he held, with one short period of detached service in Georgia, till his death, which occurred at Philadelphia on the 6th of November, 1872.

JOHN FULTON REYNOLDS.

BORN in Lancaster, Pa., 1820; admitted to the United States Military Academy at West Point, 1837; graduated June 30th, 1841, and appointed a brevet-second-lieutenant of artillery July 1st, 1841, being commissioned second-lieutenant in the Third Artillery during the subsequent month of October. Was placed on garrison duty until the breaking out of the Mexican War, and given the first-lieutenancy of his regiment on the 18th of June, 1846. Distinguished himself in the defense of Fort Brown, and at the battles of Monterey and of Buena Vista, for his "gallant and meritorious conduct" in which he received the brevets of captain and of major. After his return from Mexico he was engaged in garrison and on frontier duty in California and along the Pacific Coast. Was appointed aid to General Worth in 1852, and aid to General Twiggs in 1853; promoted to the captaincy of the Third Artillery in 1855; and appointed commandant of the Cadets at the West Point Military Academy in 1860. At the commencement of the Civil War he assisted Governor Curtin in organizing State troops, and under the Act of the Legislature of May 15th, 1861, aided materially in the formation of the Pennsylvania Reserve Corps, having in the meantime been transferred to the Fourteenth United States Infantry, with the rank of lieutenant-colonel. For his services in raising the above-named organization, he was presented with a sword of honor by his native State. On the 20th of August, 1861, he was appointed a brigadier-general of Volunteers, and placed at the head of the First Brigade of the Pennsylvania Reserve Corps, then commanded by General G. A. McCall. With this force he assisted in the construction of Fort Pennsylvania at Tenallytown, and afterward joined the Army of the Potomac, participating in the battles of Mechanicsville (Ellison's Mills), Gaines's Mill, (Chickahominy, Cold Harbor), Savage's Station and White Oak Swamp (Charles City Cross Roads, Frazier's Farm, Glendale, Nelson's Farm, New Market Cross Roads, Turkey Bend). He took command of the division after McCall was made a prisoner, during the last engagement, and was himself soon captured and taken to Richmond. For his gallantry in the aforenamed battles he received the brevets of colonel and of brigadier-general in the Regular Army. He was exchanged in August, 1862, and placed in command of a division at the second battle of Bull Run, and in the subsequent campaign in Maryland, being likewise given command of the Pennsylvania Militia called out for the defense of that State. He was afterward in command of the First Corps of the Army of the Potomac, which took part in the battle of Fredericksburg under General Franklin, and was promoted to be a major-general of Volunteers, with commission dating November 29th, 1862. His corps formed part of the reserve at Chancellorsville, where it was not allowed to participate in the battle, and was afterward taken to Gettysburg, figuring in the opening engagement of the first day. Reynolds had then command of the left wing of the army, consisting of the First, Third and Eleventh Corps. He had turned over the command of his First Corps to General Abner Doubleday, and was indefatigable in the preparations made to resist the advance by the Confederates, especially in the defense of a piece of woods which was deemed the key of the position, just beyond Seminary Ridge. Reynolds was making observations along Willoughby's Run, and was in the act of urging on his men to the charge he had ordered, when he was struck in the neck by the bullet of a Confederate sharpshooter, which passed through his head and caused immediate death. A very fine monument was erected to his memory in Philadelphia on the 1st of July, 1884.

including Spottsylvania. Mustered out of service, July 21st, 1864. Wounded at Monterey, Mexico, Gettysburg, Pa., and Spottsylvania, Va. At the time of writing (1885) occupies the prominent position of Clerk of the Superior Court of New York city.

EDWARD EVERETT CROSS.

Born at Lancaster, N. H. Commenced life as a journeyman printer. Removed to Cincinnati, Ohio, in 1852, and connected himself with the newspaper press, and in 1854 he canvassed the State for the Native American Party. He subsequently went to St. Louis, where he was employed by the St. Louis and Arizona Mining Company, and became a large stockholder in the concern. He made several trips across the plains, taking the first steam-engine that ever crossed the Rocky Mountains. In 1861 he organized the Fifth New Hampshire Regiment, went to the front as its colonel, and served with distinguished valor, notably in the Peninsular campaign, and with Pope, Burnside, Hooker and Meade. At the battle of Fair Oaks he succeeded to the command of the First Brigade of the Second Army Corps, on the disability of General O. O. Howard from being wounded. In a charge, which he was gallantly leading, he was struck with a rifle ball in the thigh, and disabled. He was especially commended by General Howard. He won especial mention at Fredericksburg and Chancellorsville, and was mortally wounded at Gettysburg, while leading his gallant Fifth New Hampshire to a charge, July 2d, 1863.

JOHN SEDGWICK.

Born in Cornwall, Conn., September 13th, 1813; entered the United States Military Academy at West Point in July, 1833, and graduated therefrom twenty-fourth in a class of fifty members, which included Generals French, Hooker,

BRANDY STATION, VA.

FROM SKETCHES BY EDWIN FORBES.

HEALTON STATION, VA.

J. H. HOBART WARD.

Born in the city of New York, June 17th, 1823. At the age of eighteen he enlisted in the Seventh United States Infantry, and after passing through various grades, was appointed sergeant-major, in August, 1845. While at Corpus Christi, Tex., participated in the siege of Fort Brown and the battles about Monterey under General Worth; subsequently under General Scott at Vera Cruz, Cerro Gordo and Huamantla. At the conclusion of the Mexican War returned to New York, and was appointed assistant-commissary general of New York; served five years in that capacity; promoted to be commissary-general in 1855, and retired by expiration of service in 1859.

In the late Civil War he recruited the Thirty-eighth New York Volunteers, and was its first colonel. Was engaged at the first battle of Bull Run, in which the regiment lost 126 men. Participated in all the battles of the Peninsula under McClellan, including Yorktown, Williamsburg, Fair Oaks (Seven Pines), Glendale and Malvern Hill to the James River. On the return of the army from the Peninsula was engaged during the various battles at second Bull Run, Groveton and Chantilly. On October 4th, 1862, promoted to be brigadier-general, and assigned to the Army of the Potomac. Commanded Second Brigade, First Division, Third Corps, at Fredericksburg, Chancellorsville, Auburn Mills, and first day at Gettysburg. Commanded First Division on second and third days at Gettysburg, Kelley's Ford and Wapping Heights. Commanded brigade at Mine Run, Locust Grove, Wilderness, and the several daily engagements up to and

Benham, Arnold, Bragg, Pemberton and Early. He entered the army as second-lieutenant of artillery, took part in several engagements against the Seminole Indians, and was subsequently engaged upon frontier duty along the Canadian border, as well as on garrison and recruiting duty, until the year 1846. He entered the Mexican War as first-lieutenant of artillery, participating in the siege of Vera Cruz, and in the battles of Cerro Gordo, Churubusco, Molino del Rey, Chapultepec, and in the assault upon the capital. For his gallantry in the above-named actions, he received the brevets of captain and of major, and in the year 1855 was transferred to the Second Cavalry, with the full rank of major, becoming its lieutenant-colonel in March, 1861. On the 25th of April following he was appointed colonel of the First Regular Cavalry, whence he was transferred to the Fourth Cavalry four months later, receiving the commission of brigadier-general of United States Volunteers on the 31st of August. In the Virginia Peninsular campaign of 1862 he commanded a division of Sumner's Second Corps, with which he took part in the siege of Yorktown, and at the head of which he subsequently pursued the Confederates up the Peninsula. He especially distinguished himself at the battle of Fair Oaks, where, after a toilsome march, he succeeded in bringing his troops in position to decide the success of the day. He also figured very prominently in the battles of Savage's Station, of Glendale, and of Antietam, where he was twice wounded. He was on the 23d of December appointed major-general of Volunteers, to date from July 4th, 1862, and when fully recovered from his wounds was placed in command of the Ninth Corps, from which he was transferred to the command of the Sixth Corps in February, 1863. While at the head of the latter, during the Rappahannock campaign, he was ordered by General Hooker to carry Marye's Heights, in the rear of Fredericksburg, and to effect a junction with the main army at Chancellorsville. On the morning of Sunday, the 3d of May, 1863, he executed Hooker's orders, after a series of engagements in which his loss was nearly 5,000 men. Continuing his march toward Chancellorsville, in pursuance of his instructions, his further advance was checked at Salem Heights by the force which General Lee was able to detach for this purpose, after the repulse of Hooker in the morning. After battling all the afternoon with varying success, Sedgwick was ordered to withdraw at dark across the Rappahannock. In the Pennsylvania campaign of 1863, the Sixth Corps formed the right wing of the army following the movements of Lee, at the time the latter attempted his second invasion, and was brought into position upon the battlefield of Gettysburg after a forced march of thirty-five miles in twenty hours, afterward participating in the battle, and also in the pursuit of the enemy, July 5th. At the battle of Rappahannock Station, Sedgwick again commanded the right wing of the army, composed of the Fifth and Sixth Corps, as he likewise did in the engagement at Mine Run, November–December, 1863. During the Richmond campaign of 1864, he continued in command of the Sixth Corps, and was conspicuous for his bravery at the battles of the Wilderness and of Spottsylvania Court House. While directing the placing of some artillery in an advanced position, during the last-named engagement, he was struck in the head by a bullet from a sharpshooter, and instantly killed. A monument wrought of cannon captured by the Sixth Corps was erected to his memory, upon the grounds of the United States Military Academy at West Point, in 1868.

JUDSON KILPATRICK.

Born near Deckertown, N. J., January 14th, 1837; graduated at the United States Military Academy at West Point, and entered the army as second-lieutenant of artillery on the 6th of May, 1861; commissioned captain of the Fifth New York Volunteers, May 9th, and wounded at the battle of Big Bethel, June 10th, 1861. Upon his recovery he was made lieutenant-colonel of the Second New York Volunteer Cavalry, becoming its colonel in December of the following year, and receiving the promotion of brigadier-general of Volunteers in June, 1863, for services rendered throughout the Rappahannock, as well as in Pope's and the Maryland campaigns. He especially distinguished himself while in command of a brigade of Stoneman's cavalry, leading his force to within a distance of two miles of the Confederate capital, and destroying many thousand dollars worth of property inside and about the fortifications, as well as much of the line of the Richmond and Fredericksburg Railway, besides capturing many prisoners. He also took a leading part in many expeditions connected with the pursuit of the Confederates, at the time of Lee's second invasion, and at the battle of Gettysburg was in command of the Third Division of the Cavalry Corps. In April, 1864, he was ordered to duty with Sherman in the West, and was severely wounded at the battle of Resaca the following month. During General Sherman's march to the sea, and his subsequent campaign through the Carolinas, he had command of the cavalry, and took part in many important engagements. He was promoted to be a major-general of Volunteers in June, 1865. He resigned his commission in the Regular Army in December of the same year, and his Volunteer commission on the 1st of January, 1866, having meanwhile received the appointment of United States Minister to the Republic of Chili by President Johnson in 1866, and recalled in 1868. He was subsequently reappointed to the same mission by President Hayes, and served during the Chili-Peruvian War. President Garfield, by reason of reported rumors of dissatisfaction with certain partisan acts of the respective American Ministers to Peru and Chili, sent a Commissioner, in the person of W. H. Trescott, to convey the instructions of Secretary Blaine in reference to the position of the Government toward the belligerents, and before his arrival Minister Kilpatrick died at Santiago, December 4th, 1881.

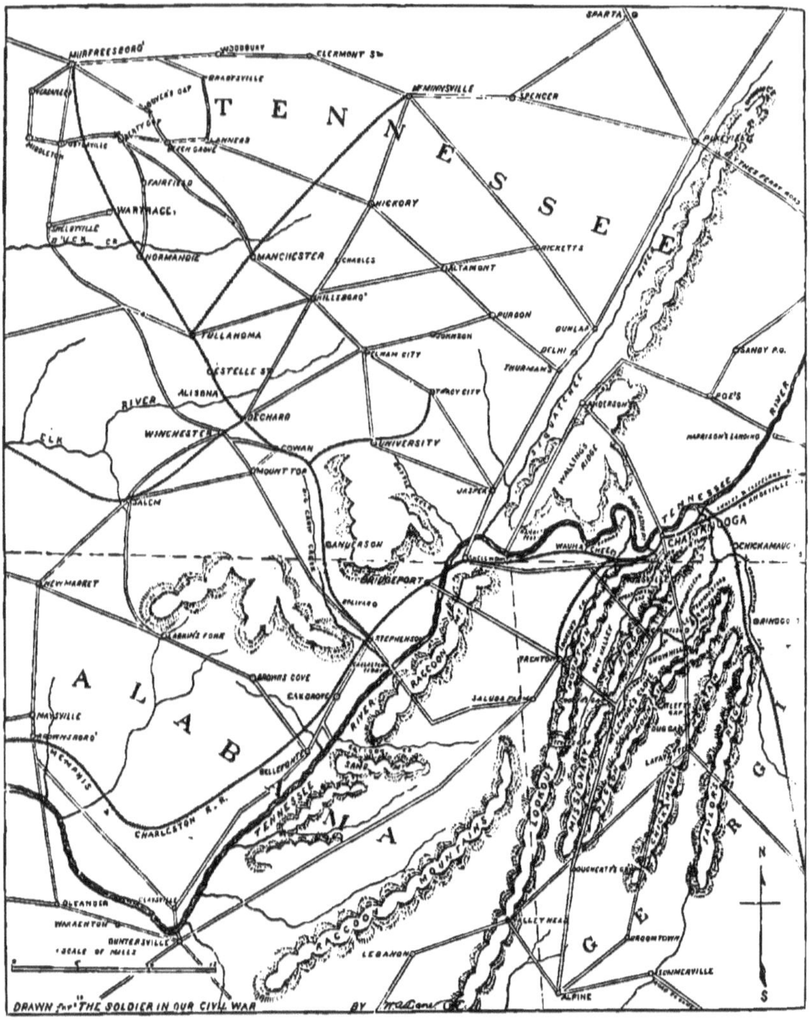

MAP

OF THE

SCENE OF OPERATIONS OF THE ARMY OF THE CUMBERLAND IN TENNESSEE, GEORGIA AND ALABAMA,

SHOWING THE LOCATION OF

THE BATTLES OF CHICKAMAUGA, CHATTANOOGA, LOOKOUT MOUNTAIN AND MISSIONARY RIDGE

THE ARMY OF THE CUMBERLAND.

CHICKAMAUGA—CHATTANOOGA—LOOKOUT MOUNTAIN—MISSIONARY RIDGE.

PENDING the resumption of the active operations by the Army of the Cumberland, several engagements worthy of special mention followed close upon the reorganization of both Rosecrans's and Bragg's armies after the battle of Murfreesboro', or Stone River.

On the 3d of February, 1863, an unsuccessful attempt was made, by Generals Wheeler, Forrest and Wharton, to recapture Fort Donelson, then held by Colonel A. C. Harding. The assailants numbered fully forty-five hundred, while the garrison did not exceed six hundred effective men, with five guns; yet after an encounter of about five hours' duration, in which the Federal gunboat *Fair Play* took part, the Confederates were driven away, with the loss of nearly six hundred in killed, wounded and prisoners.

On the 5th of March, Van Dorn and Forrest attacked Colonel John Colburn's force of thirteen hundred men, near Spring Hill. Colburn was compelled to surrender to the Confederates, who were, however, defeated in turn by General Sheridan at Thompson's Station, whence Van Dorn was driven across the Duck River with a loss of one hundred prisoners, the Federal loss being fifteen killed and wounded.

On the 18th of the same month, General John Morgan was wounded during a three-hours' fight which followed his attack upon Colonel A. S. Hall's force at Vaught's Hill (Milton). Morgan had with him about two thousand men—six hundred more than Hall. The fight lasted nearly four hours, but the assault was so determined on part of the Confederates against Hall's strong position that they lost nearly one-fifth their number, while the Federal loss was barely sixty killed and wounded.

On the 10th of April, Van Dorn made a second attack upon the Federals at and near Franklin. The Confederates were defeated by Gordon Granger's force, after a brilliant engagement with Stanley's cavalry, although the latter comprised but twenty-seven hundred men, which, with the sixteen hundred of Baird's and Gilbert's divisions, made a total of forty-three hundred, as against Van Dorn's nine thousand.

Ten days later General J. J. Reynolds, with a force under Colonels Wilder and Minty, advanced upon and attacked a Confederate post at McMinnville, capturing one hundred and thirty prisoners, and destroying much valuable railway and other property, with the loss of only a few wounded.

On the 3d of May the Confederates effected the capture of what remained of the "Independent Provisional Brigade" under Colonel A. D. Streight, which consisted of the Fifty-first (Streight's) Indiana Regiment, the Seventy-third Indiana, Eightieth Illinois, Third Ohio, and part of the Second Tennessee. This force had set out from Murfreesboro' on the 10th of the previous month, reaching Nashville the following day, for the purpose of operating in Northern Georgia. After engaging in quite a number of skirmishes and destroying much property, Streight reached Eastport, Ala., where he was joined by General Dodge's force; but after capturing Tuscumbia, the two commands had separated, Dodge entering upon a raid through Northern Alabama, before going to Corinth, while Streight made his way toward Rome and Atlanta. When near the first-named city, Streight's detachment, then consisting of thirteen hundred and sixty-five men, was surrounded by and compelled to surrender to the forces led by Generals Forrest and Roddy, numbering fully four thousand men.

Toward the middle of June, Rosecrans became satisfied that Bragg was sending reinforcements to Johnston, who was operating in the rear of Grant's army, then investing Vicksburg. He accordingly determined to attack Bragg, then at Shelbyville, and to relieve East Tennessee by driving him into Georgia.

The Federal advance began on the 23d. The next day, in the midst of an extraordinarily heavy rainstorm, General McCook's Twentieth Corps, consisting of the divisions of Sheridan, Johnson and Davis, and occupying the extreme right, moved directly upon Shelbyville. It was ordered that demonstrations be made against the latter place, while Crittenden's Twenty-first Corps would take the extreme left, upon a long *détour* by way of McMinnville; and while Thomas's Fourteenth Corps was proceeding toward Manchester by way of Hoover's Gap, Granger's Reserves were to advance from Triune in support of both the right and centre.

JUNE, 1863.

When nearly on a line with Liberty Gap, the divisions of Davis and Johnson (late Sill's) left the Shelbyville Road and proceeded to the Gap, intending to move thence along the Fairfield and Normandy Roads. Willich's brigade, leading Johnson's force, entered the Gap, where it had quite a serious encounter with part of Cleburne's force, which it defeated with the subsequent assistance of Miller's brigade.

The Federals bivouacked for the night at the northern end of the Gap, and were attacked the following day by the Confederates, who appeared from the southern entrance. The latter were again repulsed after another prolonged fight, in which Colonel J. F. Miller, then commanding one of the Federal brigades, was mortally wounded. The Confederates had to fall back to Bellbuckle, in the direction of Wartrace, where a large force of Bragg's army was then stationed.

Thomas's corps had in the meantime been ordered to seize and hold Hoover's Gap. Wilder's mounted infantry, which led the advancing column, found the entrance to the Gap unprotected, and instead of awaiting there the arrival of Reynolds's division, he moved ahead, meeting with no resistance until he reached Beech Grove. The latter was occupied by the remainder of Cleburne's force, with which Reynolds had an encounter, and which for a while threatened by its superior numbers to overcome him; but after a sharp engagement he fell back in time to a point along a ridge of woods to the right, where Reynolds had meanwhile strongly posted all of his force. With the reinforcements brought by Reynolds and Rousseau, the Confederates were afterward driven out of the woods, and the possession of the Gap was made secure against all possible further attacks.

Granger had in the meantime been joined by Stanley at Christiana, whence they had proceeded together and afterward taken Guy's Gap, after a

A SOUTHERN CARICATURE.—"GENERALS WHEELER AND WHARTON FALLING SLOWLY BACK, CONTESTING EVERY FOOT OF THE WAY."
FROM A SKETCH BY AN OFFICER OF GENERAL BRAGG'S ARMY.

BIRD'S EYE VIEW OF CHATTANOOGA, TENN., AS SEEN FROM LOOKOUT MOUNTAIN.

two hours' engagement. They had then moved upon and occupied Shelbyville, which Bragg had abandoned for Tullahoma, and whence the Confederates, under General Wheeler, were driven across Duck River, with the loss of about five hundred prisoners, three guns and a large quantity of provisions.

Wilder's brigade had at about the same time surprised and captured the town of Manchester, where Reynolds's entire division immediately followed him, and where Rosecrans was thus enabled to establish his headquarters during the afternoon of the 27th. Two days later the entire army was encamped at the same place.

The day following his arrival at Manchester, Rosecrans ordered Wilder to destroy the bridge over the Elk River, and the railway between Cowan and Decherd, in Bragg's rear; but Wilder's force, under Colonel Munroe, found the bridge strongly guarded by Wither's division, which prevented its

Of McCook's corps, Johnson's division was to move to Salem, where Sheridan's division was to join it from Cowan, and to proceed with it to Bellefonte, while Davis's division would go by the way of Mount Pop and the Big Crow Creek to Stevenson.

August, 1863.

Crittenden's corps was to proceed along the northern part of the Sequatchie Valley; Palmer's division crossing the mountains at Dunlap, and Wood's division at Thurman's; while Minty's cavalry would go by Sparta, in order to cover Van Cleve's left flank, after which it was to move on Pikeville. Crittenden was to send heavy detachments, under General Hazen, from the Valley over Wallings's Ridge, to make demonstrations above Chattanooga, so as to lead Bragg to believe that Rosecrans contemplated giving battle at the last-named place.

Of Thomas's corps, Reynolds and Brannan were ordered to go from University along the Battle Creek, taking position near the latter's mouth, and relieved by the reserves under General Granger then but a short distance away.

Four days after the crossing was completed, Chattanooga was entirely abandoned by Bragg, who took his forces through the gaps of Missionary Ridge, and posted them along the West Chickamauga River, between Lafayette and Lee and Gordon's Mill, opposite the eastern slope of Pigeon's Mountain.

Crittenden occupied Chattanooga early on the 9th, and leaving Wood in charge of the place with one of his brigades, he advanced late the same afternoon in pursuit of the Confederates with the remainder of the corps, taking the Rossville and Ringgold Road. His advance was, however, arrested by the appearance of a heavy Confederate force along the Chickamauga Creek.

McCook was ordered at the same time to move in the direction of Alpine and Summerville, Ga., so as to be in a position to attack Bragg's left.

LOOKOUT MOUNTAIN, NEAR CHATTANOOGA, TENN., OCCUPIED BY GENERAL ROSECRANS.
FROM A SKETCH BY AN ENGINEER OF BRAGG'S ARMY.

burning, and part of which pursued the Federals so actively that they were forced to go in the direction of Tantalon and Anderson, reaching Manchester again during the afternoon of the 30th.

That same night Bragg's army abandoned all its earthworks at Tullahoma, and retreated over the Cumberland Mountains and across the Tennessee River at Bridgeport to Chattanooga, where it arrived a few days later.

Rosecrans's army immediately occupied Tullahoma, but could not pursue the Confederates by reason of the start they had had, and owing to the almost unprecedented rains, which rendered the roads all but impassable. The advance finally reached the foot of the Cumberland Mountains, the railway was put in running order, and by the middle of August the army was in readiness to cross the mountains with Chattanooga as its objective point.

With all the necessary ponton and other bridges needed to cross the Tennessee River at Bellefonte, Caperton's Ferry, Bridgeport, Battle Creek and Shellmount, orders were issued for a general advance, which finally took place on the 16th.

Negley and Baird were to follow the Big Crow Creek, and take position between Anderson and Stevenson.

To the extreme right three brigades of cavalry were to be sent out as far as Athens and Whitesburg, thus making the entire movement cover the Tennessee as far as Blythe's Ferry, a line nearly one hundred and fifty miles in extent.

All these movements were completed late on the 20th. The entire army was across the Cumberland Mountains, and Crittenden at once sent out reconnoissances across Wallings's Ridge to Harrison's Landing, whence Hazen advanced his force against Chattanooga. The town was bombarded the next day from the opposite side of the river, and the shelling was so severe that the Confederates withdrew from the place beyond the range of Hazen's guns.

The Federals began crossing the river on the 29th, and by the 4th of September the whole army occupied the southern bank of the Tennessee, Baird's brigade alone remaining to guard the railway until it could be

September, 1863.

Thomas's force had meanwhile reached Trenton, in the Lookout Creek Valley, and taken possession of both Cooper's (Frick's) and Stevens's Gaps, the most important passes into McLemore's Cove, situated between Missionary Ridge and Pigeon Mountain. It was then taken through Dug Gap, in the last-named mountain, to engage the flank of the Confederates, then supposed to lie at Lafayette, the capital of Walker County, distant about thirty-two miles from Chattanooga.

The Federals soon found that the enemy did not intend falling back to Rome, as had been erroneously supposed, but that a stand was to be made in the vicinity of Lafayette, where Bragg had posted such a strong force of infantry, cavalry and artillery, that Thomas's force thought best to rejoin the main body. Rosecrans therefore ordered the concentration of his army into the Chickamauga Valley, near Crawfish Spring, and by evening of the 18th he had formed a strong line extending northwardly from Lee and Gordon's Mill, with heavy reserves on both his extreme right and left. He also placed strong forces at Rossville and at the

BATTLE OF CHICKAMAUGA, GA., FOUGHT SEPTEMBER [illegible] 20th, 1863. [illegible]

CUMBERLAND HEIGHTS FROM THE KENTUCKY SIDE.—From a Sketch by an Engineer of Bragg's Army.

Dougherty and the Bluebird Gaps, leading into the Broomtown Valley.

Information having reached Thomas that a Confederate brigade was then standing close by Reed's Bridge, apparently without immediate protection, he ordered Baird, early on the 19th, to move part of his force toward Alexander's Bridge, while Brannan would advance along the road leading to Reed's Bridge, which latter had been destroyed the day previous by a small detachment under Colonel D. McCook.

At about ten o'clock Croxton's brigade, of Brannan's division, encountered Forrest's cavalry, which was deployed across Reed's Bridge, and with which it had a sharp engagement, finally driving it back half a mile. Forrest was reinforced by Colonel Wilson's brigade, of Walker's division, and the two then engaged Croxton more fiercely than ever; but Thomas had in the meantime ordered forward Baird's division to the latter's support.

Baird came upon the scene with the remainder of Brannan's force just as another of Walker's brigades, under General Ector, had joined Wilson. The fight continued about an hour longer, when, Croxton's ammunition being exhausted, Baird and Brannan went to the front, and in a short time drove the Confederates away with heavy loss.

The victory proved, however, but a temporary one, for General Liddell's division, and the remains of Walker's division, under General Gist, were soon thrown against the Federals, whose ranks were broken, and in turn finally driven away, with the loss of about 500 prisoners and two full batteries.

Johnson's division of McCook's corps then came up on Baird's right, and was followed by Palmer's and Reynolds's divisions, which were successively posted to the extreme right. The line thus formed lost no time in advancing against Walker's flank, while Brannan's division was engaging the enemy's front, and the attacks were so furiously made that the Confederates were forced back in great disorder to their line of reserves, near Chickamauga Creek, and were compelled to abandon the two batteries which Baird had previously lost.

Cheatham's heavy division next came up to Walker's assistance and assailed the Federal left, which was made to yield its position after an obstinate resistance. The retirement of Johnson was followed by that of Palmer's division, and finally by Van Cleve's, which had come up to Palmer's support. Then Reynolds was attacked, and he also had to give way before the superior numbers which Bragg had thus been enabled to bring up, and which bid fair to sweep the entire Federal force off the field.

But with Davis's appearance all was changed. He advanced his men rapidly to the front, and succeeded in checking the Confederate advance while the disordered lines were being promptly re-formed. By the time this was done, Wood came up, as did likewise Sheridan, and the Federals once more bent their energies toward destroying the apparently ever-increasing Confederate lines.

Assault upon assault followed in rapid succession, each being apparently more furiously made as they progressed, and division after division was brought to the front, rendering the result uncertain upon either side, until a final effort made by the Federal left gave it the victory. The Confederates were again forced to yield the ground, with the loss of a number of guns and of many prisoners.

Shortly before three o'clock a lull in the battle took place, and during the interval Rosecrans posted a heavy force of artillery especially along his more exposed centre, while Bragg ordered forward J. B. Hood's division and Bushrod Johnson's division, of Buckner's corps. The other division belonging to the latter, and commanded by General A. P. Stewart, had already reached the field when Davis made his successful attack in conjunction with the forces of Wood and Sheridan, while General Preston's division remained posted upon Bragg's extreme left.

The Confederates were the first to renew the conflict, by hurling their masses against the right Federal centre, held by the troops under Van Cleve and Reynolds. They were met by the heavy grape and canister fire from Rosecrans's well-posted artillery, as well as by steady volleys from his infantry, all which opened immense lanes into their serried ranks; but regardless of the frightful losses to which they were thus being subjected, the Confederates held their own admirably, dealing as they advanced a fire which likewise told severely upon their enemy.

The battle raged furiously, the assailants manifesting a high degree of bravery, and making charge after charge upon the Federal centre, until the latter was broken, and they were unable to enter the road leading to Lafayette. Seeing this, Rosecrans immediately ordered the divisions of Generals Brannan and Negley to leave respectively the extreme left and right and to go to Reynolds's assistance. The centre, thus reinforced, arrested the progress of the Confederates, who, after bitterly contesting the ground until nightfall, were obliged to return to their former positions.

GEORGE H. THOMAS.

The succession of charges and counter-charges which signalized this day's events along the Chickamauga Creek were, however, not yet at an end. Late in the evening Cheatham's division and part of Hill's corps, under General Cleburne, were ordered to advance from Bragg's right across Tedford's Ford, and attack the new lines which Rosecrans had just formed upon his extreme left. The Confederates fell heavily upon Johnson and Baird, but the Federal artillery was once more brought rapidly and effectively into play, and they had to retire after suffering additional heavy losses. General Preston Smith, of Cheatham's force, was killed at the commencement of the action.

During the ensuing night a council of war was held at the Widow Glenn's house, where Rosecrans's headquarters had been established, and preparations were made to offset the heavy attacks which could not but follow in the morning for the possession of the Chattanooga Road. Bragg was reinforced by Hindman's division as well as by two brigades of McLaws's Virginia Veterans, and his army was divided into two commands, given to Lieutenant-generals Polk and Longstreet.

To the last-named, who reached the field at eleven o'clock in the evening, was given the left wing, embracing the six divisions of Generals Lafayette McLaws, J. B. Hood, T. C. Hindman, A. P. Stewart, William Preston, and Bushrod R. Johnson; while Lieutenant-general Polk was placed in command of the right wing, made up of the five divisions of Generals B. F. Cheatham, P. R. Cleburne, John C. Breckinridge, W. H. T. Walker and S. J. R. Liddell. The Cavalry, under Major-general Joseph Wheeler, embraced the divisions of W. T. Martin and John A. Wharton, and Forrest's corps was made up of the divisions of Brigadier-generals John Pegram and F. C. Armstrong.

Rosecrans's army consisted of McCook's Twentieth Corps, embracing the divisions of Generals Davis, Johnson and Sheridan; of Crittenden's Twenty-first Corps, embracing the divisions of Van Cleve, Wood and Palmer; and of Thomas's Fourteenth Corps, embracing the divisions of Reynolds, Baird, Brannan and Negley. The Reserve, under Gordon Granger, was made up of the divisions of Generals R. S. Granger, James B. Steedman and James D. Morgan. The Cavalry Corps embraced the divisions of General George Crooke and of Colonel E. M. McCook, and was in charge of General R. B. Mitchell, as General D. S. Stanley was at that time too ill to take the field.

A heavy fog enveloped the valley during the entire night, but by the time it cleared away, at about nine o'clock on the morning of the 20th, all preparations for meeting the impending struggle had long been completed on both sides.

SEPTEMBER, 1863.

Upon the Federal line stood Baird, covering the road to Lafayette, on the extreme left; then came Johnson and Palmer, stretching from Baird's right to Reed's Bridge Road, with Wood and Van Cleve in reserve, followed, in the order named, by Reynolds, Brannan, Negley, Davis, and Sheridan, on the extreme right.

Upon the Confederate right stood Breckinridge's force, slightly overlapping Baird's, and next to Cleburne's division, with Cheatham, Walker and Liddell in reserve, followed in order by the divisions of Stewart, Johnson and Hindman. The latter occupied the extreme Confederate left, and was supported by Preston's force, while Hood's division stood a little in the rear, about midway between Stewart and Johnson, where McLaws's force was likewise formed as soon as it reached the field.

Shortly before ten o'clock the Confederates opened battle, after nearly a full hour's heavy skirmishing, especially along the extreme Federal left. Beatty's brigade, which had been brought up on Baird's left, was strongly assailed by two of Breckinridge's brigades, consisting mainly of Florida and Louisiana regiments, under Generals Stovall and Adams. The latter force occupied Breckinridge's extreme right, and fell upon Beatty so heavily that the Federals were driven back in disorder, the Confederates pressing forward to attack Baird's rear simultaneously with an attack upon Thomas's front by Breckinridge's remaining brigade, under General Helm, as well as by part of Cleburne's division.

Before the rear could be gained, however, the force operating upon Baird's and Johnson's front had been so thoroughly beaten back, and reinforcements had come up from the divisions of Negley and Brannan so rapidly upon the Federal left, that the contemplated advance of Breckinridge's troops in that direction was promptly foiled.

Such was also the case with the attack upon Thomas's right and centre, which followed closely the assault upon the extreme left. After two hours' of steady fighting, the divisions of Palmer and Reynolds, as well as the reinforcements sent especially from Sheridan's division in support of Thomas, forced the Confederates back along their entire front, with the loss of one of their best commanders,

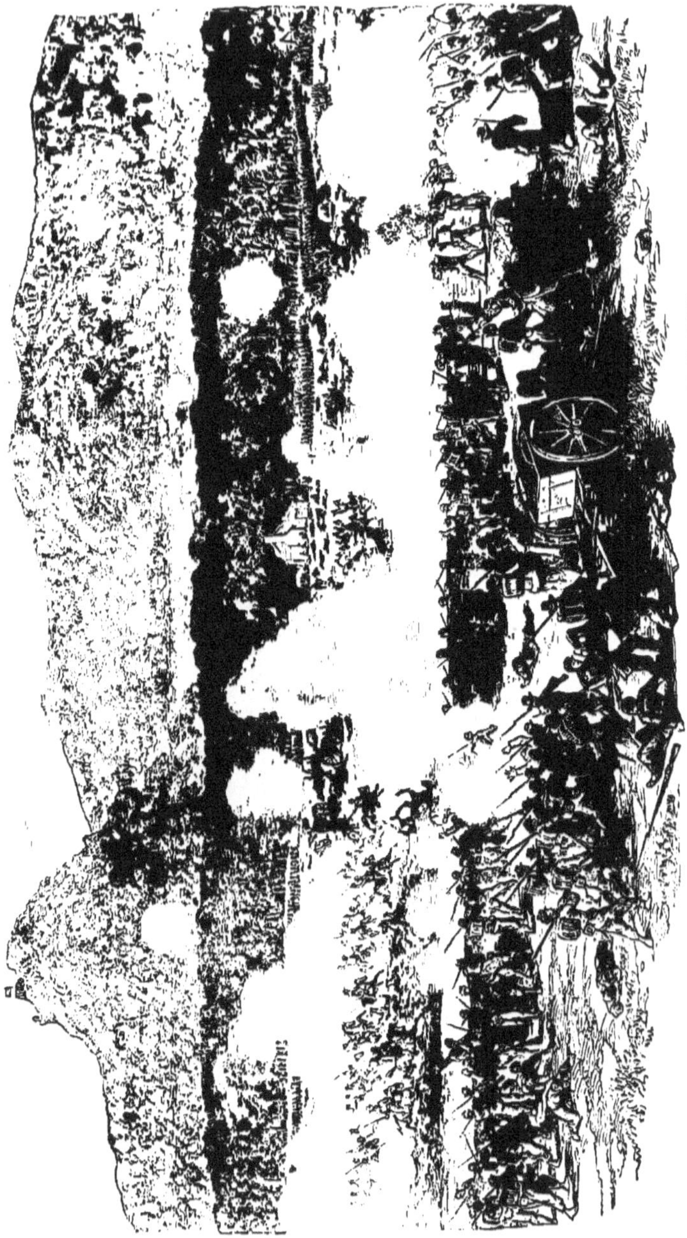

BATTLE OF CHICKAMAUGA, GA.—REPULSE OF THE CONFEDERATES AT CRAWFISH CREEK.

General James Deshler, belonging to Cleburne's division.

While all this was going on, the Confederates had been enabled to sever the Federal right from the main body, and in defeating it with heavy loss. General Wood, who had been ordered early in the day to take Negley's place on the right of Brannan's force when the former went over to the left, was afterward directed by Rosecrans to fill up a gap reported as existing in the line where Brannan first stood, Rosecrans then ignoring the fact that Brannan had retired *en échelon* to a line of woods situated but a little distance from the front, and that Reynolds's right was thus in reality still protected.

Upon receiving the order, Wood took position in Brannan's rear, where Reynolds was then posted, thus creating a worse gap in the front, to which Longstreet's attention was immediately attracted. Into this gap Hood's force was quickly sent, before Wood had deployed all of his troops, and before Davis's men could reach the spot, in accordance with McCook's orders.

Hood was supported by Stewart, and thrust himself so promptly into the opening that the Federals were soon thrown into disorder by the much superior numbers that were opposing them, through the subsequent accession of Hindman's and Johnson's forces. A determined stand was attempted, notably on the part of both Davis's and Sheridan's divisions; but it proved useless. The tide swept all before it, and in a short time the entire right wing was sent flying in the direction of Rossville and Chattanooga, losing many guns, and sustaining heavy losses in killed, wounded and prisoners.

Thomas alone remained in his original position, with Baird, Johnson, Palmer and Reynolds, as well as such troops of Brannan's and Wood's divisions as had not succumbed to Hood's vigorous attack. Thomas had asked for additional reinforcements from Sheridan's division while steadily repelling renewed assaults upon his left, just as Hood broke into the Federal right, and not knowing of the disaster which had befallen the latter, he had again sent for assistance.

His aid returned finally with the information that a large force of the enemy was approaching him from the rear of Reynolds's position. General Harker was directed to take his brigade and resist the advance, while Thomas formed a new line of battle along the "Horseshoe Ridge," between the Dry Valley and Lafayette Roads, where he promptly erected breastworks and brought together all his artillery. Here he was quickly attacked by the Confederates, who had abandoned the pursuit of the retreating right wing through the Dry Valley. A very prolonged encounter took place, and charge after charge was brilliantly repulsed by Thomas's inferior numbers, who were assailed in turn upon their flanks and rear. In these repeated attacks, Brannan's division especially distinguished itself, while Wood's force did scarcely less meritorious work in its defeat of Johnson's and Anderson's united movement upon the crest held by his force.

JOSEPH WHEELER.

The most determined and final assault of the day followed the union of Hindman's and Kershaw's divisions with Johnson's force. This was just after three o'clock in the afternoon. An almost overwhelming mass debouched from a gorge leading to Thomas's rear just as another heavy force was advancing against his flanks—a movement which, though ever so well resisted by a greatly inferior and wellnigh exhausted force, must needs have resulted disastrously for General Thomas's troops but for the timely arrival of General Steedman with two brigades of his division.

Upon hearing the noise of battle increasing upon the Federal left, General Granger, then at Rossville, had taken upon himself to send as heavy a force as he could spare to Thomas's assistance. The two brigades of Generals Whittaker and Colonel Mitchell were advanced forward under General Steedman, accompanied by Granger himself, who had left the force under Colonel Daniel McCook to protect the Ringgold Road and the approaches to Thomas's position.

Granger's troops were posted on Brannan's right, whence they were ordered to charge upon and dislodge the Confederates already swarming along the crest of the ridge. This was done so impetuously, under Steedman's leadership, that in a short time the Confederates were driven with great loss from the summit of the ridge. They returned once more to the attack, and assaulted the Federals again and again, until finally, after a most desperate hand-to-hand fight, in which the two sides again lost heavily, both the ridge and the gorge remained in possession of the Federals.

Thomas had in the meantime been equally successful, and had repelled a serious attack upon his centre, through which Longstreet had expected to force a passage to McFarland's Gap. The grape and canister that met the Confederates from six pieces of artillery which Thomas had posted along his immediate front did such effective work, in conjunction with the well-directed fire from the infantry, that when the ammunition was wellnigh exhausted, and a final bayonet-charge was ordered, the Confederates were driven away just before sunset with the loss of many prisoners.

Thus for nearly six hours Thomas had battled manfully against more than double his own numbers, and by a masterly disposition of his troops, and the display of a courage rarely equaled, secured the safety of Rosecrans's entire army. Well indeed did he deserve the sobriquet of "Rock of Chickamauga," which was then bestowed upon and has ever since attached to him.

The troops which had been driven back from the extreme right and centre had attempted to effect a junction with Thomas's force, but this being found impracticable, Rosecrans had them rallied along the Dry Valley Road, whence they were finally taken to Rossville. There a stand was ordered to be made, while Rosecrans himself went to Chattanooga to make arrangements for holding the place in case his army should be compelled to fall back upon it.

He then sent General Garfield with orders for Thomas to assume command of all the troops at the front, and to withdraw his army to Rossville. Thomas maintained his position until nine o'clock in the evening, when he began withdrawing his troops as directed, and as soon as he saw this nearly completed, he repaired to Rossville, in company with Generals Granger and Garfield, and established a new line of defenses around the last-named town.

He deployed McCook's corps from Chattanooga

B. F. CHEATHAM.

Creek to the Dry Valley Road, whence Reynolds's division extended to the right of Negley's force, posted upon the Ringgold Road, and to the left of which latter stood the whole of Crittenden's corps. All the other troops were held in reserve.

No effective pursuit could well be made by the badly punished Confederates, nor was any attempted either during the ensuing night or the following day. At about six o'clock on the evening of the 21st, the Federals began retreating to Chattanooga, completing the movement, without loss, early the next morning.

Rosecrans immediately set to work strengthening the defenses around the town, under the able direction of General J. St. Clair Morton, and Bragg took possession of Lookout Mountain, as well as of the whole front of Missionary Ridge, and massed his troops into the Chattanooga Valley.

The entire Federal losses were reported at 1,687 killed, 9,394 wounded, and 5,255 missing—total 16,336; those of the Confederates being fully as large, if not actually greater, some footing them up as high as 20,000.

ROSTER OF THE CONFEDERATE ARMY

ENGAGED AT THE

BATTLE OF CHICKAMAUGA, GA.

RIGHT WING.

Lieutenant-general Leonidas Polk.

MAJOR-GENERAL B. F. CHEATHAM'S DIVISION.

Jackson's Brigade: Brigadier-general J. K. Jackson—First Confederate Battery, Fifth Georgia, Second Georgia Battery, Fifth Mississippi, Eighth Mississippi, Scogin's (Georgia) Battery.

Maney's Brigade: Brigadier-general George Maney—First Tennessee, Twenty-seventh Tennessee, Fourth Tennessee, Sixth Tennessee, Ninth Tennessee, Maney's (Tennessee) Battalion, Smith's (Mississippi) Battery.

Smith's Brigade: Brigadier-general Preston Smith, Colonel A. J. Vaughan—Eleventh Tennessee, Twelfth Tennessee, Forty-seventh Tennessee, Thirteenth Tennessee, Twenty-ninth Tennessee, One Hundred and Fifty-fourth Tennessee, Scott's (Tennessee) Battery.

Wright's Brigade: Brigadier-general M. J. Wright—Eighth Tennessee, Sixteenth Tennessee, Twenty-eighth Tennessee, Thirty-eighth Tennessee, Fifty-first Tennessee, Fifty second Tennessee, Carnes's (Tennessee) Battery.

Strahl's Brigade: Brigadier-general O. F. Strahl—Fourth Tennessee, Fifth Tennessee, Nineteenth Tennessee, Twenty-fourth Tennessee, Thirty-first Tennessee, Thirty-third Tennessee, Stanford's (Mississippi) Battery.

HILL'S CORPS.

Lieutenant-general D. H. Hill.

MAJOR-GENERAL P. R. CLEBURNE'S DIVISION.

Polk's Brigade: Brigadier-general L. E. Polk—First Arkansas, Third Confederate, Fifth Confederate, Second

WHEELER'S CONFEDERATE CAVALRY CAPTURING A SUPPLY-TRAIN NEAR JASPER, TENN.

From a Sketch by J. F. E. Hillen.

Tennessee, Thirty-fifth Tennessee, Forty-eighth Tennessee, Calvert's (Tennessee) Battery.

Wood's Brigade: Brigadier-general S. A. M. Wood—Sixteenth Alabama, Thirty-third Alabama, Forty-fifth Alabama, Thirty-second Mississippi, Forty-fifth Mississippi, Hankin's Battalion, Semple's (Alabama) Battery.

Deshler's Brigade: Brigadier-general James Deshler, Colonel R. Q. Mills—Nineteenth Arkansas, Twenty-fourth Arkansas, Sixth Texas, Tenth Texas, Fifteenth Texas, Seventeenth Texas, Eighteenth Texas, Twenty-fourth Texas, Twenty-fifth Texas, Douglas's (Texas) Battery.

MAJOR-GENERAL JOHN C. BRECKINRIDGE'S DIVISION.

Helm's Brigade: Brigadier-general B. H. Helm, Colonel J. H. Lewis—Forty-first Alabama, Second Kentucky, Fourth Kentucky, Sixth Kentucky, Ninth Kentucky, Cobb's (Kentucky) Battery.

Adams's Brigade: Brigadier-general Daniel Adams, Colonel R. L. Gibson—Thirty-second Alabama, Thirteenth Louisiana, Twentieth Louisiana, Sixteenth Louisiana, Twenty-fifth Louisiana, Nineteenth Louisiana, Austin's (Louisiana) Battalion, Slocomb's (Louisiana) Battery.

Stovall's Brigade: Brigadier-general M. A. Stovall—First Florida, Third Florida, Fourth Florida, Forty-seventh Georgia, Sixtieth North Carolina, Mebane's (Tennessee) Battery.

MAJOR-GENERAL W. H. WALKER'S DIVISION.

Gist's Brigade: Brigadier-general S. R. Gist, Colonel P. H. Colquitt—Forty-sixth Georgia, Eighth Georgia Battalion, Sixteenth South Carolina, Twenty-fourth South Carolina, Ferguson's (South Carolina) Battery.

Ector's Brigade: Brigadier-general M. D. Ector—Alabama Battalion (Stone's), Mississippi Battalion (Pound's), Ninth Texas, Tenth Texas Cavalry, Fourteenth Texas Cavalry, Thirty-second Texas Cavalry, Battery.

Wilson's Brigade: Colonel C. C. Wilson—Twenty-fifth Georgia, Twenty-ninth Georgia, Thirtieth Georgia, First Georgia Battalion, Fourth Louisiana Battalion, Battery.

BRIGADIER-GENERAL S. J. R. LIDDELL'S DIVISION.

Liddell's Brigade: Colonel D. C. Govan—Second Arkansas, Fifteenth Arkansas, Fifth Arkansas, Thirteenth Arkansas, Sixth Arkansas, Seventh Arkansas, Eighth Arkansas, First Louisiana, Swett's (Mississippi), Battalion.

Walthall's Brigade: Brigadier-general E. C. Walthall—Twenty-fourth Mississippi, Twenty-seventh Mississippi, Twenty-ninth Mississippi, Thirtieth Mississippi, Thirty-fourth Mississippi, Fowler's (Alabama) Battery.

LEFT WING.

Lieutenant-general James Longstreet.

MAJOR-GENERAL LAFAYETTE M'LAWS'S DIVISION.

Kershaw's Brigade: Brigadier-general J. B. Kershaw—Second South Carolina, Third South Carolina, Seventh South Carolina, Eighth South Carolina, Fifteenth South Carolina, Third South Carolina Battalion.

Wofford's Brigade: Brigadier-general W. T. Wofford—Sixteenth Georgia, Eighteenth Georgia, Twenty-fourth Georgia, Third Georgia Battalion, Cobb's (Georgia) Legion, Phillips's (Georgia) Legion.

Humphreys's Brigade: Brigadier-general B. G. Humphreys—Thirteenth Mississippi, Seventeenth Mississippi, Eighteenth Mississippi, Twenty-first Mississippi.

Bryan's Brigade: Brigadier-general Goode Bryan—Tenth Georgia, Fiftieth Georgia, Fifty-first Georgia, Fifty-third Georgia.

MAJOR-GENERAL J. B. HOOD'S DIVISION.

Law's Brigade: Brigadier-general E. M. Law, Colonel Sheffield—Fourth Alabama, Fifteenth Alabama, Forty-fourth Alabama, Forty-seventh Alabama, Forty-eighth Alabama.

Robertson's Brigade: Brigadier-general J. B. Robertson—Third Arkansas, Eighteenth, Fourth, and Fifth Texas.

Anderson's Brigade: Brigadier-general George T. Anderson—Seventh Georgia, Eighth Georgia, Ninth Georgia, Eleventh Georgia, Fifty-ninth Georgia.

Benning's Brigade: Brigadier-general H. L. Benning—Second Georgia, Fifteenth Georgia, Seventeenth Georgia, Twentieth Georgia.

Artillery: Major Frank Huger—Fickling's (Virginia) Battery, Jordan's (Virginia) Battery, Moody's (Louisiana) Battery, Parker's (Virginia) Battery, Taylor's (Virginia) Battery, Woolfolk's (Virginia) Battery.

MAJOR-GENERAL T. C. HINDMAN'S DIVISION.

Anderson's Brigade: Brigadier-general Patton Anderson, Colonel J. H. Sharp—Seventh Mississippi, Ninth Mississippi, Tenth Mississippi, Forty-first Mississippi, Forty-fourth Mississippi, Ninth Mississippi Battalion, Garrity's (Alabama) Battery.

Deas's Brigade: Brigadier-general Z. C. Deas—Nineteenth Alabama, Twenty-second Alabama, Twenty-fifth Alabama, Thirty-ninth Alabama, Fiftieth Alabama, Seventeenth Alabama Battalion, Dent's (Alabama) Battery.

Manigault's Brigade: Brigadier-general A. M. Manigault—Twenty-fourth Alabama, Twenty-eighth Alabama, Thirty-fourth Alabama, Tenth South Carolina and Nineteenth South Carolina consolidated, Water's (Alabama) Battery.

BUCKNER'S CORPS.

Major-general S. B. Buckner.

MAJOR-GENERAL A. P. STEWART'S DIVISION.

Johnson's Brigade: Brigadier-general B. R. Johnson, Colonel J. S. Fulton—Seventeenth Tennessee, Twenty-third Tennessee, Twenty-fifth Tennessee, Forty-fourth Tennessee, Ninth Georgia Artillery, Battery "E."

Brown's Brigade: Brigadier-general J. C. Brown—Eighteenth Tennessee, Twenty-sixth Tennessee, Thirty-second Tennessee, Forty-fifth Tennessee, Newman's (Tennessee) Battalion, Dawson's (Georgia) Battery.

Bate's Brigade: Brigadier-general W. B. Bate—Fifty-eighth Alabama, Thirty-seventh Georgia, Fourth Georgia Battalion, Fifteenth Tennessee, Thirty-seventh Tennessee, Twentieth Tennessee, Oliver's (Alabama) Artillery.

Clayton's Brigade: Brigadier-general H. D. Clayton—Eighteenth Alabama, Thirty-sixth Alabama, Thirty-eighth Alabama, Humphreys's (Arkansas) Battery.

BRIGADIER-GENERAL WILLIAM PRESTON'S DIVISION.

Gracie's Brigade: Brigadier-general A. Gracie, Jr.—Forty-third Alabama, First Alabama Battalion, Second Alabama Battalion, Third Alabama Battalion, Sixty-third Tennessee Battery.

Trigg's Brigade: Colonel R. C. Trigg—First Florida Cavalry, Sixth Florida, Seventh Florida, Fifty-fourth Virginia, Peeple's (Georgia) Battery.

Kelly's Brigade: Colonel J. H. Kelly—Sixty-fifth Georgia, Fifth Kentucky, Fifty-eighth North Carolina, Sixty-third Virginia, Battery.

BRIGADIER-GENERAL B. R. JOHNSON'S DIVISION.

Gregg's Brigade: Brigadier-general John Gregg, Colonel C. A. Sugg—Third Tennessee, Tenth Tennessee, Thirtieth Tennessee, Forty-first Tennessee, Fiftieth Tennessee, First (Twentieth) Tennessee Battalion, Seventh Texas, Bledsoe's (Missouri) Battery.

McNair's Brigade: Brigadier-general E. McNair, Colonel D. Coleman—First Arkansas Rifles, Second Arkansas Rifles, Fourth Arkansas, Twenty-fifth Arkansas, Thirty-fifth Arkansas, Culpeper's (South Carolina) Battery.

CAVALRY.

Major-general Joseph Wheeler.

BRIGADIER-GENERAL JOHN A. WHARTON'S DIVISION.

First Brigade: Colonel C. C. Crews—Seventh Alabama, Second Georgia, Third Georgia, Fourth Georgia.

Second Brigade: Colonel T. Harrison, Third Confederate, First Kentucky, Fourth Tennessee, Eighth Texas, Eleventh Texas, White's (Georgia) Battery.

BRIGADIER-GENERAL W. T. MARTIN'S DIVISION.

First Brigade: Colonel J. T. Morgan—First Alabama, Third Alabama, Fifty-first Alabama, Eighth Confederate.

Second Brigade: Colonel A. A. Russell—Fourth Alabama*, First Confederate, Wiggins's (Arkansas) Battery.

BRIGADIER-GENERAL P. D. RODDEY'S BRIGADE.

Fourth Alabama*, Fifth Alabama, Fifty-third Alabama, Forrest's (Tennessee) Regiment, Ferrell's (Georgia) Battery.

FORREST'S CORPS.

Major-general N. B. Forrest.

BRIGADIER-GENERAL F. C. ARMSTRONG'S DIVISION.

Armstrong's Brigade: Third Arkansas, First Tennessee, Second Tennessee, McDonald's Battalion.

——— *Brigade:* Fourth Tennessee, Eighth Tennessee, Ninth Tennessee, Tenth Tennessee, Eleventh Tennessee, Freeman's (Tennessee) Battery, Morton's (Tennessee) Battery.

BRIGADIER-GENERAL JOHN PEGRAM'S DIVISION.

Davidson's Brigade: Brigadier-general H. B. Davidson—First Georgia, Sixth Georgia, Sixty-fifth North Carolina, Rucker's Legion, Huwald's (Tennessee) Battery.

Scott's Brigade: Colonel J. S. Scott—Tenth Confederate, First Louisiana, Fifth Tennessee, Twelfth Tennessee Battalion, Sixteenth Tennessee Battalion, Louisiana Battery (one section).

WILDER'S MOUNTED INFANTRY PASSING THE BLOCKHOUSE OF THE NASHVILLE AND CHATTANOOGA RAILROAD.

FROM A SKETCH BY J. F. E. HILLEN.

---

* Two regiments of the same designation. Lieutenant-colonel Johnson commanded that in Roddey's brigade.

RESERVE ARTILLERY.

Barret's (Missouri) Battery, Darden's (Mississippi) Battery, Havis's (Alabama) Battery, Le Gardeur's (Louisiana) Battery, Lumsden's (Alabama) Battery, Massenburg's (Georgia) Battery.

WHILE the Federals were fortifying the approaches to Chattanooga, Bragg was cutting off all its communications, and in a short time the only road left open to the Federals for replenishing their much-reduced supplies was that over Walling's Ridge, toward the Sequatchie Valley.

On the 16th of October, Rosecrans's Department of the Cumberland, Burnside's Department of the Ohio, and Grant's Department of the Mississippi, were, by order of the Secretary of War, consolidated into the "Military Division of the Mississippi," and Major-general U. S. Grant was given chief command.

General W. T. Sherman was placed at the head of the Army of the Tennessee, and General Thomas was appointed commander of the Army of the Cumberland in place of General Rosecrans, who was relieved of his command, as had already been Generals Crittenden and McCook, the last two being ordered to await a Court of Inquiry, which was to look into their conduct during the battle of Chickamauga. Simultaneously with the order relieving Crittenden and McCook was one consolidating the Twentieth and Twenty-first Army Corps into one, called the Fourth Army Corps, which was given in command of Gordon Granger.

LOOKOUT MOUNTAIN AND ITS VICINITY, FROM THE POSITION OF THE ELEVENTH ARMY CORPS.

FROM A SKETCH BY SERGEANT J. E. TAYLOR, SEVENTY-THIRD PENNSYLVANIA REGIMENT.

The new organization of the Army of the Cumberland, under Major-general George H. Thomas, was as follows:

FOURTH ARMY CORPS.

Major-general G. Granger.

MAJOR-GENERAL J. M. PALMER'S DIVISION.

First Brigade: Brigadier-general Charles Cruft—Twenty-first Illinois, Thirty-eighth Illinois, Twenty-ninth, Thirty-first and Eighty-first Indiana; First Kentucky, Second Kentucky, Ninetieth and One Hundred and First Ohio.

Second Brigade: Brigadier-general W. C. Whitaker—Ninety-sixth Illinois, One Hundred and Fifteenth Illinois, Thirty-fifth Indiana, Eighty-fourth Indiana, Eighth Kentucky, Fortieth Ohio, Fifty-first Ohio, Ninety-ninth Ohio.

Third Brigade: Colonel William Grose—Fifty-ninth Illinois, Seventy-fifth Illinois, Eighty-fourth Illinois, Ninth Indiana, Thirtieth Indiana, Thirty-sixth Indiana, Twenty-fourth Ohio, Seventy-seventh Pennsylvania.

Artillery: Fifth Indiana Battery, Fourth United States Artillery, Company "H"; Fourth United States Artillery, Company "M."

MAJOR-GENERAL P. H. SHERIDAN'S DIVISION.

First Brigade: Brigadier-general J. B. Steedman—Thirty-sixth, Forty-fourth, Seventy-third, Seventy-fourth and Eighty-eighth Illinois; Twenty-second Indiana, Twenty-first Mich., Second and Fifteenth Missouri, Twenty-fourth W[illegible]

Second Brigade: Brigadier-general G. D. Wagner—[illegible] Hundredth Illinois, Fifteenth Indiana, Fortieth Ind[illegible] Fifty-seventh Indiana, Fifty-eighth Indiana, Thir[illegible] Michigan, Twenty-sixth Ohio, Ninety-seventh Ohio.

Third Brigade: Colonel C. G. Harker—Twenty-second, Twenty-seventh, Forty-second, Fifty-first, and Se[illegible] ninth Illinois; Third Kentucky, Sixty-fourth, Sixty-fifth and One Hundred and Twenty-fifth Ohio.

Artillery: First Illinois Artillery, Company "M"; T[illegible] Indiana Battery; First Missouri Artillery, Company "[illegible]

BRIGADIER-GENERAL T. J. WOOD'S DIVISION.

First Brigade: Brigadier-general A. Willich—Twenty-[illegible] Illinois, Thirty-fifth Illinois, Eighty-ninth Illinois, Thir[illegible] second Indiana, Sixty-eighth Indiana, Eighth Kansas, Fifteenth Ohio, Forty-ninth Ohio, Fifteenth Wisconsin.

Second Brigade: Brigadier-general W. B. Hazen—Sixth Indiana, Fifth Kentucky, Sixth Kentucky, Twenty-third Kentucky, First Ohio, Sixth Ohio, Forty-first Ohio, Ninety-third Ohio, One Hundred and Twenty-fourth Ohio.

Third Brigade: Brigadier-general S. Beatty—Forty-fourth Indiana, Seventy-ninth Indiana, Eighty-sixth Indiana, Ninth Kentucky, Seventeenth Kentucky, Thirteenth Ohio, Nineteenth Ohio, Fifty-ninth Ohio.

Artillery: Bridge's Battery, Illinois Artillery, Sixth Ohio Battery, Twenty-sixth Pennsylvania Battery.

ELEVENTH AND TWELFTH ARMY CORPS.

Major-general Joseph Hooker commanding.

ELEVENTH ARMY CORPS.

Major-general O. O. Howard.

BRIGADIER-GENERAL A. VON STEINWEHR'S DIVISION.

First Brigade: Thirty-third New Jersey, One Hundred and Thirty-fourth New York, One Hundred and Fifty-fourth New York, Twenty-seventh Pennsylvania, Seventy-third Pennsylvania.

New York, One Hundred and Fiftieth New York, Third Wisconsin.

BRIGADIER-GENERAL JOHN W. GEARY'S DIVISION.

First Brigade: Fifth Ohio, Seventh Ohio, Twenty-ninth Ohio, Sixty-sixth Ohio, Twenty-eighth Pennsylvania, One Hundred and Forty-seventh Pennsylvania.

Second Brigade: Twenty-ninth Pennsylvania, One Hundred and Ninth Pennsylvania, One Hundred and Eleventh Pennsylvania.

Third Brigade: Sixtieth New York, Seventy-eighth New York, One Hundred and Second New York, One Hundred and Thirty-seventh New York, One Hundred and Forty-ninth New York.

Artillery: First Battalion Tenth Maine Volunteer Infantry; First New York Artillery, Company "M"; Pennsylvania Battery, Company "E"; Fourth United States Artillery, Company "F"; Fifth United States Artillery, Company "K."

LIEUTENANT-COLONEL HUNTON, UNASSIGNED ARTILLERY.

Second Kentucky Battery, First Michigan "E" and "M" Twentieth Indiana Battery, First Kentucky Battery, First Ohio Artillery, Company "E"; Tenth Wisconsin Battery.

Second Brigade: Brigadier-general J. Beatty—Third East Tennessee, Fifth East Tennessee, Sixth East Tennessee, Seventy-eighth Illinois, Ninety-eighth Ohio, One Hundred and Thirteenth Ohio, One Hundred and Twenty-first Ohio.

Third Brigade: Colonel D. McCook—Eighty-fifth Illinois, Eighty-sixth Illinois, One Hundred and Tenth Illinois, One Hundred and Twenty-fifth Illinois, Fifty-second Ohio, Twenty-second Michigan.

Artillery: Second Illinois Artillery, Company "I"; Second Minnesota Battery, Fifth Wisconsin Battery.

BRIGADIER-GENERAL A. BAIRD'S DIVISION.

First Brigade: Brigadier-general J. B. Turchin—Eighty-second Indiana, Eleventh Ohio, Seventeenth Ohio, Thirty-first Ohio, Thirty-sixth Ohio, Eighty-ninth Ohio, Ninety-second Ohio.

Second Brigade: Colonel James George—Seventy-fifth Indiana, Eighty-seventh Indiana, One Hundred and First Indiana, Second Minnesota, Ninth Ohio, Thirty-fifth Ohio, One Hundred and Fifth Ohio.

Third Brigade: Colonel E. H. Phelps—Tenth Indiana, Seventy-fourth Indiana, Fourth Kentucky, Tenth Kentucky, Eighteenth Kentucky, Fourteenth Ohio, Thirty-eighth Ohio

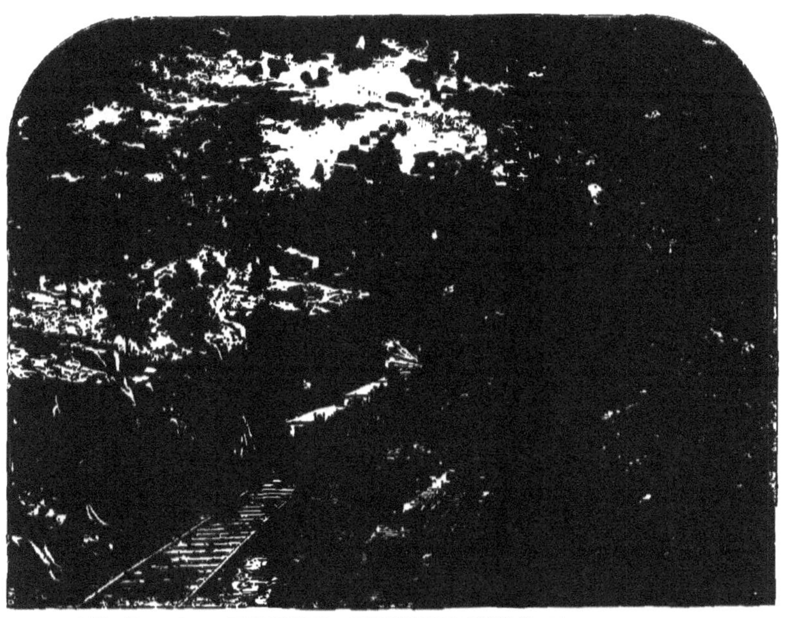

ATTEMPT OF THE CONFEDERATES TO BLOW UP A SUPPLY-TRAIN NEAR CUMBERLAND TUNNEL, OCTOBER 25TH-26TH, 1863.

FROM A SKETCH BY J. F. E. HILLEN.

Second Brigade: Thirty-third Massachusetts, One Hundred and Thirty-sixth New York, Fifty-fifth Ohio, Seventy-third Ohio.

MAJOR-GENERAL C. SCHURZ'S DIVISION.

First Brigade: Eighty-second Illinois, Forty-fifth New York, One Hundred and Forty-third New York, Sixty-first Ohio, Eighty-second Ohio.

Second Brigade: Fifty-eighth New York, Sixty-eighth New York, One Hundred and Nineteenth New York, One Hundred and Forty-first New York, Seventy-fifth Pennsylvania, Twenty-sixth Wisconsin.

Artillery: First New York Artillery, Company "I"; Thirteenth New York Battery, Independent Company, Eighth New York Volunteer Infantry; First Ohio Artillery, Company "I"; First Ohio Artillery, Company "K"; Fourth United States, Company "G."

TWELFTH ARMY CORPS.

Major-general H. W. Slocum.

BRIGADIER-GENERAL A. S. WILLIAMS'S DIVISION.

First Brigade: Fifth Connecticut, Twentieth Connecticut, Third Maryland, One Hundred and Twenty-third New York, One Hundred and Forty-fifth New York, Forty-sixth Pennsylvania.

Second Brigade: Twenty-seventh Indiana, Second Massachusetts, Thirteenth New Jersey, One Hundred and Seventh

FOURTEENTH ARMY CORPS.

(1) Major-general George H. Thomas.

(2) Major-general John McCauley Palmer.

BRIGADIER-GENERAL W. P. CARLIN'S DIVISION.

First Brigade: Colonel O. F. Moore—One Hundred and Fourth Illinois, Thirty-eighth Indiana, Forty-second Indiana, Eighty-eighth Indiana, Fifteenth Kentucky, Second Ohio, Thirty-third Ohio, Ninety-fourth Ohio, Tenth Wisconsin.

Second Brigade: Colonel M. F. Moore—Nineteenth Illinois, Eleventh Michigan, Eighteenth Ohio, Sixty-ninth Ohio, Fifteenth United States Infantry, First and Second Battalion; Sixteenth United States Infantry, First Battalion; Eighteenth United States Infantry, First and Second Battalion; Nineteenth United States Infantry, First Battalion.

Third Brigade: Colonel W. Sirwell—Twenty-fourth Illinois, Thirty-seventh Indiana, Twenty-first Ohio, Seventy-fourth Ohio, Seventy-eighth Pennsylvania, Seventy-ninth Pennsylvania, First Wisconsin, Twenty-first Wisconsin.

Artillery: First Illinois Artillery, Company "C"; First Michigan Artillery, Company "A"; Fifth United States Artillery, Company "H."

BRIGADIER-GENERAL JEFF. C. DAVIS'S DIVISION.

First Brigade: Brigadier-general J. D. Morgan—Tenth Illinois, Sixteenth Illinois, Sixtieth Illinois, Tenth Michigan, Fourteenth Michigan.

Artillery: Seventh Indiana Battery, Nineteenth Indiana Battery, Fourth United States Artillery, Company "I."

ARTILLERY RESERVE.

Brigadier-general J. M. Brannan, Chief of Artillery.

COLONEL J. BARNETT'S DIVISION.

First Brigade: First Ohio Artillery, Company "A"; First Ohio Artillery, Company "B"; First Ohio Artillery, Company "C"; First Ohio Artillery, Company "F."

Second Brigade: First Ohio Artillery, Company "G"; First Ohio Artillery, Company "M"; Eighteenth Ohio Battery, Twentieth Ohio Battery.

SECOND DIVISION.

First Brigade: Captain Sutermeister—Fourth Indiana Battery, Eighth Indiana Battery, Eleventh Indiana Battery, Twenty-first Indiana Battery.

Second Brigade: Captain Church—First Michigan Artillery, Company "D"; First Middle Tennessee Artillery, Company "A"; Third Wisconsin Battery, Eighth Wisconsin Battery.

Coburn's Brigade: Thirty-third Indiana, Eighty-fifth Indiana, Nineteenth Michigan, Twenty-second Wisconsin, Ninth Ohio Battery.

United States Forces, Gallatin, Tenn.: Brigadier-General E. A. Paine—Ninety-first Indiana (First Battalion), Fifth

A CONFEDERATE SCHOONER RUNNING INTO THE FEDERAL TRANSPORT "CHI-KIANG."

Ohio (First Battalion), Seventy-first Ohio, One Hundred and Sixth Ohio, Thirteenth Indiana Battery.

NASHVILLE, TENNESSEE.

Brigadier-general R. S. Granger commanding Post.

Ward's Brigade: Brigadier-general W. T. Ward—One Hundred and Fifth Illinois, One Hundred and Twenty-ninth Illinois, Seventieth Indiana, Seventy-ninth Ohio, First Michigan Artillery, Company "E."

A...: Eighteenth Michigan Volunteer Infantry, Twelfth Indiana Battery.

Clarksville, Tenn.: Colonel A. A. Smith commanding post—Eighty-third Illinois (First Battalion), Second Illinois Artillery, Company "H."

Chattanooga, Tenn.: Tenth Ohio Volunteer Infantry, First Battalion O. S. S.

CAVALRY.

FIRST DIVISION.

Brigadier-general R. B. Mitchell.

First Brigade: Colonel A. P. Campbell—First East Tennessee Cavalry, Second Michigan Cavalry, Ninth Pennsylvania Cavalry.

Second Brigade: Colonel E. McCook—Second East Tennessee Cavalry, Third East Tennessee Cavalry, Second Indiana Cavalry, Fourth Indiana Cavalry, First Wisconsin Cavalry.

Third Brigade: Colonel L. D. Watkins—Fourth Kentucky Cavalry, Fifth Kentucky Cavalry, Sixth Kentucky Cavalry, Seventh Kentucky Cavalry.

Artillery: Section 1, Ohio Artillery, Company "D."

SECOND DIVISION.

Brigadier-general George Crook.

First Brigade: Colonel R. L. Minty—Third Indiana Cavalry (Detachment), Fourth Michigan Cavalry, Seventh Pennsylvania Cavalry, Fourth United States Cavalry.

Second Brigade: Colonel E. Long—Second Kentucky Cavalry, First Ohio Cavalry, Third Ohio Cavalry, Fourth Ohio Cavalry.

Third Brigade: Colonel W. W. Lowe—Fifth Iowa Cavalry, First Middle Tennessee Cavalry, Tenth Ohio Cavalry, Captain Stokes's Illinois Battery, Fifteenth Pennsylvania Volunteer Cavalry, Colonel W. J. Palmer.

Miller's Brigade Mounted Infantry: Colonel A. O. Miller—Ninety-second Illinois, Ninety-eighth Illinois, One Hundred and Twenty-third Illinois, Seventeenth Indiana, Seventy-second Indiana, Eighteenth Indiana Battery.

UNITED STATES FORCES, FORT DONELSON.

Lieutenant-colonel E. C. Brott.

Eighty-third Illinois (Detachment), Second Illinois (Detachment), Second Illinois Artillery, Company "C."

UNASSIGNED INFANTRY.

Thirty-fourth Illinois, Eightieth Illinois, One Hundred and Second Illinois, Thirteenth Indiana, Fifty-first Indiana, Seventy-third Indiana, Twenty-first Kentucky, Twenty-eighth Kentucky, Third Ohio, One Hundred and Second Ohio, One Hundred and Eighth Ohio, Tenth Tennessee, Thirty-first Wisconsin.

General Hooker had been sent from the East to Rosecrans's assistance immediately after the battle of Chickamauga, and crossed on pontons at Bridgeport, October 26th, reaching Wauhatchee two days later, with General O. O. Howard's Eleventh and General H. W. Slocum's Twelfth Corps, which Halleck had, on the 23d of September, ordered detached from the Army of the Potomac. Hooker was now in position to threaten Bragg's flank after having insured the protection of the line of the Chattanooga Railroad, so that supplies could be accumulated and held at Stevenson pending their possible transmission to Chattanooga—a plan for receiving which by way of Brown's Ferry, Rosecrans had already in view.

Rosecrans's plan for opening the desired communication was not, however, fully carried out until after Grant assumed command on the 23d of October.

JOHN H. MORGAN.

Simultaneously with General Hooker's advance in the Lookout Valley, General Palmer was to take a division across the river to Brown's Ferry, and march thence through Whitesides to Rankin's Ferry, so as to protect the river communication, and General W. F. (Baldy) Smith was to leave Chattanooga at night with a force of 4,000 men, and effect a lodgment upon the range of hills commanding the road to Kelly's Ferry.

Of his force, General Smith selected 1,200 men, who were, early on the morning of the 28th, taken by General Turchin across Moccasin Point to Brown's Ferry, while the remaining 1,800 men, under General Hazen, were being floated in pontons a distance of nine miles down the river, and reached the same destination a few hours later.

Three batteries of artillery under Major J. Mendenhall protected the landing of the troops and the building of a ponton-bridge. The latter was completed at about four o'clock in the afternoon, under a continued fire from the Confederate pickets and from the batteries on Lookout Mountain. Hazen's troops having also in the meantime been subjected to an attack from a large detachment of Confederate infantry and cavalry, which had the support of three batteries of artillery. After a short but stubborn engagement, the Confederates were successfully driven away up the valley toward Chattanooga, with a loss to the Federals of 38 killed, wounded and missing, the Confederates losing nearly an equal number of killed and wounded, in addition to six prisoners, and being besides forced to abandon a large quantity of provisions.

FRANK P. BLAIR, JR.

By evening of the 28th, Howard's corps had joined Smith's force at Brown's Ferry, Geary's command being then encamped some three miles in the rear, at Wauhatchee. The formation of these two camps had been keenly watched from "Signal Rock" by McLaws's division of Longstreet's corps, then occupying Lookout Mountain, and shortly after midnight their batteries opened upon Geary's camp, while part of McLaws's force dashed furiously upon his troops. This attack of Longstreet's men was bravely withstood, and although at one time Geary was almost enveloped on three sides, he succeeded in repelling all the attacks, and in finally driving away the assailants at the point of the bayonet after an engagement of nearly three hours' duration.

Upon hearing the noise of battle, Hooker had ordered Schurz's division to Geary's assistance, but it had proceeded only a short distance when it was confronted by the remainder of McLaws's division. Another engagement followed, and the ground was here likewise so hotly contested, that Howard's remaining division, under General Steinwehr, had to be sent forward. The Confederates were charged upon along the neighboring steep hill, rising to a height of nearly two hundred feet, and were not only forced back, but pursued up to their intrenchments, which were left in the possession of the Federals after a prolonged hand-to-hand fight, lasting until half-past four the next morning, and in which heavy losses were sustained on both sides.

Among the killed in this night's engagement was Captain Geary, son of the general; the wounded embracing General Green and Colonel Underwood.

A new road from Brown's Ferry to Kelly's Ferry was completed by the 1st of the following month, and upon hearing, a few days later, that Bragg had detached the remainder of Longstreet's force to operate against Burnside in East Tennessee, Grant made preparations to attack the Confederates as soon as Sherman's force could connect with his own.

NOVEMBER, 1863.

Sherman had been ordered in September to join Rosecrans, and he had accordingly left the line of the Big Black, reaching Memphis on the 4th of October, and Bridgeport late on the 13th of the following month. On the 15th of November he was in conference with Grant at Chattanooga.

Sherman's Fifteenth Corps, then under command of General Frank Blair, was composed of four divisions, as follows:

First Division: General Peter J. Osterhaus—First Brigade, General Charles R. Woods; Second Brigade, Colonel J. A. Williamson.

Second Division: General Morgan L. Smith—First Brigade, General Giles A. Smith; Second Brigade, General J. A. D. Lightburn.

Third Division: General John E. Smith—First Brigade, General Matthies; Second Brigade, Colonel G. B. Raum; Third Brigade, Colonel J. J. Alexander.

Fourth Division: General Hugh Ewing—First Brigade, General John M. Corse; Second Brigade, Colonel Loomis; Third Brigade, Colonel J. R. Cockrell.

It was arranged that the main attack should be made on the 21st by Sherman's force, which was to march from Brown's Ferry, and cross on pontons opposite to the mouth of Chickamauga Creek, under cover of the artillery. Sherman was to take position on the northern end of Missionary Ridge, and with the aid of part of Jeff. C. Davis's force, try to seize the heights as far as the tunnel, while a demonstration was being made against Lookout Mountain in the vicinity of Trenton, and while Thomas was advancing into Chattanooga Valley.

All was made ready, and the troops were ordered forward in accordance with Grant's plans; but by reason of the very bad state of the roads consequent upon continued heavy rains, John E. Smith's division was the only one that crossed the river on the 21st. Grant accordingly delayed his plans of battle, and it was not until the morning of the 24th that Sherman's troops had the bridge in a condition to permit the crossing of the other two divisions, led by Generals Ewing and M. L. Smith. Osterhaus was prevented crossing by the renewed breaking of the bridge, and Sherman therefore asked leave to go into action with only three divisions of his corps, besides Davis's division of the Fourteenth Corps. This was allowed, and Osterhaus was ordered to report to General Hooker, whose force was to operate against Lookout Mountain.

Upon learning that Sherman's movements in Lookout Valley had been discovered by Bragg, Howard was ordered to cross into Chattanooga, so as to lead Bragg to believe that the new troops were intended to reinforce the latter place. On Monday, the 23d, Thomas ordered General Granger to make a demonstration against the Confederates, who were falsely reported as having commenced a retreat northward. The Confederates were forced back until their first line of rifle-pits was reached, when a charge took place for the possession of the batteries lining Orchard Knob, which were captured after a brief encounter, and placed in charge of General Granger's force.

During a drizzling rain Sherman's men advanced from the river at one o'clock in the afternoon of the 24th, under the command of General Francis P. Blair. His leading division, under Ewing, occupied the extreme right, while John E. Smith's column formed the centre, and Morgan L. Smith's division marched on the extreme left, along Chickamauga Creek.

November, 1863.

When they reached the summit of the first ridge, after quite a lively skirmish with the Confederate pickets, it was found that a deep hollow intervened between the hill upon which the tunnel was located, and it was then decided to intrench for the night. The Confederates, however, attacked Sherman's force while the earthworks were being thrown up, and a heavy engagement took place late in the afternoon. The assault was ably met, however, and by nightfall the Confederates had retired to their line of works around the tunnel.

Early on the 25th Sherman advanced with his right and left wings along the east and west of Missionary Ridge, and had a succession of encounters with the forces of Generals Hardee, Cheatham, Stevenson, Gist and Cleburne, against which Hooker had as yet been prevented making the intended diversion, and which by their superior numbers prevented any satisfactory headway being made toward the tunnel.

Seeing this, Thomas advanced from Orchard Knob with the centre, consisting of the divisions of Johnson, Sheridan, Wood and Baird, well supported by a strong force of reserves. At a given signal they rushed upon the force which Bragg had ordered strengthened from both his right and left, and although subjected to a most damaging fire from fifty pieces of artillery well posted upon the summit of the hill, they battled bravely until they had reached the rifle-pits at the foot of the ridge.

These being scaled at different points, a severe hand-to-hand fight followed, and the Confederates were finally driven up the ridge with great loss in killed, wounded and prisoners.

GEORGE L. HARTSUFF.

Orders had been given to hold the position, but the Federals were soon subjected to such a damaging fire from the batteries along the crest, whose fire could not be effectively returned, that the troops moved ahead, ascending the ridge of their own accord. In a short time the entire force were hurrying along its steep and rugged sides in a race for the summit. The latter was first reached by Sheridan's division, which was closely followed by the remainder of Thomas's force, all of which was soon drawn into the series of engagements that took place almost simultaneously at as many as six different points along the mountain. The ground here was bravely contested, but the Federal attacks were so fiercely made that resistance seemed useless. The contest ended in the defeat of division after division, and in the final rout of the Confederates, who, panic-stricken, were captured in large numbers.

The batteries were then turned upon the retreating Confederate centre, and Sheridan's division followed their rear-guard, afterward capturing another strong position protected by eight pieces of artillery, as well as a number of prisoners and a large quantity of stores and small arms.

In the meantime Hooker had early on the 24th, marched his force toward Lookout Mountain, but his advance was checked by the necessary building of a temporary bridge over Lookout Creek, which later had become very much swollen by heavy rain. While this was being done, he sent Geary with a strong force to effect a landing at Wauhatchee. A thick mist hanging over the mountain enabled Geary to reach the right bank of Lookout Creek and to fall upon the Confederate pickets, with which a lively skirmish took place before the alarm was given to the troops under General Stevenson, then guarding the strong line of earthworks which stretched along the entire northern ridge, and protecting all the approaches from either the Lookout or Chattanooga Valleys.

A second bridge was built by the time Geary reached the enemy's flanks, and Hooker first sent over Wood and G... who joined their forces with Geary's on the right bank, while Hooker's artillery was placed in position to cover the preliminary movements against the Confederate position. The remainder of Hooker's command crossed shortly after, and by noon the Confederates had been so fiercely engaged that Geary's advance succeeded in driving them around the highest peak, while the brigades of Freeland, Cobham, Creighton and Whittaker had marched from the Palisades, and were operating close by the Craven House. Although the clouds of heavy mist overhanging the mountain and the rugged nature of the ground made it impossible to execute any thoroughly defined movement, there was almost incessant fighting and with varying success until about one o'clock, when by a well-concerted effort the Confederates were driven from the crest toward the Chattanooga Valley.

Hooker now rested his force for a while and communicated with General Thomas, who sent Carlin's brigade to Hooker's assistance, the thick mist having meanwhile settled so low as to prevent all further advance.

Earthworks were thrown up, and the troops remained in position during the ensuing night, being only a short time subjected to a heavy fire upon the extreme right, where an attempt to enter Hooker's lines was bravely repulsed by the force under General Carlin. Early on the morning of the 25th, small detachments were sent toward the summit of the mountain to find any Confederates still occupied at any point; but none were found, and at sunrise the Eighth Kentucky Regiment hoisted the Stars and Stripes upon the topmost height.

It was soon found that Stevenson had abandoned the summit of the mountain, and had proceeded by way of Summertown toward Rossville. Hooker was ordered in pursuit, and at about ten o'clock in the morning he reached the Chattanooga Creek, where he found that the Confederates had destroyed the bridge. The advance under Osterhaus managed, however, to cross upon the stringers, and drove the Confederate pickets toward Rossville, whence the force under Wood and Williamson afterward compelled the main body of the enemy to fly with the loss of a large number of wagons and other property.

The Federals pressed on, Geary's force advancing toward the valley

JOHN A. LOGAN.

west of Missionary Ridge, while Osterhaus's force marched in an easterly direction, and Cruft took the centre. The latter soon reached the line of earthworks which Thomas had ordered thrown up after the battle of Chickamauga, and which were then occupied by General Stewart's force.

A charge was made upon the works, and was so brilliantly executed that Stewart's men were compelled to fly in all directions. A great many were captured by Geary's forces, while others fell into the hands of Osterhaus's men, and nearly all of the remainder submitted to capture, or succumbed to the blows heavily dealt by Cruft's successful troops, who kept up a running fight till late in the night.

Before morning the Confederates were withdrawn burne's force, covering Bragg's retreat. This engagement, called by many the battle of Ringgold, lasted several hours, and resulted in the defeat of the Confederates, with a loss to them of about 150 men, while the Federal loss was nearly 430 killed and wounded.

On the 28th the pursuit was ended. Hooker's and Palmer's forces soon afterward returned to Chattanooga, and Sherman made reconnoissances northward as far as the Hiawassee River, after which he was ordered to take additional command of that part of Thomas's force under Granger, as well as of the cavalry under General W. L. Elliott which had been sent to aid Burnside, and to move at once toward Knoxville.

The last-named place was reached on the 6th of formed part of the Chattanooga campaign. He had retired to Providence, R. I., after being relieved of the command of the Army of the Potomac in January, 1863 (Vol. II., page 13). On the 15th of March following he was called to take the place of General Horatio G. Wright at the head of the Department of the Ohio.

He had then taken with him the Ninth Army Corps from Newport News, and during the month of May it was arranged that while Rosecrans was advancing toward Chattanooga, Burnside would move into East Tennessee. On the 2d of June, the latter's headquarters were transferred from Cincinnati to Lexington, and shortly after the Ninth Corps was detached from Burnside's command to assist Grant's operations before Vicksburg.

FEDERAL PICKETS APPROACHED BY CONFEDERATES DISGUISED IN CEDAR BUSHES, NEAR CHATTANOOGA, TENN.

FROM A SKETCH BY C. F. H. BOSWELL.

from Sherman's front, and part of Thomas's force was joined to Sherman's, while the rest was sent to reinforce Burnside at Knoxville. Early on the

NOVEMBER, 1863.

26th the Federals started in pursuit of Bragg's army, then flying in the direction of Ringgold, Sherman going by way of Chickamauga Station, while Hooker and Palmer proceeded by the road leading to Graysville. Upon the latter an engagement took place toward evening with the rear Confederate guard, resulting in the capture of a large number of prisoners and of three guns by the Federals.

Sherman directed Howard's force to destroy the line of railway between Dalton and Cleveland, so as to delay, if not altogether prevent, Bragg going in the direction of Knoxville, and on the 27th ordered the destruction of the Atlanta Railroad from Graysville to the State line.

On the same day Hooker had a severe engagement close by Taylor's Ridge with part of Cle the following month, two days after Longstreet

DECEMBER, 1863.

had abandoned it upon his retreat to Northern Virginia. Part of Granger's corps was left to pursue Longstreet, and Sherman returned with the remaining troops to Chattanooga, whence he soon moved into Northern Alabama and placed his troops in winter-quarters.

The total losses in the engagement upon Lookout Mountain and Missionary Ridge, as well as in those immediately following them, were reported to be 757 killed, 4,529 wounded and 330 missing—a total of 5,616 for the Federals, as against a total of nearly 9,000 on the part of the Confederates, who lost besides 40 guns, 7,000 stand of small arms, many wagons, and a large quantity of other property. The Federal list of killed embraced the names of Colonels Putnam, Torrance and O'Meara; the wounded, Generals Matthias, Corse and Giles A. Smith, as well as Colonels Wangeline and Baum.

Burnside's operations around Knoxville properly

The East Tennessee campaign was postponed, and Burnside's force remained guarding all Federal communications at and about Lexington nearly two months. During that interval several raids were made, and a considerable amount of Confederate property was damaged and captured, the most important expedition being that led by Colonel H. S. Saunders, which succeeded in breaking up much of the line of the Virginia and Tennessee Railway, and in burning the long bridge spanning the Holston River at Strawberry Plains, where he also captured 10 guns and nearly 400 prisoners.

When Burnside was called upon in August to directly assist Rosecrans's operations through the Chattanooga region, he collected his forces at Crab Orchard, and moved thence in five columns by way of Somerset, Jamestown and Montgomery, as well as through Mount Vernon, London and Williamsburg, Ky., across the Cumberland Mountains into the Valley of the Tennessee.

Buckner, who was in command of the 20,000 Confederate troops guarding the Valley, retreated to the line of the Tennessee River before the advance of Burnside's army, which occupied Knoxville on the 3d of September, after capturing about 2,500 prisoners, 3 locomotives, 11 guns, and a larg quantity of small arms and ammunition. In fourteen days Burnside had thus covered a distance of nearly 250 miles, along heavy roads and across the rugged peaks of the Cumberland Mountains, sustaining but small losses in skirmishes at London and at other places along the way.

As Burnside reached Knoxville, the Confederate guerrilla chief John H. Morgan, who had commanded a cavalry squadron at Pittsburg Landing, and who had afterward created much annoyance to the Federals by his bold and successful operations throughout Kentucky and Ohio—more especially at Lebanon, Cynthiana and Clarksville—was carrying out an extensive raid upon which he had embarked as early as the 27th of June.

General Morgan had started from Sparta, Tenn., with General Basil W. Duke second in command, taking two brigades of about 3,000 cavalry, with 6 guns, and, after crossing the Cumberland River at Burkesville, had moved upon Columbia. There his advance was checked by a small party of cavalry under Captain Carter, who lost his life during

CAISSONS AND HORSES ON THE FIELD AFTER THE BATTLE.

FROM A SKETCH BY EDWIN FORBES.

the three hours' fight that followed. He then made an unsuccessful attempt to destroy the Green River Bridge at Tebbs's Bend, where he was repulsed by Colonel Orlando H. Moore's force after incurring a loss of more than 200 killed and wounded.

From the line of the Green River, Morgan moved northwardly to Lebanon, the capital of Marion County, Ky., then garrisoned by 400 men of the Twentieth Kentucky, under Colonel Harrison, whose surrender was asked and refused. The town was then attacked, and after a desperate fight of nearly seven hours' duration, and in which Morgan's brother was killed, the Federals had to surrender.

The Confederates then rapidly moved upon Springfield, Shepherdsville, Bardstown and Brandenburg. Morgan's advance reached the last-named place on the 7th of July, and captured the steamers *McCombs* and *Alice Dean*, both of which were the next day made to convey the Confederates across the Ohio River, after which the *Alice Dean* was burned and the *McCombs* abandoned. Late on the 9th the Confederates reached Corydon, the capital of Harrison County, Ind., where they captured and destroyed much valuable mill and other property, and then advanced through Greenville and Palmyra upon Salem, the capital of Washington County.

After likewise pillaging the latter place, and capturing 350 Home Guards, besides burning the Louisville and Chicago Railway Depot and other buildings, as well as three bridges, Morgan moved along the line of the Madison and Indianapolis Railroad to Canton, and then to Vienna, whence part of his force went to Old Vernon, and the rest to Madison. Morgan demanded the surrender of Old Vernon, then held by 1,200 men, under Colonel Lowe (Barkham). The Federals not only refused to surrender, but moved out to engage Morgan's force, which was, however, found to have retreated toward Versailles.

From the last-named locality the Confederates moved in separate parties, and visited successively the towns of Osgood, Harrison, Van Wedder's, Glendale, Springdale, Sharon, Reading, Montgomery, Miamiville, Williamsburg, Sardinia, Winchester, Piketon, and finally Jackson, where Morgan was joined by his entire force.

While the Confederates had thus been raiding the States of Indiana and Ohio—everywhere doing all the damage they could possibly inflict upon the Federals and their property—a very heavy force of infantry, cavalry and artillery, taken from the commands of Generals Hobson, Shackleford, Judah and Wolford, was assembled at Lebanon on the 6th of July, and placed by General Burnside in charge of General Hobson with orders to pursue Morgan and endeavor to overtake him.

The Federals reached Shepherdsville on the 7th, and on the following day crossed the Ohio, which latter was being patrolled by gunboats brought up mainly from Louisville by Lieutenant-commander Fitch, so as to prevent Morgan's escape south of the river. General Judah's force advanced from Portsmouth along the river road, and the remainder of Hobson's command proceeded through the interior, while the militia was everywhere congregating to check Morgan's further progress.

After continued forced marches the Federals came upon Morgan's party in the vicinity of Chester, close by the Buffington Ford, where a severe engagement took place on the 19th of July. Morgan was simultaneously attacked in flank and rear by Hobson's land forces, while the gunboats near Buffington Island opened upon his front, and after an hour's engagement Generals Basil Duke and Dick Morgan were compelled to surrender with nearly 800 men, and to abandon all the plunder they had brought along with them.

General John H. Morgan escaped with the remainder of his force up to Belleville, where he attempted to cross the river, but was prevented by the gunboat *Moore*. He then proceeded northward, and after losing a large number of his men during a skirmish near Kyger's Creek, struck for New Lisbon; but Hobson and Shackleford followed close upon him, and with the aid of the gunboats compelled the surrender of Morgan himself and of his force, on the 26th, near Wellsville, where he had hoped to cross the river.

General Morgan, Colonel Chike, Captain Hines and the other officers, were taken to Columbus, Ohio, where they were confined in the Penitentiary. There they remained until the 27th of the following November, when General Morgan, Captain Hines and five other officers, named McGhee, Barnet, Shelton, Taylor and Hookersmith, succeeded in cutting their way through a sewer, and in escaping to the Confederate lines. Morgan subsequently engaged in a number of raids, and finally attempted an extensive one into Tennessee, during which he was surprised by Federal cavalry and killed near Greenville on the 4th of September, 1864.

The Federals rejoined Burnside's army, which, during the absence of the expedition against Morgan, had invested and taken Cumberland Gap after an exciting skirmish at Tazewell, capturing General Frazier, with 2,000 men and 14 pieces of artillery.

Two days after the surrender of Cumberland Gap, the following message was sent by General Halleck:

"HEADQUARTERS OF THE ARMY, WASHINGTON, D.C.
September 11th, 1863.

"*Major-general Burnside, Cumberland Gap:*

"I congratulate you on your success. Hold the gap of the North Carolina Mountains, the line of the Holston River, or some point, if there be one, to prevent access from Virginia, and connect with General Rosecrans, at least with your cavalry. General Rosecrans will occupy Dalton, or some point on the railroad, to close all access from Atlanta, and also the mountain passes in the West. This being done, it will be determined whether the movable force shall advance into Georgia and Alabama, or into the Valley of Virginia and North Carolina.

"H. W. HALLECK, *General-in-Chief.*

This was followed by other dispatches on the 13th and 14th, which resulted in Burnside remaining in Eastern Tennessee.

The Federals had several encounters with the many bodies of Confederates swarming throughout the district, notably at Bristol on the 21st, and at Blue Springs, near Bull's Gap, where a large force under General Sam. Jones made a demonstration against Burnside's left early the following month. On the 10th of October, 1863, the Ninth Corps, supported by a strong force of Shackleford's cavalry and by General Wilcox's division, advanced against the Confederates and engaged them in front, while Colonel Foster's cavalry was sent in their rear by way of the Rogersville Road.

Jones's force was defeated, with the loss of many killed and wounded, after a desultory fight which lasted until into the following day, and finally escaped Colonel Foster's attack by withdrawing from Blue Springs during the ensuing night. General Shackleford pursued the Confederates until they had entered into Virginia, nearly ten miles beyond Bristol, losing, all told, about 100 men, as against the loss by the Confederates of nearly twice as many killed and wounded, besides 150 prisoners.

The Confederates then encamped at Rogersville, Jonesboro' and Greeneville. Colonel Garrard's force, which occupied Rogersville, was surprised on the 6th of November by a body of nearly 2,500 Confederate cavalry, under General W. E. Jones, which completely routed the Federal garrison, and captured 750 men, 4 guns and 30 wagons. Fearing similar attacks by the much superior forces of the enemy then reported to be congregating in the vicinity, the Federals returned to Bull's Gap.

Burnside's main body had meanwhile been distributed at several points along the southern side of the Holston and the Tennessee Rivers; but the garrisons were threatened so continually by the heavy detachments of Confederate skirmishers throughout the entire section, and General Wolford's force near Philadelphia suffered so heavily from an attack made by part of Longstreet's force on the 20th of October, that it was deemed best to concentrate along the north side of the river at and near London.

Here Burnside transferred his headquarters on the 28th, and remained until the 31st, when all immediate danger of further attacks being apparently passed, he again withdrew to Knoxville, which was then being strongly fortified under the direction of

HOSPITAL SCENE.—BRINGING IN THE WOUNDED AFTER THE BATTLE.

FROM A SKETCH BY EDWIN FORBES.

Captain O. M. Poe. While at Knoxville he was visited by the Assistant Secretary of War, Charles A Dana, and by Colonel Wilson, of Grant's staff, both of whom consulted with him regarding further plans of action.

It was soon learned that 12,000 infantry and 5,000 cavalry had been detached from Bragg's army to operate against Burnside, who thereupon moved his advanced post toward London.

After a forced march, Longstreet had crossed the Tennessee River at Hough's Ferry at early morning of November the 14th. He at once sent a strong body of cavalry under Wheeler and Forrest by way of Marysville to take possession of the heights overlooking Knoxville, and endeavored to occupy that place during Burnside's absence, thus compelling the latter's retreat, while he himself would operate directly with his main force.

Longstreet's further advance was checked at Lenoir's, where General Potter was stationed with Brigadier-general Julius White's division, of the Twenty-third Corps, and with part of the Ninth Corps, which had been hurried forward from Kentucky. General White had a warm and prolonged encounter with Longstreet's advance, and drove it back nearly two miles.

Wheeler and Forrest had meanwhile failed to carry the heights by reason of the gallant conduct of Brigadier-general W. P. Sanders, who was in immediate command of the troops, while General Parke remained within Knoxville. The Confederates were repulsed after a bitter contest, wherein the Third Michigan, Twelfth Kentucky, Forty-fifth Ohio and One Hundred and Twelfth Illinois Regiments took a prominent part, and in which General Sanders was wounded by a sharpshooter's bullet, which caused his death the following day.

Burnside made his preparations for attacking Longstreet on the 15th, but late on the previous evening he received orders from Grant to withdraw slowly toward Knoxville, so as to draw Longstreet upon the latter place, and take him further away from Chattanooga. Burnside accordingly withdrew his forces, and on the 16th reached Campbell Station, where a determined and successful stand was made by General Hartranft with a portion of the Ninth Corps, while the main body proceeded by way of the Loudon Road, and formed within the Knoxville lines of fortifications.

Longstreet followed closely, and on the 18th Knoxville was completely invested by the Confederates. An almost incessant fire was kept up against the Federal lines till near midnight of the 28th, when a desperate attempt was made to capture Fort Sanders, commanding the Kingston Road, and then held by the Twenty-ninth Massachusetts and Seventy-ninth New York, as well as by detachments from the Twentieth Michigan and Second and Twentieth Massachusetts Regiments.

The main assault was made by a force embracing part of Humphreys's, Anderson's and Bryant's brigades, as well as those of Generals Cobb, Phillips and Wolford, belonging to McLaws's division; but all efforts to scale the sides of the fort proved useless. General Ferrero's guns and Roemer's and Benjamin's batteries did such effective work that the assailants had finally to withdraw after losing fully 200 in killed and wounded, besides many prisoners, while the Federal loss was only 43 killed, wounded and missing.

Apart from another less important and equally unsuccessful assault upon the position held by Shackleford's command on the southern side of the Holston River, no other attempts were made to dislodge the Federals. During the night of the 4th of December, Longstreet raised the siege and fell back to Morristown, on the line of the East Tennessee and Georgia Railway, whence he shortly after entered Northern Virginia.

On the 7th of December, President Lincoln issued a thanksgiving proclamation for "the great advancement of the national cause" thus just attained, and on the following day sent a complimentary letter to General Grant, who shortly after received the thanks of the United States Congress, and a gold medal voted by that body.

GEORGE HENRY THOMAS.

BORN on his father's plantation in Southampton County, Va., July 31st, 1816, of wealthy parents, who were of Welsh descent on his father's, and of Huguenot-French stock on his mother's, side. He began the study of law, but in 1836 he was given a cadetship at West Point, and entered the United States Military Academy, graduating therefrom twelfth in a class of forty-two, on the 1st of July, 1840, and being appointed a second-lieutenant in the Third Artillery. After a brief service in garrison in New York Harbor, he was sent to Florida, where he served with distinction against the Indians for nearly two years, participating in Major Wade's capture of 70 Seminoles on the 6th of November, 1841, and being brevetted a first-lieutenant for gallantry. He was placed on garrison duty from January, 1842, until 1845—at New Orleans; Fort Moultrie, in Charleston Harbor; Fort McHenry, Baltimore; and Corpus Christi, Texas. He took part in the Mexican War, and engaged in the battles of Monterey and of Buena Vista, for his distinguished services in both of which he received the brevets of captain and major. After the battle of Buena Vista he went into garrison at the mouth of the Rio Grande, and remained there until the close of the war, when he was ordered to Fort Adams, Newport, R. I., and was subsequently transferred to Florida. In December, 1850, he was given command of Fort Independence, Boston Harbor, and in March of the following year was assigned to duty at West Point as instructor of cavalry and artillery. On the 24th of December, 1853, he was promoted to a full captaincy; and in 1854 was ordered to Fort Yuma, California, remaining there with his regiment until May, 1855, when he was appointed major of the newly organized Second Cavalry. Of this justly celebrated organization Albert Sidney Johnston was the colonel; Robert E. Lee, the lieutenant-colonel; and William J. Hardee, the senior major; while among the younger officers were Van Dorn, Kirby Smith, Hood, Fitzhugh Lee, and many others who afterward became celebrated on the Confederate side. With the Second Cavalry he was assigned to Jefferson Barracks, Mo., and served in Texas upward of five years. He took part in many important expeditions, and during a skirmish with Indians, near the Clear Fork headwaters of the Brazos River, in August, 1860, received a severe wound in the face. He went East on a leave of absence during the following November, and while visiting his native State, received from the Commonwealth of Virginia a splendid sword in token of its appreciation of his services in the War with Mexico. After a short leave of absence—the second in more than twenty years—he was ordered to Carlisle Barracks, Pa., where his regiment, which in the following August became the Fifth Cavalry, had been sent in a disorganized condition and without its equipments, which had been confiscated by the commander of the Division, General Twiggs. Thomas lost no time in reorganizing the regiment, of which he became the lieutenant-colonel and colonel, on the 25th of April and the 3d of May respectively. During the last-named month he was transferred to the field of active operations in the Shenandoah Valley, and was assigned to the command of a brigade in General Patterson's army. When that general was mustered out, Thomas served in the same capacity under General Banks. He took part in the engagements at Falling Waters, Martinsburg and Bunker Hill, and on the 17th of August was promoted to be a brigadier-general of Volunteers. On the 26th of the same month he was ordered to report to General Robert Anderson, then commanding the Department of the Cumberland, and upon his arrival in Louisville, on September 6th, was given the command of Camp Dick Robinson, in Southern Kentucky, where he set about mustering and organizing the First Brigade, which formed the nucleus of the First Division of the Army of the Ohio. He soon established a new camp, designated Camp Wild Cat, and on the 26th of October fought the battle of the same name, under General Schoepf. He made preparations to advance into East Tennessee, but before this could be completed, he was ordered by General Buell to

HOOKER'S BATTLE ABOVE THE CLOUDS, AND CAPTURE OF THE CONFE

FROM A SKETCH

HOOKER'S BATTLE ABOVE THE CLOUDS AND CAPTURE OF THE CONFEDERATE POSITION AT LOOKOUT MOUNTAIN, TENN. NOVEMBER 24th, 186[illegible]
[illegible]

proceed to Lebanon, Ky., there to prepare for an active campaign. He was given the command of the First Division of the Army of the Ohio when Buell was assigned to the command of the new Department of the Ohio, and early in January, 1862, fought the battle of Mill Springs, which resulted in the defeat of General George B. Crittenden, C.S.A., and was the most important victory yet attained in the West. He remained in command of his division until September 30th, 1862, except during the advance upon and siege of Corinth, when he commanded the right wing of the Army of the Tennessee. He was engaged in the movement on Nashville, and also took part in the Tennessee and Mississippi campaign, as well as in the march on Pittsburg Landing (Shiloh), where his force constituted the reserve. On April 25th, 1862, he was commissioned a major-general of Volunteers, and on the 1st of the following month was transferred to the Army of the Tennessee by order of General Halleck. He remained there but a short time, however, and was re-transferred to the Army of the Ohio, being appointed second in command of the latter upon its advance into Kentucky. He commanded the right wing at the battle of Perrysville and in the subsequent pursuit of Bragg's army. In the latter part of October, 1862, the Army of the Cumberland became known as the "Fourteenth Army Corps." General Rosecrans was placed at its head, and organized it into three grand divisions. Thomas was assigned to the centre, and in the battle of Stone River, or Murfreesboro', stopped some 50,000 men of all arms, but his advance was skillfully resisted at Duck River and Spring Hill. On November 30th occurred the battle of Franklin, and on the 15th-16th of the ensuing month was fought the battle of Nashville, which was Thomas's crowning triumph, and was recognized by many as the Federal "victory of victories." Thomas was next appointed a major-general in the Regular Army, and at its subsequent meeting Congress tendered him a vote of thanks, while the Legislature of Tennessee presented him a magnificent gold medal in recognition of his distinguished services. After the close of the Civil War he commanded the Military Division of the Tennessee (1865-66); the Department of the Tennessee (1866-67); the Third Military District (Georgia, Florida and Alabama), and the Department of the Cumberland (1867-69). From November, 1868, to May 15th, 1869, he was president of a court of inquiry in the case of General Dyer, chief of ordnance; after which he commanded the Military Division of the Pacific, with headquarters at San Francisco, where his death occurred, March 28th, 1870. Congress passed resolutions of sympathy, and military honors were paid him at Troy, N. Y., where his remains were interred.

JOSEPH WHEELER, JR.

Born in Augusta, Ga., September 10th, 1836; educated in the North. Was appointed to the United States Military Academy at West Point, from Georgia, in 1854, and graduated therefrom in 1859. Entered the United States Army as brevet-second-lieutenant of cavalry, July 1st, 1859, and attached to the First Dragoons. Transferred to the Mounted Riflemen, with full rank of second-lieutenant, and sent to the frontier. He resigned his commission, April 22d, 1861, and joined the Confederate Army. He became an *attaché* of Bragg's staff at Pensacola Navy Yard. He was promoted to a colonelcy, and assigned to General L. P. Walker's staff, which commission gave him the command of the Nineteenth Alabama Volunteers, which he organized at Huntsville, Ala. He greatly distinguished himself as its commander, and at General Bragg's request was promoted, receiving a commission as brigadier-general in the Provisional Army. After some correspondence between the Confederate Senate and General Bragg, caused by the extreme youth of the proposed brigadier-general, during which Bragg offered to appoint him on his personal staff as adjutant general, President Davis deciding that if General Bragg had so high an opinion of the young soldier, he would make a safe brigadier-general with a command, gave him the appointment. Commanded the First Brigade, Second Corps, Second Grand Division, Army of the Mississippi, under General Leonidas Polk, 1862. Took a prominent part at the battle of Shiloh, or Pittsburg Landing, in April, 1862; and at Farmington, Miss., May 10th, 1862, commanded the advance-guard of Withers's division, belonging to the Army of the Mississippi, and toward the end of the same month was placed at the head of the First Brigade, near Baldwin, Miss. On the 29th of the ensuing December, Wheeler's cavalry brigade gained the rear of Rosecrans's army, and destroyed several hundred wagon-loads of supplies and baggage, made the circuit of the enemy, and joined on the right. On February 3d, 1863, he led the unsuccessful attack upon the Federal garrison, under Colonel Harding, at Fort Donelson, and afterward opposed the advance on Dalton, Ga. July 22d, 1863, he occupied Decatur, Ga., by making a wide circuit in Sherman's rear, and subsequently cutting the railroad at Atlanta, returned up the road to Chattanooga, and did much damage both at Chattanooga and Knoxville. After the battle of Chickamauga he crossed into Tennessee with 5,000 cavalry and artillery, and marched in a northerly direction, destroying 200 wagons belonging to the Fourteenth Corps, loaded with ammunition and supplies, which he overtook in the Sequatchie Valley, about twenty miles in the rear of Rosecrans's army. As he was leaving, Colonel Edward McCook's cavalry came up and gave him a running fight to Dunlap, Coffee County, in which he lost 150 men. He then advanced on McMillan, sacked the town, and captured the Fourth Tennessee Regiment. He then proceeded to Murfreesboro' and Shelbyville, at which latter place, after firing the town, he was attacked by Colonel Crook, who killed 120 of his men, capturing 800 prisoners and 3 pieces of artillery. He retired to Fayetteville, and was again overtaken and lost 800 more prisoners, retreating across the Tennessee. He opposed Howard at Oconee Bridge, Georgia Railroad, and forced him to cross at the ford eight miles below. Participated in many important skirmishes with Kilpatrick on the march of Sherman toward Savannah, and was the means of greatly obstructing the progress of the

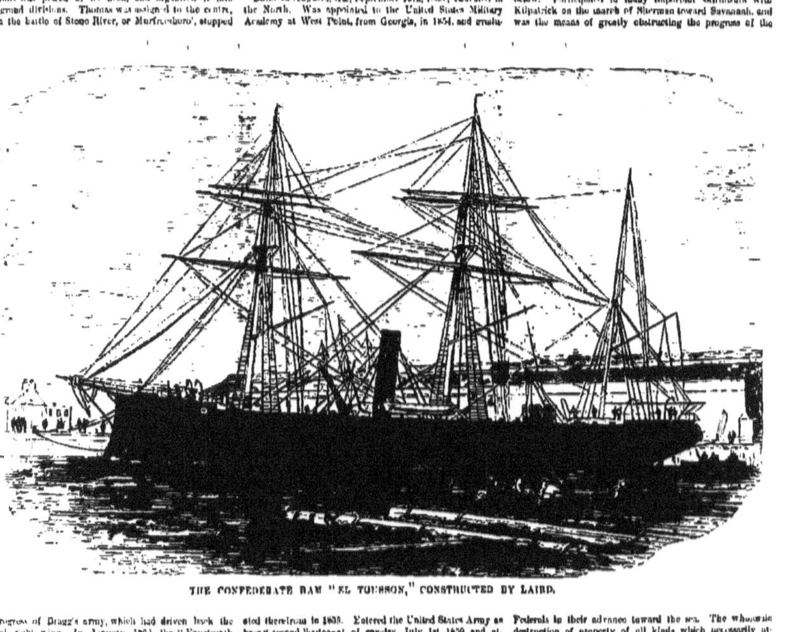

THE CONFEDERATE RAM "EL TOUSSON," CONSTRUCTED BY LAIRD.

the progress of Bragg's army, which had driven back the Federal right wing. In January, 1863, the "Fourteenth Army Corps" (Army of the Cumberland) was divided into three separate corps, known as the Twentieth, Twenty-first and Fourteenth. Thomas was assigned to command the last-named, with which he engaged in the campaign of Middle Tennessee. At the battle of Chickamauga he especially distinguished himself while in command of the extreme left, with which he succeeded in maintaining his hold of the Rossville Road, leading to Chattanooga, for the possession of which the battle was actually fought.

After this battle, where he won the title, "Rock of Chickamauga," he retired upon Chattanooga, and was soon placed in command of the Army of the Cumberland, receiving, on the 27th of October, the commission of brigadier-general in the Regular Army. He also took a prominent part in the storming of Missionary Ridge, as well as throughout the ensuing campaign, resulting in the capture of Atlanta. On the 27th of September, 1864, Thomas was detached from the main army in Georgia and given a prominent command in Tennessee, with large discretionary powers, it being at this time a matter of doubt what were the real intentions of the Confederate general Hood, who was moving northward in the hope of causing Sherman's withdrawal from Georgia. Sherman, having determined to cut loose from his communications and strike for the coast, detached the Fourth and Twenty-third Corps to Thomas's support, leaving the latter to look out for Hood and drive him out of Tennessee should he attempt invasion, or to follow him closely in event of his turning on Sherman. By November 5th, Hood was encamped along the banks of the Tennessee with a force of

Federals in their advance toward the sea. The wholesale destruction of property of all kinds which necessarily attended Sherman's successful movements brought about the following correspondence between Wheeler and the Federal commander, which is worthy of notice:

"GRAHAMS, S. C., February 7th, 1865.

"GENERAL: I have the honor to propose that, if the troops of your army be required to discontinue burning the houses of our citizens, I will discontinue burning cotton.

"As an earnest of the good faith in which my proposition is tendered, I leave at this place about three hundred bales of cotton unburned, worth in New York over a quarter of a million, and in our currency one and a half millions.

"I trust my having commenced will cause you to use your influence to insure the acceptance of the proposition by your whole army.

"I trust that you will not deem it improper for me to ask that you will require the troops under your command to discontinue the wanton destruction of property not necessary for their sustenance.

"Respectfully, general, your obedient servant,

"J. WHEELER, *Major-general, C.S.A.*"

"O. O. HOWARD, *Major-general U.S.A., commanding, etc.*"

"HEADQUARTERS MILITARY DIVISION OF THE MISSISSIPPI,
In the Field, February 8th, 1865.

"GENERAL: Yours, addressed to General Howard, is received by me. I hope you will burn all cotton and save us the trouble. We don't want it, and it has proven a curse to our country. All you don't burn, I will.

"As to private houses occupied by peaceful families, my orders are not to molest or disturb them, and I think my orders are obeyed. Vacant houses, being of no use to anybody, I care little about, as the owners have thought them of no use to themselves. I don't want them destroyed, but do not take much care to preserve them.

"I am, with respect, yours truly,

"W. T. SHERMAN, *Major-general commanding.*"

"J. WHEELER, *Major-general commanding Cavalry Corps.*"

BENJAMIN FRANKLIN CHEATHAM.

BORN in Robertson County, Tenn., where his family gained some distinction. During the Mexican War, raised a company of Volunteers; was commissioned captain in Colonel W. B. Campbell's First Tennessee Volunteer Regiment, which was received by the Government in May, 1846, for twelve months' service; became distinguished at Medelin, under Colonel Harney, on the 25th of March, 1847, and was honorably discharged at the end of the term of service. On the disbanding of this organization he raised the Third Tennessee Volunteer Regiment, which enlisted for the war, and of which he was appointed colonel in October, 1847, remaining its commander until the close of hostilities with Mexico. Upon the breaking out of the Civil War he tendered his services to the Confederate Government, and was appointed a brigadier-general. During September, 1861, General Cheatham was in command at Mayfield, Ky.; but fell back when General Grant occupied Paducah. He led the charge at Belmont on November 7th, 1861, and afterward was in command at Columbus, Ky. In 1862 he was made a major-general, and placed in command of the Fourth Division of Bragg's army. General Cheatham took an active part in the battle of Perryville in October, 1862, and drove McCook till checked by Starkweather. At the battle of Murfreesboro', December, 1862, he commanded the First Division of Bragg's army, and retained the same position during the retreat from Tullahoma, 1863. Previous to the battle of Chickamauga, he moved rapidly with his forces to Lafayette, and opened the action at Crawfish Springs. He supported Walker and Buckner in the attack on General Thomas. In this action he suffered heavily, General Preston Smith losing his life, and over 400 men of the brigade of General Wright being placed *hors de combat*. He afterward took a conspicuous part in the battles along Lookout Mountain and Missionary Ridge, as well as at Franklin, Spring Hill, and Nashville, from November, 1864, to January, 1865. He is now (1885) living on his plantation in Tennessee.

FRANCIS PRESTON BLAIR, JR.

BORN at Lexington, Ky., February 19th, 1821, and graduated at Princeton in 1841. He then began the study of law, and was admitted to the Bar in 1843, entering soon after the political field, being elected in 1850 a member of the United States Congress by the Free Soil party of St. Louis, Mo. He offered his services to the Federal Government upon the breaking out of the Civil War, and was authorized to complete the organization of the Home Guards in the vicinity of St. Louis. It was while at the head of a body of these troops that, in conjunction with a similar force under Sigel, he aided General Lyon in breaking up Governor Jackson's camp of State Guards, then under General Frost. At Vicksburg he distinguished himself while in command of a brigade of General Sherman's corps, and was subsequently assigned to the Fifteenth Corps, with which he again did excellent service during the Chattanooga campaign. In 1864 he was given command of the Seventeenth Corps, of the Army of the Tennessee, and with the latter took part in the campaign which resulted in the capture of Atlanta in September of that year. After the cessation of active hostilities he was selected as a candidate for the Vice Presidency by the Democratic Convention that nominated Horatio Seymour for the Presidency. He was subsequently sent to the Missouri Legislature, and in January, 1871, was elected to fill a vacancy in the United States Senate. He took his seat, January 25th, and retired at the end of his term in '73. Resuming his residence in St. Louis, he was appointed State Superintendent of Insurance, and held that position till his death, which occurred at St. Louis, Mo., on the 8th of July, 1875.

JOHN H. MORGAN.

BORN at Huntsville, Ala., June 1st, 1826. Served in a cavalry regiment during the Mexican War, and subsequently became a manufacturer of bagging at Lexington, Ky. At the time the Civil War broke out he was a planter of considerable means, and left his plantation to take place in the division of Brigadier-general William J. Hardee. In September, 1861, he organized the Lexington Rifles, with whom he joined General Buckner in the Confederate service; commanded a squadron of cavalry at Shiloh, or Pittsburg Landing, and soon afterward began a series of raids through the portions of Kentucky held by the Federal forces, destroying railroads, bridges, and supplies, valued at several million dollars, and gaining a wide celebrity. In July, 1863, he crossed the Ohio River upon a bold raid, and successfully visited the towns of Lebanon, Cynthiana and Clarksville. He was finally captured with the remainder of his command near Wellsville, and was confined in the Columbus (Ohio) Penitentiary, with Colonel Cluke, Captain Hines, and others of his officers. He succeeded on the 20th of November, 1863, in escaping, with Captains McGhee, Burnett, Shelton, Hockersmith and Taylor, and again undertook a raid in Tennessee, but was surprised during the night by Federal cavalry at a farmhouse near Greenville, and killed while attempting to escape, on the 4th of September, 1864.

GEORGE L. HARTSUFF.

BORN at Tyre, Seneca County, N. Y., May 28th, 1830; graduated at the United States Military Academy at West Point, and entered the army as brevet-second-lieutenant of artillery, July 1st, 1852. In this capacity he did duty in garrison and on the Texas frontier until 1853, when he was promoted to be full second lieutenant, and was engaged in Florida (1854–56) on topographical duty. In a skirmish with the Seminoles he was severely wounded, one ball remaining in his chest until his death. From 1856 to 1859 he was on duty at West Point as assistant instructor of artillery tactics. From 1859 to 1860 he served on frontier duty at Fort Mackinac. While in execution of his duty he was a passenger on the steamer *Lady Elgin*, which was wrecked on Lake Michigan, his escape being made by seizing a piece of floating timber, on which he was washed ashore. In March, 1861, he was promoted to a captaincy and made assistant adjutant-general. In the following month he was sent to Fort Pickens with the secret expedition under General Brown, and in the ensuing July became chief of staff to General Rosecrans in Western Virginia. He participated in the action at Carnifex Ferry, September 10th, 1861, and in the subsequent operations of the campaign. In April, 1862, he was appointed a brigadier-general of Volunteers, and assigned to special duty in the War Department. In May he was given command of a brigade, and was engaged at the battles of Cedar Mountain and Manassas, taking also a conspicuous part in the battles of South Mountain and Antietam. He was severely wounded in the last-named action, and was incapacitated from duty in the field until April, 1863, serving in the meantime as member of a board which was appointed to revise the rules and articles of war, and to prepare a code for the government of armies in the field. Having been promoted to be major-general of Volunteers, November, 1862, he commanded the Twenty-third Army Corps in the West from April to November, 1863, when he was compelled to relinquish his command from incapacity arising through the wound he had received at Antietam, and was employed on Bureau duty till March, 1865. He then commanded the

GRENVILLE M. DODGE.

Bermuda front of the siege-works before Petersburg, assuming command of that city on its capture, and subsequently of the District of Nottoway, which command he held till he was mustered out of the Volunteer service in August, 1865. He afterward resumed duty in the adjutant-general's department, with the rank of lieutenant-colonel, and served in various military districts and divisions until June, 1871, when, still suffering from his wound, he was retired from active service on the full rank of major-general, United States Army. After some time he went abroad, and interested himself in bringing American improvements in artillery to European attention. His death occurred at New York, May 16th, 1874.

JOHN A. LOGAN.

JOHN A. LOGAN was born in Jackson County, Ill., on the 9th of February, 1826. He is the son of Dr. John Logan, an Irish physician, and had few opportunities of acquiring an education when a boy. In 1840 he was for a short time one of the students of an academy called Shiloh College. When the War with Mexico was declared he enlisted as a private in the First Regiment of Illinois Volunteers, soon afterward became lieutenant of one of the companies, and was subsequently made adjutant of the regiment. Returning home in October, 1848, with an excellent record, he began to study law in the office of his uncle, Alexander M. Jenkins, formerly Lieutenant-governor of Illinois, and in the following year was elected Clerk of his native county. In 1851 he was admitted to the Bar, after following a course in the Louisville Law School, and formed a partnership with his uncle. In 1852 he was chosen Prosecuting Attorney of the Third Judicial Circuit, and in the Fall of the same year was elected to the State Legislature, being re-elected in 1853 and 1857. He made his mark as a good speaker, and in 1856 was elected a Presidential Elector on the Buchanan ticket. He went on the stump, and his speeches gave him a reputation which in 1858 sent him to Congress. His term of office expired March 3d, 1861, and, having obtained a re-election during 1860, he was entitled to take his seat during the Thirty-seventh Congress, but resigned to take part in putting down the rebellion. He left his seat in the halls of the Legislature during the extra session of July, 1861, to enter the ranks of Colonel Richardson's regiment of Michigan Volunteers, and exhibited great bravery during the first battle of Bull Run, July 21st, 1861. He returned to Congress after that battle, and urged upon the Government the necessity of raising a sufficient force to put down the Confederates in arms. He then, at the close of the session, went to his native State and energetically called upon his countrymen to rally around the flag of their country and put down the rebellion. The citizens of his district readily responded to the call, and the Thirty-first Regiment of Illinois Volunteers was raised and organized at Cairo on September 18th, 1861. He was chosen colonel of the regiment, with a commission dating from August 18th, 1861, and took part shortly afterward in the sanguinary battle of Belmont, where he led a bayonet-charge which broke the Confederate lines, and saved a portion of the command from falling into the hands of the enemy. He was at the capture of Fort Henry, and with several hundred cavalry pursued and captured eight of the enemy's guns. He also took an active part in the reduction of Fort Donelson, where, notwithstanding severe wounds, he held his position until reinforcements arrived. Shortly after he was attacked with a serious illness, and for some time hopes of his recovery were given up. He reported for duty as soon as able to do active service, and joined Grant at Pittsburg Landing, having meanwhile been promoted to be a brigadier-general of Volunteers on the 5th of March, 1862. In the following May he showed himself a brave and skillful general in the siege of Corinth, and after its occupation his brigade guarded the rail communications with Jackson, Tenn.

During the Summer of 1862 he was importuned to become again a candidate for Congress, but declined in a letter in which he said: "I have entered the field to die, if need be, for this Government, and never expect to return to peaceful pursuits until the object of this war of preservation has become a fact established." He displayed such skill and bravery in Grant's campaign of Northern Mississippi in 1862 and 1863, that he was made a major-general, the commission dating from November 29th, 1862. As the commander of the Third Division, Seventeenth Army Corps, under General McPherson, he took part in the battle of Port Gibson, fought with distinguished personal bravery at the battle of Raymond on the 12th of May, helped drive the Confederates out of Jackson two days later, and was in the battle of Champion's Hill, May 16th. He led the centre of General McPherson's command at the siege of Vicksburg, and his column first entered the city after the surrender, July 4th, 1863. He was appointed military governor of the city, where a gold medal was presented to him—the badge of honor of the Seventeenth Army Corps. He visited the North in the Summer of that year, and made several eloquent Union speeches. As a specimen of these speeches the following extract from one delivered at Duquoin, Ill., may be quoted: "The Government is worth fighting for. It is worth generations, and centuries of war. It is worth the lives of the best and noblest men in the land. We will fight for this Government for the sake of ourselves and our children. Our little ones shall read in the history of the men who stood by the Government in its dark and gloomy hours, and it shall be the proud boast of many that their fathers died in this glorious struggle for American liberty. I believe to-day—I believe it honestly—that if the people of the North were united and all stood upon one platform, as we do in the army, this rebellion would be crushed in ninety days. I want to show you the reason why more troops ought to be raised. We can crush this rebellion. I know it. Why, we have marched a little army clear from Cairo to Vicksburg; below, a small one has marched from New Orleans to Port Hudson. We have opened the Mississippi River. We have split the Confederacy in two, leaving on one side Texas, Louisiana, Arkansas and Missouri—more territory than is on the eastern side. We have made a gulf that is impassable for them. We can hurl our strength upon one half, and whip them; then upon the other, and whip that."

He was stationed at Huntsville, Ala., the following Winter, having succeeded General Sherman as commander of the Fifteenth Army Corps. Early in the Summer of 1864, the Division of the Mississippi was making ready for "Sherman's March to the Sea." General Logan led the Army of the Tennessee upon the right of the grand march, and was successively engaged in the battle at Resaca, in the repulse of Hardee's forces at Dallas, at Little Kenesaw Mountain, and in the desperate battle of Peach Tree Creek, where General McPherson fell. General Logan took the latter's place, and successfully led the Federals in the many important engagements that followed. In fact, he participated in every battle of that historic campaign, from Missionary Ridge to the fall of Atlanta, on the 2d of September. After these momentous events, General Logan returned to Illinois, and during the Fall months of the Presidential campaign of that year made many speeches for Lincoln in the Western States. He joined his command again at Savannah, and marched with Sherman through the Carolinas, and, after Johnston's surrender, to Washington. On the 23d of May, 1865, he was appointed to succeed General Howard in the command of the Army of the Tennessee.

In the Autumn of 1865 President Johnson offered him the position of Minister to Mexico, which he declined, and in 1866 he was nominated by the Republicans of Illinois to represent the State at large in the Fortieth Congress, and was elected by over 60,000 majority. He was one of the Managers on the part of the House in the impeachment trial of Andrew Johnson, in the Spring of 1867. He was returned to the House of Representatives by re-elections in 1868 and 1870; but in 1871 was elected to the United States Senate to succeed Senator Yates, and, later on, to the seat of Richard J. Oglesby. In the Senate he has introduced and supported many Hills concerning rewards to soldiers, and army matters in general. At military reunions he has always been active. He was one of the founders of the Grand Army of the Republic, which originated at Decatur, Ill., and was its first national Commander. He was nominated for Vice President upon the ticket led by James G. Blaine at the Republican Convention held at Chicago in 1884.

GRENVILLE M. DODGE.

Born in Danvers, Mass., on April 12th, 1831. He studied under Alden Partridge at Norwich, Vt., receiving a thorough scientific and military education. During the year 1851 he removed to Illinois, where he was employed in the surveys of the principal railroads of that State until 1854, when he temporary command of the District of the Mississippi, and superintended the reconstruction of the Mississippi and Ohio Railroad after the battle of Corinth. October, 1862, he was placed in full command of the district. In December was attached to the Seventeenth Army Corps, under McPherson. During Grant's operations before Vicksburg, General Dodge held command of the left wing of the Sixteenth Corps, and at the beginning of 1864, commanded the Second Division of the same corps, operating in Northern Alabama.

During Sherman's Georgia campaign of May, 1864, General Dodge commanded the Sixteenth Army Corps, and behaved so gallantly at Resaca that he was promoted to the rank of major-general. General Dodge originated the famous Donkey Brigade, which during 1862 operated so successfully in the mountains of Northern Alabama.

of fortifying and holding the strategical points on the Mississippi River, and President Davis offered him a commission as major-general. He took advice of Bishop Meech of Virginia, who referred him to Robert E. Lee. The latter unhesitatingly advised him to accept the commission, which he did, and was placed in command of the army operating on the Mississippi River, with headquarters at Memphis. He effected the seizure of Hickman and Columbus. At the battle of Shiloh, or Pittsburg Landing, he commanded the First Corps of the Army of the Mississippi. He also figured prominently at the battles of Murfreesboro' and Chickamauga, ranking in these engagements as lieutenant-general. At the battle of Chickamauga he was relieved of his command by General Bragg for disobedience of orders during the battle, and ordered to Atlanta. Soon after, he was given command

WOMEN OF THE SOUTH COMPELLED BY HUNGER TO APPLY TO THE FEDERAL COMMISSARY FOR FOOD.

was engaged in a similar capacity in the State of Iowa. At the commencement of the Civil War he was sent to the National Capital by the Governor, in order to procure arms and equipments for the Volunteer troops of Iowa. In June 17th, 1861, he was commissioned colonel of the Fourth Iowa Volunteers—one of the best regiments from that State.

Colonel Dodge's regiment served in Missouri during the early part of 1861, and was in February, 1862, attached to the column which marched under General Curtis to Northwestern Arkansas. At the battle of Pea Ridge, March 6th, 7th and 8th, 1862, Colonel Dodge commanded a brigade on the extreme right of the Federal lines, and although severely wounded, continued to hold his place in the field until the final rout of the whole of the Confederate forces. For his gallantry on this occasion he was promoted to the rank of brigadier-general of Volunteers, with a commission dating from March 31st, 1862.

General Dodge was, during the following June, placed in

LEONIDAS POLK.

Born at Raleigh, N. C., in 1806; was admitted to the United States Military Academy at West Point, and upon graduating from it, entered the army as a lieutenant of artillery in July, 1827; but, having been induced by Bishop McIlvaine, then chaplain at West Point, to study for the ministry, he resigned from the service, December 1st of the same year; received his ordination in the Protestant Episcopal Church during the year 1831, and during the following ten years was Missionary Bishop both of Arkansas and of part of the Indian Territory, and given provisional charge of the Dioceses of Alabama, Mississippi, and Louisiana, as well as of Missions in the Republic of Texas. From 1841 to 1861 he was Bishop of Louisiana, having resigned all other charges. He took an active part in the project of establishing a Southern Confederacy, he being a strong sympathizer with the doctrine of secession. He urged upon Jefferson Davis and the Confederate Congress the importance

of the camp of prisoners paroled at Vicksburg and Port Hudson, and in the Winter of 1863-64 had temporary command of the Department of the Mississippi. Here he displayed great skill in the disposition of his troops, and was soon afterward restored to full command, when he united his forces with Johnston at Resaca. He was killed during action at Pine Mountain, Ga., June 14th, 1864, while reconnoitring upon the eminence, in the company of Generals Joseph E. Johnston and William J. Hardee. It is said that when General Thomas observed this group he ordered Knapp's Battery to fire in its direction, immediately causing the retirement of the three generals to a place of greater safety; General Polk returned, and was struck and killed by another shell, which, like the first shot, was fired by William Atwell, of Allegheny City, Pa., of the same battery. On taking possession of the eminence, affixed to a stake was found a paper, on which was written: "Here General Polk was killed by a Yankee shell." He was buried in the yard of the Episcopal Church at Augusta, Ga.

CHARLESTON—1863-1864.

Shortly after the attack of the rams *Palmetto State* and *Chicora* upon the blockading fleet (Vol. II., page 311), General Beauregard issued the following proclamation:

"HEADQUARTERS NAVAL AND LAND FORCES,
"CHARLESTON, S. C., January 31st, 1863.

"At the hour of five o'clock this morning the Confederate States naval forces on this station attacked the United States blockading fleet off the harbor of the City of Charleston, and sunk, dispersed or drove off and out of sight, for the time, the entire hostile fleet. Therefore we, the undersigned commanders, respectively, of the Confederate States Naval and Land Forces in this quarter, hereby formally declare the blockade by the United States of the said City of Charleston, S. C., to be raised by a superior force of the Confederate States, from and after this 31st day of January, A.D. 1863.

"G. T. BEAUREGARD,
"*General Commanding.*
"D. N. INGRAHAM,
"*Commanding Naval Forces in South Carolina.*

"(Official.) THOMAS JORDAN, *Chief of Staff.*"

The erroneous report of the dispersion of the fleet and of the consequent raising of the blockade, was likewise communicated by the Confederate Secretary of State through circulars addressed to all the foreign consuls in the Confederacy. A full refutation was, however, immediately issued by the commanders of the United States steamers *Housatonic, Flag, Quaker City, Memphis*, and *Stettin*, the last-named having come upon the scene after the rams had disappeared over the bar.

The blockade was rigidly kept up, and during the months of February and March, 1863, preparations were made for a renewed attack against Charleston. As fast as vessels could be got ready for the proposed expedition, they were ordered to rendezvous at the mouth of the North Edisto River, and by evening of Sunday, the 5th of April, Rear-admiral Dupont had nine monitors and five armored gunboats in position for the contemplated attack, to be directed chiefly upon Fort Sumter.

It was intended that about 4,000 men, taken from Hunter's force, should operate in conjunction with Dupont's vessels, and they were accordingly sent upon Folly Island, close by Lighthouse Inlet, in charge of Hunter's chief of staff, General Truman Seymour. This land force was provided with artillery and with a number of pontons, with which it was intended they should dash across Morris Island immediately upon the reduction of the forts. The squadron, as will be seen, failed to reduce the Confederate defenses, and General Seymour's force could therefore take no part in the operations.

Early on the 6th of April the fleet approached the line of the blockading squadron, and the monitor *Keokuk* (Commander Rhind) was sent with the Coast Survey schooner *Bibb* (Commander Boutelle) to buoy out the bar. By nine o'clock on the morning of the 7th the fleet was posted in the main channel, about a mile from shore, having taken advantage of the prevalence of a thick mist to get into position. Shortly after noon the mist had cleared away sufficiently for the pilots to discover the main obstructions, and the fleet moved, in accordance with Rear-admiral Dupont's orders, as follows:

"The squadron will pass up the main ship-channel without returning the fire of the batteries on Morris Island, unless signal should be made to commence action.

"The ships will open fire on Fort Sumter when within easy range, and will take up a position to the northward and westward of that fortification, engaging its left or northwest face at a distance of from one thousand to eight hundred yards, firing low, and aiming at the centre embrasure.

"The commanding officers will instruct their officers and men to carefully avoid wasting a shot, and will enjoin upon them the necessity of *precision* rather than *rapidity* of firing.

"Each ship will be prepared to render every assistance possible to vessels that may require it.

"The special code of signals prepared for the ironclad vessels will be used in action.

"After the reduction of Fort Sumter it is probable the next point of attack will be the batteries on Morris Island.

"The order of battle will be the line ahead in the following succession:

"1. *Weehawken*, with raft, Captain John Rodgers; 2. *Passaic*, Captain Percival Drayton; 3. *Montauk*, Commander John L. Worden; 4. *Patapsco*, Commander Daniel Ammen; 5. *New Ironsides* (flagship), Commodore Thomas Turner; 6. *Catskill*, Commander George W. Rodgers; 7. *Nantucket*, Commander Donald McN. Fairfax; 8. *Nahant*, Commander John Downes; 9. *Keokuk*, Commander Alexander C. Rhind.

"A squadron of reserve, of which Captain J. F. Green will be the senior officer, will be formed outside the bar and near the entrance buoy, consisting of the following vessels: *Canandaigua*, Captain Joseph F. Green; *Unadilla*, Lieutenant-commander S. P. Quackenbush; *Housatonic*, Captain William R. Taylor; *Wissahickon*, Lieutenant-commander J. G. Davis; *Huron*, Lieutenant-commander G. A. Stevens; and will be held in readiness to support the ironclads when they attack the batteries on Morris Island.

"S. F. DUPONT,
"*Rear-admiral Com. South Atlantic Blockade Squadron.*"

Nearly an hour's delay was caused by the fouling of the grappling-irons attached to the *Weehawken's* torpedo-raft, which became entangled with her anchor-cable, but after that the advance continued unbroken.

The fleet passed by Morris Island unmolested, but when, shortly before three o'clock, the vessels came within range of Fort Sumter, and of the batteries along James and Sullivan's Islands, the signal was given for the opening of a concentrated fire from Forts Moultrie, Sumter, Putnam and Beauregard, and from the entire line of batteries. All appeared at first to be concentrating upon the *Weehawken*, in whose immediate vicinity a torpedo had exploded without, however, doing any damage. The *Weehawken* replied vigorously with twenty-six shots from her eleven and fifteen inch guns, and after escaping a dangerous entanglement in the obstructions covering most of the distance between Fort Sumter and Sullivan's Island, she was headed for the ocean.

The *Weehawken* was closely followed by the *Passaic*, the *Montauk* and the *Patapsco*, which fired respectively thirteen, twenty-seven, and ten shots, from their 11-inch, 15-inch, and 150-pounder rifled guns, being subjected in return to heavy firing that temporarily disabled the turret of the *Passaic*, as had already been that of the *Weehawken*, and for a time likewise disabled the *Patapsco's* 15-inch rifle. Although struck fourteen times, the *Montauk* suffered comparatively little injury.

As the last-named vessel was about turning seaward, she suddenly refused to obey her helm. The progress of the *Patapsco* was therefore impeded, and she was naturally subjected in consequence to an additional heavy battering from the forts until the *Montauk* could be driven ahead, though without experiencing any material damage.

The *Catskill*, *Nahant* and *Nantucket* meanwhile passed the *New Ironsides*, which latter had become altogether unmanageable in the strong tide, and had in consequence raised the signal to "disregard the motions of flagship." The *Keokuk* had followed the others, and by reason of the narrowness of the channel had found it necessary to advance the *Nahant* at about half-past three o'clock. For nearly an hour both vessels were subjected to a terrible fire.

THE FEDERAL IRONCLAD "WEEHAWKEN" ATTACKS FORT SUMTER, APRIL 7TH, 1863

FROM A SKETCH BY W. T. CRANE

FEDERALS.—A. Keokuk. B. Nahant. C. Nantucket. D. Catskill. E. Ironsides. F. Patapsco. G. Montauk. H. Passaic. K. Weehawken.——CONFEDERATES.—1. Morris Island Sand Battery. 2. Fort Wagner. 3. Battery Bee, on Cumming's Point. 4. Fort Johnson. 5. Fort Ripley. 6. Fort Sumter. 7. Charleston City. 8. Castle Pinckney. 9. Fort Redan. 10. Fort Moultrie. 11. Moultrie House. 12. Fort Beauregard. 13. Harbor Obstruction. 14. Cooper River. 15. Ashley River.

PANORAMIC VIEW OF CHARLESTON HARBOR.—ADVANCE OF IRONCLADS TO THE ATTACK, APRIL 7TH, 1863.

NIGHT AFTER THE FIGHT.—THE IRONCLADS AT ANCHOR OFF FORT [illegible].—[illegible] SKETCH BY W.T. CRANE.

The *Nahant* fired both shot and shell from her 11 and 15 inch guns, and suffered great damage to her turret, which received nine shots, and finally became unmanageable, as did likewise her steering gear, while the *Keokuk* had her 6-inch turrets completely riddled, and had besides her hull so thoroughly pierced in nineteen different places that she commenced sinking. At about five o'clock the *Keokuk* was taken close by Lighthouse Inlet, where, despite all efforts to save her, she went to the bottom early the following morning.

During the action the fleet was enabled to fire but 139 shots at Fort Sumter, as against as many as 3,000 sent by the Confederates. Of the latter number the fleet received 515, distributed as follows *Weehawken*, 60; *Passaic*, 53; *Montauk*, 20; *Patapsco*, 15; *New Ironsides*, 65; *Catskill*, 54; *Nantucket*, 51; *Nahant*, 80; *Keokuk*, 90.

BOMBARDMENT OF FORT SUMTER AS SEEN FROM THE LOOKOUT OF THE TURRET OF THE IRONCLAD "WEEHAWKEN."

The damage done to Fort Sumter was scarcely perceptible; but that sustained by the Federals extended, as has been seen, to the entire fleet. The casualties in the latter were 26 wounded, principally on the *Nahant* and *Keokuk*; the Confederates losing 3 killed and 11 wounded.

In his able report of the military operations of General Beauregard, Mr. Roman gives the following details concerning the most important works opposed to the progress of Dupont's fleet:

"First among them was Fort Sumter, under Colonel Alfred Rhett, with Lieutenant-colonel J. A. Yates commanding the . . . guns, and Major Ormsby Blanding in charge of the casemate batteries. The garrison consisted of seven companies of the First South Carolina Artillery (Regulars), under Captains D. G. Fleming, F. H. Harleston, J. C. King, J. C. Mitchel, J. R. Macbeth, W. H. Peronneau and C. W. Parker. The guns brought into action were: two 7-inch Brooke, four 10-inch columbiads, two 9-inch Dahlgrens, four 8-inch columbiads, four 8-inch navy guns, seven banded and rifled 42-pounders, thirteen smooth-bore 32-pounders, and seven 10-inch seacoast mortars—in all, forty-four guns and mortars.

"Next in importance was Fort Moultrie, under Colonel William Butler, assisted by Major T. M. Baker, with five companies of the First South Carolina Infantry (Regulars), commanded by Captains T. A. Huguenin, R. Press Smith, B. S. Burnett, C. H. Rivers and Lieutenant E. A. Erwin. The guns engaged were: nine 8-inch columbiads, five rifled and banded 32-pounders, five smooth-bore 32-pounders, and two 10-inch mortars—in all, twenty-one guns and mortars.

"Battery Bee, on Sullivan's Island, was under Lieutenant-colonel J. C. Simkins, with three companies of the First South Carolina Infantry (Regulars), Captains R. de Treville, Warren Adams and W. Tabourne. The guns it used against the fleet were: five 10-inch and one 8-inch columbiads—in all, six guns.

"Battery Beauregard was under Captain J. A. Sitgreaves, First South Carolina Artillery (Regulars), with two companies, one from Fort Sumter, the other from Fort Moultrie. The first was commanded by Lieutenant W. E. Erwin, the second by Captain J. H. Warley. The guns engaged were: one 8-inch and two 32-pounders, rifled.

"Battery Wagner was under Major C. K. Huger, with two companies belonging to the First South Carolina Artillery (Regulars). One gun was engaged—a 32-pounder, rifled.

"At Cumming's Point Battery, Lieutenant H. R. Lesesne commanded, with a detachment of the First South Carolina Artillery (Regulars). The guns engaged were: one 10-inch columbiad and one 8-inch Dahlgren—two guns."

Rear-admiral Dupont being satisfied that no real progress could be made without the co-operation of a strong land force, took the whole fleet, with exception of the *New Ironsides*, to Port Royal, on the 12th of April. Three days later he addressed the following to the Navy Department in justification of his failure to renew the attack upon the Charleston Harbor defenses:

". . . . . . Any attempt to pass through the obstructions I have referred to would have entangled the vessels and held them under the most severe fire of heavy ordnance that has ever been delivered, and while it is barely possible that some vessels might have forced their way through, it would only have been to be again impeded by fresh and more formidable obstructions, and to encounter other powerful batteries, with which the whole harbor of Charleston has been lined. I had hoped that the endurance of the ironclads would have enabled them to have borne any weight of fire to which they might have been exposed; but when I found that so large a portion of them were wholly or one half disabled by less than an hour's engagement, before attempting to overcome the obstructions, or testing the power of the torpedoes, I was convinced that persistence in the attack would only result in the loss of the greater portion of the ironclad fleet, and in leaving many of them inside the harbor to fall into the hands of the enemy. The slowness of our fire, and our inability to occupy any battery that we might silence, or to prevent its being restored under cover of the night, were difficulties of the gravest character, and until the outer forts should have been taken, the army could not enter the harbor, or afford me any assistance . . . . . ."

As Admiral Dupont had been instructed by President Lincoln to hold his "position inside the bar," and not to "allow the enemy to erect new

THE FEDERAL FLEET, COMMANDED BY ADMIRAL DUPONT, OPENING FIRE ON FORT SUMTER, APRIL 7th, 18[illegible]

VIEWS FROM FOLLY ISLAND, CHARLESTON HARBOR.

FROM SKETCHES BY LIEUTENANT CHARLES C. COLEMAN, ONE HUNDREDTH NEW YORK VOLUNTEERS.

batteries or defenses on Morris Island," he caused the latter section to be carefully watched, leaving the *New Ironsides* to aid materially in this service.

On the 3d of June, 1863, General Q. A. Gillmore relieved General Hunter of the command of the Department of the South, and reached Hilton Head just as Dupont was advised of an intended raid by the new ram *Atlanta* upon the blockading squadron in Warsaw Sound. It was ascertained that the swift English blockade-runner *Fingal*, which had entered the Savannah River early in 1862, and had since made several ineffectual attempts to get to sea, was now transformed into a Confederate ram called the *Atlanta*, and that she was in command of Lieutenant W. A. Webb, formerly of the United States Navy, who had a large crew and an armament of two 7-inch and two 6 4-10-inch rifled guns.

Dupont sent the monitors *Weehawken* and *Nahant* to watch the ram, and at dawn on June 17th the *Atlanta* was seen coming down the Wilmington River, in company with two gunboats. The *Weehawken* and *Nahant* turned and apparently retreated, seeing which, the *Atlanta* followed rapidly, ever, taken suddenly ill, and died in New York City on the 26th of June. Admiral John A. Dahlgren was then ordered to relieve Dupont of the command of the squadron, and reached Port Royal on the 4th of the following month.

Preparatory to the attack on Charleston, Gillmore had caused the erection, through General J. Vodges, of strong batteries south of Lighthouse Inlet on Folly Island, to cover those of the Confederates on the southern end of Morris Island. Immediately after their completion, the attention of the Confederates was detracted from Morris Island by an expedition consisting of about thirty-nine hundred men, under General A. H. Terry, which was sent up the Stono River, while another expedition, made up from General Saxton's force at Beaufort, and placed in command of Colonel Higginson, proceeded up the Edisto River to cut the Confederate communications by way of the Charleston and Savannah Railroad.

The feint was successful. It drew the enemy's attention from Morris to James Island, and the Confederates were completely taken by surprise, when, at about four o'clock on the morning of the the Third New Hampshire, Sixth and Seventh Connecticut, Ninth Maine, Seventy-sixth Pennsylvania, and the Forty-eighth and One Hundredth New York Regiments. The Federals reached the parapets, but, as General Gillmore reported, "the supports recoiled under the fire to which they were exposed, and could not be got up." The assailants were, in fact, met by such a terribly destructive fire, that they could not do otherwise than fall back, and this they were, fortunately for them, able to do without a very serious loss.

General Beauregard had meanwhile received fresh troops from Virginia, which had been sent to meet the Federal force then established on James Island, and early on the 16th of July an attempt was made to capture Terry and his command. The Confederates, led by Brigadier-general Hagood, advanced from Secessionville and succeeded in driving in the Federal pickets; but after a short engagement, in which Terry had the assistance of the gunboats *Pawnee*, *Huron*, *Marblehead*, *Mayflower*, and *John Adams*, all which lay in the Stono and Folly Rivers, Hagood's force was repulsed, with the loss of about 200 killed and wounded, the Fed-

ADMIRAL DUPONT'S MACHINE-SHOP IN CHARLESTON HARBOR, S. C.

FROM A SKETCH BY W. T. CRANE.

and soon fired a rifle shell, which, however, did no damage. She then stopped her engines, and the *Weehawken* advanced toward her, and, when about three hundred yards distant, opened upon the ram with her 15-inch gun. The first shot carried away part of the *Atlanta's* pilot-house, wounding two of the pilots, and was followed during the ensuing quarter of an hour by four more shots, at an average distance of about one hundred yards, all of which did much damage to her four-inch armor and thick oak planking, and the last of which killed one man and wounded seventeen others. Lieutenant Webb then hauled down his flag, and raised a white one in token of surrender. Captain Rodgers took possession of the ram, as well as of her 21 officers and crew numbering 121 men, and the *Atlanta* was sent to Port Royal the following day.

Immediately after his arrival at Hilton Head, General Gillmore made preparations for a renewed attack against Charleston. This was to be done upon a basis totally at variance with the expressed views of Rear-admiral Dupont, who could foresee but failure from the proposed new lines of assault. Dupont was relieved, and Rear-admiral A. H. Foote was appointed his successor. The latter was, how-10th of July, Vodges's batteries opened upon Morris Island in conjunction with a heavy fire, mainly directed against Fort Wagner, from the monitors *Catskill* (flagship), Commander G. W. Rodgers; *Weehawken*, Commander E. R. Colhoun; *Montauk*, Commander D. McN. Fairfax; and *Nahant*, Commander John Downes.

After an incessant bombardment of nearly two hours' duration, a strong force under General George C. Strong was thrown against the Confederate earthworks. A prolonged and hotly contested fight ensued, and the Confederates were compelled to fall back toward Fort Wagner, with the loss of eleven guns and much of their camp equipage. Strong pursued the enemy until within musket-range of Fort Wagner, when his men rested, and the monitors, which had moved in a line parallel to the advance of the troops, kept up a bombardment of the forts and batteries. The latter replied until about noon, when Dahlgren withdrew the monitors for about an hour, and then renewed the bombardment until nearly six o'clock in the afternoon.

At daybreak on the 11th, General Strong led in person a charge upon Fort Wagner with his own and General T. Seymour's brigade, consisting of erals losing about half that number. On the other hand, Colonel Higginson's expedition failed in its attempt to cut the Charleston and Savannah Railway, having at the outset met a much superior force of Confederates, and been compelled to return to its original position.

In the meantime Gillmore set about making preparations for a combined land and naval attack upon Fort Wagner. Terry's command was withdrawn from James Island, and batteries were erected across Morris Island, mounting 29 heavy Parrott guns and 14 large mortars. These were placed in position to bear directly upon Fort Wagner at distances of from 1,300 to 1,900 yards.

Shortly before noon of the 18th the batteries opened upon Fort Wagner simultaneously with heavy firing from the monitors and from the gunboats. The monitors

JULY, 1863.

were led by the *Montauk* (flagship), Commander Fairfax; the latter being closely followed by the *New Ironsides*, Captain Rowan; the *Catskill*, Commander Rodgers; the *Nantucket*, Commander Beaumont; the *Weehawken*, Commander Calhoun; and the *Patapsco*, Lieutenant-commander Badger; while the gunboats *Paul Jones*, Commander Rhind, and the *Ottawa*, *Seneca*, *Chippewa*, and *Wissahickon*

VIEW IN BEAUFORT, S. C., HEADQUARTERS OF THE DEPARTMENT OF THE SOUTH.
FROM A SKETCH BY W. T. CRANE

respectively in charge of Lieutenant-commanders Whiting, Gibson, Harris and Davis, stood off, and at long range used their guns upon the fort.

The bombardment of Fort Wagner thus continued all day almost without intermission, the Confederates replying only at intervals, and awaiting under cover of their bomb-proofs the land attack which they expected soon to follow. Just before dark the firing of the fleet was observed to cease, and in the midst of an unusually heavy thunderstorm the troops were formed along the beach for the grand assault.

The storming party, in charge of General Truman Seymour, advanced in two columns, led by General George C. Strong and by Colonel—acting Brigadier-general—H. L. Putnam, of the Seventh New Hampshire. The leading column under Strong was composed of the Third New Hampshire, Colonel Jackson; the Sixth Connecticut, (with part of the Seventh Connecticut), Colonel Chatfield; the Ninth Maine, Colonel Emory; the Forty-eighth New York, Colonel Barton; the Fifty-fourth (colored) Massachusetts, Colonel Shaw; and the Seventy-sixth Pennsylvania, Colonel Strawbridge.

Strong's force moved slowly up the beach until within about half a mile of Fort Wagner, when the Federals were put on the double-quick; but before they came within musket-range of the fort their advance was checked by a tremendous discharge of shot, shell and canister from the Wagner bastions, as well as from the guns of Fort Sumter and Battery Gregg, supplemented by volleys of musketry from the garrison, and by the throwing of hand grenades from the parapet.

The Federal progress was arrested but for a short time. Strong led his men up to the ditch, then containing about four feet of water. It was crossed under a continued heavy fire, the colored Massachusetts regiment taking the lead and soon reaching the parapet, where a frightful hand-to-hand encounter followed. Colonel Shaw was one of the first to fall, mortally wounded, and Color-sergeant Carney received a severe wound in the thigh while in the act of planting the regimental standard upon the parapet. The Confederates, were, however, in such large numbers that the Fifty-fourth was compelled to fall back after the loss of half their number. The Sixth Connecticut, Ninth Maine, Third New Hampshire, and other regiments, followed in turn, but the furious storm of fire that was hurled against them proved so destructive that

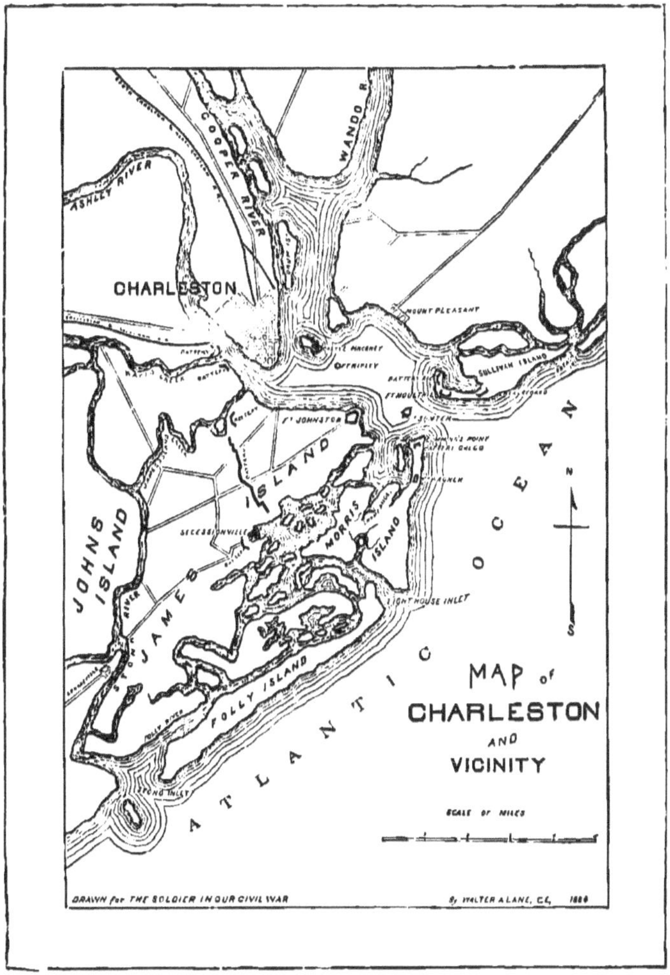

Bombardment of Fort Moultrie.

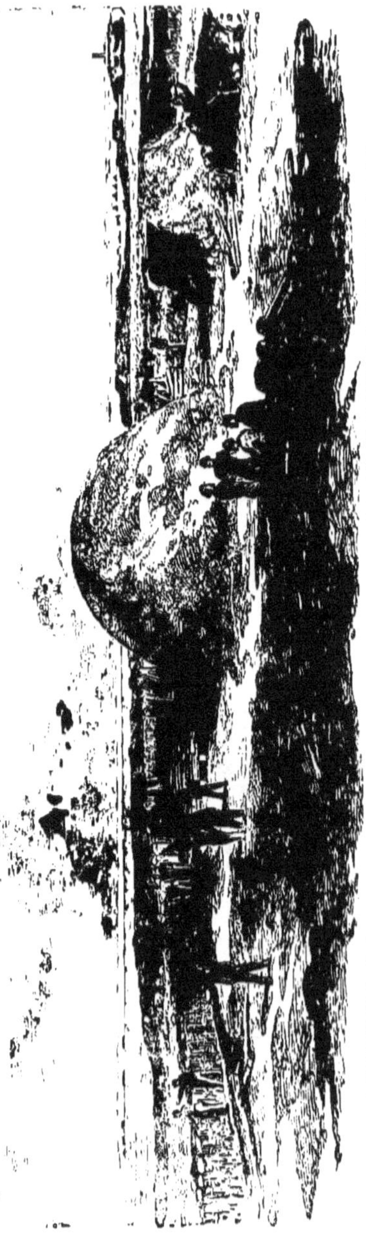

1. BOMBARDMENT OF FORT MOULTRIE AND BATTERIES BEE AND BEAUREGARD, CHARLESTON HARBOR, S. C., SEPTEMBER 7TH-8TH, 1863.

General Strong was compelled to order the troops to retire.

The commanding-general and Colonel Chatfield were mortally wounded, and Colonels Green, Barton and Jackson received such severe injuries that they were compelled to leave the field. The command of the brigade devolved upon Major Plympton, of the Third New Hampshire.

Colonel Putnam's column—made up of his own regiment, the Seventh New Hampshire; the One Hundredth New York, Colonel Dandy; the Sixty-second Ohio, Colonel Steele; and the Sixty-seventh Ohio, Colonel Voorhees—then came forward.

For nearly half an hour the contest was once more kept up, the parapet being again scaled, and many severe hand-to-hand fights carried on; but the Federals succeeded only in driving the Confederates between the traverses, and were then charged upon so furiously by fresh troops that they were expelled with great losses. The latter included Colonel Putnam, who was killed while at the head

ENGINEERS' DEPOT, MORRIS ISLAND, CHARLESTON HARBOR, S. C.
FROM A SKETCH BY W. T. CRANE.

of his troops, General Seymour having been wounded earlier in the day.

The Federals reoccupied their original position, and General Gillmore ordered the lines of batteries to be advanced, and more formidable earthworks erected. By the 17th of August Gillmore's preparations for another attack were complete. He had caused the construction of a series of parallels extending from the beach on the right to the marsh on the left.

August, 1863.

The first of these was located about 4,000 yards from Fort Sumter and some 1,200 yards from Fort Wagner; the second stood at a distance of from 600 to 700 yards from Fort Wagner; and the third was nearly 300 yards in advance of the last-named. All contained Parrott guns of the heaviest calibre, the first parallel holding in addition two 200-pound Whitworth rifles.

On the left of these parallels were constructed additional powerful batteries, and still farther to the left, on the marsh, there was erected another earthwork directly facing Fort Sumter, in which was mounted a single 8-inch 200-pound rifle Parrott gun, named "The Swamp Angel." The construction and erection of all these works and batteries had to be done chiefly at night, and even then under an active fire from the Confederate fortifications; yet the casualties among the Federals was comparatively small.

Gillmore exchanged some heavy fire with the Confederates upon different occasions, and late on the 16th ordered seven shots directed against Fort Sumter by way of experiment, but only four of those struck the outer wall, and caused some damage.

Early on the 17th Gillmore opened upon Fort Sumter and Battery Gregg from all his batteries, while Admiral Dahlgren opened upon Fort Wagner with the *Weehawken* (flagship), *New Ironsides*, *Catskill*, *Nahant*, and *Montauk*, supported by the *Canandaigua*, *Cimarrone*, *Dai Ching*, *Lodona*, *Mahaska*, *Ottawa* and *Wissahickon*.

Forts Moultrie, Sumter, Wagner and Gregg replied vigorously for a time to the attack from the fleet and the batteries; but after a couple of hours Wagner was silenced, Gregg partly so, and Sumter's wall considerably injured. Just before noon Admiral Dahlgren transferred his flag to the *Passaic*, and accompanied by the *Patapsco*, advanced up to within 2,000 yards of Fort Sumter, upon which the two vessels opened fire from their rifled 150-pounders. Later in the day both these vessels were taken opposite Fort Wagner, whence they dispersed a number of workmen who were endeavoring to repair damages previously sustained.

During the day's engagements, Commander Rodgers and Paymaster Woodbury were killed on board the *Catskill*, and Captain J. M. Wamplar, of Virginia, belonging to the Engineer Department, was mortally wounded by the explosion of a 15-inch shell. The firing was renewed and kept up by the Federals every day until the 24th, with the result given in the subjoined daily Confederate reports:

"CHARLESTON, Thursday, August 20th, 1863.

"The firing of the Parrott guns upon Fort Sumter to-day was exceedingly heavy, but not so accurate as heretofore. About noon the flag was shot away, but soon replaced.

"The battery of Parrott guns is distant from Sumter two and five-eighth miles.

"The missiles used are 200-pound bolts, eight inches in diameter, two feet long, with flat heads of chilled iron. Shells of the same dimensions are also used.

"Up to Wednesday night, the third day of the attack, 1,072 of these missiles struck Sumter, and, including to-day, 2,500 have struck.

"The damage is of course considerable, and for the last two days all the guns on the south face of the fort have been disabled."

"CHARLESTON, Friday, August 21st.

"The fire of the enemy's land batteries has been heavier than ever to-day. A new battery of Parrott guns opened on Sumter this morning, and the fires have been concentrated upon the east battery and its guns. The south wall of the fort is now a pile of rubbish. On the north the wall is also crumbling into a heap of ruins. The flag has been shot away twice to-day, and six times during the attack. The flagstaff is shot off, and the flag flies from the ruins of the south wall."

"CHARLESTON, Saturday, August 22d.

"From 5 o'clock A.M. until 7 o'clock P.M. yesterday the enemy's fire on Fort Sumter was very heavy. Nine hundred and twenty-three shots were fired, and 704 struck the fort, either outside or inside. The eastern face of the fort is badly battered. Some guns on the east and northeast face were disabled. The flag was shot down four times. Five privates and two negroes were wounded. The enemy's fire on Wagner caused five casualties, including Captain Robert Pringle, killed. About 2 o'clock this morning the enemy began throwing shells into the city from a battery on the marsh between Morris and James Islands, and distant five miles from the city. Twelve 8-inch Parrott shells fell in the city, but caused no casualties. The shelling had a good effect in hastening the exodus of non-combatants. At daylight this morning the enemy opened fire vigorously on Sumter. The *Ironsides* has since opened. Sumter is replying. Wagner is firing briskly on the enemy's advanced works, 450 yards from our battery."

"CHARLESTON, August 22d.

"The fire of the enemy's land batteries has been kept up on Fort Sumter, and more guns disabled. There was only one casualty. There was also a heavy fire on Battery Wagner from the fleet and land, also on Battery Gregg. The casualties at Wagner were one officer and four privates."

"CHARLESTON, Sunday, August 23d.

"To-day the land batteries opened from south to the north, and the monitors from east to west, coming close up. The fire was very damaging. The east wall was cracked and breached and the shot swept through the fort. A man

OBSERVATORY, MORRIS ISLAND
BUILDING BA
HAULING SIEGE GUNS
WRECK OF THE BLOCKADE RUNNER RUBY
ADMIRAL J. A. DAHLGREN

ADMIRAL J.A. DAHLGREN

SINKING OF THE MONITOR "WEEHAWKEN" AT THE SIEGE OF CHARLESTON, DECEMBER 7TH, 1863.
FROM A SKETCH BY W. T. CRANE.

burst, wounding Lieutenant Boylston, Colonel Rhett and three other officers. The fort is now in ruins. Colonel Rhett is ordered to hold this outpost even as a forlorn hope, until relieved or taken. Colonel Gaillard was killed.

"General Gillmore sent a communication at 11 o'clock giving notice that at 11 o'clock to-morrow he would open fire on Charleston."

"CHARLESTON, Monday, August 24th.

"The enemy's fire on Sumter slackened to-day. The fleet has not participated. At 12 o'clock last night the enemy's guns opened on the city, firing fifteen 8-inch Parrott shells. No casualties resulted. Non-combatants are leaving the city in continuous streams."

Colonel Alfred Rhett, commanding Fort Sumter, made the following record of shots fired at the fort from August 16th to August 23d, 1863:

	16th	17th	18th	19th	20th	21st	22d	23d
Struck outside	30	447	472	408	404	445	280	320
Struck inside	10	230	244	241	206	270	216	237
Missed	8	270	180	131	175	219	185	158
Total	48	948	876	780	879	924	681	693

a communication was received at these headquarters, dated 'Headquarters Department of the South, Morris Island, S. C., August 21st, 1863,' demanding the immediate evacuation of Morris Island and Fort Sumter by the Confederate forces, on the alleged ground that 'the present condition of Fort Sumter, and the rapid and progressive destruction which it is undergoing from my batteries, seem to render its complete demolition within a few hours a matter of certainty,' and if this letter was not complied with, or no reply was received within four hours after it was delivered into the hands of my subordinate commander at Fort Wagner for transmission, a fire would be opened on the City of Charleston from batteries already established within easy and effective range of the heart of the city. This communication to my address was without signature, and, of course, returned. About half-past one o'clock one of your batteries did actually open fire and throw a number of heavy shells into the city, the inhabitants of which, of course, were asleep and unwarned. About 9 o'clock the next morning the communication alluded to was returned to these headquarters, bearing your recognized official signature, and it can now be noticed as your deliberate and official act. Among nations not barbarous the usages of war prescribe that when a city is about to be attacked, timely notice shall be given fixed a limit for receiving an answer to your demand, which made it almost beyond the possibility of receiving any reply within that time, and that you actually did open on, and threw a number of the most destructive missiles ever used in war into the midst of, a city taken unawares and filled with sleeping women and children, will give you a bad eminence in history—even in the history of this war. I am only surprised, sir, at the limits you have set to your demand. If, in order to obtain the abandonment of Morris Island and Fort Sumter, you feel authorized to open fire on this city, why did you not include the works on Sullivan and James Islands?

"Since you have felt warranted in inaugurating this method of reducing batteries in your immediate front which were otherwise found to be impregnable, and a mode of warfare which I confidently declare to be atrocious and unworthy of a soldier, I now solemnly warn you that if you fire again on the city from your Morris Island batteries without giving a somewhat more reasonable time to remove the non-combatants, I shall feel impelled to employ such stringent means of retaliation as may be available during the continuance of this attack.

"Finally, I reply that neither the works on Morris Island nor Fort Sumter will be evacuated on the demand which you

ORDNANCE DEPOT, MORRIS ISLAND, CHARLESTON HARBOR, S. C.
FROM A SKETCH BY W. T. CRANE.

On the 21st of August a demand was made for the evacuation of Morris Island and of Fort Sumter, leading to the following correspondence:

"HEADQUARTERS DEPARTMENT OF THE SOUTH,
MORRIS ISLAND, S. C., August 21st, 1863.

"*General G. T. Beauregard, Commanding Confederate Forces about Charleston, S. C.*

"GENERAL: I have the honor to demand of you the immediate evacuation of Morris Island and Fort Sumter by the Confederate forces.

"The present condition of Fort Sumter, and the rapid and progressive destruction which it is undergoing from my batteries, seem to render its complete demolition within a few hours a matter of certainty. All my heaviest guns have not yet opened. Should you refuse compliance with this demand, or should I receive no reply thereto within four hours after it is delivered into the hands of your subordinate at Fort Wagner for transmission, I shall open fire on the City of Charleston from batteries already established within easy and effective range of the heart of the city.

"I am, general, your obedient servant,
"Q. A. GILLMORE,
"*Brigadier-general Commanding.*"

"HEADQUARTERS SOUTH CAROLINA, GEORGIA AND FLORIDA, CHARLESTON, S. C., August 22d, 1863.

"SIR: Last night, at fifteen minutes before 11 o'clock, during my absence on a reconnoissance of my fortifications, by the attacking commander, in order that non-combatants shall have an opportunity of withdrawing beyond its limits. Generally the time allowed is from one to three days; that is, time for the withdrawal in good faith of at least the women and children. You, sir, gave only four hours, knowing that your notice, under existing circumstances, could not reach me in less than two hours, and not less than that time would be required for an answer to be conveyed from this city to Battery Wagner.

"With this knowledge, you threaten to open fire on this city, not to oblige its surrender, but to force me to evacuate those works which you, assisted by a great naval force, have been attacking in vain for more than forty days.

"Batteries Wagner and Gregg and Fort Sumter are nearly due north from your batteries on Morris Island, and in distance therefrom ranging from half a mile to two and a quarter miles.

"This city, on the other hand, is to the northwest, and quite five miles distant from the battery which opened against it this morning. It would appear, sir, that, despairing of reducing these works, you now resort to the novel measure of turning your guns against the old men, women, and the hospitals of a sleeping city—an act of inexcusable barbarity, from your own confessed point of sight, inasmuch as you allege that the complete demolition of Fort Sumter within a few hours by your guns seems a matter of certainty.

"Your omission to attach your signature to such a grave paper must show the recklessness of the course upon which you have adventured. While the facts that you knowingly have been pleased to make. Already, however, I am taking measures to remove all non-combatants, who are now fully aware of and alive to what they may expect at your hands.

"Respectfully, your obedient servant,
"G. T. BEAUREGARD.

"*To Brigadier-general Q. A. Gillmore, Commanding United States Forces on Morris Island.*"

"HEADQUARTERS DEPARTMENT OF THE SOUTH,
MORRIS ISLAND, S. C., August 22d, 1863—9 P.M.

"*General G. T. Beauregard, Commanding Confederate Forces, Charleston, S. C.*

"SIR: I have the honor to acknowledge the receipt of your communication of this date, complaining that one of my batteries has opened on the City of Charleston, and thrown 'a number of heavy shells into the city, the inhabitants of which, of course, were asleep and unwarned'.

"My letter to you demanding the surrender of Fort Sumter and Morris Island, and threatening, in default thereof, to open fire upon Charleston, was delivered near Fort Wagner at 11:15 o'clock A.M. on the 22d instant, and should have arrived at your headquarters in time to have permitted your answer to have reached me within the limit assigned, viz., four hours. The fact that you were absent from your headquarters at the time of its arrival may be regarded as an unfortunate circumstance for the City of Charleston, but one for which I clearly am not responsible. This letter bore date at my headquarters, and was officially delivered by an officer of my staff.

REVOLVING THE TURRET

THE ANCHOR WELL

THE CABIN.

THE BERTH DECK.

INTERIOR VIEWS OF THE UNITED STATES MONITOR "MONTAUK."

INTERIOR OF THE TURRET OF THE UNITED STATES IRONCLAD MONITOR "MONTAUK."—From a Sketch by W. T. Crane.

"The inadvertent omission of my signature doubtless affords ground for special pleading, but is not the argument of a commander solicitous only for the safety of sleeping women and children and unarmed men.

"Your threat of retaliation for acts of mine, which you allege to be in violation of the usages of civilized warfare, except as to length of time allowed as notice of my intention, are passed by without comment.

"I will, however, call your attention to the well-established principle, that the commander of a place attacked, but not invested, having its avenues of escape open and practicable, has no right to expect any notice of an intended bombardment other than that which is given by the threatening attitude of his adversary. Even had this letter not been written, the City of Charleston has had, according to your own computation, forty days' notice of her danger.

"During that time my attack on her defenses has steadily progressed. The ultimate object of that attack has at no time been doubtful. If, under the circumstances, the life of a single non-combatant is exposed to peril by the bombardment of the city, the responsibility rests with those who have first failed to remove the non-combatants, or to secure the safety of the city, after having held control of all its approaches for a period of nearly two years and a half, in the presence of a threatening force, and who afterward refused to accept the terms upon which the bombardment might have been postponed.

"From various sources, official or otherwise, I am led to believe that most of the women and children of Charleston were long since removed from the city; but upon your assurance that the city is still 'full' of them, I shall suspend the bombardment until 11 o'clock P.M. to-morrow, thus giving you two days from the time you acknowledge to have received my communication on the 21st instant.

"Very respectfully, your obedient servant,

"Q. A. GILLMORE,

"*Brigadier-general Commanding.*"

The "Swamp Angel" had in the meantime been made completely ready, and as General Beauregard did not reply to Gillmore's last communication, fifteen shells were thrown from the gun into the City of Charleston. This shelling was continued at intervals until the thirty-sixth round was fired, when the monster gun burst into fragments.

General Gillmore determined to compel the surrender. He moved forward all his approaches and advanced his guns, under protection of part of the fleet, occasionally firing upon the Confederates, and finally subjecting them on the 5th of September to a forty-two hours' bombardment, which did considerable damage.

Late on the 6th all was ready for an assault to be made the following morning upon Fort Wagner, but during the night the Confederates evacuated both the last-named fortification and Battery Gregg, which gratifying intelligence was communicated to the General-in-Chief as follows:

"DEPARTMENT OF THE SOUTH, HEADQUARTERS IN THE FIELD, September 7th, 1863.

"*Major-general H. W. Halleck, General-in-Chief.*

"GENERAL: I have the honor to report that Fort Wagner and Battery Gregg are ours. Last night our sappers mined the counterscarp of Fort Wagner on its sea point, unmasking all its guns, and an order was issued to carry the place by assault at 9 o'clock this morning, that being the hour of low tide.

"About 10 o'clock last night the enemy commenced evacuating the island, and all but seventy-five of them made their escape from Cumming's Point in small boats.

"Captured dispatches show that Fort Wagner was commanded by Colonel Keitt, of South Carolina, and garrisoned by 1,400 effective men, and Battery Gregg by between 100 and 200 men. Fort Wagner is a work of the most formidable kind. Its bombproof shelter, capable of containing 1,800 men, remains intact after the most terrific bombardment to which any work was ever subjected. We have captured 19 pieces of artillery and a large supply of excellent ammunition.

"The City and Harbor of Charleston are now completely covered by our guns.

"I have the honor to be, general, very respectfully, your obedient servant,

Q. A. GILLMORE,

"*Brigadier-general Commanding.*

The surrendered fort and battery were at once enlarged, and several earthworks were erected so as to command Fort Sumter as well as the City of Charleston, into which shells were so effectually thrown that much of the city had to be abandoned by its inhabitants.

SEPTEMBER, 1863.

On the night of the 7th of September the *Weehawken* was ordered to enter the channel between Fort Sumter and the Cumming's Point Battery, in order to see if the obstructions could be cleared, but in so doing she grounded, and was subjected to a severe fire from Forts Moultrie and Sumter, as well as from the Sullivan Island batteries. The *Weehawken* was struck 24 times, and fired in all 46 shells at Fort Sumter, besides 36 at Fort Moultrie and at Battery Bee. She had 3 men wounded, but caused the death of 16 and the wounding of 12 men by the explosion of a magazine at Fort Moultrie. The *Weehawken* was got afloat by the vessels of the squadron, led by the *New Ironsides*, upon which the admiral had raised his flag, all of which were in turn subjected to a severe battering by the Confederates.

Late on the 8th an unsuccessful attempt was made to capture Fort Sumter by a boat expedition in charge of Lieutenant-commander T. H. Stevens, of the *Patapsco*. The flotilla consisted of five divisions, of five and six boats each, commanded respectively by Lieutenant-commander E. P. Williams, Lieutenants Preston, Remey and Higginson, and Ensign Craven. A detachment of marines under Captain McCawley likewise formed part of the expedition, numbering in all about 400 men.

At about 10 o'clock in the evening the expedition reached the vicinity of Fort Sumter, and the crews of three of the boats scaled the ruins in expectation of completely surprising the garrison. They, however, counted without their host, for Major S. Elliott had received intimation of what was going on, and as the Federals advanced they were met by a perfect shower of musket-balls and hand-grenades from the garrison, as well as by the fire from neighboring batteries. The Federals were compelled to fall back to their boats, which had in the meantime been attacked and been made to suffer by Confederates on board of vessels, who captured many prisoners and colors, and prevented the escape of more than half the original number.

Nothing else of moment occurred in Charleston Harbor, aside from the continual and very destructive bombardment of Fort Sumter, until the 5th of the following month, when Lieutenant Glassell, with the cigar-shaped torpedo boat *David*

THE CITY OF CHARLESTON, S. C., FIRED BY EXPLOSIVE SHELLS FROM GENERAL GILLMORE'S GUNS IN FORT PUTNAM, JANUARY 5th, 1864.

FROM A SKETCH BY W. T. [illegible]

THE DISABLING AND CAPTURE OF [illegible] PASS, TEXAS, SEPTEMBER 8TH, 1863.

From a Sketch by an Officer.

made an attempt to blow up the *New Ironsides*, then watching the main ship-channel. The boat was hailed at a quarter past 9 o'clock in the evening, but failed to answer, and immediately discharged a torpedo, which, however, caused but little damage.

Exactly three weeks after the last-named attempt the Federals opened upon Fort Sumter from their batteries on Morris Island, in conjunction with a cross-fire from the heavy guns on board the *Lehigh* and *Patapsco*. On the 6th of December the *Weehawken* sank while attached to one of the mooring-buoys off Morris Island. This was owing to the bad trim in which she was left after the addition of quite a heavy weight of ammunition, and in consequence of which a large volume of water was admitted through the ports as well as under the turret. The *Weehawken* carried down with her 4 officers and 20 men before the proper assistance could reach the sinking vessel.

The operations in Charleston Harbor were, during the remainder of the year and throughout 1864, confined to an occasional firing upon one of the Confederate works, and to the enforcement of a rigid blockade of the harbor, during the observance of which several important blockade-runners were destroyed by the fleet. The Confederates made repeated attempts to blow up some of the blockading vessels; but, aside from the destruction of the *Housatonic* by a "fish torpedo boat" on the 19th of February, they were all unsuccessful.

The engineering ability displayed by the rival commanders, Beauregard, on the part of the defense, and Gillmore, in managing the operations of the besieging army, was unsurpassed by any engineering skill mentioned in the world's history. The heavy guns employed in the unsuccessful attempt to reduce the Confederate forts, and then the novel use of ironclads, and the planting of heavy batteries on swampy ground, had never before been witnessed. The peculiar construction of the battery known as the "Swamp Angel" was the work of Colonel E. W. Serrill, First New York Volunteers, assisted by Captain McKenna and Lieutenants Parsons and Edwards, who, under hot fire from the Confederate batteries, erected, in a swamp where an iron rod by its own weight would bury itself, this monster battery, which threw shells in the streets of Charleston, five miles distant. This triumph of engineering skill was variously called by the soldiers, "Swamp Angel," "Mud Lark" and "Marsh Croaker."

NOTE.—It is due to Mr W. T. Crane, who furnished the sketches from which our illustrations of the siege of the Charleston forts have been taken, that the following letter be here published:

"HEADQUARTERS DEPARTMENT OF THE SOUTH,
"MORRIS ISLAND, S. C., August 28th, 1863

"Having found it necessary to employ Mr. W. T. Crane to make sketches of the progressive demolition of Fort Sumter by our batteries, I most cheerfully bear testimony to the general accuracy of his delineations.

"Q. A. GILLMORE,
"*Brigadier-general Commanding.*"

GEORGE CROCKETT STRONG.

BORN at Stockbridge, Vt., in 1832. His father died when he was but eight years of age, and he was adopted by his uncle, A. S. Strong, of Easthampton, Mass., through whom he first entered Union College, and afterward the United States Military Academy at West Point. He graduated among the first five in the class, on the 30th of June, 1857; was appointed a brevet second lieutenant in the ordnance corps of the army, and given charge of the Bridesburg Arsenal, being thence transferred to Fortress Monroe and to Mount Vernon, Ala. He subsequently had charge of the Watervliet Arsenal at West Troy, N. Y., and upon the breaking out of the Civil War was placed on the staff of General McDowell as ordnance officer. In this capacity he distinguished himself at the first battle of Bull Run, and afterward served on the staff of General McClellan until September, 1861, when he was transferred to the staff of General Butler, then operating in the Department of the Gulf. He had, in 1859, been made a lieutenant in the Regular Army, and in October, 1861, was appointed assistant-adjutant-general of Volunteers, with the rank of major. He at once entered upon the organization of the New Orleans expedition, which he accompanied, and commanded the successful expedition from Ship Island to Biloxi, Miss., as well as the perilous adventure up the Tangipahoa River. Among the first to enter New Orleans, he shortly after became General Butler's chief of staff, but sickness soon compelled him to return North.

In November, 1862, he was appointed a brigadier-general of Volunteers, and in June, 1863, was assigned to command the brigade which, in the operations against Charleston, effected the landing on Morris Island, July 10th, 1863. General Strong led the party which captured eight Confederate batteries at the sea end of that island, as well as the ineffectual assault made on Fort Wagner the following morning. On July 18th his brigade led the second assault on that work, and it was while at its head, directing the movements of the troops, that he was so severely wounded as to have to be taken from the field. He died of lockjaw on the 30th of July, 1863, at the residence of his father-in-law, Mr. W. A. Budd, in New York City.

GEORGE CROCKETT STRONG.

CHARLES P. STONE.

CHARLES P. STONE.

BORN in Greenfield, Mass., in 1824; entered the United States Military Academy at West Point, 1841; and, having graduated in 1845, was commissioned brevet-second-lieutenant of ordnance; served through the Mexican War, and, for distinguished services, as well as for special gallantry at Molino del Rey, September 8th, and at Chapultepec, September 13th, 1847, received the brevets of first-lieutenant and of captain. Studied the great armies of Europe in 1848–49–50. In 1851 was placed in charge of the Ordnance Department of the Division of the Pacific. Selected the site and commenced the construction of Benicia Arsenal, California. Served in the Division of the Pacific until 1856, when he resigned his commission and entered civil life. Was appointed in 1857 chief of the scientific commission for the survey and exploration of Sonora, and in 1859 for Lower California, in which position he continued until called into the military service as Inspector-general of the District of Columbia, January 1st, 1861, and mustered into service January 2d, 1861, on special application of Lieutenant-general Scott.

He was the first man mustered into service for the defense of the national capital. He mixed, organized, drilled, and commanded all the Volunteer troops of the District of Columbia in the Winter of 1861—all the force which the Government had for maintaining the capital in its possession up to April 24th, 1861, when the National Guards of New York, Massachusetts, and Pennsylvania, began to arrive. Was commissioned colonel of the Fourteenth Infantry, May 14th, 1861, and brigadier-general of Volunteers, May 17th of the same year. Held command of all the outposts of Washington from April 10th, 1861, to June 7th, same year.

General Stone commanded the advance-guard in the passage of the Potomac for the capture of Alexandria, May 24th, 1861; and commanded at Alexandria, Va., during two days after its capture. Commanded the Rockville expedition, June–July, 1861. Joined General Patterson with his command, July 8th, 1861, and led the advance of Patterson's left column during his advance; commanded the rear-guard of General Patterson's army during his retreat to Harper's Ferry. In August, 1861, he was given command of a special corps of observation on the right flank of the Army of the Potomac. In October, 1861, a portion of his forces, under the command of Colonel Baker, became engaged in the disastrous combat of Ball's Bluff, in which, on the Federal side, 49 officers and soldiers were killed, 158 were wounded, and 714 were missing; of the latter, 710 were taken prisoners and 4 drowned. The enemy lost 36 killed, 117 wounded, and 1 missing, who was taken prisoner. For this result, greatly exaggerated and misrepresented in the newspapers of the day, General Stone, though not responsible for the disaster, was taken severely to account. In order to allay all possible clamor and determine the responsibility, he immediately proposed to General McClellan a court of inquiry, which, however, was deemed unnecessary, as was also the subsequent inquiry suggested by the House of Representatives.

In face of the blame apparently attached to General Stone throughout the country, McClellan not only deemed it just to retain him in his former command, but showed his full confidence in Stone's loyalty, ability, and earnestness of purpose, by increasing his force to 12,000 men. The Secretary of War, however, yielding to political pressure, ordered the arrest of General Stone, which took place at midnight, February 8th, 1862. It was especially ordered that he be allowed no communication with any person, and no reason was assigned for the arrest. Stone immediately demanded exhibition of charges and trial, but got no reply. He was hurried off to Fort Lafayette, and there held a close prisoner nearly two months, constantly demanding knowledge of any charges, and opportunity to meet them, but always without an answer. Then he was transferred to Fort Hamilton, where he was allowed air exercise and communication with his friends, but his demands for investigation and charges were disregarded. Finally, after more than six months of this extraordinary treatment, he was, on the 16th of August, 1862, fully released from arrest, without a charge, or even an allegation of wrong, having been made against him. In September, 1862, General McClellan applied to the War Secretary for General Stone's services in the Antietam campaign, but was refused. The following Winter, General Hooker applied for him as his chief of staff; General Stone accepted, but the War Department refused.

In May, 1863, General Stone was ordered on duty in the Department of the Gulf, then under the command of General Banks, and served before Port Hudson, where he was the senior officer named on the commission to receive the surrender of the place. He also commanded the forces sent from Port Hudson for the relief of Donaldsonville, when it was attacked by General Green's forces. In August, 1863, he was appointed, by General Banks, chief of the staff of the Department of the Gulf, and in that capacity he served faithfully and efficiently, taking part notably in the campaign of the Teche, and in the battles of Sabine Cross Roads and Pleasant Hill. He also served before Petersburg in 1864, where he contracted a malarious fever that compelled his retirement from the army.

In 1870 he entered the military service of the Khédive of Egypt as brigadier-general and chief of staff, when he organized the Egyptian Army on a footing of 60,000 men, with military schools and proper establishments; and organized and directed many expeditions into the Soudan and Central Africa. He was there promoted to the grade of lieutenant-general in 1873, and remained in that service until 1883, receiving high decorations* from the Khédive, the Sultan and the King of Italy. He was in attendance on the Khédive during the bombardment of Alexandria by the British fleet, in July, 1882, and was subsequently selected to command the military expedition against the

* Grand Officer, Order of Osmanieh; Grand Officer, Order of Medjidieh; Commander, Order of Crown of Italy; Knight, Star of Egypt.

Mahdi, in the Soudan, in October, 1882; but, as his estimates of the force necessary to accomplish the destruction of the pretender were regarded as too high by those then ruling the destinies of Egypt, and the proper amount of force was refused, he declined the mission, considering it worse than useless to attempt the work with only 10,000 men, while he deemed 27,000 necessary.

The fate of Colonel Hicks, who accepted the mission with 10,000 men, has since proved the justice and accuracy of General Stone's estimate.

General Stone is now (1885) Engineer-in-Chief engaged in erecting at Bedloe's Island, New York Harbor, the pedestal for the colossal statue of "Liberty Enlightening the World," a gift from the people of the Republic of France to the people of the United States of America.

He holds (1885) the position of Grand Marshal of the Grand Army of the Republic in the City of New York. He is an Honorary Corresponding Member of the Royal Geographical Society of London, and of the Imperial and Royal Geographical Society of Vienna; Honorary Member of the Geographical Societies of Rome, of Lisbon, and of Eastern Switzerland; Academician of the Royal San Fernando Academy of Fine Arts, of Madrid, etc., etc.

THE FLORIDA, TEXAS AND RED RIVER EXPEDITIONS.

On the 22d of December, 1863, General Gillmore was advised that in consequence of there being no prospect of the early resumption of active operations in the vicinity of Charleston, he was free to organize such expeditions in the Department as Admiral Dahlgren and himself might decide upon. Availing of this discretion, and acting under the additional authority given him one month later, Gillmore made arrangements for the occupation of the St. John's River, and for the establishment of permanent military depots throughout Florida.

By the 5th of February an expedition was organized and placed in command of General Truman Seymour. It consisted of twelve regiments, who were the next day embarked at Hilton Head upon twenty steamers and eight schooners, and proceeded down the coast under convoy of the gunboat *Norwich*, landing at Jacksonville late on the 7th, without much opposition. General Seymour was accompanied by Major John Hay, and was soon followed by General Gillmore.

February, 1864.

During the afternoon of the next day, Seymour commenced his march toward the interior. His force was divided into three columns, commanded respectively by Colonel Seammon, who took the road upon the extreme right; Colonel J. R. Hawley, who occupied the one on the extreme left; and Colonel A. O. Barton, who took the main road in the centre of the advancing force. The three columns proceeded in the direction of Baldwin, uniting later on upon the line of the railroad, and during the ensuing night made a dash upon a Confederate camp, which they surprised, and where they took 4 guns, several prisoners and a quantity of equipage and stores.

At Baldwin, eighteen miles from Jacksonville, they captured, early on the 9th, one 3-inch rifled cannon, several cars, and property estimated worth about five hundred thousand dollars. Colonel Guy V. Henry proceeded thence, with an advance-guard, to the south fork of the St. Mary's River, in order to ascertain the exact position of the enemy, and found a small force of Confederates defending it. A skirmish followed, in which the Federals had 4 killed and 13 wounded, the Confederates losing about as many. Late in the afternoon, the Federals reached the village of Sanderson, located about forty miles west of Jacksonville, which was found abandoned, and where they rested until the following day.

It was soon ascertained that General Joseph Finnegan, who commanded the Confederate troops in the district, had withdrawn to Lake City, and Colonel Henry was ordered to pursue him; but before reaching the last-named place he was recalled, and directed to report at Sanderson.

General Gillmore returned to Hilton Head on the 15th, after ordering the concentration of troops at Baldwin, and advising Seymour not to proceed further in the interior. On the 18th Seymour took upon himself the responsibility of advancing toward the Suwanee River, and notified General Gillmore of his intended movements. The latter protested against the advance, and sent his chief of staff, General Turner, with a written message to that effect; but when Turner reached Jacksonville, on the 20th, he found to his surprise that the Federals had marched that morning sixteen miles beyond Barber's Station, and that they were already engaged with the Confederates, who had advanced from Lake City to Olustee.

The Federals had been moved forward in three columns, commanded, as before, by Colonels Seammon, Hawley, and Barton; and at about 2 o'clock in the afternoon, the Seventh Connecticut and Colonel Henry's cavalry, which were in the advance under Colonel Hawley, came upon the Confederate pickets about three miles east of the Olustee Station. Active skirmishing followed, but it soon became evident, from the sudden attacks to which the Federals were on all sides subjected, that General Finnegan had disposed quite a large force in ambush through both the swampy ground and the surrounding forest.

The Federals were soon forced into a series of severe hand-to-hand encounters, which for a while bid fair to result in the extermination of the whole of Seymour's force. This was alone prevented by the prompt arrival of Colonel Abbott's Seventh New Hampshire, accompanied by Elder's, Langdon's, and Hamilton's batteries, which respectively occupied the right, left and centre, and all of which opened with canister at short range.

Additional Confederate troops soon reached the scene, and the engagement then developed into a battle which raged furiously until dusk. The Eighth United States Colored Regiment bravely maintained its ground at the outset in support of Colonel Abbott's force, until its commander, Colonel Fribley, fell mortally wounded, when it retired in a disorderly state, giving place to a part of Colonel Barton's force. The whole of the latter's brigade finally became engaged, and was followed in turn by Colonel Montgomery's colored troops. These fought admirably, and although losing successively all their leading officers, maintained their ground so well in the immediate front that a determined charge on part of the enemy was arrested, and Seymour was meanwhile enabled to reorganize his forces for a renewal of the conflict.

Finally, after battling successfully against great odds, and finding his troops completely exhausted by the day's work, Seymour reluctantly ordered a retreat, which was conducted in successive lines of battle until it was found that the Confederates made no efforts to follow.

Seymour's loss was nearly 1,250 killed, wounded, and missing, or about twice that sustained by the Confederates. A temporary halt was made at Sanderson, and after destroying nearly all of his stores in order to prevent their falling into the hands of the enemy, Seymour took his force to Jacksonville, whence a number of raids were afterward made in different directions throughout the Department.

BANKS'S ARMY CROSSING VERMILION BAYOU, OCTOBER 10TH, 1863.
From a Sketch by C. E. F. Bonwill.

The Texas and the Red River expeditions were determined upon shortly after the surrender of Vicksburg and of Port Hudson. Their organization was left entirely to General Banks, who, with the assistance of Admiral Farragut, completed his arrangements on the 4th of September, 1863, for an important demonstration by way of the Sabine Pass.

To Major-general W. B. Franklin was given command of the land forces, numbering about 4,000 men, while the naval force was placed in charge of Lieutenant Frederick Crocker, who made his own gunboat *Clifton* the flagship, and who was accompanied by the *Sachem*, Lieutenant Amos Johnson; the *Granite City*, Acting Master C. W. Lamson; and the *Arizona*, Acting Master H. Tibbets.

The expedition sailed from New Orleans, September 5th, and two days later arrived off Sabine Pass, crossing the bar early on the 8th. Late in the afternoon the gunboats *Clifton*, *Sachem* and *Arizona* moved up the eastern channel to attack the strong earthworks defending the Pass, while the *Granite City* proceeded along the western channel to protect the landing of a division of troops under General Weitzel.

The attack of the gunboats was not responded to until they were abreast of the earthworks, when a fire from eight guns was opened fiercely upon them. A few moments later both the *Clifton* and *Sachem* were struck in their boilers, and immediately became so enveloped in steam that they got aground, and had to hoist a white flag in token of surrender. The *Arizona* also grounded, but was finally got off, and with the *Granite City* recrossed the bar by order of General Franklin, who with his diminished force abandoned all further attack, and took the expedition to Brashear City, whence it proceeded to New Orleans on the 11th.

Pass were successively occupied by the troops under General T. E. G. Ransom, the last-named point being taken by assault between the 17th and 18th of November, after a spirited contest, in which the Confederates lost about one hundred prisoners and three guns.

Corpus Christi, at the southern end of Mustang Island, was likewise occupied, and on the 19th, General C. C. Washburne moved upon Pass Cavallo, defended by an extensive work called Fort Esperanza, then garrisoned by about 2,000 men. The fort was immediately invested, and several important skirmishes took place up to the 30th, when the Confederates blew up the magazine and retreated to the mainland.

receive such additional forces as might be spared from Grant's army to aid him in the proposed operations.

The objective point was the town of Shreveport, close by the line separating Texas from Louisiana. Preparations were to be hastened so as to take advantage of such a rise in the Red River as would permit the passage of both the gunboats and the heavy transports over the falls above Alexandria, and also in order to enable the troops to take part in the movements which were to follow throughout the country east of the Mississippi.

The principal force of the Confederates was at Shreveport, under General Richard Taylor. General Price's line extended from Monroe, in Louisiana, through Camden to Arkadelphia in Arkansas, whence it could check any possible movement of Steele in a southernly direction, while General Morton's force lined the country to the southwest from Monroe to the Red River, and a division under General Walker covered the Red River and the Atchafalaya from Fort de Russy to Opelousas. General Magruder's large force, estimated at about 15,000 men, was so disposed as to protect both Houston and Galveston.

A CHARACTERISTIC ARMY SCENE.—WEIGHING RATIONS PREPARATORY TO A CONTEMPLATED MOVEMENT.
FROM A SKETCH BY EDWIN FORBES.

Another expedition was soon after organized, and sailed from New Orleans, on the 26th of October, directly for the Rio Grande. It consisted of 3,500 men, under command of Major-general Napoleon J. T. Dana, and was accompanied by General Banks, as well as by the three gunboats *Monongahela*, *Owasco*, and *Virginia*, in charge of Captain James H. Strong.

After being scattered by quite a severe gale, the fleet arrived off Brazos Santiago, and the latter point was occupied on the 2d of November. A skirmish followed with the Confederate cavalry stationed in the immediate vicinity, and the Federals succeeded in driving the Confederates beyond Brownsville, which was taken possession of on the 6th. Point Isabel, Mustang Island and Aransas

The Federals took possession of the fort and of the whole pass guarding the entrance to Matagorda Bay, the light-draught gunboats *Estrella* and the *Granite City* being afterward sent inside the peninsula.

An important foothold having thus been obtained in Texas, General Banks left General Dana to guard the Rio Grande, and returned to New Orleans in order to perfect plans for the repossession of Galveston, as well as of the works held by the Confederates at the mouth of the Brazos River. While completing his arrangements for another expedition, Banks received a dispatch from General Halleck informing him that it had been decided to make a joint land and naval demonstration against Texas by way of the Red River, and that he would

The months of January and February, 1864, were consumed in preparing for the contemplated movement. General Sherman left his army at Canton on the 28th of the last-named month, and after stopping at Vicksburg, proceeded to New Orleans, where a conference was held with General Banks

FIVE LOCOMOTIVES [illegible] OF COLONEL [illegible] McPHERSON'S STAFF

From a Sketch by [illegible]

and Admiral Porter. It was agreed between them that while General Steele's force was advancing from Little Rock on either Shreveport or Natchitoches, Banks would proceed from Franklin by way of Opelousas to Alexandria, which latter place it was believed could be reached by the 17th of March, and where he would be met by Porter's fleet as well as by the troops called for from the Army of the Tennessee.

Sherman returned to Vicksburg on the 6th of March, and at once ordered Brigadier-general Andrew J. Smith to proceed up the river, on transports, with about 7,500 men taken from the First and Third Divisions of Hurlbut's Sixteenth Corps, and about 2,500 men taken from the First and Fourth Divisions of McPherson's Seventeenth Army Corps.

March 9, 1864

On the 17th, Smith reached the mouth of the Red River, and there met Admiral Porter, who had with him the most formidable fleet ever seen in Western waters. This consisted of the following vessels:

Essex, Commander Robert Townsend.
Eastport, Lieutenant-commander S. L. Phelps.
Black Hawk, Lieutenant-commander K. R. Breese.
Lafayette, Lieutenant commander J. P. Foster.
Benton, Lieutenant-commander J. A. Greer.
Louisville, Lieutenant-commander E. K. Owen.
Carondelet, Lieutenant commander J. G. Mitchell.
Osage, Lieutenant commander T. O. Selfridge.
Ouachita, Lieutenant Commander Byron Wilson.
Lexington, Lieutenant G. M. Bache.
Chillicothe, Lieutenant S. P. Couthouy.
Pittsburg, Lieutenant W. R. Hoel.
Mound City, Lieutenant A. R. Langthorne.
Neosho, Lieutenant Samuel Howard.
Ozark, Lieutenant G. W. Browne.
Fort Hindman, Lieutenant John Pearce.
Cricket, Master H. H. Gorringe.
Gazelle, Master Charles Thatcher.

Early on the 12th of March the fleet was divided into two squadrons. One, accompanied by Admiral Porter, and consisting of the *Benton*, *Pittsburg*, *Louisville*, *Carondelet*, *Gazelle*, *Chillicothe*, *Lexington*, *Ouachita*, and *Mound City*, proceeded up the Atchafalaya, while the other, in charge of Lieutenant-commander Phelps, moved up the Red River.

After removing the obstructions in the channel, the troops were enabled to land at Simmesport on the 13th, compelling the retirement of the Confederates within Fort de Russy, which latter was assaulted the following day by both the land and naval forces, and captured after a short though quite stubborn resistance of the garrison, then under General Dick Taylor. The Federal loss was 4 killed and 30 wounded; that of the Confederates being but 5 killed and 4 wounded, in addition to 224 prisoners, and a large quantity of stores, ammunition and small arms.

After destroying the Confederate works, the fleet was ordered to proceed to Alexandria. The advance reached the last-named place and occupied it late on the 15th, after a brief resistance, the remaining vessels of the fleet coming up the day following with Admiral Porter and about 7,500 of Smith's troops.

On the 19th, General Charles P. Stone, chief of Banks's staff, arrived with a division of cavalry under General A. P. Lee, and reported that Banks was then at Opelousas. Banks's forces had been placed in charge of General W. B. Franklin, who had not received his orders until the 10th, too late to reach Alexandria by the 17th, as originally intended. He was able to leave the Teche only on the 13th, and the last of his troops reached Natchitoches between the 2d and 3d of April, after engaging in several skirmishes with the Confederates.

April, 1864

The latter had meanwhile been driven back by Smith's troops under Brigadier-general John A. Mower, who had encountered serious opposition throughout the entire route, but more particularly at Henderson's Hill, where the Confederates were surprized and lost some 250 prisoners, 200 horses and several guns.

As the river was too low to admit of the ready passage of the larger vessels, Smith's force was mainly conveyed by land, and on the 3d of April it reached Grand Ecore, situated about four miles to the north of Natchitoches. Leaving temporarily both Lieutenant-commander Phelps and General T. Kilby Smith at Grand Ecore with about 2,000 men to protect the movements of the transports, Admiral Porter and General A. J. Smith went ahead on the 7th with the light-draught gunboats *Cricket*, *Osage*, *Chillicothe*, *Hindman*, *Neosho*, *Lexington*, and a few other vessels. Their aim was to reach Loggy Bayou, opposite the Springfield Landing, on the 10th, at about the time it was supposed Banks would be there by way of Pleasant Hill and Mansfield.

General Franklin, in charge of Banks's force, advanced from Natchitoches, preceded by General Lee's cavalry, which latter was ordered to attack the Confederates wherever found, without, however, bringing on a general engagement. General Lee maintained a constant skirmish with the enemy until when about two miles beyond Pleasant Hill, where the main body of the Confederate cavalry, under General Thomas Green, was met by the brigade under Colonel H. Robinson. After a two-hours' fight Green was compelled to fall back on St. Patrick's Bayou (Bayou de Paul) where a much superior force of Confederate infantry and artillery was found to be stationed.

Colonel Robinson decided to await reinforcements, and halted for the night. Upon the arrival of Colonel Landrum's brigade, belonging to the Fourth Division of the Thirteenth Corps, he moved upon the Confederates the next afternoon, and drove them a distance of seven miles into the woods, close by Sabine Cross Roads. This was about three and a half miles south of Mansfield, and the main Confederate army, under General Dick Taylor, was found partly concealed in the dense woods bordering the Shreveport Road.

Some heavy skirmishing followed, but no decided engagement was developed until late in the afternoon of the 8th, after General Ransom had come up with the remaining brigade of the Fourth Division of the Thirteenth Corps, and had taken position upon Landrum's extreme left. The Federal skirmishers were then being driven in by the heavy Confederate lines, under Generals Taylor, Green, Mouton, and Kirby Smith, who, shortly after four o'clock, fiercely assaulted the Federals along their entire front.

Their attack was soon directed mainly upon the Federal right and centre, and to meet this the left had necessarily to be weakened. This was observed by the Confederates, who strengthened their right, and then fell heavily upon Banks's extreme left, which was driven back with great losses in killed and wounded, and was compelled to abandon three of the guns belonging to Nims's battery, nearly every horse belonging to which had been shot down early in the action.

BATTLE OF GRAND COTEAU, LA., NOVEMBER 3d, 1863.—FURIOUS ATTACK OF THE SIXTIETH INDIANA REGIMENT, COLONEL OWENS.
From a Sketch by C. E. H. Bonwill.

CAPTURE OF [illegible] FORCES UNDER GENERAL ANDREW JACKSON SMITH.

The Federal centre and extreme right were next heavily assaulted, but managed to hold their ground well in face of the superior forces hurled against them, until General Cameron's brigade of Indiana troops belonging to the Third Division of the Thirteenth Corps reached the field and advanced to the front. With the latter accession to their forces, the battle raged more furiously than ever, but notwithstanding the great encouragement afforded the troops by the presence of General Franklin and of his staff along the advanced lines, the Federals were finally compelled to retire.

They fell back slowly and in comparative good order until their line of baggage-trains was reached, the brigade, under Colonel Lewis Benedict, being placed to the extreme left of General Dwight's First Brigade, which stood across the road, while the Second Brigade, under General McMillan, was held at a close distance in reserve. The One Hundred and Sixty-second was driven back upon the main body, and General Dwight's force was next assailed so vigorously that McMillan's reserves had to be called up. The entire line was soon engaged, and efforts were repeatedly made to flank Emory's force, but unavailingly. For nearly one and a half hours the ground was bitterly contested at all points, and at about eight o'clock a final charge was made by the One Hundred and Sixty-second and the One Hundred and Seventy-third New York Regiments, which brought the fight to an end.

METROPOLITAN SANITARY FAIR—GENERAL BURNSIDE MAKING PURCHASES

General Emory's division thus actually saved the army from a terrible disaster, which might well have extended to that part of the navy then close by on the river. In view of the rapid falling of the river it was thought advisable to fall back, fifteen miles in the rear, to Pleasant Hill, which was done very quietly just before midnight, while the Confederates were being withdrawn in the direction of Mansfield.

The day's engagements resulted in a loss on each side of about 3,000, killed, wounded and missing. The list of killed embraced the names of General Mouton, C.S.A., Colonel Vance, of the Ninety-sixth Ohio, Lieutenant-colonel Webb, of the Seventy-seventh Ohio, and Captain Dickey of General Ransom's staff, among the wounded being Generals Franklin and Ransom and Colonel Robinson. The Federals lost in addition 30 field-pieces and howitzers and over 200 wagons.

The troops were joined by General A. J. Smith's force at Pleasant Hill, and early on the 9th, lines were formed to meet the possible immediate advance of the Confederates.

Upon hearing of the retreat, the Confederates pursued with cavalry, which did not, however, meet Emory's pickets until close by Pleasant Hill, where an important skirmish took place shortly before one o'clock in the afternoon. A large force of the Confederates appeared at about half-past four o'clock and opened upon General Emory's extreme right as a preliminary to the attack along the whole line which soon followed the first assault.

when further attempts on the part of the Confederates to gain the Federal rear could no longer be successfully checked by Lee's cavalry, and a panic seized the troops. They fled through the mass of wagons and lines of mules which crowded the narrow road, and all efforts on the part of General Banks himself and of the other officers to stop them proved unavailing.

The Confederates pursued the fast-retreating troops about two and a half miles, when they came upon General W. H. Emory's First Division of the Nineteenth Corps, which Franklin had ordered to form in line of battle at a place called Pleasant Grove.

Colonel Kinsey had the One Hundred and Sixty-second New York Regiment, belonging to the Third Brigade, deployed as skirmishers, the remainder of

The Confederates had been strengthened by the addition of Churchill's division, consisting mainly of Arkansas troops. Those were placed upon the extreme right of the advancing columns, and next to these came the troops under Generals Walker, Polignac (late Mouton's), and Green, the last-named occupying the extreme left. To these were opposed McMillan's brigade upon the extreme Federal right, and next to it came Dwight's brigade, slightly in advance of Benedict's, which occupied the extreme left. The artillery was distributed in the immediate rear, four pieces being placed upon an eminence commanding the left of the road, close by Colonel Benedict's position. General Smith's

JOSEPH E. BROWN.

BATTLE OF WILSON'S PLANTATION, LA., BETWEEN

THE BATTLE OF PLEASANT HILL, LA., BETWEEN GENERAL BANKS

[illegible] BROWN.

BATTLE OF WILSON'S PLANTATION, LA., BETWEEN GENERAL LEE AND GENERAL GREEN, APRIL 7TH, 1864.

WILLIAM G. BROWNLOW.

THE BATTLE OF PLEASANT HILL, LA., BETWEEN GENERAL BANKS AND THE CONFEDERATE GENERAL DICK TAYLOR, APRIL 9TH, 1864.
[illegible]

BANKS'S ARMY, IN THE ADVANCE ON SHREVEPORT, CROSSING CANE RIVER, LA., MARCH 31st, 1864.—From a Sketch by C. E. H. Bonwill.

troops, under command of General Mower, were massed in two lines of battle, fifty yards apart, and held in reserve a short distance off, while Ransom's disordered troops were directed to proceed toward Grand Ecore.

When ready for the grand assault, the Confederates burst suddenly from the woods and advanced on all sides at the double-quick, falling most heavily upon the Thirtieth Maine, the One Hundred and Sixty-second, the One Hundred and Sixty-fifth, and the One Hundred and Seventy-third New York Regiments, which formed Benedict's brigade. The wildly into the opening, where they were unexpectedly met by General Smith's reserve. The latter opened upon the Confederates from all of their guns, and soon threw their ranks into confusion. This was followed immediately by a counter-charge of the infantry, by which the Confederates were rapidly driven back into the woods with great losses in killed, wounded and prisoners. The Confederates were pursued until dark, and the Federals recaptured the four guns previously lost on Benedict's left, as well as two of the guns that had been taken from Nims's battery.

many difficulties in navigating through the crooked and narrow channel, and had overcome the numerous obstructions lining the one hundred and ten miles they had sailed over; but when they reached the Landing they found the most formidable of all obstructions, and a decided check to all further progress, in the shape of a large steamer sunk across the river. They were deliberating as to the best means for its removal when they were notified of the retreat of the army, and were at the same time ordered by Banks to return promptly to Grand Ecore. On the 11th they reached Coushatta

CONFEDERATE ATTACK ON GENERAL LEE'S WAGON TRAIN AT MANSFIELD, LA., APRIL 8TH, 1864.

FROM A SKETCH BY C. E. F. BOSWELL.

utter poured into the enemy's ranks volley after volley at close quarters, notably from the guns they had judiciously placed upon a neighboring elevation, and fought with a bravery rarely equaled against the almost overwhelming numbers against them; but after experiencing heavy losses, and having lost their commander, Colonel Benedict, who was killed while trying to rally his men for a charge, they retreated, to guard against a flank movement, being obliged in this movement to abandon four of their guns.

Emory's right and centre were next most fiercely engaged, and after a gallant fight were compelled to fall back close by the Sixteenth Corps, which was just in rear of the crest. This admitted of the free passage of the assailants, who rushed

The casualties were very heavy on both sides, the official report showing an increased total on each side of nearly 4,000 for all the engagements of the 7th, 8th and 9th of April.

The decided success obtained by the Federals at the last-named battle induced Banks to order for the next day a renewed advance in the direction of Shreveport; but at a conference of officers held in the evening it was deemed best to retire to Grand Ecore, which place was reached on the 11th, and where a line of extensive earthworks was at once thrown up.

The naval force and the transports had meantime beaten their way up the Red River, and reached Springfield Landing late on the 10th. Admiral Porter and General Kilby Smith had encountered

(Coushatta) Chute, at which place they were subjected, by the sharpshooters and other bodies of Confederates lining the banks, to the first of a series of attacks which were to be kept up all the way to their destination.

At Coushatta (Coushatta) the boats received the fire of General Liddell's and Colonel Harrison's forces, numbering together nearly 2,500 men, from both the high northern and southern banks; but although the Confederates were to a great extent enabled with impunity to fire down upon the decks, the protection afforded by a judicious arrangement of bales of hay, of mattresses, boxes and other articles covering the fire of rifled cannon, rendered the losses on board the vessels a comparatively small one.

The following day was to witness a still more important attack. After Admiral Porter had gone ahead with several of the vessels, the gunboat *Osage* and the transport *Alice Vivian* got aground just as the transport *Hastings* was about running into the bank for repairs. Seeing this, General Thomas Green, with about 2,000 men and 4 guns, suddenly opened upon the vessels. A severe fire was exchanged for two hours, and resulted in the withdrawal of the Confederates, who suffered great losses, especially from two 13-inch Rodman guns on board the *Emerald*, and from the four single guns which had been placed upon the decks of the *Rob Roy*. The canister shot proved so destructive that the Confederates were reported to have lost as many as 700 in killed alone, the latter including General Green, whose head was blown off by a shell early in the action.

Further attacks were made, but none of them were of sufficient consequence to materially delay the progress of the vessels, which reached Grand Ecore on the 14th and 15th. Lieutenant-commander Phelps had already moved most of his vessels over the bar, and these were followed shortly after by the division which had been left in charge of Lieutenant-commander Selfridge, which likewise moved toward Alexandria.

While on its way down, the *Eastport* was sunk by a torpedo, but she was raised on the 21st with the aid of two pump-boats, and managed to go a distance of about twenty miles. She grounded several times afterward, and was on each occasion floated off, until the 26th, when her condition became hopeless. Her crew was then transferred to Lieutenant Pearce's vessel, the *Fort Hindman*, and the *Eastport* was fired and abandoned.

April, 1864.

As the remaining vessels were about proceeding down the river, they were opened upon by about 1,200 Confederates, who rushed forward to seize the *Cricket*, then lying close to the bank. A steady fire of grape and canister, however, prevented their capture, and the boats met with no further molestation until they had reached a point about five miles above the mouth of Cane River, when the *Cricket*, in the advance, was opened upon from 18 guns mounted upon the right bank.

Almost every shot went through her, and at the second fire her decks were almost cleared by the explosion of a shell; but Porter ordered her to run the battery, which she did successfully, after receiving in all 38 shots, and losing half her crew. She soon came upon the *Osage* and *Neosho*, which were found engaging another battery of the enemy, and was shortly after followed by the *Fort Hindman* and the *Juliet*, both which successfully passed the Cane Creek battery during the ensuing night, the pump-boat *Champion* having alone been destroyed.

The army left Grand Ecore on the 22d, after engaging in a number of skirmishes during the encampment at that place, and early on the 23d the advance cavalry under General Arnold, accompanied by Captain Classon's artillery, engaged a strong Confederate force, led by General Bee, at Monet's Bluff, on the Cane River. A severe encounter of several hours' duration followed, in which the main body took part, and in which Colonel Fessenden was wounded. It resulted in the defeat of the enemy, and the Bluff was left in possession of the Federals, whose rear-guard had the same morning defeated a party of Confederates after a three-hours' fight near a place called Cloutierville, located on the same river.

On the 26th the army reached Alexandria, where Banks found General Hunter with orders from General Grant to close up the campaign as speedily as possible, for Sherman was anxious to have all the troops he could get together for his intended Eastern operations. It was, however, found impossible to comply at once with Grant's orders, as the river had fallen so much that the vessels could not get below the rapids.

There seemed to be no way out of the difficulty until Lieutenant-colonel Joseph Bailey, of the Fourth Wisconsin Volunteers, then acting chief engineer of Franklin's Nineteenth Corps, was allowed to enter upon the construction of a large dam, which was completed on Sunday, the 8th of May, when the *Osage*, *Neosho* and *Fort Hindman* went safely through. These were followed by the *Lexington*, and on the 11th and 12th the water was high enough to admit of the passage of the *Carondelet*, *Mound City*, *Pittsburg*, *Ozark*, *Louisville*, *Chillicothe* and other vessels.

May, 1864.

For the invaluable services which Lieutenant-colonel Bailey thus rendered the expedition, he received the thanks of Congress, and was given the commission of brigadier-general of Volunteers.

The Confederates had in the meantime proceeded below Alexandria, and were once more subjecting the vessels to continued attacks from the opposite banks. With the exception of the loss of the light-draught gunboats *Covington* and *Signal*, which were attacked by a very large force of Confederates and had to be surrendered to them, with the transport *Warner*, which they were convoying, no serious loss was experienced by the fleet.

While at Alexandria the army had been strengthened by General John A. McClernand's force, brought from Matagorda Bay, where General Fitz Henry Warren remained in command.

On the 14th of May the army left Alexandria for Simmesport, where it arrived two days later, and on the 20th it crossed the Atchafalaya upon a bridge which had been hurriedly constructed by lashing transport steamers together. Morganzia Bend was reached on the 21st, the entire march having been completed without meeting any serious opposition, except at Mansura, close by Marksville, and at the Yellow Bayou, from both of which places the Confederate attacks were repulsed with small loss.

On the 20th, General Edward R. S. Canby relieved General Banks, who at once proceeded to New Orleans, and General A. J. Smith's force embarked for Memphis, which it reached after engaging and driving back into the interior a large party of the enemy found located near Columbia.

Admiral Porter descended the Red River and re-entered the Mississippi, where he remained until relieved during the ensuing Summer, the command first devolving upon Captain Pennock, and being afterward given to acting Rear-admiral S. P. Lee, who retained it until the Mississippi Squadron was dissolved, on the 14th of August, 1865.

General Steele had remained at Little Rock and in its immediate vicinity from the time of its capture by him, on the 10th of September, 1863, after a series of engagements, which had reduced his army from 12,000 to about 7,000 effective men. This was, however, mainly the result of sickness arising from the swampy nature of the ground through which the march was made, from the time Steele was ordered to Helena during the previous July. The Federal forces in the district led by Generals Davidson, True, Brown, Blunt, and Colonel Clayton, were nevertheless able to cope successfully with the large bodies of troops raiding the country, under such men as Price, Marmaduke, Holmes, Quantrell, Shelby and Coffee, and had before the middle of the ensuing October occupied Brownsville, Fort Smith, Pine Bluff and Arrow Rock.

In accordance with General Grant's instructions, Steele, commanding the Seventh Army Corps, had moved with his 7,000 infantry and 3,000 cavalry, under General Carr, from Little Rock, Ark., on the 23d of March, 1864, for Arkadelphia, where General Thayer was to join him with 5,000 men from Fort Smith. Steele reached his destination after engaging in a number of skirmishes with the Confederates, whose large cavalry detachments, under Generals Marmaduke and Cabell, were raiding the country in all directions, and remained at Arkadelphia two days, waiting for Thayer, who had been detained on the way by several important encounters into which the latter's force had been drawn, and which could not unite with Steele until after the latter had started in the direction of Washington. The most important engagements fought by Steele took place on the 10th of April, at Prairie d'Anne, where General Price's force was badly defeated, after a series of encounters extending over two entire days.

April, 1864.

The news of the Sabine Cross Roads disaster soon reached Steele, and since it had become impossible

CITY OF MATAMORAS, MEXICO, OPPOSITE BROWNSVILLE, TEXAS.

From a Sketch by L. Avent.

to reach Shreveport, he determined to move upon Camden, which latter place was also the objective point of Colonel Powell Clayton, then advancing with a small force taken from Pine Bluffs.

The Confederate General Fagan succeeded in drawing the Federals into many engagements, but they nevertheless reached Camden on the 15th. Steele remained there, however, only a short time, for it was learned that the Confederates had been very strongly reinforced by General E. Kirby Smith, and were making preparations to attack Little Rock.

Late on the 26th of April, Steele crossed the Washita and commenced a retreat, which was, however, checked four days later by Smith's force at Jenkins's (Jenkinson's) Ferry, just as fully one-half of the Federal force had passed the Sabine River.

The Confederates were led by Generals Smith, Price, Walker, Churchill and others. They first attacked the Federal rear, covered by the Thirty-third Iowa, and pressed it back, as they did also the Ninth Wisconsin, the Twenty-ninth Iowa, and the Fiftieth Indiana, which had been successively called up to assist the first-named. The attack took such proportions that the remaining troops were hurried back from the opposite side of the river. After an engagement of several hours' duration, in which the Confederates made unavailing efforts to flank the Federals, led by Generals Rice, Salomon, Thayer, Ingleman, and Colonel Benton, and during which charge after charge was made and repulsed, General Smith's force was driven away, and Steele was enabled to continue his march on Little Rock, which he reached on the 2d of the following month. The

MAY, 1864.

Federal loss was reported at 700 killed and wounded, that sustained by the Confederates being fully three times greater.

Seven days after his return to Little Rock, the following address was issued:

"HEADQUARTERS DEPARTMENT OF ARKANSAS,
"LITTLE ROCK, May 9th.

"To you troops of the Seventh Army Corps, who participated in the recent campaign designed to co-operate with General Banks's movement against Shreveport, the major-general commanding tenders his earnest and grateful thanks. Although you were compelled to fall back without seeing the main object of the expedition accomplished, you will have the satisfaction of knowing that you have beaten the enemy wherever he has met you in force, and extricated yourselves from the perilous position in which you were placed by the reverses of the co-operating column. These let loose upon you a superior force of the enemy, under one of their best generals, causing the loss of your trains and the total interruption of your communications, rendering it impossible for you to obtain supplies. You have fallen back over rivers and swamps while pressed by a superior force of the enemy. This you have done successfully, punishing the enemy severely at the same time.

The patience with which you have endured hardships and privations, and your heroic conduct on the battlefield have been brought to the notice of the Government, and will furnish a page in the history of this war in which you may well be proud.

"F. STEELE, *Major-general Commanding.*"

RAIDS IN MISSISSIPPI, TENNESSEE AND KENTUCKY.

GENERAL SHERMAN remained in Northern Alabama (Vol II., page 163) with his command stationed at different parts along the line of the Memphis and Charleston Railway, between Huntsville and Scottsboro', until late in January, 1864.

JANUARY, 1864.

He was then ordered to proceed to Vicksburg for the purpose of organizing expeditions whose first duty would be the destruction of the railroads at and about Meridian, in conjunction with another force operating directly from Memphis against the line of the Mobile and Ohio Railway.

To Brigadier-general William Sooy Smith was given the command of all the cavalry, and with the latter he was ordered to advance, on the 1st of February, from Memphis and through Pontotoc, Okolona, and Columbus to Meridian, while at the same time endeavoring, whenever possible, to anticipate and check the depredations of the Confederate General Forrest, who had entered upon an extensive raid through Northern Mississippi and Southern Tennessee. Demonstrations were meanwhile to be made by Brigadier-general Hawkins in the rear of Vicksburg, toward the Big Black River, and possibly by a joint land and naval expedition, under both Colonel Coates and Lieutenant-commander Owen, along the Yazoo and its tributaries.

Sherman left Vicksburg on the 3d of February,

FEBRUARY, 1864.

with a force made up of the divisions of Generals Crocker and Leggett, belonging to McPherson's Seventeenth Corps, and of the divisions of Generals Veatch and A. J. Smith, belonging to Hurlbut's Sixteenth Corps, to which were added a brigade of infantry under Colonel Chambers, a brigade and a battalion of cavalry under E. F. Winslow and Captain Foster, besides two pioneer corps and seven batteries of artillery. This force moved in two columns, Hurlbut's by the railway, and McPherson's by way of Messenger's. Sherman accompanied the last-named column.

The Big Black River was crossed, and after engaging in almost a continual skirmish from the time Hurlbut reached Joe Davis's plantation, and McPherson passed Champion Hills, they entered Jackson late on the 5th. The following day the united columns, led by McPherson, crossed the Pearl River upon pontoons which had been abandoned by the Confederates when Jackson was occupied, and marched successively through Brandon and Morton, at which latter place McPherson's force remained to destroy the railroads in the vicinity, and Hurlbut took the lead.

The army then marched through Hillsboro' and Decatur, and after completing a new bridge over the Oktibbeha River to replace the former one, which had but recently been burned by the retreating Confederates, Meridian was occupied late in the afternoon of the 14th. Sherman's force had thus marched 150 miles in eleven days without meeting much opposition from the 9,000 infantry under Generals Polk, French, and Loring, or the 4,000 cavalry led by Generals Adams, Lee and Ferguson, all which evacuated Meridian upon the approach of the Federals.

It was found impossible to make a judicious pursuit of the Confederates upon their retreat across the Tombigbee River, and the army therefore rested on the 15th, when the following order was issued:

"HEADQUARTERS DEPARTMENT OF THE TENNESSEE,
"MERIDIAN, MISS., February 16th, 1864.

"1. The destruction of the railroads intersecting at Meridian is of great importance, and should be done most effectually. Every tie and rail for many miles in each direction should be absolutely destroyed or injured, and every bridge and culvert should be completely destroyed. To insure this end, to General Hurlbut is intrusted the destruction east and north, and to General McPherson the roads west and south. The troops should be impressed with the importance of this work, and also that time is material, and therefore it should be begun at once, and be prosecuted with all the energy possible. Working parties should be composed of about one-half the command, and they should move by regiments, provided with their arms and haversacks, ready to repel the attacks of cavalry. The other half in reserve will be able to watch the enemy retreating eastward.

"2. Colonel E. F. Winslow, commanding cavalry, will keep his cavalry in advance of the parties working eastward, and will act as though this army was slowly pursuing the enemy.

"3. Special instructions will be given as to the general supply train; and the troops now in Meridian will, under proper brigade parties, collect meal, meat and supplies. The destruction of buildings must be deferred till the last moment, when a special detail will be made for that purpose.

"By order of

"W. T. SHERMAN,
"*Major-general Commanding.*"

In accordance with the above, a wholesale work of destruction began on the 16th, and every description of Confederate property was burned or otherwise destroyed and rendered useless. This continued for five days, during which period the Federals placed beyond all immediate possibility of repair about 120 miles of railway, 61 bridges, 20 locomotives, many cars, saw-mills, depots, and everything else connected with the railways for twenty miles around the place.

General W. S. Smith had not been able to leave

FEBRUARY, 1864.

Memphis and Collierville before the 11th of February, when he started out with General Grierson and three brigades of

INTERIOR OF THE CITY OF MATAMORAS, MEXICO, FROM THE CHURCH-TOWER.
FROM A SKETCH BY L. AVERY.

McPHERSON'S ARMY CROSSING BIG BLACK RIVER AT MESSENGER'S FERRY, OCTOBER 15TH, 1863.
From a Sketch by F. B. Schell.

cavalry under Colonel Waring, of the Fourth Missouri; Lieutenant-colonel Hepburn, of the Second Iowa; and Colonel McCrellis, of the Third Illinois Regiments, accompanied by a brigade of infantry and some artillery.

Smith crossed the Tallahatchie at New Albany, and proceeded along the Mobile and Ohio Railroad in the direction of Okolona, which they surprised and entered. Thence General Grierson was sent with a brigade to make a demonstration against Columbus, while Smith took the remainder of his force in the direction of West Point. Before reaching the latter place he was informed that the Confederates, under Forrest, Chalmers and Lee, occupied it with a large force, and he therefore concluded best not to engage the enemy, whose real strength, as was afterward proven, did not exceed 3,000 men, who were all under General N. B. Forrest.

As soon as Smith commenced falling back, [illegible] was engaged by the Confederates, but managed [illegible] hold his own until he reached Okolona, where [illegible] was so bitterly assailed on the 22d, that, after [illegible] prolonged contest, which lasted until dark and [illegible] which he lost five guns, he fell back toward Pontotoc. After losing about 200 men and a number of horses, Smith and Grierson continued their retreat, [illegible] reached Memphis during the night of the 25[illegible]

STEVENSON, ALA., DEPOT FOR GENERAL ROSECRANS'S ARMY
From a Sketch by J. F. C. Hillen.

having during their thirteen-days' march covered about 350 miles, and destroyed several hundred thousand dollars worth of property.

Not hearing from Smith up to the 20th, Sherman ordered McPherson to return along the main road, while he himself would proceed in a northerly direction with Hurlbut's column and the cavalry. The latter passed through Marion and Muckalusha (Old Town) to Union, and after dispatching cavalry toward Columbus, principally by way of Philadelphia and Louisville, the main body moved to Hillsboro', where it was joined by McPherson's column on the 23d. From Hillsboro' the return was made across the Pearl River, at Edwards's Station and at the Ratcliffe Ferry, to Canton, the last-named place being reached February 26th.

During the progress of both these expeditions, Porter made an attack upon Yazoo City. Several gunboats given in charge of Lieutenant-commander Owen, and a detachment of troops under Colonel Osband, who took Colonel Coates's intended place, were sent up the Yazoo River, and the city was assaulted, but Porter failed to capture it, and after losing about fifty men he had to return to the place of departure.

The raid entered upon by Forrest proved to be a much more important one. After the repulse of Generals Smith and Grierson at Okolona, his force was increased to about 6,000 men, with which he moved northwardly, along the line of the Mobile and Ohio Railway, into West Tennessee. After capturing Jackson on the 23d of March, his force proceeded to Union City, and demanded its surrender on the following day. Colonel Hawkins then held the post with nearly 500 men belonging to the Eleventh Tennessee Cavalry, and succeeded in repulsing four separate attacks from the much superior forces surrounding him, before capitulating.

Hickman, Ky., was next occupied, and Forrest afterward moved upon Paducah, in company with Generals Buford and A. P. Thompson. Paducah was held by Colonel S. G. Hicks, with the troops of Colonel Cunningham, Major Barnes, and Major Chapman, belonging respectively to the First (colored) Kentucky Artillery, the Sixteenth Kentucky Cavalry, and the One Hundred and Twenty-second Illinois Infantry, in all about 650 men.

As soon as Hicks learned of Forrest's approach, he drew all of his force into Fort Anderson, where he made a stand with the aid of the two gunboats *Peosta* and *Paw Paw*, under Captain Skirk, U.S.N. On the 25th of March the following correspondence was exchanged:

"HEADQUARTERS FORREST'S CAVALRY CORPS,
"PADUCAH, March 25th, 1864.

"*To Colonel Hicks, Commanding Federal Forces at Paducah.*

"Having a force amply sufficient to carry your works and reduce the place, in order to avoid the unnecessary effusion of blood I demand a surrender of the fort and troops, with all the public stores. If you surrender, you shall be treated as prisoners of war; but if I have to storm your works, you may expect no quarter.

"N. B. FORREST,
"*Major-general Commanding.*"

Colonel Hicks replied as follows:

"HEADQUARTERS POST PADUCAH,
"PADUCAH, KY., March 25th, 1864.

"*Major-general N. B. Forrest, Commanding Confederate Forces.*

"I have this moment received yours of this instant, in which you demand an unconditional surrender of forces under my command. I can answer that I have been placed here by my Government to defend the post. In this, as well as all other orders from my superior officers, I feel it my duty as an honorable officer to obey, and must therefore respectfully decline surrendering, as you require.

"Very respectfully.

"S. G. HICKS,
"*Commanding Post.*"

The houses and other buildings in the immediate vicinity were then occupied, and two successive attacks were made upon the fort, and kept up until half-past eleven o'clock at night, when the assailants retired before the steady fire of both the garrison and gunboats. In the assaults the Federals lost 14 killed and 46 wounded, and the Confederates lost nearly 1,500 men, including General Thompson, who was killed by the explosion of a shell.

Forrest remained two days at Paducah, when he was informed of the near approach of Federal reinforcements from Cairo, and hurried off to Fort Pillow, located about seventy miles above Memphis, on the Mississippi River. The fort was then held by Major L. F. Booth, with 550 men of the Sixth United States Heavy Artillery and the Second United States Light Artillery, both colored, as well as of the Thirteenth (white) Tennessee Cavalry. The colored troops were under the immediate command of Major Booth, and the white troops under Major W. F. Bradford.

Early on the 12th Forrest approached Fort Pillow, and suddenly attacked the intrenchments outside the fortification, with Bell and McCulloch's brigades of General Chalmers's division, which were led by Generals J. R. Chalmers and himself. The Federal pickets were driven in, and a sharp encounter followed immediately before the outworks, until about nine o'clock in the morning, when the garrison was called into the fort by Major Bradford, who had just succeeded to the chief command upon the death of Major Booth.

APRIL, 1864.

With the aid of the gunboat No. 7, *New Era*, Captain Marshall, of the Mississippi Squadron, which was now enabled to shell the Confederates thus drawn near to the river, the defense was steadily kept up until between two and three o'clock in the afternoon, when the Confederates, finding that they had gained no decisive success, stopped their fire and sent in a flag of truce, calling for the unconditional surrender of the fort within the ensuing twenty minutes.

GENERAL McPHERSON ENTERING CLINTON, MISS., ON HIS RAID FROM VICKSBURG.

FROM A SKETCH BY C. E. H. BONWILL.

In reply, Major Bradford asked an hour's delay in order to consult with his officers and those of the *New Era*. A second demand for the surrender rapidly followed. General Forrest offered to allow twenty minutes in which to move the troops from the fort, adding that if the latter was not evacuated in that time he would order a general assault.

Major Bradford refused the surrender, and immediately thereafter, at bugle-sound, some of Forrest's men, who had concealed themselves along the ravines and in the neighboring buildings while the negotiations for a surrender were going on, made a dash in different directions, and obtained possession of the fort, with the cry of "No quarter!" But little opportunity was offered for resistance. The Federals threw down their arms and sought escape down the high bluffs upon which the fort was situated, as well as throughout the town. They were pursued, and an indiscriminate slaughter followed.

Inside and outside the fort nearly all were murdered. Pollard, in his "Third Year of the War," says: "There is no doubt that for some moments the Confederate officers lost control of their men,

THE NEGRO IN THE WAR.—VARIOUS

who were maddened by the sight of negro troops opposing them. It is to be remarked, too, that the Yankees and negroes at Fort Pillow neglected to haul down their flag. In truth, relying upon their gunboats, the Yankee officers expected to annihilate our forces after we had entered the fortifications. They did not intend to surrender at the first fire. After Forrest's men scaled the walls, many of the negroes threw down their arms, and fell as if they were dead. They perished in the pretense, or could only be restored at the point of the bayonet. To resuscitate some of them, more terrified than the rest, they were rolled into the trenches made as receptacles for the fallen."

The scenes that followed the capture of Fort Pillow became the subject of a Congressional investigation, during which one of Forrest's men testified that, while being led a prisoner toward Jackson, Tenn., Major Bradford was one day taken some distance from the line of march and deliberately shot down.

From Fort Pillow, General Buford was sent to Columbus, and upon his arrival there issued the following summons:

"HEADQUARTERS C. S. A.,
"BEFORE COLUMBUS, KY., April 13th, 1864.

To the Commander of the U. S. Forces, Columbus, Ky.

"Fully capable of taking Columbus and its garrison by force, I desire to avoid shedding blood. I therefore demand the unconditional surrender of the forces under your command. Should you surrender, the negroes now in arms will be returned to their masters. Should I be compelled to take the place by force, no quarter will be shown negro troops whatever; white troops will be treated as prisoners of war.

"I am, sir, yours,
"A. BUFORD,
"*Brigadier-general.*"

THOMAS E. G. RANSOM.

The surrender was refused, and General Buford retired without making any attack. He soon joined Forrest, and the two rapidly retreated into Mississippi upon hearing that a force of about 12,000 men under General S. D. Sturgis had been ordered to intercept them.

Sturgis was too late, however, for by the time he left Bolivar, on the 30th of April, the Confederates had already crossed Wolf River. But some weeks later he started again for Memphis, upon learning that Forrest was getting together the largest force he had ever commanded.

APRIL, 1864.

This time Sturgis was accompanied by Grierson, and by nearly the whole of the remainder of A. J. Smith's division, recently brought from the Red River. He marched southeasterly, and struck the Mobile and Ohio Railroad at Guntown, where Grierson's cavalry, in the advance, met and drove back a large force under General Forrest, on the 10th of June.

His first assault rapidly led to such a sharp encounter that Grierson called for the assistance of Sturgis's troops, then about six miles in the rear. The latter were pushed forward as rapidly as the hot sun would permit, and at once joined in the fight, endeavoring to defeat the enemy in the immediate front, without, however, making any attempt at flanking.

JUNE, 1864.

The result was most disastrous to

M'PHERSON'S TROOPS FORAGING AT THE HEADQUARTERS OF THE CONFEDERATE GENERAL WHITFIELD.

FROM A SKETCH BY F. B. SCHELL.

the Federals. They had been given no time for rest, and were subjected to such a galling fire from the artillery with which Forrest had lined the most commanding ridges, that their columns soon gave way, and in a short time the entire Federal force of cavalry and infantry was driven so rapidly toward Ripley that it lost about 3,000 in killed, wounded and prisoners, together with the whole of the wagon-train, which had been injudiciously brought within range of the Confederate artillery.

The Federals made a stand at Ripley, which served as a temporary check to the pursuit, and finally continued on their way until Memphis was again reached.

On the 7th of July another expedition was organized against Forrest. It consisted of about 12,000 men, under General A. J. Smith, and advanced in the direction of Tupelo, skirmishing all the way to that place, and reached it on the 14th, after defeating the Confederates in quite a severe cavalry attack upon Mower's train shortly after its leaving Pontotoc.

July, 1864.

JAMES B. McPHERSON.

At Tupelo, Forrest was reported to have about 14,000 effective men. As soon as the Federals approached the town they were attacked by heavy numbers, but succeeded in repulsing every assault, and in at last compelling the withdrawal of the Confederates, who were followed up and again badly punished the following day in a cavalry fight close by the Old Town Creek. Forrest rapidly withdrew his forces, and Smith fell back to Memphis, whence he once more went in search of Forrest on the 4th of the ensuing month.

Smith moved by way of Holly Springs, and reached the line of the Tallahatchie River on the 17th, but failed to ascertain the whereabouts of Forrest, and again returned to Memphis, where he learned that during his absence Forrest had, on the 18th, made a dash upon the place with about three thousand men, and charging through the city, had first visited the Gayoso House, where he expected to find Generals Hurlbut, Buckland and Washburne.

August, 1864.

They were, however, absent at the time, and he took away a number of other officers and about three hundred soldiers as prisoners. Forrest made an unsuccessful attempt to liberate the Confederates in Irving Prison, and before he left town was drawn into a skirmish in which he lost a great many men. He then retreated into Mississippi, and did not again engage upon any extended raid until toward the end of the ensuing September, when, under the direction of General Hood, he made a dash across the Tennessee River.

GENERAL McPHERSON DRIVING THE CONFEDERATES FROM THEIR POSITION ON THE CANTON ROAD, NEAR BROWNSVILLE, MISS.

From a sketch by F. B. Schell.

THOMAS EDWARD GREENFIELD RANSOM.

Born at Norwich, Vt., November 29th, 1834. Left an orphan early in life, he had to struggle for the means of subsistence like the most of the boys of that period. Yet, by industry and thrift, he managed to acquire a good education, and started forth to carve out his own career in the world. He first taught mathematics in a school at Middletown, Conn.; then was employed to survey the Connecticut River, and afterward was engaged as a teacher at a military school in New Jersey; again at Fayetteville, N. C., and at Washington, Ga.; at Pensacola, Fla., he was Professor of Mathematics in the United States Navy. He was afterward employed as chief engineer on the public works of Illinois, and finally drifted back almost to the point whence he had started—Norwich, Vt.—where he became the principal of Captain Allen Partridge's Military School, then, as since, an academy of great renown. This military school at one time almost rivaled the United States Military Academy at West Point. Upon the breaking out of the Civil War he enlisted, on the 20th of April, 1861, in Company E, Eleventh Illinois Infantry, and was at once elected captain of his company. As soon as the companies of the regiment had assembled, on the 3d day of May of the same year, he was elected major, and went with his regiment to the capital of his State (Springfield), and on to Cairo and Bird's Point. Here, on the 30th of July, the three months for which the regiment had been enlisted expired, and it re-enlisted for three years; Ransom was elected lieutenant-colonel, and subsequently, on the 15th of February, 1862, when his colonel, W. H. L. Wallace, was made brigadier-general, he (Ransom) became the colonel of the Eleventh Illinois Infantry. In November of the same year he was himself made a brigadier-general, and was breveted a major-general in September, 1864.

While at the head of the Eleventh Illinois, Ransom shared in every engagement with General Grant about Cairo, at Forts Henry and Donelson, at Shiloh and Corinth, and as brigadier-general was at Oxford and Vicksburg. He was wounded in Southeast Missouri on the 19th of August, 1861; at Donelson, February 16th, 1862; and again at Shiloh, April 6th, 1862.

After the capture of Vicksburg, Ransom was ordered to Louisiana and Texas. In the Banks expedition up the Red River, early in 1864, he commanded two divisions of the Thirteenth Corps, and at Sabine Cross Roads, April 8th, on the skirmish line, he was again wounded (for the fourth time), and so severely that he was sent to the rear, and had to return to Chicago for treatment. But so impatient was he to do his full share of work, that he applied for duty, and was ordered to report to General Sherman in Georgia. This was on the 3d day of August, in the midsummer of 1864, when operations were being so vigorously pushed against the City of Atlanta. He was then assigned to duty with the Army of the Tennessee, with which he had formerly been connected, and he fell to the command of the Fourth Division of the Sixteenth Corps, then commanded by General G. M. Dodge. Shortly afterward—on the 20th of August—General Dodge himself received a disabling wound, which compelled him to leave, and the command of that corps devolved on the youthful General Ransom, who commanded it at the battle of Jonesborough, and at the capture of the City of Atlanta.

He was soon after given command of the Seventeenth Corps, and although unable to ride his horse by reason of a severe illness he was then suffering from, insisted upon being carried to Rome, Ga., where he died, on the 29th of October, 1864. Observing fatal symptoms his kind attendants had carried him to a farmhouse by the roadside, and there, lying on a bed, he said: "As a soldier I have tried to do my duty. I do not claim that all I have done was owing to patriotism alone, though I believe I have as much of that as most of men. Patriotism and inclination have led me the same way to do all in my power for my country."

From Rome, Ga., his body was sent to his home in Chicago, where it is now buried. The Society of the Army of the Tennessee has decreed a monument to be raised to his memory, and his name has been given to several prominent Posts of the Grand Army of the Republic throughout the different States.

JAMES BIRDSEYE McPHERSON.

Born in Sandusky County, O., November 14th, 1828; graduated at the United States Military Academy at West Point at the head of his class, July 1st, 1853, and was appointed a brevet second lieutenant in the corps of engineers. His superior qualifications caused him to be retained at the Academy as an assistant instructor of engineering until September, 1854, when he was assigned to duty in New York as assistant engineer on the defenses of that harbor and of the improvement of the Hudson River. In December, 1854, he was appointed a full second-lieutenant of engineers; three years later he was placed in charge of the construction of Fort Delaware, and subsequently of the defenses on Alcatraz Island, San Francisco Harbor, Cal. In 1858 he was promoted to be a first-lieutenant, and early in 1861 was ordered to Boston, Mass., where he gave his attention to the organization of a corps of engineer troops, being made a captain of engineers in August, 1861. During the subsequent November he was chosen by General Halleck as aid-de-camp and assistant engineer of the Department of Missouri, with the rank of lieutenant-colonel, being promoted to a colonelcy in May, 1862. He was shortly after made a brigadier-general of United States Volunteers, and appointed general superintendent of military railways in the District of West Tennessee during the ensuing month of June. For his gallantry at Corinth he was promoted to be a major-general of Volunteers, with commission dating from October 8th, 1862. His brilliant career, from the capture of Fort Henry in 1862 up to the surrender of Vicksburg in 1863, is fittingly told by General Grant in his letter recommending McPherson to be a brigadier-general in the Regular Army, of which the following is an extract:

"He has been with me in every battle since the commencement of the rebellion, except Belmont. At Forts Henry and Donelson, Shiloh, and at the siege of Corinth, as a staff officer and engineer, his services were conspicuous and highly meritorious. At the second battle of Corinth his skill as a soldier was displayed in successfully carrying reinforcements to the besieged garrison when the enemy was between him and the point to be reached. In the advance through Central Mississippi, General McPherson commanded one wing of the army with all the ability possible to show, he having the lead in the advance, and the rear, retiring. In the campaign and siege terminating with the fall of Vicksburg he has filled a conspicuous part. At the battle of Port Gibson it was under his direction that the enemy was driven, late in the afternoon, from a position they had succeeded in holding all day against an obstinate attack. His corps, the advance always under his immediate eye, were the pioneers in the movement from Port Gibson to Hawkinson's Ferry. From the north fork of the Bayou Pierre to Black River it was a constant skirmish, the whole skillfully managed. From Hawkinson's Ferry to Jackson, the Seventeenth Army Corps marched on roads not traveled by other troops, fighting the entire battle of Raymond alone; and the bulk of Johnston's army was fought by this corps entirely under the management of General McPherson. At Champion Hills the Seventeenth Corps and General McPherson were conspicuous. In the assault of the 22d of May on the fortifications of Vicksburg, and during the entire siege, General McPherson and his command took unfading laurels. He is one of the ablest engineers and most skillful generals. I would respectfully but urgently recommend his promotion to the position of brigadier-general in the Regular Army."

Upon this recommendation General McPherson was, on the 1st of August, 1863, appointed to the desired position, and soon after surprised the Confederate camp at Canton, Miss. In February, 1864, he accompanied General Sherman's famous raid to Meridian as second in command, and in March was assigned to command the Department and Army of the Tennessee, to the reorganization of which he devoted several weeks, preparatory to the invasion of Georgia. During this famous campaign his services were invaluable. At Resaca, Dallas, and throughout the almost daily severe fight-

MASSACRE OF THE FEDERAL TROOPS AFTER THE CAPTURE OF FORT PILLOW, APRIL 12TH, 1864.

ing up to and including Kenesaw Mountain, he was conspicuous and greatly distinguished himself. In the battles before Atlanta he commanded the Left Grand Division, and it was while at Decatur, Ga., that he was killed by a shot fired from an ambuscade, on July 22d, 1864. On the 24th of the same month General Sherman addressed Adjutant-general Thomas as follows: "It is my painful duty to report that Brigadier-general James B. McPherson, U. S. Army, major-general of Volunteers and commander of the Army of the Tennessee in the field, was killed by a shot from ambuscade about noon yesterday. At the time of this fatal shot he was on horseback, placing his troops in position near the City of Atlanta, and was passing by a cross-road from a moving column toward the flank of troops that had already been established on the line. He had quitted me but a few minutes before, and was on his way to see in person to the execution of my orders. About the time of this sad event the enemy had sallied from his intrenchments of Atlanta, and by a circuit had got to the left and rear of this very line, and had begun an attack which resulted in a serious action; so that General McPherson fell in battle, booted and spurred, as the gallant knight and gentleman should wish. Not his the loss but the

General Grant had already, on the 4th of March, been notified of the passage by Congress of an Act appointing him Lieutenant-general,

March, 1864.

and upon receipt of the President's order, he proceeded, on the 19th, from Nashville to Washington, where he joined the Army of the Potomac, with which he was destined soon to achieve the most brilliant successes of the War. As will be seen by the orders,* Halleck was made chief of staff of the Army, and Generals Sherman and McPherson were respectively assigned to the command of the Military Division of the Mississippi and of the Department and Army of the Tennessee.

The Military Division of the Mississippi which was thus transferred from General Grant to General Sherman comprised the Departments of the Cumberland, of the Tennessee, of the Ohio and of the Arkansas. The Army of the Cumberland, then at

NEGRO RECRUITS TAKING THE CARS FOR MURFREESBORO', TENN., TO JOIN THE FEDERAL ARMY.

From a Sketch by C. E. F. Hillen.

country's, and this army will mourn his death and cherish his memory as that of one who, though comparatively young, had risen by his merit and ability to the command of one of the best armies which the nation had called into existence to vindicate its honor and integrity. History tells of but few who so blended the grace and gentleness of the friend with the dignity, courage, faith and manliness of the soldier. His public enemies, even the men who directed the fatal shot, never spoke or wrote of him without expressions of marked respect; those whom he commanded loved him even to idolatry; and I, his associate and commander, fail in words adequate to express my opinion of his great worth. I feel assured that every patriot in America, on hearing this sad news, will feel a sense of personal loss, and the country generally will realize that we have lost not only an able military leader, but a man who, had he survived, was qualified to heal the national strife which had been raised by designing and ambitious men. His body was sent North in charge of Major Willard, Captains Steele and Gile, of his personal staff."

RESACA AND ATLANTA.

Two weeks after General Sherman's return to Canton—on the 12th of March, 1864—President Lincoln retired Major-general Halleck as General-in-Chief of the Armies, and appointed in his stead Ulysses S. Grant.

braced the Fifteenth Corps, General Logan; the Sixteenth Corps, General Dodge; and, later on, the Seventeenth Corps, General Blair. The Army of the Ohio, encamped at Red Clay, about ten miles northeast of Ringgold, was made up alone of the Twenty-third Corps, commanded by General J. M. Schofield, as the Ninth Corps, formerly belonging to it, had left East Tennessee between the 17th and 23d of March, and proceeded to Annapolis, joining the Army of the Potomac, and once more falling under command of General Burnside. The Army Department of the Arkansas was at first commanded by Major-general Steele, and then by General Canby, with headquarters at Little Rock.

On the 10th of April, Sherman was ordered by Grant to advance against the Confederate forces under General Joseph E. Johnston, then at and about Dalton, it being understood that Grant was to make a simultaneous movement from Culpepper.

Ringgold, under the command of General George H. Thomas, comprised the Fourth Corps, General Howard; the Fourteenth Corps, General Palmer; and the Twentieth Corps, General Hooker. The Army of the Tennessee, stationed at Lee and Gordon's Mill, under General J. B. McPherson, em-

* War Department, Adjutant-general's Office, Washington, March 12th, 1864.

(General Order No. 98.)

The President of the United States orders as follows:

(1) Major-general Halleck is at his own request relieved from duty as General-in-Chief of the Army, and Lieutenant-general U. S. Grant is assigned to the command of the Armies of the United States. The headquarters of the Army will be in Washington, and also with Lieutenant-general Grant in the field.

(2) Major-general Halleck is assigned to duty in Washington as chief of staff of the Army, under the direction of the Secretary of War and the Lieutenant-general commanding. His orders will be obeyed and respected accordingly.

(3) Major-general W. T. Sherman is assigned to the command of the Military Division of the Mississippi, composed of the Departments of the Ohio, the Cumberland, the Tennessee and the Arkansas.

(4) Major-general J. B. McPherson is assigned to the command of the Department and Army of the Tennessee.

(5) In relieving Major-general Halleck from duty as General-in-Chief, the President desires to express his approbation and thanks for the zealous manner in which the arduous and responsible duties of that position have been performed.

By order of the Secretary of War, E. D. Townsend, Assistant-adjutant General.

with Richmond as the objective, while Sherman's was to be the City of Atlanta.

Johnston's army was arranged into three infantry corps, numbering about 50,000 men, under Generals Hardee, Hood and Polk, and a cavalry corps of about 10,000 men, led by General Wheeler. Against these forces Sherman had opposing Johnston a total of about 98,000 men.

Sherman's preparations for the advance were not completed until late on Friday, the 6th of May,

May, 1864.

and early the following day Thomas advanced the Fourth, Fourteenth, and Twentieth Corps into Dogwood Valley at and about Trickum, while McPherson moved toward Ship's Gap and Villanow, and Schofield marched the Twenty-third Corps in the direction of Lee's and Catoosa Springs.

After meeting some opposition in front of Buzzard's Roost Gap, where Newton's and Geary's divisions had a skirmish with the Confederates, Thomas occupied Tunnel Hill on the 7th, McPherson reaching the Snake Creek Gap on the 8th, while Schofield took a position on the Dalton Road just south of Red Clay. McPherson advanced no

BROWNSVILLE, TEXAS, OCCUPIED BY THE ARMY UNDER GENERAL BANKS, NOVEMBER, 1863.—From a Sketch by L. Avery

MAMMOTH CANNON CAST AT FORT PITT FOUNDRY IN 1863, KNOWN AS THE 20-INCH RODMAN GUN.

the 9th through the Snake Creek Gap, and with Kilpatrick's cavalry suddenly came upon the Resaca earthworks late in the afternoon; but he found the place so strongly fortified, and so well guarded by Canty's brigade, that it would have been unwise to risk an attack with his then small force, and he therefore returned to a strong position at the southern end of the Gap.

There was almost continued skirmishing between the opposing armies until the night of the 11th, when orders were issued for a general advance at daybreak the following morning. With the exception of Howard's Fourth Corps, and some cavalry which remained in front of Buzzard's Roost to divert the enemy's attention, the entire army advanced at sunrise on the 12th through Snake Creek Gap upon Resaca, Kilpatrick's cavalry taking the lead, and being closely followed by McPherson's central column along the main road, as well as by Schofield and Thomas upon the extreme right and left.

Part of Wheeler's cavalry force, which had the day before entered upon an extended reconnoissance against Schofield's left, which it had unsuccessfully engaged, now attacked Kilpatrick, when the latter was about two miles distant from Resaca, and a spirited engagement followed, in which Kilpatrick was so badly wounded that he had to turn his command over to Colonel Murray. Wheeler's men were promptly dispersed, and McPherson afterward struck the infantry pickets, which he drove within their intrenchments, being thus enabled to take up a strong position upon a ridge, with his left abreast the town, and his extreme right resting upon the Oostenaula River. General Thomas then brought up his force upon McPherson's left, and Schofield placed the Twenty-third Corps upon a group of hills to the south of Tilton, on the Dalton and Resaca Road.

It was then ascertained that General Johnston had on the 9th dispatched three of Hood's divisions to Resaca, and that the remainder of his army had since followed, leaving Dalton in possession of Howard's force, which had afterward for a time pursued the Confederates, without, however, bringing on any general engagement.

Sherman was not prepared to attack until the 14th, when he ordered a ponton-bridge to be laid across the Oostenaula River in the direction

May, 1864

of Calhoun. The latter place was to be threatened by Sweeny's division of the Sixteenth Corps at the same time that General Garrard's cavalry would proceed toward Rome to destroy the line of railway below Calhoun and above Kingston, and while the main army would attack Resaca from different points.

The Confederate army was in a strong position behind Camp Creek. It occupied the forts as well as a high hill, whence Johnston's artillery could command the railway and all the bridges thrown across the Oostenaula—the extreme left, under Polk, resting upon the latter river, and connecting with the centre, under Hardee; while the extreme right, under Hood, extended around Resaca in a north-easterly direction to the Connasauga.

During the afternoon of the 14th, Sweeny and Garrard entered upon the proposed movements, while McPherson got across Camp Creek and drove away Polk's force from his commanding position, where he promptly secured a good lodgment for his artillery. Thomas followed closely along the Camp Creek Valley, where Schofield met him late in the day, and took position upon his left, close to Resaca, after marching most of his force by way of the Rome and Dalton Road.

Orders were issued by Johnston to attack the next morning, but when it was learned that Calhoun was threatened, and that Polk could not well maintain the position to which McPherson had driven him, Walker's division was sent to Calhoun, and what promised to develop into an important battle was confined to a series of infantry skirmishes, lasting until the afternoon. These occurred mainly upon the extreme left, where the artillery could not be used, owing to the rough nature of the ground, and by reason of the dense woods, and where General Hooker's force had been shifted, while the troops under Howard, Schofield and Palmer had taken position upon the Federal right.

Shortly after one o'clock Butterfield's division, supported by those of Generals Geary and Williams, was sent forward to test the enemy's strength along the front, and soon came upon Hood's advance, under Stevenson, whose guns occupied quite a leading position. The attack, though promptly met and ably contested by the Confederates, was made so impetuously that Stevenson had no time to withdraw four 12-pounders, which were captured by the Federals, and brought in by the Fifth Ohio, under Colonel Kilpatrick, after a bitter contest, lasting until nightfall. In this engagement the Confederates lost a large number in killed and wounded, besides about 200 prisoners, and the battle-flags of the Thirty-fifth and Thirty-eighth Alabama Regiments.

The total loss was about 800 while in front of Dalton, and about 2,000 before Resaca, the latter

JOHN M. SCHOFIELD.

being nearly equally divided between the Army of the Cumberland and two divisions of the Army of the Ohio. The Confederates reported their total loss at about 2,200.

Another ponton-bridge had in the meantime been thrown at Lay's Ferry, close by the mouth of Snake Creek, and Sherman's lines were gradually being drawn so closely around Resaca, that, with the threatening of the railway at Calhoun, Johnston saw no likely chance of extricating himself should he attempt a farther stand against the heavy force opposing him. He therefore abandoned Resaca during the night of the 15th, and burning the railroad bridge behind him, retreated across the Oostenaula in the direction of Calhoun.

Early on the 16th, Sherman entered the town of Resaca and set about repairing bridges and sending his troops across the river. The cavalry divisions of Generals Stoneman

May, 1864

and McCook were dispatched in pursuit of the enemy, and General Thomas's force crossed at Resaca, while McPherson's crossed the Oostenaula at Lay's Ferry, and Schofield's forded the Connasauga at Fite's Ferry, and the Coosawattee at McClure's Ferry.

With the exception of Jefferson C. Davis's division, which moved alone to Rome, where, without much opposition, it succeeded in taking possession of several heavy guns, and in capturing as well as destroying much valuable property, the whole army marched southward by different roads, and after engaging in several skirmishes with the Confederate rear-guard at Adairsville and elsewhere, besides preparing to give battle at Kingston and at Cassville, where the enemy appeared disposed to make a stand, Sherman rested his troops along the banks of the Etowah River.

Early on the 23d, Sherman ordered an advance. The troops and wagons were provided and loaded with subsistence for twenty days, and garrisons were left both at Rome and Kingston, which latter was announced as a temporary base of supplies. The Federals then crossed the Etowah River, and marched in three columns; Thomas in the centre *via* Euharlee and Burnt Hickory; McPherson crossing on the right at the mouth of the Connasene Creek, near Kingston, and *via* Van Wert; and Schofield taking the Cassville Road, so as to come in upon Thomas's left. General Davis's division was ordered to move directly from Rome for Dallas by way of Van Wert.

In order to ascertain definitely whether Sherman's whole army had abandoned the line of the Etowah, Johnston ordered Wheeler to make a reconnoissance toward Cassville. This was done late in the evening of the 23d. Wheeler succeeded in eluding Kilpatrick by crossing several miles to the right, and took advantage of the opportunity to attack the small force left in charge of the Federal supply-trains at Cassville. There could be but little resistance offered to Wheeler's heavy force of cavalry, and, after destroying all the property they could not take away, the Confederates carried off a number of negroes and teams, as well as nearly one hundred prisoners.

Wheeler returned and reported that Sherman's army was on its way to Dallas, where the Federals knew Johnston had concluded to make another stand, and the Confederate lines were at once disposed to meet the coming force. Hardee was already near New Hope Church, with his left across the Stilesboro', Dallas and Atlanta Road, south of Dallas, and Polk was placed in the centre, with Hood upon the extreme right, the latter's centre being directly at New Hope Church.

Hooker's corps led the advance, and when near Owen's Mills, on the Pumpkin-vine Creek, Geary's division came upon a body of Confederate cavalry, which it drove back a distance of nearly two miles, when it met Hood's advance infantry, under Colonel Bush Jones, and consisting of Austin's sharpshooters and of the Thirty-second and Fifty-eighth Alabama Regiments.

A sharp conflict took place, and Sherman hurried to the front, but as the divisions of Generals Ward and Williams, also belonging to Hooker's corps, were on different roads, it was nearly five o'clock in the afternoon before Sherman could get the troops well in hand. Hooker was then ordered to take possession of New Hope Church, located at the meeting of the Acworth, Dallas and Marietta Roads. Hood's position was violently assaulted, but under cover of their earthworks the Confederates were enabled to successfully resist every attack along the neighboring ridge and dense woods, and at dark the Federals had to beat a retreat. During the ensuing stormy night they retired behind the ridge and gathered up their dead and wounded, which were reported as numbering nearly 600.

The following morning Johnston was found still more strongly intrenched, with well-developed lines extending from Dallas to Marietta. Sherman had meanwhile brought up Howard's Fourth Corps to Hooker's support, and ordered McPherson's to Dallas, upon which Davis was then advancing to take position on McPherson's left, while Schofield was directed to leave Hovey's division to protect the trains, and to advance with the other divisions to Owen's Mills. The cavalry under Stoneman was

GENERAL GEARY'S HEADQUARTERS AT ATLANTA.

THE CITY HALL, ATLANTA.

RUINS OF A CONFEDERATE FORT ON THE SOUTHEAST OF ATLANTA, WITH CHEVAUX-DE-FRISE AND ABATIS IN FRONT.

THE CAPTURE OF BUZZARD'S ROOST, AT HOVEY GAP, GA.

THE BATTLE OF RESACA, FOUGHT MAY 14TH, 1864.
FROM A SKETCH BY C. E. F. HILLEN.

to aid Schofield, and Garrard was to operate in conjunction with McPherson, while McCook's cavalry was to protect the rear.

The continued storm had rendered the roads so d, and the troops had to cross such thick woods, at it took many days to get the men into the oved positions. They were besides all the time ased by the enemy's sharpshooters, and were the same time drawn into many a skirmish at different points.

While these movements were being perfected, the immediate front of both armies was likewise kept on the alert. On the 26th, McCook's cavalry had quite a lively tilt with Wheeler's force, from which latter it captured nearly 50 prisoners; and on the 27th, reconnoissances by the divisions of Newton, Stanley and Wood led to quite a lively encounter in the vicinity of Pickett's Mill. The Federals were bravely met by the divisions of Generals Cleburne, of Hardee's corps, and Hindman, of Hood's corps, strongly supported by part of Wheeler's cavalry, and after losing about 1,500 killed and wounded, besides nearly 150 prisoners, they retired to their former position.

May, 1864

On the 28th, McPherson was boldly attacked by part of Hardee's force, just as he was bringing up his troops upon Thomas's left, the better to envelop the enemy's right; but the temporary earthworks erected by the Federals enabled them to successfully repulse the assault without much loss. McPherson was again attacked during the night of the 29th. Johnston pushed his skirmish lines close to those of the Federals, at the same time opening upon Sherman's works from nearly all his batteries on the neighboring hills; but after a little over an hour's exchange of artillery, the pickets were left to continue in the dark their desultory firing until the morning.

On the 30th, Sherman gave orders for the shifting of the entire Federal line to the left, and by the 1st of June the movement was effected. The roads to Allatoona and Acworth were seized, and General

GEARY'S SECOND BRIGADE CHARGING UP THE MOUNTAIN AT THE BATTLE OF RESACA.
FROM A SKETCH BY ASSISTANT-SURGEON J. S. TREXLER, SEVENTY-THIRD PENNSYLVANIA.

CAPTURE OF LOST MOUNTAIN, GA., BY GENERAL HOOKER, JUNE 15th, 1864.

From a Sketch by C. E. F. Hillen.

KINGSTON, ON THE ETOWAH RIVER, GA., OCCUPIED BY SHERMAN, MAY 14th, 1864.

FROM A SKETCH BY C. E. F. HILLEN.

...oneman's cavalry was sent toward Allatoona, at ... eastern end of the Pass, while Garrard's horse ...ceeded in the rear by the west end, thus turn... the Pass and compelling its evacuation.

The total Federal losses for the month of May ...e now reported at about 2,000 killed and ...0 wounded and missing. Johnston gave the ...mber of his killed at 700, and of his wounded at ...ut 4,700, to which must be added some 3,250 ...oners taken by the Federals, making the total ...ualties nearly equal on both sides.

Orders were immediately given to reconstruct the ...way from Kingston to the Etowah, as well as ... bridge at Etowah Station, and on the 4th Sher...n commenced moving directly upon the railway ... Acworth, which he took possession of two days ...er.

Seeing this, Johnston was compelled to abandon ...e works at Hope Church, wherein Sherman had ...ft him, and to move his army toward the hills ...otecting Marietta, where the next stand was to ...e made.

At Acworth, Sherman was joined on the 8th by General Frank P. Blair, Jr., who had with him Colonel Long's brigade of Garrard's cavalry, and ...wo divisions of the Seventeenth Corps—in all ...bout 9,000 men—which were at once attached to McPherson's corps, already occupying the railway.

On Wednesday, the 9th of June, Sherman advanced toward Big Shanty, a station on the railway about equidistant from Acworth and Kenesaw.

Between Acworth and Marietta intervenes a very mountainous district, having three detached and well-defined summits, the most easterly of which is called Kenesaw Mountain, whilst the one to the southwest, on the road to Dallas, bears the name of Lost Mountain, and the third, situated half a mile further to the north, and nearly midway between the other two, is called Pine Mountain.

Upon each of these mountains the Confederates had well-appointed signal-stations, and quite an extensive line of strong abatis, as well as several successive lines of intrenchments. Behind the latter lay a force sufficient to check and materially damage any advance toward the Kenesaw, which was the controlling point of the whole region, as it completely commanded both the line of railway and the town of Marietta.

Along the summit of the mountains, notably on the Kenesaw, rising to a height of nearly 1,200 feet, Johnston had placed a heavy line of artillery, and under its cover lay his infantry, then consisting in all of nine divisions of about 7,000 each. The latter were well supported by the Georgia Militia, called out by Governor Brown, and placed in charge of General G. W. Smith.

Hardee's corps held the extreme Confederate left, resting upon Lost Mountain; Polk's corps, the centre; and Hood's corps, the right, extending across the Acworth and Marietta Road. The cavalry, estimated at about 15,000 men, was left to operate on the flanks and in the Federal rear.

Sherman's army advanced as before in three columns, Schofield toward Lost Mountain, McPherson toward Marietta, and Thomas on Kenesaw and Pine Mountains. From the 9th to the 14th the Federal lines were gradually closed up toward the Confederate position, Sherman's first object being to break the line between the Kenesaw and Pine Mountains.

During the afternoon of the 14th there was a temporary cessation of the drenching rains which had lasted almost continuously since the beginning of the month, and the whole front was advanced close to the Confederate works, wherein the enemy's pickets were rapidly driven from the outposts. The right of Palmer's force and the left of Howard's were pushed forward between Pine Mountain and the works east of it, General Hooker's troops afterward taking place upon Howard's right.

JUNE, 1864.

Like all the other movements of the army, this advance was accompanied by almost incessant skirmishing, and when the Federals came within

TROOPS STARTING FROM RINGGOLD, GA., FOR THE FRONT.

FROM A SKETCH BY C. E. F. HILLEN.

ENGAGEMENT AT KULP (CULP'S) HOUSE, JUNE 22D, 1864.—THE FEDERAL ARTILLERY DRIVING HOOD'S MEN BACK TO THEIR EARTHWORKS.

FROM A SKETCH BY C. E. F. HILLEN.

range of the guns upon the hills overlooking their lines, they were once more subjected to a very damaging fire from the enemy.

At one time several groups of Confederate officers appeared reconnoitring along Pine Mountain, and General Thomas ordered the artillery to open upon them, which was done with apparently good effect, as all instantly disappeared. It was afterward ascertained that one of these groups was composed of Generals Johnston, Hardee and Polk, who had come together at the suggestion of General Hardee, who justly felt concerned at Sherman's movements.

One of the shells from Knapp's battery, fired by William Knapp, of Allegheny City, Pa., had caused the dispersion of the group; but it appears that Polk again returned for further observation, and was then struck by the fragments of another shell fired from the same battery, which caused his instant death. The command of Polk's corps then temporarily devolved upon the senior division commander, General William W. Loring, whose division was given to General W. S. Featherstone, until General S. D. Lee took permanent command of the army of the centre.

On the 15th, Thomas found that Johnston had drawn back his centre to a strong line of intrenchments in the hills, connecting the Lost and Kenesaw Mountains, having practically abandoned Pine Mountain. The latter was immediately taken and Williams's centre, at the same time Hascall was attacked by Stevenson, and the onslaught was made with such impetuosity that for a while the Federals were driven back in the somewhat marshy ravine separating the forces of Williams and Geary.

The advantage thus gained was but temporary, however, for a converging fire of grape-shot and canister directed by the Woodbury and Winegar batteries of rifled guns, as well as by the Thirteenth New York Artillery, proved so destructive that Hood's men had to fall back, and were finally driven to their earthworks with the loss of nearly 1,000 men. The Federal loss was reported at about 400 in killed and wounded.

Two days after the engagement at "Kulp (Culp's) House" an assault was ordered to be made, on Monday, the 27th, simultaneously at two points south of the Kenesaw, upon Johnston's left centre. McPherson was to attack the Little Kenesaw, while Thomas would operate a mile to the southward.

The movement was executed as intended at about nine o'clock on the morning of the 27th. After a most rigorous cannonade, the Federals advanced upon the enemy, falling most heavily upon the forces of Generals Hardee and Loring; but after a very hotly contested engagement of a little over an hour's duration, the assailants had to retire with the loss of about 3,000 men, as against one-sixth the number lost by the Confederates. Among the

The official reports of losses on each side, from the 1st of June to the 3d of July, were as follows:

Army of the Cumberland.	*Killed and Missing.*	*Wounded.*	*Total.*
Howard's Fourth Corps...	603	1,543	2,144
Palmer's Fourteenth Corps.	353	1,466	1,819
Hooker's Twentieth Corps.	323	1,246	1,568
Army of the Tennessee.			
Logan's Fifteenth Corps...	179	687	866
Dodge's Sixteenth Corps...	53	157	209
Blair's Seventeenth Corps..	47	213	260
Army of the Ohio.			
Schofield's Twenty third Corps................	105	362	467
Cavalry..................	130	68	198
Grand Total.........	1,790	5,740	7,530
Hardee's Corps	200	1,433	1,633
Hood's Corps.............	140	1,121	1,261
Loring's (Polk's) Corps....	128	926	1,054
Grand Total.........	468	3,480	3,948

Johnston prevented Sherman's intended attack upon his flank and rear by making a forced march to the railway crossing, and erecting there some earthworks, besides opposing an intrenched line across the road at Smyrna Church, with flanks resting behind the Rottenwood and Nickajack Creeks. This position was, however, abandoned late on the 4th, when Sherman's army came up, and after capturing the entire line of rifle pits

NORTHERN VIEW OF HOVEY GAP, GA., SHOWING JOHNSTON'S RESERVE CAMPS.

FROM A SKETCH BY C. E. F. HILLEN.

possession of by the Federals. The remainder of the 15th was occupied with almost incessant skirmishing, which extended as well throughout the 16th and up to the time the Federal army advanced upon Johnston's intrenchments on the 17th.

The Confederates were so heavily pressed at all points that they soon had to abandon Lost Mountain, as well as the long line of breastworks connecting it with Kenesaw Mountain. Their centre was transferred to the latter, while Hood's force, on the right, was made to cover Marietta, and their left, under Hardee, was bent still more behind Noses Creek, so as to protect the line of railway communicating with the Chattahoochee.

The lines were every day drawn tighter around the Confederate position until the 22d, when the customary skirmishing gave place to quite a sanguinary engagement at what was known as the "Kulp (Culp's) House," southwest of Marietta. Schofield had just taken position upon Hooker's right, which had been considerably advanced toward the Confederate works, when the two divisions of Hood's corps, led by Generals Hindman and Stevenson, suddenly appeared and drove the skirmishers upon the main line.

JUNE, 1864.

Hooker and Schofield promptly ordered up the divisions of Generals Williams, Geary and Hascall, and these began the throwing up of breastworks; but they had made little progress by the time the enemy came upon them. Hood's extreme right, under Hindman, struck both Geary's right Federal killed were Generals C. G. Harker and Daniel McCook, and Colonel Barnhill, of the Fortieth Illinois Regiment; the wounded including General G. D. Wagner and Colonel Elliott W. Rice.

On the 1st of July, Sherman ordered Hooker and Schofield to advance some two miles to the right, whither they were followed the next day by General McPherson, whose place in front of the Kenesaw had been taken by Garrard's cavalry, while Stoneman's horse was sent ahead to strike the river near Turner's Ferry, about four miles below the railroad bridge, and thus threaten the Confederate rear.

JULY, 1864.

General Johnston saw that Sherman's plan was to completely turn the Confederate left, thus cutting him off from Atlanta, and he, therefore, concluded to abandon his strong position upon the Kenesaw so as to fall back upon the Chattahoochee. The movement was commenced late on the 2d, and early the following morning the Federal pickets occupied the crest of the mountain.

Orders were at once given to pursue the fast-retreating Confederates. General Thomas moved forward along the railroad to Marietta, and thence, in a southwardly direction, to the Chattahoochee, while General Logan's force was ordered to Marietta by the main road, and the remainder of the army pressed on rapidly toward the Nickajack Creek so as to attack the Confederates both in flank and rear. General Sherman, accompanying the Army of the Cumberland, entered Marietta at nine o'clock on the morning of the 3d. along the main road, began demonstrations along Nickajack Creek, as well as in the direction of Turner's Ferry.

Johnston's army fell back to the Chattahoochee, and Sherman decided to turn it by sending General Schofield's force along the Sandtown Road to effect a lodgment along the elevated eastern bank of the river, near the mouth of Soap's Creek, while cavalry demonstrations were being made at Roswell and elsewhere.

Schofield crossed the Chattahoochee at Powell's Ferry, and established himself upon the east bank after capturing a gun and a number of prisoners. Garrard occupied Roswell, where he destroyed several woolen and cotton mills, as well as other property, while another detachment of Federals were operating with nearly equal success as far as Campbelltown, nearly fifteen miles below the bridge. General Schofield strongly intrenched himself and began the construction of ponton and trestle bridges, while Howard was building a bridge at Power's Ferry, about two miles below Schofield's position.

General Newton's division having been sent to hold the ford at Roswell, the Federals were enabled to cross at three different points on the Chattahoochee, just above the Confederate lines. Seeing that this movement would flank him, Johnston crossed the river during the night of the 9th, and took up a new position covering Atlanta, his line extending from the Chattahoochee to Peach Tree Creek.

CAPTURE OF MISSION RIDGE NEAR [illegible] BY GENERAL THOMAS NOVEMBER [illegible]

[illegible]

ROSTER OF THE FEDERAL FORCES.

MILITARY DIVISION OF THE MISSISSIPPI.

Major general Wm. T. Sherman commanding.

ARMY OF THE CUMBERLAND.

Major-general George H. Thomas commanding.

FOURTH ARMY CORPS.

(1) Major-general Oliver O. Howard.
(2) Major-general David S. Stanley.

FIRST DIVISION.

(1) Major-general D. S. Stanley.
(2) Brigadier-general Nathan Kimball.

First Brigade: (1) Brigadier-general Charles Cruft; (2) Colonel Isaac M. Kirby.

Second Brigade: (1) Brigadier-general Walter C. Whitaker; (2) Colonel Jacob E. Taylor.

Third Brigade: Colonel William Grose.

Artillery: Battery "B," Independent Pennsylvania, and the Fifth Indiana Artillery.

SECOND DIVISION.

(1) Major-general John Newton.
(2) Brigadier-general George D. Wagner.

First Brigade: Brigadier-general Nathan Kimball.

Second Brigade: Colonel John G. Mitchell.

Third Brigade: (1) Colonel Daniel McCook; (2) Colonel Caleb J. Dilworth.

Artillery: Second Minnesota, "I" Second Illinois, and Fifth Wisconsin Batteries.

THIRD DIVISION.

Brigadier-general Absalom Baird.

First Brigade: (1) Brigadier-general John B. Turchin; (2) Colonel Morton C. Hunter.

Second Brigade: (1) Colonel F. Van Derveer; (2) Colonel Newell Gleason.

Third Brigade: Colonel George P. Este.

Artillery: Seventh Indiana and Nineteenth Indiana Batteries.

TWENTIETH ARMY CORPS.

(1) Major-general Joseph Hooker.
(2) Major-general Henry W. Slocum.

FIRST DIVISION.

Brigadier-general Alpheus S. Williams.

First Brigade: Brigadier-general Joseph F. Knipe.

Second Brigade: Brigadier-general Thomas H. Ruger.

Third Brigade: (1) Brigadier-general H. Tyndale; (2) Colonel James S. Robinson.

Artillery: Batteries "M" and "I," First New York.

ARMY OF THE TENNESSEE.

(1) Major-general James B. McPherson commanding.
(2) Major-general Oliver O. Howard commanding.

FIFTEENTH ARMY CORPS.

Major-general John A. Logan.

FIRST DIVISION.

(1) Brigadier-general Peter J. Osterhaus.
(2) Brigadier-general Charles R. Woods.

First Brigade: (1) Brigadier-general Charles R. Woods; (2) Colonel William B. Woods.

Second Brigade: Colonel James A. Williamson.

Third Brigade: Colonel Hugo Wangelin.

Artillery: Battery "F," Second Missouri, and Fourth Ohio Independent.

SECOND DIVISION.

(1) Brigadier-general Morgan L. Smith.
(2) Brigadier-general J. A. J. Lightburn.
(3) Brigadier-general William B. Hazen.

First Brigade: (1) Brigadier-general Giles A. Smith; (2) Colonel J. S. Martin; (3) Colonel Theodore Jones.

Second Brigade: (1) Brigadier-general J. A. J. Lightburn; (2) Colonel Wells S. Jones.

Artillery: Battery "H," First Illinois, and "A," First Illinois.

KNAPP'S PENNSYLVANIA BATTERY SHELLING PINE MOUNTAIN, SCENE OF THE DEATH OF THE CONFEDERATE GENERAL POLK.

Second Brigade: (1) Brigadier-general G. D. Wagner; (2) Colonel Emerson Opdycke.

Third Brigade: (1) Brigadier-general C. G. Harker; (2) Colonel Luther P. Bradley.

Artillery: Batteries "G," First Missouri and "M," First Illinois.

THIRD DIVISION.

Brigadier-general Thomas J. Wood.

First Brigade: Colonel William H. Gibson.

Second Brigade: (1) Brigadier-general William B. Hazen; (2) Colonel P. Sidney Post.

Third Brigade: (1) Brigadier-general Samuel Beatty; (2) Colonel Frederick Knefler.

Artillery: Sixth Ohio, and Bridges's Illinois Batteries.

FOURTEENTH ARMY CORPS.

(1) Major-general John M. Palmer.
(2) Brevet-major-general Jefferson C. Davis.

FIRST DIVISION.

(1) Brigadier-general Richard W. Johnson.
(2) Brigadier-general John H. King.

First Brigade: Brigadier-general William P. Carlin.

Second Brigade: (1) Brigadier-general John H. King; (2) Colonel William L. Stoughton.

Third Brigade: (1) Colonel James M. Neibling; (2) Colonel Benjamin F. Scribner.

Artillery: Batteries "A," First Michigan, and "C," First Illinois.

SECOND DIVISION.

(1) Brigadier-general Jefferson C. Davis.
(2) Brigadier-general James D. Morgan.

First Brigade: Brigadier-general James D. Morgan.

SECOND DIVISION.

Brigadier-general John W. Geary.

First Brigade: Colonel Charles Candy.

Second Brigade: (1) Colonel A. Buschbeck; (2) Colonel Patrick H. Jones.

Third Brigade: Colonel David Ireland.

Artillery: Battery "E," Independent Pennsylvania, and Thirteenth New York.

THIRD DIVISION.

(1) Major-general Daniel Butterfield.
(2) Brigadier-general William T. Ward.

First Brigade: (1) Brigadier-general William T. Ward; (2) Colonel Benjamin Harrison.

Second Brigade: Colonel John Coburn.

Third Brigade: Colonel James Wood, Jr.

Artillery: Batteries "C," First Ohio, and "I," First Michigan.

CAVALRY.

Brigadier-general W. L. Elliott, Chief of Cavalry.

FIRST DIVISION.

Colonel Edward M. McCook.

First Brigade: Colonel A. P. Campbell.

Second Brigade: Colonel O. H. La Grange.

Third Brigade: Colonel L. D. Watkins.

Artillery: Eighteenth Indiana.

SECOND DIVISION.

Brigadier-general Kenner Garrard.

First Brigade: Colonel William B. Sipes.

Second Brigade: Colonel R. H. G. Minty.

Third Brigade: Colonel A. O. Miller.

Artillery: The Chicago Board of Trade Battery.

THIRD DIVISION.

Brigadier-general John E. Smith.

First Brigade: Colonel Jesse I. Alexander.

Second Brigade: Colonel Green B. Raum.

Third Brigade: Colonel Jabez Banbury.

FOURTH DIVISION.

Brigadier-general William Harrow.

First Brigade: Colonel Reuben Williams.

Second Brigade: Colonel Charles C. Walcutt.

Third Brigade: Colonel John M. Oliver.

Artillery: First Iowa Battery.

SIXTEENTH ARMY CORPS.

Major-general Grenville M. Dodge.

SECOND DIVISION.

(1) Brigadier-general Thomas W. Sweeny.
(2) Brigadier-general John M. Corse.

First Brigade: Colonel Elliott W. Rice.

Second Brigade: (1) Colonel P. E. Burke; (2) Colonel August Mersy; (3) Lieutenant-colonel Phillips; (4) Colonel R. N. Adams.

Third Brigade: (1) Colonel M. M. Bane; (2) Brigadier-general William Vandever.

Artillery: Battery "H," First Missouri Light Artillery.

FOURTH DIVISION.

(1) Brigadier-general James C. Veatch.
(2) Brigadier-general John W. Fuller.

First Brigade: Brigadier-general John W. Fuller.

Second Brigade: Colonel John W. Sprague.

Third Brigade: (1) Colonel John Tillson; (2) Colonel James S. Howe.

Artillery: Fourteenth Ohio Battery.

SEVENTEENTH ARMY CORPS.

Major-general Francis P. Blair, Jr.

THIRD DIVISION.

Brigadier-general Mortimer D. Leggett.

First Brigade: (1) Brigadier-general Manning F. Force; (2) Colonel George E. Bryant.

Second Brigade: (1) Colonel Robert K. Scott; (2) Lieutenant-colonel G. F. Wiles.

Third Brigade: Colonel Adam G. Malloy.

Artillery: Third Ohio, Battery "D"; First Illinois, Eighth Michigan Battery.

FOURTH DIVISION.

(1) Brigadier-general Walter Q. Gresham.
(2) Brigadier-general Giles A. Smith.

First Brigade: (1) Colonel William L. Sanderson; (2) Colonel B. F. Potts.

Second Brigade: Colonel George C. Rogers.

Third Brigade: Colonel William Hall.

Artillery: Company "F," Second Illinois.

Besides the artillery above mentioned, the following batteries were in the Army of the Tennessee, viz.: Illinois, batteries "E," "F" and "G" of the First Light Artillery; batteries "F" and "G" of Second Light Artillery, and Cogswell's Battery. Indiana, Third, Ninth and Fourteenth. Michigan, Second Battery. Minnesota, First Battery. Ohio, Seventh, Eighth, Tenth, Fifteenth and Twenty-sixth batteries. Wisconsin, Sixth, Seventh and Twelfth. Only part of them were at any one time with the moving column. They were under the direction of Colonel Andrew Hickenlooper, Chief of Artillery.

ARMY OF THE OHIO.

TWENTY-THIRD ARMY CORPS.

Major-general John M. Schofield commanding.

FIRST DIVISION.

Brigadier-general Alvin P. Hovey.

First Brigade: Colonel Richard F. Barter.

Second Brigade: (1) Colonel John C. McQuiston; (2) Colonel Peter T. Swaine.

SECOND DIVISION.

(1) Brigadier-general Henry M. Judah.
(2) Brigadier-general Milo S. Hascall.

First Brigade: (1) Brigadier-general Nathaniel C. McLean; (2) Colonel Joseph A. Cooper.

Second Brigade: (1) Colonel John R. Bond; (2) Colonel William E. Hobson.

Third Brigade: Colonel Silas A. Strickland.

Artillery: Shields's Nineteenth Ohio and Paddock's Sixth Michigan Batteries.

THIRD DIVISION.

Brigadier-general Jacob D. Cox.

First Brigade: Colonel James W. Reilly.

Second Brigade: (1) Brigadier-general M. D. Manson; (2) Colonel Daniel Cameron; (3) Colonel John S. Casement.

Third Brigade: (1) Brigadier-general N. C. McLean; (2) Colonel Robert K. Byrd; (3) Colonel Thomas J. Henderson.

Artillery: Harvey's Fifteenth Indiana; Wilber's Twenty-third Indiana and "D" First Ohio (Cockerill's).

CAVALRY—ARMY OF THE OHIO.

Major-general George Stoneman commanding.

FIRST DIVISION.

Colonel Israel T. Garrard.

The cavalry of the army, though nominally connected with the three subordinate armies was, during the active campaign, organized into four commands, which were assigned to duty by General Sherman as circumstances required, and as will be seen by the narrative of the campaign. One division was usually upon each flank and one covering the communications at the rear, whilst the fourth was ready for expeditions in front which might be ordered. The nearest subordinate army commander usually exercised authority over the cavalry co-operating with him.

In the War Department records for June, they are stated as follows:

Principal Cavalry Commanders.—Major-general George Stoneman, Brigadier-general Judson Kilpatrick, Brigadier-general Kenner Garrard, Brigadier-general Edward M. McCook.

ROSTER OF THE CONFEDERATE ARMY.

ARMY OF TENNESSEE.

GENERAL JOSEPH E. JOHNSTON COMMANDING.

HARDEE'S ARMY CORPS.

Lieutenant-general William J. Hardee.

MAJOR-GENERAL B. F. CHEATHAM'S DIVISION.—*Brigades*—Maney's, Wright's, Strahl's, Vaughn's.

MAJOR-GENERAL W. H. T. WALKER'S DIVISION.—*Brigades*—Mercer's, Jackson's, Gist's, Stevens's.

MAJOR-GENERAL PAT. R. CLEBURNE'S DIVISION.—*Brigades*—Polk's, Lowry's, Govan's, Smith's.

MAJOR-GENERAL W. B. BATE'S DIVISION.—*Brigades*—Tyler's, Lewis's, Finley's.

HOOD'S ARMY CORPS.

Lieutenant-general J. B. Hood.

MAJOR-GENERAL T. C. HINDMAN'S DIVISION.—*Brigades*—Deas's, Colonel J. G. Coltart commanding; Manigault's; Tucker's, Colonel J. H. Sharp commanding; Walthall's, Colonel Sam Benton commanding.

MAJOR-GENERAL C. L. STEVENSON'S DIVISION.—*Brigades*—Brown's, Cummings's, Reynolds's, Pettus's.

MAJOR-GENERAL A. P. STEWART'S DIVISION.—*Brigades*—Stovall's, Clayton's, Gibson's, Baker's.

WHEELER'S CAVALRY CORPS.

Major-general Joseph Wheeler.

MAJOR-GENERAL WILLIAM T. MARTIN'S DIVISION.—*Brigades*—Allen's, Iverson's.

BRIGADIER-GENERAL J. H. KELLEY'S DIVISION.—*Brigades*—Anderson's, Dibbrell's, Hannon's.

BRIGADIER-GENERAL W. Y. C. HUMES'S DIVISION.—*Brigades*—Ashby's, Harrison's, Williams's.

ARTILLERY.

Brigadier-general F. A. Shoup.

BATTALIONS ATTACHED TO HARDEE'S CORPS (3 batteries in each battalion—Colonel M. Smith).—*Battalions*—Hoxton's, Hotchkiss's, Martin's, Cobb's.

BATTALIONS ATTACHED TO HOOD'S CORPS (Colonel R. F. Beckham).—*Battalions*—Courtney's, Eldridge's, Johnston's.

WHEELER'S CORPS (Lieutenant-colonel F. W. Robertson).—Five batteries.

RESERVE BATTALIONS.—Eight batteries—Williams's, Palmer's, and Waddell's battalions.

DETACHMENTS.

ESCORTS (CAVALRY).—General Johnston's Headquarters Company "A" and Company "B." Headquarters—Cheatham's, Cleburne's, Walker's, Bate's, Hardee's, Hindman's, Stevenson's, Stewart's. One company each.

ENGINEER TROOPS (Major J. W. Green).—*Divisions*—Cheatham's, Cleburne's, Stewart's, Hindman's, Buckner's. Detachment of Sappers and Miners. One company each.

ARMY OF MISSISSIPPI.

Major-general W. W. Loring.

MAJOR-GENERAL S. G. FRENCH'S DIVISION.—*Brigades*—Ector's, Cockrell's, Sears's.

MAJOR-GENERAL W. W. LORING'S DIVISION (Brigadier-general W. S. Featherstone).—*Brigades*—Adams's, Featherstone's, Scott's.

MAJOR-GENERAL ED. C. WALTHALL'S DIVISION.—*Brigades*—Quarles's, Canty's, Reynolds's.

CAVALRY.

Brigadier-general W. H. Jackson.

BRIGADIER-GENERAL W. H. JACKSON'S DIVISION.—*Brigades*—Armstrong's, Ross's, Ferguson's.

ESCORTS (CAVALRY).—Three companies.

ARTILLERY.

Brigades—Storrs's, Meyrick's, Preston's, Waddell's. Three batteries each.

THE MILITARY COLLEGE, MARIETTA, GA. FROM A SKETCH BY D. R. BROWN, TWENTIETH CONNECTICUT.

JOHN M. SCHOFIELD.

BORN in Chautauqua County, N. Y., September 29th 1831; graduated at the United States Military Academy, and promoted brevet second-lieutenant of the Second Artillery, July 1st, 1853, and captain of First Artillery, May 14th, 1861. From 1855 to 1861 he was Professor of Natural and Experimental Philosophy at West Point, and at the outbreak of the Civil War was filling the chair of Physics in Washington University, St. Louis, Mo. Appointed major of the First Missouri Volunteers, April 26th, 1861, he served with General Lyon as chief of staff in the operations in Missouri, participating in the battles of Dug Spring and Wilson's Creek. Commissioned brigadier-general of United States Volunteers, and of Missouri Militia, November, 1861, he commanded the State troops and the District of St. Louis, and in October 1862, he was placed in command of the Army of the Frontier. Promoted to be major-general, United States Volunteers, November 29th, 1862, he commanded the District and Department of Missouri until January, 1864, when he was appointed to command the Army of the Ohio; was in the immediate command of the Twenty-third Corps in Sherman's Georgia campaign, participating in the almost constant severe fighting, ending with the capture of Atlanta, September 2d, 1864. In November, 1864, he was placed in command of the forces detached from General Sherman's army to strengthen General Thomas at Nashville, being constantly engaged with Hood's invading army in Tennessee, and defeated it at the battle of Franklin, Nov. 30th, 1864; joined General Thomas the next day, and commanded the Twenty-third Corps at the battle of Nashville and in subsequent pursuit of Hood's army. For his services at Franklin he was appointed brigadier-general in the Regular Army. Transferred with his command to North Carolina, and placed in command of that Department, February 9th, 1865, he occupied Wilmington, February 22d, fought the battle of Kinston

THE OCEAN MONITOR "DICTATOR."

DOUBLE-TURRETED MONITOR "MONADNOCK" AND THE MONITOR TORPEDO-BOAT "NAPA," IN FIGHTING TRIM.

ONE OF THE TORPEDO-BOATS.

LIGHT-DRAUGHT MONITOR "TUNXIS."

PICKET-BOATS.

FEDERAL IRONCLADS.—NEW PATTERNS ADOPTED BY THE GOVERNMENT DURING 1864.

VIEW OF THE BATTLEFIELD, NEAR ATLANTA, GA., WHERE GENERAL McPHERSON WAS KILLED.

VIEW OF THE JAIL AT DECATUR, GA., IN WHICH FEDERAL PRISONERS WERE CONFINED.

March 8th–10th, and joined General Sherman at Goldsboro', March 23d, 1865. Upon the surrender of General Johnston's army (April 26th), he was appointed to execute the terms of the Convention. In command of the Department of North Carolina until June, 1865, and of the First Military District of Virginia, 1866–67; Secretary of War *ad interim*, May, 1868—March, 1869, when he was promoted to be major-general, United States Army, and assigned to command the Department of Missouri. In May, 1870, he entered command of the Division of the Pacific. Served Superintendent of the United States Military Academy at West Point from September 1st, 1876, to January 21st, 1881, when he was appointed to the command of the Department of Texas, with headquarters at San Antonio. On November 1st, 1883, he was appointed to the command of the Division of the Missouri—on the promotion of General Sheridan to the command of the Army—with headquarters at Chicago, Ill., his jurisdiction embracing the Departments of the Platte, Dakota, Missouri and Texas.

JAMES C. LANE.

Born in New York City ("Greenwich Village"), July 23d, 1823. After prosecuting a thorough line of scientific studies, he made a specialty of architecture and of civil engineering in all its branches, establishing them in a successful business, which he carried on in his native State until the year 1851. He was then called to aid in the construction of the Illinois Central Railroad, under Colonel R. B. Mason, and was prominently connected with that enterprise until late in 1852, when he entered the United States Coast Survey at Washington, D. C. By leave of the latter, and at the express solicitation of President F. M. Kelley, of the Interoceanic Canal Association, he led several important explorations in New Granada. He was afterward engaged in mineralogical surveys in San Domingo, Porto Rico, and Cuba, up to the time of the breaking out of the Civil War, when he tendered his services to the United States Government, and was shortly after commissioned major of the One Hundred and Second Regiment of New York Volunteers. As such, he took charge of McCall's camp at Dranesville and of the defenses of Harper's Ferry during the months of April and May, 1862, being promoted to the lieutenant-colonelcy of his regiment on the 10th of the ensuing July. In the following month he commanded the regiment at the battle of Cedar Mountain, where, during a bitter encounter of less than two hours' duration, the One Hundred and Second lost 137 men and 11 officers. He afterward participated in many of the battles attending Pope's retreat, and

JAMES C. LANE.

was in command of the regiment at the second Bull Run battle, as well as at Chantilly and Antietam, in September, 1862. Three months later he received the colonelcy of the regiment, and with it took a leading part in the battle of Chancellorsville, where the regiment remained in the rifle-pits with the Sixtieth New York, when all the rest of the Third Brigade, Twelfth Corps, had retired on account of the terrible artillery fire which enfiladed them. The Confederates, yelling like devils, rushed down upon the Federals and the Twelfth Georgia Regiment sprang in among the One Hundred and Second, calling out, "You are our prisoners." "Not by a d—n sight!" shouted the boys of the One Hundred and Second; and they disarmed the Georgia Twelfth, taking their stand of colors, and in the midst of the fight marching them off prisoners of war. While this was going on, a Confederate officer jumped in among them, and seeing them mixed—half butternuts and half blue-jackets—called out, "What regiment is this?" "The One Hundred and Second New York." "H—l!" said he; "I suppose I am your prisoner then. Well, bully for you! I am a New York boy myself." The One Hundred and Second New York Regiment was organized in the Fall of 1861, and proceeded to the seat of war, March 10th, 1862. It was in the thickest of the fight at White Sulphur Springs, Antietam, Chancellorsville, Gettysburg, Lookout Mountain, Ringgold and the second Bull Run.

At the decisive battle of Gettysburg, General Lane was in command of a brigade, and during the three days' fight he received a severe wound in the right arm from a sharpshooter's rifle. He was then sent West with Generals Hooker and Slocum, and led the advance on Lookout Mountain, taking likewise a prominent part in the engagement along Missionary Ridge; as well as in many of the principal battles constituting the Georgia campaign. While forming part of Geary's brigade, his regiment captured four Napoleon brass guns at Resaca, and made important reconnoissances, notably at Snake Gap, Dallas, Allatoona Creek, and at Pine Hill. Was mustered out of service by consolidation of regiments, at Atlanta, July 12th, 1864, having received the brevets of brigadier-general and of major-general of Volunteers; and since the close of the war has been engaged in mineralogical surveys in California, Arizona, Nevada, and Lower California, as well as in topographical surveys in Palestine east of the River Jordan, and as chief engineer of the South Side and of the New York, Woodhaven and Rockaway Railroads of Long Island, besides engaging in the practice of general mining and civil engineering. At the time of writing (1885) he is engaged as engineer of the Commission appointed by the Supreme Court for appraising new parks for New York City.

VIEW OF ALLATOONA, GA., SCENE OF THE BATTLE ON THE 5TH OF OCTOBER, 1864.

PRESENTATION OF COLORS TO THE TWENTIETH UNITED STATES COLORED INFANTRY, COLONEL [illegible], IN NEW YORK CITY, MARCH 5th, 1864.

THE ARMY OF THE POTOMAC.

MEADE'S VIRGINIA CAMPAIGN.

ASIDE from the reoccupation of Harper's Ferry by General French, the capture of Falling Waters, and a cavalry skirmish at Shepherdstown, Va., no movements of importance were made by Meade's army after Lee's second repulse from Maryland and Pennsylvania (Vol. II., page 133) until the 17th of July.

JULY, 1863.

The skirmish at Shepherdstown resulted in the loss of about 100 men on both sides, and in the defeat of a body of cavalry under the immediate command of General Fitzhugh Lee, who was attacked on the 16th by General Gregg's force, taken from the Tenth New York, and the First, Fourth and Sixteenth Pennsylvania Cavalry. But the Confederates then marching through the Chester Gap to Culpepper.

General French had been ordered on the 22d to march to Manassas Gap as soon as a sufficient force could be got together, it being Meade's intention to flank Lee's army before it could proceed further on its retreat. But there was so much delay at the Gap by reason of a series of engagements with the rear-guard of the Confederate army, under General Ewell, that the attack could not be brought on as intended.

Longstreet's corps was enabled to reach Culpepper Court House on the 24th, and was immediately followed there by Hill's force, while Ewell was thus barring the Federal progress, and the latter succeeded in reaching Front Royal after a brisk engagement, called by many the battle of Wapping Culpepper Court House, which they set about strengthening in every way, while the Confederates were intrenching themselves upon a new and more advantageous line along the southern side of the Rapidan. Meade was about attacking the latter position when Howard's Eleventh and Slocum's Twelfth Corps were taken from him on the 23d, and sent to aid that part of the Army of the Cumberland then operating against Chattanooga (Vol. II., page 161).

Pending the arrival of reinforcements, Meade remained on the defensive until the 10th of the following month, when he felt himself strong enough for an advance, and sent Buford's cavalry to reconnoitre in different directions.

OCTOBER, 1863.

Meade was soon informed that Lee had likewise

EXPLOSION OF A TORPEDO UNDER THE "COMMODORE BARNEY," ON JAMES RIVER, AUGUST 4TH, 1863.

FROM A SKETCH BY C. E. H. BONWILL.

affair at Falling Waters, two days previous, was of far greater consequence. In this, the entire Third Division of Cavalry of the Army of the Potomac was engaged, and succeeded in capturing some 1,500 prisoners, 2 guns, 2 caissons, 2 battle-flags, and a large number of small-arms; the Confederates losing in addition General J. J. Pettigrew, who was shot early in the action, and whose body remained in the hands of Meade's troops.

On the 17th of July, the Federals began crossing the Potomac on ponton-bridges at Berlin and at Harper's Ferry, and after passing through Lovettsville (19th), Union (20th), Upperville (22d), Markham Station (23d), and Salem (24th), they reached Warrenton on the 25th. Meade had taken possession of the Blue Ridge Gaps, and had advanced so rapidly that a day's halt had to be made at Union, lest his right should be left unprotected, and be subjected to an attack from the strong bodies of Heights, in which the troops under Generals J. H. Hobart Ward, Prince, and Spinola, succeeded, with the aid of Buford's cavalry, in driving back the Confederates with heavy loss.

The latter engagement came to an end at nightfall, and when Meade decided to press on his advantage the following day, it was found that the Confederates had continued on their retreat during the night, and that all were then on their way to Culpepper. Meade thereafter withdrew that portion of his army already at the Gap, and made his way slowly toward the Rappahannock, crossing the latter only on the 16th of September, upon learning, through reconnoissances made by Kilpatrick, Buford and Gregg, that Longstreet's corps had been detached and sent to the assistance of General Bragg in Tennessee.

SEPTEMBER, 1863.

Lee's army fell back without bringing about any general engagement, and the Federals occupied determined to assume the offensive, and that the Confederates were already advancing by way of Madison Court House to attack Meade's right; but it was not until later in the day that he became satisfied as to Lee's real intentions. Meade's advanced posts at (Robertson's Run) James City, then held by part of the Third Corps, and a detachment from Kilpatrick's cavalry, were attacked during the afternoon by a strong force under General Stuart, and after a spirited contest the Federals were driven back to Culpepper with the loss of many killed, wounded and prisoners.

Realizing the danger he was in, Meade abandoned Culpepper early on the morning of Sunday, the 11th, and after recrossing the river, destroyed the Rappahannock Station Bridge, continuing his retreat along the line of the railroad running to Alexandria. On the 12th, however, he was informed that Lee had not gone beyond Culpepper, and as

CULPEPPER COURT HOUSE, VA.

it was possible that a stand was intended to be made at that place, Meade ordered the Third Corps to take position at Freeman's Ford, while General Gregg's cavalry watched the Upper Rappahannock, and he sent back the Second, Fifth and Sixth Corps, with Buford's cavalry division, in the direction of Brandy Station, where it was found that Lee had abandoned Culpepper and entered upon another flanking movement.

It proved that Lee had advanced from Culpepper in two columns, the better to intercept Meade's retreat along the Orange and Alexandria Railway at some point north of the river. Late on the 12th, Lee arrived at Sulphur Springs, and the advance of his army crossed the Rappahannock at that place, as well as at Waterloo and Warrenton, compelling Meade's farther retreat toward Catlett's Station, after subjecting Gregg's cavalry to a severe attack and defeat at a place called Jeffersonton. The opposing forces were now marched rapidly and by almost parallel roads toward Alexandria.

Late on the 13th, Stuart's cavalry had hurried forward to such an extent that it suddenly found itself between the force holding the heights of Cedar Run, at which place Caldwell's division had three batteries admirably posted, and the rear-guard consisting of the Second Corps under Genera

CHARACTERISTIC VIRGINIA SCENE—A FARMER ON HIS WAY TO THE MILL.

FROM A SKETCH BY EDWIN FORBES.

CAPTURE OF STUART'S CONFEDERATE GUNS, NEAR CULPEPPER, BY GENERAL CUSTER'S CAVALRY BRIGADE, SEPTEMBER 14th, 1863.

VIRGINIA FARMERS' FAMILIES ON THEIR WAY TO THE FEDERAL COMMISSARY FOR PROVISIONS.

FROM A SKETCH BY EDWIN FORBES.

Warren, supported by Kilpatrick's cavalry. There being apparently no chance for escape without encountering a heavy loss from the superior numbers about him, Stuart hid his men the best way he could throughout the intervening thickets, and managed to send messengers through the Federal lines asking for reinforcements.

The latter were promptly sent, and as soon as the noise of musketry reached his ears, before daylight the following morning, Stuart opened so fiercely and suddenly upon Caldwell from his place of concealment, that the Federals fell back to the opposite side of the hill. There, however, another attack was made upon them from the Warrenton Road, along which Ewell was marching toward Greenwich. The Confederate advance struck Warren's troops, and for a while it looked as if the latter would be completely swept off the field between the two fires; but General Hays rapidly threw across the northern side of Cedar Run two regiments from his advance division—the One Hundred and Twenty-sixth New York and the Twelfth New Jersey—who bravely and at great loss held the enemy in check until the remainder could be brought up.

Ewell's troops were driven away, and Stuart managed to escape without much suffering; but the cavalry, led by Colonel Thomas Ruffin, was less fortunate. It was throughout sharply engaged by Hays's men, and during its fight with the One

CELEBRATING WASHINGTON'S BIRTHDAY BY A BALL AT THE SECOND CORPS HEADQUARTERS.

FROM A SKETCH BY EDWIN FORBES.

VIRGINIA DURING THE WAR—SCENES IN THE AR

VIRGINIA DURING THE WAR—SCENES IN THE [illegible] THE POTOMAC, SEPTEMBER AND OCTOBER [illegible]

INTERIOR AND EXTERIOR OF THE OPERA HOUSE ERECTED BY THE SECOND BRIGADE, FIRST DIVISION, FIRST ARMY CORPS, COMMANDED BY GENERAL RICE.

CAPTURE OF A TRAIN, NEAR MEADOW BRIDGE, VA., BY GENERAL STONEMAN.

GENERAL MEADE RECROSSING THE RAPPAHANNOCK, OCTOBER, 1863, BEFORE LEE'S ADVANCE.

From a Sketch by Edwin Forbes.

Hundred and Twenty-sixth New York Regiment, lost its commander, as well as many of its bravest officers.

Both armies soon resumed their march, Meade forcing the way along the railroad toward Centreville, where he had decided to halt and give battle. Lee made Bristoe Station his objective point in order to anticipate the arrival of the Federal troops. Meade's army had, however, except Warren's corps, which brought up the rear, passed Bristoe Station before Hill's forces came up. Hill, therefore, attacked the rear of the Fifth Corps as they were crossing Broad Run. Warren had already engaged Ewell at Auburn, and now suddenly came upon Hill, in the location he had expected to find Sykes. His position was critical, as Hill turned his batteries from Sykes's retreating forces upon Warren's advance, before he could get his men into position.

When Warren got ready, however, an artillery duel followed, in which the Federals certainly obtained the advantage. The batteries of Arnold, Brown and Ricketts were brought to bear upon the Confederates from the rear of an embankment, whence they could inflict heavy losses upon their assailants. The first attack had fallen mainly upon Colonel Heath's First Brigade and General Mallon's Third Brigade of General Webb's division, as well as upon General Owen's Third Brigade of General Hays's division who had been ordered forward upon the first attack.

SAMUEL COOPER.

In a short time the Confederates were driven back, with the loss to them of nearly 500 prisoners, several pieces of artillery and two battle-flags. The loss on the Federal side was 51 killed and 329 wounded, General James E. Mallon being among the killed. While this was a temporary advantage to Warren, he was not able to hold the position, and it was dangerous to withdraw, as Ewell's corps coming up brought Lee's entire force in front of the Second Corps. Night saved Warren, as under cover of darkness he withdrew, and the next morning joined at Centreville the main body. As Lee had failed to gain Meade's rear, he did not follow him and press the Federal troops beyond the heights of Centreville, within the Washington fortifications, not deeming it prudent to assault the enemy in position. He, therefore, threw forward a thin line as far as Bull Run, thus covering his designs to destroy the Orange and Alexandria Railroad, and make a retrograde movement beyond the Rappahannock. Meade followed the next day (19th), but failed to overtake Lee. Except cavalry skirmishes, there was no serious encounter. Stuart covered Lee's movements, and on October 19th Kilpatrick's division skirmished

BATTLE OF MINE RUN, VA.—POSITION OF THE ARMIES OF LEE AND MEADE, DECEMBER 1ST, 1863.

FROM A SKETCH BY EDWIN FORBES

warmly with Hampton's division. He forced the crossing of Broad Run at Buckland Mills, on the south bank of which Hampton was posted. Stuart directed the manœuvre of falling back slowly toward Warrenton, thus permitting Fitzhugh Lee's cavalry division to come up to Auburn and attack the Federal cavalry in flank and rear. This charge forced Kilpatrick's command to give way, and he retreated in confusion. At Warrenton General Meade halted and repaired the Orange and Alexandria Railroad, accomplishing it by the 7th of November, and then in two columns he continued his advance toward the Rappahannock.

heavy batteries, and opened a lively fire. Late in the afternoon a storming party, formed of Russell's and Upton's brigades, of the Sixth Corps, carried the works by assault, capturing 1,500 prisoners, 4 guns and 8 standards. Sedgwick lost about 300 killed and wounded. This advantage was not followed up, and Lee availed himself of the opportunity to withdraw to the Rapidan. Meade then advanced to the same position he occupied before the retreat. The campaign was attended by much toil and suffering to both armies, and resulted in no decided advantage to either.

General Meade being eager for action, watched

of November. The Fifth Corps, followed by the First Corps, was to cross the Rapidan at Culpepper Mine Ford and proceed to Parker's Store. The Second Corps was to cross at Germanna Ford and proceed to Robert's Tavern. The Third Corps, followed by the Sixth Corps, was to cross at Jacob's Mills Ford and gain the same place.

Owing to delays of the Third Corps, under General French, the whole army was detained [illegible] three hours; a second obstacle being a blunder on the part of the engineers in underestimating the width of the Rapidan, so that the ponton bridges were too short. In consequence, the army,

GENERAL CUSTER'S FIFTH REGULARS, COLONEL ASH, CHARGING INTO J. E. B. STUART'S CAMP, NEAR CHARLOTTESVILLE, VA.

From a Sketch by Edwin Forbes.

The left wing, under General French, crossed the Rappahannock at Kelley's Ford, and the right, under General Sedgwick, at Rappahannock Station. Lee held his army at Culpepper, with outposts at Kelley's Ford and Rappahannock. The Third Corps advanced on Kelley's Ford, and General Birney crossed over a division without waiting for a ponton-bridge, and the Fortieth New York, First and Twentieth Indiana, One Hundred and Tenth Pennsylvania, and the Third and Fifth Michigan, carried the rifle-pits and captured 500 prisoners. In the meantime Early held the north bank of the river at Rappahannock Station, defended by works built some time before by the Federal troops. He had 2,000 men of his division. General Sedgwick gaining the rear of the works, they planted

for a favorable opportunity to deliver battle. Near the end of November he planned the operation known as the "Mine Run Move." Lee, while resting his army on the Rapidan, near Morton's Ford, had left the fords of the river at Ely's, Culpepper Mine, Germanna and Jacob's Mills, uncovered. Ewell's corps held position from Morton's Ford to Orange Court House; Hill's corps was south of that point along the railroad to near Charlottesville, leaving an interval of several miles between the two corps.

Meade planned to cross the Rapidan at the lower fords, turn the Confederate right, and advancing toward Orange Court House, connect that place with Fredericksburg. November 1863

The movement was begun at dawn on the 26th

instead of making the passage of the river [illegible] the day, was not across until the following [illegible]. On the 27th the corps were again in motion. [illegible] while the intention was fully disclosed, and [illegible] as may be supposed, was not inactive. The Confederate line was drawn along a prominent ridge extending north and south for six or eight miles.

The 28th of November was passed in [illegible] reconnoissances, which were not completed until late on Sunday, the 29th. So it was resolved to make the attack on Monday morning. Early [illegible] the 30th the sound of Sedgwick's cannon [illegible] rolling along the line, but not an echo from Warren on the left. The presence of Warren's troops had attracted Lee's attention to his right, and he had powerfully strengthened that flank by placing artil

…es in position and infantry behind …tworks and abatis. Warren saw …at an attack was useless, and re…ed to sacrifice himself rather …an his command. He assumed …responsibility of suspending the …ack.

General Meade afterward became …vinced that the judgment of Gen…l Warren was correct. The troops …being nearly exhausted, and their …ons limited, General Meade dur… the following night withdrew the …y across the Rapidan, and it re…ned its old camps. Lee did not …empt to follow.

The movement of Mine Run ter…ated for the season the operations …Virginia, and the army established …elf into winter-quarters for the …t three months. During this …iod of dullness there were one or …cavalry expeditions planned with …aim of capturing Richmond. …first was devised by General …tler. Believing that Richmond …been stripped of its garrison …the purpose of strengthening the …nfederate force operating in North …olina under General Pickett, Gen… Butler formed the design of …oping down on the Confederate …pital with a cavalry raid by way …New Kent Court House, on the Peninsula. …raiding column, under General Wistar, left …w Kent Court House on February 5th, and …ached the Chickahominy at Bottom's Bridge on the following day. On the 5th, General Sedgwick temporarily commanding the Army of the Potomac in the absence of General Meade, threw Kilpatrick's cavalry division across the Rapidan at Ely's Ford, and Merritt's division at Barnett's Ford, while two divisions of the Second Corps made the passage at Germanna Ford by wading. The raid amounted to nothing. General Wistar found Bottom's Bridge blockaded, and after reconnoitring the position he returned.

WILLIAM W. AVERELL.

A few weeks later a bold expedition was fitted out, with the view of releasing the large body of Federal prisoners held at Richmond. This enterprise was under command of General Kilpatrick, with some three or four thousand cavalry, seconded by Colonel Ulric Dahlgren, a young officer of extraordinary dash and daring. It set out on the 28th of February, after Sedgwick's corps and Custer's cavalry had made a demonstration on Lee's left. Crossing the Rapidan at Ely's Ford, the force marched to Spottsylvania Court House. Here Colonel Dahlgren, with 500 picked men, pushed forward toward the James River. The column under General Kilpatrick struck the Virginia Central Railroad at Beaver Dam Station, whence parties were sent out to damage the road. While engaged in this work a train of troops arrived from Richmond, but after a short skirmish these retired. The main column then advanced with little opposition, and on March 1st drew up before the fortifications of Richmond. In the meantime, Colonel Dahlgren had arrived at the James River, where he obtained

SHAVING IN CAMP.—A SCENE IN GENERAL MEADE'S ARMY, NEAR CULPEPPER.

FROM A SKETCH BY EDWIN FORBES.

THE SOLDIERS OF MEADE'S ARMY DISCOVERING UNBURIED FEDERAL DEAD ON THE BATTLEFIELD OF GROVETON.

From a Sketch by Edwin Forbes.

a guide to lead the party to a ford not far from Richmond, but who treacherously conducted the column to near Goochland Court House, a full day's march from the intended point. The guide was hanged on the nearest tree, and Dahlgren moved toward Richmond, in front of which he arrived late on March 1st.

General Kilpatrick, hearing nothing of Dahlgren's column, became fearful as to his safety, and decided to fall back down the Peninsula. Dahlgren being thus isolated from the main body, decided also to retreat, as the country was now thoroughly aroused.

During the night of the 3d, while on the retreat, Colonel Dahlgren, with a hundred horsemen, became separated from the rest of his command, and falling into an ambush, he was killed, with some of his men, the remainder surrendering. The other portion succeeded in reaching Kilpatrick's column, which returned to the Army of the Potomac by way of Fortress Monroe. Both armies now

major-general, June 22d, 1863, he engaged in the numerous actions preceding Gettysburg, where he also commanded in chief the cavalry. Transferred to Missouri in 1864, he drove the invading forces of General Price from the State. Mustered out of the Volunteer service, January 15th, 1866, he resigned in 1868 his commission in the Regular Army, and for several years was United States Collector of Internal Revenue.

RICHARD STODDARD EWELL.

Born in the District of Columbia, October, 1816; graduated at West Point in 1840, served on the Western frontier, 1840-45, on coast duty, 1846, in the War with Mexico, 1846-48, engaged at Vera Cruz, Cerro Gordo, Contreras, Churubusco, Molino del Rey, and Chapultepec. Became captain of Dragoons in 1849; did frontier duty in New Mexico, 1850-51; and engaged in the Gila and Pinal Apache expeditions, 1857-59, encountering the Apaches on the Gila River in a skirmish. Resigning, May 7th, 1861, from the United States Army, he joined the Southern forces in the Civil War, serving in the Manassas campaign, 1861; engaged at White Oak Swamp, Cedar Mountain, Kettle Run and Manassas, 1862, in the Maryland campaign, 1862, in which he was severely wounded; became lieutenant general in 1863, and succeeded Stonewall Jackson at his request, being in

"for meritorious conduct." On July 15th, 1852, Colonel Cooper was promoted to the grade of adjutant-general of the whole Army of the United States. On March 7th, 1861, three days after the inauguration of President Lincoln, Colonel Cooper resigned, and offered his services to the Confederacy; he was at once appointed to the head of their Adjutant-general Department. After the battle of Bull Run he was created a general of the Confederate States Regular Army, and ranking officer next to the Confederate President. Died at Cameron, Va., November, 1876.

WILLIAM W. AVERELL.

Born in the State of New York in 1832; graduated at West Point in 1855; appointed lieutenant, Mounted Riflemen, served on frontier and fighting Indians till 1859, when wounded. During the Civil War he was present at the battle of Bull Run, July, 1861; colonel, Third Pennsylvania Cavalry, 1861; commanded cavalry brigade about Washington, D.C. In the Virginia Peninsula campaign, 1862, was engaged at Yorktown, Williamsburg, Fair Oaks, Malvern Hill. In 1862 he was appointed brigadier-general of Volunteers; engaged at Fredericksburg, December, 1862; in command of Kelley's Ford, March, 1863; participated in Stoneman's cavalry expedition toward Richmond, April and

SOLDIERS LOOKING AT A SHOW, NEAR CULPEPPER, VA.

From a Sketch by Edwin Forbes.

settled down into Winter cantonments to recuperate from the trying season of 1863. At the beginning of the Spring campaign of 1864, General Grant assumed command of the Army of the Potomac.

ALFRED PLEASONTON

Born in the District of Columbia, December, 1823; graduated at the United States Military Academy, West Point, July, 1844, when he was appointed brevet second-lieutenant of First Dragoons. He took part in the War against Mexico, winning the brevet of first-lieutenant for gallantry at Palo Alto and Resaca de la Palma; subsequently, prior to 1861, served on frontier duty with his company, and as acting assistant adjutant-general. In February, 1861, he was appointed major of the Second Cavalry. In the Civil War he commanded his regiment on its march from Utah to Washington, with which he continued to serve throughout the Virginia Peninsula campaign of 1862; appointed brigadier-general of Volunteers, July 16th, 1862, he commanded in September the division of cavalry (Army of the Potomac) following Lee's army invading Maryland; engaged at Boonsboro, South Mountain, Antietam, and subsequent pursuit, and constantly engaged the enemy's cavalry at Fredericksburg. At Chancellorsville, by his brilliant action, he staid the advance of Stonewall Jackson's corps, which threatened to carry all before it. Promoted for this valuable service to be

command of the Second Corps at Winchester, Gettysburg, Wilderness, and subsequent operations of the campaign, and was captured, April 6th, 1865, at Sailor's Creek. He was a bold, blunt, honest soldier, and on the collapse of the Confederacy, accepted in good faith its results. Died, January 25th, 1872, near Spring Hill, Tenn.

SAMUEL COOPER.

Born in the State of New York in 1798; graduated at West Point on December 10th, 1815, and was appointed brevet-second-lieutenant of Artillery, being attached to the Light Artillery Corps. On the 15th of December, 1817, he was fully commissioned a second-lieutenant of that branch of the United States service, and when the Regular Army of the country was reorganized, on the 1st of June, 1821, Lieutenant Cooper was retained as a second-lieutenant of the First United States Artillery. On July 6th, 1831, he was breveted captain "for ten years' faithful service in one grade of rank" in the United States Army. During 1836 Captain Cooper published a work entitled, "A Concise System of Instruction for the Militia and Volunteers of the United States." In 1838 he was promoted an assistant adjutant-general, with the brevet rank and pay of major. In 1847 he was appointed lieutenant-colonel. During the War with Mexico, Lieutenant-colonel Cooper devoted himself with great determination to the accomplishment of the object of the war, and was after the close of the same breveted colonel

May, 1863; engaged in, and in command of, skirmishes, actions and raids in West Virginia, Tennessee and Shenandoah Valley; at Opequon, September 19th, 1864, and Fisher's Hill, September 22d, 1864; captain, Third Cavalry, United States Army, July, 1862, and breveted successively major, lieutenant-colonel, brigadier-general and major-general, United States Army; resigned May 18th, 1865; appointed United States Consul-general to Canada, 1866; at present, president of a manufacturing company in New York.

ULYSSES S. GRANT.

Born, April 27th, 1822, at Point Pleasant, Clermont County, O. His father was of Scotch descent, and a dealer in leather. At the age of seventeen young Grant entered the Military Academy of West Point, and four years later graduated twenty-first in a class of thirty-nine, receiving the commission of brevet-second-lieutenant. He was assigned to the Fourth Infantry, and remained in the Army eleven years. Was engaged in every battle of the Mexican War, except that of Buena Vista, and received two brevets for gallantry. In 1848 he married Julia, daughter of Frederick Dent, a prominent merchant of St. Louis. He engaged in farming, but met with small success, and in 1860 he entered the leather trade with his father at Galena, Ill. When the Civil War broke out in 1861, Grant was thirty-nine years of age, but entirely unknown to public men, and without any personal acquaintance with great affairs. The President's

EDWARD FERRERO.

ALFRED PLEASONTON.

BATTLE AT RAPPAHANNOCK CROSSING, VA., NOVEMBER 7TH, 1863.—A PORTION OF SEDGWICK'S

EDWARD FERRERO

ALFRED PLEASONTON

R. S. EWELL

J. T. SPRAGUE

BATTLE AT RAPPAHANNOCK CROSSING, VA., NOVEMBER 7TH, 1863—A PORTION OF SEDGWICK'S CORPS AND THE SKIRMISHERS OF THE FORTY-FOURTH NEW YORK CHARGING THE CONFEDERATE WORKS

THE ELEVENTH PENNSYLVANIA CAVALRY COVERING THE ESCAPE OF FEDERAL PRISONERS FROM LIBBY PRISON, RICHMOND, VA.

first call for troops was made on the 15th of April, and on the 19th Grant was drilling a company of Volunteers at Galena. He also offered his services to the adjutant-general of the Army, but received no reply. The Governor of Illinois, however, employed him in the organization of Volunteer troops, and at the end of five weeks he was appointed colonel of the Twenty-first Illinois Infantry. He took command of his regiment in June, and reported to General Pope in Missouri. On August 7th he was commissioned a brigadier-general of Volunteers, the appointment being made without his knowledge. He had been unanimously recommended by the Congressmen from Illinois, none of whom had he personally known. On September 1st, he was placed in command of the District of Southeast Missouri, with headquarters at Cairo; and on the 6th, without orders, he seized Paducah, at the mouth of the Tennessee River, commanding the navigation both of that stream and of the Ohio. This stroke secured Kentucky to the Federal cause. Early in November he was ordered to make a demonstration in the direction of Belmont, a point on the west bank of the Mississippi, about eighteen miles below Cairo. The object of the demonstration was to prevent the crossing of the Confederate troops into Missouri. Grant received his orders on the 5th, and moved on the 6th, with 3,100 men, on transports. On the 7th, he landed at Belmont, broke up and destroyed the camp under a heavy fire from Columbus, and was returning to his transports, when large reinforcements arrived from the eastern bank to intercept him. But Grant, charging the enemy, cut his way out, reached the steamers, and returned to Cairo, having fully obeyed his orders, and accomplished the object of the expedition. In the affair of Belmont the Confederates had 7,000 men engaged against Grant's 3,000. Their loss was 642, and his 485. Early in February 1862, after repeated applications to General Halleck, his immediate superior, he was finally allowed to move up the Tennessee River against Fort Henry, in conjunction with a naval force. The gunboats silenced the fort, which surrendered on the 6th, before the troops arrived. Grant immediately made preparations to attack Fort Donelson, about twelve miles off, on the Cumberland River. Without waiting for orders he moved his troops to the latter point, and on the 12th began the siege. This position was extremely strong, and the garrison numbered 21,000. There was hard fighting on three successive days, and on the 15th, Grant carried by assault the works which were the key to the place. On the 16th, the Confederates surrendered unconditionally.

This was the first important success won by the Federal troops during the War. Its strategic results were marked; the entire States of Kentucky and Tennessee at once fell into Federal hands, and the navigation of the Mississippi, the Tennessee and the Cumberland Rivers was opened for [illegible] miles. Grant was made a major-general of Volunteers, and placed in command of the District of West Tennessee. In March he was ordered to move up the Tennessee River toward Corinth, where the Confederates were concentrating a large army; he was directed, however, not to attack. His forces, numbering 38,000, were accordingly encamped near Shiloh, or Pittsburg Landing, on the west bank of the Tennessee, waiting the arrival of General Buell. On April 6th, the Confederates came out from Corinth and attacked Grant violently, hoping to overwhelm him before Buell could arrive. Both sides fought fiercely, but the Federal forces were pushed back to the river. There, however, Grant held out till dark, when the head of Buell's column came upon the field. There was no more heavy fighting that night; but on the 7th, the combined Federal armies attacked and drove the Confederate force, who retreated as far as Corinth, nineteen miles. Grant was senior in rank to Buell, and commanded on both days. His entire loss was 12,217; that of Beauregard was 10,617; but the ground remained in the hands of Grant, and the object of the attack was unattained. Two days afterward Halleck arrived at the front and assumed command of the army, Grant remaining at the head of the right wing and the reserve. On May 30th, Corinth was evacuated by the Confederates, although no fighting had occurred since Shiloh. In July, Halleck was made General-in-Chief, and Grant succeeded him in command of the Department of the Tennessee. On September 19th, he fought the battle of Iuka. The strategy of this battle was Grant's; the tactics were those of Rosecrans and Ord. Subsequently Grant fortified Corinth, and directed the operations which resulted in the repulse of the Confederates from that place on the 3d and 4th of October, and in the battle of the Hatchie on the 5th, the commanders under him being again Rosecrans and Ord.

Immediately after the victory of Corinth, Grant proposed to the General-in-Chief the capture of Vicksburg, and receiving no answer, on November 2d he began a movement into the interior of Mississippi. While he threatened Vicksburg from the rear, Sherman was sent, by way of the Mississippi River, to attack it in front. Grant advanced as far as Oxford—fifty miles—when Holly Springs, his principal base of supplies, was surrendered by Colonel Murphy, who was dismissed from the army in consequence. This compelled the abandonment of the campaign, and Grant returned to the neighborhood of Corinth. Sherman's assault on Vicksburg failed at about the same time. In January, 1863, Grant took command in person of all the troops in the Mississippi Valley, and moved by the river to a point opposite Vicksburg. There he spent several months in fruitless efforts to turn the place. One plan was to build a canal in sight of Vicksburg, but out of reach of its guns, through which the army could pass to a point below; another, to divert the Mississippi River from its course; a third, to find or make a circuitous passage to the rear of the town through the tortuous streams on the north and east. But all these failed, and in April, Grant marched his army through the swamps on the western bank to a place below Vicksburg, while the gunboats and the transport fleet ran the batteries under a terrible fire. On April 30th he crossed the river, and landed at Bruinsburg, thirty miles south of Vicksburg.

There were now two armies opposed to him. Pemberton defended Vicksburg, and Johnston, with a smaller but rapidly increasing force, was at Jackson, fifty miles further east. Grant at once abandoned all communications with the river, and pushed into the interior between the two hostile armies.

On the 1st of May he met and defeated a portion of Pemberton's command at Port Gibson; then, advancing eastward, on the 12th he fell upon and destroyed a force coming out from Jackson to resist him; and on the 14th he captured the latter city, and scattered Johnston's army. Turning the same day to the Mississippi, on the 16th he utterly routed

ULRIC DAHLGREN.

JAMES B. FRY.

WILLIAM T. CLARK.

ULYSSES S. GRANT

THE ENTHUSIASM OF THE FEDERAL ARMIES—RE-ENLISTMENT OF THE SEVENTEENTH ARMY CORPS.

Pemberton's entire force at Champion's Hill; on the 17th, pursuing hotly, he came up with the enemy, and beat him again at Black River Bridge; and on the 18th drove him into Vicksburg, encamping in his rear, with his own base on a point on the Mississippi.

On the 19th and 22d he made unsuccessful assaults, and on the 23d began a regular siege. On the 4th of July the place surrendered, with 31,600 men and 172 cannon, at that time the largest capture of men and material ever made in war. During the entire campaign the Confederates had lost 30,000 prisoners, besides 12,000 in killed and wounded, and about 8,000 by disease and straggling—altogether an army of 60,000 men. Grant's entire loss was 8,873.

The great river was thus opened to the sea, and no more important fighting occurred in the Mississippi Valley, Grant being made a major-general in the Regular Army, and placed in command of the Military Division of the Mississippi, which included the Armies of the Ohio and the Cumberland, as well as that of the Tennessee.

Chattanooga was at this time beleaguered and almost surrounded by hostile forces, and the Army of the Cumberland, which defended it, was in imminent danger of starvation or capture. Grant reached this place on October 23d, and on

stead, and for some months was a member of Mr. Johnson's Cabinet. In 1868 he was elected President of the United States; on the expiration of the term of office in 1872, he was re-elected by the largest majority received by any candidate since the United States became a nation. After his second term he retired to private life and on the 17th day of May, 1877, started on his renowned tour around the world. He made the circuit of the globe in 914 days, arriving at Philadelphia, the point of his departure, on the 16th day of December, 1879, having visited all the important centres and nations of Europe, Asia, and Africa, and receiving the hospitality of the several rulers, as no previous American traveler had been honored.

In 1880 he was placed before the people as a candidate for renomination for the Presidency by the Republican party, but as the popular feeling against a third term overtopped the universal desire to honor Grant, he failed of the renomination, and entered into the banking business in New York City, which resulted disastrously; and, reduced in health and fortune, he is now, March, 1885, living in retirement in the City of New York.

On March 4th, 1885, the last official act of President Arthur was to "nominate Ulysses S. Grant, formerly General

Capitol. With the Ninth Corps under General Burnside at the siege of Knoxville where he defended Fort Sanders against the assault of Longstreet's veterans; and his name will ever be associated with the gallant defense of the capital of Tennessee. Returned to the Army of the Potomac, and commanded a division of colored troops at the siege of Petersburg which he led with great skill; and on December 2d, 1864, was made major-general by brevet. He was mustered out of the Volunteer service, August 24th, 1865, and is now engaged (1885) in business in New York City.

ULRIC DAHLGREN.

Born in 1842, he was the son of Rear-admiral John A. Dahlgren. He entered the Navy as a midshipman, before the breaking out of the Civil War. At the time of the attack upon Fort Sumter, he was traveling in the South. Hastening home, he assisted his father in the Ordnance Department, who sent him to place the guns in position on Maryland Heights, and to take charge of the battery. He executed his duty with great skill, and when General Sigel relieved General Saxton of his command, he found young Dahlgren at his post as captain of artillery, and took him at once upon his staff.

RECEPTION OF THE SECOND NEW YORK FIRE ZOUAVES, COLONEL BURNS, BY CHIEF DECKER AND THE NEW YORK FIRE DEPARTMENT, FEBRUARY 9TH, 1864.

On 27th the battle of Lookout Valley, fought under his direction, relieved the Army of the Cumberland. On November 23d, 24th and 25th he fought the battle of Chattanooga, defeating Bragg, capturing over 6,000 prisoners and 40 pieces of artillery. The victory of Chattanooga overthrew the last important hostile force west of the Alleghanies, and opened the way for the Federal armies into Georgia.

In February, 1864, Grant was made lieutenant-general, and assumed command of the armies of the United States. Sending Sherman into Georgia, he directed Sigel to penetrate the Valley of Virginia, and Butler to capture Richmond. He fought his own way from the Rapidan to the James. On May 4th he could put into battle 110,000 soldiers. Lee confronted him with 75,000. The battles of the Wilderness, Spottsylvania, North Anna and Cold Harbor were the hardest Grant ever fought, but after each he advanced, and Lee withdrew. When the final campaign began, Lee had collected 73,000 men at Richmond. Grant had 110,000 in the works before Petersburg and Richmond. Petersburg fell on April 2d, and Richmond on the 3d, Lee retreating toward Lynchburg, and on being surrounded, he surrendered on the 9th of April, 1865, at Appomattox Court House. All the other Confederate armies soon after surrendered, and the greatest civil war in history was at an end.

Grant returned to Washington to superintend the disbandment of the armies. Upon President Johnson's suspending Mr Stanton the Secretary of War, Grant was placed in his

Commanding the Armies of the United States, to be General on the Retired List of the Army, with the full pay of such rank," which nomination was unanimously confirmed by the Senate.

EDWARD FERRERO.

Born in Madrid, Spain, in 1832. Came to the United States in 1834. He inherited a military inclination, and entered the Militia of New York State as soon as his age would allow, and soon became a field officer of the Eleventh Regiment, New York National Guard. In the Summer of 1861 he recruited the Fifty-first Regiment, New York State Volunteers, known as the "Shepherd Rifles." He led his regiment at the battles of Roanoke Island and New Berne with great dash and effect, and won the promotion to the command of a brigade, distinguishing himself again at the second battle of Bull Run and in covering the retreat of the Federal army the next day at Chantilly. After the death of Reno, at South Mountain, Ferrero took command of a brigade and on the battlefield of Antietam received promotion to brigadier-general. In the desperate fight at Fredericksburg, out of the 1,700 men that he took into the fight, he lost 570, killed and wounded. At the attack on Vicksburg his brigade made up part of the Ninth Corps, and occupying the extreme right, was not brought into the fight. He pursued Johnston, and defeated him at Jackson, Miss., where he planted his brigade colors on the dome of the

He served in Fremont's mountain campaign, distinguishing himself at Cross Keys, and served through Pope's campaign, acting as chief of artillery under Sigel at the second battle of Bull Run. In 1862 he was engaged under General Stahl, and when the Army of the Potomac moved down into Virginia in November, 1862, he made an attack upon Fredericksburg, at the head of Sigel's bodyguard. For his gallant act, General Burnside detailed him as a special aid upon his staff. He rejoined General Sigel when the army went into winter-quarters, and when that general was relieved of command, General Hooker applied to have Captain Dahlgren transferred to his staff. He again distinguished himself at the battle of Chancellorsville; was with General Pleasonton in all of the cavalry raids in the Bull Run Mountains, and at Aldie. When General Meade succeeded General Hooker he requested Captain Dahlgren to remain upon his staff. Before the battle of Gettysburg he obtained from General Pleasonton a hundred picked men, with a roving commission, scoured the country in search of a bearer of dispatches whom he knew to be on his way from Jefferson Davis to General Lee, captured him and his escort, secured the dispatches, and by the most skillful manœuvring, succeeded in reaching General Meade's tent after the first day's battle, and laid these important papers before him. On Lee's retreat he led the famous charge into Hagerstown, where of five officers in the charge two were killed; he was wounded. He was brought to Washington, and his leg amputated. For his gallantry in

GENERAL KILPATRICK SETTING OUT ON HIS CAVALRY RAID TO RESCUE

GENERAL KILPATRICK SETTING OUT ON HIS CAVALRY RAID TO RESCUE THE FEDERAL PRISONERS CONFINED IN LIBBY PRISON AND ON BELLE ISLE

Colonel W. Krzyzanowski, 58th N.Y. — Lieutenant-colonel R. Avery, 102d N.Y. — Colonel O. H. Morris, 66th N.Y.
Colonel P. Kelly, 88th N.Y. — Colonel G. L. Prescott, 32d Mass. — Lieutenant-colonel J. McConihe, 169th N.Y.

COLONELS OF VETERAN REGIMENTS WHO RE-ENLISTED FOR THE WAR.

this campaign he was made colonel, and as soon as he was able to move he returned to active service. In connection with General Kilpatrick, he planned the raid toward Richmond, hoping to release the Federal prisoners then suffering so terribly at Libby Prison and Belle Island. Accepting the most dangerous part of the duty, he was led into the midst of the enemy by his treacherous guide, and was killed while endeavoring to fight his way out. With exultant comments, the Confederates published papers, which they asserted were found on his person, giving instructions to his men to burn Richmond, and even photographed these papers, and sent copies to England. His friends asserted that they were base forgeries.

WILLIAM T. CLARK

Born in Connecticut and settled in Iowa. Entered the Army at the breaking out of the Civil War, and served as adjutant-general and chief of staff to General Grant, with the Seventeenth Army Corps, with the rank of lieutenant-colonel. At the siege of Vicksburg he distinguished himself, and was promoted successively colonel, brigadier-general, and brevet-major-general, and accompanied Sherman in his march through Georgia, and from Savannah to Washington, being in command of the First Brigade, Third Division, of the Fifteenth Army Corps. Was mustered out of the Volunteer service, February 1st, 1866.

until the Bureau terminated by law, August 28th, 1866," is published in Parts I. and II. as a Congressional document. Promoted through various grades to lieutenant-colonel in the Adjutant-general's Department and brevet major-general in the United States Army, served since 1868 as adjutant-general of the Military Divisions of the Pacific, the South and the Atlantic. Was retired from active service at his own request on July 1st, 1881, after over thirty years' service in the United States Army. He is now (1893) in New York City.

JOHN T. SPRAGUE.

Born at Newburyport, Mass. While a mere lad, his father, who was a surgeon in the United States Army, settled in Detroit, Mich., where young Sprague became a favorite of General Cass, and accompanied him to Washington when he was called to the War Department by President Jackson. Sprague was attached to that department till 1834, when he was appointed a lieutenant in the Marine Corps. Served in the Creek and Florida Wars, and was appointed quartermaster and commissary of troops in the field. General Jessup, on assuming active operations, made him an aide-de-camp. At the close of hostilities, Lieutenant Sprague led 2,000 of the Indians to Fort Gibson, Ark. When Colonel Worth organized the Eighth Infantry, Sprague was made first-lieutenant. Under General Macomb he joined in the Florida campaign against Wild Cat in 1839, and soon became adjutant to General Worth. Received the brevet of captain for gallantry at Pilaklikaha, in which engagement Halleck was defeated.

In 1846 Captain Sprague's regiment was sent to Texas, and he was assigned to the command of the Department of Florida. He wrote a history of the Florida War, which is ranked as one of the great histories of the country. In 1848 he was breveted major and sent to Texas, and was actively employed in New Mexico. When the Civil War broke out he was on furlough, and at once reported for duty, and asked the War Department not to order him back to Texas under General Twiggs; but his request was disregarded, and on his way back he was arrested in San Antonio, in March, 1861, and included in General Twiggs's capitulation. He was subsequently paroled, and was placed on duty at Albany, N. Y., as mustering and disbursing officer. He became Adjutant-general of the State under Governor Seymour.

English flag at the fore, of the English-built steamer *Alabama*, or ("290"), in the harbor of the Azores, and started on a cruise which lasted nearly two years, and during which time she sunk, burned and destroyed, or captured and ransomed, among others, the following-named vessels, sailing under the United States flag: The ship *Ocmulgee*, of Martha's Vineyard; barks *Alert*, *Virginia*, *Elisha Dunbar*, *Lafayette*, *Nye*; schooner *Kingfisher*; ships *Golden Rule*, *Levi Starbuck*, and *Benjamin Tucker*, of New Bedford; ships *Thomas B. Wales*, *Punjaub*, *Morning Star*, *Nora*, *Charles Hill*, *Anna F. Schmidt*; barks *Sea Bride*, *Amazonian*, *Olive Jane*, *Parker Cook*, *Lauretta*, *Lamplighter*; brigantine *Chastelain*, and schooner *Starlight*, of Boston; bark *Ocean Rover*, of New London; schooners *Weathergauge* and *Courser*, of Provincetown; brigantine *Altamaha*, of Sippican; ship *Lafayette*, of New Haven; brigantine *Baron de Castine*, of Castine; schooner *Crenshaw* and bark *Justina*, of Baltimore; ship *Express*, of Portsmouth; ship *Tonawanda* and bark *Conrad*, of Philadelphia; ship *John Scott*, of Bucksport; ships *Jonas Hatch* and *Bethiah Thayer*, of Rockland; brigantine *Kate Cory*, of Westport; ship *John A. Parks*, of Hallowell; ships *Talisman*, *Gildersleeve*, *Sea Lark*, *Dorcas Prince*, *Washington*, *Manchester* and *Brilliant*; barks *Wave Crest*, *Golden Rule* and *Union Jack*; schooners *Palmetto* and *Crenshaw*; brigantine *Dunkirk* and steamer *Ariel*, of New York; and the United States steamer *Hatteras*. On June 19th, 1864, the United States steamer *Kearsarge*, Captain John A. Winslow, destroyed the *Alabama* off Cherbourg, but her commander escaped through the assistance he received from the yacht *Deerhound*. When the *Alabama* was sinking, the *Deerhound* appeared, steaming up to the *Kearsarge*. On being asked to try and pick up the scores of the Confederate ship's crew and officers who were swimming about, he lowered his yacht-boats. One of them, commanded by a man named Adams, was steering directly into a group of a dozen struggling persons, when it passed a drowning man with an officer's cap on. One of the men in the boat cried out, "That is Semmes!" and the drowning man said: "I am the captain; save me; I cannot keep up any longer." Adams succeeded in dragging him into the boat. Semmes then said: "For God's sake, don't put me on board the *Kearsarge*, but put me on board your yacht."

Adams promised to do so, and laid Semmes down in the bottom, and covered him with a sail, to conceal him from the *Kearsarge's* boats, which were evidently anxiously searching for him. When Adams had saved a boatload, he took them on board the yacht, and Semmes was at once placed below. As soon as all that were seen in the water were picked up, the *Deerhound* steered to Southampton.

It is said that the day before the engagement Captain Semmes had handed over to the Brazilian Consul at Cherbourg sixty-six chronometers, his will, his money and the bills of ransomed vessels, and induced the yacht *Deerhound* to follow him. This latter statement has been denied.

SINKING OF THE "ALABAMA" ("290"), CAPTAIN SEMMES, AFTER AN HOUR'S ENGAGEMENT WITH THE "KEARSARGE," CAPTAIN WINSLOW, OFF CHERBOURG, JUNE 19TH, 1864.

JAMES B. FRY.

Born, February 22d, 1827, in Carrollton, Greene County, Ill.; graduated at the United States Military Academy in 1847; was commissioned as brevet-second-lieutenant in the Third United States Artillery, and joined it in the City of Mexico during the Mexican War; served as assistant-instructor of artillery at the Military Academy in 1847, and again in 1853-54, and as adjutant of the Military Academy in 1854-59; appointed assistant-adjutant-general, 1861, taking part in the first battle of Bull Run; chief of staff to General McDowell during his campaign of 1861; as chief of staff to General Buell in 1861-62, taking part in the battle of Shiloh, the advance upon and siege of Corinth, the operations in Northern Alabama and the battle of Perryville; provost-marshal-general of the United States from 1863 to 1866 under the Enrollment Act of 1863, passed to enforce military service after the system of voluntary enlistment had proved inadequate. As provost-marshal-general he put into the Army, by conscription, substitution, and voluntary enlistment, 1,120,621 men; arrested and returned to the Army 76,562 deserters; made an exact enrollment of the National forces, showing that there remained in the country, liable to conscription but not called out, 2,254,063 men; and collected, under a money-commutation clause of the Enrollment Act, $26,366,316 78. His "Final Report of the Operations of the Bureau of the Provost-marshal-general of the United States from the commencement of the business, March 17th, 1863,

THE "ALABAMA," OR "290."

On Sunday, the 24th of August, 1862, Captain Raphael Semmes, with John Low, of England, as first officer; C. S. Tullam, Bull, England, as second officer; D. B. Llewellyn, Easton, Wilts, England, as surgeon; C. R. Yonge, Savannah, Ga., as paymaster; J. McNair, England, as chief engineer, with 26 officers and 85 men, two-thirds of whom were English, hoisted the Confederate flag at the peak, and the

THE RUSSIAN SQUADRON IN THE HARBOR OF NEW YORK, OCTOBER, 1863, ON A SU

THE RUSSIAN SQUADRON IN THE HARBOR OF NEW YORK OCTOBER, 1863, ON A SUPPOSED SECRET MISSION BY SPECIAL ARRANGEMENT WITH THE FEDERAL GOVERNMENT

HORSESHOEING IN THE ARMY.—From a Sketch by Edwin Forbes.

GENERALS MEADE AND GRANT IN CONSULTATION DURING THE BATTLE OF THE WILDERNESS.

FROM A SKETCH BY J. C. FITZPATRICK.

THE BATTLE OF THE WILDERNESS.

GENERAL GRANT having been commissioned Lieutenant-general on March 2d, 1864, and placed in supreme command of the Federal Army, he gave over the control of the West to General William T. Sherman, and for himself reserved the special field of Virginia. He imagined that Lee and the Army of Northern Virginia could be overcome by the same means he had employed against Pemberton and Bragg, and he set himself the task to make the Army of the Potomac do that which he thought it never yet had done. At this time he openly gave his preference to hard blows over manœuvring. "Continuous hammering" was his motto.

Grant's objective was Lee's army, and as long as General Lee held to the defense of Richmond, that city was the goal. "On to Richmond!" meant nothing; the real object being to destroy Lee's army. In reorganizing the Army of the Potomac, the Second, Fifth and Sixth Corps were consolidated into two divisions. The First and Second Divisions of the Third Corps were transferred to the Second Corps, preserving their badges and distinctive marks. The Third Division of the Third Corps was transferred permanently to the Sixth Corps. The three divisions forming the old First Corps, consolidated into two divisions, were transferred to the Fifth Corps, preserving their distinctive marks. The reorganized army th stood as follows:

FIFTH CORPS.

Major-general Gouverneur K. Warren.

Inspector-general and Chief of Staff—Lieutenant-colonel Henry C. Bankhead.

Chief of Artillery—Colonel Charles S. Wainwright.

First Division: Brigadier-general Charles Griffin.
First Brigade—Brigadier-general James Barnes.
Second Brigade—Brigadier-general Joseph J. Bartlett.
Third Brigade—Brigadier-general Romeyn B. Ayres.
Second Division: Brigadier-general John C. Robinson.
First Brigade—Colonel Hiram Leonard.
Second Brigade—Brigadier-general Henry Baxter.
Third Brigade—Colonel Andrew W. Denison.
Third Division: Brigadier-general Samuel W. Crawford.
First Brigade—Colonel William McCandless.
Second Brigade—Colonel Joseph W. Fisher.
Fourth Division: Brigadier-general James S. Wadsworth.
First Brigade—Brigadier-general Lysander Cutler.
Second Brigade—Brigadier-general James C. Rice.
Third Brigade—Colonel Roy Stone.

SECOND CORPS.

Major-general Winfield Scott Hancock.

Inspector-general and Chief of Staff—Lieutenant-colonel Charles H. Morgan.

Chief of Artillery—Colonel John C. Tidball.

First Division: Brigadier-general Francis C. Barlow.
First Brigade—Colonel Nelson A. Miles.
Second Brigade—Colonel Thomas A. Smyth.
Third Brigade—Colonel Paul Frank.
Fourth Brigade—Colonel John R. Brooke.
Second Division: Brigadier-general John Gibbon.
First Brigade—Brigadier-general Alexander S. Webb.
Second Brigade—Brigadier-general Joshua T. Owen.
Third Brigade—Colonel Samuel S. Carroll.
Third Division: Major-general David B. Birney.
First Brigade—Brigadier-general J. H. Hobart Ward.
Second Brigade—Brigadier-general Alexander Hays.
Fourth Division: Brigadier-general Joseph B. Carr.
First Brigade—Brigadier-general Gershom Mott.
Second Brigade—Colonel William R. Brewster.

1. THE BATTLE OF THE WILDERNESS, BETWEEN GENERAL GRANT AND GENERAL LEE, MAY 5th, 1864
THE FIGHT ON THE LEFT—BURNSIDE'S AND HANCOCK'S

1. THE BATTLE OF THE WILDERNESS BETWEEN GENERAL GRANT AND GENERAL LEE, MAY 6th, 1864.—From a Sketch by Edwin Forbes. 2. THE BATTLE OF SPOTTSYLVANIA COURT HOUSE, MAY 10th, 1864—THE FIGHT ON THE LEFT—BURNSIDE'S AND HANCOCK'S CORPS ENGAGING THE ENEMY.—From a Sketch by J. Becker.

BATTLE OF SPOTTSYLVANIA COURT HOUSE, VA. MAY 8th, 1864.

From a Sketch by Edwin Forbes

GENERAL BUTLER LANDING AT FORT POWHATAN, ON THE JAMES RIVER, VA.

SIXTH CORPS.

Major-general John Sedgwick.

Inspector general and Chief of Staff—Lieutenant-colonel Martin T. McMahon.

Chief of Artillery—Colonel C. H. Tompkins.

First Division: Brigadier-general Horatio G. Wright.
First Brigade—Brigadier-general Alfred T. A. Torbert.
Second Brigade—Colonel Emory Upton.
Third Brigade—Colonel Hiram Burnham.
Fourth Brigade—Brigadier-general Alexander Shaler.
Second Division: Brigadier-general George W. Getty.
First Brigade—Brigadier-general Frank Wheaton.
Second Brigade—Colonel Lewis A. Grant.
Third Brigade—Brigadier-general Thomas H. Neill.
Fourth Brigade—Brigadier-general A. Henry Eustis.
Third Division: Brigadier-general Henry Prince.
First Brigade—Brigadier-general William H. Morris.
Second Brigade—Brigadier-general David A. Russell.

The Army of the Potomac was at and in the vicinity of Culpepper. The Army of Northern Virginia was at Orange. Grant had in theory favored moving on Richmond by way of the James River. The overland route he deemed too costly in time and men. But eventually he adopted a plan savoring of both.

The Army of the Potomac, under Meade, and the Ninth Corps, under Burnside, was to take the overland route on the east of Richmond. Butler, with 30,000 men (the Army of the James), was to move up the James River. Sigel and Crook were to operate from the debouches of the Shenandoah. Meade had under his immediate command the Second Corps, under Hancock, the Fifth, under Warren, and the Sixth, under Sedgwick. These, with the Ninth, numbered 122,000 men, and 359 guns; headquarters at Culpepper Court House. Lee confronted this army with the corps of Longstreet, Hill and Ewell—in all, some 62,000 men, and over 200 guns.

Grant's purpose was to turn Lee's right. Two days sufficed to put 100,000 men across the Rapidan. Warren led, Sedgwick followed, over Germanna Ford. Hancock crossed at Ely's Ford, further east. Burnside was to remain in camp a day later. Grant's route was through the Wilderness, due south. Lee made no effort to dispute Grant's crossing, but purposed to attack him while in these dreary woods.

Meeting with no opposition in crossing the river, Grant supposed that Lee had retreated to more

GENERAL MEADE CROSSING THE RAPIDAN, MAY 5TH, 1864.

From a Sketch by Edwin Forbes.

SKETCH ON THE LINE OF THE SECOND CORPS AT THE BATTLE OF THE WILDERNESS, VA., MAY 10th, 1864—WAITING FOR THE ENEMY.

From a Sketch by Edwin Forbes.

THE FIFTH CORPS HOSPITAL AT THE BATTLE OF SPOTTSYLVANIA COURT HOUSE, VA.

FROM A SKETCH BY EDWIN FORBES

favorable ground. He had no idea of fighting here, in the forest which had proved so nearly fatal to Hooker. On the night succeeding the passage of the Rapidan, both armies camped near by each other, Grant unsuspicious of the close presence of the enemy. Next day Ewell attacked Warren as he moved by the flank through the wood roads. Grant and Meade, at Old Wilderness Tavern, supposed this to be the attack of a simple rear-guard. Before Sedgwick could come up on Warren's right, Ewell had inflicted a loss of 3,000 men upon the Fifth Corps.

Grant being ready to accept battle here, Sedgwick was ordered to join Warren's right, and Hancock was summoned from Chancellorsville. On his

DOUBLE LINE OF BREASTWORKS THROWN UP ON THE NIGHT OF MAY 6TH, 1864, IN THE WILDERNESS, BY THE FIFTH ARMY CORPS. THE FOURTEENTH NEW YORK REGIMENT AWAITING THE ENEMY.

FROM A SKETCH BY J. BECKER.

1. HANCOCK'S SECOND CORPS CHARGING LEE'S RIGHT IN FRONT OF SPOTTSYLVANIA COURT HOUSE, VA., MAY 12TH, 1864. 2. GUNS CAPTURED IN HANCOCK'S CHARGE.

arrival he promptly attacked Hill. The Warren-Ewell and Hancock-Hill combats were isolated.

Both Grant and Lee determined to attack on the morrow. Burnside was ordered up to take position between Warren and Hancock. Lee awaited the arrival of Longstreet, whom he wanted to place opposite Hancock's right.

Grant ordered an attack along the whole line at 5 A.M. Lee determined to turn Grant's left and throw him back upon the river. Hancock fell upon Hill at five o'clock, and drove him over a mile down the Plank Road, when he stopped to rearrange his troops. While thus pausing, Longstreet came upon the field and attacked him. Hancock, by the suddenness of this attack, was driven back to his old lines on the Brock Road. Here he rallied his men, and Longstreet being wounded, the violence of the Confederate attack subsided.

In the afternoon Lee again attacked Hancock; night once more supervened. Nothing had been decided. Grant lost 15,000 men. Lee's loss was less by several thousand

beyond a cavalry fight by Sheridan against J. E. B. Stuart, there were no further operations on this ground. Both armies were exhausted. Neither had gained anything but respect for the other's valor.

SPOTTSYLVANIA—YELLOW TAVERN.

GENERAL GRANT's determination to move southward from the Wilderness was formed early on Saturday, the 7th of May, intending to plant his army between General Lee and Richmond by a movement upon Spottsylvania Court House, fifteen miles southeast of the battlefield of the Wilderness. The infantry were not to march until nightfall, but the immense trains were withdrawn in the middle of the afternoon, and sent to Chancellorsville. This movement of the trains apprised the Confederates of Grant's withdrawal, but not of his objective; and it was by a mere accident that Anderson's Confederate corps marched toward Spottsylvania that night. Lee, seeing that Grant was moving off somewhere, but not knowing whether toward Fredericksburg or Spottsylvania, instructed Anderson, who had temporary command of Longstreet's corps, to draw out his corps from the breastworks and camp it in readiness to move to Spottsylvania *in the morning*. Anderson, not finding a good place to bivouac (the woods being on fire), *began the march that night*, about ten o'clock.

MAY, 1864.

The direct route to Spottsylvania Court House is by the Brock Road, via Todd's Tavern. On this road the Fifth Corps, under General Warren, was to take the advance, and by a rapid march seize Spottsylvania Court House. Hancock's corps was to follow on the same line, while Sedgwick and Burnside were to move on an exterior route, by way of Chancellorsville. The route of Lee, in order to foil his antagonist's design of planting himself between the Confederate army and Richmond, was by the road from Parker's Store to Spottsylvania Court House, which runs parallel to the Brock Road, a few miles to the west. The distance in each case is nearly equal.

THE CONFEDERATE GENERALS EDWARD JOHNSON AND G. H. STEWART TAKEN TO THE REAR BY NEGRO CAVALRY, MAY 12TH, 1864.

BATTLE AT JERICHO FORD, ON THE NORTH ANNA RIVER, VIRGINIA, MAY 23D, 1864.

FROM A SKETCH BY EDWIN FORBES.

BATTLE OF THE WILDERNESS, FRIDAY, MAY 6TH, 1864.—FEDERAL FORCES UNDER GENERAL

BATTLE AT JERICHO FORD, ON THE N[illegible] ANNA RIVER, VIRGINIA, MAY [illegible] 1864.

BATTLE OF [illegible] COURT HOUSE [illegible] OF GRANT'S LINE AWAITING ORDERS.

BATTLE OF THE WILDERNESS, FRIDAY, MAY 6th, 1864—FEDERAL FORCES UNDER GENERAL U. S. GRANT, CONFEDERATE FORCES UNDER GENERAL ROBERT E. LEE.—[illegible]

GENERAL BUTLER'S ARMY, SOUTH OF THE JAMES—TROOPS IN POSITION AWAITING AN ATTACK PREVIOUS TO THE ARRIVAL OF GRANT'S ARMY, JUNE 3d, 1864

From a sketch by E. F. Mullen.

SOLDIERS HURRIEDLY RESUMING THEIR POSITIONS ON HEARING THE FIRST GUN ANNOUNCING THE RE-OPENING OF HOSTILITIES.

The vital interest of this movement centred in the march of Warren to seize Spottsylvania Court House. Warren's corps advanced at 9 P.M. on the 7th. Reaching Todd's Tavern, he was delayed for an hour and a half by the cavalry escort of General Meade blocking the way. On the 8th he was again detained by the cavalry division of General Merritt, who had been engaged in fighting and driving Stuart's cavalry, whom Lee had sent to block the Brock Road, and who still barred further advance.

Merritt, after two hours' of ineffectual effort, gave way to Warren, who advanced to clear his own path. The advance brigades, under Robinson, were deployed in line of battle, while the remainder of the corps followed in column.

At 8 A.M. of the 8th the column emerged from the woods into a clearing, two miles north of Spottsylvania Court House. Anderson (Longstreet's corps) had in the meantime arrived at the same place. Warren waited for Sedgwick to come up before making an attack. Before the latter arrived, night had fallen. As a consequence of all these incidents, Lee had managed to place himself across Grant's path, and having drawn upon the Spottsylvania Ridge a bulwark of defense, he was able to hold the Army of the Potomac in check. The Army of the Potomac on the following morning—Monday, May 9th—filed into line in front of Lee's position; in order from the right, Hancock, Warren, Sedgwick, Burnside. One of the first misfortunes on this fatal ground was the death of the gallant Sedgwick, the beloved chief of the Sixth Corps, who was shot while standing in the breastworks along his line, and almost instantly killed. General Horatio G. Wright succeeded to the command.

Hancock crossed the River Po in the hope of capturing a Confederate wagon-train, which was observed filing along the road leading into Spottsylvania, but on account of the darkness the attempt was unsuccessful. Next morning, the 10th, Hancock was ordered to withdraw two divisions from the south side of the Po to assist in an assault upon the enemy on Warren's front. In obedience to this order, the divisions of John Gibbon and D. B. Birney were retired, Barlow's division alone remaining, and as the Confederates showed a desire to attack, Hancock was instructed to withdraw also. The point against which the attack was designed to be made was a hill held by the Confederates in front of Warren's line, known as Laurel Hill. The attack upon this position had already been essayed by both the Second and Fifth Corps, with most unpromising results; the first attack being made by the brigades of Webb and Carroll, of Gibbon's division, at 11 A.M., in which they suffered severe loss. At 3 P.M. the divisions of Crawford and Cutler, of Warren's corps, had also made a preliminary attack; but they also failed, and were repulsed with heavy sacrifice.

When Hancock's division joined the Fifth, an assault was made by both corps, at five o'clock; but it met with a repulse. Among the killed was General James C. Rice, of the Fifth Corps. On the left of Warren an assault by part of the Sixth Corps met with more success. Colonel Emory Upton's brigade in a vigorous charge carried the first line of intrenchments, capturing 900 prisoners and several guns; but being unsupported, the advantage could not be maintained; so after nightfall Upton withdrew, leaving the guns behind.

Thus far the attacks had been mainly directed against Lee's left, so now it was resolved to make a sudden sally against his right centre. Hancock's

SOLDIERS COMING OUT OF THEIR RESPECTIVE RIFLE-PITS ON CESSATION OF FIRING, AND EXCHANGING CIVILITIES AND "YANKEE NOTIONS" DURING THE INVESTMENT OF PETERSBURG.

CAVALRY FIGHT AT YELLOW TAVERN, NEAR RICHMOND, VA., MAY 11TH

CAVALRY FIGHT AT YELLOW TAVERN, NEAR RICHMOND, VA., MAY 11th, 18[illegible], BETWEEN THE FORCES OF PHIL. H. SHERIDAN AND J. E. B. STUART.

corps was selected for this operation, which was to be supported by the rest of the army. The 11th of May was passed in preparing for this; after dark the Second Corps were moved to the place decided on for the assault. Hancock disposed his troops as follows: Barlow's division in two lines of masses—Brooke's and Miles's brigades in the first line; Brown's and Smythe's brigades in the second line, each regiment forming double column on the centre; Birney formed in two deployed lines on Barlow's front; Mott's division supported Birney, and Gibbon's division was held in reserve.

At half-past four A.M., Thursday, May 12th, Hancock moved forward; Barlow's division, formed on cleared ground, extending up to the Confederate lines, advanced at quick time for some distance; his heavy column without firing a shot marching over the Confederate pickets. When half-way toward the hostile line the men broke into a ringing cheer, and on the double-quick rolled like a the service performed by the Sixth Corps during the day was of the first importance.

At eight o'clock Burnside and Warren were ordered to make a general attack, and to relieve Hancock and Wright. The assault was made as directed, but made no impression. Seeing that nothing could be hoped for from this, two of Warren's divisions (those of Cutler and Griffin) were detached and sent to aid the Second and Sixth Corps.

Lee seemed to be determined to retake at any cost the line wrested from him, and throughout the day made five heavy assaults, being repulsed each time. At midnight, after twenty hours' of combat, Lee drew back his lines and re-formed them on his interior position; the loss on the Federal side being over 8,000, and on the Confederate side nearly as great.

During the succeeding week various movements were made from flank to flank in the hope of Corps, promptly met this attack, and succeeded in driving the Confederates from the road and into the woods beyond. On the 20th the Federal army, moving by the left, once more took up its march toward Richmond.

May, 1864.

General Philip H. Sheridan, with his cavalry, consisting of the divisions of Merritt, Wilson and Gregg, which cut loose from the Army of the Potomac on the 9th of May, reached the crossing of the North Anna on the 10th, where he destroyed ten miles of the railroad-track, two locomotives, three trains of cars, and a million and a half of rations. He also recaptured 400 Federal prisoners on their way to captivity in Richmond.

The South Anna was crossed at Ground-squirrel Bridge. Capturing Ashland Station on the 11th, destroying large quantities of stores, Sheridan resumed his march toward Richmond. To meet this advance, Stuart had succeeded in placing himself between the assailants and the Confederate capital,

COLD HARBOR, THE SCENE OF STONEWALL JACKSON'S FLANK MOVEMENT AND OF GRANT'S OPERATIONS.

FROM A SKETCH BY EDWIN FORBES.

resistless wave into the Confederate works, and in spite of a desperate resistance carried the line at all points.

Inside the intrenchments there ensued a hand-to-hand combat with the bayonet and clubbed muskets, which resulted in the capture of nearly 4,000 prisoners, comprising the whole of Johnson's division of Ewell's corps, including Major general Edward Johnson and Brigadier-general G. H. Stewart, 20 pieces of artillery, and 30 stands of colors. Flushed with success, the troops could not be restrained; they pushed the flying enemy through the forest toward Spottsylvania Court House. At some distance they came upon a fresh line of breastworks, where the Confederates had quickly rallied on their reserves, and, assuming the offensive, threw back their pursuers on the captured line. The Confederates, who had been re-enforced by heavy masses, began an assault to retake the lost line; but at this moment the Sixth Corps reached the ground and relieved the Second Corps from the front to the right. Its arrival was timely, and finding a spot where the lines could be broken; the Confederates extending their line to correspond with the shifting of the Army of the Potomac, and every assault made was repulsed.

Grant continued to throw out toward the left in the hope of breaking in the Confederate right flank; so that, instead of occupying a line extending four or five miles to the northwest of Spottsylvania Court House, it had at the end of ten days assumed a position almost due east from that place, the left resting at Massaponax Church, a distance of four miles. After twelve days' effort the carrying of the position was seen to be hopeless, and General Grant abandoned the attempt, and resolved by a flanking movement to dislodge Lee from a position seen to be unassailable. Preparations were begun on the 19th; but Lee, observing this, retarded its execution by a bold demonstration against the Federal right. Ewell crossed the Ny River above the right flank, seized the Fredericksburg Road, and captured an ammunition-train. Robert Ogden Tyler, in command of the heavy artillery of the Second and had massed all his available cavalry at Yellow Tavern, a few miles north of Richmond. Here Sheridan attacked him on the 11th, and gained possession of the Turnpike, driving Stuart back toward Ashland and across the North Fork of the Chickahominy. In this passage of arms between the ablest cavalry leaders of the rival armies, the dashing Confederate cavalry leader, J. E. B. Stuart, was killed. Pursuing his advantage gained at Yellow Tavern, General Sheridan made a bold dash upon the outer defenses of Richmond. The first line was carried, Custer's brigade capturing a section of artillery and over 100 prisoners. The second line being too strong to assail, and as the garrison rallied for the defense, Sheridan retired toward the Chickahominy. Crossing at Meadow Bridge, he drove the Confederates from his front, and repulsed an attack upon his rear by Confederate infantry from the city. Destroying the railroad bridge over the Chickahominy, Sheridan moved to Haxall's Landing, which he reached on the 14th of May. Here he remained three days to

BUILDING BREASTWORKS AT HAWES'S STORE, VA., MAY 29TH, 1864.
FROM A SKETCH BY EDWIN FORBES.

refit, when he returned by way of Baltimore Store, White House and Hanover Court House, rejoining the Army of the Potomac, the 25th of May, on the Pamunkey.

The following dispatches will indicate the feeling of the respective commanders after the six-days' struggle:

"WASHINGTON, MAY 11th, 11:30 P.M.

"*Major-general John A. Dix:*

"Dispatches from General Grant, dated at eight o'clock this morning, have just reached this department. He says: 'We have now ended the sixth day of very hard fighting. The result to this time is much in our favor. Our losses have been heavy, as well as those of the enemy. I think the loss of the enemy must be greater. We have taken over 5,000 prisoners in battle, while he has taken from us but few except stragglers. *I propose to fight it out on this line if it takes all Summer.*' The Government is sparing no pains to support him.

"EDWIN M. STANTON,
"*Secretary of War.*"

The following dispatch of General Lee was sent to Richmond:

"SPOTTSYLVANIA COURT HOUSE, *via* GUINEY'S,
"May 10th, 1864.

"*The Honorable Secretary of War:*

"General Grant's army is intrenched near this place, on both sides of the Brock Road. Frequent skirmishing occurred yesterday and to-day, each army endeavoring to discover the position of the other. To-day the enemy shelled our lines and made several assaults with infantry against different points, particularly on our left, held by General R. H. Anderson; the last, which occurred after sunset, was the most obstinate, some of the enemy leaping over the breastworks. They were easily repulsed, except in front of General Doles's brigade, where they drove our men from their position, and from a four-gun battery there posted. The men were soon rallied, and by dark our line was re-established and the battery recovered.

"A large body of the enemy moved around our left on the evening of the 9th, and took possession of the road about midway between Shady Grove Church and the Court House. General Early, with a part of Hill's corps, drove them back this evening, taking one gun and a few prisoners. Thanks to a merciful Providence, our casualties have been small. Among the wounded are Brigadier-generals Hays and H. H. Walker.

"R. E. LEE."

OPERATIONS OF THE ARMY OF THE JAMES.

THE Army of the James, under command of General Benjamin F. Butler, was, during the month of April, 1864, at Yorktown and Gloucester Point, on the York River. It was composed of the Eighteenth Corps, under General W. F. Smith, and the Tenth Corps, under General Q. A. Gillmore. The Eighteenth Corps was composed of two divisions of white troops, under Generals William T. H. Brooks and Godfrey Weitzel, and a division of colored troops, under General Edward W. Hinks. The Tenth Corps was composed of three divisions, under Generals Alfred H. Terry, Adelbert Ames and John W. Turner. General Butler had in addition a cavalry division, under General Alfred V. Kautz, at Norfolk and Portsmouth.

On May 1st, Butler sent a detachment of his force by water to West Point, across the Peninsula. Kautz with his cavalry was ordered to move northward from Suffolk to the south side.

On the night of May 4th Butler's entire command went down the York River on transports, passing Fortress Monroe, and ascended the James River, convoyed by a fleet of gunboats. On the 5th they landed on the south side of the James—a detachment at City Point, another at Fort Powhatan; but the main body about two miles above City Point, at Bermuda Hundred.

General Grant had instructed General Butler to make Richmond his objective point. On May 6th the landing of the forces was completed, and as Butler had orders from General Grant to intrench, the construction of a defensive front across the narrow neck of Bermuda Hundred was immediately commenced. This line was drawn within three miles of the Richmond and Petersburg Railroad, which Butler desired to destroy.

On the 7th of May, General Beauregard with his army reached Petersburg, and

MAY, 1864.

when a column of five brigades moved out to destroy the Richmond and Petersburg Railroad on that morning, they found the Confederates in a position covering that road, from Walthal Junction north to Chester Station. Brooks attacked and drove the Confederates some distance, but they soon rallied and pushed back his right; finally both parties withdrew. Another advance was made on the 9th. The Confederates were soon encountered and driven to Swift Creek, three miles from Petersburg, on the right bank of which was a strong line of earthworks. Having destroyed the railroad, Butler intended crossing Swift Creek and crowding the Confederates into Petersburg; but receiving accounts from Washington that Lee was "in full retreat to Richmond," he turned northward, in order to aid in the investment of the Confederate capital. A general advance was ordered two days afterward in the direction of Richmond. Encountering the Confederates, they were driven back to a position on the left bank of Proctor's Creek. On the morning of the 13th, the Confederates withdrew from the creek to an intrenched line in the rear, which General Gillmore succeeded in turning, holding its extreme right.

The flanks fell back on the Confederates' left to the James River and Drury's Bluff. Butler's force was much strung out, and the assault ordered for the following morning had to be abandoned

GIBBON'S DIVISION, HANCOCK'S CORPS, REPELLING AN ATTACK BY LEE'S

FROM A SKET

GIBBON'S DIVISION, HANCOCK'S CORPS, REPELLING AN ATTACK BY LEE'S FORCES, BEFORE DAYLIGHT, ON THE MORNING OF THE 3d OF JUNE, 1864.

From a Sketch by [illegible]

THE EIGHTEENTH ARMY CORPS STORMING THE FORT ON THE RIGHT OF THE CONFEDERATE LINE BEFORE PETERSBURG, JULY 15TH, 1864

THE TWENTY-SECOND NEGRO REGIMENT, DUNCAN'S BRIGADE, CARRYING THE FIRST LINE OF CONFEDERATE WORKS BEFORE PETERSBURG.

It was then determined to make an attack on the morning of the 16th. Before dawn, the sleeping camp was suddenly aroused by a savage outburst of musketry and artillery fire along the whole line. General Beauregard had anticipated Butler, and had begun the execution of a plan of offensive action himself. Butler's force was disposed along a front excessively extended, and though General William Smith endeavored to reach as far as possible by drawing out his corps in one thin line, there was still some distance between his right flank and the James.

To make his stroke still more sure, General Beauregard, moving up with his main force from Petersburg to Butler's front, had left one of his divisions, under General William H. C. Whiting, a considerable distance to the rear of Butler's left. The right of Smith's line, where the shock of the flanking column was first felt, was held by the brigade of General Charles A. Heckman. The suddenness of the assault nearly overwhelmed them; but, fortunately, General Butler had assigned three regiments of General Adelbert Ames's division, of General Q. A. Gillmore's corps, to General Smith as a reserve to his line. Two of these—the One Hundred and Twelfth New York and Ninth Maine—met the Confederates at a point where the road on which they were moving crosses the road running back to Bermuda Hundred. The Confederates aimed to seize the latter road, but were foiled by the stubborn resistance of the two regiments above named. While this movement was going on, General Beauregard assailed the front of Smith's line, held by the divisions of Brooks and Weitzel, but was again repulsed.

Finding that the Federal force was prepared to resist any attack from the front, Beauregard decided to make a move in heavier force against the right flank. The force at General Smith's disposal was too small to resist a serious effort in that direction, for the Confederates had but to swing their left well round in order to attain a lateral road leading back to Bermuda Hundred. On learning of this new movement—which threatened the trains, the communications, and even the depot on the James River—General Smith ordered a retirement to a position in the rear, where he could better cover what was of value behind him. While Smith was thus engaged, Gillmore's corps was on the left, and his right barely felt the effect of the attack. When Smith's corps was withdrawn, General Gillmore conformed to the movement. General Butler then withdrew the whole force within the lines of Bermuda Hundred. Finding himself so situated that he could not operate against Richmond, he decided to pass on the south side of the Appomattox and seize Petersburg, but receiving orders from General Grant to detach the larger part of his force to the assistance of the Army of the Potomac, he gave up this plan, and joined Grant on the Chickahominy.

HINKS'S DIVISION OF NEGRO INFANTRY BRINGING IN THE GUNS CAPTURED FROM THE CONFEDERATES AT BAYLOR'S FARM, NEAR PETERSBURG, VA., JUNE 15TH, 1864.—FROM A SKETCH BY E. F. MULLEN.

OPERATIONS IN THE SHENANDOAH VALLEY.

THE Army in the Shenandoah Valley and West Virginia was divided into two columns, one under General George Crook, consisting of a force of infantry, and a division of cavalry under General William W. Averell; the other, under General Franz Sigel. The first was to move by the Kanawha to operate against the East Tennessee and Virginia Railroad; the latter, to advance as far as possible up the Virginia Valley. Both movements began on the 1st of May. Moving up the Shenandoah Valley, Sigel met the Confederates, on the 15th, at Newmarket, and after a fierce engagement, retired behind Cedar Creek. Sigel was then relieved, and General David Hunter placed in command. He immediately took up the offensive, under orders from General Grant to move on Staunton and destroy the railroad thence toward Charlottesville. On the 5th of June, Hunter encountered the Confederates at Piedmont, capturing 1,500 prisoners and three pieces of artillery. Hunter formed a junction with Crook and Averell at Staunton, on the 8th, from which place they moved toward Lynchburg by way of Lexington. Finding

THE BATTLE OF COLD HARBOR, VA., JUNE 1st, 1864.—THE EIGHTEENTH CORPS DRIV…

BATTLE BETWEEN CRAWFORD'S DIVISION, OF WARREN'S CORPS, AND RODES'S DIVISION

THE BATTLE OF COLD HARBOR, VA., JUNE [illegible] —THE EIGHTEENTH CORPS DRIVING [illegible] REBEL FORCES FROM THEIR FIRST LINE OF RIFLE PITS.—FROM A SKETCH BY [illegible]

WATER SKIN, AND MODE OF CARRYING IT.

SIGNALING WITH A PIECE OF LOOKING-GLASS.

CUTTING [illegible] FORAGE INTO CHAFF.

HOW TO SECURE A PRISONER.

SLED MADE OUT OF A BOUGH.

BRIDGING ACROSS A GAP.

SECTION OF TENT WITH FIREPLACE.

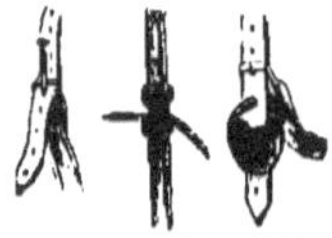

1. A BROKEN TONGUE MENDED. 2. FASTENING ROPES. 3. A STRAP PADLOCKED.

FRAMEWORK FOR SMALL TENT.

UNDERGROUND TENT WITH TWO STORIES.

DESCENDING A STEEP HILL.

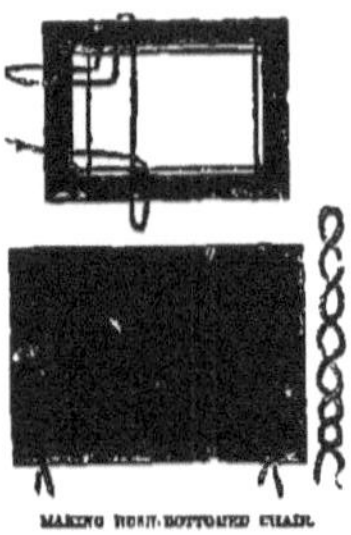

MAKING RUSH-BOTTOMED CHAIR.

SHELTER AGAINST A DRIVING WIND.

MODE OF DISTILLING SEA-WATER.

SAFE MODE OF SLEEPING WITH A LOADED GUN.

HINTS TO SOLDIERS IN THE CAMP AND ON CAMPAIGN.

Lynchburg well fortified, and reinforcements arriving by railroad from Lee's army to the Confederates, while his own supplies were nearly exhausted, he decided to return, which he did by way of the Alpine region of West Virginia.

SPOTTSYLVANIA TO THE CHICKAHOMINY.

ON May 20th, General Grant ordered Hancock to withdraw the Second Corps from the right, under cover of the remaining troops, and to march east to Massaponax Church. On the following day he headed southward, pushing his advance seventeen miles to Milford Station. The cavalry, under General A. T. A. Torbert, met General Kemper *en route* from Richmond to Spottsylvania to reinforce Lee, who held the bridge across the Mattapony. Torbert dislodged the brigade, and captured 66 prisoners. At Bowling Green Hancock remained until the morning of the 23d. Lee, instead of acting on the aggressive during this While Griffin repulsed the first attack, the Confederate commander, holding Griffin's front by three brigades, detached Brown's brigade to assault the flank. He fell upon Cutler's division, on the right of Griffin. Cutler gave way, and the division was thrown into confusion. Bartlett's brigade came up, reëstablished the line, and repulsed the Confederates with a loss of 350 killed and wounded. Meanwhile Hancock's corps were opposed by a part of McLaws's division, of Longstreet's corps, who were intrenched and commanded the bridge and plain. Birney's division was the storming party. Colonel Tidball placed three sections of artillery to reply to the enemy's fire. Pierce and Egan's brigades made the assault, swept across the plain, captured the works and planted the flag on the redan. On the following morning the Confederates abandoned their works on the southern bank of the river. Burnside, on attempting to cross at the centre, was repulsed. Both Hancock and Warren were separated from the centre by the river, and from the other wing by Lee's army.

former on the Tolopotomoy, and the latter on the road to Shady Grove Church. At this last place the whole of Ewell's corps held position. The Confederates soon afterward threatened to turn Warren's left by a move by the Mechanicsville Pike. General Samuel W. Crawford directed the brigade of Reserves, under Colonel Martin D. Hardin, to cover that road. Reaching Bethesda Church, on the Mechanicsville Pike, a division of Ewell's corps, under General Robert E. Rodes, moving up that road, assailed them furiously on the flank. General Crawford brought up the remainder of the Reserves, and with the brigade of Colonel J. Howard Kitching, took up a good position, and repulsed the impetuous assault of Rodes.

BATTLE OF COLD HARBOR, OR NEW COOL ARBOR.

SHERIDAN'S cavalry had, on the 31st, after a severe action, seized Cold Harbor—a place of strategic value, being a centre of roads leading to

BUILDING A CORDUROY ROAD IN THE WOODS, NEAR THE WELDON RAILROAD, VA.

FROM A SKETCH BY A. McCALLUM

flank movement of the enemy, sent Longstreet on a parallel road in the direction taken by Hancock. When Warren started to follow Hancock, on the morning of the 21st, Lee ordered General R. S. Ewell to follow Longstreet; Burnside and Wright brought up the rear after Warren, and Hill's corps followed Ewell's. When the Army of the Potomac reached the North Anna, on the 23d, the Army of Northern Virginia were there to receive them, having taken a shorter route. Hancock, with the left column, struck the North Anna near the railroad crossing; the right, under Warren, at the Jericho Ford. Bartlett's brigade, at the head of Warren's corps, waded the river, which was breast-high, and formed on the opposite side, thus covering the laying of the ponton-bridge, over which the balance of the corps crossed. A line of battle was then formed, with Cutler's division on the right, Griffin's on the centre, and Crawford's on the left. They were opposed by a single brigade of Wilcox's division, of Hill's corps, under command of Colonel Brown. This small force was soon reinforced by the brigades of Scales, Gordon and Thomas, and, shortly afterward, by Heth's entire division. Griffin, before he could retreat, was furiously assailed by the whole of the Confederate force, in double lines of battle.

The Army of the Potomac, on the 26th, withdrew from this unfavorable position, speedily but cautiously; the Second Corps acting as the rear-guard while the movement was carried out. The entire army reached Hanover Town on the 27th and crossed the Pamunkey. But Lee was again on hand, covering the line of the Chickahominy.

MAY, 1864.

There are two roads leading from Hanover Town direct to Richmond; these Lee defended with his entire force. His position could not well be broken, so Grant moved on the 28th across the Tolopotomoy Creek and toward Cold Harbor. Lee did the same, and, as usual, moved with greater rapidity. The armies now were on the old ground, being near Gaines's Mill and Mechanicsville. Fair Oaks could be reached in an hour, and Richmond was less than ten miles off. On the 29th, the Sixth Corps was directed to Hanover Court House; the Second Corps, on the road from Hawes's Store, toward the same point; the Fifth Corps toward Shady Grove Church, and the Ninth Corps in position to support either the Second or Fifth. General Horatio G. Wright, with the Sixth Corps, reached Hanover Court House; but both Hancock and Warren were brought to a halt, the

both Richmond and White House. General H. G. Wright, with the Sixth Corps, was dispatched with orders to hold it. At the same time General Smith arrived with a force of 16,000 men, made up of four divisions taken from the Tenth and Eighteenth Corps of the Army of the James, and was ordered to coöperate with General Wright. General Smith had moved this force on transports down the James and up the York and Pamunkey Rivers. Lee had kept informed of these manœuvres, and moved Longstreet to the same cross-roads, where Wright and Smith found him occupying a commanding position. They gave him battle and drove him beyond Cold Harbor. The occupancy of the first line of rifle trenches—June 1st, 1864—cost Wright and Smith 2,000 men: they rested on their arms before the second line of trenches. Hancock, on the morning of the 2d, moved the Second Corps to Wright's left.

MAY, 1864.

JUNE, 1864.

Warren remained on the right, extending his line nearly four miles, with Burnside in supporting distance on the right and rear. The lower fords of the Chickahominy and the roads leading toward the White House, which was now the depot of supplies to the Army of the Potomac, were protected by

1. THE ARMY OF THE POTOMAC CROSSING THE JAMES RIVE
2. THE FORTS AND BREASTWORKS, NEAI

1. THE ARMY OF THE POTOMAC CROSSING THE JAMES RIVER AT DOUTHARDS NEAR FORT POWHATAN ON A PONTON BRIDGE CONSTRUCTED BY GENERAL BENHAM, JUNE 14th, 1864.
2. THE FORTS AND BREASTWORKS, NEAR PETERSBURG, CAPTURED BY THE EIGHTEENTH ARMY CORPS, GENERAL W. F. SMITH, JUNE 15th, 1864.

EARTHWORKS ON THE LEFT OF THE CONFEDERATE LINE, IN FRONT OF PETERSBURG, CAPTURED BY THE EIGHTEENTH ARMY CORPS, GENERAL W. F. SMITH

From a Sketch by Edwin Forbes

BURNSIDE'S CORPS CHARGING THE CONFEDERATE POSITION ON THE RIGHT OF THEIR LINE OF DEFENSE

From a Sketch by Edwin Forbes

Sheridan's cavalry. Burnside, in moving to the support of Warren on the afternoon of the 2d, was attacked by the Confederates, his skirmish line driven through the swamp, and many captured. Lee then penetrated Warren's line, between his battle and skirmish line, and captured over 400 prisoners. This threw Warren on the defensive. General J. J. Bartlett's Second Brigade, however, stopped the progress of the Confederates. Warren and Burnside formed a line of battle awaiting the morrow. Lee, as usual, had secured an excellent position for defense, and was ready for the morrow.

and several hundred prisoners and three guns were captured and turned upon the retreating enemy; but Barlow's second line failing to come up promptly, the Confederates were reinforced and drove Barlow's troops out of the captured fortifications. Gibbon's command, in moving forward, became separated, but both sections advanced close up to the works. Col. James P. McMahon with his regiment reached the parapet, where he planted his colors, but fell immediately afterward mortally wounded. General Robert O. Tyler was wounded, and Colonels Orlando H. Morris, 66th N.Y.V., while

ment, to men; but nobody stirred, the silent but emphatic verdict being against further slaughter. The loss on the Federal side was over 13,000 while the Confederate loss was less than as many hundred. Next day, siege operations were begun, but this work also ended in a few days. On the 4th, Col. Lewis O. Morris, 7th N. Y. H. Art., was killed while reconnoitring with General F. C. Barlow.

From May 5th to June 10th General Grant had fought a succession of sanguinary battles, and the losses to the Federal army in killed, wounded and missing amounted in the aggregate to 54 55!

LIEUTENANT-GENERAL GRANT IN A COUNCIL OF WAR AT MASSAPONAX CHURCH, VA.

The Federals were drawn up in the following order: Hancock on the left: the Sixth Corps, under Wright, next: then Smith's command, with Burnside and Warren on the right—the latter rested on the Totopotomoy Creek, and the former on Dispatch Station Road. Two divisions of cavalry under Sheridan held the lower fords of the Chickahominy and the roads to the White House. The other cavalry divisions, under General James H. Wilson, were stationed on the right flank. In the early morning of the 3d, an attack along the whole line was ordered. The attack on the left, supported by Birney, was made by the divisions of Barlow and Gibbon, of Hancock's corps. After a severe struggle the Confederates were driven back,

leading charge of 1st Brig., composed of 7th N. Y. H. Art., 5th N. H., 146th Pa. and 5th Del. Vols., Franklin A. Haskell, 36th Wis., and Peter A. Porter, 8th N.Y. H. Art., were killed. The advance of the 6th Corps on the right of Hancock, and that of Smith on the right of the 6th, met with no better success. Every assault was repulsed with great slaughter.

The Fifth Corps, on the right, held its own, but no more. The Ninth Corps, under Burnside, engaged the Confederates on the Shady Grove Road. Some hours after the failure of the first assault, General Meade instructed his corps commanders to renew the attack without reference to the troops on the right or left. The order was issued from corps to division to brigade, to regi-

officers and men. The losses were: At the Wilderness, May 5th to 12th, 269 officers and 3,019 enlisted men killed; 1,017 officers and 18,261 enlisted men wounded; 177 officers and 6,667 enlisted men missing. At Spottsylvania, May 12th to 21st, 114 officers and 2,032 enlisted men killed; 259 officers and 7,697 enlisted men wounded; 31 officers and 248 enlisted men missing. At North Anna, May 21st to 31st, 12 officers and 138 enlisted men killed; 67 officers and 1,063 enlisted men wounded; 3 officers and 324 enlisted men missing. At Cold Harbor, June 1st to 10th, 144 officers and 1,561 men killed; 421 officers and 8,621 men wounded; 51 officers and 2,355 men missing. This battle General Grant acknowledged a great mistake

ADMIRAL PORTER'S FLEET PASSING THROUGH COLONEL BAILEY'S DAM, ABOVE ALEXANDRIA

FROM A SKETCH BY

THE SIEGE OF PETERSBURG.—ADVANCE OF THE FED

FROM A SKETCH BY

ADMIRAL PORTER'S FLEET [illegible] THROUGH COLONEL BAILEY'S DAM ABOVE ALEXANDRIA [illegible] ARKANSAS, MAY, [illegible] AFTER [illegible] THE RAPIDS BY [illegible]

[illegible]

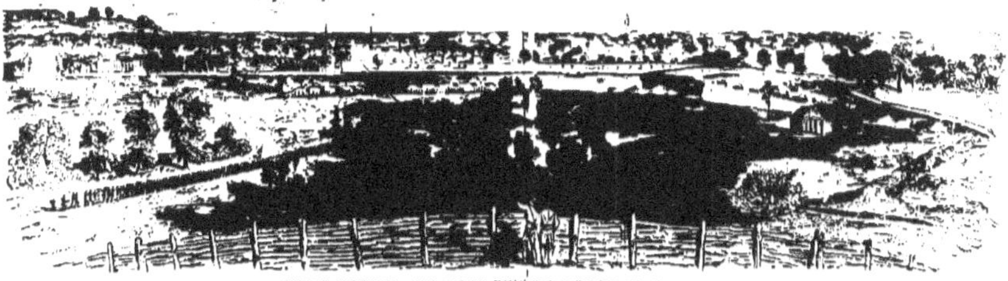

THE SIEGE OF PETERSBURG—ADVANCE OF THE [illegible] AGAINST THE CITY JUNE [illegible]

A REGIMENT OF THE EIGHTEENTH CORPS CARRYING A PORTION OF BEAUREGARD'S LINE IN FRONT OF PETERSBURG.
From a Sketch by E. F. Mullen.

SIEGE OF PETERSBURG.

GENERAL GRANT having determined on a change of base, transferred the army, by a flank movement, to the south side of the James River.

Immediately after the battle of Cold Harbor, the Ninth Corps, then holding the extreme right of the line, had been withdrawn from its position, and posted between the Fifth and Eighteenth Corps. The Fifth then became the right of the line. On the 6th of June the Fifth Corps was retired and massed in the rear of the centre, the Ninth Corps again becoming the right of the line.

The Second Corps, on the 7th, formed the left of the line, being stretched to the Chickahominy. The Fifth was transferred to that flank, to extend it as far as Dispatch Station, on the York River Railroad. On the same day, General Sheridan and two divisions of cavalry were sent to destroy the Central Railroad.

This disposition of the troops placed the army within easy march of the lower crossings of the Chickahominy—General Warren being about ten miles from Long Bridge.

During the night of June 12th, 1864, the movement to the James was commenced. Wilson's cavalry division took the lead, followed by Warren, who seized the crossings of the Chickahominy at Long Bridge. Hancock's corps then followed the Fifth, and marched to Wilcox's Landing, on the left bank of the James. Wright and Burnside crossed at Jones's Bridge, and marched to Charles City, on the James. General Smith's commands returned to Bermuda Hundred *via* White House.

Lee discovered the withdrawal early on the 13th, and soon after retired toward Richmond. The Federal army had in the meantime reached the James River, near Harrison's Landing. A delay was caused here by the non-arrival of the ponton-bridges; but Hancock's corps crossed at Wilcox's Landing, near Windmill Point.

By noon on the 16th the whole army was on the south side of the James, having crossed it at Douthard's, a few miles below Hancock's crossing. At the point selected by General Weitzel, who was the chief engineer of the Department of Virginia and North Carolina, the channel was thirteen fathoms deep, and the ponton-bridge had to be floated to cover two thousand feet in length, the width of the river at this point. The first section was launched during the forenoon of the 14th, and the entire bridge completed by midnight, under the direction of Brigadier-general Benham.

On the 10th of May, Butler had sent out an expedition, under General Gillmore in command of the infantry, and General A. V. Kautz in command of the cavalry, to assault the Confederate works constructed around Petersburg by General Beauregard. The cavalry carried the works on the south side, and gained an entrance almost to the city, but was forced to retire. General Gillmore, on approaching the defenses, found them so skillfully constructed and so well manned that he deemed an assault useless, and he retired the whole force to Bermuda Hundred.

On the 14th General Butler determined to make another effort to capture Petersburg, and to that end, at midnight, he ordered General Smith, who had just debarked his force at Bermuda Hundred, to move against the city. The cavalry division of General Kautz, and a division of colored troops, under General E. W. Hinks, passed on a ponton-bridge to the south side of the Appomattox, and on the morning of the 15th took up the seven-mile march to Petersburg. Kautz, with the cavalry on the extreme left, was to threaten the fortifications near the Norfolk and Petersburg Railroad, and be at the same time a protection to the left flank of the infantry. Hinks's division, in the rear of Kautz, was to take position as near as possible to the enemy's works; Brooke's division to take position on the right of Hinks; Martindale's division, on the extreme right, was to strike the City Point Railroad. Two miles out, at Baylor's Farm, the cavalry confronted a line of rifle-pits, near the City Point Railroad. The cavalry withdrew to the left, and Hinks's division was ordered to carry the line, which it did promptly, capturing a gun. This delayed the whole column, the advance of which did not reach the fortifications about Petersburg until noon of the 15th, and the whole force was up and deployed in position about 3 P.M.

JUNE, 1864.

In the meantime General Beauregard had, on learning of the movement of Smith and Hancock against Petersburg, withdrawn from his Bermuda Hundred line of intrenchments General Bushrod R. Johnson's division, and at about 10 P.M. on the 16th, the reinforcement arrived within the Petersburg fortifications. The cavalry pickets and the skirmish line left by Johnson was the force driven off by Hinks in the morning. Beauregard had just completed, at Howlett's House, a battery of heavy guns from Richmond. This he determined to evacuate, and his chief engineer, Colonel Harris, dismounted and carefully buried the guns, carriages and chassis in the vicinity of the battery, so well concealing the spot that the enemy failed to discover it. On the 18th, when Pickett's division drove off the Federals from the line, these guns and apparatus were uncovered, mounted and used against the Federal ironclads and other vessels on the river.

THE FORTY-EIGHTH PENNSYLVANIA, COLONEL PLEASANTS, MINING THE CONFEDERATE WORKS IN FRONT OF PETERSBURG, JULY 15TH–20TH, 1864.

THE FEDERAL ARMY INTRENCHED BEFO

FROM

THE FEDERAL ARMY INTRENCHED BEFORE PETERSBURG.—A NIGHT SCENE IN THE TRENCHES

[illegible]

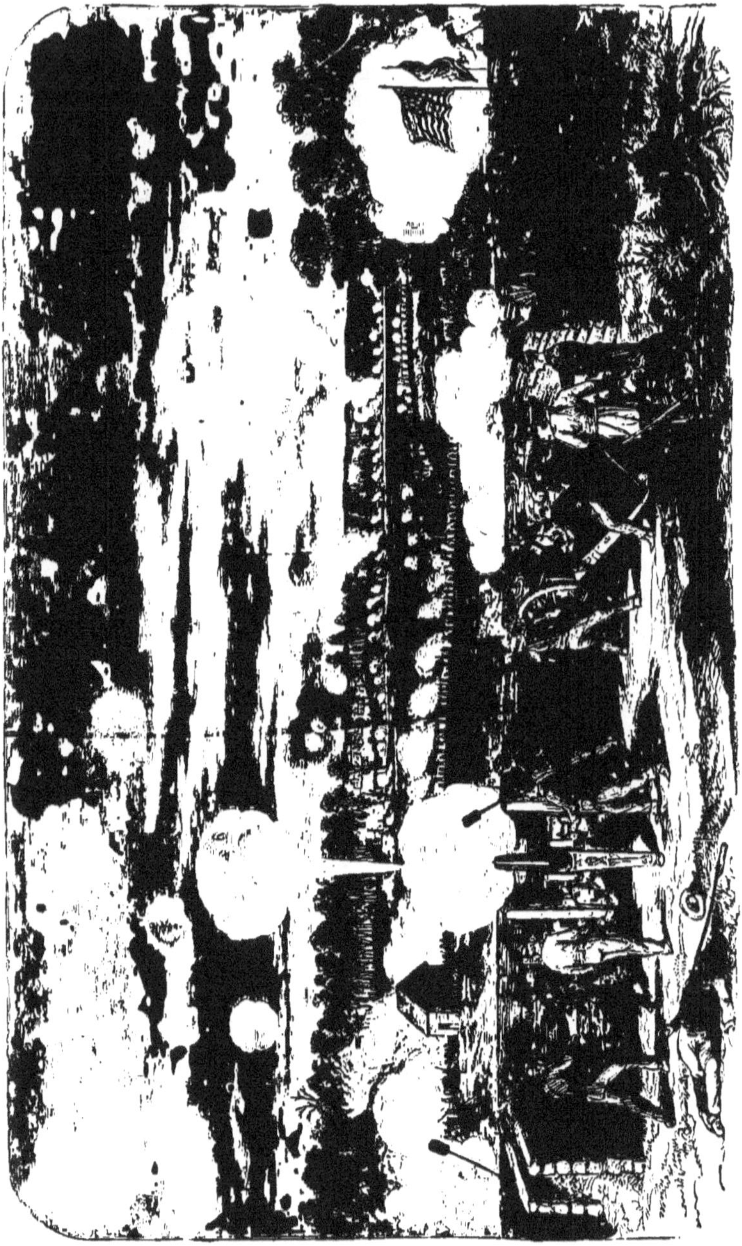

ROEMER'S THIRTY-FOURTH NEW YORK AND TWITCHELL'S SEVENTH MAINE BATTERIES, THIRD DIVISION, NINTH ARMY CORPS, SHELLING PETERSBURG, VA.

From a Sketch by A. McCallum.

General Beauregard now had about 10,000 men confronting the Federal army, consisting of Hancock's Second Corps and Smith's Eighteenth, in all about 40,000 men. Burnside's Ninth Corps came up about noon of the 16th, and then, by instructions from General Meade, Hancock ordered an assault the same evening. For three hours the whole strength of the three Federal corps was directed against the Confederate works, and finally Egan's brigade, of Birney's division, effected a lodgment. The contest continued long in the night, and then gradually slackened.

Warren's Fifth Corps did not reach Petersburg until night, and took no part in the assault of the 16th.

The Federal forces now assailing Petersburg numbered fully 90,000, and Beauregard's force had not been reinforced beyond his 10,000 men. On the morning of the 17th the assault was resumed, and Hancock succeeded in capturing the hill on which the Hare House stood. Burnside directed his attack against that part of the Confederate line which had not been already assailed, and he succeeded in capturing a redoubt, four guns and several hundred prisoners. Another attack was made in the afternoon by Burnside, assisted by Barlow's division, of the Second Corps, but met with a heavy loss in killed, wounded and prisoners. Burnside, however, succeeded in getting across the enemy's line, his force being at right angles with the Confederate line. Crawford's troops were brought up to support the left, but became bewildered in the ravine. After dark, Beauregard, having been reinforced by Gracie's brigade, of Johnson's division, made another desperate sortie, leaped the breastworks Burnside had captured, and drove the Ninth Corps out, capturing about 2,000 prisoners. The Federal forces had, however, established an integral line of defense, and were ready for a general assault on the 18th. Smith's corps had been relieved and sent to the aid of Butler at Bermuda Hundred, and the Sixth Corps took its place, except Martindale's division, which continued to hold the extreme right. Advancing on the morning of the 18th, the Federal skirmishers found the line of defense abandoned, and Beauregard's forces concentrated behind an inner line, which he had marked out during the progress of the fight, and occupied the same night, leaving his camp-fires brightly burning, and sentinels well thrown out. Before morning he had constructed a new line of defense in the face of an enemy numbering almost ten to one, and daylight found him in possession of a position which proved almost impregnable, as the same line, further strengthened, repelled the continuous assaults of the Federal army, until evacuated near the close of the War.

General Meade had ordered an attack for four o'clock on the morning of the 18th, but the new line of defense made it necessary to re-dispose the troops, and it was 3:30 P.M. before the assault was made. Warren's corps confronted Beauregard's extreme right, which was but a thin skirmish line, until Kershaw's division arrived with 5,000 men, which then resisted the persistent attacks of Warren's corps. With the additional reinforcement of Field's division, and the presence of General Lee on the field, the Confederate troops were greatly encouraged, and with a force of about 20,000 men they repulsed Meade at every point. With the arrival of fresh troops from Richmond, augmenting the Confederate army to 60,000 men, General Grant, convinced that the capture of the place by assault was vain, ordered his army to intrench. By the 21st they had so fortified their line that the Second and Sixth Corps were withdrawn from the right to the left flank to more closely invest Petersburg on that side, and the cavalry of Wilson and Kautz were sent to cut the Weldon and Southside Railroad. Wilson met and defeated W. H. F. Lee's division of cavalry; Kautz destroyed miles of the railroad, burning the stations and rolling-stock. On the return, on the 28th, Wilson met a strong force under General Wade Hampton, from whom he barely escaped within the Federal lines with a remnant of his shattered force.

JUNE, 1864.

Both armies devoted their energies toward strengthening their positions, and until the 30th of July no direct outbreak occurred. On the 25th of June, General Burnside detailed the Forty-eighth Pennsylvania Regiment, composed mostly of Schuylkill miners, under direction of their colonel, Pleasants, himself an accomplished engineer, to mine the enemy's works. Starting within the line of rifle-pits, the mine extended under Taylor's Creek, and terminated 170 yards to a point under Elliott's salient; then lateral galleries extended right and left thirty-seven feet each, thus mining the Confederate lines in a concave line seventy-four feet. In these lateral galleries were four magazines, containing about 8,000 pounds of powder, equally distributed. On the 26th of July, General Hancock's Second Corps, with two divisions of Sheridan's cavalry, crossed the Deep Bottom, with instructions to proceed rapidly to Chapin's Bluff to destroy Lee's ponton-bridges, which were the means of communication between the army at Richmond and the forces defending Petersburg, and Sheridan was to operate toward Richmond and capture the thinly-held lines. General Foster's occupation of Deep Bottom was disputed by Lee. Hancock sent Miles's brigade, of Barlow's division, consisting of the One Hundred and Eighty-third Pennsylvania, Twenty-eighth Massachusetts and Twenty-sixth Michigan, under Colonel J. C. Lynch, to dislodge them, which they accomplished, capturing four guns. Lee, however, sent a large force from Petersburg, which drove Sheridan back and checked the purpose of Hancock. General Grant determined, in the absence of this force of Lee, to assault Petersburg. Hancock was ordered to withdraw secretly from his lines on the north side of the James, and again took position on the lines temporarily vacated on the 18th, and Sheridan, assembled at Deep Bottom, was to move against the Confederate right by the roads from the south and west leading to Petersburg. The ponton-trains were held in readiness under Major Duane, and engineer officers assigned to each corps. The forces made disposable for this assault consisted of about 50,000 men, exclusive of the cavalry.

JULY, 1864.

The order to spring the mine was made for 3:30 A.M., on the 30th of July. The match was applied, but with no attendant effect, and a brave lieutenant and sergeant of the Forty-eighth Pennsylvania volunteered to descend and inspect the cause of failure. They found the fire had died out, and they relit the extinguished fuse, and at 4:44 A.M. the explosion occurred. Bushrod R. Johnson's command was alone defending the trenches, as the balance of Beauregard's and Lee's armies was either on the road to oppose Hancock's demonstration north of the James, or held in readiness to march. Elliott's salient, the immediate scene of the explosion, was defended by

JULY, 1864.

THE FIFTH ARMY CORPS AWAITING THE ORDER TO ADVANCE, AFTER THE EXPLOSION OF THE MINE, PETERSBURG, JULY 30TH, 1864.

THE NINTH ARMY CORPS CHARGING THE CONFEDERATE WORKS, BEFORE PE

THE NINTH ARMY CORPS CHARGING THE CONFEDERATE WORKS BEFORE PETERSBURG IMMEDIATELY AFTER THE EXPLOSION OF THE MINE, JUNE 30th 1864

SCENE OF THE FIGHT BETWEEN DETACHMENTS OF THE SIXTH CORPS, GENERAL WRIGHT, AND RODE'S AND GORDON'S DIVISIONS OF EWELL'S CORPS, AT FORT STEVENS, WASHINGTON, D.C., JULY 12TH, 1864.

FROM A SKETCH BY E. F. MULLEN.

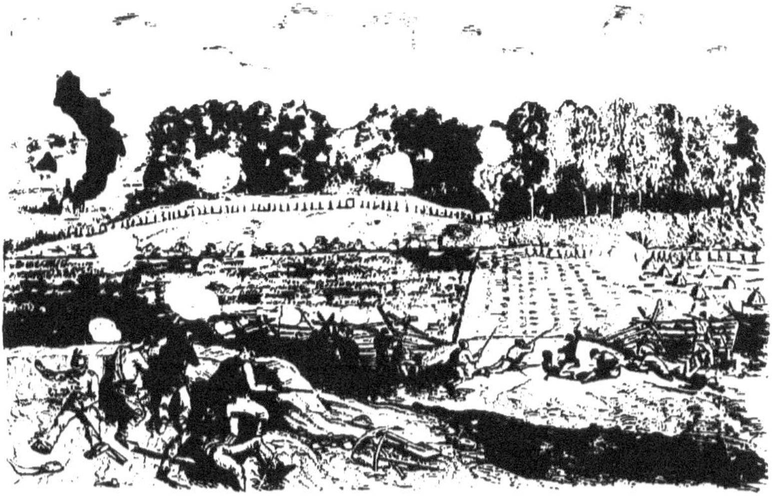

CONFEDERATE ASSAULT ON THE WORKS NEAR WASHINGTON REPULSED BY DISMOUNTED CAVALRY AND MILITIA, JULY 12TH, 1864.

FROM A SKETCH BY GEORGE H. DURKEE.

his own brigade, and embraced the Seventeenth, Eighteenth, Twenty-second, Twenty-third and Twenty-sixth South Carolina Volunteers, with Ransom's brigade on the left, Wise's brigade on the right and Colquitt's on the extreme right. The Federal assaulting party was chosen from the Ninth Corps by lot, and fell upon the First Division, General James H. Ledlie, possibly a selection that prudence and military judgment would not have approved. As the smoke lifted from the line of the explosion, which had been accompanied by a simultaneous outburst of artillery fire from all the Federal batteries, silencing the batteries of the Confederates not directly affected by the explosion, Ledlie's division advanced to the charge. On reaching the site of the fort, it was found to have been converted into a yawning crater, 135 feet long, 97 feet wide and 30 feet deep. The explosion had buried the guns of Pegram's battery and a part of the Eighteenth and Twenty-second South Carolina Regiments. The crater divided Elliott's brigade, and a panic seized the men who had been so suddenly aroused from their sleep, and they rushed in all directions. Their officers, however, soon rallied them, and Beauregard directed the remaining guns of his batteries toward the assaulting party, now fairly in the crater. Wilcox's division followed

NIGHT ATTACK ON FORT STEVENS, JULY 11TH, 1864, WHILE PRESIDENT LINCOLN WAS THERE.

HORATIO G. WRIGHT. JOHN A. RAWLINS. U
GOUVERNEUR K. WARREN. DAVID B. BIRNEY. BENJAMIN F. BUTLER.

UNION
GRANT
AND THE
GENERALS
ARMY
POTOMAC

CONTRABANDS COMING INTO THE FEDERAL CAMP IN VIRGINIA.

From a Sketch by Edwin Forbes.

Ledlie, and then Potter's, while the Federal artillery opened all along the lines, concentrating its fire on the right and left of the crater. Beauregard had directed, in case of any breach by assault, that his whole army should concentrate at that point, leaving the other lines of defense in charge of pickets. This was promptly executed by General Bushrod R. Johnson, division commander. General Elliott was severely wounded, and on Colonel F. W. McMaster devolved the command of the defense of the crater. A hand-to-hand fight ensued, the Federal soldiers, under General Potter, gaining the parapet and main trench, but were quickly driven out by a cross-fire from the batteries on either side of the crater, and, owing to want of support, were compelled to fall back. General Ledlie and occupied the crater for two hours, and Burnside advantage of a favorable opportunity for the men to retire with the least possible sacrifice of life. Hancock's and Warren's corps had taken no part in the attack, and they received orders at the same time—9:30 A.M.—"to suspend all offensive operations." The same order was given to General Ord.

At 11:30 General Wright's brigade, of Mahone's division, drove the Federals from the trenches on the right of the crater, which they had captured, but the Federals soon re-occupied them. Beauregard then concentrated all his available batteries upon the crater and adjacent trenches, and prepared the combined forces of Mahone and Johnson for a charge; but the cross-fire from the batteries had so effectually emptied the crater that the Confederate batteries slackened their fire, and only thirty men and three stands of colors were captured.

of invasion, down the Shenandoah Valley to Martinsburg, where he arrived on the 3d of July.

JULY, 1864

Sigel, who held the post, retreated across the river by way of Shepherdstown. Weber, in command of Harper's Ferry retired to Maryland Heights. Early reached Frederick City, July 7th, from which point he could operate either against Baltimore or Washington. Lew Wallace was in command of a small force at Baltimore. Grant, on learning of the rapid movement of Early, detached the Sixth Corps, forwarding it by transports to Washington. General Emory had just arrived at Hampton Roads from New Orleans with the Nineteenth Corps. Without leaving their transports, they were sent up the Potomac to Washington. Rickett's division, of the Sixth Corps, joined Wallace, and took position on the Monocacy

CONFEDERATE CAVALRY RANSACKING THE TOWN OF NEW WINDSOR, MD.

FROM A SKETCH BY FREDERICK DIELMAN.

found that the more troops he threw in, the greater the confusion. Yet he ordered General Ferrero at 7:30 to push through the breach and carry Cemetery Hill with his negro division. Ferrero passed the crater, advanced toward the crest, met a fierce artillery and musketry fire, but his men broke in disorder. Their commander partly reorganized them, but they soon broke again, fleeing in wild confusion into and out of the crater, back to the remotest of Burnside's lines. This stampede effectually disheartened the remainder of the party, who gathered within the crater, where they were exposed to a murderous fire from left and right, and General Grant, riding to the scene of action, exclaimed, "These troops must be immediately withdrawn; it is slaughter to leave them there!" and, returning to Meade's headquarters, a peremptory order was given by Meade at 9:45 to withdraw his troops, which, however, was so modified as to leave to Burnside's discretion the time, in order to take

Beauregard gives the Confederate loss as 1,172, of which Johnson's division, including Colquitt's brigade, temporarily attached to it, bore of this loss 922; Elliott's brigade alone losing 672, 256 of whom were victims of the explosion. General Meade reported his loss to be 4,400, killed, wounded and missing. General Badeau, in his "Life of General Grant," characterizes this affair as "one of the most discreditable to the National arms that occurred during the War."

In order to divert the army of General Grant from further combined operations against Richmond from the south, General Lee determined to make a demonstration against the Federal capital, and thus draw a portion of Grant's army to its defense. General Hunter, after his defeat at Lynchburg, had retreated by way of West Virginia, and thus left the road to Washington and the North uncovered. Lee detached a body of 12,000 men, under General Early, over the already beaten track to oppose the advance of Early. On the 8th of July they were attacked, and after a gallant stand were forced to retire toward Baltimore. This opened

JULY, 1864.

the route to Washington, and Early pushed forward in that direction, first sending a cavalry force toward Baltimore, which destroyed the railroad and burned the viaduct, effectually cutting off communication with the North and securing their rear. On the 9th of July, Early reached Rockville, fourteen miles from Washington. The next day, resuming the march, his advance force reached the northern approaches to Washington, defended by Forts Stevens and Massachusetts. On the 11th the Confederate force had invested these forts, which were almost undefended. The department clerks and citizen volunteers, however, made a good show, and Early hesitated to attack, and by the afternoon the Sixth Corps, followed by the Nineteenth, effectually manned the fortifications and saved Washington.

INVASION OF MARYLAND, 1864.—DRIVING OFF CATTLE A

FROM A

INVASION OF MARYLAND, 1864—DRIVING OFF CATTLE AND PLUNDER TAKEN FROM THE FARMERS BY EARLY'S CAVALRY

CHARGE OF THE SECOND DIVISION, NINTH ARMY CORPS, INTO THE CRATER CAUSED BY THE EXPLOSION OF THE MINE IN FRONT OF PETERSBURG, JULY 30TH, 1864.

From a Sketch by A. McC[illegible]

The two armies kept up a skirmishing fire, but made no violent demonstration until, on the afternoon of the 17th, a brigade of both corps fell upon Early and drove him about a mile, sustaining and inflicting about the same loss—300 in killed and wounded.

The same night Early withdrew by way of Edwards' Ferry, taking with him a good supply of booty. General Wright pursued the retreating Confederates, but did not come up to them until they reached the Valley. A short skirmish took place at Snicker's Ferry, when Early beat a hasty retreat southward. The Sixth and the Nineteenth Corps were sent to the Valley, where General Phil. Sheridan took command.

As Grant withdrew but one corps—the Sixth—from before Petersburg, notwithstanding the urgent demands of the War Department at Washington, General Lee had failed in his effort, and Petersburg was still besieged by Grant's main army, and with support Mott. Barlow, however, kept up his junction with Mott's right, and was thus obliged to string his men over a long line to cover the Confederate line, and his thin line was in no condition to form a storming party. He made an effort with one brigade, but failed to dislodge the enemy. General Birney, on the other side of the creek, broke through the Confederate lines—they having weakened their right to oppose Barlow—and captured four guns. On the 15th, Birney undertook to find the enemy's left flank and turn it with the support of Gregg's cavalry. Not getting far enough to the left, the movement failed for the day. On the next morning he made a direct attack with Terry's division, and captured the line, with three colors and nearly three hundred prisoners. The Confederates, however, rallied and drove Terry back. On the 20th, Hancock withdrew to his old camp before Petersburg. The Federal loss in this expedition exceeded 1,500 men.

great confusion. Twenty-five hundred prisoners were captured, including General J. Hays. Wilcox and White, of the Ninth Corps, came up to the aid of Warren, who then re-formed his lines and regained his lost position. On the 21st the Confederates opened an artillery fire along the line, crossing their fire at right angles over Warren's position. They then attacked the front, and at the same time made an effort on the left flank. Warren repulsed A. P. Hill's forces in front. Haygood's brigade, supported by five brigades of Mahone's division, was to make up the flanking force. Mahone failed to come up, and Haygood found himself before a strongly intrenched line, stretching far to both the left and right. The small force pressed forward, gaining the parapet of the works, expecting support, but soon found its retreat cut off. Captain Daly, of General Cutler's staff, boldly rode forward, seizing the regimental colors. Haygood, on foot, demanded their return, and ordering his

SCENE OF THE LOCALITY WHERE SHIELDS FOUGHT STONEWALL JACKSON IN 1862, AND WHERE CROOK WAS DEFEATED IN AUGUST 1864.

FROM A SKETCH BY J. E. TAYLOR.

Sheridan in the Valley, Lee saw no hope of further successful raids North.

On the 12th of August was set on foot by General Grant a repetition of the manœuvres of July, on the north bank of the James River. Hancock again took charge of the expedition, and in addition to his own corps, he took the Tenth Corps, now under General Birney, and the cavalry division of General

August, 1864.

Gregg, and embarked on transports at City Point to better cover up his design, trusting that Lee would believe the troops *en route* for Washington. During the night he steamed up the stream, landing with much difficulty the next morning at Deep Bottom, where an intrenched camp had been held by General Foster since the last expedition. Hancock moved by the Malvern Hill and New Market Roads to Bailey's Creek, where a month ago he had encountered a reverse. Here he found the enemy intrenched, and with Mott's division fronting their line, Barlow, with two divisions, numbering about 10,000 men, assaulted on the extreme right, with instructions to carry the position, and then move to the left to

While Hancock was on the north side of the James, Warren was dispatched to take possession of the Weldon Railroad. Establishing himself on the road early on the 18th, and leaving Griffin's division to guard the point seized, he continued with the

August, 1864.

balance of his force northward along the railroad. He proceeded to within a mile of Petersburg, where a Confederate line of battle opposed his further progress. Placing Crawford's division to the right, and Ayres on the left, he gave battle. The result was the withdrawal of Ayres's force, with a loss of 200 of the Maryland Brigade, prisoners. The Fifteenth New York Heavy Artillery covered the retreat and prevented a rout. Wilson still held possession of the Weldon Road, but his loss had been over 1,000 men, killed, wounded and prisoners. Lee had now only the Danville Road as a means of communication and supply between Petersburg and Richmond, and on the 19th made an unsuccessful effort to dislodge Warren, who had intrenched. Warren's flank was turned, the Confederates gaining the rear of Crawford's line, and swept down on Warren's left, causing

men to fall back, he seized Daly's horse, and shooting the gallant captain through the body, he mounted his horse as Daly's body fell from it; his orderly seized the captured flag, and thus mounted, the intrepid commander ordered a charge on the Federal lines in the rear and made good his retreat. The road remained in the hands of Warren, who strongly intrenched his line. He had lost in this expedition, he reported, an aggregate of 4,455 men, killed, wounded and missing.

Hancock, on the 21st, was ordered to the left, in the rear of Warren's position. This he accomplished, and his troops destroyed the railroad as far south as Ream's Station. By the 24th they had destroyed three miles beyond, and returned to the intrenchments. On the 25th, Gibbon's division was to continue the destruction as far as Rowanty Creek. He had scarcely left the intrenchment at Ream's Station when he was attacked by a Confederate force under Generals A. P. Hill and Wade Hampton. Hancock withdrew Gibbon's division within the intrenchments, placing it on the left of the First Division, commanded by General Miles.

BEFORE PETERSBURG, JULY 30TH, 1864.—EXPLOSION OF THE MINE,

BEFORE PETERSBURG, JULY [illegible], [illegible]—EXPLOSION OF THE MINE, A[illegible] ON THE CONFEDERATE WORKS—[illegible] ANDREW McCALLUM

VIEW OF THE CONFEDERATE WORKS AFTER THE EXPLOSION OF THE M[illegible] AND THE BATTLE OF JULY 30th, 186[illegible] From a sketch by E. F. M[illegible]

BATTLE OF REAM'S STATION, VA.—EFFORTS OF THE CONFEDERATE FORCES TO REGAIN POSSESSION OF THE WELDON RAILROAD AUGUST 25TH, 1864.

From a Sketch by Joseph Becker.

The Confederates fell on Miles, who speedily repulsed them. A second and a third attack, more vigorously executed, were likewise checked. The Confederates then concentrated a powerful artillery fire on the Federal position, and owing to the faulty construction of the breastworks (which were occupied but not built by Hancock), General Heth's division, of A. P. Hill's corps, by an impetuous rush, broke through Miles's line, and the command gave way in confusion. With no reserve but a brigade of Gibbon's division, under Colonel Rugg, which failed to support, the Confederate storming party seized the artillery, and the batteries of McKnight, Perrin and Sleeper were captured. Hancock ordered Gibbon's division to retake the guns and position lost. They made a feeble effort, but were obliged to fall back, and but for the splendid fight of Miles's division, and the gallantry of their commander, who succeeded in rallying a portion of the sixty-first New York, and forming it at right-angles intrenched on Preble's Farm carried a line of rifle-pits, capturing one gun and about one hundred prisoners. At the same time Ayres's division captured a work on Squirrel Level Road. Parke, on Warren's left, was fiercely assailed and forced back in disorder. Griffin came to his support, and regained the ground. On the morning of the 1st, Gregg met the enemy's cavalry and forced it back.

October, 1864.

In the afternoon Gregg was assailed on the Duncan Road, which he held in order to guard the left and rear of the operating forces, but held his position. On the 2d the whole force advanced, to find the enemy had withdrawn to their main intrenchments, and the Federal forces at once made defensive the new position, which had been gained with a loss of about 2,500 men.

In the meantime General Butler had been operating against the defenses of Richmond, capturing Fort Harrison, fifteen pieces of artillery and the defenses of the New Market Road. On the 8th of September this brilliant movement had been accomplished by the corps of Birney and Ord. They next were repulsed in an attack on Fort Gilmer, in front of Chapin's Farm, losing about 300 men.

HOSPITAL STEWARD FILLING SURGEONS' ORDERS AT THE ARMY DRUG STORE.

From a Sketch by Joseph Becker.

to the breastworks, checking the advance of the Confederates, retaking McKnight's guns, and recovering a portion of the lost line, the disaster would have been much greater.

Hancock failed to receive reinforcements, and he withdrew from Ream's Station with a loss of 2,400 killed, wounded and missing, out of a command of only 8,000. The loss to the Confederates was probably as severe.

It was near the end of September before any further offensive operations were made by General Grant, the army in the meantime having thoroughly intrenched, and connected the advance lines with the main body before Petersburg. General Grant ordered two divisions of the Fifth Corps, under Warren, and two divisions of the Ninth, under Parke, to move from the left toward Poplar Spring Church and Preble's Farm, with a view of preventing the Confederates reinforcing the troops operating against General Butler. Gregg's cavalry moved to the left and rear of Warren's and Parke's forces. Griffin's division struck the Confederates

On the 23d of September, General Beauregard was ordered by President Davis to Charleston, South Carolina, to take charge of the defenses of that city and the Atlantic coast, which he had left seven months before in charge of General Ripley to go to the assistance of Lee in the defense of Petersburg, the key to the Confederate capital. This task he had thoroughly accomplished, and as the bad roads and Virginia Winter were unfavorable to aggressive movements, Davis no longer feared an active campaign on the part of Grant.

The Federal commander, however, determined on one more effort to capture Petersburg before Winter set in. His plan was to turn the extreme right of the enemy's intrenched line, and seize the Southside Railroad, which was now Lee's principal means of communication between Richmond and Petersburg. Leaving a sufficient force to hold the lines in front of Petersburg, he dispatched the greater part of his three army corps to carry out this design.

The left flank of the Federal army occupied a position about two miles beyond (west of) the Weldon Railroad. General Lee had extended his right flank so as to cover the Boydton Plank Road, below where it crosses Hatcher's Run. This wing was intrenched, and protected the Southside Railroad, which ran parallel to and two miles distant from the Plank Road.

The Ninth Corps, supported by the Fifth, was to attack the extreme right of the intrenched line of the Confederates, while the Second Corps was to cross to the west side of Hatcher's Run by a swinging movement, strike the Boydton Plank Road, and advance to seize the Southside Railroad.

October, 1864.

This movement was begun on the early morning of the 27th. After a march of three miles westward, Parke and Warren confronted the right of the Confederate intrenched line on the east bank of Hatcher's Run. Parke was on the right, Warren on the left. Hancock moved by the Vaughan Road, which lies south of the line of march of the Ninth and Fifth Corps. He forced a crossing of Hatcher's Run, advanced northwestward, passed Dabney's Mill, and gained the Boydton Plank Road. He then was to cross at White Oak Bridge, two miles above, march four miles, and strike the Southside Railroad in the rear of the enemy's extreme right. Gregg's cavalry division covered his left. At one o'clock in the afternoon, while driving a small force of the enemy across Hatcher's Run, at Burgess's Mill, in order to mask his movement, he received an order from General Meade to halt on the Boydton Plank Road. This order was a surprise to Hancock, and was prompted by a failure of the Ninth Corps, which had attacked the enemy's front and been repulsed, and Meade had directed Warren to make an effort to turn the line. He ordered Crawford's division, supported by Ayres's brigade, across Hatcher's Run, at Armstrong's Mill, and they marched up the stream.

THE SECOND CORPS, UNDER GENERAL HANCOCK, FLANKING THE CONFEDERATE WORKS AT ARMSTRONG'S MILL, ON HATCHER'S RUN, VA., OCTOBER 27TH, 1864.

AGENTS OF NORTHERN MEN DRAFTED IN THE ARMY PROCURING NEGRO SUBSTITUTES AT NORFOLK, VA.

Meade's order of halt to Hancock was so as to allow time for Warren's troops to reach and support him, as in his position at Burgess's Mill he was isolated from the main army by five or six miles, and separated from Warren and Parke by Hatcher's Run. Crawford found a difficult march, and his men became separated and lost in the dense woods; in fact, regiments lost trace of their divisions, and companies of their regiments. It took three hours to reach the right flank of the intrenched enemy opposed to the remainder of the Fifth and Ninth Corps, with the Run between them. Warren found the maps defective and the country strange. He therefore ordered a sucesso of operations until he could consult Meade. Warren's force was now about one mile from Burgess's Mill, but it was several hours before the respective forces found out the position of the other. In the meantime Hancock had been attacked by Hill's Confederate corps, while he had sent General ..., in command of Gibbon's division, to the ... ut of the Boydton Plank Road, who deployed and faced southward. Smythe's and Willett's brigades, of Egan's division, McAllister's brigade, of Mott's division, and De Trobriand's brigade and Kerwin's dismounted cavalry, combined in the assault. Egan's charge was irresistible, and the Confederates lost their captured guns, two colors and 1,000 prisoners. In their retreat they were lost in the woods, and several hundred were captured within Crawford's line.

Had Crawford then made an attack, the Federal victory would have been decisive, but he had no orders, as Warren thought Ayres's division could reach Hancock more easily than Crawford, as the latter was in the dense woods, and with no road. Ayres, however, was able only to reach Armstrong's Mill, where he halted for the night. While the fight was going on on the right. General Wade Hampton, with five brigades of Confederate cavalry, assailed Gregg's mounted division, which held the left and rear of Hancock's forces. The attack was so furious that Hancock had to use all the force not engaged on the right to repel the gallant Confederate, of the enemy. The division of Gregg moved by the Jerusalem Plank Road to Ream's Station, thence westward across Rowanty Creek, marching rapidly on Dinwiddie Court House. The Fifth Corps passed to the west side of the creek to take position on the right of the Second Corps, which marched down the Vaughan Road toward Hatcher's Run. The Second Division of Humphreys's Second Corps, under Smythe, turned abruptly to the right, taking a path that led to Armstrong's Mill, where Smythe found the enemy intrenched. He took up a position making a connection between the two other divisions of the same corps. In the afternoon the Confederates assailed Smythe, endeavoring to turn his flank; but Smythe's division, aided by McAllister's brigade, of Mott's division, resisted repeated attacks, which were continued until dark. The next day the Fifth Corps, together with Gregg's cavalry, reinforced the Second Corps. Warren's left, under Crawford, advanced to Dabney's Mill and drove out Pegram. The Confederates, finding this flank exposed, sent a force by the Vaughan

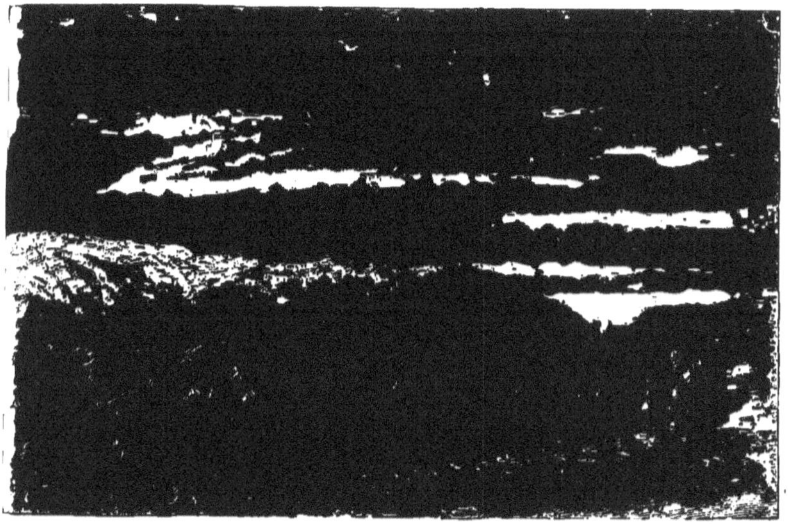

THE SIEGE OF PETERSBURG.—GOING TO THE TRENCHES.

FROM A SKETCH BY E. F. MULLEN.

two brigades far to the right, and subsequently two regiments still further in the woods, in order to find Crawford's force. They failed to form a connection, the distance between them really being nearly three-fourths of a mile. Lee's original design was to cross the Run above Burgess's Mill and fall on Hancock's left flank. Hancock anticipated him, and carried the bridge over the dam; and Lee, to save the Heights, ordered Hill to cross where h. was and attack Hancock's right. The crossing was effected at a point directly midway between the forces of Crawford and Hancock, and Hill, passing close to Crawford's skirmishers, but not being discovered owing to the woods, about 4 P.M. suddenly fell on Mott's division of Hancock's corps. The troops being disposed so as to receive an attack in the opposite quarter, were fired upon on their rear. Pierce's brigade, of Mott's division, gave way, a section of artillery was captured, and a rout was imminent. Hancock ordered Egan to the front to resist the victorious troops. The brave commander had already anticipated his superior's orders, and swept upon the flank of the Confederates, who had failed to comprehend the situation, and pushed across the road Hancock lost about 1,500 men in this fight, and the Confederates fully as many. The result was no advantage to the Federal side, and the expedition was unfortunate in plan, while the execution was in every way brilliant. Hancock, reluctant to leave the field, found his men worn out and without ammunition, and, with no prospect of Ayres reaching him in time for an early morning attack, he withdrew, and by morning the whole force was within the Federal lines before Petersburg. Lee had massed his forces—15,000 infantry and Hampton's entire cavalry—ready for an assault at daylight of the 28th, but the morning found no enemy.

There were no further active operations during the year. Hancock was ordered North to raise the new First Corps, and Humphrey assumed command of the Second Corps.

A second attempt was made early in February, 1865, to gain possession of the Southside Railroad. The Federal forces had during the Winter extended their line of defenses westward to Hatcher's Run. The Fifth Corps, with the Second Corps under Humphreys, and Gregg's cavalry, under cover of a heavy bombardment from all the Federal batteries before Petersburg, intended to engage the attention Road to reach Crawford's rear, and fell upon Gregg's cavalry, which they drove back to Hatcher's Run, while at the same time they opened an attack in front. Ayres's division, while moving in column to the support of Crawford, was attacked and driven back, and the victors then attacked Crawford and threw his division back in great confusion, with heavy loss. This success they followed up with an attack on Wheaton's division of the Sixth Corps, which was moving to the support of the left, and the entire left retreated toward the position occupied by the Second Corps at Hatcher's Run. Elated by their success, the Confederate force pushed to the front of the Second Corps, where Humphreys met them with a sharp fire from his temporary intrenchments, which forced the Confederate troops to retire. The Federal loss was 2,000, the greatest proportion being of Crawford's division. The Confederates lost 1,000; their commander, General John Pegram, was killed. Except an expedition under Warren with the Fifth Corps, Mott's division of the Second Corps, and Gregg's mounted division, to destroy the Weldon Railroad, which was only partially successful, there were no further movement ... fore Petersburg until the Spring campaign.

BATTLE OF POPLAR SPRING CHURCH, VA.—GALLANT CHARGE OF A PART OF THE FIFTH CORPS ON THE CONFEDERATE FORT.

DAVID A. RUSSELL.

Born in Washington County, N. Y., in 1824; entered the Military Academy at West Point in 1841; and graduated in July, 1845. Was assigned to the Fourth Regular Infantry, and stationed on the Pacific Coast, where he remained ten years, acquiring the rank of captain. When the Civil War broke out he was chosen colonel of the Seventh Massachusetts Regiment, and led the same with honor through the memorable campaign of the Peninsula, under General McClellan. He was appointed brevet-major in the Regular Army for distinguished services at the battle of Williamsburg. He fought gallantly at Fair Oaks (or Seven Pines), and was made a full major of the Eighth Infantry, and subsequently for general good conduct throughout the Peninsula campaign was made lieutenant-colonel by brevet in the Regular Army. In November, 1862, he was made brigadier-general of Volunteers. He commanded his brigade on the left of the line at Fredericksburg, in December, 1862; at Salem Heights in May, 1863; in the expedition to Beverly and Kelly's Fords in June; and at Gettysburg in July of the same year. He presented to the War Department the colo which his brigade captured on the Rappahannock, and w highly complimented by Secretary Stanton for his gall conduct and important services while in command of t brigade. President Lincoln at once promoted him to be major-general by brevet, and in November, 1863, he w placed in command of a division, and conducted the F Division of the Sixth Army Corps through the battles the Wilderness, Spottsylvania, Cold Harbor, and befo Petersburg. Called to the defense of the National Capi against the threatening operations of Early, General Rus with his division rendered signal service, and was activ prominent in pushing the gallant Confederate cavalry ha back into Virginia and up the Valley, until at Winches Sheridan's signal victory proved the beginning of a spee and to the daring raids that had thrown the whole Nor into consternation. At the battle of Opequan (or Winchest September 19th, 1864, General Russell was instantly kill by a cannon-ball while at the head of his division. His lo was deeply lamented by his fellow-soldiers.

DAVID A. RUSSELL.

THE NINTH CORPS PASSING POPLAR SPRING CHURCH, SEPTEMBER 30TH, 1864.—CONFEDERATE PRISONERS COMING IN UNDER GUARD.

From a Sketch by Joseph Becker.

ALEXANDER S. WEBB.

ALEXANDER HAYS.

ALEXANDER S. WEBB.

Born in New York city on the 15th day of February, 1835, son of General James Watson Webb, and a grandson of General Samuel B Webb, who was an aide-de-camp to General Washington, and later a colonel and brigadier-general in the Connecticut Line of the Revolutionary Army. In his youth he attended the school of Mr. Churchill, a graduate of West Point. Among his schoolmates were the Kings, Leavenworths, Barnwells, Dodge, Graces, Cheney, Hoffmans, Van Rensselaers, and others well known in every department of life. Leaving there he was prepared for entrance to West Point by Professor Ross, of the Free Academy, now the College of the City of New York. He entered West Point 1851, and graduated in 1855, in the 21st year of his age. Among his classmates were such men as Comstock, Weitzel, Torbert, Governor F. R. T. Nicholls, Averill, Hazen, [illegible], and others who gained distinction during the Civil War of 1861-65. In November, 1855, he married Anna Remsen, daughter of Henry Rutgers Remsen, of New York City, and the following month left for Florida to serve under Colonel Harvey Brown against the Seminole Indians.

He served with the Army of the Potomac from Bull Run to Appomattox Court House under the following commissions: First lieutenant, Second United States Artillery; captain, Eleventh United States Infantry; major, First Rhode Island Artillery; lieutenant-colonel, United States Volunteers, and inspector-general, Fifth Army Corps; brigadier-general, United States Volunteers; brevet-major general, United States Volunteers; and meanwhile received brevet commissions in the United States Army as major, lieutenant-colonel, colonel, brigadier-general and major general. Under the last-mentioned he was, after the surrender of the Confederate armies, appointed by the President Military Governor of the First Military District of Virginia. The significant wording of each brevet commission, "for gallant and meritorious services," and "gallant and distinguished conduct at Gettysburg, Bristoe Station, Wilderness, and Spottsylvania," attest the character of his services. The list of engagements in which he participated, commencing with Bull Run and ending at Appomattox Court House, comprises every one of magnitude, except Cold Harbor, fought by the Army of the Potomac. Wounded at Gettysburg while stemming the tide of Pickett's grand assault, he nevertheless remained on the field and witnessed the magic disappearance of that charging column of 18,000 men. Of his color guard, composed of a sergeant and seven corporals, all were killed or wounded but one, who, while carrying the colors of the Second Division of the Second Corps, under the command of General Webb, at Spottsylvania, ended his military career. At Spottsylvania General Webb was severely wounded in the head, but recovered and served as chief of staff to Major-general Meade, commanding the Army of the Potomac, to the end of the Virginia campaign. The following letter from General Meade attests the value of his services:

"Headquarters Department of the East, Philadelphia, Pa.,
"November 1st, 1866.

"*Brevet-major-general A. S. Webb, U. S. A., West Point, N. Y.*

"General: The Union League of Philadelphia have furnished me with a few copies in bronze of the elegant gold medal which was presented to me recently in commemoration of the battle of Gettysburg. In selecting those to whom I should distribute these medals, I know no one general, who has more claims than yourself either for 'distinguished personal gallantry' on that ever-memorable field, or for the cordial, warm and generous sympathy and support so grateful for a commanding general to receive from his subordinates. Accept therefore the accompanying medal, not only as commemoration of

SAMUEL D. STURGIS.

GEORGE SYKES.

the conspicuous part you bore in the great battle, but as an evidence on my part of reciprocation of the kindly feelings that have always characterized our intercourse, both official and social.

"Very truly, yours, George G. Meade,

"Major-general, United States Army."

In 1869 he was elected President of the College of the City of New York, which position he now holds (1885); and he has during the intervening seventeen years so administered the affairs of his office as president, that the institution to-day takes rank with nearly all the older American colleges.

LOUIS FITZGERALD.

Born in New York City on May 31st, 1838, and after completing a thorough course of studies entered mercantile pursuits. In 1857 he joined the famous Seventh Militia Regiment of New York, and marched with that command, in 1861, to the defense of Washington. After the expiration of the term for which it had enlisted, the regiment returned to New York, and young Fitzgerald entered the United States service as first-lieutenant in the Eleventh Regiment, New York Volunteers (Ellsworth Fire Zouaves), and was promoted to be captain, for gallantry at the first battle of Bull Run, as stated in orders.

After the disbandment of the Zouaves he was commissioned first-lieutenant in the Fortieth New York (Mozart), and for gallantry in the battle of Fair Oaks was again promoted to a captaincy. He was one of the sufferers by the *Hiram Barney* disaster. He had been sent on the vessel to make a reconnoissance of the Confederate fortifications along the river, and was standing on the bow at the time of the explosion. Bruised and unconscious, he was picked up by a tugboat, and cared for by his comrades; but it was a long time before he was able to resume his duty.

During the Peninsula campaign he served as provost-marshal and as aid-de-camp on the staff of the gallant General Phil Kearny, and is one of the few officers entitled to wear the Kearny Cross. After the death of that great soldier, Captain Fitzgerald served as aid-de-camp to General D. B. Birney in the Third Corps. He was subsequently ordered to General J. G. Foster, commanding the Eighteenth Corps, and accompanied the latter officer in all the campaigns in North Carolina, South Carolina, Kentucky and Tennessee. In 1864 he was promoted major, and subsequently lieutenant-colonel, of the First Mississippi. Colonel Fitzgerald served with distinction in many departments, and his gallantry was conspicuous in the many battles and skirmishes in which he was engaged. He was wounded at Bull Run, Williamsburg and Fair Oaks. At the close of the War he was breveted lieutenant-colonel in the National Guard of New York "for faithful and meritorious services during the War," and was immediately returned to his old favorite, the Seventh Regiment, as its adjutant. Was for ten years considered the model adjutant in the State of New York. In 1875 he was elected lieutenant-colonel of the Seventh Regiment, and in 1882 was appointed a brigadier-general, and placed in command of the Second Brigade, comprising the Seventh, Sixty-ninth, Eighth and Seventy-first Militia Regiments of New York. He is at present (1885) connected with many prominent corporations in his native city, having held for several years the Presidency of the New York Mercantile Trust Company.

LOUIS FITZGERALD.

EDWARD L. MOLINEUX.

Born in England, October 12th, 1833. He first became identified with the National Guard of the State of New York in 1854, when he joined the celebrated "Brooklyn City Guard," and passed through the several grades of non-commissioned rank, his membership being terminated by his acceptance of an important mission to South America. On the outbreak of the Civil War he was one of the first to volunteer in defense of the Union, enrolling himself as a member of the Second Company of the Seventh Regiment, and serving throughout the preliminary campaign in which that regiment was engaged. He was one of the foremost promoters of the Twenty-third Regiment of Brooklyn; as brigade inspector he was largely instrumental in organizing the Eleventh Brigade, N. G. S. N. Y., and was subsequently unanimously elected lieutenant-colonel of the Twenty-third Regiment. In August, 1862, he raised the One Hundred and Fifty-ninth Regiment, New York Volunteers, as lieutenant-colonel; was mustered into the United States service in November following as full colonel, and, with the regiment, assigned to the Banks Expedition, the One Hundred and Fifty-ninth subsequently being the first regiment to land at Baton Rouge, La. He commanded a detachment of General Banks's army, protecting the right wing of the main body during the feint against Port Hudson. At the battle of Irish Bend (April 14th, 1863), while leading a charge, Colonel Molineux was severely wounded, a rifle-ball entering his mouth just as he uttered the rallying-cry, "Forward New York!" taking off a large piece of his upper jaw, and passing out at the centre of the left cheek. The "Draft Riots" (August, 1863) occurring while he was home, wounded, he offered his services to General Butler, and did effective duty on "boat patrol" on the river-front during those troubles. Returning to active duty in the field during the ensuing month of July, he was appointed assistant-inspector-general on the staff of Major-general Franklin, being subsequently made acting provost-marshal-general and commissioner for the exchange of prisoners. In the Spring of 1864 he was made military commander of the La Fourche District, La.; was afterward assigned the duty of organizing "State Troops," or independent companies of Louisiana scouts; and upon the construction of the celebrated Dam at Alexandria, was given command of all the United States forces north of the Red River. Ordered North with his command, he joined General Butler at Bermuda Hundred, July 25th, 1864; but ten days afterward, having in the meantime organized a provisional division, reinforced General Sheridan in the Valley, participating in all the engagements and battles of that campaign, and being promoted brigadier-general by brevet for conspicuous gallantry and zeal at Fisher's Hill, Winchester and Cedar Creek. Returning to the Department of the South early in 1865, General Molineux was placed in charge of the works at Savannah, and later given command of Fort Pulaski and Tybee. While here he was instrumental in saving the ship *Lawrence*, in recognition of which service the New York Board of Underwriters voted him a service of plate. In June ensuing he was made military commander of the District of Northern Georgia, with headquarters at Augusta. He seized and secured to the United States Government Confederate coin and bullion to a very large amount, capturing $188,000 from Jefferson Davis, over 70,000 bales of cotton, quartermaster and commissary stores aggregating $10,000,000, and Government buildings and factories of great value. His administration of affairs was marked by firmness and wisdom, and by his uniform courtesy and kindness, coupled with his bold administration of military law, he won the esteem of the whole community.

On the termination of active hostilities, General Molineux returned to civil life, with the rank of major-general by brevet "for gallant and meritorious services during the War." He is now (1885) major-general of the Second Division, N. G. S. N. Y.

EDWARD L. MOLINEUX.

SAMUEL DAVIS STURGIS.

Born at Shippensburg, Pa., in 1822, graduated at West Point, July 1st, 1846; appointed as second-lieutenant of Second Dragoons; served in the Mexican War; was made a prisoner while on a reconnoissance just before the battle of Buena Vista; subsequently served in California, New Mexico and on the frontiers; and was made captain, March 3d, 1855. At the breaking out of the Civil War he was in command of Fort Smith, Arkansas; all his officers resigning, he abandoned the fort, thus saving his command and most of its material. In May, 1861, was made colonel of Volunteer Cavalry, serving in Missouri; in August, a brigadier-general and assigned to the Army of the Tennessee; afterward to the command in Kansas; and in 1862 to that of the fortifications at Washington; subsequently serving in the field at the battle of Fredericksburg, and in the South and West. On March 13th, 1865, he was breveted brigadier-general and major-general. Was mustered out of the Volunteer service, August 24th, 1865. His rank in the Regular Army is colonel. Now (1885) in command of the Seventh United States Cavalry.

GEORGE SYKES.

Born at Dover, Del., October 9th, 1822; graduated at the United States Military Academy in 1842, when appointed a brevet second-lieutenant in the Third Infantry, his first service being against the Seminoles in Florida. In the War with Mexico he served with credit from Vera Cruz to the Mexican capital, gaining the brevet of captain for gallantry at Cerro Gordo. From 1848 to 1861 he was almost constantly with his regiment on the frontier, serving on numerous expeditions, and being engaged in frequent actions with hostile Indians. In 1855 he attained the rank of captain, and in the early part of 1861 was serving with his company in Texas. Hastening north, he was in May appointed major of the newly authorized Fourteenth Infantry, and in July commanded the battalion of Regular troops in the battle of Bull Run. Commissioned a brigadier-general of Volunteers in September, he commanded the Regular infantry in the defenses of Washington during the Winter of 1861-62, and in the Virginia Peninsula campaign of 1862 the division of Regulars (Porter's corps) which so stubbornly maintained its position on the right of Gaines's Mill. In the succeeding campaigns he continued in command of this division at the second battle of Bull Run, Antietam, Fredericksburg and Chancellorsville; and on the appointment of General Meade to the command of the Army of the Potomac (June, 1863), Sykes succeeded to that of the Fifth Corps, which a week later was engaged at Gettysburg, and at the head of which he continued during the ensuing operations of the Army of the Potomac, until April, 1864, when ordered to duty in the Department of Kansas. For gallantry at Gaines's Mill he was breveted colonel, brigadier-general for Gettysburg, and major-general for gallant services during the Civil War. Mustered out of the Volunteer service in January, 1866, returned to duty with the Fifth Infantry, of which he had been appointed lieutenant-colonel in October, 1863. In January 1868, he became colonel of the Twentieth Infantry.

ALEXANDER HAYS.

Born at Pittsburg, Pa., in 1820; graduated at the West Point Military Academy, July 1st, 1844, and entered the Army as brevet-second-lieutenant of Infantry; appointed second-lieutenant, June, 1846; served on frontier duty, 1844-46; and in the Mexican War was engaged in the battles of Palo Alto and Resaca de la Palma, being breveted first-lieutenant for gallantry. Ordered to Pennsylvania on recruiting duty, he quickly enlisted a large number of men, and returned to the seat of war, being engaged in various actions. On the 12th of April, 1848, he resigned from the Army, and engaged in the manufacture of iron at Venango, Pa., subsequently adopting the profession of civil engineer, which he followed until the outbreak of the Civil War, when he was appointed major of the Twelfth Pennsylvania Volunteers, and in the following month a captain in the Sixteenth United States Infantry. In August, 1861, he was commissioned colonel of the Sixty-third Pennsylvania Volunteers, and led his regiment in the Virginia Peninsula campaign of 1862, through most of the battles from Yorktown to Malvern Hill, receiving the brevets of major and lieutenant-colonel. In the second battle of Bull Run he was severely wounded and disabled till September 29th, 1862, when he was promoted to be brigadier-general of Volunteers, and assigned to duty in the defenses of Washington. At the battle of Gettysburg he was in command of a division of the Second Corps, and subsequently led it at Auburn, Bristoe Station and the Mine Run affair. In the Richmond campaign of 1864 he fell at the head of his command in the battle of the Wilderness, May 5th, 1864.

SHERMAN'S CAMPAIGN IN GEORGIA.

Prepared for "The Soldier in Our Civil War" by a Confederate officer of General Johnston's army and participant in the campaign.

THE battle of Missionary Ridge, Tenn., in November, 1863, so disastrous to the Confederate forces, was followed by a long cessation of active fighting. This period was one of preparation for the decisive campaign of 1864 in Georgia, which resulted in quartering the Confederacy by Sherman's March to the Sea, the halving process having already taken place in Grant's capture of Vicksburg.

During the Winter of 1863–64 both armies were gathering strength for the momentous conflict impending. The Federal army was quartered at and near Chattanooga, Tenn., and the Confederate army at and near Dalton, Ga. General W. T. Sherman, of the Federal army, assumed command of the Military Division of the Mississippi, which included this territory, on the 18th of March, 1864. General Joseph E. Johnston took command of the Confederate Army of the Tennessee on the 27th of December, 1863, at Dalton.

General Sherman had organized a magnificent force, and, with remarkable foresight, made all his arrangements for the campaign. He tells with great glee in his "Memoirs," how, needing locomotives and 1,000 cars to transport supplies, he had held on to and secured trains from every northern road, and adds that he never learned how the railroads recovered their stock. He started the campaign May 1st, 1864, with 98,797 infantry, and 254 cannons. These were divided into: Army of the Cumberland, Major-general Thomas, 60,773 men and 130 guns; Army of the Tennessee, Major-general McPherson, 24,465 men and 96 guns; and Army of the Ohio, Major-general Schofield, 13,559 men and 28 guns. The cavalry amounted to 12,000 men and horses, under Generals Stoneman, Garrard, E. McCook and Kilpatrick. The Federal army aggregated 110,000 men.

General Joseph E. Johnston took command of General Bragg's army, discouraged and depleted by the defeat of Missionary Ridge, and spent the entire Winter in bringing up the demoralized organization. The position at Dalton had not been selected for its strength, but was the point where the Confederate army happened to be after the battle of Missionary Ridge. General Johnston's labors in reorganizing the army were very valuable. Both he and the Confederate War Department were anxious to get ready and assume the offensive, but it was not found practicable to do so. General Johnston's Confederate force, on the 2d of May, 1864, was 42,464 infantry and artillery, with 2,392 cavalry, aggregating 44,856 men. These troops were under command of Lieutenant-generals Hardee, Polk and Hood as corps commanders, and the division commanders, Stewart, Bate, Cheatham, Walker, Stevenson, Hindman and Cleburne. General Wheeler led the cavalry. General Thomas, of the Federal army, was at Ringgold, on the Western and Atlantic Railroad; Schofield was at Red Clay, on the East Tennessee, Virginia and Georgia Railroad; while McPherson moved down to the right to cut Johnston's communications at Resaca. Thomas moved on Tunnel Hill, and Schofield pressed down from Red Clay. Sherman's idea was to push Johnston with Schofield and Thomas, and hold the Confederate forces engaged while McPherson struck the rear at Resaca. The Western and Atlantic Railroad runs from Dalton due south, and parallel with it on the right, looking south, is Rocky Face Ridge.

Thomas's attack on the State Road was successfully resisted by Lieutenant-general Hardee, who with Pettus's and Brown's brigades, and Stewart's and Bate's divisions, held his place at Mill Creek Gap.

General McPherson, with 23,000 Federals, slipped through Snake Creek Gap in Rocky Face Ridge, the march being made down to the Gap under the protection of the Ridge, and attacked Lieutenant-general Polk with Loring's division a mile out from Resaca. A reconnoissance by General Wheeler around the northern end of Rocky Face Ridge, in which he had quite a skirmish with the Federal cavalry, disclosed the fact that Sherman was moving his whole army down through Snake Creek Gap. Johnston ordered Hardee's and Hood's corps down to Resaca, evacuating Dalton.

The battle of Resaca was fiercely contested. Sherman's line of battle deployed against Resaca had McPherson on the right, Thomas in the centre and Schofield on the left. This deployment was finished May 13th. The Confederate army at Resaca was in two lines; Polk's corps was left of Hardee's corps, and both corps were west of Resaca and the railroad facing to the west, Polk's left resting on the Oostenaula River. Hood's corps extended from Hardee's right across the railroad to the Connasauga, facing to the northwest.

On the 14th, Sherman closed in, enveloping the town, and skirmishing occurred all day. On the afternoon of the 14th, about six o'clock, Lieutenant-general Hood, with Stewart's and Stevenson's divisions, engaged Schofield's corps, and drove it some little distance. But Lieutenant-general Polk's advanced troops on the left had been driven from a hill in front of his left by McPherson's troops. This hill commanded the Confederate bridges at short range.

General Sherman did another sharp thing. The town of Calhoun is six miles below Resaca. At Calhoun was Johnston's base and reserves. The Oostenaula River runs by Calhoun down to within a mile of the town, when it turns and goes in the direction of Rome. At Tanner's Ferry, two and a half miles from Calhoun, where the river bends, Colonel J. W. Avery, of the Fourth Georgia Cavalry, was stationed with a brigade of cavalry and a battery of artillery, defending two miles of the river. Brigadier-general John T. Morgan's cavalry brigade was in reserve, and at Calhoun General W. H. T. Walker's division of infantry was stationed. It was a shrewd step in Sherman to gain possession of this ferry, which put him three and a half miles nearer to Calhoun than was Johnston with his army. A heavy force, the afternoon of the 14th, effected the crossing, to which Colonel Avery's brigade, extending two miles along the river, presented a thin line of defense. Both General Morgan and General Walker were sent for, but arrived only after the Federals had driven Colonel Avery back with a loss of half of his brigade, after several hours' fighting, and intrenched on this side of the river. The movement was communicated to General Johnston that night; but the next morning General Walker, deceived by the Federal quiet, and against the opinion of the cavalry in his front, dispatched General Johnston that the report of the passage of the Oostenaula was unfounded. He, however, threw a brigade against the intrenched Federals, and met a quick and bloody repulse, and immediately notified General Johnston.

On the 15th, heavy fighting continued all day. McPherson and Hooker's corps were actively engaged on the Federal side, while Hindman's and Stevenson's divisions had some very stubborn fighting, the latter assaulting the Federal left. Under General Walker's inaccurate information that the Federals had not crossed at Tanner's Ferry (called Lay's Ferry in Sherman's "Memoirs"), General Johnston arranged for Lieutenant-general Hood to make a strong attack on the Federal left; but on the reception of the correct intelligence, he abandoned the idea, and wisely left Resaca with his army, the night of May 15th.

McPherson and Hardee had quite a brush on the Tanner's Ferry Road, a mile and a half south of Calhoun. Hardee's object being to check the Federal advance, to allow the Confederates time for an easy retreat.

THE SIXTEENTH ARMY CORPS FORDING THE CHATTAHOOCHEE AT ROSWELL'S FERRY, JULY 10TH, 1864.

FROM A SKETCH BY GEORGE D. SAYLER, SECOND IOWA INFANTRY.

HOWLETT'S CONFEDERATE BATTERY ON THE JAMES [illegible] LABORERS ON THE DUTCH GAP CANAL.

it will be seen that General Johnston's persistent policy was to stand on the defensive, to spare the blood of our soldiers by fighting under cover habitually, and to attack only when bad position or division of the Federal forces might give the Confederates advantages counterbalancing that of superior numbers.

Johnston, on the 17th of May, fell slowly back to Adairsville, Polk's and Hood's corps on the left, and Hardee on the right. Thomas's column came up with the Confederates that evening, and a sharp skirmishing was kept up between his troops and Cheatham's Confederate division and Wheeler's cavalry until nightfall. That night the Confederates retired. Hardee's corps reached Kingston the 18th, and Polk's and Hood's stopped within a mile of Cassville.

McPherson was coming on a road four miles west of Kingston, Thomas was four miles east of Kingston, while Schofield and Hooker were marching direct to Cassville. With the Federal columns some eight miles apart, General Johnston's plan was to give battle at this point, regarding the conformation of ground as especially favorable. It was shows his losses to have been a total of 3,268 killed and wounded, 445 of the former, and 2,043 of the latter. His reinforcements were Canty's, Loring's and French's infantry divisions, 12,000 men, and Martin's and Jackson's cavalry divisions, 7,400 men—total, 19,400, making his whole army 64,456, from which, taking his losses, he crossed the Etowah with 61,068 men.

General Sherman gives his losses to the 1st of May, including those of the battle of New Hope Church, at 9,299 killed and wounded, 1,863 of the former, and 7,436 of the latter. Johnston's losses, including those of New Hope, were 5,393, of which 721 were killed, and 4,672 wounded.

General Sherman rested a few days, and then planned to flank the Allatoona Pass by a movement in the direction of Dallas, Polk County. General Johnston sent General Wheeler across the Etowah River, who, on the 24th of May, captured quite a wagon-train of the Federals near Cassville.

General Johnston moved his army to New Hope Church, General Hardee's corps reaching it the afternoon of the 24th, and Hood's corps early on the 25th, of May. Hood's corps was formed oppo-

This battle of New Hope Church continued almost incessantly until the 4th day of June. Sherman had McPherson on the right, Hooker in the centre, and Thomas and Schofield on the left, who steadily extended their line, overlapping Johnston's right toward the railroad. Hardee was on the left, Hood in the centre, and Polk on the right. Cleburne's division, of Hardee's corps, was placed on Polk's right on the 27th, and that afternoon the Federal Fourth Corps attempted again to turn the Confederate right; Granberry's Confederate brigade, with Wheeler's cavalry, and Lowry's brigade and two regiments of Govan's brigade, repulsed the movement. The desperation of this attack is shown by the fact that 700 dead Federals were counted before the Confederate intrenchments, while Cleburne's Confederate division reported 85 killed and 365 wounded.

Major-general Bate threw his division against McPherson's corps at Dallas, on the 28th, with considerable loss. From the 1st to the 4th of June there was steady skirmishing. On the 4th, Sherman withdrew his army to a position in front of Allatoona, occupying the railroad from Allatoona

FEDERAL FORCES, AT JONESBORO, DESTROYING THE MACON RAILROAD

From a Sketch by George D. Sayler, Second Iowa Infantry

Sunday, the 19th of May, late in the afternoon, that General Johnston's battle order was read to the Confederate army. The effect was inspiriting. The men were loath to give up their homes to the Federals, and the prospect of a decisive battle was joyfully welcome. Sherman discovered the purpose to fight, and cheerfully accepted the gage.

At a council of war with his lieutenant-generals, held that evening by General Johnston, General Hood and General Polk both declared their inability to hold their positions, though General Hardee, who had the weakest place on the line, expressed his entire confidence of being able to maintain his own ground. Acting on this declaration of the majority of his corps commanders, General Johnston reluctantly, and against his better judgment, gave up the idea of a battle, and in the night retired from his well-chosen positions. It illustrated the Confederate soldiers' confidence in Johnston that this renunciation of the cherished plan did not demoralize his troops. Johnston's army crossed the Etowah River about noon of the 20th of May, Colonel I. W. Avery, of Wheeler's command, burning the bridges, and being the last man to cross under heavy fire.

The official report of General Johnston's army site the church, Polk's next on the left, and Hardee joining Polk. Sherman had to depend on his wagons in this movement. Hooker arrived first, and attempted, on the afternoon of May 25th, about an hour and a half before sunset, to capture New Hope. The attack was made on Stewart's division, of Hood's corps, and was fiercely pressed in two determined assaults, both of which were repelled. The Federals called this peaceful church "Hell Hole," from the bloody fighting there. McPherson, on the 26th, reached Dallas, four miles from New Hope, and was held there until the 1st of June, when he joined Hooker. On the afternoon of the 28th, Sherman made a strong attempt to turn Johnston's right. Colonel Avery, of the Fourth Georgia Cavalry, was thrown at the double-quick to check the movement until troops could get up to thwart it. General Johnston says of this dangerous attempt of a corps to cut him from his base: "Finding himself confronted by the advance-guard of several divisions of Federal troops, Colonel Avery fought against overwhelming numbers until the needed reinforcements came up. Although severely wounded, he remained in his saddle, supported by a soldier, and thus accomplished his grand self-imposed task for duty's sake."

and Acworth forward to Big Shanty, in sight of the famous Kenesaw Mountain. McPherson was on the left at Acworth, with Thomas joining, and Schofield on the right. General Blair joined Sherman, with two divisions of the Seventeenth Corps, with effective strength of 9,000 men. Sherman estimates his three armies at 100,000 effective men. Sherman, on the 10th, moved his whole army to Big Shanty, and on the 11th had the railroad repaired, the Etowah Bridge rebuilt, and cars running up to his skirmish lines.

Johnston's losses through the New Hope battles were 2,439, of which 369 were killed and 2,070 wounded.

General Johnston had Hardee's corps near Pine Mountain, with Bate's division on the summit, Polk's corps near the Acworth and Marietta Road, and Hood to the right. It was on the morning of the 14th of June, when Johnston went out with Polk and Hood to reconnoitre Pine Mountain, and had determined to abandon that eminence, that General Polk was killed by a shell fired at the party. General Sherman from his own elevation saw the group of Confederate generals, and ordered them to be fired upon, ignorant as to whom they were. Major-general Loring succeeded General

CITIZENS OF ATLANTA LEAVING THE CITY IN COMPLIANCE WITH GENERAL SHERMAN'S ORDERS.

POSITION OF THE FIFTEENTH AND SEVENTEENTH ARMY CORPS, IN THEIR ATTACK O

FROM A SKETC

CITIZENS OF ATLANTA LEAVING THE CITY IN COMPLIANCE WITH GENERAL SHERMAN'S ORDERS.

GENERAL SHERMAN'S WAGON TRAIN PASSING THROUGH RESACA, GA., AT NIGHT.

POSITION OF THE FIFTEENTH AND SEVENTEENTH ARMY CORPS IN THEIR ATTACK ON THE CONFEDERATE BATTERIES LOCATED ON KENESAW MOUNTAIN, GA., JUNE 27th, 1864.

AN INCIDENT OF BATTLE—A FAITHFUL DOG WATCHING THE DEAD BODY OF HIS MASTER.

A BAGGAGE TRAIN CROSSING THE MOUNTAINS OF GEORGIA IN A STORM.

FROM A SKETCH BY C. E. F. HILLEN.

Polk in the command of the corps. The bridges and ferries on the Chattahoochee River were guarded by a division of State Militia under Major-general Gustavus W. Smith.

On the 19th of June, Johnston made some changes in his line, and formed an alignment that included the crest of Kenesaw Mountain. Hardee's corps was placed nearly south, across Lost Mountain, on the left; Cheatham, Cleburne, Bate and Walker, placed from left to right; Loring's corps next, in the centre, with French's, Walthall's, and Featherstone's divisions in order; while Hood's corps was on the right, between the railroad and the Marietta Road.

Sherman extended his line to the right, toward the Chattahoochee River. General Hood's corps was transferred to the Confederate left, joining Cheatham's division.

On the 20th of June, Garrard's Federal cavalry and Wheeler's Confederate horsemen had a sharp affair, in which Garrard was repulsed, and lost 50 killed, 160 captured, and two standards; Wheeler had 15 killed and 50 wounded.

Sherman says: "At all points the enemy met us with determined courage." Loring's corps was struck by McPherson's army; Hardee's corps, by Thomas. The principal efforts of the Federals were against Scott's brigade, of Featherstone's division, in Loring's corps. Some of the Federals charged clear into General Quarles's rifle-pits, where most of the Federals were either killed or captured. Cockrell's Missouri Brigade, of French's division, was heavily pressed. About 80 of Walker's men were bayoneted in their rifle-pits by the Federals. The most resolute assault of the day was made on Cheatham's division and the left of Cleburne's division, of Hardee's corps. The Federal dead lay up against the Confederate breastworks. The assault was over and failed by 11:30 A.M. Brigadier-general Harker and Brigadier-general Daniel McCook, Federals, were both fatally wounded in this fight. General Johnston reports his loss at 808, and General Sherman his loss at 2,500.

A truce was granted on the 29th of June to allow the Federals to bury their dead.

Satisfied of the bloody cost of attacking intrenched

10th of June up to the passage of the Chattahoochee, at 7,530, of which 1,790 were killed, and 5,740 wounded. Johnston's losses were 8,948—killed, 468; wounded, 3,480. The total losses of the campaign so far reported by General Sherman were 16,829—killed, 3,653; wounded, 13,173. General Johnston reported: Total loss, 9,450—killed, 1,221; wounded, 8,229.

Lieutenant-general Stewart took command of the Polk corps on the 7th. On the 17th of July the whole Federal army crossed the Chattahoochee between Roswell and Power's Ferry. The same day General Johnston received a telegram from Richmond relieving him of the command of the Confederate army, and putting General J. B. Hood in charge. General Johnston's removal was a shock to the Confederate army and to the people. General Hood was a brave fighter, but not the equal of Johnston in military ability. General Sherman himself greeted the change with satisfaction, and said with relief that "heretofore the fighting has been as Johnston pleased, but that hereafter it would be as he pleased."

THE FEDERAL ARMY CROSSING THE COOSA RIVER, ALA., ON ITS RETURN FROM THE PURSUIT OF THE CONFEDERATES UNDER HOOD.

FROM A SKETCH BY STANLEY FOX.

The men of the two armies learned the value of intrenchments, and whenever they occupied new ground they raised parapets with ditches in front, and made long crests cut into each other. General Sherman cleverly organized a negro corps to dig these intrenchments at night while the soldiers were sleeping, paying them $10 a month. The weather was very bad during these operations. Up to the 21st of June, General Sherman reported nineteen days of rain, the roads impassable and the fields and woods becoming quagmires. There was continual fighting of serious character. In the main, the Federals assumed the aggressive. Hood struck Hooker's corps on the 22d, but was repulsed. Hardee's corps was assaulted on the 24th, and Stevenson's division on the 25th. On the 27th of June, Sherman made a general attack along the whole line. For ten miles the fighting was simply furious. Sherman's idea was to make a breach somewhere, thrust in it a strong head of column, and, holding one Confederate wing in check, overwhelm the other in flank. General Johnston says of this attack: "At several points the characteristic fortitude of the Northwestern soldiers held them under a close and destructive fire long after reasonable hope of success was gone." General

lines, General Sherman resumed his flanking operations, and began to move to General Johnston's left. That wary leader, in anticipation of such a movement, prepared a new line of defense ten miles south of Marietta, while for some time works were constructed around Atlanta. On the 3d of July, Johnston moved his army back, near the Chattahoochee, crossing the road to Atlanta at right angles, placing Loring's corps on the right of the road, Hardee's corps on the left, and Hood's corps left of Hardee's. Sherman, on the 4th of July, turned Johnston's left, and in consequence, the Confederate army withdrew on the morning of the 5th to a line of redoubts on the high ground near the Chattahoochee River, which General Sherman declared to be one of the strongest pieces of field fortification he ever saw.

In the fight of the 4th, General Noyes, afterward Governor of Ohio, lost a leg. Sherman tried Johnston in his Chattahoochee redoubts. On the 9th, Sherman crossed Schofield's troops at Soap's Creek, while Garrard's cavalry crossed the Chattahoochee at Roswell. General Johnston that night withdrew his army across the Chattahoochee, and established a line two miles from the river.

General Sherman reported his losses, from the

Johnston turned over to General Hood an experienced army of 50,627 veteran soldiers. General Sherman says, when he learned of Hood's appointment as the general he was to oppose, he asked Schofield, who was Hood's classmate at West Point, about his character, and learned he was bold to rashness, and inferred that the change meant "fight."

Hood received the order assigning him to the command of the Confederate army at 11 P.M. on the 17th of July, 1864. He lost no time in assuming the aggressive. Sherman on the 19th moved McPherson on the Georgia Railroad, between Stone Mountain and Decatur, about seven miles below Decatur, whence he marched toward Atlanta, destroying the road. Thomas was crossing Peachtree Creek on the right, in line of battle, and Schofield between them, connecting Thomas and McPherson near Decatur.

Hood arranged promptly for a fight on the 20th, beginning his arrangements on the night of the 18th. He placed Stewart's corps on the left, facing Thomas, Hardee in the centre, and Cheatham on the right. General Smith's Georgia State troops were placed on the right of Cheatham. Peach-tree Creek is directly North of Atlanta, and Decatur

VIEW OF THE CITY OF ATLANTA, GA., LOOKING SOUTH. TAKEN ON THE EVE OF ITS EVACUATION BY GENERAL SHERMAN, NOVEMBER 12TH, 1864.

EVACUATION OF ATLANTA, GA., BY THE [illegible] TO [illegible]

a little north of east. Hood's attack on Thomas with Hardee's and Stewart's corps was ordered at 1 o'clock P.M., the 20th of July, but was delayed until 4 P.M. The Federals were taken by surprise. Stewart's corps struck Hooker's corps on the 20th, Johnston's division of the Fourteenth Corps, and Newton's division of the Fourth Corps. The Federals were resting, and the two forces fought hand-to-hand in some cases. Thomas got some batteries to work, and the Confederates were finally driven back. Hood claimed that Hardee's corps only skirmished, and thus the movement failed. Hooker's corps lost 1,500 men.

Sherman closed up his lines, overlapping the Confederate right. McPherson had the Fifteenth Corps across the Georgia Railroad, and the Seventeenth Corps next, on the left of the Fifteenth. On the right of the Fifteenth Corps was Schofield, and next to him Howard's, Hooker's and Palmer's Corps, on the Federal extreme right. Dodge's Sixteenth Corps was back of McPherson's right.

Hood resolved to make another sally immediately. He had a new line of fortifications constructed (General Blair's) in the rear. Hardee's line also struck Dodge's Corps in motion, so opportunely on hand, through McPherson's provision of danger. Hardee did brilliant fighting, capturing 6 guns and 13 stands of colors. Two Brigades of the Fifteenth Federal Corps joined in, and the Federal line falling back, joined Leggett's division of the Seventeenth Corps. General Sherman informed General Logan of McPherson's death, Logan being the ranking officer, and the command of the Army of Tennessee thereby devolved on him. General Cheatham made an attack, taking temporarily some Federal defenses, but afterward yielding them, capturing five guns and six stands of colors. General C. R. Wood's division, of the Fifteenth Corps, participated handsomely in the battle, and General Schofield used twenty guns to the left front of the Howard House, where Sherman was stationed.

This battle of the 22d is called the battle of Atlanta, and extended for nearly seven miles. Hardee broke the Federal lines, but his movement was finally checked. And Sherman claims that he used only the Army of the Tennessee in thwarting lead of Hood's corps, that Cheatham had been commanding.

General Sherman was quiet a few days. His plan was to move the Army of the Tennessee, under Howard, to the right, to strike the Macon Railroad, and to throw his cavalry, both right and left, against the same railroad, lower down about Jonesboro'. The plan was changed, allowing Stoneman with the cavalry to go on to Macon. The Federal Army of the Tennessee began this movement to the right (the Confederate left) on the 27th. Hood discovered it on the 28th, and sent out Lee's corps to intercept the movement. Hood sent Stewart to Lee's reinforcement, and the battle raged at Ezra Church the entire afternoon. The Confederates failed to dislodge the Federals from their position. The Federal loss was reported at 572. Among the Confederates the slight wounding of Generals Stewart, Brown, Loring and Johnson happened. General McCook's Federal cavalry was defeated near Newman by General Wheeler, some 950 prisoners, 2 cannon and 1,200 horses being captured; while General Stoneman surrendered with 500 men to

UNITED STATES SOLDIERS, AT ATLANTA, GA., TEARING DOWN BUILDINGS SHATTERED DURING THE BOMBARDMENT.

closer to Atlanta, and his plan was to move into them the night of the 21st, and have Hardee's corps move to the rear and left flank of McPherson's troops. Wheeler was to take his cavalry with Hardee, Stewart was to watch Thomas and keep him engaged, and Cheatham was to strike Schofield.

The morning of the 22d of July was designated as the time for the attack. General Hardee was delayed in getting into position, and when he did, he found that General McPherson had in excess of caution strengthened his extreme left flank with Dodge's Corps, and sent intrenching-tools there to erect batteries. General Sherman relates that he and General McPherson were talking together at General Sherman's headquarters when the sound of artillery in the direction of Decatur indicated the battle opened, and alarmed both of these officers. General McPherson left immediately to look into matters, and had ordered troops to the pressed point; and then, his staff all sent off, alone had cut across a wooded valley which he thought safe, and had been shot, his horse going back wounded and riderless. Hardee pressed the Federals, striking Giles A. Smith's division of the Seventeenth Corps the attempt. General Hood claimed that the result was beneficial; that it improved the *morale* of his troops, and defeated the effort of McPherson and Schofield on the Confederate communications. As the Federals lost a brave and useful general in McPherson, so the Confederates suffered a similar loss in Major-general William H. T. Walker. The fighting was resumed with fury at four o'clock, and continued until night, when the Confederates withdrew into Atlanta.

This was a most desperate battle. The Federal loss was 3,521, and the Confederate loss larger.

General Rousseau and General Garrard, of the Federal cavalry, made successful raids, the former to Opelika, Ala., and the latter to Covington, Ga. One incident of the fighting around Atlanta was the wounding of Colonel Reynolds, of the Federal army, an Irish officer, shot in the leg. He saved his limb from amputation by wittily arguing that it was an "imported leg," too valuable to be cut off.

General O. O. Howard was assigned to the command of McPherson's Federal army, and General Stanley placed in command of Howard's corps. Lieutenant-general Stephen D. Lee was given the General Iverson near Macon. During July the Confederate losses were 8,841—killed, 1,341; wounded, 7,500. The Federal losses, 9,719—killed and missing, 3,804; wounded, 5,915. This does not include the cavalry losses of the Federals, which, according to Sherman, amounted to 1,300, making the Federal loss aggregate 11,019. General Wheeler, of the Confederate cavalry, was very active, and performed most effective service, seriously crippling the cavalry of the Federal army. Sherman, however was the superior of Hood in every element of generalship, and under his powerful and masterly lead the tide of Federal success steadily continued.

General Sherman determined to extend his line to the Macon Road with infantry. He had Schofield make this movement with the Twenty-third Corps, and Palmer's Fourteenth Corps, under command of General Jeff C. Davis. Sherman kept up a constant attack in front of the Confederate lines. On the 5th of August, General Reilly's Federal command made a vigorous assault on General Bate's division, but was repulsed. On the 10th of August, Sherman received some Parrott 30-pound cannon, and began to make it lively, throwing

VIEW OF THE CAPITOL AT MILLEDGEVILLE, GA.—FEDERAL SOLDIERS HOISTING THE STARS AND STRIPES.

equate to the work, and Hardee was repulsed. Sherman pressed his advantage actively. He tore up the railroad. On the evening of the 1st of September, Davis's Fourteenth Corps closed down on the north front of Jonesboro', connecting on his right with Howard, his left reaching the railroad, on which Stanley's Fourth Corps was moving, followed by Schofield. Davis assaulted and captured a part of Govan's brigade, with some cannon. Two divisions of Blair's Seventeenth Corps were sent to get in the rear of Jonesboro' and cut the railroad. Stanley was ordered to lap Jonesboro' on the east, and thus surround Hardee. But the wary Hardee was too sharp to be caught, and that night he slipped out of the toils and left Jonesboro', falling back to Lovejoy's Station.

General Lee had moved his corps from Jonesboro' to Rough and Ready on the 1st of September, about 2 P. M., and protected the evacuation of Atlanta, which began at 6 P. M. that day, amid exploded magazines and burning stores. Hood joined Hardee at Lovejoy's Station with Stewart's and Lee's corps.

The loss of Atlanta was an inspiriting matter for the Federal cause, and proportionately discouraging to the Confederates. Its moral effect cannot be estimated. Lee, in Virginia, had steadily repulsed Grant with loss. Early, in the Valley, had won victory. The North was gloomy. A convention clamored for peace. The people growled. More troops were drafted. In this discouragement, Atlanta, the heart of the Confederacy, fell—the key

THE PRISON PEN AT MILLEN, GA., IN WHICH FEDERAL PRISONERS WERE CONFINED.

shell into Atlanta. The women and children were driven to the cellars. Wheeler made a raid, going as far as Dalton, and doing considerable damage. Kilpatrick's Federal cavalry made quite a successful raid about Jonesboro'.

On the night of August 25th, Sherman began his move against the Macon Railroad with infantry. He placed the Twentieth Corps at the Chattahoochee Bridge to protect it. On the 28th he struck the West Point Railroad, and spent the 29th in tearing up the track from East Point to Fairburn. On the 31st, Schofield reached Rough and Ready; General Howard was within two miles of Jonesboro', and Thomas between them.

General Hood had sent General Brown's division to Rough and Ready, and Reynolds's and Lewis's brigades to Jonesboro'. Hardee, on the 30th, had been near Rough and Ready, with Lee's corps on his right, near East Point. Hardee moved to Jonesboro' late that day, and Lee was ordered to follow him late that night. Lewis's brigade had repulsed a Federal attack near Jonesboro' that day. General Hardee was ordered to attack the Federal forces at daylight on the 31st. General Hardee made the attack, striking the Federals with tremendous vigor. A bloody fight ensued. Major-general Patton Anderson and Brigadier-general Cummings, of Hardee's command, were badly wounded. But the Confederate forces were inad-

GOVERNOR'S HOUSE AT MILLEDGEVILLE, GA.—FEDERAL SOLDIERS HOISTING THE STARS AND STRIPES.

to workshops, granories, railroads and arsenals. The triumph re-inspired the Union cause, and gave a stunning shock to Southern hope. It also made certain Lincoln's re-election.

General Sherman took possession of Atlanta. His troops were given a period of rest. On the 8th of September, General Sherman himself rode into Atlanta. He immediately determined to convert the city into a purely military station. With this view he ordered the citizens to leave. A tart correspondence took place between General Sherman and General Hood, who protested against the course. But Sherman was immovable, and some 1,700 persons were sent back into the Confederacy.

The casualties of this Georgia campaign are reported by each side officially as follows up to this time:

Federal army, total	31,687
Confederate army, total	21,996
Federal army, killed	4,423
Confederate army, killed	3,044
Federal army, wounded	22,822
Confederate army, wounded	18,879
Federal army, missing	4,442
Confederate army, missing	(not reported.)

General Sherman reports as captured by his troops 12,983 Confederates.

The strength of the two armies is officially reported as follows:

GENERAL SHERMAN'S SOLDIERS HAILING GENERAL FOSTER'S FLAGSHIP.

Federal army		May 1st, 1864	98,797
"	"	June 1st, 1864	112,819
"	"	July 1st, 1864	106,030
"	"	August 1st, 1864	91,675
"	"	September 1st, 1864	81,758
Confederate army		May 1st, 1864	44,866
"	"	June 10th, 1864	59,248
"	"	July 1st, 1864	52,080
"	"	July 17th, 1864	50,627
"	"	July 31st, 1864	41,405
"	"	September 20th, 1864	40,403

KING'S BRIDGE, GA., HEAD OF NAVIGATION OF THE OGEECHEE RIVER, DESTROYED BY THE CONFEDERATES, BUT REBUILT BY GENERAL SHERMAN'S FORCES IN THIRTY-SIX HOURS.

The Confederate situation was not promising. General Hood, in addition to his continued disasters, distrusted his army, and especially General Hardee, and asked for the removal of that valuable officer. Hood requested Mr. Davis, the President of the Confederacy, to visit and confer with him. On the 25th of September, Mr. Davis arrived at Palmetto. Hood's feelings were harshly grated upon by some of the brigades on review calling to Mr. Davis: "Give us General Johnston." As a result of the conference, General Hardee was assigned to the command of South Carolina and Florida, and General Hood started off on that erratic movement into Alabama and Tennessee which finally ended in the practical annihilation of the Confederate Army of Tennessee at Franklin and Nashville, reducing it to 23,053 men, December 10th, 1864.

General Hood's army captured small garrisons at Big Shanty and Acworth. General French failed to carry Allatoona. Hood marched up to Resaca and Dalton, captured 1,000 men at the latter place, and destroyed the track between Resaca and Tunnel Hill. On the 15th, Hood reached Cross Plains, nine miles south of Lafayette. Sherman had sent General Thomas to Chattanooga with two divisions. When Hood started on his movement, Sherman's idea was to make for Savannah. Sherman, however, took his army up as far as Resaca, and then went over to the Chattanooga Valley, near Gadsden, and reached Gaylesville by the 21st of October. On the 26th, learning that Hood's army was at Decatur, Sherman resolved to leave Hood for Thomas to grapple with, and began to make arrangements for his March to the Sea, to make which he had been for some time endeavoring to got the approval of the authorities at Washington. On November 2d, 1864, Sherman received Grant's assent to this step. He sent back extra stores from Atlanta and other points to Chattanooga. General Corse burned all the mills and factories at Rome that could be useful to the Confederates. On the morning of the 12th of November, 1864, General Sherman had at Cartersville his last telegraphic communication with General Thomas at Nashville, and his wires were cut and his communications ceased with the rear. General Sherman truly said, "It surely was a strange event—two hostile armies marching in opposite directions."

By November 14th all the detachments of Sherman's army along the railroad had destroyed the track and arrived at or near Atlanta. General Sherman divided his army into two wings: the right, under General O. O. Howard, and the left, under General H. W. Slocum. The right wing had the Fifteenth Corps, General P. J. Osterhaus, with four divisions, under Brigadier-generals C. R. Woods, W. B. Hazen, J. E. Smith, and J. M. Corse; and the Seventeenth Corps, General F. P. Blair, with three divisions, under Major-general J. A. Mower, and Brigadier-generals M. D. Leggett and O. A. Smith.

The left wing had the Fourteenth Corps, General Jefferson C. Davis, with three divisions, under Brigadier-generals W. P. Carlin, J. D. Morgan, and A. Baird; and the Twentieth Corps, Brigadier-general A. S. Williams, with three divisions, under Brigadier-generals N. J. Jackson, J. W. Geary and W. T. Ward.

The cavalry consisted of a division under Brigadier-general J. Kilpatrick, with two brigades, led by Colonels E. H. Murray and S. D. Atkins.

INCIDENT ON THE OGEECHEE RIVER, NEAR FORT McALLISTER — OPENING COMMUNICATION BETWEEN ADMIRAL DAHLGREN AND GENERAL SHERMAN, DECEMBER 13TH, 1864.

THE SIEGE OF ATLANTA—CONFEDERATE ATTACK ON GENERAL LOGAN'S CORPS, JULY 28TH, 1864.

PONTON-BRIDGE ON SAVANNAH RIVER, OVER WHICH THE CONFEDERATES CROSSED ON THE EVACUATION OF SAVANNAH, DECEMBER 21ST, 1864.

DESTRUCTION OF THE MACHINE-SHOPS OF THE GEORGIA STATE ROAD AT ATLANTA, NOVEMBER 14TH, 1861.

ARSENAL AT MILLEDGEVILLE, GA., DESTROYED BY THE FEDERAL FORCES, NOVEMBER 14TH, 1864.

The army had 62,204 men: 55,329 infantry, 5,063 cavalry and 1,812 artillery. It would be hard to organize a better army of healthy, trained soldiers, well armed, equipped and organized. There was one cannon to every 1,000 men, or 65 altogether, in batteries of four guns. The army had 2,500 wagons, with six mules each, or 15,000 mules altogether, and 600 ambulances with two horses each. Each soldier had 40 rounds of ammunition, and the wagons carried 160 more rounds to the man, and 200 rounds of assorted ammunition were carried to each cannon. Each corps had about 800 wagons, stretching out five miles on the march.

The night of the 14th Atlanta was in flames, and out of 5,000 houses all but 600 were burned, the churches escaping however. On the morning of the 15th, Sherman's army started on its march; Howard, with the right wing and the cavalry, taking the Jonesboro' Road, and Slocum, with the Twentieth Corps, going down the Georgia Railroad by Decatur to Madison. General Sherman left Atlanta the morning of the 16th, with the Fourteenth Corps and the rear-guard of the right wing. At Covington, Davis's Fourteenth Corps turned to the right to go to Milledgeville. General Slocum, with the Twentieth Corps, went to Madison. Geary's division burned the bridges over the Oconee, and then marched for Milledgeville by way of Eatonton.

ONE OF THE CAVES MADE BY THE CITIZENS OF ATLANTA, TO PROTECT THEIR FAMILIES FROM THE SHELLS DURING THE BOMBARDMENT.

Sherman started with 1,200,000 rations, enough for twenty days for the men, and five days' forage for stock, and a good supply of beef cattle. A methodical and effective system of local foraging was adopted. Squads of foragers, fifty to each brigade, were started every morning on foot off of the line of march some five or six miles. They impressed stock and cattle, and wagons and carriages, and loaded up with everything good to eat—poultry, ham, vegetables, flour, meal, molasses, bacon, potatoes, etc.—and brought in their truck at night, which was then lumped together and issued to the men.

The negroes as a general thing gave a cordial welcome to the Federal army, and numbers went along.

The Legislature of Georgia was in session at Milledgeville when Sherman started for Atlanta. The news of the approach of the Federal army, as can well be imagined, created a commotion. The Legislature adjourned for dinner and did not return, even leaving Bills for legislation and other matters lying on the desks. The members immediately cleared out for home. A good deal of the public property was removed by General Foster, the State Quartermaster-general. The Penitentiary convicts were organized into a company, under Dr. Roberts, a felon, and did good service. A company of cadets from the Georgia Military Institute was in Milledgeville, and fought

HEADQUARTERS OF GENERAL SHERMAN AT ATLANTA, GA.

HEADQUARTERS OF GENERAL H. A. BARNUM AT ATLANTA, GA.

GENERAL SHERMAN RECEIVED BY GENERAL FOSTER ON BOARD THE REVENUE CUTTER "NEMAHA," IN THE OGEECHEE RIVER, GEORGIA, DECEMBER 14TH, 1864.

GENERAL GEARY ISSUING PASSES TO CITIZENS OF SAVANNAH, GA.

BURNING OF THE RAILROAD ROUND-HOUSE AT ATLANTA, NOVEMBER 14TH, 1864.—FEDERAL SOLDIERS AT WORK ALONG THE RAILROAD TRACK.

gallantly, going to Savannah and thence into South Carolina. The Federals held a mock session of the Legislature in the Capitol, and repealed the Secession Act. Many of the records were destroyed.

Sherman entered Milledgeville, November 23d, and communicated with the other wings of his army. There was constant skirmishing between the Federal cavalry and Wheeler's body of Confederate cavalry. Macon was not entered, though at Griswoldville, ten miles below, General Gustavus W. Smith, with a division of Georgia Militia, had a sprightly little brush with General C. R. Woods's division of the Fifteenth Corps, commanded by General Osterhaus. The main fighting in this little affair was done by Walcutt's brigade, Walcutt being wounded in the leg.

Sherman left Milledgeville on the 24th of November; Howard, with the right wing, went down the Central Railroad, tearing up the track; Slocum marched down the Louisville Dirt Road; Kilpatrick was ordered by Millen to rescue some prisoners.

Wheeler with his Confederate cavalry moved to the front of the Federals, and had some right lively fighting with Kilpatrick about Waynesboro'. At Millen, Sherman determined to continue on to Savannah, and not to take in Augusta.

General Hardee organized such force as he could gather to defend Savannah. At Ogeechee Church, about fifty miles from Savannah, General Sherman found some fresh earthworks that had been thrown up by the Confederate infantry, who were, however, in too small force to offer resistance. Wheeler kept pegging away persistently at Kilpatrick. On the night of the 8th of December, Sherman reached Pooler's Station, eight miles from Savannah. On the 9th and 10th of December, the Federal army surrounded the defenses of that city, that had been constructed by General Hardee. The Fourteenth Corps, General Davis, was placed on the left, touching the river; the Twentieth Corps, General Williams, next; then the Seventeenth, General Blair, and the Fifteenth, General Osterhaus, on the extreme right. The cavalry were transferred to the south bank of the Ogeechee, with orders to open up communication with the Federal fleet awaiting in Ossabaw Sound.

General Hazen's division of the Fifteenth Corps was sent down the right bank of the Ogeechee with instructions to carry Fort McAllister by assault. The garrison of Fort McAllister consisted of 250

BURNING OF THE GEORGIA CENTRAL RAILROAD BRIDGE OVER THE OGEECHEE RIVER, NOVEMBER 30TH, 1864, BY THE FEDERAL FORCES UNDER COLONEL P. H. JONES.

THE SANITARY FAIR, BROOKLYN, N. Y.—HEAVY GOODS DEPARTMENT. AUDITORIUM. KNICKERBOCKER HALL.

THE SANITARY FAIR, BROOKLYN, N. Y.—HEAVY GOODS DEPARTMENT.—AUDITORIUM.—KNICKERBOCKER HALL.

VIEW OF SAVANNAH, GA., LOOKING EAST TOWARD FORT JACKSON.—SKETCHED FROM THE TOWER OF THE EXCHANGE BY W. T. CHASE

BURNING OF THE NAVY YARD AT SAVANNAH BY THE CONFEDERATES, DECEMBER 21st, 1864.

troops, under Major George W. Anderson, a gallant young officer. General Hazen had General Sherman's old division, which he had commanded at Shiloh and Vicksburg. General Hazen made the assault about an hour before night, on the 13th of December. The assault was by three parties: one from below, one from above the fort, and the third directly in the rear. Fort McAllister is about sixteen miles from Savannah and six miles from Ossabaw Sound, on the Great Ogeechee River, on Genesis Point, near where the Savannah, Florida and Western Railroad passes. It is an earthwork commanding the river. It had successfully resisted attacks on June 29th, 1862; November 2d and 19th, 1862; January 27th, 1863; February 1st, 1863, 28th of February, 1863; and March 3d, 1863.

Major Anderson had his men strengthening his position for forty-eight hours, and they were much fatigued. The land front had parapet, ditch, and *chevaux-de-frise* made of branches of live oak, but the trunks of the trees had not been removed, and afforded protection to the Federal skirmishers. The Federals stormed the works and overpowered the garrison. The Confederates lost 17 killed and 31 wounded—48 total.

General Sherman had watched the storming from the roof of a shed attached to a mill. With characteristic impatience, he incurred risks of torpedoes and every other peril, and in the night in an open boat, picked his way through forest and river, to find the commander of the fleet awaiting the arrival of his army with rations and clothing.

General Sherman finished his environment of Savannah, and on the 17th of December demanded of General Hardee the surrender of the city, stating that he should feel justified in resorting to the harshest measures. General Hardee refused to surrender, saying, that as to the threats conveyed in the demand, he had conducted his military operations according to civilized warfare, and should regret any course by General Sherman that would force him to deviate from it.

PROVOST MARSHAL'S OFFICE, ATLANTA.—CITIZENS GETTING PASSES TO GO NORTH AND SOUTH, IN CONSEQUENUE OF GENERAL SHERMA'S ORDER FOR THE DEPARTURE OF ALL CITIZENS.

TABLEAUX IN CHILDREN'S DEPART.

CLOSING THE ARMS & TROPHIES DEP'T

CHILDREN'S DEPARTMENT

STALL IN INTERNATIONAL DEPART.

THE KNICKERBOCKER KITCHEN.

METROPOLITAN SANITARY FAIR, NEW YORK CITY—[illegible] AND INCIDENTS IN THE VARIOUS DEPARTMENTS

BURNING OF THE PENITENTIARY AT MILLEDGEVILLE, GA., NOVEMBER 23D, 1864.

CONFEDERATE PRISONERS, UNDER ORDER OF GENERAL SHERMAN, TAKING UP TORPEDOES IN FRONT OF FORT McALLISTER, CAPTURED BY THE FEDERAL FORCES, DECEMBER 13TH, 1864.

FROM A SKETCH BY W. T. CRANE.

VIEW OF FORT McALLISTER, ON THE OGEECHEE RIVER, GEORGIA, CAPTURED BY GENERAL SHERMAN, DECEMBER 13TH, 1864.

General Hardee had about 10,000 men in the city, and was not prepared with food to stand a siege. He had under him Generals H. W. Mercer, H. R. Jackson, W. R. Boggs, J. F. Gilmer and G. P. Harrison. General Hardee found the defense of the place impracticable, and on the night of December 20th he crossed his small army into South Carolina, and yielded up Savannah to the Federal force.

General Sherman telegraphed to President Lincoln the capture of Savannah as a Christmas gift. He obtained 250 siege-guns, 31,000 bales of cotton, and vast quantities of stores.

The capture of Savannah ended Sherman's campaign in Georgia. His losses from Atlanta to Savannah were 1,338—killed, 103; wounded, 424; missing, 278; captured, 530.

Sherman's success in Georgia gave a blow to the Confederate cause from which it never recovered. It was rightfully regarded by the people of the North as foreshadowing the fall of the Confederacy. Congress thanked Sherman and his army for its decisive achievement. Georgia for 400 miles in length and 40 miles in width, an area of 16,000 square miles, was devastated. The Confederacy was quartered, the basis of supplies destroyed, and the spirit of the Southern cause broken.

It was a fateful thing that the first act of hostility—the seizure of Fort Pulaski—took place on Georgia soil; that the decisive campaign of the War—the Sherman march—was in Georgia; and that finally, the capture of President Davis, the last blow to the Confederacy, occurred in this State.

SHERIDAN'S OPERATIONS IN THE VALLEY.

GENERAL SHERIDAN, of all the officers of the Army of the Potomac best fitted to carry out a dashing, aggressive campaign against such accomplished cavalry commanders as Jubal A. Early and Fitzhugh Lee, leaders of the Confederate forces in the Valley, was selected by General Grant to preserve the "granary of the Confederacy"—the Shenandoah Valley—and prevent the frequent raids of Early and his men on the fertile fields of Pennsylvania.

The Sixth and Nineteenth Corps, and the infantry and cavalry of West Virginia, under Crook and Averell, and two divisions of cavalry under Torbert

THE FIGHT AT CEDAR CREEK, VA., FRIDAY, AUGUST 12TH, 186[illegible]

From a Sketch by J. E. Taylor.

BATTLE OF FISHER'S HILL, VA., SEPTEMBER 23D, 1864, BETWEEN TH

BATTLE OF FISHER'S HILL, VA, SEPTEMBER 22d, 1864, BETWEEN THE [illegible] OF GENERALS PHILIP H. SHERIDAN AND JUBAL E. EARLY.

THE FEDERAL FORCES FALLING BACK THROUGH CHARLESTOWN, AUGUST 21st, 1864, 9 A.M.—Sketched from Judge Hunter's Yard by J. E. Taylor

SIEGE OF PETERSBURG—CONFEDERATE ATTEMPT, AUGUST 29th, 1864, TO REGAIN THE WELDON RAILROAD—From a Sketch by Joseph Becker

VIEW OF THE FRONT FROM THE FEDERAL LINE ON JACKSON HILL, VA.

and Wilson—making an effective force of 40,000 men—were placed under his command on the 7th of August, 1864. He at once asked privilege to make an aggressive warfare, but General Grant, knowing that defeat would mean an open road for the Confederate forces to Pennsylvania and the North, held his lieutenant in check, and confined him to careful defensive movements until September, when by a personal visit the Commanding General found Sheridan so confident of success that he gave him full rein. Early held the west bank of the Opequan Creek, covering Winchester. Sheridan's forces lay in front of Berryville, twenty miles south of Harper's Ferry. This situation was such as to admit of either army bringing on a battle at any moment. Leaving Fitzhugh Lee with one division of infantry and his cavalry to defend Winchester, Early threw the bulk of his army forward by his left to Bunker Hill, distant twelve miles north of Winchester. On the the 18th he reconnoitred as far north as Martinsburg. Sheridan at

SEPTEMBER, 1864.

Berryville was twelve miles east of Winchester, and on the 19th advanced on that place. Wilson's cavalry carried the intrenched skirmish line of Lee on the west bank of the Opequan, four miles west of the town. The Kanawha infantry and the Sixth Corps crossed the ford and took position two miles nearer. The main force of Early was ten miles off. The Federal advance waited for the Nineteenth Corps, under Emory, who had followed behind the baggage-train of the Sixth, which blocked the road, thus giving Early time to hurry southward from Bunker Hill in order to meet the attack. Sheridan formed a line of battle with the Sixth Corps on the left, covered by Wilson's cavalry, the Nineteenth Corps in the centre, and the Kanawha infantry on the right, flanked by Merritt's division of cavalry. Averell's cavalry had pressed on the retiring Confederates from Bunker Hill, and now succeeded in closing in on the Federal right. The Federal forces, with two full divisions of cavalry on the right of their line, extended about four miles, enveloping Winchester from the north and east. Early's left rested behind fortified hills to the northwest of the town. Early had 8 900 infantry, three battalions of artillery, and about 3,000 cavalry. Sheridan had upward of 10,000 cavalry and 25,000 infantry. After several hours' fighting between the infantry with no decisive advantage, Sheridan ordered a general advance at 4 P.M., and the cavalry of Merritt and Averell, overlapping Early's left, easily carried the fortified hill, while the infantry pressed hurriedly on the centre, and the cavalry under Wilson, on the right, broke the Confederate lines, and they fled through the streets of Winchester, closely followed by the Federal troops. Night prevented further pursuit, and Sheridan rested with 2,500 prisoners, five pieces of artillery and nine battle-flags as his trophies of victory. The Confederates lost among their killed Generals Rodes and Godwin. The Federals lost the gallant leader of the First Division of the Sixth Corps, General David A. Russell. The Confederates designated this as the battle of Winchester; Grant, as the battle of Opequan.

Early did not halt in his retreat southward until he had placed thirty miles between himself and Sheridan. He rested at Fisher's Hill, which commanded the narrow Strasburg Valley, between the Shenandoah River and North Mountain. In front of this position Sheridan arrived on the 22d, and made ready for a direct attack. He sent two divisions of cavalry, under Torbert, by the Luray Valley, to gain New Market, twenty miles to Early's rear. The direct attack was ineffectual, and a cavalry dash was made for the right, under cover of which a corps of infantry moved to that flank and carried the Confederate left on North Mountain. A general attack in front then broke the line of Early, and he retired in confusion, leaving several hundred prisoners and sixteen pieces of artillery in the hands of Sheridan. Early was not prepared for this attack, as he was about evacuating his position, fearing the flank movement of Torbert, who, however, was held in check at Milford by a small Confederate cavalry force under Colonel Munford. But for this fact the Confederates acknowledged Sheridan would have annihilated Early between Newmarket and Fisher's Hill. As it was, Early lost half his army, and retreated to the lower passes of the Blue Ridge, closely pursued as far as Staunton by Sheridan, who then returned and took position at Cedar Creek, near Strasburg. Sheridan laid

BATTLE BETWEEN GENERAL WILSON'S CAVALRY AND THE CONFEDERATES UNDER FITZHUGH LEE, AUGUST 21st, 1864

GENERAL SHERIDAN RIDING ALONG THE LINES OF THE

GENERAL SHERIDAN'S RIDING ALONG THE LINES OF THE [illegible] ARMY AFTER THE BATTLE OF [illegible]

BATTLE OF WINCHESTER.—POSITION OF THE NINETEENTH CORPS, GENERAL EMORY, SEPTEMBER 19TH, 1864—THE CENTRE.—FROM A SKETCH BY J. E. TAYLOR.

BATTLE OF WINCHESTER.—CHARGE OF CROOK'S EIGHTH CORPS—THE RIGHT.—FROM A SKETCH BY J. E. TAYLOR.

FIGHT OF DUFFIE'S CAVALRY, NEAR HUNTER'S HOUSE, CHARLESTOWN, VA., COVERING THE RETREAT OF THE FEDERAL FORCES.

waste all the country south of Strasburg. The desolation of the region was complete.*

A committee of citizens and magistrates of Rockingham County appointed to estimate the damage, reported the loss in that county to be $25,000,000.

Early was soon reinforced by 600 cavalry from Lee's army and by Kershaw's division of infantry, and made his way northward over the track of destruction left by Sheridan, and took up his position again on Fisher's Hill. Sheridan confronted him on the north bank of Cedar Creek. Frequent cavalry combats took place, but no decisive movement until October 19th. At this time Sheridan's infantry lay along the east bank of the creek, behind intrenchments thrown up on rising, rolling ground; Crook's Eighth Corps on the left, Emory's Nineteenth Corps in the centre, and the Sixth Corps, under Ricketts, on the right and somewhat in the rear. Custer's and Merritt's cavalry guarded the right flank; Averell's (under Powell) guarded the left, and picketed the whole line of the North Fork from Cedar Creek to Front Royal. Sheridan was at Washington, and the command devolved on Wright. Early awaited an opportunity to surprise the Federal forces, as he well knew that he could not make an open attack with his small force. Soon after midnight of the 18th–19th of October, he made a feint on the right, and at the same time marched one column southeasterly from Strasburg along the Manassas Gap Railroad past the Federal left flank; a second column massed behind the picket line for a direct attack. The first column forded the North Fork one mile east of its confluence with Cedar Creek, and before dawn gained the rear of Crook's corps, then closed in upon and captured the pickets, attacked the camp and captured the men before they had time to form. Early with the second column emerged from the hills west of Cedar Creek at the same time, and struck the troops directly on Crook's right. The whole Federal left and centre became demoralized, and were driven along the main turnpike, eighteen captured guns having been turned upon the fleeing troops. The Sixth Corps being to the right and rear, changed front and gallantly stood to receive the shock of the victorious Confederates. This it did, checking their progress, and serving to cover the general retreat that Wright now ordered as the only practicable means of recovering command of his troops. The Federal force fell back in the best order they could maintain until they reached Middletown, where they formed a line of battle, but the force of Early dashed on, and, threatening to overlap Wright's left flank, he again fell back. As Early's force pressed less impetuously, Wright obtained better control over his men, and as he slowly retreated, re-formed the scattered regiments. Between Middletown and Newtown, Wright halted, and, with his troops in a compact line, was prepared to resist further attack. This was at half-past 10 o'clock A.M. Sheridan had returned from

* "I have destroyed over 2000 barns filled with wheat and hay and farming implements; over 70 mills filled with flour and wheat; have driven in front of the army over 4,000 head of stock, and have killed and issued to the troops no less than 3000 sheep. This destruction embraces the Luray and the Little Fort Valley as well as the main Valley."—*Sheridan's Despatch.*

WILSON'S CAVALRY FORAGING IN THE SHENANDOAH VALLEY.

From Sketches by J. E. Taylor.

DEFEAT, AT MOUNT JACKSON, OF THE CONFEDERATE GENERAL ROSSER, TH
DESPERATE EFFORT OF ROSSER TO SA

THE ARMY OF THE SHENANDOAH AT WOODSTOCK, ON THE MOVEMENT FRO

DEFEAT, AT MOUNT JACKSON, OF THE CONFEDERATE GENERAL ROSSER, THE [illegible] OF THE VALLEY, BY SHERIDAN'S FORCES UNDER GENERAL TORBERT. DESPERATE EFFORT OF ROSSER TO SAVE [illegible] LAST GUN.—From a Sketch by J. E. Taylor.

THE ARMY OF THE SHENANDOAH AT WOODSTOCK, ON THE MOVEMENT FROM [illegible]SONBURG AFTER DEVASTATING THE VALLEY.—From a Sketch by J. E. Taylor.

THE CONFEDERATE ARMY, UNDER GENERAL EARLY, DRIVING BACK THE SIXTH, EIGHTH AND NINETEENTH FEDERAL CORPS, UNDER GENERAL WRIGHT AT CEDAR CREEK, VA., ON THE MORNING OF OCTOBER 19TH, 1864.—FROM A SKETCH BY J. E. TAYLOR.

BATTLE OF MIDDLETOWN, ON THE 19TH OF OCTOBER, 1864.—REPULSE OF GENERAL EARLY BY THE SIXTH CORPS, GENERAL WRIGHT.—FROM A SKETCH BY J. E. TAYLOR.

Washington, and slept the previous night at Winchester. Hearing the artillery-firing from the south, he started on his famous ride, and arrived in time to co-operate with Wright in his design to recover the lost position and turn defeat to victory. Sheridan's appearance on the field and his personal magnetism exerted its influence all along the lines, and the troops were determined to regain their lost prestige. Early's men had abandoned their position and turned their attention to obtaining the booty they found in the captured Federal camps. The re-formed Federal line pressed on the retreating Confederates and drove them back to Fisher's Hill. In the retreat, Early abandoned much of his captured booty, and 23 additional guns and 1,500 prisoners. The next morning the Confederate forces continued their retreat southward, and Early gave up further aggressive cavalry operations in the Valley, and his infantry rejoined the forces at Petersburg. General Grant recalled the Sixth Corps to the Army of the Potomac. In this last engagement Early lost 1,860 men, killed and wounded, and 1,200 prisoners. In the beginning of the battle he had captured 1,420 prisoners, whom he had immediately dispatched toward Richmond, where they arrived in a few days. Sheridan's loss was 5,764. The Sixth Corps lost 2,215; the Nineteenth Corps, 2,468; the West Virginia troops, 847; and the cavalry, 214. Colonels Joseph Thoburn and Charles R. Lowell, Jr., and General Daniel D. Bidwell, were killed; Colonel J. Howard Kitching was fatally wounded; Generals Wright, Grover and Ricketts, and Colonels Mackenzie and W. H. Penrose, were wounded. President Lincoln, on receiving news of the battle, sent to General Sheridan the following message: "With great pleasure I tender to you and your brave army the thanks of the nation, and my own personal admiration and gratitude, for the month's operations in the Shenandoah Valley, and especially for the splendid work of October 19th, 1864."

A few weeks later the President appointed Sheridan a major-general "for the personal gallantry, military skill, and just confidence in the courage and patriotism of your troops, displayed by you on the 19th day of October at Cedar Run, whereby, under the blessing of Providence, your routed army was reorganized, a great national disaster averted, and a brilliant victory achieved over the rebels for the third time in pitched battle within thirty days." These words were dictated by Abraham Lincoln.

OPPOSING FORCES IN THE SHENANDOAH VALLEY.

1.—*Organization of the Army of the Shenandoah, in the Middle Military Division, commanded by* MAJOR-GENERAL PHILIP H. SHERIDAN, *date, August 31st, 1864.*

(General Headquarters Escort, Sixth United States Cavalry.)

CAVALRY FORCES.*

Brigadier-general Alfred T. A. Torbert commanding.

FIRST DIVISION (A. P. C.).

Brigadier-general Wesley Merritt.

First Brigade: Brigadier-general George A. Custer—First Michigan, Fifth Michigan, Sixth Michigan, Seventh Michigan.

Second Brigade: Colonel Thomas C. Devin—Fourth New York, Sixth New York, Ninth New York, Seventeenth Pennsylvania, First United States Artillery, Batteries K and L.

Third Brigade: Colonel Charles R. Lowell, Jr., First Maryland (P. H. B.), Second Massachusetts, Twenty-fifth New York.

Reserve Brigade: Colonel Alfred Gibbs—First New York Dragoons, Sixth Pennsylvania, First United States, Second United States, Fifth United States, Second United States Artillery, Battery D.

THIRD DIVISION (A. P. C.).

Brigadier-general James H. Wilson.

First Brigade: Brigadier-general J. B. McIntosh—First Connecticut, Third New Jersey, Second New York, Fifth New York, Second Ohio, Eighteenth Pennsylvania.

Second Brigade: Brigadier-general G. H. Chapman—Third Indiana (det.), First New Hampshire, Eighth New York, Twenty-second New York, First Vermont.

Reserve Horse Artillery Brigade: Captain La Rhett L. Livingston—First United States Artillery, Battery I, Second United States Artillery, Battery A; Second United States Artillery, Batteries B and L; Second United States Artillery, Battery M; Third United States Artillery, Battery C; Fourth United States Artillery, Batteries C and E.

FIRST DIVISION (W. VA. C.).

Brigadier-general Alfred N. Duffié.

First Brigade: Colonel William B. Tibbits—Second Maryland, P. H. B. (Company F); First New York (Lincoln); First New York (Veteran); Twenty-first New York; Fourteenth Pennsylvania.

Second Brigade: Colonel John E. Wynkoop—Fifteenth New York, Twentieth Pennsylvania, Twenty-second Pennsylvania.

SECOND DIVISION* (W. VA. C.).

Brigadier-general William W. Averell.

Eighth Ohio, First West Virginia, Second West Virginia, Third West Virginia, Fifth West Virginia. Fifth United States Artillery, Battery L.

SIXTH ARMY CORPS.

Major-general Horatio G. Wright commanding.

FIRST DIVISION.

Brigadier-general David A. Russell.

First Brigade: Colonel W. H. Penrose—Fourth New Jersey, Tenth New Jersey, Fifteenth New Jersey.

Second Brigade: Brigadier-general Emory Upton—Second Connecticut Heavy Artillery, Sixty-fifth New York, Sixty-seventh New York (det.), One Hundred and Twenty-first New York, Ninety-fifth Pennsylvania, Ninety-sixth Pennsylvania.

Third Brigade: Colonel Oliver Edwards—Seventh Massachusetts (det.), Tenth Massachusetts (det.), Thirty-seventh Massachusetts, Twenty-third Pennsylvania (det.), Forty-ninth Pennsylvania, Eighty-second Pennsylvania, One Hundred and Nineteenth Pennsylvania, Second Rhode Island Battalion, Wisconsin Battalion.

SECOND DIVISION.

Brigadier-general George W. Getty.

First Brigade: Brigadier-general Frank Wheaton—Sixty-second New York, Ninety-third Pennsylvania, Ninety-eighth Pennsylvania, One Hundred and Second Pennsylvania, One Hundred and Thirty-ninth Pennsylvania.

Second Brigade: Brigadier-general Lewis A. Grant—Second Vermont (det.), Third Vermont (det.), Fourth Vermont, Fifth Vermont, Sixth Vermont, Eleventh Vermont.

Third Brigade: Brigadier-general Daniel D. Bidwell—Seventh Maine, Forty-third New York, Forty-ninth New York, Seventy-seventh New York, One Hundred and Twenty-second New York, Sixty-first Pennsylvania.

THIRD DIVISION.

Brigadier-general James B. Ricketts.

First Brigade: Colonel William Emerson—Fourteenth New Jersey, One Hundred and Sixth New York, One Hundred and Fifty-first New York, Eighty-seventh Pennsylvania, Tenth Vermont.

Second Brigade: Colonel J. Warren Keifer—Sixth Maryland, Ninth New York Heavy Artillery, One Hundred ...

SOLDIERS, AT THE APPROACH OF THE PRESIDENTIAL ELECTION, NOVEMBER, 1864, READING POLITICAL HANDBILLS.

FROM A SKETCH BY JOSEPH BECKER.

* The cavalry divisions of Averell and Duffié are transferred to this head from the roster of the West Virginia troops, on which they are borne, inasmuch as they were under Torbert's orders. Of Duffié's division, four days prior to August 31st, some troops had been given to Averell, others to the post at Harper's Ferry, and the remainder were sent to Cumberland to remount. Custer afterward received Wilson's division; Powell, Averell's; and Lowell, the reserve brigade.

* The returns for this division are obviously imperfect in the roster from which the foregoing is compiled. Colonel Powell and Major Gibson commanded the brigades, and there was afterward a third brigade.

EXCITING SCENE IN THE HOUSE OF REPRESENTATIVES, JANUARY 31st, 1865, ON THE

EXCITING SCENE IN THE HOUSE OF REPRESENTATIVES, JANUARY [illegible], ON THE [illegible] OF THE AMENDMENT TO THE CONSTITUTION ABOLISHING SLAVERY FOR EVER

"WASHERWOMEN" IN THE ARMY OF THE SHENANDOAH.—A LAUNDRY ESTABLISHMENT.
FROM A SKETCH BY JOSEPH BECKER.

tenth Ohio, One Hundred and Twenty-second Ohio, One Hundred and Twenty-sixth Ohio, Sixty-seventh Pennsylvania, One Hundred and Thirty-eighth Pennsylvania.

Artillery Brigade: Colonel Charles H. Tompkins—Maine Light Artillery, Fifth Battery; First Massachusetts Light Artillery, Battery A; New York Light Artillery, First Battery; First Rhode Island Light Artillery, Battery C; First Rhode Island Light Artillery, Battery G; Fifth United States, Battery M.

NINETEENTH ARMY CORPS.

Brigadier-general William H. Emory.

FIRST DIVISION.

Brigadier-general William Dwight.

First Brigade: Colonel George L. Beal—Twenty-ninth Maine, Thirtieth Massachusetts, Ninetieth New York, One Hundred and Fourteenth New York, One Hundred and Sixteenth New York, One Hundred and Fifty-third New York.

Second Brigade: Brigadier-general J. W. McMillan—Twelfth Connecticut, Thirteenth Maine, Fifteenth Maine, One Hundred and Sixtieth New York, Forty-seventh Pennsylvania, Eighth Vermont.

Third Brigade: Colonel L. D. H. Currie—Thirtieth Maine, One Hundred and Thirty-third New York, One Hundred and Sixty-second New York, One Hundred and Sixty-fifth New York, One Hundred and Seventy-third New York.

Artillery: New York Light Artillery, Fifth Battery.

SECOND DIVISION.

Brigadier-general Cuvier Grover.

First Brigade: Brigadier-general Henry W. Birge—Ninth Connecticut, Twelfth Maine, Fourteenth Maine, Twenty-sixth Massachusetts, Fourteenth New Hampshire, Seventy-fifth New York.

Second Brigade: Colonel Edward L. Molineux—Thirteenth Connecticut, Third Massachusetts Cavalry (dis.), Eleventh Indiana, Twenty-second Iowa, One Hundred and Thirty-first New York, One Hundred and Fifty-ninth New York.

Third Brigade: Colonel Jacob Sharpe—Thirty-eighth Massachusetts, One Hundred and Twenty-eighth New York, One Hundred and Fifty-sixth New York, One Hundred and Seventy-fifth New York, One Hundred and Seventy-sixth New York.

Fourth Brigade: Colonel David Shunk—Eighth Indiana, Eighteenth Indiana, Twenty-fourth Iowa, Twenty-eighth Iowa.

Artillery: Maine Light Artillery, First Battery.

Reserve Artillery: First Rhode Island Light Artillery, Battery D; Indiana Light Artillery, Seventeenth Battery.

ARMY OF WEST VIRGINIA.

Brigadier-general George Crook commanding.

FIRST DIVISION.

Colonel Joseph Thoburn.

First Brigade: Colonel George D. Wells—Thirty-fourth Massachusetts, Fifth New York Heavy Artillery (4 Companies), One Hundred and Sixteenth Ohio, One Hundred and Twenty-third Ohio.

Second Brigade: Colonel William G. Ely—Eighteenth Connecticut, Second Eastern Shore, Md.; First West Virginia, Fourth West Virginia, Twelfth West Virginia.

Third Brigade: Colonel Jacob M. Campbell—Twenty-third Illinois, Fifty-fourth Pennsylvania, Tenth West Virginia, Eleventh West Virginia, Fifteenth West Virginia.

SECOND DIVISION.

Colonel Isaac H. Duval.

First Brigade: Colonel Rutherford B. Hayes—Twenty-third Ohio, Thirty-sixth Ohio, Fifth West Virginia, Thirteenth West Virginia.

Second Brigade: Colonel Daniel D. Johnson—Thirty-fourth Ohio, Ninety-first Ohio, Ninth West Virginia, Fourteenth West Virginia.

MILITARY DISTRICT OF HARPER'S FERRY.

Brigadier-general John D. Stevenson.

Cavalry: Twelfth Pennsylvania, Virginia Rangers, Loudoun Independent Company.

Artillery: Indiana Light Artillery, Seventeenth Battery; Kentucky Light Artillery, First Battery; Maryland Light Artillery, Battery A; Maryland Light Artillery, Baltimore Battery; Fifth New York Heavy Artillery; New York Light Artillery, Thirtieth Battery; New York Light Artillery, Thirty-second Battery; Ohio Light Artillery, First Battery; First Ohio Light Artillery, Battery L; First Pennsylvania Light Artillery, Battery G; First West Virginia Light Artillery, Battery A; First West Virginia Light Artillery, Battery F.

Infantry: First Maryland P. H. B., Second Maryland P. H. B., One Hundred and Thirty-fifth Ohio, One Hundred and Sixtieth Ohio, One Hundred and Sixty-first Ohio.

FORCES WEST OF SLEEPY CREEK.

Brigadier-general Benjamin F. Kelley.

Cavalry: Ohio Third Independent Company, Sixth West Virginia.

Artillery: First Illinois, Battery L; First West Virginia, Battery H; First Maryland, Battery B.

Infantry: One Hundred and Twenty-second Ohio, Sixth West Virginia, One Hundred and Sixty-fifth Ohio.

KANAWHA VALLEY FORCES.

Brigadier-general Jeremiah C. Sullivan.

Seventh West Virginia Cavalry; First Pennsylvania Light Artillery, Battery D; Pennsylvania Acting Engineers Independent Company; Virginia Exempts, Independent Company A; Veteran Reserve Corps, One Hundred and Thirty-second Company, Second Battery; First West Virginia Light Artillery, Battery D; First West Virginia Light Artillery, Battery E; Fifth United States Artillery, Battery B.

II.—*Organization of the Army of the Valley District, commanded by* Lieutenant-general JUBAL A. EARLY, *date, September* 30th, 1864.

RODES'S DIVISION.*

Major-general S. D. Ramseur commanding.

Grimes's Brigade: Brigadier-general Bryan Grimes—Thirty-second North Carolina, Colonel D. G. Cowand; Forty-third North Carolina, Colonel J. H. Winston; Forty-fifth North Carolina, Colonel J. R. Winston; Fifty-third North Carolina, Colonel D. G. Cowand; Second North Carolina Battalion, Colonel D. G. Cowand.

Cook's Brigade: Brigadier-general Philip Cook—Fourth Georgia, Lieutenant-colonel W. H. Willis; Twelfth Georgia, Captain James Everett; Twenty-first Georgia, Captain H. J. Battle; Forty-fourth Georgia, Lieutenant-colonel J. W. Beck.

Cox's Brigade: Brigadier-general W. R. Cox—First North Carolina, Captain W. H. Thompson; Second North Carolina, Captain T. B. Beall; Third North Carolina, Captain W. H. Thompson; Fourth North Carolina, Colonel Ed. A. Osborn; Fourteenth North Carolina, Captain Joseph Jones; Thirtieth North Carolina, Captain J. C. McMillan.

Battle's Brigade: Brigadier-general C. A. Battle—Third Alabama, Colonel Charles Forsyth; Fifth Alabama, Lieutenant-colonel E. L. Hobson; Sixth Alabama, Captain J. Green; Twelfth Alabama, Captain P. D. Ross; Sixty-first Alabama, Major W. E. Pinckard.

GORDON'S DIVISION.*

Major-general John B. Gordon commanding.

Hays's Brigade:† Colonel William Monaghan—Fifth Louisiana, Major A. Hart; Sixth Louisiana, Lieutenant-colonel J. Hanlon; Seventh Louisiana, Lieutenant-colonel T. M. Terry; Eighth Louisiana, Captain L. Prados; Ninth Louisiana, Colonel William R. Peck.

Stafford's Brigade:† Colonel Eugene Waggaman—First Louisiana, Captain Joseph Taylor; Second Louisiana, Lieutenant-colonel M. A. Grogan; Tenth Louisiana, Lieutenant-colonel H. D. Monier; Fourteenth Louisiana, Lieutenant-colonel David Zable; Fifteenth Louisiana, Captain H. J. Egan.

Evans's Brigade: Colonel E. N. Atkinson (October 30th, Brigadier-general C. A. Evans)—Thirteenth Georgia, Colonel John H. Baker; Twenty-sixth Georgia, Lieutenant-colonel James S. Blain; Thirty-first Georgia, Colonel John H. Lowe; Thirty-eighth Georgia, Major Thomas H. Bomar; Sixtieth Georgia, Captain Milton Russell; Sixty-first Georgia, Captain E. F. Sharpe; Twelfth Georgia Battalion, Captain J. W. Anderson.

Terry's Brigade:‡ Brigadier-general William Terry—Second Virginia, Fourth Virginia, Fifth Virginia, Twenty-seventh Virginia, Thirty-third Virginia (Stonewall Brigade, Colonel J. H. S. Funk; October 30th, Colonel A. Spengler); Twenty-first Virginia, Twenty-fifth Virginia, Forty-second Virginia, Forty-fourth Virginia, Forty-eighth Virginia, Fiftieth Virginia (J. M. Jones's Brigade, Colonel R. H.

---

* "I would call attention to the great scarcity of officers in the entire command. The best and most efficient officers in nearly every brigade have for the most part been either killed or wounded during this campaign. . . . Cox's brigade had not a single field officer present, and the Fourth Regiment in it is commanded by a second lieutenant."—From Inspection Report of Rodes's Division, September 30th.

* From inspection returns of August.

† These brigades were united under General Zebulon York, succeeded by Lieutenant-colonel D. Zable.

‡ Composed of the "fragmentary remains of fourteen of the regiments of Johnson's division, most of which was captured by the enemy, May 12th, 1864." The inspection report of August 31st says that the fusing of Hays's and Stafford's brigades into one, under York, and the consolidation of three brigades, "the remains of fourteen regiments," into one, under Terry, produced a bad effect on the discipline of the troops, who lost their chance of perpetuating their brigade history; and that Evans's brigade had lost by casualty so many valuable officers as to interfere seriously with its good management.

gregan; October 30th, Colonel W. A. Witcher); Tenth Virginia, Twenty-third Virginia, Thirty-seventh Virginia (G. H. Steuart's Brigade, Lieutenant-colonel S. H. Saunders; October 30th, Lieutenant-colonel Martz).

EARLY'S DIVISION.*

Brigadier-general John Pegram commanding.

Pegram's Brigade: Colonel John S. Hoffman—Thirteenth Virginia, Captain Felix Heiskell; Thirty-first Virginia, Lieutenant-colonel J. S. K. McCutchen; Forty-ninth Virginia, Captain John G. Lobban; Fifty-second Virginia, Captain J. M. Humphreys; Fifty-eighth Virginia, Captain L. C. James.

Johnston's Brigade: Brigadier-general Robert D. Johnston—Fifth North Carolina, Colonel John W. Lea; † Twelfth North Carolina, Colonel Henry E. Coleman; † Twentieth North Carolina, Colonel T. F. Toon; Twenty-third North Carolina, Colonel C. C. Blacknall.†

Godwin's Brigade: Lieutenant-colonel W. T. Davis—Sixth North Carolina, Lieutenant-colonel S. McD. Tate; Twenty-first North Carolina, Major W. J. Pfohl; Fifty-fourth North Carolina, Captain A. H. Martin; Fifty-seventh North Carolina, Captain M. L. Hunter; First North Carolina Battalion, Captain R. E. Wilson.

WHARTON'S DIVISION.

Brigadier-general G. C. Wharton commanding.

Echols's Brigade: Captain Edmund S. Read—Twenty-second Virginia, Captain Henry S. Dickerson; Twenty-third Virginia, Captain John M. Pratt; Twenty-sixth Virginia, Captain Frank S. Burdett.

Wharton's Brigade: Captain R. H. Logan—Forty-fifth Virginia, Major Alexander M. Davis; Fifty-first Virginia, Colonel August Forsberg; ‡ Thirtieth Virginia Battalion, Lieutenant-colonel J. Lyle Clarke.‡

Smith's Brigade: Colonel Thomas Smith—Thirty-sixth Virginia, Lieutenant Jackson Vin; Sixtieth Virginia, Captain A. G. P. George; Forty-fifth Virginia Battalion, Captain W. B. Hensley; Thomas Legion, Lieutenant-colonel J. R. Love.

KERSHAW'S DIVISION.

Major-general J. B. Kershaw commanding.

Wofford's Brigade: Colonel C. C. Sanders—Sixteenth Georgia, Major J. S. Gholston; Eighteenth Georgia, Colonel Joseph Armstrong; Twenty-fourth Georgia, Colonel C. C. Sanders; Third Georgia Battalion, Lieutenant-colonel N. L. Hutchins; Cobb's Legion, Lieutenant-colonel L. J. Glenn; Phillips's Legion, Lieutenant-colonel J. Hamilton.

Kershaw's Brigade: Brigadier-general Conner—Second South Carolina, Colonel J. D. Kennedy; Third South Carolina, Colonel W. D. Rutherford; Seventh South Carolina, Captain E. J. Goggans; Eighth South Carolina, Colonel J. W. Henagan; Fifteenth South Carolina, Colonel J. B. Davis; Twentieth South Carolina, Colonel S. M. Boykin; Third South Carolina Battalion, Lieutenant (Col.) W. G. Rice.

Humphreys's Brigade: Brigadier-general B. J. Humphreys—Thirteenth Mississippi, Lieutenant-colonel A. G. O'Brien; Seventeenth Mississippi, Captain J. C. Cochran; Eighteenth Mississippi, Colonel T. M. Griffin; Twenty-first Mississippi, Colonel D. N. Moody.

Bryan's Brigade: Brigadier-general Goode Bryan—Tenth Georgia, Colonel W. C. Holt; Fiftieth Georgia, Colonel P. McGlashan;* Fifty-first Georgia, Colonel E. Ball;* Fifty-third Georgia, Colonel J. P. Simms.

ARTILLERY DIVISION.

Colonel T. H. Carter commanding.

Braxton's Battalion: Lieutenant-colonel C. M. Braxton—Alleghany Artillery, Va., Captain J. C. Carpenter; Stafford Artillery, Va., Captain W. P. Cooper; Lee Battery, Va., Lieutenant W. W. Hardwick.

Cutshaw's Battalion: † Major W. E. Cutshaw—Orange Artillery, Va., Captain C. W. Fry; Staunton Artillery, Va., Captain A. W. Garber; Courtney Battery, Va., —— L. F. Jones.

McLaughlin's Battalion: Major William McLaughlin—Bryan's Virginia Battery, Chapman's Virginia Battery, Lowry's Virginia Battery.

Nelson's Battalion: Lieutenant-colonel William Nelson—Amherst Artillery, Va., Captain T. J. Kirkpatrick; Fluvanna Artillery, Va., Captain J. L. Massie; Milledge's Artillery, Ga., Captain John Milledge.

CAVALRY FORCES

LOMAX'S DIVISION.

Major-general J. J. Lomax.

McCausland's Brigade: Brigadier-general J. McCausland—Fourteenth Virginia, Sixteenth Virginia, Seventeenth Virginia, Twenty-fifth Virginia, Thirty-seventh Virginia Battalion.

Johnson's Brigade: Brigadier-general B. T. Johnson—Eighth Virginia, Twenty-first Virginia, Twenty-second Virginia, Thirty-fourth and Thirty-sixth Virginia Batteries.

Jackson's Brigade: Brigadier-general H. B. Davidson—First Maryland, Nineteenth Virginia, Twentieth Virginia, Forty-sixth and Forty-seventh Virginia Battalions.

Imboden's Brigade: Colonel George H. Smith—Eighteenth Virginia, Twenty-third Virginia, Sixty-second Mounted Infantry.

LEE'S DIVISION.

Major-general Fitzhugh Lee.

Wickham's Brigade: Brigadier-general W. C. Wickham—First Virginia, Colonel Carter; Second Virginia, Colonel Munford; Third Virginia, Colonel Owen; Fourth Virginia, Colonel Payne.

Lomax's Brigade: Brigadier-general L. L. Lomax—Fifth Virginia, Colonel H. Clay Pate; Sixth Virginia, Colonel Julian Harrison; Fifteenth Virginia, Colonel C. R. Collins.

Rosser's Brigade: Brigadier-general Thomas L. Rosser—Seventh Virginia, Colonel R. H. Dulany; Eleventh Virginia, Colonel O. R. Funsten; Twelfth Virginia, Colonel A. W. Harman; Thirty-fifth Virginia Battalion, Lieutenant-colonel E. V. White.

[NOTE.—For the foregoing rosters we are indebted to the War Records Office. In the original returns the Federal regimental commanders are not indicated. The troops of General Stevenson, Kelley and Sullivan, though reckoned on the official Department Returns, were in garrison, not in the marching army.]

* Commanded by Ramseur, until he took Rodes's division, after the battle of the Opequon.

† These officers absent, and actual commanders not indicated. October 31st, after the battle of Cedar Creek, the officers in place of Lea, Coleman, and Blacknall, respectively, were Captains E. M. Dugald, Kemp, Plummer and Albert D. Peace.

‡ These officers absent, and actual commanders not indicated. The Fifteenth Virginia, Vanderventer's, is ascribed to this brigade in a roster of October 31st.

* Absent wounded, and actual commanders of these regiments not stated. The foregoing organization is for August, when Kershaw arrived in the Valley.

† In an earlier roster Fry's Orange Battery is ascribed to Carter's battalion, and in its place appears the Charlottesville Artillery, Captain J. M. Carrington.

MOBILE.

ON JANUARY 18th, 1864, Admiral Farragut desired to make use of his squadron, then lying off Mobile Harbor, in attacking the defenses of the place, and preventing the completion of the ironclads in course of construction by the Confederates. Having no available land force—the troops being engaged in the Red River expedition—Farragut was obliged to await the co-operation of the military arm of the Federal Government to successfully reduce the forts commanding the harbor, and he maintained an effective but tiresome blockade with his wooden ships, awaiting the repeatedly-asked-for troops and the assistance of such ironclads as were ready for service, until July, when the arrival of the Monitor ironclads and the promised co-operation of General Canby's forces were assured. Our map shows the position of the defenses of the harbor and the city. The fleet of Farragut is indicated at the entrance of the bay. Fort Morgan, on Mobile Point, and Fort Gaines, on Dauphin Island, with Fort Powell, on Tower Island, commanded the entrances to the harbor, and were heavily mounted with columbiads, rifled guns and howitzers for siege and flank defense. Fort Morgan was the most formidable, being built to carry both barbette and casement guns, and its armament was fully up to the best standard of modern cannon. In the harbor, Admiral Franklin Buchanan commanded the fleet, made up of the ram *Tennessee*; the gunboat *Morgan*, commanded by Commander George W. Harrison; the *Gaines*, commanded by Lieutenant J. W. Bennett; and the *Selma*, commanded by Lieutenant P. U. Murphy. There were three or four ironclads of light draught

CHIMNEY ARCHITECTURE.—SOLDIERS AT THEIR CAMP-FIRES.

FROM A SKETCH BY A. McCALLUM.

and armament near the city. The *Tennessee* was built by the Confederates (begun at Selma, Ala., in 1863) from timber just cut near her dock, and clad with iron, the ore of which was dug, smelted and forged, during her construction, in mines near Atlanta, Ga. Six inches of iron, sheathing twenty-four inches of wood, defended her gunners; the iron, carried down two feet below the water-line, presenting an angle which was proof against the enemy's prow, and at the same time converted her into a powerful ram. She carried six Brooke guns that threw 90 and 110 pound solid shot. She was in charge of Commander J. D. Johnston. The harbor was farther protected by torpedoes planted across the main ship-channel, went into the fight with their topsail-yards across; the others sent down their yards and topmasts. The wooden ships were lashed in couples, the lighter vessels on the off hand; the four Monitors in a column inshore and abreast the leading ships, the *Tecumseh* leading slightly in advance of the column. Admiral Farragut had intended to lead with the *Hartford*, but deferred by persuasion to Captain Alden with the *Brooklyn*.

The attack was made in the following order:

STARBOARD COLUMN—MONITORS.

Tecumseh, Commander Thomas A. M. Craven, 2 guns.
Manhattan, Commander J. W. A. Nicholson, 2 guns.
Winnebago, Commander Thomas H. Stevens, 4 guns.
Chickasaw, Lieutenant-com'r George H. Perkins, 4 guns.

At five o'clock on the morning of August 5th, 1864, the signal was given for the fleet to get under way. The *Brooklyn* weighed at once; the other vessels followed in order. At 6:30 the order for battle was formed, all the ships hoisted the United States flag from the peak and the three mast-heads, and the first two shots were fired by the *Tecumseh* at the fort. At five minutes before seven the fleet was sent ahead; at five minutes after seven the *Brooklyn* received the fire from the fort and responded with her bow-gun, and immediately after the action became general between the fort and the Monitors and the bow-guns of the fleet. At the same time Admiral Buchanan moved out with his gunboats from behind Fort Morgan

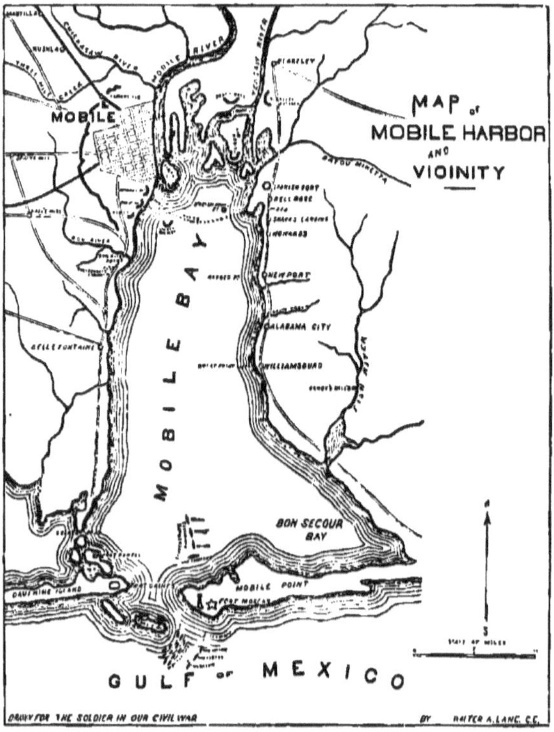

except a narrow passage of about one hundred yards, marked by a red buoy, left open for blockade-runners, and through which the Federal admiral planned to pass his fleet.

Farragut took personal charge of the fleet off Mobile Bay the last week in July, and prepared to force an entrance thereto. It was the 4th of August before his wooden ships had been sufficiently strengthened and equipped for the undertaking. General Gordon Granger was to land his troops on Dauphin Island and invest Fort Gaines on the 4th. Farragut was to pass Fort Morgan and enter the bay the same morning. Granger landed, but Farragut was delayed. The Confederates threw more troops into Fort Gaines to resist Granger. This was an advantage to the Federals, as they captured them two days later. The *Hartford* and *Brooklyn*

PORT COLUMN—WOODEN SHIPS.

{ *Brooklyn*, Captain James Alden, 24 guns.
{ *Octorara*, Lieutenant-com'r Charles H. Greene, 6 guns.
{ *Hartford*, { Rear-admiral David G. Farragut. Captain Percival Drayton, 21 guns.
{ *Metacomet*, Lieutenant-com'r James E. Jouett, 6 guns.
{ *Richmond*, Captain Thornton A. Jenkins, 20 guns.
{ *Port Royal*, Lieutenant-com'r Bancroft Gherardi, 6 guns.
{ *Lackawanna*, Captain John B. Marchand, 8 guns.
{ *Seminole*, Commander Edward Donaldson, 8 guns.
{ *Monongahela*, Commander James H. Strong, 8 guns.
{ *Kennebec*, Lieutenant-com'r William P. McCann, 5 guns.
{ *Ossipee*, Commander William E. Leroy, 11 guns.
{ *Itasca*, Lieutenant-com'r George Brown, 5 guns.
{ *Oneida*, Commander J. R. M. Mullany, 9 guns.
{ *Galena*, Lieutenant-com'r Clark H. Wells, 10 guns.

The *Octorara*, *Metacomet* and *Port Royal* were side-wheel double-enders; the others were screw-ships. All had been built for the naval service.

and formed in line of battle across the channel from east to west, just inside the line of torpedoes. This position enabled him to pour a raking fire upon the Federal fleet until it passed the fort and buoy. The *Tecumseh*, after firing the two first guns, turned her turret and loaded again with steel shot and sixty pounds of powder. Her commander's game was the *Tennessee*, and he steered quietly on, unmindful of the shot from the fort, a little ahead of the *Hartford*, until he neared the buoy. Craven, from the pilot-house, saw the buoy so near the beach that he turned to his pilot and said: "It is impossible the admiral means us to go inside that buoy: I cannot turn my ship." He then saw that the *Tennessee*, which had lain to the eastward of the buoy, was steaming to the westward of it, and either afraid she would get away, or fearing to par-

through the narrow channel, Craven gave the order, "starboard!" and pushed the *Tecumseh* straight at the *Tennessee*. The *Tecumseh* had gone but a few yards, and the officers of the *Tennessee* were watching Lieutenant Wharton with lock-string in hand, ready to fire into the *Tecumseh* as soon as the two ironclads touched. At this moment a torpedo exploded. The *Tecumseh* lurched, careened, and sat down headforemost, her screw visible from the lookout of the *Tennessee*, not 200 yards off, on the other side of the fatal line. Craven and the pilot were in the pilot-house, above the turret; both rushed for the narrow hatchway. Craven, with the true instinct of an officer and soldier, drew back, with "After you, pilot," and waved his companion through the narrow opening. The pilot was saved, but Craven went to the bottom with his ship, passing outside the fatal buoy over the line of torpedoes, whose cases knocked against the bottom of the ship, but did not explode. The admiral, in the midst of the anxiety as to the success of his fleet, did not forget the drowning men on the *Tecumseh*, and from his position in the port main rigging of the *Hartford* he hailed Captain Jouett, who stood on the starboard wheelhouse of the *Metacomet*, and asked if he had a boat that he could send to their rescue. The captain manned a boat and placed it in the charge of Ensign H. C. Neilds, a volunteer naval officer, who pulled around under the *Hartford's* stern and broadside across the bows of the *Brooklyn*, toward the wreck, where he saved John Collins, the pilot, and nine of the ship's company. Ensign Neilds was but a mere lad. He heeded not the shot flying thick past him, and in swung her around, so she presented her broadside to the fort, upon which she poured a heavy fire, driving the gunners out of the water battery. She finally brought her head in the right direction, and steamed on, following the flagship. The *Brooklyn* followed with the other ships of the port column. When the heavier ships were out of range of the fort, the Confederate gunners returned to their posts and severely punished the smaller of the fleet. The *Oneida* was so disabled that her consort, the *Galena*, had to tow her past the fort. As the *Hartford* advanced, the smaller gunboats of Admiral Buchanan kept up a heavy raking fire, to which the *Hartford* could only reply with her bow guns, as the channel was narrow. She suffered severely, her forward division losing ten killed and five wounded by one shot, and her quarters became a slaughter-

THE NAVAL COMBAT IN MOBILE HARBOR.—THE FLAGSHIP "HARTFORD" ENGAGING THE CONFEDERATE RAM "TENNESSEE."

FROM A SKETCH BY E. B. HOUGH.

The *Brooklyn* was 300 yards astern; the *Hartford* following on her port quarter; the *Richmond* behind her and in the *Brooklyn's* wake. The *Winnebago* and *Manhattan* were skirting the beach, steering to pass inside the buoy, as they were ordered. They kept their course, occupying the attention of the guns on shore, which were raking the Federal fleet. The officers of the *Brooklyn*, espying objects in the water ahead, stopped, and began with her consort to back, coming down on the *Hartford*, whose engines were stopped. The admiral hailed to learn the cause of the movement. "Torpedoes ahead!" was the reply. Without apparent hesitation, Farragut ordered his own ship with her consort ahead, and gave the signal, "Close order!" The *Brooklyn* having drifted so as to close the channel inside the buoy, the *Metacomet* was backed, and Farragut went ahead with the flagship; their heads were turned, and they passed to the westward, his position, with the rudder in hand, he, looking back, noticed that the flag was flying from the boat. He stooped, took it from its cover, unfurled and planted it in its place. This was done just as the ensign of the forecastle division of the *Hartford* had trained one of his 100-pounders upon the boat, thinking it an enemy or torpedo in disguise. One of the ship's company caught his arm and stopped the gunner. The *Hartford* having passed, Neilds placed the rescued men on the *Winnebago*, and with his crew he boarded and served on the *Oneida* during the rest of the action. Of the crew of the *Tecumseh*, 21 were saved out of over 100 souls on board when the fatal torpedo sent her to the bottom.

The *Brooklyn* was lying bow to the fort, and received a raking fire, her position enabling her to use only her bow guns. In backing down she feared a collision with the *Richmond* and consort, whose engines had stopped. A fortunate tide pen. The Confederate admiral waited with the *Tennessee* until the Federal vessel drew past her, and as the ram started, intending to run her wooden antagonist down, the *Hartford* put her helm to starboard, and having the greater speed, avoided the collision. Two shots fired from the ram missed their mark, and the *Hartford* proceeded up the bay, closely followed by the *Tennessee* for about a mile, when she gave up the pursuit and turned to meet the other wooden vessels, which were advancing in close order, the *Brooklyn* leading. The *Tennessee* made for Captain Alden's ship, intending to ram, but sheered off, passed on her starboard side at less than 100 yards, fired two guns, whose shot passed through and through the *Brooklyn*, which gave the ram the contents of her broadside in return. The *Tennessee* then passed down the line to the *Richmond*, which gave her a broadside, and her musketeers poured a brisk fire into the *Tennessee's* open ports. The Confederate ironclad returned two shots, which passed over and did no harm. The *Tennessee* next passed the *Lackawanna* on the starboard side. Captain Strong, of the *Monongahela*, seeing her intention to ram down the *Lackawanna*, undertook to strike her at right angles, but having the *Kennebec* in tow, she swung too far around and struck a glancing blow on her port quarter. This threw the *Tennessee's* stern around, and she collided with the *Kennebec*, leaving one of her boats and its davits as mementos. As she passed she fired a shell which seriously wounded an officer and four men. The *Ossipee* came up, struck and righted the *Tennessee*, which passed at close quarters between the two vessels, giving the *Ossipee* two shots nearly together. The ram then passed the crippled *Oneida* and endeavored to give her a broadside, but her guns missed fire and she passed to the rear, delivering a raking fire, which struck the *Oneida's* stern, and seriously wounded Commander Mullany, who lost an arm. The ironclad *Winnebago* then came up and took position between the combatants, saving the *Oneida*, whose crew jumped on the rail and cheered their old commander, Stevens, who had been assigned to the Monitor before the fight. The *Tennessee* then took position under the guns of Fort Morgan. The *Hartford* was still being followed by the lesser ironclads, who kept up a hot fire. A shot disabled the Confederate vessel *Gaines*, and Admiral Farragut directed the *Metacomet* to cast off and chase the gunboats, and prevent their escape up to Mobile. The *Selma* soon hauled down her flag. The *Morgan* ran under protection of Fort Morgan, and then escaped to Mobile. The *Gaines* was burned. The *Hartford* anchored four miles from Fort Morgan, and her crew breakfasted. Admiral Buchanan had ordered Captain Johnston to follow the Federal fleet up the bay, and ere the crew of the Federal admiral's flagship were seated at mess, the approach of the *Tennessee* was announced. The *Hartford* was at once cleared for action, and the ironclads were signaled to engage the ram while the *Monongahela*, *Lackawanna* and *Ossipee* were to run her down. The *Monongahela* struck her fairly amidships, on the starboard side, at the same time receiving two shells which passed through the berth-deck. The ram then passed to the starboard of the *Monongahela*, receiving a broadside at ten yards. The *Lackawanna* then struck the *Tennessee* a square blow on the port side, causing her to list over and swing round. The *Hartford* then made an attack as a ram, and struck so that the port bow of each vessel came in contact, doing little damage. As they swung loose the *Hartford* poured a broadside against the *Tennessee* at ten feet, with no perceptible effect. The Confederate ram tried to return the fire, but the primers failed again, and but one gun went off. This was the last shot of the *Tennessee*. The *Hartford* made a circuit, to ram the Confederate vessel, when the *Lackawanna* struck her near where the admiral was standing, who barely escaped, and his vessel was cut down within two feet of the water-line. The Monitors then came up, and the *Chickasaw* followed, and pouring shot into the stern of the ram, soon disabled her steering apparatus. Her iron shutters were so jammed that her guns could not be used. Her smokestack came down, filling the gun-deck with smoke. In this plight she headed down the bay, followed by the *Chickasaw*, pounding with her heavy shot the after-end of the shield. The *Manhattan* and *Winnebago* were also at work, while the *Hartford* and *Ossipee* were seeking a chance to ram her. Admiral Buchanan personally superintended the sighting of the guns, until an iron splinter broke his leg; then Captain Johnston hauled down the flag. As it had been shot away before, the Federals did not stop firing until Captain Johnston climbed to the roof of the *Tennessee* and raised a white flag.

The fight lasted only a little over an hour. The *Tennessee's* loss was two killed and ten wounded. The loss of the Federal fleet from the forts and the Confederate squadron was 52 killed and 170 wounded.

The *Chickasaw*, which had so persistently stuck to the ram, took her in tow and anchored her near the flagship, after which she steamed down to Fort Powell. The fort had been built to resist an attack from the front, and was not prepared to meet on

THE CONFEDERATE RAM "BALTIC," DEFENDING MOBILE HARBOR.

CHASING A BLOCKADE-RUNNER AT NIGHT, DURING THE INVESTMENT OF MOBILE HARBOR

From Sketches by E. B. Hough

coming like this from the rear. It was soon evacuated and blown up. On the 6th the *Chickasaw* went down and shelled Fort Gaines, which surrendered on the 7th; but Fort Morgan still held out. General Granger's force was transferred from Dauphin Island to Mobile Point, and a siege-train, sent from New Orleans, was landed in the rear of the fort, on the 17th. On Monday, the 22d, at early dawn, the bombardment commenced from the batteries, the three Monitors, and the ships outside as well as inside the bar. The fort surrendered on the 23d. Mobile, as a port for blockading-running, was thus sealed. In the meantime Admiral D. G. Farragut went North in December, leaving Commodore Palmer in command of the squadron until the following February, when he was relieved by Rear-admiral H. K. Thatcher. Palmer, however, staid, by his own wish, until the city fell.

The works around the city, inland, were very strong, but it was not approached from that side. General Canby, commanding the Army of West Mississippi, began to move against it in March, 1865. One corps marched from Fort Morgan, up the head of the bay to attack the city, which was immediately given up, the Confederate troops having already been withdrawn.

FRANKLIN—NASHVILLE—FORT FISHER.

GENERAL GRANT, in his plan for a final campaign, included the driving out by Thomas of Hood from Northern Georgia and Tennessee, and the accomplishment of a raid through Alabama to join with Canby in forming a new base at Mobile, destroying in his path the factories, mills and munitions of war. In Nashville, Thomas encountered the double task of shaping discordant elements into an army, and with that army meeting the disappointed Confederate chieftain Hood, who had so unwittingly been eluded by Sherman, and who now sought to recover his standing in the Confederacy by a brilliant feat of arms. This determination was shared by some of his officers who had been censured by Hood, and were determined to regain the good opinion of the army by an extraordinary display of valor and prowess on their part. Thomas had an army made up of the Fourth Corps, under T. J. Wood; the Twenty-third Corps, under J. M. Schofield; three divisions of the Army of the Tennessee, under A. J. Smith; Wilson's cavalry forces; and an unwieldy and inexperienced body of recruits, of questionable utility in a fight—making up an army of 40,000 strong. Hood's army consisted of S. D. Lee's, A. P. Stewart's and B. F. Cheatham's corps, ably supported by N. B. Forrest's horsemen—in all a force of about 36,000 men. Schofield held his line south of the Duck River. Hood flanked him, and Schofield retired, under the general directions given by Thomas, to the north side. Forrest moved around Schofield's left to Spring Hill, where a slight interchange of hostilities between the retiring forces of Schofield, protected by Wilson's cavalry, and Forrest took place; but Hood did not push his advantage, and Schofield took position at Franklin. He lacked pontons to cross the Harpeth River, as he wished, and therefore formed his line south of the town, and set at work to intrench and also to improve the fords and rebuild the bridges.

NOVEMBER, 1864.

When he had carried his artillery across and planted the guns in Fort Granger—a fort previously constructed on the hill, and commanding his line on the other side of the river—he got his trains beyond danger, and began moving his army to the north side. About six o'clock in the afternoon, with the Fourth Corps partly across the river, a general attack was precipitated by the Federal rear-guard, which, instead of retiring in good order when attacked by the advancing Confederates, as directed by the commander, gave them a warm reception, and provoked a desperate charge on the isolated brigades of General Wagner. With a tremendous yell the Confederates swept away the opposing forces, and on the heels of the panic-stricken regiments overran the Federal parapets and drove their defenders from the centre of the line. The Federal forces, reinforced by the reserve, established a new line within twenty-five yards of the one just lost. The combat lasted until nearly nine o'clock, and prevailed along the whole line. It was a desperate and sanguinary fight, but without much advantage to either party. As Schofield's position was not secure, he withdrew his forces during the night to the north side of the river without further loss. Hood in this, the battle of Franklin, lost about 6,300 men and 32 battle-flags; Schofield lost 2,326 men. Thomas complimented Schofield and his men for their gallant stand against double their number, and ordered the troops to withdraw to Nashville.

ADMINISTERING THE OATH OF ALLEGIANCE TO CONFEDERATE PRISONERS.
FROM A SKETCH BY E. F. MULLEN.

the east side of the bay to a small stream called Fish River; the remainder of the army was then brought to the same point by transports. General Steele left Pensacola about the same time and marched to Blakely. A short distance below Blakely was Spanish Fort, upon the defense of which the fate of the city rested. The gunboats had not yet crossed Dog River bar on account of low water. On the 27th the fleet moved up and the bar was safely crossed by the *Octorara*, Captain W. W. Low; and ironclads *Kickapoo*, Captain M. P. Jones; *Osage*, Captain William M. Gamble; *Milwaukee*, Captain James H. Gillis; *Winnebago*, Captain W. A. Kirkland; and the *Chickasaw*, Captain George H. Perkins. They opened that day on the Confederate works, which were invested by the army the same night.

The siege lasted until the evening of the 8th of April, when Spanish Fort surrendered. On the 12th, Commander Palmer, with the *Octorara* and the ironclads, moved up the Blakely to the point where it branches off from the Tensaw and down the latter stream, coming out about a mile from Mobile, within easy shelling distance. At the same time Admiral Thatcher, with the gunboats, and 8,000 troops under General Granger, crossed

The Confederate loss of commissioned officers was very heavy, and among the general officers* they lost Adams, Quarles, Cleburne, Strahl, Gist, Stafford, Granberry, Scott and Cockrell.

With his army safely within the lines of Nashville, General Thomas took time to prepare his army for further operations against Hood. The War Department at Washington, the President, General Grant, and the entire people of the North, insisted upon an immediate movement against the enemy.

DECEMBER, 1864.

Grant ordered Thomas either to move at once on Hood, or to turn his command over to Schofield. Thomas quickly replied that he would cheerfully turn over his command, but would not attack Hood until himself satisfied that the time was ripe. In the meantime Hood was devastating Tennessee, recruiting his army by forced conscription among the young men, and spreading terror throughout all

* Walthall reported that in Quarles's brigade the ranking officer on coming out of the fight was a captain.

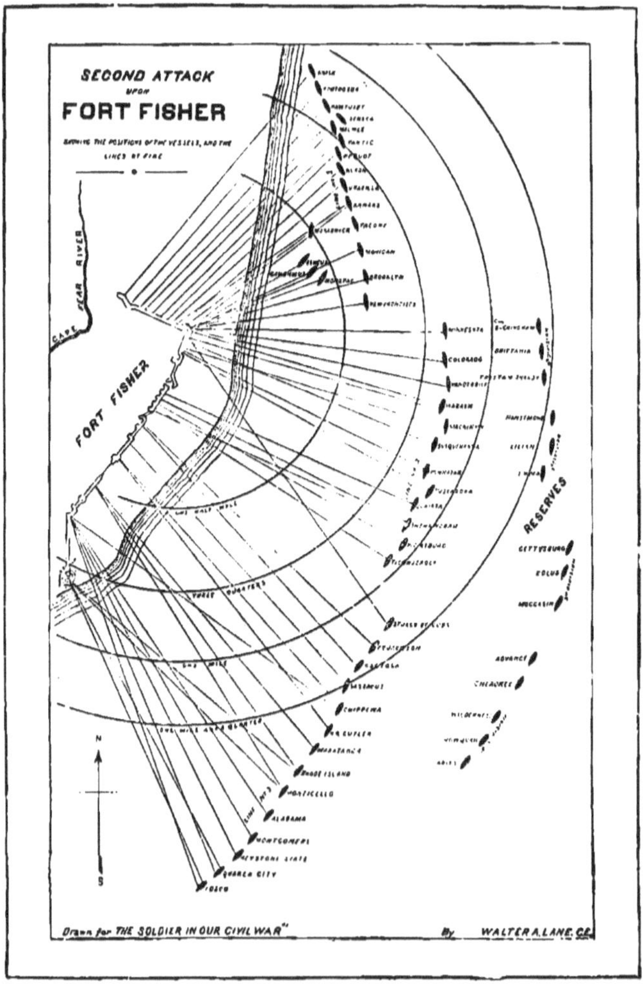

the region. Grant therefore ordered General Logan to Nashville to supplant Thomas.

Thomas had on the 1st of December, 1864, at Nashville, 6,000 infantry and artillery, and 3,000 cavalry, mostly dismounted. General A. J. Smith's force of about 9,000 men reached Nashville about the same time. Thomas received up to December 14th reinforcements making up a division, placed under command of General Cruft, of over 5,000 men. Hood led against Nashville an army of about 38,000 men, which had been depleted at Franklin and discouraged by its severe losses. He placed Lee's corps in the centre, across the Franklin Turnpike; Cheatham took the right and Stewart the left of the line. Forrest occupied the country between Stewart and the river. Hood at the same time attempted to repair the railroad from Corinth to Decatur, and thence by Pulaski to his rear, for a line of retreat if necessary, and to provide supplies.

Thomas posted his troops upon the heights surrounding Nashville; Smith's divisions on the right; the Fourth Corps, Wood commanding, in the centre; Schofield's Twenty-third Corps on the left. Steedman on his arrival was placed in front of Schofield's left, on the Nolansville Pike, and the next day on the extension of Schofield's line, on the arrival of Wilson's cavalry, who were sent over the river to Edgefield on the north bank. The position of the Confederate army placed Smith's corps obliquely to their line of battle, and the commanding general took advantage of it. He was supported by Schofield, and they successfully captured the field-works of Lee's main lines and reserves, and crushed Stewart's on the left, turning the Confederate flank. On the 15th of December, Wood, with the Fourth Corps, made a successful assault on Hood's right, compelling Cheatham to use all his reserves to prevent a rout. Night put a stop to the fight. During the night Hood withdrew Cheatham from the right to sustain the left which had fallen to the rear of the centre line. The morning of the 16th found Hood's army massed upon the hills back of his former line, with both wings somewhat refused. Thomas sent Wilson to work, unobserved, around the extreme left flank, now thus thrown back. It was 4 P.M. when another general assault was made along the whole line. Wood, on the left, did not meet with success. Smith, on the right, however, broke down the left centre, and not allowing even breathing-time to his troops, pushed them forward, driving the Confederates in wild disorder from the field. Wilson's cavalry in the meantime fell, dismounted, on the rear and flank of the retreating troops of Hood, and increased the confusion and rout. This enabled Wood to join in the pursuit, and all organization was lost in Hood's army as it fled across the country toward Franklin. The necessity for relieving Thomas was thus fully overcome, and the War Department, the President and the people united with General Grant in giving all honor to the successful general, and a generous acknowledgment that the commander at Nashville and his lieutenants knew best the necessities for success and the time to strike. Hood's loss in the battle of Nashville has never been officially stated, and probably was about 4,000 killed and wounded. Thomas captured 4,500 prisoners and 53 pieces of artillery. Among the prisoners were Generals Johnson, Smith, Jackson and Rucker. Thomas lost 3,057, of which less than 400 were killed.

It was Thomas's intention to rest his troops after the battle, but orders from Washington carrying out Grant's plans to finish up the work of conquering the territory claimed by the Confederates, and bringing the war to their very homes, kept his army on the move. The Fourth Corps was ordered to Huntsville, Ala. Generals Schofield, Smith and Wilson were to concentrate at Eastport, Miss. Schofield's Twenty-third Corps, on reaching Clifton, on the Tennessee, was ordered to the Atlantic Coast, where, with the Tenth Corps, under Terry, and the Twenty-third, under Cox, he was to reduce Wilmington, N. C., and advance from that city and from New Berne to Goldsboro' to make a junction with Sherman's forces on their way from Savannah. Wilmington was defended from the sea by Fort Fisher, on Federal Point. It was the last of the Confederate ports open to blockade-runners, Savannah, Charleston and Mobile having been closed. The Federal Government had prepared a naval force—the largest fleet that had ever sailed under its flag—to proceed to the rendezvous, twenty-five miles east of Fort Fisher. The command of the naval force was assigned to Admiral D. D. Porter, and General Grant had selected Godfrey Weitzel as the officer to accompany him, with about 6,500 men from the Army of the James. General Butler as commander of the land forces accompanied the expedition, and insisted on carrying out a scheme to blow up the magazine of the fort by exploding a powder-boat near by. As senior officer, he controlled its operations. On December 13th, the fleet was arranged in a semicircle and opened a bombardment which silenced the fort after two days' firing. The second day 3,000 men under General Weitzel landed, awaiting the explosion, which proved a complete failure, producing no effect. However, the land forces advanced and would probably have captured the place had not General Butler, evidently chagrined at the failure of his scheme, ordered the troops to withdraw, as he was unwilling to sacrifice the lives of his men in an assault on so strong a fort. The failure of Butler's effort produced a profound sensation throughout the North, and the news caused a panic on the Gold and Stock Exchanges of Wall Street, gold commanding a premium of 285 per cent.

DECEMBER, 1864.

Threatening weather prevented the embarking of the troops for Fortress Monroe until the 27th, when General Butler reported the impregnable character of the fort, and the impossibility of carrying it by assault. The vessels not engaged in the blockade were withdrawn to Beaufort to await orders. The Confederates claimed they had driven off the great fleet and gained a decisive victory.

At the suggestion of President Lincoln, Secretary Welles invited General Grant to a military co-operation with the navy, which, he asserted, had already been proved by Admiral Porter to be sure to effect the capture of Fort Fisher. General Terry arrived at Beaufort, N. C., January 8th, 1865, with a co-operative army force. On the 12th, after delays from severe storms, the fleet, accompanied by transports, left Beaufort in three lines, comprising 48 vessels and 5 ironclads, and on the morning of the 13th the first line took position, with the ironclads nearest the fort, and formed a right wing to the array of men-of-war. Line No. 2 took the centre, and Line No. 3 the left wing, and before night all along this line a destructive fire of shot and shell was being poured against Fort Fisher and the woods and land batteries surrounding. Under protection of this fire General Terry had landed 6,000 men and twelve days' provisions on the peninsula two miles north of the fort, and threw up defenses. Early on the morning of the 14th, Admiral Porter detailed 1,600 sailors and 400 marines to accompany the troops in the assault, the sailors to attack the sea face, while the troops assailed the land side. During the day the small gunboats directed their fire against the north front of the fort, to dismount the guns bearing along the intended line of assault. The entire fleet kept up a bombardment until the hour of assault. On the 15th, at 9 A.M., the signal was given—the ships sent their quotas of men on shore. On landing, by some oversight there was no commander, and the men were huddled on the beach in some confusion. The time was being lost, and the several officers commanding the details hastily arranged a plan of action, and organized three divisions, with Cushman, Parker and Selfridge in command—Parker, the senior officer, the ranking

ALFRED H. TERRY.

commander. Soon Lieutenant-commander Breeze came from General Terry carrying the admiral's flag, and assumed command. Parker outranked him, but, out of deference to the admiral's letter, taking second place. At three o'clock the signal came, the vessels changed their guns in the direction of the upper batteries; all the steam-whistles were blown, and the troops dashed ahead, the sailors taking the beach, while the troops pushed through the palisades, now leveled by the vessels' shot, and mounted the parapet. The sailors were subjected to a long march on the low beach under shot and shell from the fort and bastion, and were obliged to retreat to the protection of the pits and trenches. Being armed only with revolvers and cutlasses, the sailors and marines were at a great disadvantage, as the Confederate troops swarmed the parapets of the fort, and with their rifles and musketry easily prevented an assault. They bravely rallied three times, under the personal encouragement of their commanding officers, but failed to gain much ground. The Federal soldiery, however, carried seven of the traverses of the fort with aid of the shells from the *New Ironsides* and Monitors. But they had desperate men to face, for, the Confederates, flanked by a destructive fire of shells, had no alternative but to fight; and the Federals had to abandon traverse after traverse or be killed in their tracks. The vessels kept up the bombardment, however, and General Bragg failing to bring up Hoke's division, which was along the peninsula, and had a march of two miles, exposed to the fire from the Federal gunboats, at ten o'clock resistance in Fort Fisher ceased. The Confederate defenders being out of ammunition, retired to the innermost point of the fort, and such as had means of transportation escaped. A shower of rockets from the Federal fleet illuminated the sky, and proclaimed to the defenders of the other defenses of the entrance to the river that Fort Fisher had fallen. On the next morning, the 16th, soon after sunrise, the magazine of the fort was mysteriously blown up, and over 200 brave men, equally divided between the late opposing forces, were killed. The losses on the side of the Federals in killed and severely wounded were about 700. They took 112 Confederate officers and 1,971 enlisted men prisoners. The remaining defenses on Smith's Island, Fort Caswell, and elsewhere, were burned, and the magazines blown up by the Confederates, on their retiring toward Wilmington. General Sherman had been delayed in his march from Savannah by the rains, and General Bragg opposed the march of General Terry toward Wilmington. General Schofield, on the 17th of February, advanced from Smithfield, and Admiral Porter, having made his way up the river after carefully removing the torpedoes planted to dispute his passage, on the 18th reduced Fort Anderson, situated on the Cape Fear River, half-way to Wilmington. On the 20th and 21st the fleet proceeded slowly up the river, removing torpedoes and obstructions, meeting with and reducing the land batteries. On the 22d the Federal troops fired a national salute in the City of Wilmington, which had been evacuated by General Bragg, and as the day was the anniversary of the birth of Washington, the salute was doubly suggestive.

THROUGH THE CAROLINAS.

GENERAL SHERMAN'S plan before leaving Atlanta was to march from Savannah direct through Columbia, S. C., to Goldsboro', N. C., and as Grant was to extend his lines west of Petersburg and prevent Lee from turning the Army of Northern Virginia against him, his route was selected along the watershed where the streams could be forded; but at this season even these little streams were swollen, and the Confederates did not expect Sherman to move his army during January. They supposed he would compliment the cities of Augusta, Ga., and Charleston, S. C., with a call, and therefore Beauregard and Hardee kept these cities prepared for an attack, instead of concentrating their forces, by evacuating Charleston and Augusta, which they had planned to do early in February, but General Sherman made feints on each to prevent such a design, and conducted his main army, in spite of mud and rain, over corduroy roads nearly the whole distance to Columbia, S. C. This undertaking was accomplished with vast labor, and Sherman's troops were afterward complimented by General Johnston as being "the toughest and most ready army since Julius Cæsar commanded the Roman legions." On the 17th of February the army reached Columbia, having laid waste the country through which they passed, destroying all factories and mills, and sparing only educational and private property. The Confederates burned the cotton in the streets of Columbia on the approach of the Federal army, as they were also prepared to do in both Charleston and Augusta should these cities have been reached. These fires, with possibly the carelessness of the invading army, ignited the buildings, and the city was burned despite the efforts of General Sherman to save it. The commanding general then provisioned and sheltered the homeless inhabitants, and at once pushed his army on to the north, continually skirmishing with small bodies of retiring Confederates, as he had been on the whole march. General Wheeler had drawn from Beauregard, at Augusta, a small force of cavalry, infantry, and some light batteries, and by burning bridges and holding the causeways through the swamps had caused some annoyance; but Sherman's army, with its 2,500 wagons, rolled on.

JANUARY, 1865.

Beauregard left the Georgia Militia to garrison

SHERMAN'S "BUMMERS" FORAGING IN SOUTH CAROLINA.—From a Sketch by J. E. Taylor.

Augusta, and led the remnant of the Army of Tennessee by country roads through Newberry and Chester to Charlotte, N.C. Hardee, still reluctant to give up Charleston to Dahlgren and Foster, who had been so long pounding at its doors, delayed evacuating Fort Sumter and the City of Charleston. On the night of the 17th and morning of the 18th of February, General Lafayette McLaws, who was in command, in the absence of General Hardee, who was on sick leave, received the news of the abandonment of Columbia, and was directed to carry out the instructions as to the evacuation of the fort and city as given by General Beauregard to General Hardee. He withdrew the army and took the railroad, by way of Cheraw, to join Lieutenant-generals Hampton and Beauregard at Greensboro', between which place and Raleigh Beauregard had from the first advised a concentration of all the scattered forces in the Carolinas, as well as the army of General Lee, but which delay of Hardee and want of co-operation from the War Department and General Lee had prevented. General Hardee burned the cotton in the warehouses at Cheraw, and destroyed the powder and ammunition stored there, the explosion resulting in the killing of [illegible] of the inhabitants gathered to witness the fire. General Howard, on

JOHN A. WINSLOW.

the 3d of March, entered the place, driving out Hardee's forces. Hampton's cavalry moved toward Charlotte, and joined Hardee's forces at Fayetteville on the 11th, retreating before Slocum, who entered the place with the Fourteenth (Davis') Corps on that day. Hampton and Kilpatrick had a series of cavalry combats, in which first one and then the other had the advantage. At Fayetteville, Sherman destroyed the arsenal, and here first received news of Schofield's progress against Wilmington.

On February 25th, General Joseph E. Johnston was, by order of General Lee, assigned to the command of the Confederate forces in the Carolinas, General Beauregard continuing, at the request of Johnston, to concentrate the troops and carry out his already advanced plans. General Bragg had retreated from Wilmington with 8,000 men toward Goldsboro' to form a junction with Johnston's army, which he did not accomplish until Sherman had united his forces with Schofield. At Kinston, General Cox with three divisions had, on the 8th inst., to withstand a severe onslaught by General Bragg, with a loss of [illegible] prisoners. On the [illegible]th of March, Sherman's whole army was on its march to Goldsboro', first sending out the left wing up the river as if aiming at Raleigh, thus to delay a speedy concentration of the Confederate forces. General Johnston, fearing for the safety of Raleigh, collected a portion of his forces

FINAL AND TRIUMPHANT ASSAULT ON FORT FISHER, NEAR WILMINGTON, N.C., ON THE EVENING OF JANUARY 15TH, 1865.

BATTLE OF BENTONVILLE, MARCH 19TH, 1865. GENERAL MOWER, COMMANDING FIRST DIVISION, SEVENTEENTH ARMY CORPS, TURNING THE CONFEDERATE LEFT.

CAPTURE OF CONFEDERATE RIFLE-PITS, ON JAMES ISLAND, S. C., FEBRUARY 9TH, 1865, SHORTLY BEFORE THE EVACUATION OF CHARLESTON.

FROM A SKETCH BY W. T. CRANE.

at Smithfield. Hardee moved from Fayetteville to Raleigh, with part of his cavalry on the Goldsboro' Road and part of it on the road leading to Raleigh.

On the 16th, five miles south of Averysboro', Hardee was attacked by Jackson's and Wood's divisions of the Twentieth Corps, with Kilpatrick's cavalry on the right. General Sherman personally conducted the attack. Rhett's brigade, with a battalion of artillery, and Hampton's cavalry, received two successive assaults without losing their line. After several hours' stubborn fighting, Taliaferro's division fell back to the second line, which he held with the aid of McLaws's division, which was intrenched. Hardee, however, being weak on

CITIZENS OF CHARLESTON, S. C., TAKING THE OATH OF ALLEGIANCE SOON AFTER THE EVACUATION OF THE CITY BY GENERAL HARDEE.

SCENE OF THE NEGOTIATIONS BETWEEN GENERALS SHERMAN AND JOHNSTON, APRIL 18TH, 1865.
JAMES BENNETT'S HOUSE, WHERE THE INTERVIEW WAS HELD.—GENERAL KILPATRICK, WITH CONFEDERATE GENERAL HAMPTON AND STAFF, DISCUSSING THE CAMPAIGN.

SHERMAN'S SEVENTEENTH ARMY CORPS CROSSING THE SOUTH EDISTO RIVER ON PONTONS, FEBRUARY 9TH, 1865.

the flank, which was threatened, retired during the night toward Smithfield. Johnston, at the commencement of this occurrence, to avoid any misunderstanding, announced Beauregard as second in command to himself, and in the conduct of the defensive operations had his full confidence and advice. As the forces of S. D. Lee, B. F. Cheatham, and the cavalry of Generals Butler and Wheeler, were not present at the battle of Averysboro', Johnston decided to concentrate his forces and strike a blow. Sherman's army, by reason of the heavy rains and bad roads, had become much strung out, and Johnston, under cover of the cavalry of Hampton, gathered his army at Bentonsville. He mustered 15,000 strong, Cheatham, with 2,000 men, and Wheeler's and Butler's cavalry, not coming up in time. Within a day's march of him was Slocum with the Federal left wing, while Sherman was with his right wing, extended to open communication with Schofield. On the morning of the 19th, two divisions of Davis's Fourteenth Corps were eight miles from Bentonsville. Two divisions of Williams's Twentieth Corps were eight miles further to the rear. Kilpatrick was to the left and rear of Williams. Howard, with four divisions, was six to ten miles to the southward, on a parallel road. The trains with their guards were still in the rear of Howard. Sherman, who believed Johnston to be concentrating his troops at Raleigh to defend the capital, was anxious to reach Goldsboro' and cooperate with Schofield, supposing the left amply able to take care of Hardee. Johnston knew the exact location of both the Federal armies, and struck at Bentonsville, hoping to overwhelm Sherman's left, and then attack his right by the flank before a junction with Schofield could be made.

Davis's corps encountered Hampton's cavalry on the morning of the 19th, and Hardee opened the battle, forcing Davis back. Slocum ordered the Twentieth Corps to his support, in the meantime falling back about a mile, losing three guns before the Twentieth came up. Then Slocum took the offensive, the

MARCH, 1865.

Confederates maintaining their ground until dark. Sherman's troops were unaccustomed to defeat, and fought with desperate energy, successively capturing and retiring from the same line of breastworks. During the night Sherman sent reinforcements from the right wing, and Howard, Logan and Kilpatrick had come up. The Fifteenth Corps was ordered to move down from Goldsboro' and threaten Johnston's left flank and rear. On the 20th and 21st, Sherman was on the field, and finding Johnston's intention to maintain his strongly-fortified position until he could carry off his wounded and open the way of retreat to Smithfield, he drew his lines together and pressed the Confederate position. On the 21st, after noon, the extreme right of Sherman's line, under General Mower, succeeded in gaining Johnston's rear, and was attacked by Wheeler's cavalry and Cheatham's division, under Lowry, which had just come up. Howard had not been apprised of the intended movement, and did not support Mower until he heard the firing, when he

SHERMAN'S SEVENTEENTH ARMY CORPS ENTERING CHERAW, S. C., AND DRIVING OUT THE CONFEDERATES.

Phil. H. Sheridan

CAPTAIN H. M. BRAGG, OF GENERAL GILLMORE'S STAFF, RAISING THE FLAG OVER FORT SUMTER, FEBRUARY 18TH, 1865, ON A TEMPORARY STAFF FORMED OF AN OAR AND BOAT-HOOK.

From a Sketch by W. T. Crane.

ordered Blair to the right, and advanced Logan's line to make a strong demonstration in the front. Logan's men intrenched within fifty yards of Bragg's line. Sherman, however, ordered Mower back, as he did not want to take the risk of a general engagement in the swamps and he felt sure Johnston must retreat and give him the opportunity to unite his whole army in the open country north of the Neuse, with chance of better success with less loss of life. Johnston retired on the night of the 21st, and Sherman resumed his march on the 22d. Schofield entered Goldsboro' on the 21st. Terry reached the Neuse on the same day, and laid a pontoon-bridge. On the 23d, Sherman rode into Goldsboro', bringing together a combined army now numbering about 90,000. The Federal army had lost at Averysboro' and Bentonville, 1,604 men, of which 1,196 were in Slocum's command. The Confederates, according to General Beauregard's "Military Operations," put their total loss at 2,343.

Stoneman's cavalry operated about Greensboro' and on the Danville Railroad, keeping Wheeler and Beauregard on the alert to prevent the destruction of Lee's lines of retreat. Lee on the 3d of April evacuated Richmond, intending to take temporary refuge at Danville.

The line of Confederate defences around Petersburg was broken on the 2d of April in the morning, and the troops fell back to their inner works, and, simultaneously with the troops in Richmond, evacuated the city. President Davis removed to Danville and awaited the arrival of Lee and his force, and with no news from him for several days, fearing for the safety of the temporary seat of Government, he sent for Beauregard, who, with Johnston, was equally ignorant of the whereabouts of the Army of Northern Virginia. On April 9th all the plans of concentration of the armies of the Confederacy for a final stand, so long advocated by Beauregard, were frustrated by the surrender of General Lee. President Davis, his Cabinet and Government officials, left Danville for Greensboro, N. C., where they learned of the desperate situation of Johnston's army; of the advance of the Federal cavalry under Wilson, on Selma and Montgomery; of the capture of Mobile; of the movements through Mississippi, and the hopeless condition of the Confederacy. President Davis proposed keeping up the conflict and marching the remnant of the army to join Kirby Smith across the Mississippi. The

APRIL, 1865.

Beauregard and Johnston both discouraged, and accepting the inevitable, prepared to make the best terms possible with

SURPRISED ON PICKET

THE ROAD TO ANDERSONVILLE

CAMP SUMTER
ANDERSONVILLE PRISON 1864

SURPRISED ON PICKET
THE ROAD TO ANDERSONVILLE
CAMP SUMTER
ANDERSONVILLE PRISON 1864
IN THE PEN
FORT SUMTER
CHARLESTON
THE EXCHANGE 1864

CAPTAIN H.

ordered Blair to the right
line to make a strong dem
Logan's men intrenched
Bragg's line. Sherman, l
back, as he did not wan
general engagement in the
Johnston must retreat and
nity to unite his whole ar
north of the Neuse, with
with less loss of life. Jo
night of the 21st, and Sher
on the 22d. Schofield on
21st. Terry reached the
and laid a ponton-bridge.
rode into Goldsboro', bring
army now numbering abo
army had lost at Avery
1,604 men, of which 1,196

LIBBY PRISON, RICHMOND, VA.

GENERAL SCHOFIELD'S ARMY ON ITS MARCH TOWARD GOLDSBORO', N.C.—CONFEDERATE WORKS IN THE REAR OF WILMINGTON.

Sherman, and stop the war. On the 13th, Raleigh was occupied by General Sherman, and on the same day President Davis dictated, Mr. Mallory wrote down, and General Johnston signed, a letter,* which was intrusted to Lieutenant-general Wade Hampton, and delivered to General Sherman the succeeding day, opening negotiations for peace.

General Sherman's answer, dated the 14th of April, reached General Johnston on the 16th:

"I have this moment received your communication of this date. I am fully empowered to arrange with you any terms for the suspension of further hostilities between the armies commanded by you and those commanded by myself, and will be willing to confer with you to that end. I will limit the advance of my main column to-morrow to Morrisville, and the cavalry to the University, and expect that you will also maintain the present position of your forces until each has notice of a failure to agree.

"That a basis of action may be had, I undertake to abide by the same terms and conditions as were made by Generals Grant and Lee at Appomattox Court House, on the 9th inst., relative to our two armies; and furthermore to obtain from General Grant an order to suspend the movements of any troops from the direction of Virginia. General Stoneman is under my command, and my order will suspend any devastation or destruction contemplated by him. I will add that I really desire to save the people of North Carolina the damage they would sustain by the march of this army through the central or western parts of the state."

* "The results of the recent campaign in Virginia have changed the relative military condition of the belligerents. I am therefore induced to address you in this form the inquiry, whether, in order to stop the further effusion of blood and devastation of property, you are willing to make a temporary suspension of active operations, and to communicate to Lieutenant-general Grant, commanding the armies of the United States, the request that he will take like action in regard to other armies, the object being to permit the civil authorities to enter into the needful arrangements to terminate the existing war."

BATTLE NEAR KINSTON, N. C. MARCH 8TH, 1865

BLOWING OUT THE BULKHEAD OF THE DUTCH GAP CANAL

From a Sketch by J. E. Taylor.

In view of the assurances given by General Sherman, Hardee was ordered to halt his command, and an order to suspend movements was extended to all the commands without explanation. The suspense made the men uneasy, and fearing they would be soon surrendered, the Confederate troops did not wait for permission, but thousands of them, especially in the cavalry, started for "home."

Through the instrumentality of General Hampton, Sherman and Johnston met at noon, on the 17th, at Durham Station; but it was the next day before the negotiations were drawn up, accepted and signed by the two commanders:

"Memorandum of basis of agreement made this 18th day of April, A. D. 1865, near Durham Station, in the State of North Carolina, by and between General Joseph E. Johnston, commanding the Confederate army, and Major-general William T. Sherman, commanding the army of the United States in North Carolina, both present.

"1st. The contending armies now in the field to maintain the *status quo* until notice is given by the commanding general of any one to its opponent, and reasonable time—say forty eight (48) hours allowed.

"2d. The Confederate armies now in existence to be disbanded and conducted to their several State capitals, there to deposit their arms and public property in the State Arsenal; and each officer and man to execute and file an agreement to cease from acts of war, and to abide the action of the State and Federal authority. The number of arms and munitions of war to be reported to the Chief of Ordnance, at Washington City, subject to the future action of the Congress of the United States, and, in the meantime, to be used solely to maintain peace and order within the borders of the States respectively.

"3d. The recognition, by the Executive of the United States, of the several State Governments, on their officers and Legislatures taking the oaths prescribed by the Constitution of the United States, and, where conflicting State Governments have resulted from the war, the legitimacy of all shall be submitted to the Supreme Court of the United States.

"4th. The re-establishment of all the Federal Courts in the several States, with powers as defined by the Constitution and laws of Congress.

"5th. The people and inhabitants of all the States to be guaranteed, so far as the Executive can, their political rights and franchises, as well as their rights of person and property, as defined by the Constitution of the United States and of the States respectively.

"6th. The Executive authority of the Government of the United States not to disturb any of the people by reason of the late war, so long as they live in peace and quiet, abstain from acts of armed hostility, and obey the laws in existence at the place of their residence.

"7th. In general terms, the war to cease; a general amnesty, so far as the Executive of the United States can command, on condition of the disbandment of the Confederate armies, the disposition of the arms, and the resumption of peaceful pursuits by the officers and men hitherto composing said armies.

"Not being fully empowered by our respective principals to fulfill these terms, we individually and officially pledge ourselves to promptly obtain the necessary authority, and to carry out the above programme.

"J. E. JOHNSTON,

"*General Commanding Confederate States Army in North Carolina.*"

"W. T. SHERMAN,

"*Major-general Commanding Army of the United States in North Carolina.*"

Beauregard carried a copy of the agreement to President Davis, at Greensboro', on the 19th, who, however, had gone to Charlotte without waiting for the conclusion of the conference. Five days elapsed without a decision from the Confederate President. General Johnston, from Greensboro', published General Order No. 14, suspending operations pending negotiations between the two Governments. A like order was issued by General Sherman On the 24th, President Davis

GEORGE CROOK.

approved the action of General Johnston. On the same day General Sherman received from Secretary Stanton instructions overruling the judgment of the general commanding, and ordering him to confine his agreement to the unconditional surrender of the military forces of General Johnston. President Lincoln had just been assassinated, and the Secretary of War and President Johnson, with overstraining and embittered zeal, destroyed the work of peace attempted by General Sherman. On the 26th the opposing generals met at the same place, and at Bennett's house concluded the final surrender of the Confederate forces in North Carolina on the terms accorded to General Lee by General Grant at Appomattox. As the Confederate Government had abandoned Generals Johnston and Beauregard, and could not be reached for consultation or advice, the surrender of their army to General Sherman on these terms was a purely military act, and effectually ended the existence of the Army of the Confederate States of America.

GEORGE A. CUSTER.

BORN in Ohio in 1840; graduated at the United States Military Academy, West Point, in 1861; lieutenant-colonel, Seventh Cavalry, July 28th, 1866; and brigadier-general, United States Volunteers, April 15th, 1865. He served in the Civil War in the Manassas campaign, 1861, engaged at Bull Run; in the Virginia Peninsula, 1862, engaged at Yorktown, and aide-de-camp to Major-general McClellan in the subsequent operations of the campaign; in the Maryland campaign, 1862, engaged at South Mountain and Antietam; in the Rappahannock campaign, 1863, engaged on "Stoneman's raid" and at Brandy Station; in Pennsylvania campaign, 1863, engaged at Gettysburg and various minor actions; in operations in Central Virginia, 1863-64, engaged in numerous skirmishes, etc.; in the Richmond campaign, 1864, engaged at the Wilderness, Todd's Tavern, Yellow Tavern, Meadow Bridge, Hawe's Store, Cold Harbor, Trevillian Station, etc.; in the Shenandoah campaign, 1864-65, engaged at Opequan and Cedar Creek. About this time was breveted brigadier-general, U. S. Volunteers. He was in command of the cavalry division in the pursuit of Lee's army, 1865; engaged at Dinwiddie Court House, Five Forks, Sailor's Creek and Appomattox. Being breveted major-general, he commanded the cavalry division in the Military Division of the Southwest and Gulf, 1865; as chief of cavalry in the Department of Texas, 1865-66. After the war he was on Western frontier duty, and was killed, June 25th, 1876, with a part of his command, by Sioux Indians, under Sitting Bull, in the battle of the Little Big Horn.

GEORGE CROOK.

BORN near Dayton, O., September 8th, 1828; graduated at West Point, July, 1852, as brevet-second-lieutenant, Fourth Infantry; July 7th, 1853, second-lieutenant; March 11th, 1856, first lieutenant; May 4th, 1861, captain, Fourth Infantry; July 18th, 1866, major, Third Infantry; July 28th, 1866, lieutenant-colonel, Twenty-third Infantry; October 29th, 1873, brigadier-general in the Regular Army. In the Volunteer service he entered the War as colonel of the Thirty-sixth Ohio Regiment, September 13th, 1861; made brigadier-general, September 7th, 1862, for gallant and meritorious service in the field, brevet-major-general, July 18th, 1864; major general, October 21st, 1864; mustered out of the Volunteer service, January 15th, 1866.

General Crook's Civil War record is a succession of promotions gained on the battlefield. In 1861-2, in the operations in West Virginia, wounded at Lewisburg (breveted major). In 1862 was in the Northern Virginia campaign; engaged at South Mountain and Antietam (brevet-lieutenant-colonel). In 1862-63, in West Virginia. In 1863, in the Tennessee campaign, engaged at Tullahoma, Hoover's Gap, Chickamauga, and in pursuit of Wheeler (brevet-colonel). In 1864, in Northern Virginia, in pursuit of Early, and constant raids (brevet-brigadier-general, Regular Army, and brevet major-general of Volunteers). In Sheridan's Shenandoah campaign, 1864, engaged at Berryville, Fisher's Hill (brevet-major-general, Regular Army); Strasburg, Opequan and Cedar Creek. In command of the cavalry of the Army of the Potomac, 1865; engaged at Dinwiddie Court House, Jettersville, Sailor's Creek, Farmville and Appomattox Court House, and in command of the District of Wilmington, N. C., 1865-66. Since the War he has been prominently engaged in quelling disturbances with the Indians, and has gained the respect of the leading chiefs of all the Indian tribes, many of whom he has met and defeated on the battlefield. General Crook is probably better informed as to the true policy in managing these "wards of the nation" than any other civil or military officer in the United States.

He is now (1885) in command of the Department of Arizona.

GEORGE A. CUSTER.

THE FEDERAL ARMY [illegible]

THE FALL OF RICHMOND AND SURRENDER OF LEE

We must now go back to the operations of the Army of the Potomac, under the personal leadership of General Grant. Sheridan had, on the 27th of February, left Winchester and pushed up the Shenandoah Valley with 10,000 cavalry. Early, with 2,500 men, still hovered over the Valley, and at Waynesboro', March 3d, made an effort to dispute the progress of Sheridan. He was broken in pieces, losing two-thirds of his army, artillery-train and colors. Sheridan then passed to Charlottesville,

PRESIDENT LINCOLN RIDING THROUGH RICHMOND, APRIL 4TH, 1865, IMMEDIATELY AFTER THE EVACUATION OF THE CITY BY GENERAL LEE

FROM A SKETCH BY JOSEPH BECKER

destroying the railroads to Richmond and Lynchburg, and burning the two large bridges. He made a demonstration toward Lynchburg, intending to join Sherman southwest of Danville, and cut off Lee's escape; but, finding the river swollen and bridges destroyed, he decided to strike across the country to White House, and effect a junction with General Grant before Petersburg. He reached White House on the 19th of March, rested and refitted, and on the 24th marched across the Peninsula to James River, and on the 27th joined the army before Petersburg, where the meditative Grant sat, silent, in his wooden tent, awaiting his time to complete the destruction of the Confederate army—and end the War.

On the morning of the 25th of March, General Lee carried into effect an effort to break through Grant's left flank, and open a retreat to join Johnston. Fort Steadman was the point of attack selected. General John B. Gordon led the two divisions in the advance, General Lee holding all the remaining available troops (about 20,000) ready to support. The Confederate troops, with the mist of the morning to cover their movements, gained the ground in front of the fort, and, with a rush, surprised and captured the guns and part of the Fourteenth New York Foot-artillerists and of the Third Brigade, First Division, Ninth Corps. Those who escaped capture were thoroughly routed. The captured guns were then turned on the neighboring Federal troops, and the Ninth, Tenth and Eleventh Batteries were soon occupied by the Confederates. The Federal works were, however, so planned, that the capture of one line exposed the occupants to the fire from both flanking works. But General Gordon, not being promptly supported, lost his advantage, as a counter assault, led by Hartranft's division, drove the Confederates back, and exposed them to the rain of fire from the commanding batteries, and 2,000 men surrendered rather than to submit themselves to the deadly peril. The loss on each side was about 2,500.

Lee's plan was well conceived, but the Army of Northern Virginia had lost its prowess, and its leader could no longer command its obedience to his will.

General Grant had, when he went into winter quarters, fixed upon the 29th of March as the date on which to resume the campaign against Lee. He determined to throw his whole available force, including Sheridan's army and the Army of the James, now commanded by General Ord, against Lee's right, leaving a sufficient force in the forts on the Richmond side of the James to prevent their ready capture and to deter Longstreet from leaving their front to support Lee. The Ninth Corps was used as the pivot to the manœuvre. Early on the morning of the 29th, Warren and Humphreys moved their corps to the rear and left, passed Hatcher's Run, and then faced northward to lead the advance. Lee's intrenched line ran southwest from Petersburg, across and west of Hatcher's Run along the White Oak Road, thus covering the South Side Railroad. Four miles farther west of this intrenched front a detached line along White Oak Road covered Five Forks—a point of strategic importance. Warren pursued his advance march, driving the Confederate skirmishers before him; and, when about two miles from the position of Lee, Griffin's division was assailed by a line of battle. Chamberlain's brigade bore the brunt of the conflict, and repulsed the Confederates, who left their dead and wounded and 160 prisoners in his hands. The Federals lost 370 killed and wounded. Warren pressed on, and soon drew the fire from the

THE LAST NIGHT BOMBARDMENT OF PETERSBURG, VA

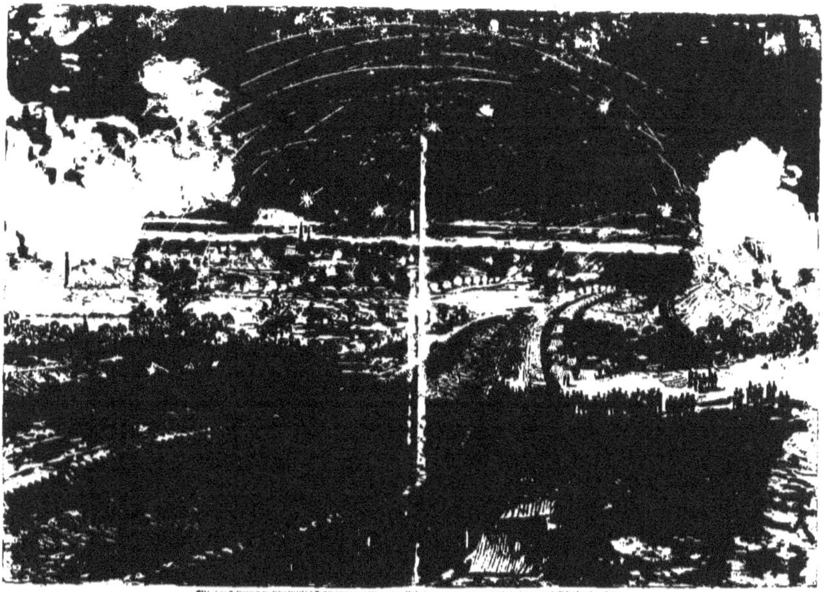

THE LAST NIGHT BOMBARDMENT OF PETERSBURG, VA., [illegible] 186[illegible], PREPARATORY TO A GENERAL ASSAULT.

VIEW OF RICHMOND, VA., FROM THE PRISON CAMP ON BELLE ISLE, JAMES RIVER

JEFFERSON DAVIS, UNDER ARREST, ENTERING AN AMBULANCE, EN ROUTE FOR FORTRESS MONROE.

From a Sketch by One of his Captors.

intrenched line on the White Oak Road. Humphreys, on the right of Warren, pushed through a dense wood, and reached the enemy's front just as the night stopped further progress; Sheridan, meanwhile, advancing still further to the left, and occupying Dinwiddie Court House in the evening. This was six miles southwest of, and detached from, Warren and Humphreys's position. The line of Grant now extended from Appomattox to Dinwiddie Court House, in the order from right to left: Parke, Wright, Ord, Humphreys, Warren, Sheridan. On the morning of the 30th, Sheridan was to cut loose from this line, and operate against the South Side and Danville Railroad. Grant, however, directed Sheridan to stay on the line, and wrote him as follows: "I now feel like ending the matter, if it is possible to do so, before going back. I do not want you, therefore, to cut loose and go after the enemy's roads at present. In the morning, push around the enemy, and get on to his right rear. We will act all together as one army here, until it is seen what can be done with the enemy." General Lee, in the meantime, had been fully alive to the intention of Grant, and he was too good a soldier not to prepare for the assault by strengthening his right and defending the lines on which he depended for his daily supply of food. From left to right he had thirty-five miles of breastworks to guard, with less than 35,000 muskets. Grant had deceived him as to the troops in front of Longstreet and Mahone, and he did not disturb them; Lee, however, drew from Wilcox, Pickett, Bushrod Johnson, and Gordon, all he dared, and with 15,000 men he hurried to defend his right. In the Petersburg intrenchments he left 5,000 men strung out like sentinels along nine miles of breastworks. Fitzhugh Lee's cavalry took, during the night, position in front of Warren and Humphreys's corps, where darkness had halted them. The night was dark, and a heavy rain set in, and continued throughout the next day (the 30th). The swampy ground was flooded, the roads

SHERMAN'S "BUMMERS" PASSING GENERAL AUGUR'S HEADQUARTERS, WASHINGTON, D. C., MAY [illegible], 1865.

From a Sketch by J. E. Taylor.

GRAND REVIEW OF THE ARMIES OF THE UNITED STATES, AT WASHINGTON, D. C., MAY 23D, 1

FROM A SKE

GRAND REVIEW OF THE ARMIES OF THE UNITED STATES AT WASHINGTON, D. C., MAY 23d, 1865—TROOPS MARCHING UP PENNSYLVANIA AVENUE BEFORE PASSING THE REVIEWING STAND

were impassable, and the aggressive movement planned for that day had to be suspended. Lee's infantry could tramp through mud and rain, as it was unincumbered by wagon-trains or artillery, and the delay enabled the Confederate commander to complete preparations for Grant's onslaught. All the Federal commander could do was to advance the Second Corps close to the front of the Confederate line. The 31st still found an advance impracticable; and while Grant waited, Lee precipitated the action by falling on Warren's corps, occupying the extreme left, and having no cavalry to protect its flanks—Sheridan being six miles further to the left. Warren, however, disposed his troops in masses, *en échelons*, so that they could be prepared for attack from any quarter. To further secure his position, Warren threw forward Winthrop's brigade as skirmishers to get possession of the White Oak Road and develop the strength and movements of Lee. The Confederate general anticipated the movement, and at half-past ten fell heavily on Warren, from both the north and west. Ayres's troops, in the thick woods, at once gave way, and, falling on Crawford's division, disorganized that command, which, too, broke. On gaining the clear ground, encouraged by Griffin's division, they re-formed, and soon checked the Confederate onset. Miles's division, of Humphreys's corps, came to the assistance of Warren, posted on his right, and assailed the Confederate left flank, while Warren attacked the front and drove the soldiers of Lee back to their original line.

Lee now prepared to oppose the advance of Sheridan, who, with Devin's division, and Davies's, Smith's and Gregg's brigades, of Crook's division, had occupied Five Forks, threatening Lee's line of supplies and the safety of his right flank. Two divisions of infantry, under Pickett and Bushrod Johnson, fell upon Sheridan and drove him out of Five Forks, and back toward Dinwiddie Court House. Sheridan was at a disadvantage, as the range of the Confederate rifles baffled the cavalry, who were forced to dismount and take refuge behind hastily-constructed breastworks, when they returned the fire with their carbines until night relieved them. Warren hastened to the succor of the cavalry; but the Confederates having destroyed the bridge over Gravelly Run, Ayres was obliged to halt and build an infantry bridge. This occupied until 2 A.M. of April 1st. In the meantime Lee, finding it imprudent to maintain his ground, as he was out of position for the defense of the Confederate line, and also menaced by Warren's corps, withdrew to Five Forks. Sheridan followed at early dawn, and Warren's two divisions met him across the country, midway between Dinwiddie Court House and Five Forks, at 7 A.M., April 1st. Warren was by this disposition under Sheridan's orders.

This movement left the Confederate line, from Appomattox to Hatcher's Run, sparsely defended, as the calls for troops to strengthen the right flank left but one man to every five yards of breastworks. Parke's, Wright's, Ord's and Humphreys's corps had been unbroken, and thus confronted the Confederate line. It was surely no military necessity to fight the battle of Five Forks to gain possession of Petersburg; but Grant and Sheridan cared more to capture or destroy Lee's army, and prevent its escape to join Johnston, thus to capture and occupy a city. Sheridan used the cavalry as a mask, behind which he manœuvred the infantry, thus avoiding the peril his first occupation of Five Forks developed. He directed Merritt to demonstrate against the Confederate right, while Warren

PRESIDENT JOHNSON, LIEUTENANT-GENERAL GRANT AND SECRETARY STANTON REVIEWING SHERMAN'S ARMY, ON PENNSYLVANIA AVENUE WASHINGTON, D. C., MAY 24TH, 1865.—SHERMAN SALUTING AT THE HEAD OF HIS STAFF.

FROM A PHOTOGRAPH BY BRADY.

brought the full pressure of the infantry against the left. McKenzie was sent to prevent reinforcements from Petersburg, and Warren, at 4 P.M., advanced to attack the left wing of the Confederates, while the cavalry enveloped their front and right, and gained their rear. The Confederate forces with desperate valor met the double onset; but Warren sweeping down toward the White Oak Road, and simultaneously the cavalry charging the road with resistless force, and carrying the centre, as he had carried the left, the Confederates, assailed in front, flank and rear, threw down their guns. Two divisions remained, and continued the combat. The gallant Warren, seeing his men fire without advancing on the new line, dashed forward, calling on those near him to follow, and led the van of the rushing lines. Within a few feet of the breastworks his horse was shot under him, and the gallant Colonel Richardson, of the Seventh Wisconsin, seeing the danger, sprang between his beloved commander and the enemy, and while himself wounded, saved from hurt the victorious leader of the Fifth Corps.

enable darkness to cover his purpose to abandon Petersburg and Richmond.

Lee retired the whole Confederate front by the north bank of the Appomattox River, and at Chesterfield Court House was joined by the army holding the front at Bermuda Hundred, when the whole Confederate army headed westward, and before dawn of Monday, April 3d, had put sixteen miles between it and Grant's forces at Petersburg. When the morning mists lifted from the city, its evacuation was discovered. On the same gray morning General Weitzel beheld the sky above Richmond lighted with a lurid glare, accompanied with rapid explosions; and, throwing forward his cavalry, it entered undisputed into the city and hoisted its flag on the Capitol.

Lee's army reached Amelia Court House, thirty-eight miles west of Richmond, on April 4th, and found that the commissary stores ordered there had, by the mistaking of an order by President Davis, been sent to Richmond, and destroyed in the conflagration. This forced Lee to forage for provisions, and delayed his retreat, thus giving Sheridan time

the Army of Northern Virginia in this struggle. I feel that it is so, and regard it as my duty to shift from myself the responsibility of any further effusion of blood, by asking of you the surrender of that portion of the Confederate States army known as the Army of Northern Virginia.

"U. S. GRANT, *Lieutenant-general.*"

"*General R. E. Lee.*"

The same evening Lee replied as follows:

"GENERAL: I have received your note of this date. Though not entertaining the opinion you express on the hopelessness of further resistance on the part of the Army of Northern Virginia, I reciprocate your desire to avoid useless effusion of blood, and, therefore, before considering your proposition, ask the terms you will offer on condition of its surrender.

"R. E. LEE, *General.*"

"*Lieutenant-general U. S. Grant.*"

Before Grant received this communication, Lee had, by rapid marching all night, put a considerable distance between the opposing armies.

"APRIL 8TH, 1865.

"GENERAL: Your note of last evening, in reply to mine of the same date, asking the condition on which I will accept the surrender of the Army of Northern Virginia, is just received. In reply, I would say that *peace* being my great desire, there is but one condition I would insist upon,

VOLUNTARY DISPERSION OF KIRBY SMITH'S ARMY AT SHREVEPORT, LA., MAY 26th, 1865.

A cavalry charge completed the rout, and the remnant of Pickett's and Johnson's divisions fled, pursued many miles westward by Merritt and McKenzie. Above 5,000 prisoners were taken, of which number 3,244 were captured by the Fifth Corps. The Federal cavalry lost but a few hundred men, and the infantry 634 killed and wounded. Immediately after the battle Sheridan suspended Warren, and placed the Fifth Corps under Griffin.

As the battle of Five Forks closed, the army in front of Petersburg opened a furious night bombardment, and from all along the Federal lines the shells and bombs, bursting over the doomed city, illuminated the sky, a pæan to victory. The bombardment was kept up from nightfall of the 1st of April until four o'clock on the morning of the 2d, when Parke, Wright and Ord assaulted the Confederate lines from the Appomattox to Hatcher's Run. After desperately defending their successive works, the Confederates were finally driven within the inner lines of defense around Petersburg. General A. P. Hill, in an unsuccessful charge with Heth's division against the Ninth Corps, lost his life, and with it the Army of Northern Virginia struck its last blow in defense of Richmond, as Lee only maintained his position to

to come up with 18,000 cavalry, against which the Confederate chieftain could not hope to successfully make a stand. On the night of the 5th Lee moved from Amelia Court House. Grant's whole army was in full pursuit. The Confederate foragers were captured, and Sheridan and Custer kept up a running battle during the 5th and 6th; and although the army of Lee made many and determined stands, and contested the ground inch by inch in its retreat, the chances of escape grew less and less, and on the 7th of April General Grant opened communication with Lee, who, while Grant was awaiting a reply, kept up his retreat, and thus gained a night's march. On the 8th Grant continued the pursuit. Sheridan gained Appomattox Station, and cut off Lee's supplies, as well as his way of escape, and on the 9th General Lee requested a suspension of hostilities and an interview with General Grant.

The following is the correspondence exchanged between Generals Grant and Lee. General Grant, believing that Lee's chances of escape were now utterly hopeless, wrote from Farmville:

"APRIL 7TH, 1865.

"GENERAL: The result of the last week must convince you of the hopelessness of further resistance on the part of

namely: that the men and officers surrendered shall be disqualified for taking up arms again against the Government of the United States until properly exchanged. I will meet you, or will designate officers to meet any officers you might name for the same purpose, at any point agreeable to you, for the purpose of arranging definitely the terms upon which the surrender of the Army of Northern Virginia will be received.

"U. S. GRANT, *Lieutenant-general.*"

"*General R. E. Lee.*"

General Grant had in the meantime renewed the pursuit, and Sheridan was about to close the only means of escape left to Lee—that toward Lynchburg. Lee, nevertheless, replied as follows:

"APRIL 8TH, 1865.

"GENERAL: I received at a late hour your note of to-day. In mine of yesterday I did not intend to propose the surrender of the Army of Northern Virginia, but to ask the terms of your propositions. To be frank, *I do not think the emergency has arisen to call for the surrender of this army*, but, as the restoration of peace should be the sole object of all, I desired to know whether your proposals would lead to that end. I cannot, therefore, meet you with a view to surrender the Army of Northern Virginia, but as far as your proposal may affect the Confederate States forces under my command, and tend to the restoration of peace, I should be pleased to meet you at 10 A.M., to-morrow, on the old stage road to Richmond, between the picket lines of the two armies.

"R. E. LEE, *General.*"

"*Lieutenant-general Grant.*"

Grant, receiving this about midnight, replied in the morning in these terms:

"April 9th, 1865.

"General: Your note of yesterday is received. I have no authority to treat on the subject of peace; the meeting proposed for 10 A. M. to-day could lead to no good. I will state, however, general, that I am equally anxious for peace with yourself, and the whole North entertains the same feeling. The terms upon which peace can be had are well understood. By the South laying down their arms they will hasten that most desirable event, save thousands of human lives, and hundreds of millions of property not yet destroyed. Seriously hoping that all our difficulties may be settled without the loss of another life, I subscribe myself, etc.,

"U. S. Grant, *Lieutenant-general.*"

"*General R. E. Lee.*"

Before Lee received this, he attempted, as his only means of escape, to cut his way through Sheridan's lines. In the meantime the Army of the James was ready to attack in front, while the Army of the Potomac would strike the rear. Gordon's troops impetuously charged to carry out Lee's design, and met with apparent success until the Federal infantry arrived, when the tide of battle speedily turned, Sheridan's order to charge being met by a white flag, with a letter from General Lee asking for an interview with General Grant. The chieftains met soon after, and the following correspondence was the outcome of the meeting:

"Appomattox Court House, Va.,

"April 9th, 1865.

"General: In accordance with the substance of my letter to you of the 8th instant, I propose to receive the surrender of the Army of Northern Virginia on the following terms—to wit: Rolls of all the officers and men to be made in duplicate, one copy to be given to an officer designated by me, the other to be retained by such officer or officers as you may designate. The officers to give their individual paroles not to take up arms against the United States until properly exchanged; and each company or regimental commander to sign a like parole for the men of their commands. The arms, artillery, and public property to be parked and stacked, and turned over to the officers appointed by me to receive them. This will not embrace the side-arms of the officers, nor their private horses or baggage. This done, each officer and man will be allowed to return to his home, not to be disturbed by United States authority so long as they observe their paroles and the laws in force where they may reside.

"U. S. Grant, *Lieutenant general.*"

"*General R. E. Lee.*"

"Headquarters

"Army of Northern Virginia,

"April 9th, 1865.

"General: I have received your letter of this date containing the terms of surrender of the Army of Northern Virginia as proposed by you. As they are substantially the same as those expressed in your letter of the 8th instant, they are accepted. I will proceed to designate the proper officers to carry the stipulations into effect.

"Robert E. Lee."

"*Lieutenant-general U. S. Grant.*"

The news of the surrender soon spread through both armies and all along the lines. The long looked-for time, "When this cruel war is over," was believed to have come. General Lee rode along his lines, with tears mingling with those of his gallant soldiers. His choked utterance, "Men, we have fought through the war together; I have done the best that I could for you," recalled Manassas, Fredericksburg, Chancellorsville, and Cold Harbor, as examples of his *best.*

Three days after the surrender—days of peace—no martial array—no fear of surprise—no call to arms—victors sharing their rations with vanquished around a common camp-fire—Lee's army marched by divisions to the field near Appomattox Court House, stacked their arms and deposited their accoutrements. Less than 8,000 men presented themselves with musket in hand; 18,000 were capitulated unarmed; paroles were given to each, and the Army of Northern Virginia ceased to exist. The Federal troops retraced their steps to Richmond, where they welcomed President Lincoln on his visit to the fallen Confederate capital, and soon after were transferred to Washington, where, with the Army of the West, they passed in review before the President and his Cabinet, who, with foreign representatives and a vast concourse of people, received the victorious soldiers of our Civil War, and bid them god-speed to their several homes, there to be welcomed once again as citizens who had won for a common country the peace for which they fought.

* * * * * *

Note.—In "Around the World with General Grant," by John Russell Young, published by the American News Company, Mr. Young relates a conversation with General Grant, while sailing over a calm sea and nearing the shores of Japan, from which, by permission of the publishers, we extract the following:*

"On the night before Lee's surrender," said General Grant, "I had a wretched headache—one of the headaches to which I have been subject—nervous prostration, intense personal suffering. But suffer or not, I had to keep moving. I clearly saw, especially after Sheridan had cut off the escape to Danville, that Lee must surrender, or break and run into the mountains—break in all directions and leave us a dozen guerrilla bands to fight. The object of my campaign was not Richmond, not the defeat of Lee in actual fight, but to remove him and his army out of the contest, and, if possible, to have him use his influence in inducing the surrender of Johnston and the other isolated armies. You see, the war was an enormous strain upon the country. Rich as we were, I do not now see how we could have endured it another year, even from a financial point of view. So with these views I

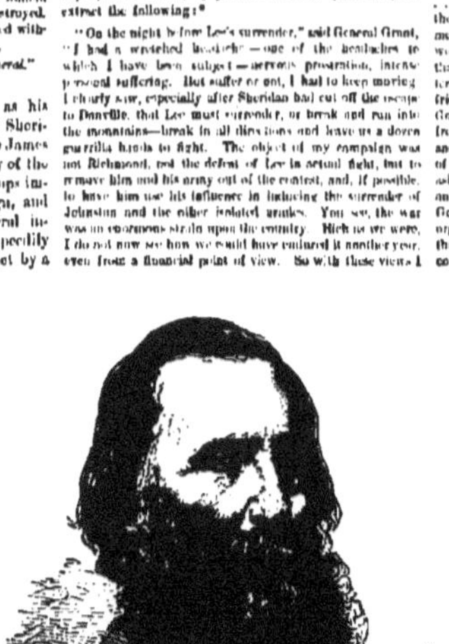

JAMES LONGSTREET.

wrote Lee, and opened the correspondence with which the world is familiar. Lee does not appear well in that correspondence, not nearly so well as he did in our subsequent interviews, when his whole bearing was that of a patriotic and gallant soldier, concerned alone for the welfare of his army and his State. I received word that Lee would meet me at a point within our lines, near Sheridan's headquarters. I had to ride quite a distance through a muddy country. I remember now that I was concerned about my personal appearance. I had an old suit on, without my sword, and without any distinguishing mark of rank, except the shoulder-straps of a lieutenant-general on a woolen blouse. I was splashed with mud in my long ride. I was afraid Lee might think I meant to show him a studied discourtesy by so coming—at least I thought so. But I had no other clothes within reach, as Lee's letter found me away from my base of supplies. I kept on riding until I met Sheridan. The general, who was one of the heroes of the campaign, and whose pursuit of Lee was perfect in its generalship and energy, told me where to find Lee. I remember that Sheridan was impatient when I met him, anxious and suspicious about the whole business, fearing there may be a plan to escape, feeling that he had Lee at his feet and wanted to end the business by going in and forcing an absolute surrender by capture. In fact, he had his troops ready for such an assault when Lee's white flag came within his lines. I went up to the house where Lee was waiting. I found him in a fine, new, splendid uniform, which only recalled my anxiety as to my own clothes while on my way to meet him. I expressed my regret that I had to meet him in so unceremonious a manner, and he replied that the only suit he had available was one which had been sent him by some friends in Baltimore, and which he then wore for the first time . . . Lee then broached the subject of our meeting. I told him my terms, and Lee, listening attentively, asked me to write them down. I took out my 'manifold' order book and pencil, and wrote them down. General Lee put on his glasses and read them over . . . I said to Lee that I hoped and believed this would be the close of the war; that it was most important that the men should go home and go to work, and the Government would not throw any obstacles in the way. Lee answered that it would have a most happy effect, and accepted the terms. We resumed our conversation about old times and friends in the armies. Various officers came in—Longstreet, Gordon, Pickett, from the South; Sheridan, Ord, and others from our side . . . The next day I met Lee on horseback, and we had a long talk . . . I urged upon Lee the wisdom of ending the war by a surrender of the other armies. I asked him to use his influence with the people of the South—an influence that was supreme—to bring the war to an end. General Lee said that his campaign in Virginia was the last organized resistance which the South was capable of making—that I might have to march a good deal and encounter isolated commands here and there; but that there was no longer any army that could make a stand. I told Lee that this fact only made his responsibility the greater, and any further war would be a crime . . . But Lee would not move without consulting Davis, and as a matter of fact, at that time or soon after, Davis was a fugitive in the woods."

JAMES LONGSTREET.

Born in South Carolina in 1820; removed at an early age with his parents to Alabama, from which State he was appointed to the United States Military Academy in 1838, graduated in 1842, entering the army as lieutenant of infantry; and, after a few years of routine life in garrison and on the frontier in the Southwest, the threatened troubles with Mexico called him into more active service. From the occupation of Texas he was engaged in all the principal battles of the war up to the storming of Chapultepec, where, in the assault upon the castle, he received severe wounds. For Contreras and Churubusco he was brevetted captain, and for Molino del Rey, major. As adjutant of his regiment he served mostly on duty at frontier posts in Texas (1847-52), when he was appointed captain, but remained in Texas until transferred to the staff in 1858 as paymaster, with the rank of major. In June, 1861, Longstreet resigned to join the Confederacy, and commanded a brigade at Bull Run the following month. Promoted to be major-general in 1862, he thereafter bore a conspicuous part, and rendered valuable service to the Confederate cause. In command of the rear guard of the army falling back from Yorktown, he passed through Williamsburg, May 5th, 1862, when he was called back to oppose the hastily advancing Federal forces, a battle lasting nearly nine hours resulting, thus allowing the escape of the main army to Richmond, himself following rapidly under cover of night. At Seven Pines he directed the main attack, and in the subsequent fighting at Gaines's Mill, Frazier's Farm, Malvern Hill, etc., his division fought bravely, losing nearly one half its numbers in killed and wounded. At the second battle of Bull Run he skillfully made the passage of the Thoroughfare Gap, and on the second day held the right of the line and contributed largely to the success of the day. At Antietam he commanded the right wing; the left, at Fredericksburg, where the assault was so fatal to the Federal army. After the battle he was temporarily detached with three divisions of his corps to operate below the James, and in April attacked General Peck at Suffolk, Va., which place he invested until recalled by General Lee, after the battle of Chancellorsville. In the organization of the army with which it was designed to invade the North, Longstreet was assigned to the command of one of its three corps, with the rank of lieutenant-general, and in the ensuing battle of Gettysburg, commanded the right of the line during the second and third days of the fight. The importance of impending operations in the West caused Lee, who felt secure against attack, to again detach Longstreet, and on this occasion the change was timely and precious, for he arrived with his corps in time to decide the fortunes of the day at Chickamauga. The following month Bragg assigned Longstreet to lead a movement against Burnside in East Tennessee, and in November he compelled that officer to seek the intrenchments of Knoxville with his army, which place Longstreet beleaguered, but was compelled to abandon the siege upon Grant's victory at Chattanooga, and hastily move eastward to Virginia, where he rejoined the army of General Lee; in the ensuing campaign he was severely wounded by his own troops in the Wilderness battle (May 6th), and disabled for months. Returning to duty in October, he commanded the defenses of Richmond, north of the James, and was partially engaged in the action around Petersburg the day of evacuation. The war ended, General Longstreet accepted the result, and having renewed his al-

* In this work we find numerous conversations on kindred subjects; and as the galley-proofs of this matter, referring personally to General Grant, were sent by the publishers to him, while in China, and by him revised and corrected before publication, they are an authoritative account of the great soldier's impressions on men and things connected with the Civil War.

giance to the General Government, and labored earnestly to obliterate all traces of war, and promote an era of good feeling between all sections of the country. Taking up his residence in New Orleans, he was appointed (in 1869) Surveyor of the Port, and has been a school commissioner. In 1878 he settled in Georgia. He was appointed United States Marshal by President Hayes, and is now (1885) living in retirement on his farm at Gainesville, Ga.

JOSEPH B. CARR.

Born in the City of Albany, N.Y., on the 16th of August, 1828. His parents came to this country from Ireland in 1824. His military education commenced in the ranks of the Troy Guards. After carrying a musket a year, he received his commission as second-lieutenant, and subsequently was promoted to the command of the Twenty-fourth Regiment, New York State Militia.

On April 15th, 1861, the Second New York Volunteer Regiment was organized, and Colonel Carr placed in command. He left Troy on the 18th, and arrived at Fortress Monroe on the 24th of May, disembarked, and marched to the north side of Mill Creek, Va., his regiment being the first to encamp on the "sacred soil." A thorough course of instruction and discipline was begun and continued up to the battle of Big Bethel, in which his regiment was engaged. He reported to General McClellan at Fair Oaks, June 10th, and was assigned to Patterson's brigade, Hooker's division, Third Corps. He commanded the Third Brigade through the series of battles which continued for seven days, and which included the sanguinary contests at Glendale and Malvern Hill, on the 2d of July. "For gallant and meritorious services in the field" and for conspicuous bravery at Bristow Station he was promoted by the President, upon the personal recommendation of General Hooker, to be brigadier-general of Volunteers, to date from September 7th, 1862.

General Carr participated in the second Bull Run and Chantilly. On the 17th of September he was transferred to the First Brigade. He took an active part in the battle of Fredericksburg, and on the 12th of January, 1863, he was intrusted with the command of an expedition to Rappahannock Bridge. He returned victorious. On May 3d following, General Carr, succeeding to the command of Hooker's old division, engaged the enemy at Chancellorsville, displaying such good judgment in the disposition of his troops, and such gallantry on the field, as to elicit special mention in the report of General Sickles, commanding the corps.

General Humphreys having assumed command of the division, General Carr returned to his brigade, and, after a march of nearly two hundred miles, participated in the memorable battle of Gettysburg. After the battle of Wapping Heights, in which he was engaged, General Carr was assigned to the command of the Third Division of the Third Corps. After participating in the battles of Brandy Station and Kelly's Ford, he crossed the Rapidan in November, and was one of the principal actors in the battles of Locust Grove, Robinson's Tavern and Mine Run. He was subsequently assigned to the command of the Fourth Division, Second (Hancock's) Corps, which position he held until directed to report to General Butler, commanding the Army of the James. He was placed in command of the exterior line of defense on the Peninsula, headquarters at Yorktown. In July, 1863, he was directed to evacuate Yorktown, and was placed in command of the First and Third Divisions of the Eighteenth Corps. On the 4th of August he com-

LOUIS BEIREL.

manded the First Division of the same corps, and occupied the right of the line in front of Petersburg. He retained this position until October 1st, when he assumed charge of the defenses of the James, remaining seven months, and building two important and serviceable forts. On the 20th of May, 1864, he was transferred to City Point, on the James River, and on the 1st of June he was promoted by the President to a brevet-major-generalship, "for gallant and meritorious services during the War.

Major-general Humphreys, Chief of Staff of the Army of the Potomac, testifies to the bravery of General Carr: "He was close to me repeatedly, and constantly under my observation during the hottest of the battle. I do not know a braver or cooler man. There can be no mistaking a man's character in that respect, who went through the fiery ordeal in the manner General Carr did at Gettysburg."

The following extract from a letter written by General

JOSEPH B. CARR.

Hooker in 1870 to General Carr, shows the estimate which "Fighting Joe" placed upon General Carr as a man and a soldier: "I formed my estimate of your civil and military character under circumstances in which I was not likely to be deceived, for if there is in all of life's situations a more searching, unerring test of character than that presented on the field of battle, I have never found it, and my opinions formed of men in these desperate struggles for life I have never had occasion to change or amend. . . . Representatives who have witnessed on the field the cost of our institutions will be likely to revere them."

The aggressive energy which wrought for General Carr an honorable military position has been no less conspicuous in molding his success as a civil officer of the State of New York. For three consecutive terms he has been chosen to fill the responsible position of Secretary of State. In 1879, by a plurality of 1,575 votes; in 1881, by a plurality of 13,022, and in 1883, by a plurality of 18,583 votes.

LOUIS BEIREL.

Born at Valparaiso, Chili, on the 15th of January, 1814. Tendered his services to the United States Government upon the breaking out of the Civil War, and mainly by his own personal unaided efforts raised a full company of Volunteers, composed entirely of New York men, and which became Company "G" of the First California Regiment. The latter won for itself a high reputation in the Virginia and Maryland campaign of 1862, notably at the battle of Ball's Bluff, where it signally distinguished itself by long maintaining its ground against superior numbers, and where its justly prominent leader, General E. D. Baker, fell by the bullet of a Confederate. Baker's death was promptly avenged by Captain Beirel, who immediately shot his assailant, and under a shower of bullets carried the general's body off the field to prevent its falling into the hands of the enemy. President Lincoln, in published orders, subsequently directed him to form part of the escort named to convey the general's remains to Washington. Beirel took part in many other battles of the Civil War, and at its termination went to New York City, where he has since resided, and where he is now (1885) occupying a position under the Commissioners for Emigration.

JOHN RAMSAY.

Born in New York city on the 7th of October, 1838. Entered the Federal Army in April, 1861, as private in Company "G," Second Regiment, New Jersey State Militia, and was subsequently promoted to a lieutenancy and to the captaincy of the company. Was discharged with the regiment at the expiration of its three months' term of service. In August, 1861, he was offered and accepted a captaincy in the Fifth Regiment of New Jersey Volunteers, then being organized, with S. H. Starr, a Regular officer, as its colonel. Gershom Mott (afterward major-general) became its lieutenant-colonel, and W. J. Sewell, the present United States Senator from New Jersey, was made one of the captains.

The regiment became a part of Hooker's division, and with Kearny's formed the Third Army Corps, under command of General Heintzelman, constituting a part of the Army of the Potomac during the war.

He took part with the Fifth New Jersey in the siege of Yorktown, and in the battle of Williamsburg, being promoted to the majorship of the regiment after the last-named engagement upon the special recommendation of Colonel Starr. He afterward took part in the battle of Fair Oaks, as well as in the subsequent so-called Seven Days' Battle around Richmond. At the end of the Peninsula campaign he joined General Pope, and took part in the battles of Bristow Station, August 27th, 1862, and of the second Bull Run, August 29th and 30th, 1862, receiving at the last named a slight wound in the leg, and being made lieutenant-colonel of the regiment. The latter was likewise engaged at Chantilly, where General Kearny was killed, September 1st, 1862, and at the battle of Fredericksburg in the coming December. He was then promoted to the colonelcy of the Eighth New Jersey Regiment of Volunteers, which he commanded at the battle of Chancellorsville, fought in May, 1863, and where he received a bullet wound through the fleshy part of the arm. At Gettysburg he received a wound in the shoulder. He afterward took a leading part in the Virginia campaign, and distinguished himself in the battles of McLean's Ford, October 15th, 1863; Mine Run, November 29th and 30th to December 1st, 1863; the Wilderness, May 5th and 6th, 1864; Spottsylvania, May 8th to 11th; Spottsylvania Court House, May 12th to 18th; North Anna River, May 23d and 24th, 1864; Tolopotomy Creek, May 30th and 31st, 1864; and Cold Harbor, June, 1864. At this time he was assigned to the command of the Second Brigade, Second Division, Second Army Corps, known as the "Corcoran Legion of New York," and was one of the commanders selected to attack Petersburg on the night of June 16th, 1864. He was seriously wounded on the latter date, but recovered sufficiently to take part in the engagements at Boydton Plank Road, October 22d, 1864, as well as in many others fought around Petersburg during the Winter of 1864-65.

By special order of President Lincoln he was made a brevet-brigadier-general, "for distinguished services in the campaign, on the 2d of December, 1864, before Richmond, Va." He was then assigned to duty in accordance with the new rank, and was shortly after given command of the First Brigade, First Division, Second Army Corps, at the head of which he remained throughout the engagements preceding the surrender of General Lee at Appomattox; after which he became commander of the First Division, Second Army Corps. On the 13th of March, 1865, he was appointed a brevet-major-general "for gallant and meritorious services during the war." He is at present (1885) engaged in manufacturing business, in Jersey City, N. J.

JOHN A. RAWLINS.

Born at East Galena, Ill., February 13th, 1831. The son of a farmer and charcoal-burner, he had but limited opportunities for obtaining an education, being obliged to assist his father. At the age of twenty he began to attend school; in November, 1854, commenced the study of law; in 1855 was admitted to the Bar, and began practice in Galena. He won success in his profession, and became a leading Democrat of the Douglas school.

Though using his best efforts to avert war, he ardently espoused the cause of his Government when it came. While engaged in raising a regiment, General Grant offered him a position on his staff as assistant-adjutant-general, with the rank of captain, which was accepted, and with the exception of two months, during illness, he was with General Grant in all of his battles and campaigns until the close of the War. He won the warmest regard and fullest confidence of his chief, and was advanced in rank from time to time, until, in 1865, he was appointed chief of staff to the Lieutenant-general, with rank of brigadier-general, United States Army, and later was breveted major-general. When General Grant was elected President, he appointed him to a place in his Cabinet as Secretary of War. In the few months of his administra-

JOHN RAMSAY.

tion he displayed the same executive ability which led to his selection. He died at Washington, D. C., September 6th 1869.

JOHN A. WINSLOW.

Born, November 19th, 1811, in North Carolina; entered the Navy as a midshipman, February 1st, 1827; became a lieutenant in 1839, a commander in 1855, captain in 1862, commodore in 1864, and rear-admiral in 1870. Served on the east coast of Mexico during our war with that country, and participated in the capture of Tuspan; but the service which placed his name on the roll of fame was that performed by him on June 19th, 1864, when, in command of the *Kearsarge*, he sent to the bottom, after an hour's action, the Confederate steamer *Alabama*, which had made such havoc among American merchantmen. The fight was about as fair a one as had ever been fought at sea, "the vessels being well matched in size, speed, armament and crew," and the Secretary of the Navy but expressed the public sentiment when, in his dispatch of July 6th, 1864, he wrote: "The battle was so brief, the victory so decisive, and the comparative results so striking, that the country will be reminded of the brilliant actions of our infant navy, which have been repeated and illustrated in this engagement."

A story which was for some time current, that the *Kearsarge* was an "ironclad," had its foundation, most probably, in the fact that her executive officer had had her sheet-cables "stopped up and down her sides, so as to cover her midship section"; and as this expedient had often been resorted to before, by Federal naval orders, for the protection of one of the vital parts of a ship (her motive power) from projectiles, it seems somewhat singular that it should not have suggested itself to any one on board the *Alabama*.

Rear-admiral Winslow died September 29th, 1873.

HENRY WHITNEY BELLOWS.

Born in Walpole, N. H., June 11th, 1814; graduated at Harvard in 1832, and from the Divinity School at Cambridge in 1837. He became pastor of the First Congregational Church in the City of New York in 1838. The place of worship was, during the progress of the city, removed twice, and became the Unitarian Church of All Souls, in which he continued to minister, up to the time of his death, forty-four consecutive years. He gained distinction as an eloquent public speaker, and lectured on a variety of subjects, especially social, educational and patriotic enterprises. In 1846 he was one of the founders of the *Christian Examiner*. Among his works are "Lectures on the Treatment of Social Diseases" (1857), and "The Old World in its New Face" (1868). He was the principal promoter and the first president of the United States Sanitary Commission, established in 1861 for the relief of the sick and wounded soldiers in the army, and which spread its branches in every division of the service, and made its influence for good felt through the world. Dr. Bellows's efforts made this organization a success. He died in the City of New York, January 30th, 1882.

HENRY WHITNEY BELLOWS.

ALFRED HOWE TERRY.

Born in Hartford, Conn., November 10th, 1827; educated at schools in New Haven, and at the Law School of Yale College; entered upon the practice of law in 1848, and was clerk of the Superior and Supreme Courts of Connecticut from 1854 to 1860. For some years prior to the Civil War he had been an active member of the State Militia, and since 1854 in command of the Second Connecticut Militia, which regiment was mustered into the service of the United States in response to a call for three months' troops, and, with Terry still in command, was engaged in the first battle of Bull Run.

Returning at the expiration of the three months, Terry then organized the Seventh Connecticut Volunteers, of which regiment he was appointed colonel, in September, 1861, and which he commanded in the expeditionary corps of General T. W. Sherman, at the capture of Port Royal, S. C. At the siege of Fort Pulaski he was commended for zeal, and placed in command of that work upon its capture. Promoted to be brigadier-general of Volunteers in April, 1862, he served in the operations about Charleston, in making a successful demonstration up the Stono River, during the descent on Morris Island, and in the siege operations of Forts Wagner and Sumter. In the Virginia campaign of 1864 he commanded a division in the Army of the James, and was engaged at Drury's Bluff, Bermuda Hundred, and the siege of Petersburg, being in command of the corps, May–July, 1864. Upon the failure of the first attempt to capture Fort Fisher, N. C., Terry was selected in January, 1865, to command the new expedition, which successfully carried that work by assault, January 15th. For his services on this occasion, he was promoted to be a major-general of Volunteers, and made a brigadier-general in the Regular Army, and Congress passed a vote of thanks to him and his command. In the capture of Wilmington he rendered efficient aid, and in March, 1865, was placed in command of the Tenth Corps, serving during the subsequent operations of the campaign in North Carolina. In June, 1865, he was placed in command of the Department of Virginia. He commanded the Department of the South, 1869-72, from which he was transferred to the Department of Dakota, and is still (1884) in command of the Department, with headquarters at Fort Snelling, Minn.

STEPHEN C. ROWAN.

Born December 25th, 1808, in Ireland; emigrated to the United States, 1818; entered the Navy as a midshipman, February 1st, 1826; became a passed midshipman in 1832, a lieutenant in 1837, a commander in 1855, a captain in 1862, a rear-admiral in 1866; distinguished for capacity, conduct and courage during the Mexican War as a captain in the siege of Angeles de Pales, and with a marine corps on the Pacific Coast. In the Florida War he gained much reputation for the United States Navy. On the breaking-out of the Civil War, he commanded the

FITZHUGH LEE.

STEPHEN C. ROWAN.

Pawnee, and in 1862 the Federal fleet off North Carolina, capturing New Berne and Elizabeth City, and received the thanks of Congress. He commanded the *Ironsides* in the siege of Fort Sumter, and for his long, honorable and gallant service, was made vice-admiral of the Navy, August 15th, 1870. His service in the Navy covers a period of sixty years, and the veteran is still (1885) doing excellent service as chairman of the Lighthouse Board at Washington, D.C.

THE UNITED STATES SANITARY COMMISSION.

The history of our Civil War will ever have associated with it the work of this great organization, prompted by soldiers was the average daily ministration in these homes—over 800,000 in one single year. A Claim Agency, a Back-pay Agency, and a Pension Agency, were supported, and with no cost to the soldiers whose interests were protected and served. A Hospital-directory costing $20,000 per year was sustained, in which anxious relatives and friends could readily find the sick and wounded. They had sixty hospital-inspectors constantly in the field, and trains of hospital-cars, on which the disabled soldiers were carried to homes and hospitals, and provisions returned to the battle-fields. They would expend vast sums of money to meet the exigencies of a great battle. After Murfreesboro', Antietam, Gettysburg, Chattanooga, Vicksburg, and Port Hudson, the Commission

THE SANITARY COMMISSION MINISTERING TO THE WOUNDED AND DYING AFTER THE BATTLE.

divine charity, guided by Providence, and without a parallel in human annals.

The institution sprung from a meeting of a few New York ladies, guided by that clear-headed, great hearted man, Rev. Dr. Henry W. Bellows. One million dollars in cash reached their treasury the first three years, of which sum three-quarters came from the Pacific Coast. Fifteen-sixteenths of this sum was expended for supplies and transportation; the other sixteenth, for the support of its homes, lodges, hospital-directory, hospital and camp inspection, and in the machinery of distribution. The officers and members of committees gave their services and time gratuitously. They supported more than forty Soldiers' Homes, scattered over the whole field of war. Two thousand three hundred sick and wounded expended from three to ten dollars for the comfort of each wounded soldier. Nor was such an expense extravagant, considering the blessings and comforts thus dispensed at the very moment most needed, and when the General Government could ill spare the money or machinery to carry out so beneficent a scheme.

FITZHUGH LEE.

Born in Virginia in 1835. He was the eldest son of Sidney Smith Lee, who was an officer in the United States Navy, and brother of Robert E. Lee, the Confederate general.

Fitzhugh Lee was entered at West Point as a cadet from Virginia in 1852; graduated in July, 1856, and was commissioned second lieutenant in the Cavalry. He acted as adjutant to General Earl Van Dorn in the celebrated expedition against the Comanche Indians, and distinguished himself in the action of May 13th, 1859. On the outbreak of the Civil War he resigned his commission in the United States Army until Virginia was made the battle-field, when he joined the Confederacy, and distinguished himself as a daring and gallant cavalry leader, operating in the Valley and in the various battles before Richmond and Petersburg, finally surrendering at Appomattox. He is now (1885) engaged in agricultural pursuits on his farm at Richland, Va., and doing his share toward building up the fortunes of his native State, so thoroughly devastated by the iron heel of war during the four years of terrible conflict. He is also president of the Board of Managers of the Confederate Soldiers' Home, near Richmond, Va., which was established through the efforts of the Robert E. Lee Camp, Confederate Veterans, and formally opened, May 20th, 1885, the Confederate Camp being assisted by the Aaron Wilkes Post, G. A. R., of Trenton, N. J.

The sons of General Robert E. Lee are also settled in Virginia. W. H. Fitzhugh Lee, with whom the subject of our sketch is often confused, and who served also as a cavalry leader, but was not educated at West Point, is now engaged in farming; and Custis Lee succeeded his father in the presidency of the Washington and Lee University at *Lexington*, Va., where the people of Virginia make yearly pilgrimages to the tomb of their great military captain, and offer as a memorial the early flowers of springtime.

THE WOMAN'S RELIEF CORPS,

AUXILIARY TO THE GRAND ARMY OF THE REPUBLIC.

THE Woman's Relief Corps, Auxiliary to the Grand Army of the Republic, dates its organization, as a National Order, to July 25th, 1883. General Order No. 11 of Commander-in-chief Van Dervoort, issued at Omaha, Neb., under date of May 1st, 1883, convening the Grand Army of the Republic in Seventeenth Annual Encampment at Denver, Col., July 25th, 1883, contained this clause:

"V. The representatives of Woman's Relief Corps and Auxiliary Societies of the Grand Army of the Republic are cordially invited to meet at Denver, and perfect a National Organization. They should bring their rituals, rules and by-laws of organization, and if possible agree on a uniform mode, or system, of procedure throughout the country. I pledge the noble women who compose these Societies that they will be warmly greeted and given all the encouragement possible."

In a circular issued December 16th, 1882, and in General Order No. 8, issued February 16th, 1883, and in all his Camp-fire and Reunion speeches, the Commander-in-chief had specially recommended woman's work in the Grand Army, referring Comrades to recognized leaders in the work, including Mrs. E. Florence Barker, President of the Union Board Woman's Relief Corps, Boston; Mrs. Kate B. Sherwood, President Forsyth Post Auxiliary, Toledo, O., and editor of "Loyal Woman's Work" in the *National Tribune* of Washington, D. C., as among those from whom information could be secured by Comrades desiring to form Auxiliaries. Others, specially mentioned, were Mrs. A. M. Sawyer, President Woman's Relief Corps, Portland, Me.; Mrs. Laura McNier, President of the Loyal Ladies' League, Camden, N. J.; and Mrs. Emily Thornton Charles, editor of the *Veteran*, Washington, D. C. General Order No. 8 contained the following:

"XIV. The Commander-in-chief is delighted to learn that the loyal women of the land are forming Auxiliary Societies everywhere. The grand work done by these Organizations is worthy of the highest praise. The Woman's Relief Corps of Massachusetts is hereby particularly mentioned on account of the work they have done and their perfect organization. The President of the same, Mrs. E. Florence Barker, Malden, will be happy to furnish information."

The recommendations of the Commander-in-chief induced the Comrades to write to the ladies named, and the result was that between the months of December, 1882, and July, 1883, hundreds of letters were answered and instructions sent out, Mrs. Sherwood alone, during the Winter and Spring of 1883, writing over five hundred letters, and aiding in the organization of over one hundred Auxiliaries, scattered throughout the country, from Pennsylvania westward. The necessity of a National Organization was attested by the eagerness manifested by the Comrades in following the recommendation of their Commander-in-chief.

The status of existing Societies at that time was this: Maine, Woman's Relief Corps, to which only wives, mothers, sisters, and daughters, were eligible to membership; Massachusetts, Woman's Relief Corps; Connecticut, Woman's Relief Corps; New Hampshire, Woman's Relief Corps, all united under a Union Board—wives, mothers, sisters, and daughters, and all loyal women, eligible; New Jersey, Loyal Ladies' League—wives, mothers, sisters, and daughters, eligible. All of these were secret Orders, modeled after the Grand Army of the Republic, working according to a ritual, with sign, countersign, salute, signal and password. Maine had a few scattering Corps, but no Department; New Jersey had twelve or fourteen Corps and a Department.

Besides these, there was a similar Organization at Washington, D. C., of which Mrs. Emily T. Charles was President—a single Auxiliary, confined to one Post; and still another independent Organization at Warsaw, Ind. Both were secret, and both conferred membership on the near relatives of Veterans.

On the Toledo, or Soldiers' Aid Society, plan, there was a chain of Auxiliaries, all working according to the constitution of Forsyth Post Auxiliary, but each independent of the other. All loyal women were eligible to membership, the only test being their willingness to work for the soldier. All meetings were open to visitors, and all proceedings public. But although so widely differing in the character of the organization, it is well to note that all the various Organizations were organized to care for the widows and orphans of Veterans, and to aid the Grand Army in patriotic and benevolent work.

This was the condition of affairs when the Commander-in-chief made his formal call; and many who knew the tenacity with which a woman holds to her opinion, and how slow she is to yield a pet project when once it has entered her heart, were quick to doubt the possibility of fusing all the various elements into a National Organization.

Very early in the discussion, the *National Tribune* had invited correspondence upon the subject of woman's work in the Grand Army, and, by recommendation of the Commander-in-chief, Mrs. Sherwood, in January, 1883, became a regular contributor to its columns, which position she has retained ever since, and on May 17th, 1883, she assumed editorial control of the Department of "Loyal Woman's Work," when she announced this prediction, so early to be fulfilled:

"Some months since the *Tribune* began the experiment of giving special attention to the work of the Woman's Relief Corps, and other Auxiliaries of the Grand Army of the Republic. It is needless to say that the experiment is an experiment no longer, but has grown to such proportions as to warrant its preservation as a permanent feature of the Woman's Department. Therein questions will be answered

KATE BROWNLEE SHERWOOD.

from week to week, and such subjects discussed as will facilitate the good work all along the line. That this work is but yet in its infancy is well determined. It is to no flush of enthusiasm that the loyal women of America have organized for the campaign of peace, an enthusiasm short-lived because so spontaneous. It is no fitful fever which will die out, leaving the worn-out subject colder and more corpse-like than when the icy rigors were at their destructive work. Neither is it a short-lived impulse, but a strong, healthy, normal growth, which is to warm and expand until fill the entire country with its beneficent and wholesome influence."

Following the call for the Denver Convention, a series of inquiries, looking to a National Union, were sent out, through the Woman's Department of the *Tribune*, to the President of every Corps, League and other Auxiliary, so far as the address of each could be secured. Several hundred in all were sent out. They were as follows:

First. Do you favor a National Association for the extension and perfection of woman's work in the Grand Army of the Republic?

Second. Would you confine the membership in individual Societies to the wives, mothers, sisters and daughters of soldiers, or would you allow all loyal women to become members?

Third. Would you make the Society a secret organization, with ceremonies of initiation and a ritual, or would you have the meeting conducted openly, according to rules governing parliamentary bodies?

Fourth. In case of a failure to agree on this question, would you favor the organization of a National Society, under a constitution that would allow individual Societies to accept or reject secret work, at their discretion?

Fifth. Will your Society be represented at the Denver Encampment?

The publication and circulation of these inquiries led to an animated correspondence, and prepared the way for the Union at Denver. Every Organization was given the opportunity for a full and frank expression, and nearly all availed themselves of the privilege. Mrs. E. Florence Barker, the first National President, in reviewing the Denver proceedings, in her Annual Address, writes as follows:

"With twenty-six different Organizations represented, I think the result very complimentary to women's legislation, and I cannot refrain from complimenting Mrs. Sherwood, the pioneer in national work, for the position she took on that occasion; preferring, as she said, open work, she gracefully waived a point in the interest of harmony, and advised those preferring open meeting to submit to the testimony of those having already the example of secret work. Thus, thanks to her endeavors, was one wide difference overcome."

Without the discussion in the *National Tribune*, these concessions would not so readily have been brought about, as those enlisted in woman's work in the West were strenuous advocates of open work. Mrs. Sherwood, the pioneer worker, drafted the constitution and by-laws under which the Toledo Auxiliary had been doing harmonious and efficient work since March 15th, 1878, and had been instrumental in starting the independent Auxiliary movement in the West. But the discussion had developed these facts, viz.—First, that the majority favored secret work. Second, that the majority favored the admission of all loyal women. Third, that all were desirous of forming a National Organization. Therefore it seemed to her that all that was necessary was to propose this compromise: That, in behalf of the open-work Auxiliaries, she would accept secret work, upon condition that the advocates of secret work and restricted membership would declare for the admission of all loyal women. She also remembered that the Commander-in-chief had recommended the work of Massachusetts, and, therefore, offered the following resolution:

Resolved, That we organize ourselves into a National Woman's Relief Corps, upon the basis of the Woman's Relief Corps of Boston, Mass.

The resolution was divided, each clause considered separately, and adopted. Later, it was moved and carried that the Executive officers of the Union Board Woman's Relief Corps be made the National officers for the coming year, which proposition was unanimously received, and the National Organization became a living verity, with the following officers:

President, Mrs. E. Florence Barker, Malden, Mass.
Senior Vice-president, Mrs. Kate B. Sherwood, Toledo, O.
Junior Vice-president, Mrs. E. H. Stimson, Denver, Col.
Secretary, Mrs. Sarah E. Fuller, Boston, Mass.
Treasurer, Mrs. L. A. Turner, Boston, Mass.
Chaplain, Mrs. Mattie B. Moulton, Laconia, N. H.
Inspector, Mrs. Laura McNier, Camden, N. J.
Conductor, Mrs. P. S. Runyan, Warsaw, Ind.
Guard, Mrs. J. W. Benton, Rockford, Ill.

Upon the completion of the Organization the thanks of the Convention were formally tendered to the retiring Commander-in-chief, Paul Van Dervoort, for his services in bringing about a National Organization, and a Committee of Three was appointed to convey to the Encampment a message, through Chaplain-in-chief Foster, announcing the National Organization, and asking the approval of the Grand Army of the Republic in the work which they proposed to do. The resolution, as proposed by Comrade Foster, and which was passed by a large majority, after a spirited discussion, was as follows:

Resolved, That we cordially hail the organization of a National Woman's Relief Corps, and extend our greeting to them. We return our warmest thanks to the loyal women of the land for their earnest support and encouragement, and bid them godspeed in their patriotic work.

Later, the National officers of the Woman's Relief Corps, attended by the delegates in a body, were admitted to the floor of the Encampment, to be present at the installation of the Commander-in-chief, Robert B. Beath. They were received with every mark of consideration by the Comrades, given seats on the platform, and extended a cordial greeting in behalf of the Grand Army of the Republic, to which Mrs. President Barker made a happy response. And so was conspicuously begun the great National Organization which has become recognized as the loyal left of the grand association of veterans, whose crowning jewel is Charity, the connecting-link in the golden chain between a

Fraternity born of the battle and a Loyalty that was the Nation's hope in times of danger, and its calm confidence in times of peace.

Woman's work in the Grand Army is synonymous with the Grand Army itself. It began on the red fields of war, in the camp, the hospital, and on the sanitary boats. And, although most of the Soldiers' Aid Societies disbanded with the close of the War, their members continued to work. Some, as the Soldiers' Aid Society at Portsmouth, O., never disbanded, but have since been rebaptized as an Auxiliary of the Woman's Relief Corps. We learn of an Auxiliary in Boston, Mass., dating back to 1868; of a Woman's Relief Corps at Portland, Me., dating back to 1869; and, nearly a decade later, of the formation of a Ladies' Auxiliary at Toledo, O., 1878; of the organization of a Woman's Relief Corps at Fitchburg, Mass., in 1877; and in 1879, of the formation of the Department of Massachusetts at the same place. The serious depression in business, beginning with 1874, and continuing for several years, with the great pressure brought to bear upon the Grand Army for the help of needy Comrades and the widows and orphans of Veterans, seems to have given the first great impetus to woman's work, following the War. And so it is that Corps, Leagues and Auxiliaries began to increase and multiply everywhere, sowing the seed of the bounteous ingathering which is now taking place.

The Grand Army of the Republic, in Annual Encampment, was slow to recognize a woman's Auxiliary, although as early as 1870, at the Fourth Annual Encampment, the Clara Barton Degree, agitated in several Departments, was discussed. At the Fifth Annual Encampment it came up again, but no favorable action was taken. At the Seventh Encampment it was again discussed, and referred to a committee, where it slept its last sleep.

At the Fourteenth Annual Encampment, 1880, the subject of woman's work was introduced, and a committee appointed, consisting of Comrades J. F. Lovering, George Bourne and H. Crabb, to carefully consider the subject, and report at the Fifteenth Encampment. At the Fifteenth Encampment, June 15th, 1881, held at Indianapolis, the committee reported the following, which was adopted:

> *Resolved*, That we approve of the project entertained of organizing a Woman's National Relief Corps.
>
> *Resolved*, That such Woman's Relief Corps may use, under such title, the words, "Auxiliary to the Grand Army of the Republic," by special indorsement of the National Encampment, Grand Army of the Republic.

But even with such recognition, and with Chaplain-in-chief Lovering on their side, the Woman's Relief Corps made no progress outside of the cluster of New England States noted, nor could they have done so without a national assemblage of the women of the Union, such as was the Denver Convention.

The Woman's Relief Corps, Auxiliary to the Grand Army of the Republic, is a simplified edition, so far as its general work is concerned, of the Grand Army of the Republic. It has a ritualistic service, with odes, installation and burial service, annual inspections, etc. The emblem of the Association is the Maltese Cross. The Auxiliary to a Post is known as a Subordinate Corps, and takes the name of the Post to which it is auxiliary. The Corps of a State, associated together, constitute a Department, and the State Departments, a National Convention. The officers of a Subordinate Corps are: President, Senior Vice-President, Junior Vice-President, Secretary, Treasurer, Chaplain, Conductor and Guard. The Department officers are the same, with addition of Department Inspector, and the National with the addition of National Inspector. It has codified Rules and Regulations, with a Preamble which reads as follows:

> "We, the undersigned, mothers, wives, sisters and daughters of the soldiers, sailors and marines of the late War, and other loyal women, do unite to establish a permanent association for the purposes and objects hereinafter set forth, with such amendments as we shall from time to time think proper to make.
>
> OBJECTS: *Sec. 1*—To specially aid and assist the members of the Grand Army of the Republic, and to perpetuate the memory of the heroic dead.
>
> *Sec. 2*—To inculcate lessons of patriotism and love of country, not only among our membership, but to our children also.

Upon the organization of the Woman's Relief Corps, Department of Massachusetts, in 1879, it had received direct recognition from Department-commander, Horace Binney Sargent; his adjutant, General James F. Meech, aided largely in the organization. In 1880 the New Hampshire ladies formed a Department, were recognized by the Department of New Hampshire, Grand Army of the Republic, and united in an organization with Massachusetts, known as the Union Board. In 1882 Connecticut effected a similar organization, and became a part of the Union Board. Between July, 1883, when the Union Board was merged into a National Association, and July, 1884, the following States organized Departments, and became a part of the National Organization in the order named: Ohio, Kansas, Illinois, New York, Michigan, Nebraska, Maine, Pennsylvania, Wisconsin, Colorado, Iowa, Indiana, with Subordinate Corps in Minnesota, Dakota, New Jersey, Missouri, Oregon, Washington Territory and Nevada. The rapidity with which Corps and Departments organized, and the warm and cordial indorsement extended by the Grand Army in every State and Territory, show the wisdom of the National Encampment in the recognition accorded the Woman's Relief Corps. The Relief Corps having been specially commended in general orders by Commander-in-chief Beath, and Department-commanders generally, greatly aided in the formation of Corps and Departments.

The National Secretary, Mrs. Fuller, reported

WILLIAM A. HAMMOND, SURGEON-GENERAL, U.S.A.

156 Corps organized during the year ending July 25th, 1884, and an aggregate membership of over 6,000. The National Treasurer, Mrs. Turner, reported the receipts for the year as \$4,231.35; expenditures (including assets on hand, \$1,652.23), \$4,231.35. Balance to new account, \$1,516.27.

The development of the Woman's Relief Corps has surpassed the expectations of its most sanguine friends, and commanded the support and confidence of those who were lukewarm at the first, or opposed to any Auxiliary to the Grand Army, of whatever character. The retiring Commander-in-chief, Robert B. Beath, in his address before the Minneapolis Convention, paid the Organization this fine compliment, all the more appreciated as General Beath is a recognized authority in all matters pertaining to the Grand Army:

> "I deemed it a duty to call personally on the National officers of the Woman's Relief Corps in Boston, to ask if there was any service which I could render in the prosecution of their work. I also met on several occasions their efficient Western organizer, Mrs. Kate B. Sherwood, S. V. P., and in all those interviews was deeply impressed with the fact that they had in themselves the ability and resources to carry out the details of organization, and that what they most needed from us was the expression of our hearty appreciation of their work and sympathy for their objects.
>
> "They are now much further advanced in organization in this one year than the Grand Army was in the same time.
>
> "Comrades who doubted the wisdom of our taking any action last year will soon see that this Woman's Relief Corps is to be our Grand Army Reserve, ready to respond for efficient help in all our social and charitable work."

The Second Annual Convention at Minneapolis is memorable for the good reports received; from the warm recognition accorded by Commander-in-chief Robert B. Beath and his successor, John S. Kountz, and all the leading representatives of the Grand Army, many of whom visited the Convention in a body and listened to the reports; from the wise and beneficent legislation, in aid of army nurses and other woman workers in the War, inaugurated; and from the fact that the Woman's Relief Corps were accorded an invitation to be present at the installation of Commander-in-chief Kountz before the National Encampment, and to install their officers upon the platform, to which the officers had been invited in a body. The National President, Mrs. Sherwood, was called upon, following her installation, and had the pleasure of addressing the Comrades upon the work of the Organization which she had been chosen to represent.

The National officers, Woman's Relief Corps, for the year ending July, 1885, are as follows:

Kate B. Sherwood, *National President*, Toledo, O.
Emma D. Sibley, *National Secretary*, Toledo, O.
Sarah E. Fuller, *National Senior Vice-President*, East Boston, Mass.
Lizzie Anderson, *National Junior Vice-President*, Topeka, Kansas.
Lizabeth A. Turner, *Treasurer*, Boston, Mass.
Annie Wittenmeyer, *Chaplain*, Philadelphia, Pa.
Sarah C. Nichols, *Inspector*, Auburn, N. Y.
Maggie J. Shu, *Conductor*, Pittsburg, Pa.
Jennie E. G. Walsh, *Guard*, Minneapolis, Minn.

Mrs. Wittenmeyer, the National Chaplain, is the celebrated army nurse and organizer of the Diet Kitchens, connected with the Sanitary Service of the Union Army, a woman beloved and honored by every Comrade in the land. She has been appointed by the National President as one of the Committee of Relief to devise ways and means for a proper recognition of the noble women of the War, who gave of their time and strength and means for the care of the Union sick and wounded, and for whom no provision or support has been granted by the Government.

Mrs. Kate B. Sherwood, the National President, is the wife of General J. R. Sherwood, Colonel of the 111th O. V. I., breveted brigadier-general for gallant and meritorious services at the battle of Franklin, Tenn., ex-Secretary of State of Ohio, and ex-Member of Congress.

The following is an extract from one of the many poems written by her for Army Reunions and Encampments. It was recited by Elizabeth Mansfield Irving, July 23d, 1884, at the Minneapolis Encampment:

THE GRAND ARMY.

BY KATE BROWNLEE SHERWOOD.

Methinks a vision filled the night of strong men mustering,
And two by two in solemn pride they strode with sturdy swing;
I stood upon the battlements and saw them man the guns
And fling the halyards to the breeze where dead [illegible] runs:
To right of me, to left of me, they rally, man and man,
Until, it seemed, the plains were groves, the groves like rivers ran;
I heard the scream of bugles and the throbbing of the drums,
At the murmur of the thunders that portend the storm that comes.
My pulses sting and tremble, my blood is all afire,
To see the sons go stalking forth to battle, with their sire;
"God keep my first-born darling," the mother kneels to pray,
And so our great Grand Army was mustered in that day.

* * * * * * * *

Oh, there was brave manœuvre in sight of foe and friend,
And toss of plume and feather and marching without end;
And there were banners waving, and there were songs and cheers
And for the patriot praises, and for the coward jeers.
And here the splendid Infantry [illegible] gray and blue,
And there the gleaming trappings of Cavalry in view;
And flash of scarlet guidons and riders in the line,
With gorgeous spreading epaulets and sashes red as wine.
And lo! the long processions of maidens drawing nigh,
With kisses and with flowers to say a last good-by;
And lo! the wives a-lifting their babies to the sun,
And so our great Grand Army beheld its work begun.

* * * * * * * *

Unite your ranks, O comrades, consolidate brigades!
Call in vidette and picket! unsheath your [illegible] blades!
Take home your captured cannon and mold them into stars,
To deck the breasts of veterans returning from the wars!
Swing out the tattered banners though riddled through and through
With elbow touching elbow begin your Grand Review;
Was ever seen such marching, say, comrades, 'neath the sun,
As, army meeting army, you made in Washington!
The hilltops are exultant! the streets with joy are wild,
And the veteran's heart is happy as the heart of a little child
Cheers meeting cheers resounding make up a sea of sound,
That lauds our great Grand Army wherever fame is found!

* * * * * * * *

Play up the march of Empire! play up the march of Love!
The mighty West before us! the stars and Stripes above!
Play up the South returning, play up the reveille;
Play up the true Union! play the union to be!
Play up the struggling nations whose eyes have hailed the morn
That glows above the cradle where Liberty was born!
Play up the toiling millions, their race is but begun!
Play up, play up for Lincoln! Play up for Washington!
Play up the Union rally! play up both loud and shrill:
One heart, one hope, one faith, one flag, shall be our slogan still!
Play up the "March through Georgia," your merriest music play:
Play up our great Grand Army for ever and for aye!

TWENTY YEARS AFTER

On Thursday, the 15th of May, 1884, a large party, consisting of Veterans of the First Corps, of the Army of the Potomac, several Senators and Representatives in Congress, and a considerable number of distinguished officers and military men, assembled at Fredericksburg for the purpose of General H. W. Slocum, Major Stein, historian of the First Corps, and many others.

On Thursday, the first place visited was Hamilton Crossing, the extreme right of the Confederate line at the battle of Fredericksburg. General Doubleday, and the Hon. W. W. Brown, of Pennsylvania, explained the movements and position of the Federal lines and reserves. Colonel Gats, of Alabama, tery, Colonel Herbert gave a vivid account of the operations of the Confederate forces. General Hunt pointed out the position of the Federal artillery, and gave a detailed account of the building of bridges and of the crossing of General Burnside's army. General Longstreet narrated in detail the operations of the Confederate forces and their plans both before and after the battle. "A truce was

Stein. Longstreet Rosecrans

REVISITING THE BATTLEFIELDS OF VIRGINIA IN 1884.

visiting the battlefields along the line of the Rappahannock, as well as the scenes of the Wilderness engagements and of those fought at Spottsylvania Court House.

Among the visitors were: General Rosecrans; General Bayne, of Pennsylvania; General Newton, General Hunt, General Longstreet, General Doubleday, General Ayres; General Robinson, of Ohio; W. F. Rogers, of New York; General G. W. Steele, of the Confederate Army, pointed out the position of the Confederate lines, and gave a graphic description of the death of the brave General Gregg, of South Carolina, who received his death-wound at this point. General Ayres and Mr. C. C. Coffin, the famous war correspondent, described the movements of the artillery. The party next proceeded to Marye's Heights. Upon arrival at the extreme right of the range of hills now the National Cemecalled," said General Longstreet, "after the fight, to bury the dead. I have seen a great many battlefields, but none so shocking as this. The dead were buried in numerous pits, eight feet deep and thirty feet square." General Newton and Colonel Jackson added their testimony, and then the Veterans of the First Army Corps marched back to Fredericksburg.

On the following day Chancellorsville was visited

FREDERICKSBURG, VA., IN 1885.

General Joseph Dickinson, chief of staff to General Hooker, described the position and movements of the Federal Army, the disaster that befell the Eleventh Corps, and its disastrous retreat, and also the wounding of General Hooker on the porch of the Chancellorsville House and the subsequent destruction of that house by fire, caused by the bursting of a shell. General H. W. Slocum and General John C. Robinson made eloquent defenses of the Eleventh Army Corps, and were frequently applauded. From Chancellorsville the party drove through the sombre Wilderness woods to where General Longstreet and Colonel Herbert located the lines, and to the spot where Wadsworth was killed. Midway between the Wilderness and Chancellorsville, on the left-hand side of the Pike Road going toward the Chancellorsville House, a rough, uninscribed fragment of rock, planted along the wayside brambles, marks the spot where Stonewall Jackson fell.

Saturday, the 17th of May, was devoted by the historical party to a visit to the battlefield of Spottsylvania Court House, under the lead of Generals Rosecrans, and John C. Robinson, of New York, who led the forces of General Grant in this battle; the Hon. J. H. Bagley, of New Jersey; and R. M. Murray, of Ohio. They arrived on the scene of action about eleven o'clock, and located the spot where General Robinson formed his lines. Two hundred yards to the right lay the Alsop Farm, where Sedgwick was killed. The spot where he fell was found, and Generals Rosecrans and Robinson and Major Stein, assisted by John J. J. Klimer, C. C. Coffin, Colonel J. B. Batchelder, A. J. Hunteon, S. B. Prentice, Thomas Brooks, Dr. H. Taylor, Colonel G. C. Kniffen, John C. Johnson, H. L. Stetes, and Mr. Edwards, erected a stone to mark the spot until the Sixth Corps can build a suitable monument to their gallant commander. The rest of the day was spent on the field near McCool's house, at the point known as the "bloody angle." Messrs. Johnson and Edwards came from Kansas, 1,200 miles, to be present on the occasion.

An amusing incident is related of the visit to the Alsop Farm. A member of the party handed to a son of Mrs. Alsop, who was present, a five-dollar bill, saying: "On this day twenty years ago I stole a side of bacon from your mother, and I want you to give her this to pay for it."

The chief points of historical interest in connection with the battlefields appear in our sketches. The topographical and other changes which have been wrought since the artists of ***Frank Leslie's*** *Illustrated Newspaper* went over the same ground, nearly a generation ago—when Forbes, Hillen, Becker, Taylor and Crane, with pencil held by the hand that grasped the musket, propelled by the inspiration of the stirring scenes in which they were to be the faithful pictorial historians, handed down the actions of two great armies—are often very marked, as our pictures indicate. One of the most interesting of the illustrations is that which shows Generals Rosecrans and Longstreet and Major Stein, surrounded by a group of interested spectators, examining the plan of the battle of Fredericksburg, while standing on the terrace overlooking the city and the adjacent country.

Green grass, broad tobacco-leaves and peaceful grain now wave over the historic fields of old Virginia. The battle-flags are furled, and the dove perches on the rusty cannon's mouth. Once more the veteran soldiers meet on the battle-grounds of twenty years ago, not with drawn swords, but to walk arm-in-arm amid the hallowed scenes, and tell for future generations the true story of a great struggle that developed the strength and patriotism of a nation, and educated the soldier to a just appreciation of the prowess of his brother.

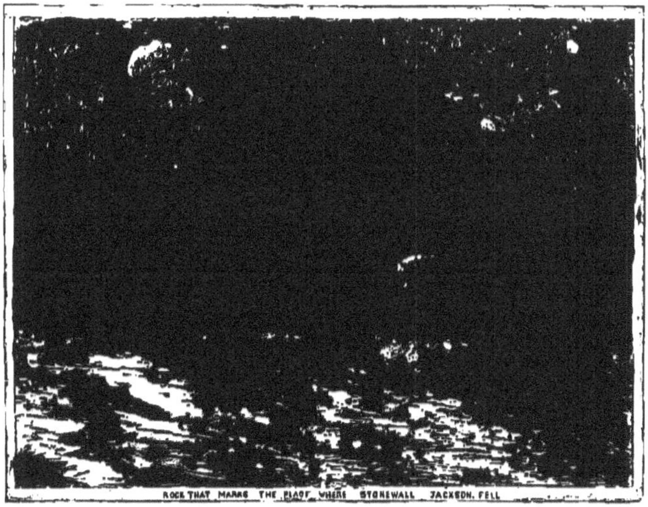

ROCK THAT MARKS THE PLACE WHERE STONEWALL JACKSON FELL.

CHANCELLORSVILLE, VA. – THE BATTLEFIELD IN 1885.

THE GRAND ARMY OF THE REPUBLIC.

BY PAUL VAN DERVOORT.

The secret work and foundation of the organization of the Grand Army of the Republic was laid by Dr. B. F. Stephenson, of Springfield, Ill. He had thought deeply upon the best way to band together, after the war, the men who wore the blue, and by degrees during the war perfected his plan.

BATTLE MONUMENT AT GETTYSBURG, PA.

Early in 1866 a Post or two had been organized, and he had communicated his idea to many of his army associates. It was decided best to call a meeting of soldiers at Springfield, Ill., July 12th, 1866. Accordingly representative soldiers were invited from all parts of the State, who met there on that day, and were duly mustered in and given authority to organize in their homes. General John M. Palmer was made the chief officer, and Stephenson, John M. Lynder, and J. C. Webber, assisted him. The State of Illinois was divided into Districts, and the organization of Posts was exceedingly rapid.

It was estimated that in less than six months 40,000 men were enrolled. Other States, hearing of the organization through correspondence, sent Comrades to Springfield, who were given the work, and at once, as if by magic, Departments were started in all the Northwestern States as follows:

Illinois was organized July 12th, 1866; Iowa, September 26th, 1866; Indiana, November 22d, 1866; Kansas, December 27th, 1866; Wisconsin, September, 1866; Connecticut, April 11th, 1867; Massachusetts, May 7th, 1867; Minnesota, August 14th, 1867; Missouri, May 16th, 1867; New York, April 3d, 1867; Ohio, January 30th, 1867; Pennsylvania, January 16th, 1867; California, July 30th, 1868; Maine, January 10th, 1868; Maryland, January 8th, 1868, Michigan, May 6th, 1868; New Hampshire, May, 1868; New Jersey, January, 1868; Virginia, February 12th, 1868; West Virginia, September 12th, 1868; Vermont, October 23d, 1868; Colorado, December 11th, 1879; Dakota, February 27th 1883; Delaware, January 14th, 1880; Florida, June 19th, 1884; Gulf, May 15th, 1884; Kentucky, January 17th, 1883; Nebraska, January 25th, 1870; New Mexico, July 19th, 1883; Oregon, September 29th, 1882; Potomac, February 11th, 1869; Tennessee and Georgia, 1884; Utah, October 16th 1881; Washington Territory, June 20th, 1883; Arkansas July 11th, 1883.

The Departments named below died, and were reorganized as follows:

Indiana, August 11th, 1879; Iowa, 1879; Kansas, March 18th, 1880; Maryland, January, 1876; Michigan, 1879; Minnesota, May 18th, 1880; Missouri, 1881; West Virginia, February 20th, 1883.

The First National Encampment met at Indinapolis on the 20th day of November, 1867, under the call of B. F. Stephenson, Commander-in-Chief, and J. C. Webber, Adjutant-general, Department of Illinois. S. A. Hurlbut, of Illinois, was elected Commander-in-Chief, and B. F. Stephenson, Adjutant-general.

The Second Annual Encampment was held at Philadelphia, January 15th, 16th and 17th, 1868. John A. Logan, of Illinois, was elected Commander-in-Chief.

The Third Annual Encampment was held at Cincinnati, Ohio. John A. Logan re-elected Commander-in-Chief.

The Fourth Annual Encampment was held at Washington, D.C., May 11th and 12th, 1870. John A. Logan again elected Commander-in-Chief—the only instance in the history of the Order where a Commander-in-Chief has held office for three terms.

The Fifth Annual Encampment, Boston, Mass., May 10th and 11th, 1871. A. E. Burnside elected Commander-in-Chief.

The Sixth Annual Encampment, Cleveland, O., May 8th and 9th, 1872. A. E. Burnside re-elected Commander-in-Chief.

The Seventh Annual Encampment, New Haven, Conn., May 14th and 15th, 1873. Charles Devens, of Massachusetts, elected Commander-in-Chief.

The Eighth Annual Encampment, Harrisburg, Pa., May 13th, 1874. Charles Devens, of Massachusetts, re-elected Commander-in-Chief.

The Ninth Annual Encampment, Chicago, Ill., May 12th and 13th, 1875. John F. Hartranft, of Pennsylvania, elected Commander-in-Chief.

The Tenth Annual Encampment, Philadelphia, Pa., June 30th, 1876. John F. Hartranft re-elected Commander-in-Chief.

The Eleventh Annual Encampment, Providence, R. I., June 26th and 27th, 1877. John C. Robinson, of New York, elected Commander-in-Chief.

The Twelfth Annual Encampment, Springfield, Mass., June 4th, 1878. John C. Robinson re-elected Commander-in-Chief.

The Thirteenth Annual Encampment, Albany, New York, June 17th and 18th, 1879. William Earnshaw, of Ohio, elected Commander-in-Chief. With him commenced the one-term idea.

The Fourteenth Annual Encampment, Dayton, O., June 8th and 9th, 1880. Louis Wagner, of Pennsylvania, elected Commander-in-Chief.

The Fifteenth Annual Encampment, Indianapolis, Ind., June 15th and 16th, 1881. George S. Merrill, of Massachusetts, elected Commander-in-Chief.

The Sixteenth Annual Encampment, Baltimore, Md., June 16th and 17th, 1882. Paul Van Dervoort, of Nebraska, elected Commander-in-Chief.

The Seventeenth Annual Encampment, Denver, Col., July 23d–25th, 1883. Robert B. Beath, of Philadelphia, Pa., elected Commander-in-Chief.

The Eighteenth Annual Encampment, Minneapolis, Minn., July 23d and 24th, 1884. John S. Kountze, Toledo, O. elected Commander-in-Chief.

Membership of Order from 1872 to 1884, quarter ending March 31st of each year, was as follows:

1872	29,174
1873	26,037
1874	25,333
1875	27,303
1876	28,123
1877	25,444
1878	29,002
1879	33,777
1880	40,000
1881	61,847
1882	85,065
1883	146,163
1884	231,385

The largest gains were made during the administrations of Comrades Van Dervoort and Beath, the first turning over a membership reported at 178,811, not counting the month of July of his work, which cannot be estimated; while Comrade Beath turned over 253,000 members at the close of his year, without estimating the month of July. By the next Encampment, which will be held in July, at Portland, Me., the Order will certainly number over 300,000 Comrades. The plan of traveling on the part of the Commander-in-Chief was first inaugurated by Commander-in-Chief Louis Wagner, of Pennsylvania. The object was to visit each Department, stir up interest and enthusiasm, increase the membership, and make known the objects of the Order to the people at large.

The above officer visited nineteen Departments, traveling 11,800 miles.

SOLDIERS' MONUMENT, NATIONAL CEMETERY, ANTIETAM BATTLEFIELD, UNVAILED BY THE GRAND ARMY OF THE REPUBLIC, DEPARTMENT OF MARYLAND, SEPT. 17TH, 1880.

The next Commander-in-Chief, George S. Merrill, of Lawrence, Mass., enlarged upon the work so grandly done by his predecessor, and visited twenty-two Departments, traveling 23,700 miles, and attending ninety-three meetings of the Grand Army and other soldier organizations.

Continuing the splendid example set by Comrades Merrill and Wagner, Comrade Paul Van Dervoort visited the following permanent Departments: Maine, New Hampshire, Vermont, Connecticut, Massachusetts, Rhode Island, New York, New Jersey, Delaware, Pennsylvania, Maryland, Potomac, Virginia, West Virginia, Ohio, Indiana, Michigan, Wisconsin, Illinois, Iowa, Minnesota, Missouri, Kentucky, Nebraska, Dakota, Kansas, Colorado, California and Oregon.

Visited the Provisional Departments of Utah and Washington. Also visited New Mexico, Arizona, Wyoming, Nevada, Idaho and Montana. In all, thirty-seven States and Territories, leaving only twelve, including Alaska, unvisited.

Visited the Departments named below more than once: Connecticut, Potomac, Illinois, Iowa, Wisconsin, Pennsylvania, Indiana, Colorado, Missouri.

Attended nine Department Encampments and two Semi-annual Encampments, and the organization of one Provisional Department.

Delivered at Reunions, Camp-fires, Banquets, Receptions, Annual and Semi-annual Encampments, 143 addresses; visited 158 Posts; traveled 40,403 miles; was absent from home over 265 days. When at home daily devoted many hours to the duties of the office; wrote over 1,000 letters, and cheerfully gave one year of his life to the work.

Comrade Beath visited seventeen Departments.

The membership of the Order by Departments on March 31st, 1884, was as follows:

Arkansas—432; California—2,800; Colorado—2,338; Connecticut—4,118; Dakota—1,470; Delaware—518; Florida—124; Gulf—280; Illinois—17,988; Indiana—14,306; Iowa—13,183; Kansas—17,251; Kentucky—800; Maine—6,733; Maryland—2,100; Massachusetts—14,711; Michigan—11,798; Minnesota—3,527; Missouri—6,692; Nebraska—6,456; New Hampshire—3,641; New Jersey—5,279; New Mexico—301; New York—27,115; Ohio—23,329; Oregon—607; Pennsylvania—31,476; Potomac—1,706; Rhode Island—940; Tennessee and Georgia—547; Utah—314; Vermont—2,350; Virginia—358; West Virginia—800; Wisconsin—6,797; Washington Territory—463. Total, 233,595.

The only Post existing outside of the United States is one at Honolulu, Hawaiian Islands, attached to the Department of California.

The amount disbursed in charity can only be given during the terms of Van Dervoort and Beath.

During Van Dervoort's administration	$106,907 74
Number of members of Order relieved	8,423
During Beath's administration	$158,804 90
Number relieved of Grand Army	6,824
Relieved of soldiers and families not members	2,518

The above does not give the private sums disbursed by members of the Order, but only the official amounts given by Posts and Departments.

A Comrade in attendance at the Minneapolis Encampment lost his leg by an accident, and $3,500 was raised in the Encampment, by donations from the National body, Departments, and individuals.

Several Departments—notably California and Massachusetts—have already, or in progress, at Yountville and Chelsea, Homes for disabled soldiers.

In Massachusetts every old soldier has been taken from the almshouses and cared for in the Home. At the last session of Congress, through the influence of the Committee of the National Encampment, a Bill was passed appropriating $250,000 to establish a National Home for Disabled Soldiers west of the Mississippi River. It was located a short time ago near Leavenworth, Kan.

The Order have a Committee on Pensions, which look after legislation in Congress. Upon the call of Comrade Van Dervoort, the members of organizations of Woman's Relief Corps, organized to aid the Grand Army in the work of charity, met at Denver in July, 1883, formed the National Woman's Relief Corps, and elected E. Florence Barker, of Malden, Mass., president. They have had unexampled prosperity, demonstrating the noble work of woman most grandly, and adding thousands of dollars to the relief funds of the Order.

The Order is, and has been for many years, strictly non-partisan, as shown by the following extract from the Address of Past Commander-in-Chief Van Dervoort:

"POLITICS IN THE GRAND ARMY.

"No case of the violation of the Rules and Regulations of our Order in reference to politics has come before me during my term of office. The case brought before the Encampment at Baltimore has been settled harmoniously by the action of the Department of Indiana.

"The early builders of our Organization wisely foresaw the insidious influence of partisanship. The grand Comrades who have preceded me in command, each referred in strong, vigorous terms to the fact that the Order, if it would be lasting, must be non-partisan.

"No principle is more firmly established. We have in our ranks men of all parties and creeds. Honorable service in the War for the Union is the only test, and we care not for the political faith of any member of our noble Order. Faithful service in the War for the Union gives an old soldier the right to believe, act and vote as he deems best.

"We stand in line to-day as we did when we marched to the front, burning with loyalty, breaking asunder the ties of party, and meeting on one common platform—waving aloft a torn and discolored honorable discharge, and exemplifying fraternity, charity and loyalty.

TWENTY-FIVE YEARS AFTER.

"I have heard the doctrine advocated that the sentence in our installation service, 'That we should stand by the soldier through the whole world assail him,' means that we should do so if our Comrade be a candidate for a political office.

"The Grand Army fetters the conscience of no member. It gives the largest liberty to all. It stands aloof from the strife and clash of parties. 'It will stand by the Comrade though the world assail him,' in sickness, in distress, when the old wounds reopen, when the wife and children are destitute. It will take old veterans from the almshouse. It will remove their dust and bones from a pauper's grave and bury them in holy ground. It will procure employment. It will lighten up the desolate home with the glowing illustration of charity; but in all political and religious affairs we will hold our independence of thought and our conscience as something we will not surrender to any order."

Hundreds of soldiers' and sailors' monuments have been erected; Orphans' Homes have been built and endowed in many States; soldiers buried in pauper graves have been re-interred, and no old soldier or widow and orphan need suffer for the necessaries of life if they will make their wants known to the Grand Army. In proportion to the means of the Order they have done more for the starving soldiers and sailors than the Government they saved by their valor. The motto of the Order is "Fraternity, Charity and Loyalty."

The badge of the Grand Army consists of an eagle and a star, connected by a ribbon representing the flag. The metal of the badge is from captured cannon. None but honorably discharged soldiers can become members of the Order.

Under the auspices of the Order thousands of camp-fires, Grand Army fairs, reunions and banquets are held. These revive the suffering and sacrifices, and recall the unwritten history, of the War. At these meetings the old songs of the War are sung again as they were in the olden days; each member is a Comrade; no rank is recognized save that conferred by the Order, and every member is eligible for any position in its gift. Each Department and the National Encampment have a countersign. The secret work is prepared by the National Encampment, and consists of a beautiful ceremony, with sufficient signs and work to enable members to recognize each other.

Eleven hundred and eighty-eight members of the Order died from July, 1882, to June 30th, 1883. Eighteen hundred and ninety-seven from June 1883, to June, 1884.

When the last member dies the Order will cease to exist. It contains to-day more than one-fourth of the survivors of the war.

Memorial Day was first instituted by Comrade John A. Logan, and on the 30th of May each year has been proudly observed. It has become a national holiday, and means to perpetuate, by floral offerings, and orations commemorative of the dead, the memory of those only who wore the Union blue, and fought in defense of the flag of our common country.

THE UNITED CONFEDERATE VETERANS.

BY COLONEL I. W. AVERY,

of Atlanta Georgia.

The organization of the United Confederate Veterans, the Southern companion body to the Northern Grand Army of the Republic, had its beginning in April, 1886, when Jefferson Davis, the ex-President of the Southern Confederacy, was invited to attend the unveiling of the statue of the Honorable Benjamin Harvey Hill at Atlanta, Georgia

Mr Hill was in his life both a Confederate States senator and a United States senator, and while holding the former position he was the confidential friend and adviser of Mr Davis and his representative in many important Confederate missions of great public importance. It was peculiarly fitting that the Confederate ex-President should come to attend the ceremonies in honor of his dead friend and closest co-laborer in the statesmanship of the South in the colossal contest.

The announcement of the coming of the Southern chieftain created a profound interest among the old surviving soldiers of the Confederacy, and arrangements were made for a gathering of the scarred old Southern veterans on a large scale to pay respect to the venerable chieftain, and to carry out this purpose the idea of an organized concert of action was suggested and immediately carried into execution.

Col. John Milledge, State librarian, and a grandson of Governor John Milledge, a Revolutionary hero and an early executive of Georgia, drafted a call for a meeting of Confederate veterans and it was held in the Court House on the night of the 8th of April, 1886. Colonel Milledge presided over the meeting, which consisted of one hundred and eighty-two soldiers. An organization was created, entitled The Confederate Veterans' Association of Fulton county, Georgia

Capt. William A Wright, the Comptroller General of the State of Georgia, a one legged soldier, was chosen president of the association and its commander; John Milledge, vice president, Captain W. T. Newman, treasurer, and Ben J. Davis, secretary. The purpose of this initial organization, thus connected with the then living and only President of the Confederacy, was thus stated

"The objects of the Association are the conservation of Confederate memories; the promotion of fellowship, and the cultivation of friendship between the surviving soldiers and officers of the army, navy, marine and signal corps, and other organizations in the service of the Confederacy; the exhibition of a loyal respect to the recollections and impulses of a Confederate past; the encouragement and practice of manly virtues, the extension of reasonable aid and sympathy to fellow members in seasons of sickness and distress, and, in case of death, burial and the rendition of suitable funeral honors."

On the next Memorial Day, after that first meeting, this Veterans' Association paraded in line for the first time, under command of Captain William A. Wright

CONFEDERATE MONUMENT, CHARLESTON, S. C

And on the unveiling of the Hill monument, when Mr. Davis was present, in whose honor the association was organized, the body was out in full force and there was an immense gathering of veterans from all parts of the State and the South. Col. J. C. C. Black, of Augusta, Ga., was the orator of the occasion; Miss Winnie Davis, the daughter of Mr. Davis, called by General Gordon the "Daughter of the Confederacy," was on the stage and Mr. Davis was introduced to the great gathering by that marvellous orator, Henry W. Grady, with the words, "Defeat hath its glories no less than victory." Mr. Davis eloquently replied with the declaration, "My friends, ours is the day of peace."

Since then the association has increased to seven hundred members, and is the largest Confederate organization in the South, and is one of the most popular and important organizations in the city of Atlanta, with membership of the best citizens. It is one of the main benevolent institutions of the State, and dispenses a large charity for the need of the poor veterans, and under its charter of incorporation it can hold property and do every kind of thing in furtherance of its benevolent franchises.

The association has a beautiful plat in West View Cemetery, where indigent deceased members are given an honorable sepulchre. In the center of the lot a handsome monument has been erected, whose ground has been deeded by the cemetery company to the association, and upon the monument are these words inscribed, "Erected by the Fulton County Confederate Veterans' Association in Memory of Their Dead Comrades."

The present officers of the association are: Col. W. L. Calhoun president and commander, chosen in 1888, and annually re-elected since; Captain Frank T. Ryan, vice president; Major John F Edwards, secretary; Dr. Amos Fox, treasurer; Rev. T. P. Cleveland, chaplain; Dr. K. C. Divine, surgeon; Judge Robert L. Rogers, historian, who has written an interesting history of the association.

An interesting incident in the record of this association, and testifying to its liberal spirit was that it sent a delegation of fifty representatives to a meeting of the "Blue and the Gray," at Kennesaw Mountain, October, 1887, in a convention of old soldiers of the Confederate and Federal armies

The next step in the progress of Georgia Confederate veteran organizations was the creation of the State "Confederate Survivors' Association" of Georgia, organized in Atlanta, Ga., August 15, 1889. The officers were, Lieutenant-General John B. Gordon, Commander in-Chief; and Commanders, General Alfred H. Colquitt, present United States Senator; General Philip Cook Secretary of State of Georgia; Major-General P. M. B. Young; and Captain John McIntosh Kell, Adjutant-General of Georgia; General Clement A. Evans, Chaplain.

On the 10th of June, 1889, a convention of delegates from different Southern States assembled in New Orleans, Louisiana, and effected a general Southern Confederate organization designated as the "United Confederate Veterans," composed of all bodies of ex-Confederate soldiers and sailors throughout the Union

Gen. John Brown Gordon, of Georgia, a lieutenant general in the Confederate army under Lee, and governor and United States senator from Georgia, was elected Commander in Chief at the organization of the brotherhood, and re elected successively at the annual conventions - at Chattanooga, Tennessee, July 4th 1890, at the first annual encampment; at Jackson, Mississippi, June 9th, 1891, at the second annual encampment; and at New Orleans, Louisiana, April 8th, 1892, at the third and last annual encampment.

The first article of the constitution makes the following declaration of purpose:

"The objects and purposes of this organization will be strictly social, literary, historical, and benevolent. It will endeavor to unite in general federation all associations of Confederate veterans soldiers and sailors, now in existence or hereafter to be formed; to gather authentic data for an impartial history of the war between the States; to preserve relics or mementoes of the same; to cherish the ties of friendship that should exist among men who have shared common dangers, common sufferings, and privations; to care for the disabled and extend a helping hand to the needy; to protect the widow and the orphan, and to make and preserve a record of the services of every member, and as far as possible of those of our comrades who have preceded us in eternity."

Article II reads thus:

"The discussion of political or religious subjects nor any political action shall be permitted within the organization of the United Confederate Veterans, and any camp that will have acted in violation of this article shall be declared to have forfeited its membership."

General Gordon appointed the following staff:

Genl Fitzhugh Lee Va, Lieutenant-General.

Genl Clement A. Evans, Ga, Adjutant-General and Chief of Staff.

Genl. Thomas H. Carter, Assistant Adjutant General, Va.

Lieut. Genl. Stephen D. Lee, Miss., Quartermaster-General.

Genl W. S. Walker, Fla., First Assistant Quartermaster General.

Genl. J. F. Shipp, Tenn., Second Assistant Quartermaster-General.

Genl. Robert F. Hoke, N. C., Inspector-General.

Genl. Wright Schaumburg, Mo., First Assistant Inspector-General.

Genl. Thomas G. Jones, Ala. Second Assistant Inspector-General.

Genl. M. C. Butler, S. C, Judge-Advocate General.

Genl. W. B. Bate, Tenn., Judge-Advocate General.

Col. W. P. C. Breckenridge, Ky. Assistant Judge-Advocate General.

Genl. Joseph Wheeler, Ala., Commissary General.

Genl. W. H. Jackson, First Assistant Commissary-General

Genl. L. I. McCollum, Tenn., Second Assistant Commissary-General.

Dr. Joseph Jones, M.D., La., Surgeon-General.

Dr. I. S Todd, M D., Ga., Assistant Surgeon General.

Rev. R. L. Dabney, Tex., Chaplain.

Aides to the General Commander:

Alfred Scales, N. C.
Basil Duke, Ky.
W. H. Rogers, La.
Genl. P. M. B Young, Ga.
James Eagle, Ark.
E. P. Fleming, Fla.
E. M. Henry, Va.
Senator R. Q. Mills, Tex.
Col. John Milledge, Ga.
Col. Joseph Hodgson, Ala.
F. A. Moses, Tenn.
Charles Marshall, Md.
Col. Wm. W. Gordon, Ga.
Col. Stoddard Johnson, Ky.
Holmes Conrad, Va.
Col. Charles C. Jones, Jr., Ga.
Col. J. A. Chaleron, La.
Col Allen D. Chandler, Ga.
W. Miller Owen, La.
W. D Kyle, Ala.
J. W. Morton, Tenn.
Henry G. Muldrow, Miss.
Thomas F. Perkins, Tenn.
J. H. Forney, Ala.
Charles E. Hooker, Miss.
William Elliott, La.
Col. John C. Calhoun, N. Y.
Senator John W. Daniel, Va.
Genl. J. B. Kershaw, S. C.
Genl. Lawrence S. Ross, Tex.
Charles M. Hayes, Miss.
William Bull, Mo.
Col. John Haskell, S. C.
E. D. Willett, La.
Capt. William A. Wright, Ga.
J. T. Leslie, Fla.
H. L. Buck, S. C.
C. W. Frazier, Fla.
S. H. Buck, Ala.
D. A. Given, La.
B. T. Johnson, Md.
Price Williams, Jr., Ala.
Henry K Douglass, Md
Col. Robert Vance, N. C.
Col. John O. Waddell, Ga.
Robert Ransom, N. C.

LEE'S MONUMENT, RICHMOND, VA.

In 1892 the following additional staff officers were appointed:

Genl. W. L. Calhoun, Atlanta, Ga. Aide-de-camp.

Genl. George A. Mercer, Savannah, Ga., Aide-de-camp.

Genl. Charles C. Jones, Jr., Augusta, Ga., Fourth Assistant Inspector-General.

Genl. A. B. Andrews, Raleigh, N. C., Aide-de-camp.

Genl. J. W. Thomas, Nashville, Tenn., Aide-de-camp.

Major-Genl. E. P. Alexander, Savannah, Ga., Inspector-General.

Genl. J. C. Breckenridge, Ky., Aide-de-camp.

In 1891, July 2d, these important appointments were made:

Major-Genl. George Moorman, New Orleans, La., Adjutant General.

Col. J. F. Shipp, Chattanooga, Tenn., Quartermaster General.

The territory of the United Confederate Veterans is divided into three Departments, viz:

1. East of the Mississippi, composed of all of the Southern States this side of the Mississippi River.

2. Trans-Mississippi all States west of the Mississippi River.

3. Northwest, recently created States in the Northwest.

I. DEPARTMENT EAST OF THE MISSISSIPPI.

Lieutenant-General E Kirby Smith, Commander, Sewanee, Tenn.

Brig Genl. Wright Schaumburg, Adjutant-General and Chief of Staff. New Orleans, La.

LOUISIANA DIVISION.

Major John Glynn, Jr., Commander, New Orleans, La.

Col. W. R. Lyman, Adjutant-General and Chief of Staff, New Orleans, La.

MARYLAND DIVISION.

Major General George H. Stewart, Commander, Baltimore, Md.

VIRGINIA DIVISION.

Major-General Thomas A. Brander, Commander, Richmond, Va.

Col. Joseph V. Bidgood, Adjutant-General and Chief of Staff, Richmond, Va.

Brig.-Genl. T. S. Garnett, Aid

Brig.-Genl. Micajah Woods, Aid.

NORTH CAROLINA DIVISION.

Major General E. D. Hall, Commander, Wilmington, N. C.

Col. Junius Davis, Adjutant-General and Chief of Staff, Wilmington, N. C.

Brig.-Genl. Rufus Barringer, Charlotte, N. C., Aid.

Brig.-Genl. W. P. Roberts, Gatesville, N. C., Aid.

SOUTH CAROLINA DIVISION.

Major-General Ellison Capers, Commander, Columbia, S. C.

Col. Thomas S. Moorman, Adjutant General and Chief of Staff, Columbia, S. C.

Brig. Genl. John Bratton, Winnsboro. S. C., Aid

Brig.-Genl Stanley S Crittenden, Greenville, S. C., Aid.

FLORIDA DIVISION.

Major General J. J. Dickison, Commander, Ocala Fla.

Col. Fred L. Robertson, Adjutant-General and Chief of Staff, Brooksville, Fla.

Brig. Genl. Geo. Reese, Pensacola, Fla., Aid.

Brig.-Genl. John M. Martin, Ocala, Fla., Aid.

Brig. Genl. S. G. French, Winter Park, Fla., Aid.

GEORGIA DIVISION.

Major General P. M. B. Young, Commander Cartersville, Ga.

ALABAMA DIVISION.

Major General J. T. Holtzclaw, Commander, Montgomery, Ala.

MISSISSIPPI DIVISION.

Lieutenant General Stephen D. Lee, Commander, Starkville, Miss.

Col. E. T. Sykes, Adjutant General and Chief of Staff, Columbus, Miss.

Brig Genl. Robert Lowry, Jackson, Miss., Aid.

Brig.-Genl. J. R. Binford, Duck Hill, Miss., Aid

TENNESSEE DIVISION.

Major-General W. H. Jackson, Commander, Nashville, Tenn.

Col John P. Hickman, Adjutant-General and Chief of Staff, Nashville, Tenn.

Brig. Genl. Geo. W. Gordon, Memphis, Tenn., Aid.

Brig.-Genl. L. E. Polk, Columbia, Tenn., Aid.

KENTUCKY DIVISION.

Major-General John Boyd, Commander, Lexington, Ky.

Col. Joseph M. Jones, Adjutant-General and Chief of Staff, Paris, Ky.

Brig. Genl. W. G. Bullitt, Paducah, Ky., Aid.

TRANS-MISSISSIPPI DEPARTMENT.

Lieutenant-General William L. Cabell, Commander, Dallas, Tex.

Brig.-Genl. W. L. Thompson, Adjutant-General and Chief of Staff, Dallas, Tex.

The State of Texas furnished the largest number of camps of any State, and the State had to be divided into five divisions:

NORTHEASTERN TEXAS DIVISION.

Major-General W. L. Bush, Commander, McKinney, Tex.

Col. J. M. Pearson, Adjutant-General and Chief of Staff, McKinney, Tex.

NORTHWESTERN TEXAS DIVISION.

Major-General Richard Cobb, Commander, Wichita Falls, Tex.

Col. Wm. Parke Skeene, Adjutant-General and Chief of Staff, Wichita Falls, Tex.

Brig.-Genl. Joseph Benedict, Graham, Tex., Aid.

Brig.-Genl. W. B. Plemmons, Amarillo, Tex., Aid.

SOUTHEASTERN TEXAS DIVISION.

Major-General W. G. Blain, Commander, Fairfield, Tex.

Col. Thomas J. Gibson, Adjutant-General and Chief of Staff, Mexia, Tex.

Brig. Genl. H. H. Boone, Navasoto, Tex., Aid.

Brig.-Genl. D. H. Nunn, Crockett, Tex., Aid.

SOUTHWESTERN TEXAS DIVISION.

Major-General W. H. Young, Commander, San Antonio, Tex.

Col. D. M. Poor, Adjutant-General and Chief of Staff, San Antonio, Tex.

Brig. Genl. Hamilton P. Bee, San Antonio, Tex., Aid.

Brig. Genl. Thomas W. Dodd, Loredo, Tex., Aid.

WESTERN TEXAS DIVISION.

Major-General E. M. Bean, Commander, Cameron, Tex.

Col. W. M. McGregor, Adjutant General and Chief of Staff, Cameron, Tex.

Brig. Genl. H. E. Shelley, Austin, Tex., Aid.

Brig. Genl. Robert Donnell, Meridian, Tex., Aid.

ARKANSAS DIVISION.

Major General Ben T. DuVall, Commander, Fort Smith, Ark.

Col. R. M. Fry, Adjutant-General and Chief of Staff, Fort Smith, Ark.

Brig.-Genl. Robert H. Crockett, Stuttgart, Ark., Aid.

Brig.-Genl. J. M. Bohart, Bentonville, Ark., Aid.

MISSOURI DIVISION.

Major General J. O. Shelby, Commander, Adrian, Mo.

INDIAN TERRITORY DIVISION.

Major-General N. P. Guy, Commander, McAlester, I. T.

Col. R. B. Colman, Adjutant General and Chief of Staff, McAllester, I. T.

OKLAHOMA DIVISION.

Major-General Sam T. Leavy, Commander, Norman, O. T.

DIVISION OF THE NORTHWEST.

Major General John C. Underwood, Commander, Chicago, Ill.

Col. Sam'l Baker, Chief of Staff, Chicago, Ill.

The objects of the Southern national organization of the United Confederate Veterans are fourfold:

1st. *Historical.* To procure complete and accurate history of the deeds of Southern soldiers and commands.

2d. *Social.* To cultivate cordial and brotherly relations between the surviving soldiers of the Confederacy.

3d. *Humane.* To take care of the disabled and indigent soldiers of the Confederacy and their helpless families.

4th. *Non-Political and Non-Sectarian.* To keep the organization rigidly out of rancor of politics and the prejudice of religious creeds, cultivating patriotism and unsectarian Christianity.

The organic constitution of the order forbids any political or sectarian discussions, and any attempt to introduce them into the body is to be punished by expulsion.

The order is an aggregation of organizations and not of individuals. No man can be a member who is not a member of some State or local organization. Any local organization can join the order singly, without reference to its State association, and while the constitution provides for organizing State associations and local associations in States, it does not interfere in any way with such organizations.

Over two hundred separate camps have united with the general organization, and there is every likelihood, if the present rate of growth is kept up, that the next annual convention will see the number of camps that belong to the order doubled. The membership now runs to 20,000 members, and the order includes every Southern State. Texas has the largest number, Louisiana the second, and Tennessee next. Since May 13, 1891 165 bodies joined the order from Texas, 75; Louisiana, 21; Florida, 16; Tennessee and Kentucky, 13 each; Mississippi, 8; Alabama, 5; Georgia, 3; South Carolina, North Carolina and Arkansas, each 2; and Oklahoma Territory and District of Columbia, each 1. Georgia has the largest single camp in the order, the Fulton County Association, with over seven hundred members.

Conventions are held annually, and each convention chooses the time and place of the next convention.

The next convention is to be held at Birmingham, Ala., July 19th, 1893.

The last of the Southern States to form a connection with the order was Virginia, which united with the veterans in June, 1892, which Southern completion of the order was made the occasion of a congratulatory order by the Commander-in-Chief, General

MONUMENT OF STONEWALL JACKSON.

Gordon, in which he used the following eloquent words:

"This patriotic action by the gallant veterans of the grand old commonwealth, whose soil was so freely watered by the blood of the brave sons of all of her sister States of the South; whose matchless record as soldiers is only equaled by their peerless citizenship, bright exemplars in peace, and worthy of imitation by all in the holy work of honoring their illustrious dead and caring for their living heroes, conspicuous for their devotion to their traditions and resplendent history from 1861 to 1865, and at the same time yielding to none in their allegiance and in their emulous and ennobling endeavor to contribute to the upbuilding and grandeur of our reunited country."

These words from the head of this order emphasize the spirit of its leaders and rank and file, that the most tender consideration of Confederate memories and virtues goes hand in hand with loyalty to the principles of the government and devotion to the welfare of the whole country.

August 15th, 1891, the Commander appointed a committee to select an official seal for the order. Thomas D. Peake was chairman. The seal recommended was approved and officially adopted October 31st, 1891, and is a gold seal, round, two and one-half inches in diameter, with a figure of Lee on horseback, pointing to the front, and over his head the words, "Deo Vindice." The figure is encircled by a wreath, and encircling the seal on its outer edge are the words, "United Confederate Veterans, 1889, 1861-1865."

The badge of the order is half an inch square, with a cross of blue, with ends at each corner, and filled with thirteen white stars, the four triangular spaces colored red.

The first annual convention of the United Confederate Veterans was held at Chattanooga, Tennessee, July 3d, 4th and 5th, 1890. The occasion was a great one. There was a vast attendance, eloquent speeches, large parades, fireworks on an extensive scale, a visit to the historic battlefields around Chattanooga, separate reunions of the surgeons and the chaplains of the Confederacy, and the complete organization of the order into working shape.

The second convention was held at Jackson, Mississippi, June 9th, 1891, and had an increased attendance and interest.

The third and last annual convention was an enormous affair, and a number of important matters were done. The place of meeting was New Orleans, La., and the time the 8th and 9th of April, 1892. Fully twenty five thousand people from a distance were in attendance, and the entire inhabitancy of the city turned out to witness the parade.

The chief feature of the convention was the great oration of that, as General Gordon called in introducing him, "unrivalled" orator, United States Senator John Warwick Daniel, of Virginia. It was masterful, eloquent and patriotic. There was not a sectional sentiment in it, but a broad catholicity of national feeling, and its Southern pride was accompanied by a noble respect for the other side of the contest. These vital sentences are alike pregnant with truth and the spirit of the order:

"There was no difference between the Confederate States and the United States in respect to those things which made or were the fruit of the revolution of 1776."

"Nature made a map of a great empire in the territory of the Union."

"In their shirt sleeves no man could have told the difference between a Union and a Confederate soldier. It was a family quarrel, between a big brother and a little one, and like most little brothers we got the worst of it."

The most important matter, perhaps, done by the convention was the passage of a unanimous resolution for the Commander to appoint an historical committee of seven to formulate a plan to secure a true and reliable history of the late Civil War, and to select a proper and truthful history of the United States for use in the schools of the South. The Commander appointed the following committee:

Lieut.-Genl. E. Kirby Smith, chairman, Sewanee, Tenn.

Prof. J. N. Stubbs, Woods Crossroads, Gloucester County, Va.

Prof. Alonzo Hill, Tuscaloosa, Ala.

Lieut.-Genl. Stephen D. Lee, Starkville, Miss.

Major-Genl. Ellison Capers, Columbia, S. C.

Col. H. L. Bentley, Abilene, Tex.

Prof. J. W. Nicholson, Baton Rouge, La.

The New Orleans Convention also passed a unanimous resolution, for the Commander to appoint a committee to memorialize the Governors and Legislatures of the States and Territories of the late Confederate States to make adequate provision for maimed and helpless Confederate veterans and their widows. This is the committee:

Lieut. Genl. Wade Hampton, chairman, Columbia, S. C.

U. S. Senator John W. Daniel, Danville, Va.
Ex Governor Robert Lowry, Jackson, Miss.
Ex Governor L. S. Ross, College Station, Tex.
Ex Governor James B. Eagle, Little Rock, Ark.

The convention also authorized by a vote of the entire body the appointment of a committee, to be composed of one delegate from each State and one from the Indian Territory, District of Columbia and District of the Northwest to raise a fund to build a monument to Jefferson Davis. This is the committee:

Lieut-Genl. W. L. Cabell, chairman Dallas, Tex.
Capt. John L. Ardmore, Galt, Ardmore, I. T.
Genl. John M. Harrell, Hot Springs, Ark.
Major-Genl. J. O. Shelby, Adrian, Mo.
Col. Charles G. Johnson, New Orleans, La.
Col. J. L. Power, Jackson, Miss.
Major-Genl. W. H. Jackson, Nashville, Tenn.
Major-Genl. John Boyd, Lexington, Ky.
Major-Genl. John C. Underwood, Chicago, Ill
Genl. Joseph Hodgson, Mobile, Ala.
Genl. W. L. Calhoun, Atlanta, Ga.
Major-Genl. J. J. Dickison, Ocala, Fla.
Dr. R. H. Holliday, Clinton, N C
Capt B. H Teague, Aiken, S. C.
Major Albert Akers, Washington, D. C.

In unison with the spirit of respect to Mr. Davis, the New Orleans convention passed a resolution unitedly to appoint a committee to memorialize the Confederate States to grant a pension to Mrs Jefferson Davis during her lifetime The committee appointed consists of the following Veterans:

Gen. George W. Gordon, chairman, Memphis, Tenn.
Hon. G W. Bolton, Pineville, La.
Maj.-Genl N B. Guy McAlester, I. T
Joseph W. Mercer, Kansas City, Mo.
Genl. A T. Watts, Dallas, Tex.
Major-Genl. Ben T. Duval, Fort Smith, Ark.
Col. and Hon. W. C. P. Breckenridge, Lexington, Ky.
Joseph F. Johnston, Birmingham, Ala.
Col. Hugh H Colquitt, Atlanta, Ga
Gov. P. P. Fleming, Jacksonville, Ala.
Col. J. B. Davis Aiken, S. C.
Genl. and Senator Matt W. Ransom, Carysburg, S C.
Major-Genl. J. M. Stone, Jackson, Miss.

An important committee on the constitution of the order was authorized to be appointed, of which Gen J A. Chalaron was made chairman.

General Gordon, in his initial address in 1889, upon first being installed as the Commander of the veterans, presented clearly the spirit of the organization, that should and will commend the order to the patriotic and country loving everywhere

He said that no misjudgments can defeat their peaceful purposes for the future. Their aspirations had been lifted by the mere force and urgency of surrounding conditions to a plane far above the paltry considerations of partisan triumphs. The honor of the American Republic, the just powers of the Federal government, the equal rights of the States, the integrity of a constitutional Union, the sanctions of the law, and the enforcement of order had no class of defenders more true and devoted than ex soldiers of the South and their worthy descendants

The truth must be realized that a people without memories of heroic deeds, heroic sufferings and sacrifices, is a people without a history; that to cherish such memories and recall such a past, whether crowned with success or consecrated in defeat, is to idealize principle, strengthen character, intensify love of country, and convert defeat and disaster into pillars of support for future manhood and noble womanhood.

Whether, he urged unanswerably, the Southern people, under their changed conditions, may ever hope to witness another civilization which shall equal that which began with their Washington and ended with their Lee, it is certainly true that devotion to their glorious past is not only the surest guarantee of future progress and the holiest bond of unity, but is also the strongest claim they can present to the confidence and respect of the other sections of the Union

CHRONOLOGICAL

LIST OF EVENTS

(1863-1865)

AND

MISCELLANEOUS STATISTICS.

COMPILED AND ARRANGED

BY

T. CAMPBELL-COPELAND,

Editor of "Modern Military Maxims," etc., etc.

FROM "OFFICIAL RECORDS OF THE FEDERAL AND CONFEDERATE ARMIES;" THE "REBELLION RECORD;" "PHISTERER'S STATISTICAL RECORD;" "HAMERSLEY'S ARMY REGISTER;" THE "OFFICIAL ARMY REGISTER"; STATISTICAL VOLUMES AND PAMPHLETS OF THE DEPARTMENT OF THE INTERIOR; "THE ANNUAL CYCLOPÆDIA;" "TWENTY YEARS OF CONGRESS;" AND SUCH OTHER THOROUGHLY RELIABLE BOOKS AND DOCUMENTS AS HAVE BEEN MADE AVAILABLE.

CHRONOLOGICAL LIST OF EVENTS (1860-1865).—Continued.

Date	Event	Location	Duration	Force F	Force C	Composition of Force	Commanders	Killed F.	Killed C.	Wounded F.	Wounded C.	Prisoners taken by F.	Prisoners taken by C.	Missing F.	Missing C.	Guns taken	Stands of arms taken	Advantage
1863																		
Sept. 21	Engagement	Bristol, Tenn.				Foster's Cavalry Brigade, Shackleford's Cav. Division of Army of the Ohio.												
	Engagement	White's Ford, Va.				Cavalry of the Army of the Potomac.												
Sept. 22	Skirmish	Johnson's Depot, Tenn.				8th Tennessee Volunteers.												
	Skirmish	Jack's Shop, Madison Court House, Va.			Cav.	1st Div., Cav. Corps, Army of the Potomac	Gen. Buford, F.	1		20		45						Federal.
	Engagement	Carter's Station, Tenn.				3rd Brig., Cav. Div., Army of the Ohio.												
	Battle	Blountsville, Tenn.	4 hours			2nd Mounted Brig., Cav. Div., Army of the Ohio	Col. Foster, F. / —— Carter, C.	5	30	12	56	60				1		Federal.
	Engagement	Rockville, Md.			Cav.	11th New York Cavalry, and Infantry	Capt. Kilgore, C.		K&W 34									Federal.
Sept. 23	Raid by Confederate Guerillas	Donaldsonville, La.		14		14th New York Cavalry							14					Conf'd.
Sept. 24	Engagement	Zollicoffer, Tenn.				3rd Brig., Cav. Div., Army of the Ohio.												
	Proclamation issued by President Lincoln raising the blockade of Alexandria, Va.																	
Sept. 25	Skirmish	Upperville, Va.			Guer 150	1st Maryland Potomac Home Brigade of Cavalry	Maj. Cole, F.		1			9						Federal.
	Skirmish	Red Bone Church, Mo.				2nd Wisconsin Cavalry.												
	Attack on Federal Garrison	Donaldsonville, La.			Guer	Federal Troops												Federal.
Sept. 26	Engagement	Calhoun, Tenn. (Hagnewood Prairie).				Cavalry of the Army of the Ohio.												
Sept. 27	Attack on Federal Troops	Moffat's Station, Ark. (Hagnewood Station)		75	Cav.	Detachment of 1st Arkansas Volunteers	Capt. Parker, F. / —— Shelby, C.	2	5	2	20	16						Federal.
Sept. 28	Engagement	McMinnville, Tenn.				(Troops not specified.)												Federal
	Consolidation of 20th and 21st Army Corps, to be called the 4th Army Corps, under Major-Gen. Gordon Granger.																	
	Capture of Confederate Cavalry	Amite and Comite Rivers, La.		80	Guer	4th Wisconsin Cavalry	Lieut. Earl, F.											Federal.
	Bombardment of Fort Sumter, S. C., by Federal Batteries on Morris Island.																	
Sept. 29	Engagement	Sterling's Farm, (Morganzia), La.	2 hours	500	4500	19th Iowa and 26th Indiana Volunteers	Col. Leake, F. / Maj. Montgomery, F. / Gen. Green, C.	K.W. & P. 400								2		Conf'd.
	Skirmish	Moor's Bluff, Big Black River				Federal Troops												Conf'd.
Sept. 30	Skirmish and Capture of Confederate Guerillas	Swallow's Bluff, Tenn.			Guer 120	7th Kansas and 7th Illinois Cavalry	Col. Rowett, F. / —— Newsome, C.	1		2		120						Federal.
	Lieut.-Gen. L. Polk, C. S. A., relieved from his command.																	
Oct. 1	Capture of General Rosecrans' Wagon-Train by Confederates, under Wheeler, near Anderson's Cross Roads, Tenn.																	
Oct. 2	Attack on Confederate Troops	Anderson's Cross Roads, Tenn.			4000	1st Wis., 2nd Ind., 1st Tenn. Cav. of the Army of the Cumberland	Col. McCook, F.		K&W 120			200						Federal.
	Cavalry Skirmish	Franklin, La.			Cav.	Federal Cavalry	Col. Davis, F. / Capt. Squires, C.		1							1		Federal.
Oct. 3	Engagement	Thompson's Cove, Tenn.				1st Brig., 2nd Div., Cav. and Wilder's Brig., Mounted Inf.												
	Engagement and Capture by Confederate Forces	McMinnville, Tenn.	1½ hours	450	19000	4th Tennessee Volunteers	Maj. Patterson, F.	7	K&W 23	W&M 31								Conf'd.
Oct. 4	(5th-1). Skirmishes	Murfreesboro' Road, Tenn.				2nd Ky. Cav. and Wilder's Brig. of Mounted Inf.	Col. Utley, F. / Gen. Forrest, C.											
	Skirmish	Newtown, La.				(Organizations not stated)		1		4								Federal.
	Skirmish	Neosho, Mo.		3 Co.		6th Missouri Militia Cavalry.												
Oct. 5	Skirmish	Stone River, Tenn.		1 Co.		10th Michigan Volunteers.												
	Scout and Skirmish	Harper's Ferry, Va.		30	Cav.	Federal Cavalry	Capt. Bean, F. / —— Imboden, C.	1		3		10						Conf'd.
	Engagement	Blue Springs, Tenn.				Portion of Gen. Burnside's Forces.												
	Skirmish	New Albany, Miss.				(Troops not specified.)												
	Raid on Federal Troops	Glasgow, Ky.				37th Kentucky Mounted Infantry	Capt. Nun, F. / Col. Hughes, C.		4		0		142				100	Conf'd.
	Skirmish	Wartrace, Tenn.				5th Iowa Cavalry.												
Oct. 6	Raid by Confederates	Baxter Springs, Ark.		100	600	Detachment 3rd Wis., 14th Kan., Cav. and 12th Kan. Vols. (83rd U. S. Colored Troops)	Gen. Blunt, F. / —— Quantrell, C.	75		6								Conf'd.
	Skirmish	Fort Blair, Ark.				Detachment 3rd Wisconsin Cavalry.												
Oct. 7	Attack on Federal Troops	Como, Miss.	3 hours		Guer.	West Tennessee Cavalry	Col. Harrison, F. / Cols. Faulkner and Wilson, C.	37										Conf'd.
Oct. 8	(6th and 8th.) Engagements	Shelbyville Pike, Tenn. (Farmington).				1st, 2nd and 4th Ohio, 2nd Ky. Cav. and Wilder's Brigade of Mounted Infantry	Gen. Crook, F. / Gen. Wheeler, C.	20	K&W 235	150		800						Federal.
	Engagement	Charlestown, Va.		1 Co.	Cavl. 400	Federal Cavalry	Capt. Somers, F. / —— Imboden, C.	10		10						4		Conf'd.
	Skirmish	Warsaw, Mo.				7th Missouri Militia Cavalry.												
	Engagement	Salem, Miss.		5000	4000	Colonels McCrellis and Phillip's Cavalry Brigades	Col. McCrellis, F. / Col. Phillips, F. / Gen. S. D. Lee, C.		K&W 16									Federal.
	Destruction of Carthage, Mo., by Confederate Troops.																	
Oct. 9	Engagement	Sugar Creek, Tenn.				3rd Brigade, 2nd Cavalry Division.												
Oct. 10	Engagements	Rapidan, Va.				1st Div., Cav., Army of the Potomac.												
	Engagement	Ingraham's Plantation, Miss.	3 hours			2nd Wisconsin Cavalry	Col. Hatch, F.		K&W 50									Federal.
	Reconnoissance and Skirmishes	James City, Va. (Robertson's Run)	1 hour		Cav	3rd Cav. Div., Army of the Potomac	Gen. Kilpatrick, F. / Gen. Stuart, C.											Conf'd.
	Engagement	Blue Springs, Tenn.				Shackleford's Cav. Div. and Inf. of the Ohio	Gen. Shackleford, F.	K&W 100				150						Federal.
	Engagement	Vermilion Bayou, La.				1st Brigade, 1st Division, 19th Corps	Gen. Weitzel, F. / Col. Paine, F.			5								Federal.
Oct. 11	Engagement	Rheatown, Tenn.				2nd Brig. Cav. Div., Army of the Ohio.												

CHRONOLOGICAL LIST OF EVENTS (1860-1865).—Continued.

Date	Event	Location	Duration	Force F.	Force C.	Composition of Force	Commanders	Killed F	Killed C	Wounded F	Wounded C	Prisoners Taken at F	Prisoners Taken at C	Missing F	Missing C	Guns	Stands of Arms	Advantage
1863																		
Oct. 11	Engagement	Henderson's Mill, Tenn	3 hours	500	2700	5th Indiana Cavalry	Col. Graham, F.; Col. Butler, F.; Gen. Williams, C.	...	30	11	...	10	...	6	...	...	...	Conf'd.
	Engagement	Collierville, Tenn	3 hours	...	...	66th Ind. Volunteers, 13th U. S. Infantry	Gen. Sherman, F.; Lieut. ——, 13th Regiment, F.	15	...	80	...	...	...	...	...	...	...	Federal.
Oct. 12	Engagement	Jeffersonton, Va	...	...	...	2nd Cav. Div., Army of the Potomac.												
	Engagement	Ingham's Mills, Miss	3 hours	...	...	2nd Brigade of Cavalry, 16th Corps	Col. Hatch, F.	...	k&w 50	...	...	...	...	...	...	...	...	Federal.
	(13th-18th). Engagement	Culpepper White Sulphur Springs, Va	...	...	...	Cavalry Corps, Army of the Potomac	Gen. Kilpatrick, F.; Col. Gregg, F.	k.w. & m. 150	...	k.w. & m. 400	...	...	...	...	...	...	...	Conf'd.
	(12th-13th). Engagement	Merrill's Crossing, Mo	...	1600	2000	1st, 4th and 7th Mo. Militia Cavalry, Enrolled Militia Infantry and 1st Mo. Militia Battery	B.-Gen. Brown, F.; L.-Col. Lazear, F.	k&w 30	63	...	70	...	...	...	...	...	...	Federal.
Oct. 13	Action	Wyatts, Miss	2 hours	2500	8000	2nd Brigade, Cavalry Division, 16th Corps	Col. Hatch, F.	k&w 40	15	...	...	76	...	...	...	...	...	Federal
	Reconnoissance	Big Black River, Miss	...	...	...	Federal Infantry and Cavalry	M.-Gen. McPherson, F.											
	Engagement	Maysville, Ala	...	...	...	1st Div., Cav. Corps, Army of the Cumberland.												
	(13th-14th). Skirmish and Engagement	Blountsville, Tenn	...	...	...	3rd Brigade Cav. Div., Army of the Ohio	Gen. Shackleford, F.; Capt. Copeland, F.	1	6	6	24	...	...	...	...	...	...	Federal.
	Attack on Federal Outpost	Bull Town, Va	...	400	...	Detachment 9th and 11th W. Va. Volunteers	Capt. Mattingly, F.; Col. W. L. Jackson, C.	...	8	...	90	...	...	...	...	...	...	Federal
Oct. 14	Battle	Bristol Station, Va	...	...	...	2nd Corps, Warren's; portions of Sykes' 5th Corps and 2nd Cav. Div., Army of the Potomac	Gen. Warren, F.; Gen. A. P. Hill, C.	81	k&w 1800	828	...	450	...	...	...	5	...	Federal.
	Engagement	Auburn, Va	...	...	...	Portion of 1st Div., 2nd Corps, Army of the Potomac.												
	Engagement	Salt Lick, Va	...	...	...	6th West Virginia Volunteers	Maj. Howe, F.; Col. W. M. Jackson, C.	...	...	...	...	...	...	...	...	...	...	Federal.
Oct. 15	Engagement and Capture by Federal Forces of	Canton, Miss	...	...	...	Portions of 15th and 17th Corps	M.-Gen. McPherson, F.	...	k.w. & p. 200	...	...	...	...	...	...	...	...	Federal.
	Engagement	McLean's Ford, Va. (Liberty Mills)	...	...	...	N. J. Brig., 3rd Corps, Army of the Potomac		3	k&w. 60	25	...	...	...	...	...	...	...	Federal.
	Capture of Confederate Troops	Hedgesville, Va	...	...	...	Detachment 1st N. Y. and 12th Penn. Cav. and 116th Ohio Volunteers	Col. Pierce, F.; —— Gilmore, C.	...	...	...	...	46	...	...	...	...	...	Federal.
	Capture of Confederate Troops	Blackburn Ford, Va	...	Cav.	...	Portion of the 2nd Corps, Army of the Potomac	Gen. Buford, F.	...	...	...	...	60	...	...	...	...	...	Federal.
Oct. 16	(16th-18th). Skirmishes	Brownsville, Miss	...	...	...	Portions of the 15th and 17th Corps	M.-Gen. McPherson, F.											
	Skirmish	Cross Timbers, Mo	...	...	...	18th Iowa Volunteers.												
Oct. 17	Destruction of Two Blockade Runners	Tampa Bay, Fla	...	...	...	Federal Gunboats *Tahoma* and *Adela*	Act. Master Harris, U.S.N.; Capt. Westcott, C.	0	...	10	...	...	5	...	...	...	...	Federal.
	Engagement	Clinton, Miss	...	...	...	Detachment of the Army of the Tennessee	M.-Gen. McPherson, F.											
	Engagement	Rapidan, Va	...	...	Cav.	1st Div., Cav. Corps, Army of the Potomac	Gen. Buford, F.	...	...	...	...	...	...	...	...	...	...	Conf'd.
	Skirmish	Humansville, Mo	...	...	...	6th Missouri Militia Cavalry.												
Oct. 18	Capture and Re-capture of	Charlestown, Va	...	...	...	9th Maryland Volunteers	Col. Simpson, F.; Col. Wells, F.; Gen. Imboden, C.	10	k&w 30	5	...	21	379	...	...	...	...	1 Con. 2 Fed.
	Engagement	Bentonville, Va	...	...	...	34th Mass. Volunteers and 17th Indiana Battery.												
Oct. 19	Action	Buckland Mills, Va	...	...	...	3rd Div., Cav. Corps, Army of the Potomac	Gen. Custer, F.; Gen. Stuart, C.	k.w. & m. 200	...	...	...	...	...	...	...	...	...	Conf'd.
Oct. 20	Engagement	Barton Station, Miss	...	500	1000	Troops of the Army of the Tennessee	Col. Sprague, F.; Gen. Ferguson, C.	15	...	...	...	...	...	...	...	...	...	Conf'd.
	(20th-22d). Engagement	Philadelphia, Tenn	4 hours	...	...	45th Ohio Mounted Infantry, 1st, 11th and 12th Ky. Cavalry and 24th Indiana Battery	Col. Wolford, F.	...	...	...	...	...	...	...	...	...	...	Conf'd.
	Pursuit of Confederate Troops, and Engagement	Philadelphia, Tenn	...	...	...	1st and 11th Kentucky Cavalry	Major Graham, F.	20	130	60	350	111	...	354	...	...	...	Federal.
Oct. 21	Engagement	Cherokee Station, Ala	1 hour	...	4000	Osterhaus' 1st Div., 15th Corps, Army of the Tenn	Gen. Osterhaus, F.; Gen. S. D. Lee, C.	k&w 100	...	...	...	...	...	...	...	...	...	Federal.
	Engagement, and Occupation of	Opelousas, La	...	...	...	Franklin's Division of Bank's Troops	Gen. Franklin, F.	...	...	...	...	...	...	...	...	...	...	Federal.
Oct. 22	Skirmish	Beverly Ford and Rappahannock Crossing, Va	...	...	Pkts.	2nd Pennsylvania and 1st Maine Cavalry	Lieut.-Col. Brinton, F.	...	...	6	...	...	...	...	...	...	...	Federal.
	Skirmish	New Madrid Bend, Tenn	...	...	...	32nd Iowa Volunteers.												
Oct. 23	Attack on Federal Supply Train	Tullahoma, Tenn	½ hour	80	...	70th Indiana Volunteers	Lieut. Campbell, F.	...	...	...	...	...	...	...	...	...	...	Federal.
Oct. 24	Skirmishes	Bealton and Rappahannock Bridge, Va	...	...	...	1st Div. Cav. Corps, Army of the Potomac.												
	Skirmish	Sweetwater, Tenn	...	...	...	Cavalry, Army of the Ohio.												
Oct. 25	Attack of Confederate Troops	Collierville, Tenn	...	...	...	(Troops not given.)		...	...	...	...	...	...	...	...	...	...	Federal.
	Engagement	Pine Bluff, Ark	5 hours	600	2300	5th Kansas and 1st Indiana Cavalry	Col. Clayton, F.; Gen. Marmaduke, C.	11	k&w 130	27	...	53	...	1	...	...	...	Federal.
	Skirmish	Creek Agency, Ind. Territory	...	...	...	1st Kansas Indian Home Guards and 2nd Ind. Battery.												
Oct. 26	Engagement	Cane Creek, Ala. (Bear Creek or Tuscumbia)	...	...	...	1st Division, 15th Corps	Gen. Osterhaus, F.	2	10	6	80	...	...	...	...	...	...	Federal
	Skirmish	Philadelphia, Tenn	...	...	...	(Organizations not recorded.)												
	Attack on Federal Troops	Vincent's Cross Roads, Miss. (Bay Springs)	...	600	...	1st Alabama Federal Cavalry	Col. Spencer, F.	...	...	...	...	...	...	...	...	...	...	Conf'd.
Oct. 27	Attack on Confederate Troops	Brown's Ferry, Tenn	...	...	...	Detachments from 5th, 6th and 23rd Ky., 1st, 6th, 41st, 93rd and 124th Ohio and 20th Ind. Vols.	Gen. W. F. Smith, F.; B.-Gen. Hazen, F.; Gen. Longstreet, C.	5	6	21	...	...	...	9	...	...	...	Federal

CHRONOLOGICAL LIST OF EVENTS (1860-1865).—Continued.

DATE.	EVENT.	LOCATION.	DURATION.	FORCE. F.	FORCE. C.	COMPOSITION OF FORCE.	COMMANDERS.	KILLED. F.	KILLED. C.	WOUNDED. F.	WOUNDED. C.	PRISONERS TAKEN BY F.	PRISONERS TAKEN BY C.	MISSING. F.	MISSING. C.	[illegible]	[illegible]	ADVANTAGE.
1863 Oct. 27	Bombardment of Fort Sumter, S. C., by four Federal Monitors																	
Oct. 28	Battle	Wauhatchie, Tenn.	3 hours.			11th Corps and 2nd Division, 12th Corps	Gen. Hooker, F.; Gen. Geary, F.; Gen. Longstreet, C.	K. W. & M. 416				100						Federal.
	(28th-29th). Engagement	Lookout Creek, Tenn.				Troops of Gen. Thomas' Command	Gen. Howard, F.											Federal.
	Skirmish	Clarksville, Ark.				3rd Wisconsin Cavalry.												
	Engagement	Leiper's Ferry, Tenn.				11th and 37th Kentucky and 112th Illinois Vols.												
	Major-Gen. B. F. Butler appointed to command 18th Army Corps, and Department of Virginia and North Carolina.																	
Oct. 29	Engagement	Cherokee Station, Ala.				1st Division, 15th Corps												Federal.
	Lieut.-Gen. Polk, C. S. A., appointed to "a new field of duty" by Jefferson Davis, who exonerates him from all blame in connection with his late command.																	
Nov. 1	Skirmish	Washington, N. C.				(Organizations not recorded.)												Federal
	Skirmish	Fayetteville, Tenn.				4th Indiana Cavalry												
Nov. 2	Occupation by Federal Forces of	Brazos de Santiago, Texas.				Troops of the 13th Corps	Col. Dwyer, F.											
Nov. 3	Skirmishes	Centreville and Pike Factory, Tenn.			Guer.	Federal Cavalry	L.-Col. Shelby, F.; — Hawkins, C.		15			60						Federal.
	Action	Grand Coteau, La.				3rd and 4th Divisions, 13th Corps	M.-Gen. Washburn, F.; Gen. Burbridge, F.; Brig. Gen. Green, C.	26.	K. W. & M. 415	12?		65		576				Federal.
	Attack by Confederate Troops on	Collierville, Tenn.				Cavalry Brigade, 16th Corps	Col. Hatch, F.											Federal.
Nov. 4	(3d-?). Engagement	Lawrenceburg, Tenn.			400	14th Michigan Mounted Infantry	Col. Fitzgibbon, F.; — Cooper, C.		8	3	7	24						Federal.
	Attack by Confederate Troops on	Moscow and La Fayette, Tenn.				Cavalry Brigade, 16th Corps	Col. Hatch, F.; Gens. Chalmers and Lee, C.	5	20	41				41				Federal.
	(8th-?). Attack on Confederate Troops	Metley's Ford, Little Tenn. River				Cavalry of the Army of the Ohio	Gen. Sanders, F.; Col. Adams, F.		40			40						Federal.
Nov. 5	Engagement	Mill Point, W. Va.				14th Pennsylvania and 3rd West Virginia Cavalry												Federal.
	Occupation of Brownsville, Texas, by Federal Troops under Major-Gen. Banks																	
Nov. 6	Skirmish	Kincaids, Tenn.				(Troops not specified.)												
	Engagement	Rogersville, Tenn.				7th Ohio Cavalry, 2nd Tenn. Mounted Infantry and 2nd Illinois Battery	Gen. Shackleford, F.	5	80	12				650				Conf'd.
	Battle	Droop Mountain, Va.				14th Penn., 2nd and 5th W. Va. Cav., 8th and 10th W. Va., 28th Ohio Vols., and Bat. B. W. Va. Art.	B.-Gen. Averill, F.; Gens. Echols and Jenkins, C.	K&W 100										Federal.
Nov. 7	Engagement	Kelly's Ford, Va.				1st U. S. Sharpshooters, 40th N. Y., 1st and 20th Ind., 3rd and 5th Mich., 110th Penn. Vols., with remainder of 3rd Corps, Army of the Potomac	Gen. Birney, F.; Col. Godwin, C.	K&W 35										Federal.
	Engagement	Stevensburg, Va.				3rd Cavalry Division, Army of the Potomac	Gen. Kilpatrick, F.											Federal.
	Occupation of Lewisburgh, Va., by Federal Forces under Gen. Duffie.																	
	Engagement	Rappahannock Station, Va.			2000		Gens. French and Sedgwick, F.; Col. Godwin, C.	K&W 400				1500				0		Federal.
Nov. 8	Skirmish	Clarksville, Ark.				3rd Wisconsin Cavalry												
	Cavalry Fight	Muddy Run, Culpepper, Va.			Cav.	1st Div., Cav. Corps, Army of the Potomac	Gen. Buford, F.; — Wilson, C.											Federal.
Nov. 9	Engagement	Bayou Sara, Miss.			Guer	Federal Cavalry			60			40						Federal.
Nov. 10	Advance of a portion of the Army of the Potomac, under General Kilpatrick.																	
Nov. 11	(13th-?). Skirmish	Natchez, Miss.			Cav. 50	58th U. S. Colored Troops (6th Mississippi)	Capt. Hitchcock, F.; — Adams and Mosby, C.	4	4	7								Federal.
	Maj. Gen. Foster, U. S. A., relieved from the command of the Department of Eastern Virginia and North Carolina.																	
	Maj.-Gen. Butler assumes command of the Departments of Eastern Virginia and North Carolina.																	
Nov. 12	Skirmish	Roseville, Ark.		2 Co's		2nd Kansas Cavalry.												Feder...
Nov. 13	Skirmish	Trinity River, Cal.		2 Co's		1st Battalion, California Mountaineer Infantry.												
	Skirmish	Mill Creek Valley, W. Va.				(Troops not specified.)												
	Skirmish	Palmyra, Tenn.		1 Co.	Guer.	Federal Mounted Infantry	Capt. Cutler, F.		2	3	5	1						Federal.
	Maj.-Gen. John A. Logan surrenders his command of the 3d Division, 17th Army Corps, to Brig.-Gen. Leggett, by order of the War Department.																	
Nov. 14	Engagement	Huff's Ferry, Tenn.				111th Ohio, 107th Ill., 11th and 13th Ky., 23rd Mich. Vols. and 24th Mich. Battery.	Gen. White, F.; Col. Chapin, F.											Federal.
	Skirmishes	Rockford, Tenn.		Pkts.		1st Ky. Cav. and 45th Ohio Mounted Infantry	Gen. Sanders, F.											Conf'd.
	Skirmish	Marysville, Tenn.				11th Kentucky Cavalry.												
Nov. 15	Skirmish	Loudon Creek, Tenn.				111th Ohio Volunteers.												
	Evacuation of Lenoirs, Tenn., by Federal Forces	Lenoirs, Tenn.				Cavalry and Infantry of the Army of the Ohio	Gen. Burnside, F.											
	Engagement	Holston River, Knoxville, Tenn.				11th Ky., 45th Ohio and 37th Ky. Mounted Infantry.												
Nov. 16	Expedition	Charles City Cross Roads, Va.				Federal Cavalry	Col. West, F.											
	Engagement	Campbell Station, Tenn.				9th Corps, 2nd Division, 23rd Corps and Cavalry, Army of the Ohio	Gen. Burnside, F.; Gen. Longstreet, C.	K&W 400	K. W. & F. 1000									

CHRONOLOGICAL LIST OF EVENTS (1860-1865).—Continued.

DATE.	EVENT.	LOCATION.	DURATION.	FORCE. F.	FORCE. C.	COMPOSITION OF FORCE.	COMMANDERS.	KILLED. F.	KILLED. C.	WOUNDED. F.	WOUNDED. C.	PRISONERS TAKEN BY F.	PRISONERS TAKEN BY C.	MISSING. F.	MISSING. C.	GUNS TAKEN.	STANDS OF ARMS TAKEN.	ADVANTAGE.
1863																		
Nov. 17	(17th–Dec. 4th). Siege 17th, Attack on outposts	KNOXVILLE, TENN.		Outpts		Army of the Ohio	Gen. Burnside, F.; Gen. Longstreet, C.	K. W. & P. 600	K. W. & P. 1600									Conf'd.
	Skirmish	WILLOW CREEK, CAL.				1st California Battalion Mountaineer Infantry.												
	Skirmish	MOUNT JACKSON, VA.				1st New York Cavalry	Col. Bayard, F.	2		8		27		8				Federal.
	Engagement and Capture by Federal Forces	MUSTANG ISLAND near ARANSAS PASS, TEX.			Bat'y	13th and 14th Me., 24th Iowa and 8th Ind Vols. and Battery F, 1st Mo. Art. and Gunboat *Monongahela*.	Maj.-Gen. Banks, F.											
Nov. 18	Skirmish	CARRION CROW BAYOU, LA.				6th Missouri Cavalry												
	Return to Harper's Ferry, Va., of Colonel Bayard's Expedition.																	
Nov. 19	Skirmish	UNION CITY, TENN.				2nd Ill. Cav. and Detachment 38th Ill. Infantry	Capt. Moore, F.		11			63						Federal.
	Consecration of National Cemetery, at Gettysburg, Pa.																	
Nov. 21	Affair at	WATERPROOF, LA.			Guer.	Federal Steamer *Welcome*.												
	Attack by Confederate Battery and Guerillas on the Steamer *Black Hawk*, near Red River Landing on the Mississippi.																	
Nov. 23	(23rd–25th). Battles	CHATTANOOGA, TENN. (including Orchard Knob, Lookout Mountain, and Missionary Ridge).		85,000	45,000	4th and 14th Corps, Army of the Cumberland, 11th Corps, Geary's Div. of the 12th Corps and 15th Corps, Army of the Tennessee	Gen. Grant, F.; Gen. Bragg, C.	757		4529		6142		330		40	7000	Federal.
	Battle	CHATTANOOGA, TENN. (Orchard Knob).				Granger's and Palmer's Corps, supported by Howard's Corps	Gen. Thomas, F.	K. W. & M. 167				169						Federal.
Nov. 24	Battle	LOOKOUT MOUNTAIN, TENN.	3 hours	9681		4th and 14th Corps, Army of the Cumberland, 11th Corps, Geary's Div. of the 12th Corps and 15th Corps, Army of the Tennessee	Gen. Hooker, F.; Gen. Bragg, C.					500						Federal.
	Skirmish	BARNWELL'S ISLAND, S. C.				33rd U. S. Colored Troops, 1st South Carolina.												
Nov. 25	Battle	MISSIONARY RIDGE, TENN.	9 hours			4th and 14th Corps, Army of the Cumberland, 11th Corps, Geary's Div. of the 12th Corps and 13th Corps, Army of the Tenn., with re-enforcements	Gen. Hooker, F.; Gen. Bragg, C.					2000						Federal.
	Attack on Confederate Camp	GREENEVILLE, N. C.				12th N. Y. Cav., 1st N. C. Vols. and 24th N. Y. Bat.	Capt. Graham, F.					50				100		Federal.
Nov. 26	Skirmish	BONFOUCA, LA.				31st Mass. Vols. and 4th Mass. Battery.												
	Engagement	SPARTA, TENN.				1st Tennessee and 9th Pennsylvania Cavalry	Lt.-Col. Brownlow, F.; Col. Murray, C.		1		2	10						Federal.
	Skirmish	BERSHEBA SPRINGS, TENN.			Guer.	Alabama and Tennessee Scouts	Capt. Brixie, F.					15						Federal.
	Engagement	WARM SPRINGS, N. C.		400	100	(Troops not specified.)	Lieut.-Col. Bryson, C.	K. & W. 20										1 Con. 2 Con. 3 Fed.
	Engagement	KINGSTON, TENN.				Cavalry, Army of the Ohio.												
	(26th–28th). Operations at (Raccoon Ford, Bartlett's Mills, Robertson's Tavern, and New Hope)	MINE RUN, VA. (Locust Grove, Payne's Tavern and Orange Grove.				1st, 2nd, 3rd, 5th and 6th Corps and 1st and 2nd Cavalry Divisions, Army of the Potomac	M.-Gen. Meade, F.; Gen. Lee, C.	100	K. W. & M. 500	400								Conf'd.
Nov. 27	Engagements	RINGGOLD. GREYSVILLE. PEA VINE CREEK. TAYLOR'S RIDGE. Ga.				Johnson's Div., 14th Corps; Osterhaus' Div., 15th Corps and Geary's Div., 12th Corps	Gen. Hooker, F.; Gen. Hardee, C.											Federal.
	Escape of General J. H. Morgan, C. S. A., from the Penitentiary at Columbus, Ohio.																	
	Engagement	CLEVELAND, TENN				2nd Brigade, 2nd Cavalry Division.												
	(27th–29th). Destruction (by Confederates) and Occupation of Fort Esperanza, Texas, by Federal Forces	FORT ESPERANZA, TEXAS				8th and 18th Ind., 33rd and 99th Ill., 23rd and 34th Iowa, 13th and 15th Me. Vols., 7th Mich., Co. F. 1st Mo. Battery, portions of 1st and 2nd Division, 13th Corps	M.-Gen Washburne	1	1	2						10		Federal.
Nov. 28	Cavalry Fight	LOUISVILLE, TENN.		225		6th Illinois Cavalry												Federal.
Nov. 29	Assault by Confederate Forces on	FORT SANDERS, KNOXVILLE, TENN.				Army of the Ohio	Gen. Longstreet, C.		K. W. & M. 800									Federal.
Nov. 30	Skirmish	SALYERSVILLE, KY.				14th Kentucky Volunteers.												
Dec. 1	Engagement	RIPLEY, MISS.				2nd Brig., Cav. Div., Army of the Tennessee.												
Dec. 2	Attack on Federal Pickets	WALKER'S FORD, CLINCH RIVER, W. VA.	3 hours		Cav.	5th Ind. and 14th Ill. Cav., 21st Ohio Battery, 65th, 116th and 118th Ind. Volunteers	Col. Graham, F.; M.-Gn. Martin, C.	7	25	23	50	28		31				Federal.
	General Braxton Bragg, C. S. A., transfers command of Confederate Forces to Lieut.-Gen. Hardee.																	
Dec. 3	Evacuation by Federal Forces of	SALISBURY, TENN.				2nd Brigade, Cavalry Division, 16th Corps												Federal.
Dec. 4	Skirmish	NIOBRARA, NEB.		1 Co.		7th Iowa Cavalry.												
	Engagement and rout	MOSCOW STATION, MISS. (Wolf River Bridge)			Cav.	Cavalry Division, 16th Corps	Col. Hatch, F.; — Chalmers and Forrest, C.	K. & W. 175					40					Conf'd.
	Siege of Knoxville, Tenn., raised by Confederate Troops.																	
Dec. 5	Maj.-Gen. Schenck, U. S. A., succeeded in command of Middle Department by Brig.-Gen. Lockwood.																	
	Destruction by fire of Georgetown, S. C.																	
Dec. 6	Attack on Confederate Cavalry	CLINCH MOUNTAIN, TENN.				Cavalry, Army of the Ohio	Maj.-Gen. Foster, F.											Federal.
	Maj.-Gen. Sherman arrived at Knoxville, Tenn.																	
	Reconnoissance of Federal Cavalry under Major Scott, to Madison Court-House, Va.																	
	Federal ironclad *Weehawken* foundered at the entrance to Charleston Harbor during a storm							30										
Dec. 7	Skirmish	NATCHEZ, MISS.		1 Co.		4th Iowa Cavalry.												
	Skirmish	CREELSBORO', KY.				13th Kentucky Cavalry.												

CHRONOLOGICAL LIST OF EVENTS (1860-1865).—Continued.

Date.	Event.	Location.	Duration	Force F.	Force C.	Composition of Force.	Commanders.	Killed F.	Killed C.	Wounded F.	Wounded C.	Prisoners Taken by F.	Prisoners Taken by C.	Missing F.	Missing C.	Guns Captured	Stands of Arms Captured	Advantage.
1863 Dec. 7	Skirmish	Celina, Tenn.				13th Kentucky Cavalry.												
	Maj.-Gen. John A. Logan assumes command of the Fifteenth Army Corps																	
Dec. 8	Engagement	Princeton, Ark				Detachment Federal Cavalry.												
	(8th-21st). Averill's Raid	Southwestern Virginia				2nd, 3rd, 4th and 8th W. Va. Mounted Infantry, 14th Penn. and Dufour's Battery, Cavalry and Battery G, W. Va. Artillery.	Gen. Averill, F.	6		6		200	94					
	Cannonade between Fort Moultrie and Battery Gregg, Charleston Harbor	Charleston Harbor, S. C.																—
	President Lincoln appends an Amnesty Proclamation to his Message.																	
	The Federal House of Representatives pass, unanimously, a Vote of Thanks to General U. S. Grant and his Army, and order that a medal be struck in his honor, "in the name of the people of the United States."																	
Dec. 10	Cavalry Skirmish	Bean's Station, Tenn.				Bond's Brigade, Cavalry, Army of the Ohio.	Col. Bond, F.					130						Federal.
	Reconnoissance and Engagement	Morristown, Tenn.	2 hours		Cav. Brig	Garrard's Brigade of Cavalry, Army of the Ohio.	Col. Garrard, F.; —— Jones, C.		8		18							Federal
	Skirmish	Mossborough, Tenn.				Cavalry, Army of the Ohio.												—
	Maj.-Gen. Grant issues Order returning his "sincere thanks and congratulations to the brave Armies of the Cumberland, the Ohio, the Tennessee, and their comrades from the Potomac."																	
	Bombardment of Charleston, S. C., by General Gillmore	Charleston, S. C.	Sev'l hours															—
	The New Volunteer Fund of New York City amounted on this day to $750,000.																	
Dec. 11	Maj.-Gen. J. G. Foster, U. S. A., assigned to command of the Army of the Ohio, vice Maj.-Gen. Burnside, resigned by order of War Department.																	
Dec. 12	Skirmish	Duvall's Bluff, Ark.				9th Missouri Cavalry.												
	Skirmish	Big Sewell and Meadow Bluff, W. Va.				12th Ohio Volunteers.												
	Engagement	Lewisburg, Va.				Federal Troops.	Gen. Scammon, F.; Gen. Echols, C.											Federal.
Dec. 13	Orders issued by Maj.-Gen. Grant, U. S. A., concerning seizure of secessionist property in his Department.																	
Dec. 14	Attack on Federal Cavalry	Bean's Station, Tenn	3 hours			Cavalry Division Army of the Ohio.	Gen. Shackleford, F.; Gen. Longstreet, C.	K. W. & M. 700	K. W. & M. 900									Conf'd.
Dec. 16	(17th-?). Raid on Federal Troops	Sangster's Station, Va.		1 Co.	Cav.	155th New York Volunteers.				1			4					—
Dec. 16	Engagement	Blain's Cross Roads, Tenn.				Army of the Ohio.												
	Maj.-Gen. Buford, U. S. A., commanding Division of Cavalry, Army of the Potomac, died at Washington, D. C.																	
Dec. 17	Engagement	Rodney, Miss				1st Miss. Marine Brigade, Cavalry and Infantry.												
	Capture of Confederate Troops	Washington, N. C.			Cav.	Detachment 50th Pennsylvania Regiment.	Capt. Blakely, F.					34						Federal.
	Attack on Federal Outposts	Fort Gibson, Ark.				Federal Troops.	—— Standwaite, C.											Federal.
Dec. 18	Engagement	Indian Town, N. C.				36th U. S. Colored Troops, 2nd N. C. and 5th U. S. Colored Troops.												
	Engagement	Fort Gibson, Ark.	5 hours	400	Guer.	Federal Troops of the Indian Brigade.	Col. Phillips, F.; —— Quantrell, C.											Federal.
	3 Military Executions in the Army of Potomac.																	
Dec. 19	Skirmish	Barren Fork, Indian Territory				1st and 3rd Kansas Indian Home Guards.												
	Maj.-Gen. Grant, U. S. A., arrives at Nashville, Tennessee.																	
Dec. 20	Trial of Mrs. Anne Johnston of Cincinnati, Ohio, as a "rebel spy."																	
Dec. 22	Raid by Confederate Troops	Cleveland, Tenn.		Pkts.	Cav. 40	Federal Troops.	Maj. White, C.	1					6					Conf'd.
	Skirmish	Fayette, Miss				Federal Troops, Gen. Ellet's Marine Brigade.	Col. Curry, F.					10						Federal.
	General Michael Corcoran, U. S. A., died at Fairfax Court-House, Va.																	
	Lieut.-Gen. Polk, C. S. A., assumes command of the Department of the Mississippi, vice General J. E. Johnston, relieved by order of Jefferson Davis																	
Dec. 23	Skirmish	Jacksonport, Ark.				3rd Missouri Cavalry.												
Dec. 24	Engagement	Rodney, Miss.				1st Miss. Marine Brigade, Cavalry and Infantry												
	(24th-25th). Battle	Bolivar and Summerville, Tenn.		500	Cav.	7th Illinois Cavalry.	Col. Prince, F.; —— Forrest, C.	8		8								Conf'd.
	Murder of Federal Foraging Party, by Guerrillas in Lincoln County, Tennessee.																	
Dec. 25	Skirmish	Lafayette, Tenn.				117th Illinois Volunteers.												
	Action	Legareville, Stono Inlet, S. C.			Batt.	Federal Gunboat *Marblehead*.												Federal.
	Colonel R. R. Livingston, U. S. A., assumes command of the District of North-Eastern Arkansas.																	
	Attack on Confederate Cavalry	Bolivar, Tenn.	3 hours			7th Illinois Cavalry	Col. Prince, F.; —— Forrest, C.											Conf'd.
Dec. 26	Engagement	Port Gibson, Miss.				Miss. Marine Brigade of Infantry and Cavalry.												
Dec. 27	(27th-28th.) Engagements	Collierville, Tenn.				Cavalry of the Army of the Tennessee.												
Dec. 28	Skirmish	Charleston, Tenn.			Cav.	Detachment of Inf. and Cav., and 4th Ohio Cav.	Col. Laibold, F.; Gen. Wheeler, C.	3		14		122		1				Federal.
Dec. 29	Battle	Talbot's Station and Mossy Creek, Tenn.				1st Brig., 2nd Div., 23rd Corps, 1st Tenn., 1st Wis., 2nd and 4th Ind. Cavalry and 24th Ind. Battery	L.-Col. Young, F.; M.-Gen. Martin, C.											Federal.
	(29th-30th). Engagement	Matagorda Bay, Tex.				3 Co.'s of 13th Me. and Federal Gunboat *Sciota*.												
Dec. 30	Attack on Federal Wagon-guard	St. Augustine, Fla.			Cav.	10th Conn. and 24th Mass. Volunteers.	Lieut. Brown, F.	4										Federal.

CHRONOLOGICAL LIST OF EVENTS (1860-1865).—Continued.

Date	Event	Location	Duration	Force F.	Force C.	Composition of Force	Commanders	Killed F.	Killed C.	Wounded F.	Wounded C.	Prisoners Taken by F.	Prisoners Taken by C.	Missing F.	Missing C.	Gen. Off. Killed	[illegible]	Advantage
1863																		
Dec. 30	Reconnoissance and Engagement	Greenville, N. C.		140		Detachment 12th N. Y., 23rd N. Y. Battery and 1st N. C. Volunteers	Col. McChesney, F.; Maj. Moore, C.	1	8	6				1		1		Federal.
	Skirmish	Waldron, Ark.				2nd Kansas Cavalry.												
1864																		
Jan. 1	Cavalry Scout and Engagement	Hectorstown, Va. (Five Points)		75	Cav.	1st Maryland Cavalry, Potomac Home Brigade		k&w 57										Conf'd.
	Capture of Colonel Hawkins, Confederate Scout, at Lick Creek, Kentucky.																	
	Federal Soldiers frozen to death at Island No. 10.																	
Jan. 3	Raid and Capture of Federal Troops	Jonesville, Va.	8 hours		400	Detachment 16th Ill. Cav. and 22nd Ohio Battery	Maj. Beers, F.; Gen. Sam Jones, C.	k&w 60	4		13		300					Conf'd.
	Affair at Lockwood's, Folly Inlet, S. C.	Folly Inlet, S. C.			Batt.	Federal Gunboat *Fah Kee*	Admiral Lee, F.											
Jan. 4	Fight with the Navajo Indians	Fort Sumner, New Mexico			Ind.	Company B, 2nd California, Apaches and Citizens			Ind. 40		Ind. 25							Federal.
	Reconnoissance of Federal Troops to	Front Royal				Cavalry, Army of the Potomac	Col. Taylor, F.											
	Rear-Admiral Farragut sails from Brooklyn in the Flag-Ship *Hartford*, to assume command of the East Gulf Squadron.																	
Jan. 5	Attack on Federal Pickets	Eldorado, Culpepper County, Va.		Pkt.	Cav.	Federal Troops, Army of the Potomac							8					Conf'd.
Jan. 6	Brig.-Gen. Wilcox, U. S. A., assigned to command of the Clinch District, (region between Cumberland and Clinch Mountains.)																	
Jan. 7	Skirmish	Martin's Creek, Ark.				11th Missouri Cavalry.												
	Occupation by Federal Forces of	Madisonville, La.				(Troops not specified.)												
	Charleston, S. C., shelled from Federal Batteries under Gen. Gillmore.	Charleston, S. C.					Gen. Gillmore, F.											—
Jan. 8	Skirmish	Petersburg, W. Va.				(Troops not specified.)												
Jan. 9	Skirmish	Turman's Ferry, Ky.				39th Kentucky Volunteers.												
	Engagement between Confederates in Fort Morgan and Federal Gunboats, in Mobile Bay	Mobile Bay, Ala.	3 hours			Federal Gunboats												—
Jan. 10	Attack on Federal Camp	Loudon Heights, Va.	1 hour			1st Maryland, Potomac Home Brigade	Maj. Cole, F.; —— Mosby, C.	2	4	18		8						Federal.
		Strawberry Plains, Tenn.				Federal Cavalry.												
	Charleston, S. C., shelled by Federal Batteries.	Charleston, S. C.																—
Jan. 12	Skirmish	Matfield, Ky.				50th Illinois Volunteers												
Jan. 13	Attack on Confederate Troops	Mossy Creek, Tenn.				Federal Cavalry	Gen. McCook, F.		14			47						Federal.
Jan. 14	Skirmish	Middleton, Tenn.				35th Iowa Volunteers.												
	Attack on Federal Cavalry	Healton, Va.		1 Co.	200	9th Massachusetts Volunteers			3	3	13							Federal.
	Capture and Re-capture of Confederate Wagon Train	Terrisville, Cony Creek, Tenn.				Detachment 18th Penn. and 10th Ohio Cavalry	Maj.-Gen. Vance, F.; Col. Palmer, C.											Conf'd.
Jan. 16	Pursuit of Confederate Forces—Expulsion from	Dandridge, Tenn.			Vid.	Gen. Sturgis's Cavalry												Federal.
Jan. 16	(10th–16th).	Grand Gulf, Miss.				Cav. and Inf. of the Miss. Marine Brigade.												
	(16th–17th). Attack on Federal Forces	Dandridge, Tenn.				Cav. Div., Army of the Ohio, and Inf., 4th Corps	Gen. McCook, F.		k&w 150									Conf'd.
Jan. 17	Cavalry Fight	Lewisburg, Ark.			Cav.	Detachment 2nd Arkansas Cavalry	Capt. Hamilton, F.; Cpt. Thompson, C.	2	6	4	6							Federal.
	Bombardment of Charleston, S. C., by Forces under General Gillmore, U. S. A.	Charleston, S. C.																—
Jan. 18	Attack on Federal Pickets	Flint Hill, Va.		Pkts.	15	Federal Troops												Federal.
	Occupation by Confederate Forces of	New Market, Tenn.																
Jan. 19	Attack on Confederate Troops	Branchville, Ark. (Ivy Ford near Pine Bluff)	½ hour		Cav.	5th Kansas Cavalry	Col. Clayton, F.; —— Shelby, C.											Federal.
Jan. 20	Engagement	Island No. 76, Miss.				Battery E, 2nd Colored Light Artillery.												Federal.
	Engagement	Tracy City, Tenn.			Guer.	Detachment 20th Connecticut Volunteers												
Jan. 21	Skirmish	Dalton, Ga.				39th Ky. Mounted Infantry and 4th Mich. Cavalry.												
Jan. 22	Skirmishes	Armstrong Ferry, Tenn.				(Troops not specified.)												
Jan. 23		Rolling Prairie, Ark.				11th Missouri Cavalry.												
	Raid by Confederate Cavalry under General Wirt Adams, into Gelvertown, Miss.												35					Conf'd.
	Raid by Federal Cavalry into Cache County, Tenn.											83						Federal.
Jan. 24	Scout and Skirmish	Baker Springs, Caddo Gap, Ark.			40	2nd and 6th Kansas Cavalry	Lieut. Williams, F.; Cpt. Williamson, C.	1	8	1	2	27						Federal.
	Engagement	Tazewell, Tenn.				34th Ky., 116th and 118th Ind. Vols., 11th Tenn. Cav. and 11th Mich. Battery.												
Jan. 25	Attack on Federal Garrison	Athens, Ala.	3 hours	100	600	(Troops not specified.)		k.w. & m. 20										Federal
	Expedition of Federal Troops, under Brig.-Gen. Graham, to Brandon Farms, James River																	
	Evacuation of Corinth, Miss., by Federal Forces.																	
	Major Burroughs, Guerilla Chief, shot while attempting to escape from Fortress Monroe, Va.																	
Jan. 26	Engagement	Florence, Ala.			Brig.	Federal Troops	Col. Miller, F.; —— Johnson, C.		15	10								Federal.
Jan. 27	Attack on Train on the Orange and Alexandria Railroad	Cameron, Va.			Guer.	Federal Cavalry	Lieut. Jackson, F.					1						—
	Cavalry Engagement	Fair Gardens, Tenn. (French Broad and Kelly's Farms)	8 hours		Cav.	Cavalry Division, Army of the Ohio	Gen. Sturgis, F.; Gen. McCook, F.		k&w 65			100				2		Federal
	Confederate Raid on Federal Pickets	Scott's Mills Roads, Tenn.		Pkts.	Cav.	13th Kentucky and 23rd Michigan Volunteers	Col. Chapin, F.	1					12					1st Conf'l; 2d Fed.
	Reconnoissance of General Davies' Division, under General Palmer, toward Tunnel Hill, Ga.								k&w 22	2		1 Co.						Federal.
Jan. 28	Capture of Confederate Cavalry	Tunnel Hill, Ga.				Part of the 14th Corps, Army of the Cumberland	Gen. Palmer, F.											Federal.

CHRONOLOGICAL LIST OF EVENTS (1860–1865).—Continued.

DATE	EVENT.	LOCATION.	DURATION.	FORCE F.	FORCE C.	COMPOSITION OF FORCE.	COMMANDERS.	KILLED F.	KILLED C.	WOUNDED F.	WOUNDED C.	PRISONERS TAKEN BY F.	PRISONERS TAKEN BY C.	MISSING F.	MISSING C.	[illegible]	[illegible]	ADVANTAGE.
1864																		
Jan. 28	Engagement	Oregon Mountains				1st California Cavalry.												
	Confederate Force under General Roddy driven to the South side of the Tennessee by Federal Force under Colonel Phillips.																	
Jan. 29	Engagement (Attack on Federal Wagon-train)	Medley, W. Va. (Williamsport)	4 hours			23rd Ill., 2nd Md. Potomac Home Brigade, 1st and 14th W. Va. Vols. and 4th W. Va. and Ringgold (Pa.) Cavalry	Col. J. W. Snyder, F.	K & W 80	K & W 100									Conf'd.
	Skirmish	Cumberland Gap, Tenn				(Troops not specified.)												
	Affair near	Islands No. 70 and 71, Miss.			Guer	21st Missouri Regiment (on Steamer.)	Maj. Moore, F.	1		6								
	Fight with Indians	Canon de Chelly				Federal Troops.	Col. Kit Carson, F.											
	Raid of Federal Cavalry into Jones and Onslow Counties, N. C.			200		Detachment 12th New York, 9th Vermont, 12th and Mix's Cavalry	Col. Jourdan, F.					80						Federal.
	Evacuation of Petersburgh, West Virginia, by Federal Troops under Colonel Thoburn.																	
	Confederate Raid	Scottsville, Ky				Federal Troops	Maj. Johnson, F. Col. Hamilton, C.		40			20						Federal.
Jan. 31	Destruction of Warsaw, N. C., by fire.																	
Feb. 1	Order issued by President Lincoln for draft of 500,000 men, "to serve 3 years or during the War."																	
	(Feb. 1st–March 8th). Expedition up the	Yazoo, Miss				11th Ill. 47th U. S. Colored Troops (8th La.), 3rd U. S. Colored Cavalry (1st Miss.) and a portion of Rear Admiral Porter's Fleet	Lt.-Com. Owen, U. S. N.											
	Engagement	Bachelors Creek, N. C.	4 hours			132nd N. Y., 9th Vt., 17th Mass., 2nd N. C. Vols., 12th N. Y. Cav. and 3rd N. Y. Artillery	Gen. Palmer, F. Gens. Pickett and Hoke, C.	K & W 60				50						Conf'd.
	Engagement	Smithfield, Va.		90		Detachment 3rd Penn. Artillery, 20th N. Y. Cav., 99th N. Y. and 21st Conn. Volunteers, and seamen from Steamer Minnesota	Gen. Graham, F. Lieu.-Com. Gillis, F.											Conf'd.
	Skirmish	Waldron, Ark				2nd Kansas Cavalry.												
	Engagement	New Creek Valley, W. Va		1 Co.		Federal Infantry												Federal.
Feb. 2	Engagement	Newport Barracks, N. C.				132nd N. Y., 9th Vt., 17th Mass., 2nd N. C. Vols., 12th N. Y. Cav. and 3rd N. Y. Artillery												
Feb. 3	Engagement	Santatia, Miss			3000	Federal Gunboats	Gen. Ross, C.											
	Expedition to	Lebanon, Ala				Detachment from Army of the Cumberland												
	Engagement	Liverpool Heights, Miss				11th Ill. Vols and 47th U. S. Colored Troops (8th La.)	Col. Coates, F.	5		25								Conf'd.
	Engagement	Newbern, N. C.				132nd N. Y., 9th Vt., 17th Mass., 2nd N. C., Vols., 12th N. Y. Cav. and 3rd N. Y. Artillery	Gen. Foster, F. Gen. Pickett, C.	K. W. & M. 212	K. W. & M. 300									Federal.
	Skirmish and Engagement	Patterson Creek, W. Va. Springfield, W. Va.			Cav. 500	(Troops not specified.) Federal Cavalry	Gen. Averill, F. Lt. Col. Thompson, F. Gen. Rosser, C.	2		10								1 Con. 3 Fed.
	(Feb. 3d–March 5th) Expedition from	Vicksburg to Meridian, Miss.				Veatch's and A. J. Smith's Divisions, 16th Corps, Leggett's and Crocker's Divisions, 17th Corps, with 5th and 11th Ill., 4th Iowa, 10th Mo., and Foster's Ohio Battalion of Cavalry	M.-Gen. Sherman, F. M.-Gen. Hurlbut, F. M.-Gen. McPherson, F.	K. W. & M. 170	K & W 400			200						
Feb. 4	Skirmish	Rolling Prairie, Mo				8th Missouri Militia Cavalry.												
	Skirmish	Hot Springs, Ark				3rd Missouri Cavalry												
	Expedition and Engagement	Big Black River, Miss. (Bolton)			Cav.	10th Mo., 4th Iowa, 5th and 11th Ill. and Foster's Battalion Ohio Cav. and a portion of 17th Corps	Gen. McPherson, F. Gen. —— Lee, C.	13		35								Federal.
	Engagement	Moorefield, W. Va.	8 hours			Portion of the Troops of the Department of W. Va.	Col. Mulligan, F. —— Rosser, C.											Federal.
Feb. 5	Engagement	Clinton and Jackson, Miss				Cavalry and a portion of 17th Corps		K & W 25										Federal.
	Attack on Confederate Camp	Quallatown, N. C. (Deep Creek)			60	Detachment 14th Illinois Cavalry	Maj. Davis, F. —— Thomas, C.	3	K & W 215	5		50						Federal.
	Attack on Guerillas	Cape Girardeau, Mo.		Scts.	Guer	2nd Missouri Militia Cavalry	Capt. Shelby, F. —— Bolls, C.		7			8						Federal.
	Expedition of Federal Troops under Colonel Jourdan, from Newport, N. C., to the White River.											25						
		Wyatts, Miss				114th Illinois Volunteers												
Feb. 6	Occupation by Federal Force of	Bolivar, Tenn.				Detachment 7th Illinois Cavalry		1	K. W. & P. 30	8								Federal.
	Occupation by Federal Forces of	Jackson, Miss.																
	Reconnaissance	Morton's Ford, Va.				Part of the 2nd Corps, Army of the Potomac	Gen. Caldwell, F. Gen. Owen, F.	K & W 250										
Feb. 7	Reconnaissance	Barnett's Ford, Va				1st Cavalry Division, Army of the Potomac	Gen. Merrill, F.											
	Attack on Federal Garrison	Vidalia, La.			Cav.	6th U. S. Colored Heavy Artillery, 2nd Miss., 64th U. S. Colored Troops, 7th La. and 30th Miss. Vols.	Col. Farrar, F. L.-Col. McCaleb, F.		6		10	8						Federal.
Feb. 8	Occupation by Federal Troops of	Morton, Miss				Cavalry of Maj.-Gen. Sherman's Forces.												
	Skirmish	Donaldsonville, La.				4th Wisconsin Cavalry.												
Feb. 9	Escape of Colonel Streight and 109 other Federal officers from Libby Prison, Richmond, Va. (48 recaptured).																	
	Skirmish	Point Washington, Fla				Detachment 7th Vermont Volunteers.												
	Engagement	Morgan's Mills, Ark. (Spring River)				Detachm't 11th Mo. and 1st Neb. Cav. and 4th Ark. Inf.												
	(9th–10th). Engagement	Baker's Place, South Fork, Fla				40th Mass. Mounted Volunteers and Independent Battalion Mass. Cavalry.												

CHRONOLOGICAL LIST OF EVENTS (1860-1865).—Continued.

DATE.	EVENT.	LOCATION.	DURATION.	FORCE F.	FORCE C.	COMPOSITION OF FORCE.	COMMANDERS.	KILLED. F.	KILLED. C.	WOUNDED. F.	WOUNDED. C.	PRISONERS TAKEN. F.	PRISONERS TAKEN. C.	MISSING. F.	MISSING. C.	GUNS TAKEN.	STANDS OF ARMS TAKEN.	ADVANTAGE.
1864																		
Feb. 10	(10th–25th). Smith's Raid	GERMANTOWN, TENN				4th Mo., 2nd N. J., 7th Ind., 10th Penn., 2nd Iowa, 2nd, 3rd, 6th, 7th and 9th Ill., 3rd Tenn., 4th U. S. and 5th Ky. Cav., 72nd Ind. Mounted Infantry and other regiments.	Gen. Smith, F.					300						
	Major-Gen. Meade, U. S. A., announces in a speech at Philadelphia, that, "Since March, 1861, when the Army of the Potomac left its lines in front of Washington, not less than 100,000 men have been killed and wounded."																	
Feb. 11	Cavalry Expedition under Generals W. S. Smith and Grierson, leave Memphis, Tenn., to co-operate with Forces under Gen. Sherman	MEMPHIS, TENN.				Federal Cavalry	Gen. W. S. Smith, F. Gen. Grierson, F.											
	Train on the Baltimore and Ohio Railroad captured and robbed by Guerillas near Harper's Ferry, Va	HARPER'S FERRY, VA.																
Feb. 12	Occupation of Decatur, Miss., by Federal Troops under General Sherman.																	
	Skirmish	ROCK HOUSE, WAYNE COUNTY, W. VA				14th Kentucky Cavalry.												
	Skirmishes	CADDO GAP and SCOTT'S FARM, ARK.				2nd Kansas Cavalry.												
	Skirmish and Evacuation by Confederate Forces of	LAKE CITY, FLA.				40th Mass. Vols. and Independent Battalion Mass. Cav.	Col. Henry, F. Gen. Finnigan, C.		2	8								Federal.
	Skirmish, and Occupation of	DECATUR, MISS				One regiment of 16th Corps (Guarding Wagon Train.)												
	Engagement	CHUNKY STATION, MISS				20th, 29th, 31st, 45th and 124th Ill. Vols., 17th Corps.												
Feb. 13	Engagement	VICKSBURG, MISS				52nd U. S. Colored Troops and 2nd Mississippi.												
	Engagement	TUNNELL HILL, MISS				Cavalry advance of Gen. Sherman's Forces.												
Feb. 14	Skirmish	ROSS LANDING, GRAND LAKE, ARK.				51st U. S. Colored Troops and 1st Mississippi.												
	Occupation of Meridian, Miss., by Federal Forces under Major General Sherman																	
	Capture and Subsequent Evacuation by Federal Troops of	GAINESVILLE, FLA.				40th Massachusetts Volunteers	Capt. Marshall, F.		10*									Federal.
	Skirmish	BRENTSVILLE, VA		Scts.	Guer'la Cav. 400	13th Pennsylvania Cavalry	Maj. Larmer, F. Col. Jackson, F.	4		1			8					Federal.
	(14th–15th). Attack of Confederate Troops on	WATERPROOF, LA.				49th U. S. Colored Troops, 11th La. and Gunboat *Forest Rose*	Capt. Johnson, F.	16 13	8 7	3 13		5						1 Fed. 3 Fed.
Feb. 16	Skirmish	LAUDERDALE SPRINGS, MISS.				32nd Wis. Vols and Ind. Regiment.												
	Engagement	GRANT'S PASS, MOBILE, ALA.				Federal Gunboats.												
Feb. 17	Skirmish	MARION, MISS.				Portion of the 17th Corps.												
	Destruction of the Federal Steam Sloop, *Housatonic*, by torpedo, in Charleston Harbor, S. C.																	
Feb. 18	Expedition of Federal Cavalry under General Gregg, from Warrenton, Va., toward Middleburgh											28						
Feb. 19	Skirmish	GROSSE TETE BAYOU, LA				4th Wisconsin Cavalry.												
	Attack on Federal Forage-Train	WAUGH'S FARM, BATESVILLE, ARK.		300	800	11th Mo. Cavalry and 4th Arkansas Infantry	Capt. Castle, F. —Rutherford, C.	8	6	3	10							Federal.
Feb. 20	Skirmish	HOLSTON RIVER, TENN.				4th Tennessee Volunteers.												
	Battle	OLUSTEE, FLA. (Ocean Pond and Silver Lake)	4 hours	5000		47th, 48th and 115th N. Y., 7th Conn., 7th N. H., 40th Mass. Vols., 1st Mass. Cavalry, 54th Mass. Colored Troops, 1st N. C. Colored Troops, 8th U. S. Colored Troops, 1st and 3rd U. S. Artillery and 3rd Rhode Island Artillery	Gen. Seymour, F. Gen. Cesar Finnegan, C. Gen. Gardner, C.	193	K. W. & M. 500	1175				460				Conf'd.
	Smith's Raid	PRAIRIE STATION, MISS.				Federal Cavalry	Gen. Smith, F.											Federal.
Feb. 21	Attack on Confederate Entrenchments (Smith's Raid)	WEST POINT, MISS				Federal Cavalry	Gen. Smith, F.	K & W 40										Federal.
Feb. 22	Engagement (hand-to-hand)	POWELL'S RIVER BRIDGE, TENN.	4 hours	2 Cos.	500	34th Kentucky Infantry	Lieut. Slater, F.											Federal.
	Skirmish	CUMBERLAND GAP, TENN.		4 Co.		91st Indiana Volunteers.												Conf'd.
	Skirmish	MULBERRY GAP, TENN. (Wyerman's Mills)				9th Tennessee Cavalry												
	Engagement	OKALONA and MOUNT IVY, MISS. (Ivy Kills)				Brig.-Gen. W. S. Smith's and B. F. Grierson's Cavalry Divisions	Gen. Smith, F. Lt.-Col. Brown, F.	K. W. & M. 350										Federal.
	Attack on Federal Troops	DRAINSVILLE, VA.		Scts. 150	Guer. 250	Detachment 2nd Massachusetts Cavalry	—— Mosby, C.	8		7				50				Conf'd.
	Engagement	LUNA LANDING, ARK				1st Miss. Marine Brigade (Missouri Volunteers.)		4				20						
	Reconnoissance and Skirmish	WILLIAMSBURG ISLAND, S. C.				55th Penn. and 4th N. H. Volunteers												
	Prisoners killed by Guerillas	JOHNSON'S MILLS, WHITE COUNTY, TENN				Detachment 5th Tennessee Cavalry.												
Feb. 23	Skirmish	CALFKILLER CREEK, TENN				5th Tennessee Cavalry.												
Feb. 25	(22d–25th)	BUZZARD ROOST and TUNNELL HILL, ROCKY FACE RIDGE, GA.				4th and 14th Corps and Cavalry Corps, Army of the Cumberland	Gen. Palmer, F. Gen. Wheeler, C.	K & W 75				200						Federal.
	Bombardment of Fort Powell, below Mobile, Alabama, by Federal Fleet	FORT POWELL, ALA.																
Feb. 27	(27th–28th). Skirmish	CANTON, MISS.				Detachments 3rd Iowa and 32nd Iowa Volunteers	Col. Winslow, F. —— Adams, C.											—
Feb. 28	Capture of Colonel Richardson, Guerilla Chief, near Nashville, South of the Cumberland River.																	
	(Feb 28th–March 4th). Kilpatrick's Raid	STEVENSBURG TO RICHMOND, VA.				Division of Cavalry, Army of the Potomac	Gen. Kilpatrick, F.					500						Federal.
	Engagement	DUKEDOM, KY				Detachment 7th Tennessee Cavalry						1						
	Skirmish	YAZOO CITY, MISS.				3rd U. S. Colored Cavalry and 1st Mississippi.												
Feb. 29	Skirmish	NEWBERN, N. C				(Troops not specified.)												
	Skirmish (Kilpatrick's Raid)	TAYLORSVILLE, SOUTH ANNA RIVER, VA.				6th New York Cavalry	Maj. Hall, F. Maj. Hall, F.											
Mch. 1	Engagement	STANARDSVILLE and BURTON'S FORD, RAPIDAN, VA.				1st, 2nd, 5th and 6th U. S., 6th Penn., 1st N. Y. and 1st N. J. Cavalry	Gen. Custer, F.			12		60						Federal.
	Capture of Confederate Pickets (Kilpatrick's Raid)	BUCK'S TURNPIKE, VA.				Cavalry, Army of the Potomac	Gen. Kilpatrick, F.											

CHRONOLOGICAL LIST OF EVENTS (1860-1865).—Continued.

DATE.	EVENT.	LOCATION.	DURATION	FORCE. F.	FORCE. C.	COMPOSITION OF FORCE.	COMMANDERS.	KILLED. F.	KILLED. C.	WOUNDED. F.	WOUNDED. C.	PRISONERS TAKEN BY F.	PRISONERS TAKEN BY C.	MISSING. F.	MISSING. C.	[illegible]	[illegible]	ADVANTAGE.
1864																		
Mch. 1	Kilpatrick's Raid	ATLEE'S, BIDDELLS CROSS ROADS, VA.				Cavalry, Army of the Potomac	Gen. Kilpatrick, F.											
	Maj.-Gen. Grant, U. S. A., nominated to Chief Command of the Army, with the rank (specially created) of Lieutenant-General.																	
Mch. 2	Kilpatrick's Raid	WALKERTOWN, VA.				2nd New York Cavalry.												
	Bombardment	HARRISONBURG, LA.				Mississippi Squadron	Rear Ad. Porter, F.											
	The "death" sentence awarded deserters to be mitigated to "imprisonment during the war" at the Dry Tortugas, Florida, by order of President Lincoln																	
Mch. 3	Attack on Federal Camp (Kilpatrick's Raid)	TUNSTALL STATION, VA.	½ hour			7th Michigan and 1st Vermont Cavalry	Col. Litchfield, F.; Col. Preston, F.											Federal.
Mch. 4	Engagement	RODNEY, MISS.				Cavalry and Infantry, Miss. Marine Brigade.												
Mch. 5	Engagement	PANTHER SPRINGS, TENN.		93	Cav.	3rd Tennessee		2	K&W. 30	8			22					
	Expedition up the Yazoo River. Attack on	YAZOO CITY, MISS.	7 hours; 3 hours			3rd U. S. Colored Cavalry (1st Miss.), 47th U. S. Colored Troops (8th La.) and 11th Ill. Vols.	—— Ross and Richardson, C.	K,W, & M 130	K,W & M 300									Federal.
	Engagement	COLEMAN'S, MISS.				Mississippi Marine Brigade.												
Mch. 6	Skirmish	FLINT CREEK, ARK.				14th Kansas Cavalry.												
Mch. 7	Capture by Federal Forces of	DECATUR, ALA.				Troops of the Army of the Tennessee	Gen. Dodge, F.											
Mch. 9	Engagement	SUFFOLK, VA.				2nd U. S. Colored Cavalry	Col. Cole, F.	K, W & M 20	25									—
	Capture of Federal Troops	BRISTOE STATION, VA.		40	Guer.	Federal Cavalry							40					Conf'd.
	Attack by Guerillas on the Federal Steamer *Hillman*, opposite Island No. 18, Miss. River.																	
	Maj.-Gen. Grant, U. S. A., formally presented with his commission as Lieutenant-General.																	
Mch. 10	Skirmish	CARLETOWN, VA.				1st New York Veteran Cavalry.												
	Occupation of Pilatka, Florida, by Federal Forces under Colonel Barton.																	
Mch. 12	Lieutenant-Gen. Grant, U. S. A., assigned to command of the Federal Army, vice Maj.-Gen. Halleck, who resigns at his own request.																	
	Maj.-Gen. Halleck, U. S. A., appointed Chief-of-Staff of the Federal Army.																	
	Maj.-Gen. W. T. Sherman, U. S. A., assigned to command of the Military Division of the Mississippi, comprising the Departments of the Ohio, the Cumberland, the Tennessee, and the Arkansas.																	
	Maj.-Gen. McPherson, U. S. A., assigned to command of the Department and Army of the Tennessee.																	
Mch. 13	(Expedition under General Wistar). Engagement	CARROLLTON STORE, VA.				1st N. Y. Mounted Rifles and 11th Penn. Cav. and 6th, 22nd and 45th U. S. Colored Troops and Batts.	Gen. Wistar, F.		20		K&W 70							Federal.
Mch. 14	Skirmishes	CHEEK'S CROSS ROADS, TENN.				Federal Cavalry	Col. Garrard, F.; Col. Gilmer, C.											Federal.
	(15th–?). Capture by Federal Forces of	FORT DE RUSSY, LA.				Detachments 16th and 17th Corps and Miss. Squadron	Gen. A. J. Smith, F.; Admiral Porter, F.	4	5	15	4		234					Federal.
	200,000 additional men called for by President Lincoln "for navy and service."																	
Mch. 15	Skirmish	CLARENDON, ARK.				8th Missouri Cavalry.												
Mch. 16	Engagement	FORT PILLOW, TENN.			1000	(Troops not specified.)			K&W 30									Federal.
Mch. 17	Attack on Guerillas	MANCHESTER, TENN.			Guer.	5th Tennessee Cavalry	Col. Stokes, F.; —— Champ Ferguson, C.		K&W 21									Federal.
	Lieut.-Gen. Grant assumes command of the Federal Armies.																	
Mch. 18	Skirmish	MONTICELLO, ARK.				7th Missouri Cavalry.												
	Attack on Guerillas	CALFKILLER RIVER, TENN.				5th Tennessee Cavalry	Col. Stokes, F.; —— Champ Ferguson, C.		5									Federal.
Mch. 20	Skirmish	BERSHEBA SPRINGS, TENN.				5th Tennessee Cavalry.												
Mch. 21	Battle	HENDERSON MILLS, LA. (Bayou Rapides)				Detachment 16th Corps and Cavalry 16th Corps	Gen. Mower, F.; Gen. R. Taylor, C.					[illegible]				8		Federal.
Mch. 22	Maj.-Gen. Lew Wallace, U. S. A., assumes command of the Middle Department, 8th Army Corps.																	
Mch. 23	Expedition of Federal Troops under General Steele, from Little Rock, Ark., in pursuit of General Price.																	
	Brig.-Gen. Nathan Kimball, U. S. A., assumes command of Department of Arkansas.																	
	The Army of the Potomac to include 2d, 5th and 6th Corps only, under Generals Hancock, G. K. Warren, and Sedgwick respectively (1st and 3rd Corps distributed into 2nd, 5th, and 6th Corps).																	
Mch. 24	Capture of Federal Troops, and Destruction by Confederate Forces of	UNION CITY, KY.		500		7th Tennessee Cavalry	Col. Hawkins, F.; Gen. Forrest, C.											Conf'd.
	Maj.-Gen. French detached from the Army of the Potomac.																	
Mch. 25	Attack on Federal Troops	FORT ANDERSON, PADUCAH, KY.		646		16th Ky. Cavalry, 122nd Ill. Infantry and 8th U. S. Colored Heavy Cavalry (1st Ky.)	Col. Hicks, F.; Gen. Forrest, C.	14	300	46	1000		80					Federal.
	Maj.-Gens. Newton and Pleasanton relieved of their commands in the Army of the Potomac (on re-organization).																	

CHRONOLOGICAL LIST OF EVENTS (1860-1865).—Continued.

DATE.	EVENT.	LOCATION.	DURATION.	FORCE F.	FORCE C.	COMPOSITION OF FORCE	COMMANDERS	KILLED F	KILLED C	WOUNDED F	WOUNDED C	PRISONERS TAKEN BY F.	PRISONERS TAKEN BY C.	MISSING F	MISSING C	GUNS LOST	[illegible]	ADVANTAGE.
1864																		
Mch. 26	Expedition and Engagement at	LONGVIEW, ARK.			1200	5th Kansas and 7th Mo. Cav. and 28th Wis. Vols.	Col. Clayton, F.; Gen. Dockery, C.	K.W. A.M 15	K&W 110			33						Federal.
	Official announcement from Washington that Illinois is 10,436 "ahead of all quotas under the calls of President Lincoln for more Troops."																	
Mch. 27	Colonel J. M. Hughes, 25th Tennessee Regt. (Confederate), surrenders his command and applies to Colonel Stokes, commanding at Sparta, Tenn., for permission to take the oath of allegiance.																	
Mch. 28	Skirmish	DANVILLE, ARK.				2nd Kansas Cavalry.												
	Skirmish	ARKADELPHIA, ARK.				Advance Cavalry, 7th Corps.												
	Attack by "Copperheads"	CHARLESTON, ILL.				Detachment 54th Illinois Volunteers.	Col. Mitchell, F.	7		11		12						Federal.
Mch. 29	Skirmish	BOLIVAR, TENN.				6th Tennessee Cavalry.												
Mch. 30	Expedition of Federal Troops	MOUNT ELBA, ARK.				7th Miss. and 5th Kansas Cav. and 28th Wis. Vols.	Col. Clayton, F.					35						
	Skirmish	GROSSE TETE BAYOU, LA.				Detachment 118th Illinois Volunteers.												
Mch. 31	Red River Expedition	NATCHITOCHES, LA.				Cavalry, 19th Corps.	Gen. Banks, F.; Gen. Taylor, C.		K&W 6			25						Federal.
	Attack by Confederate Troops	ROACH'S or BROOK'S PLANTATION, SNYDERSVILLE, MISS.	1 hour.	600	1500	3rd U. S. Colored Cavalry (1st Mississippi.)		16	K&W 10									Federal.
Apr. 1	Skirmish	NEAR THE RAPPAHANNOCK, VA.		Pat'l.		1st Connecticut Cavalry.												
	Battle	FITZHUGH'S WOODS, ARK.	4 hours.	300		3rd Minn. Volunteers and 8th Mo. Cavalry	Gen. Andrews, F.; Gen. McRae, C.	7		16				4				—
Apr. 2	Steele's Expedition	ANTOINE, ARK.				13th Illinois and 1st Iowa Cavalry.												
	Engagement. (Steele's Expedition)	SPOONVILLE, ARK. (Terre Noire Creek)				29th Iowa, 50th Ind., 9th Wis. Vols. and 1st Mo. Cav.	Brig.-Gen. Rice, F.; —— Shelby, C.											Federal.
	Red River Expedition	CRUMP'S HILL, LA. (Pine Woods)				14th N. Y., 2nd La., 2nd Ill. and 16th Mo. Cav. and 5th U. S. Colored Artillery	Gen. Lee, F.	5				60						Federal.
	Skirmish	CLEVELAND, TENN.				1st Wisconsin Cavalry.												
	Engagement (hand-to-hand)	PENSACOLA, FLA.	10 minutes	89	Cav. 80	14th New York Cavalry	Capt. Schmidt, F.; Maj. Inde ph. C.		K&W 10	8		11						Federal.
Apr. 3	Engagement (Steele's Expedition)	OKALONA, ARK.				1st Mo. and 13th Ill. Cav., and 27th Wis., 40th Iowa, 77th Ohio and 43rd Illinois Vols., of 1st and 3rd Divisions, 7th Corps	Col. Engleman, F.											Federal.
	Maj. Gen. Slocum, U. S. A., to serve with Division of the Mississippi. Maj.-Gen. Stoneman, U. S. A., to serve with the Department of the Ohio.																	
Apr. 4	Reconnaissance and Skirmish (Red River Expedition)	CAMPTI, LA.				2nd and 18th N. Y. and 3rd R. I. Cavalry, 35th Iowa and 5th Minn. Volunteers.	Col. Gooding, F.	10		19								Federal.
	(4th–6th). Steele's Expedition	ELKIN'S FORD, LITTLE MISSOURI RIVER, ARK.				43rd Ind., 29th and 36th Iowa Vols., Battery E, 2nd Mo. Artillery and 1st Iowa Cavalry	Gen. Steele, F.											
	Maj.-Gen. P. H. Sheridan, U. S. A., assigned to command of the Cavalry Corps of the Army of the Potomac.																	
	Maj.-Gen. Hooker, U. S. A., assigned to command of 1st Army Corps (consolidation of 11th and 12th Corps).																	
	Maj.-Gen. O. O. Howard, U. S. A., assigned to command of 4th Army Corps, vice Maj.-Gen. Gordon Granger, relieved.																	
	Maj.-Gen. Schofield, U. S. A., assigned to command of the 23d Army Corps.																	
Apr. 5	Engagement	ROSEVILLE, ARK.		76		2nd and 6th Kansas Cavalry.												
	Skirmish	STONE'S FARM, ARK.		26	Guer	6th Kansas Cavalry		11										
Apr. 6	Skirmish	QUICKSAND CREEK, KY.				Co. I, 14th Kentucky Volunteers.												
	Brig.-Gen. Guitar, U. S. A., relinquishes his command to Brig.-Gen. C. B. Fisk																	
Apr. 7	Red River Expedition	WILSON'S FARM, LA.				Advance Cavalry, 19th Corps.												
	Engagement	HARNEY LAKE VALLEY, OREGON				1st Oregon Cavalry.												
	Attack on Federal Troops	PLAIN'S STORE near PORT HUDSON, LA.			Cav.	Detachment 118th Ill. and 21st N. Y. Battery and 3rd Illinois Cavalry		1		4		2	6					—
Apr. 8	Attack on Federal Camp	PENDESCOTT BAYOU near OSCEOLA, ARK.		100	Guer.	Battery I, 2nd Missouri Light Artillery	Lieut. Phillips, F.	4		7								Federal.
	Destruction of Bridge by Federal Troops	WOLF RIVER, TENN.				Federal Cavalry	Gen. Grierson, F.	K&W 8				2						Federal.
	Battle	SABINE CROSS ROADS, LA. (Mansfield) and Pleasant Grove)	4 hours.	8000	12000	Cav. Div., 3rd and 4th Div's, 13th Corps, 1st Div., 19th Corps. Army of the Department of the Gulf.	Maj.-Gen. Banks, F.; Gen. A. J. Smith, F.; Gen. Dick Taylor, C.	200	K.W. & M 1500	900				1800				1 Con. 2 Fed.
Apr. 9	Red River Expedition	PLEASANT HILLS, LA.				Cav. Division, 1st and 3rd Divisions 16th Corps, 1st Division 19th Corps	Maj.-Gen. Banks, F.; Gen. A. J. Smith, F.; Gen. Kirby Smith, C.	100	K.W. & M 2000	700				200				Federal.
Apr. 10	Destruction of the Transport Steamer *General Hunter*, by torpedoes in St. John's River, Florida.																	
	(10th–13th). Steele's Expedition. Battle	PRAIRIE D'ANN, ARK.				1st Ark., 18th, 29th, 33rd, 36th and 40th Iowa, 50th Ind., 43rd Ill., 27th Wis., 12th Kan. Vols., 2nd and 3rd Mo., 13th Ill., 2nd, 6th and 14th Kan. and 1st Iowa Cav., Bat. A, 3rd Ill. and 2nd Ind. Artillery.	Gen. Steele, F.; Gen. Marmaduke, C.											Federal.
	Skirmish	LITTLE CACAPON, VA.				Company K, 54th Pennsylvania Volunteers.												
Apr. 12	Attack on Federal Troops	FORT PILLOW, TENN.	20 minutes			11th U. S. Colored Troops (6th U. S. Colored Heavy Art. and 1st Ala.), Battery F, 2nd U. S. Colored Light Art. and Bradford's Batt. of 13th Tenn. Cav.	Maj. Booth, F.; Maj. Bradford, F.; Gen. Forrest, C.	350	80	60				164		6	630	Conf'e.
	Fight with Indians	FREMONT'S ORCHARD, DENVER, COLORADO		2 Cos.		Detachment 1st Colorado Cavalry		2		4								
	Red River Expedition	PLEASANT HILL, LA. (Blair's Landing)				Ironclads *Osage* and *Lexington* and Troops of 17th Corps on Transports.												

CHRONOLOGICAL LIST OF EVENTS (1860-1865).—Continued.

DATE.	EVENT.	LOCATION.	DURATION.	FORCE F.	FORCE C.	COMPOSITION OF FORCE.	COMMANDERS.	KILLED F.	KILLED C.	WOUNDED F.	WOUNDED C.	PRISONERS TAKEN BY F.	PRISONERS TAKEN BY C.	MISSING F.	MISSING C.	Guns taken	Stands of Arms taken	ADVANTAGE.
1864																		
Apr. 13	Skirmish	Indian Bay, Ark.				56th U. S. Colored Troops (3rd Arkansas.)												
	Skirmish	Florence, Ala.				Detachment 9th Ohio Cavalry.												
	Engagement	Cleveland, Tenn.				1st Wisconsin Cavalry.												
	Steele's Raid	Moscow, Ark.				18th Iowa Vols., 2nd Ind. Battery and 6th Kan. Cav.												
	Attack on Confederate Troops	Paintsville, Ky.			1000	Kentucky Volunteers	Col. Gallup, F.; Col. True, F.		25			66						Federal.
Apr. 14	Expedition (Skirmish)	Smithfield, Va. (Cherry Grove)				9th N. J., 23rd and 25th Mass. and 118th N. Y. Vols.	Gen. Graham, F.			5		6		1		1		Federal.
	Skirmish	Half Mount, Ky.				Kentucky Volunteers	Col. Gallup, F.											
	Steele's Raid	Dutch Mills, Ark.				6th Kansas Cavalry.												
Apr. 1	Attack on Federal Pickets	Bristoe Station, Va.			Cav.	13th Pennsylvania Cavalry		1		2								Federal.
	Steele's Raid	Liberty Post Office, Ark.				29th Iowa, 50th Ind. and 9th Wis. Volunteers.												
	(15th–16th.) Occupation of	Camden, Ark.				Advance of 17th Corps.												
Apr. 16	Skirmish	King's River, Ark.				2nd Arkansas Volunteers.												
	Engagement	Scullyville, Ind. Territory				3rd Kansas Indian Home Guards.												
Apr. 17	(17th–20th.) Engagement	Plymouth, N. C. (Forts Gray, Wessells and Williams)				85th N. Y., 103rd Penn. and 16th Conn. and Fed. Navy	Gen. Wessells, F.; Lt.-Com. Flusser, U.S.N.; Gen. Hoke, C.	20	K. W. & M. 500	80				1500				Conf'd.
	Skirmish	Decatur, Ala.				23rd Wisconsin Volunteers.												
Apr. 18	Attack on Forage Train	Poison Springs, Camden, Ark.				18th Iowa Vols., 79th U. S. Colored Troops (2nd Kansas) and 6th Kansas Cavalry.												
	Skirmish	Boykin's Mills, S. C.				54th Massachusetts, U. S. Colored Troops.												
Apr. 19	Attempt of Confederate Troops to invade Kentucky	Pound Gap, Ky.			80	45th Kentucky Volunteers												Federal.
		Natchitoches, La.				4th Brigade, Cavalry Division, 19th Corps.												
Apr. 20	Skirmish	Waterproof, La.				63rd U. S. Colored Troops (9th Louisiana).												
Apr. 21	Engagement	Cotton Plant, Cache River, Ark.				8th Missouri Cavalry.												
	Skirmish	Red Bone, Miss.				2nd Wisconsin Cavalry.												
Apr. 22	Skirmish	Tunica Bend, Red River, La.		3 Cos		3rd Rhode Island Cavalry.												
Apr. 23		Swan Lake, Ark.				5th Kansas Cavalry.												
	Engagement. (Red River Expedition)	Monett's Bluff, Cane River, La.				Cavalry Division and 3rd Brigade, 1st Division, 19th Corps and 3rd Division, 13th Corps	Gen. A. T. Smith, F.; Gen. Dick Taylor, C.	K. W. & M. 350	K. W. & M. 400							9		Federal.
	(23d–24th) Red River Expedition	Cloutiersville, La.				Portions of 13th, 17th and 19th Corps.												
	Attack on Federal Pickets	Nickajack Trace, Ga.		64		Detachment of 92nd Illinois Volunteers	Lieut. Scoville, F.	9		8		1		16				—
Apr. 24	Skirmish	Jacksonport, Ark.				1st Nebraska Cavalry.												
Apr. 25	(25th–26th). Engagements	Wautauga Bridge, Tenn. (Carter's Station)				10th Michigan Cavalry.												
	Steele's Campaign. Capture of Wagon-Train by Confederates	Marks' Mills, Ark.				36th Iowa, 77th Ohio and 43rd Ind. Vols., Battery E, 2nd Mo. Light Artillery and 1st Ind. and 7th Mo. Cavalry (Wagon Train Guard.)	Col. Drake, F.						2000			4		Conf'd.
Apr. 26	Engagement	Red River, La.				Federal Gunboats *Cricket* and *Fort Hindman*	Rear-Adm. Porter, F.											
	Engagement	Moro Creek, Ark.				33rd and 40th Iowa Vols. and 6th Kansas, 2nd and 4th Mo. and 1st Iowa Cavalry.												
	Engagement	Alexandria, La.				14th N. Y. and 6th Mo. Cavalry.												
Apr. 28	Skirmish	Offett's Knob, Mo.				1st Missouri Militia Cavalry.												
	Evacuation and Destruction of Washington, N. C., by Federal Forces.																	
	Reconnoissance of Federal Cavalry under General Davis, to Madison Court-House, Va.											80						
	Brig.-General Palmer in command of the District of North Carolina, vice Major-General Peck, relieved.																	
Apr. 29	Engagement	Princeton, Ark.				40th Iowa and 43rd Ill. Vols., 2nd Ill. Battery and 6th Kansas Cavalry.												
	Skirmish	Sni Hills, Mo.				2nd Colorado Cavalry.												
	Attack on Confederate Pickets	[illegible], Va.				Federal Troops						10						1 Fed. 3 Con.
Apr. 30	Attack on Federal Forces (Banks' Expedition)	Jenkin's Ferry, Saline River, Ark.	7 hours			77th Ohio, 4th, 18th, 29th, 33rd, 36th and 40th Iowa, 1st Ark., 12th Kan., 9th and 27th Wis. and 43rd Ill. Vols., 79th (1st Kan.) and 83rd (2nd Kan.) U. S. Colored Troops, Battery A, 3rd Ill. and 2nd Ind. Battery and 1st Iowa, 2nd, 6th and 14th Kan., 1st and 2nd Mo. and 13th Ill. Cavalry, 3rd Div. of 17th Corps	Gen. Steele, F.; Gen. Fagan, C.	260	K. W. & M. 1100	955						8		—
	Expedition of Federal Troops under General Sturgis, in pursuit of Forrest.																	
	Attack on Confederate Troops	Burnt Hill County, Ky.				Detachment 45th Kentucky Regiment	Capt. Adams, F.		4; 2			46; 35						
	Expedition of Federal Fleet up the Washita River.																	
May 1	Skirmish	Jacksonville, Fla.				7th U. S. Colored Troops.												
	Engagement	Hudnot's Plantation, La.				Cavalry of the 19th Corps.												
	(1st–4th). Skirmishes	Ashwood Landing, La.				64th U. S. Colored Troops.												
	Skirmish	Clinton, La.				(Troops not specified.)												
	(1st–8th). Skirmishes	Alexandria, La.				Portions of the Cavalry of the 13th and 19th Corps.												
May 2	Occupation by Federal Forces, of	West Point, Va.				Federal Troops												Federal
	Engagement	Memphis, Tenn.				7th Kansas Cavalry.												
	Engagement	Governor Moore's Plantation, La.				83rd Ohio Volunteers and 3rd R. I. Cavalry.												
May 3	Transport *City Belle* attacked	Snaggy Point, Red River, La.				120th Ohio Vols. and 73rd U. S. Colored Troops.												
	Skirmish	Cedar Bluffs, Colorado Territory		1 Co.		1st Colorado Cavalry.												
	Engagement	Bolivar, Tenn.	2 hours	700	1000	Federal Cavalry	Gen. Sturgis, F.; —— Forrest, C.	2		10								Federal
	Engagement	Red Clay, Ga.				1st Cavalry Division, Army of the Cumberland.												
	Skirmish	Baton Rouge, La.				4th Wisconsin Cavalry.												

CHRONOLOGICAL LIST OF EVENTS (1860-1865).—Continued.

DATE.	EVENT.	LOCATION.	DURATION.	FORCE. F.	FORCE. C.	COMPOSITION OF FORCE.	COMMANDERS.	KILLED. F.	KILLED. C.	WOUNDED. F.	WOUNDED. C.	PRISONERS TAKEN BY F.	PRISONERS TAKEN BY C.	MISSING. F.	MISSING. C.	[illegible]	[illegible]	ADVANTAGE.
1864																		
Mar 3	Skirmish	Richland, Ark				2nd Arkansas Cavalry.												
May 4	Engagement	Doubtful Cañon, Ariz. Territory				Detachment 5th Cal. Vols. and 1st Cal. Cavalry.												
	(4th-19th). Yazoo City Expedition, Miss.	Yazoo City, Miss.				3rd U. S. Colored Cavalry, 11th, 72nd and 76th Ill. Vols., 5th Ill. Cav. and 7th Ohio Battery.												
	(4th-12th). Kautz's Cavalry Raid	Suffolk to City Point, Va.				5th and 11th Penn., 3rd N. Y., 1st D. C. Cavalry and 8th New York Battery	Gen. Kautz, F.	5		43		150						
May 5	Attempt to destroy the Confederate Ram *Albermarle*	Roanoke River, N. C.	3 hours			Federal Gunboats *Ceres, Commodore Hull, Mattabesett, Sassacus, Seymour, Wyalusing, Miami* and *Whitehead*	Capt. M. Smith, U.S.N.	6		26		37						Conf'd.
	Attack on Federal Troops	Dunn's Bayou, Red River, La.				Federal Steamer *Covington*, Gunboat *Signal* and Transport *Warner*, with 56th Ohio Volunteers												
	Kautz's Raid	Wall Bridge, Va.				Cavalry Division, Army of the James.												
	Engagement	Thoroughfare Gap, Va.				Portion of Gen. Burnside's Cavalry												Federal.
	Engagement	Craig's Meeting House, Va.				3rd Division Cavalry, Army of the Potomac.												
	(5th-7th). Battle	Wilderness, Va.		[illegible]	52,620	2nd, 5th, 6th, 9th and Cav. Corps, Army of the Potomac	Gen. Grant, Meade and Burnside, F.; Gen. Lee, C.	3288	3500	12037	10000	6400	8784			22		—
	(5th-9th). Engagements	Rocky Face Ridge, Ga. (includes Tunnell Hill, Mill Creek Gap, Buzzards' Roost, Snake Creek Gap and near Dalton)				4th, 14th and 20th Corps, Army of the Cumberland, 15th and 16th Corps, Army of the Tennessee, 23rd Corps, Army of the Ohio	Gen. Sherman, F.; Gen. J. Johnson, C.	200	k.w. & m. 600	837								—
	(May 5th-Sept. 8). Campaign to Northern Georgia	Chattanooga to Atlanta, Ga.				Armies of the Cumberland, Tennessee and Ohio.												
	Evacuation by Confederate Forces of	Petersburg, Va.																
May 6	Affair on the	James River near City Point, Va.				Federal Gunboat *Commodore Jones*.												
	Engagement	Princeton, W. Va.				Advance of Gen. Crook's Command.												
	(6th-7th). Destruction of	Richmond and Petersburg Railroad near Port Walthal and Chester Station, Va.				Portion of the 10th and 18th Corps, Army of the James	Gen. Brooks, F.	k&w 250										Federal.
May 7	Skirmish	Benton, Miss.			Brig.	11th, 72nd and 76th Ill. Vols. and 7th Ohio Battery	Gen. McArthur, F.; Col. Mayberry, C.											Federal.
	Red River Expedition	Bayou La Mourie, La.				Portion of the 10th Corps.												
	Maj.-Gen. Canby, U. S. A., assigned to command of the Department of Western Louisiana and Arkansas.																	
	Engagement	Tunnell Hill, Ga.			300	4th Corps and Cavalry, Army of the Cumberland	Gen. Thomas, F.; Gen. Stanley, F.			10								Federal.
	Engagements	Mill Creek and Dug Gaps, Ga.				20th Corps, Army of the Cumberland.												
	Kautz's Raid	Stoney Creek Station, Weldon Railroad, Va.		2000		5th and 11th Penn., 3rd N. Y. and 1st D. C. Cavalry and 8th N. Y. Battery	Gen. Kautz, F.; Gen. Hill, C.											Federal.
May 8	Cavalry Fight	Todd's Tavern, Va.				2nd Division, Cavalry Corps, Army of the Potomac	Gen. Merritt, F.	k&w 80										Federal.
	(8th-18th). Engagements	Spottsylvania Court House, Va.	1½ hours			2nd, 5th, 6th, 9th and Cav. Corps, Army of the Potomac	Gen. Grant, F.; Gen. Lee, C.	4177	k.w. & m. 9000	[illegible]				2377		30		Federal.
	Occupation by Federal Forces	Fredericksburg, Va.																
	Skirmish	Jeffersonville, Va. (Abb's Valley)				Cavalry of the Army of West Virginia.												
	Engagement	Buzzards Roost Gap, Ga.				4th Corps and Cavalry, Army of the Cumberland	Gen. Stanley, F.											Federal.
	Engagement	Snake Creek Gap, Ga.				15th Corps, Army of the Tennessee	Gen. McPherson, F.											
May 9	Capture by Federal Forces of	Dalton, Ga.				23rd Corps, Army of the Ohio	Gen. Sherman, F.					3000				10		Federal.
	(9th-24th.) Sheridan's Raid	Through Confederate Lines				1st and 2nd Divisions, Cav. Corps, Army of the Potomac	Gen. Sheridan, F.	k&w 600				200		150		8		
	Kautz's Raid	Jarrett's Station, Weldon Railroad, Va.				11th Penn. Cavalry and 8th N. Y. Battery.												
	Kautz's Raid	White's Bridge, Nottaway Creek, Va.				3rd N. Y. and 1st D. C. Cavalry and 8th N. Y. Battery.												
	Engagement	Varnell's Station, Ga.				1st Cavalry Division, Army of the Cumberland.												
	Sheridan's Raid	Childsbury, Va.				6th Ohio and 1st New Jersey Regiments.												
	(9th-10th). Engagements	Swift Creek, Va. (Arrowfield Church)				10th and 18th Corps, Army of the James	Gen. Heckman, F.	90	k.w. & m. 500	400								Federal.
	(9th-10th). Engagements	Cloyd's Mountain and New River Bridge, Va.		6000		12th, 23rd, 34th and 36th Ohio, 9th, 11th, 14th and 15th W. Va. Vols., and 3rd and 4th Penn. Reserves, Army of West Virginia	Gen. Crook, F.; Col. White, F.; Gen. Jenkins, C.	126	k.w. & m. 900	585		300		31		6		Federal.
	(9th-10th) Engagements	Cove Mountain, Wytheville, Grassy Lick, Va.		2000		14th Penn., 1st, 2nd and 3rd W. Va., and 34th Ohio Mounted Volunteers	Gen. Averill, F.; Gen. Jones, C.											Federal.
	Sheridan's Raid. Destruction of	Beaver Dam Station, North Anna, Va.				1st Division, Cavalry Corps, Army of the Potomac	Gen. Sheridan, F.											Federal.
May 10	Destruction of Bridge (Sheridan's Raid)	Ground Squirrel Church Bridge, South Anna, Va.				1st Division, Cavalry Corps, Army of the Potomac	Gen. Sheridan, F.											Federal.
	Skirmish	Dardanelle, Ark				6th Kansas Cavalry.												
May 11	Skirmish (Sheridan's Raid)	Ashland, Va.				1st Massachusetts Cavalry	Gen. Sheridan, F.; Gen. Davies, F.						30					Federal.
	Engagement (Sheridan's Raid)	Yellow Tavern near Richmond, Va.				1st and 3rd Divisions, Cav. Corps, Army of the Potomac	Gen. Sheridan, F.; Gen. Devens, F.; Gen. Stuart, C.									2		Federal.
May 12	Skirmish	Smith's Station, Ind. Territory				1st Nebraska Battalion Cavalry.												
	Engagement. Expedition to Yazoo City	Vaughn, Miss.				11th, 72nd and 76th Illinois Volunteers	Gen. McArthur, F.											Federal.
	(12th-16th). Engagements	Fort Darling, Drury's Bluff, Va. (including Weirbottom Church, Proctor's and Palmer's Creeks)				10th and 18th Corps, Army of Virginia and N. C.	Gen. Butler, F.; Gen. Beauregard, C.	422	k.w. & m. 2500	2380		80		210				Federal.

CHRONOLOGICAL LIST OF EVENTS (1860-1865).—Continued.

DATE.	EVENT.	LOCATION.	DURATION.	FORCE. F.	FORCE. C.	COMPOSITION OF FORCE.	COMMANDERS.	KILLED. F.	KILLED. C.	WOUNDED. F.	WOUNDED. C.	PRISONERS TAKEN BY. F.	PRISONERS TAKEN BY. C.	MISSING. F.	MISSING. C.	GUNS TAKEN.	STANDS OF ARMS TAKEN.	ADVANTAGE.
1864																		
May 12	(12th-17th). Kautz's Raid.	Petersburg and Lynchburg Railroad, Va.				Cavalry of the Army of the James.	Gen. Kautz, F.											Federal.
	Engagement (Sheridan's Raid).	Meadow Bridge, Chickahominy River, Va.				1st and 3rd Divisions, Cav. Corps, Army of the Potomac.	Gen. Sheridan, F.											Federal.
May 13	(13th-16th). Engagements and Battle. (15th?).	Resaca, Ga. (Sugar Valley or Oostenaula)		Army total. 98,797	Army total. 60,000	4th, 14th and 20th Corps, Cavalry, Army of Cumberland, 15th and 16th Corps, Army of the Tenn. and 23rd Corps, Army of the Ohio.	Gen. Sherman, F. Gen. J. Johnson, C.	600	k. w. & M. 2800	2147		1000				8		Federal.
	Skirmish.	Pulaski, Tenn.				111th U. S. Colored Troops (3rd Alabama.)												
	Engagement.	Tilton, Tenn.				1st Division, Cavalry, Army of the Cumberland.												
	Affair near.	Point Lookout, Va.				Detachment 36th U. S. Colored Troops and Seamen from the Potomac Flotilla.												Federal.
May 14	(14th-16th). Red River Expedition.	Mansura, La. (Avoyelle's Prairie, Morreauville, Marksville).				3rd Division, 16th Corps, and a portion of Cavalry Division, 19th Corps.												
	Occupation of.	Rouss Hill, Va.				Portion of the Army of West Virginia.												
May 15	Skirmish.	Mount Pleasant Landing, La.				67th U. S. Colored Troops.												
	Battle.	New Market, Va.		7000	[illegible]300	Portion of the Army of West Virginia.	Gen. Sigel, F. Gen. Breckinridge, C.	120	k. w. & M. 405	560				240				Conf'd.
	Engagement.	Ley's Ferry, Ga.				Portion of the 16th Corps, Army of the Tennessee.												
	Engagement.	Tanner's Bridge near Rome, Ga.				2nd Cavalry Division, Army of the Cumberland.												
May 16	Engagement.	Rome Cross Roads, Ga.				16th Corps, Army of the Tennessee.	Gen. McPherson, F. Gen. Dodge, F.											Federal.
	Skirmish.	Ashepoo River, S. C.				34th U. S. Colored Troops.												
	Skirmish.	Pond Creek, Pike County, Ky.				39th Kentucky Volunteers.												
	Skirmish.	Clear Creek, Mo.		2 Cos.		15th Kansas Cavalry.												
	(16th-20th).	Fredericksburg Road, Va.				Tyler's Division, 5th Corps, Army of the Potomac.												
	Action.	Smoky Hill, Colorado.				1 Co. 1st Colored Cavalry and McLain's Colorado Battery.												
	(16th-30th). Engagement and Battle.	Bermuda Hundred, Va.		38,000	20,000	10th and 18th Corps, Army of the James.	Gen. Butler, F. Gen. Beauregard, C.	200	k. w. & M. 3000	1000								—
	Kautz's Raid.	Belcher's Mills, Va.				3rd N. Y., 5th and 11th Penn. and 1st D. C. Cavalry.												
May 17	(17th-18th). Engagement.	Adairsville, Ga. (including Grave's House and Calhoun).				4th Corps, Army of the Cumberland.												
	Engagement.	Madison Station, Ala.				3rd Division 15th Corps, Army of the Tennessee.												
May 18	Occupation of.	Rome, Ga.				2nd Division, 14th Corps and Cavalry, Army of the Cumberland.	Gen. McPherson, F. Gen. Davis, F.											
	Occupation of.	Kingston, Ga.				2nd Cavalry Division, Army of the Cumberland.	Gen. Sherman, F.											Federal.
	Attack on Federal Forces (Red River Expedition).	Bayou de Glaize, La. (Old Oaks, Yellow Bayou, Simmsport and Calhoun Station).				1st and 3rd Divisions, 16th Corps, portion of the 17th Corps and Cavalry, 19th Corps.	— Polignac, C.		k. & w. 300			800						Federal.
	Skirmish.	Crooked River, Oregon.				1st Oregon Cavalry.												
May 19	Skirmish.	Fayetteville, Ark.				6th Kansas Cavalry.												
	Skirmish.	Welaka and Saunders, Fla.				Detachment 17th Connecticut Volunteers.												
	(19th-22d). Engagements.	Cassville, Ga.				20th Corps, Army of the Cumberland.												
May 20	Skirmish.	Downer's Bridge, Va.				3d New York Cavalry.												
	Occupation of.	Milford Station, Va.				1st Cavalry Division, Army of the Potomac.												Federal.
May 21	Maj.-Gen. Hunter, U. S. A., assumes command of Department of West Virginia, vice Maj.-Gen. Sigel, relieved by order of President Lincoln.																	
	Skirmish.	Snia Hills, Mo.				2nd Colorado Cavalry.												Federal.
	Maj.-Gen. McDowell, U. S. A., assigned to command of the Department of the Pacific.																	
	Skirmish.	Mount Pleasant, Miss.				4th Missouri Cavalry.												
May 22	Skirmish.	Old River, La.				6th Missouri Cavalry.												
May 23	(23d-27th). Engagements.	North Anna River, Va. (Jericho Ford and Taylor's Bridge).				2nd, 5th and 9th Corps, Army of the Potomac.	Gen. Grant, F. Gen. Lee, C.	223	k. w. & M. 2000	1460				290				Federal.
	Capture of Steam Tug *Columbine*.	Horse Landing, St. John's River, La.	1½ hours.	300		35th U. S. Colored Troops and sailors on the *Columbine*.	Lieut.-Com. Breese, F.						80					Conf'd.
May 24	Skirmish.	Holly Springs, Miss.				4th Missouri Cavalry.												
	Attack on Federal Wagon Train.	Kingston, Ga.				50th Ohio and 14th Ky. Vols. and 2nd Ky. Cav.	Col. Holman, F.											Conf'd.
	Engagement.	Wilson's Wharf Landing, Va.				1st D. C. and 10th U. S. Colored Troops and Battery B, U. S. Colored Artillery.	Gen. Wild, F. Gen. Fitz-Hugh Lee, C.	k. & w. 40	k. & w. 275			11						Federal.
	Skirmish.	Nashville, Tenn.				15th U. S. Colored Troops.												
May 25	(May 25th-June 4th). Engagements.	Dallas, Ga. (New Hope Church, Burned Hickory, Pumpkin Vine Creek, and Altoona Hills).				4th, 14th, 20th Corps and Cavalry, Army of the Cumberland, 23rd Corps, Army of the Ohio, 15th, 16th and 17th Corps, Army of the Tennessee.	Gen. Hooker, F. Gen. Hardee, C.	k. w. & M. [illegible]	k. w. & M. 3000									
	Attack on Confederate Troops.	Cassville Station, Ga.				1st and 11th Kentucky Cavalry.	Col. Holman, F.	6		5	3	1						Conf'd.
May 26	Engagement.	Burned Church, Ga.				Cavalry of the 1st Division, Army of the Cumberland.												
	Skirmish.	Lane's Prairie, Morris County, Mo.		2 Cos.		2nd Wisconsin Cavalry.												
	Skirmish.	Bachelor's Creek, N. C.				132nd and 158th N. Y. and 58th Penn. Volunteers.												
	(26th-27th). Engagement.	Decatur, Courtland Road, Ala.				1st, 3rd and 4th Ohio Cavalry, Cavalry Corps and 3rd Brigade, 4th Division, 16th Corps.												
May 27	Affair near.	San Carlos River, Cal.				Co. K, 5th California Infantry.												
	Engagement.	Hanoverton, Pamunkey River, Va.				1st and 2nd Divisions, Cav. Corps, Army of the Potomac.												
May 28	Battle.	Dallas, Ga.				Federal Troops under Gen. Sherman.	Gen. Sherman, F. Gen. McPherson, F. Gen. Longstreet, C.	200	k. & w. 2500			300						Federal.
	Skirmish.	Jacksonville, Fla.				7th U. S. Colored Troops.												

CHRONOLOGICAL LIST OF EVENTS (1860-1865).—Continued.

DATE.	EVENT.	LOCATION.	DURATION.	FORCE. F.	FORCE. C.	COMPOSITION OF FORCE.	COMMANDERS.	KILLED. F.	KILLED. C.	WOUNDED. F.	WOUNDED. C.	PRISONERS TAKEN BY F.	PRISONERS TAKEN BY C.	MISSING. F.	MISSING. C.	Guns taken.	Stands of arms taken.	ADVANTAGE.
1864																		
May 28	Engagement	Hawes' Shop, Tocopotomy Creek, Va. (Salem Church)				1st and 2nd Divisions Cavalry, Army of the Potomac	Gen. Gregg, F.; Gens. Hampton and Fitz-Hugh Lee, C.											Federal.
	Skirmish	Little Rock, Ark.				57th U. S. Colored Troops.												
	Skirmish	Pleasant Hill, Mo.				2nd Colorado Cavalry.												
	(28th-29th). Engagement	Moulton, Ala.				1st, 3rd and 4th Ohio Cavalry, Army of the Cumberland												
May 29	(29th-31st). Action near	Tocopotomy, Va.				2nd and 5th Corps, Army of the Potomac	Gen. Birney, F.					40						Federal.
May 30	Engagements	Hanover Court House, Va.; Ashland, Va.; Old Church, Va.				3rd Division, Cavalry Corps, Army of the Potomac. 3rd Division, Cavalry Corps, Army of the Potomac. 1st Division, Cavalry Corps, Army of the Potomac												Federal.
June 1	(1st-12th). Engagements and Battle. (1st.)	Cold Harbor, Va. (and vicinity)	[illegible] hours	[illegible]	[illegible]	2nd, 5th, 6th, 9th and Cavalry Corps, Army of the Potomac and 18th Corps, Army of the James	Gens. Grant and Meade, F.; Gen. Lee, C.	1705	1700	9042	8500	1500	2406					Federal.
June 2	Occupation of	Bermuda Hundred, Va.				10th Corps, Army of Virginia and North Carolina.												
	Engagements	Gaines' Mills, Va.; Salem Church, Va.; Hawes' Shop, Va.				Cavalry of the Army of the Potomac												Federal.
June 3	Skirmish	Searcy, Ark.				Detachment 3rd Missouri Cavalry.												
	Engagement	Panther Gap, W. Va.	11 hours.			Gen. Hayes' Brig., 2nd Div., Army of W. Va.												
	(3d-4th). Engagement	Ackworth, Ga.				Cavalry of the 2nd Div., Army of the Cumberland.												
June 5	Battle	Piedmont, Va. (Mount Crawford)	10 hours.			Cavalry and Infantry of the Army of W. Va.	Gen. Hunter, F.	130	400	650	1450	1600				3	3000	Federal.
June 6	Engagement	Buffalo Gap, W. Va.				Gen. Hayes' Brig. of the 2nd Div., Army of W. Va.												
	Engagement	Lake Chicot, Ark. (Old River Lake, Dutch Bayou, Columbia, Fish Bayou)				16th Corps.												
	Skirmish	Greenland Gap Road near Moorefield, W. Va.				22nd Pennsylvania Cavalry.												
June 7	Engagement (Expedition to Guntown)	Ripley, Miss.			Cav.	Cav. Advance of Maj. Gen. Sturgis Command												Federal.
June 8	Skirmish	Lafayette, Tenn.				7th Kansas Cavalry.												
	Skirmish	Point of Rocks, Md.				2nd U. S. Colored Cavalry.												
	(9th-30th). Actions at	Kenesaw Mountain, Ga. (Lost Mountain, Nose's Creek, Marietta and Big Shanty; includes Pine Mountain, Pine Knob, Golgotha, Culp's House, General Assault, 27th, McAfee's Cross Roads, Lattemore's Mills, and Powder Springs)				4th, 14th and 20th Corps, Army of the Cumberland; 15th, 16th and 17th Corps, Army of the Tenn.; 23rd Corps, Army of the Ohio		1370	1100	6500	1900	3500	900					
	Engagement	Mount Sterling, Ky.				Cavalry of the Division of Kentucky	Gen. Burbridge, F.					700						Federal.
June 10	Morgan's Raid. Attack on	Frankfort, Ky.			60	Enrolled Militia and Citizens	Col. Monroe, F.; Lt.-Col. Pryor, C.			3								Federal.
	(10th-11th). Engagement	Lexington, W. Va.				2nd Division, Army of West Virginia.												
	Skirmish	Cane Creek, Ala.			Guer	100th Ohio Volunteers.												
	Skirmish	Lexington, Ky.				4th Kentucky Cavalry.												
	Skirmish	Princeton, Ky.				(Troops not specified.)												
	Engagement	Petersburg, Va.				Cavalry Commanded by Gen. Kautz, and portion of the 10th Army Corps, Army of the James												
	Battle. (12th?)	Brice's Cross Roads near Guntown, Miss.		12,000	6000	4th Mo., 2nd N. J., 19th Penn., 7th and 9th Ill., 7th Ind., 3rd and 4th Iowa, 10th Kan. Cav., 9th Minn., 81st, 95th, 108th, 113th, 114th, and 120th Ill., 72nd and 93th O., 93rd Ind., Vol., 1st Ill., 6th Ind., and Co. F., 2nd Ill. Batteries, 59th (1st Tenn.) 55th (1st Ala.) U. S. Col. Troops, and Battery F., 2nd U. S. Colored Artillery	Gen. Sturgis, F.; Gn. Kirby Smith, C.; Gen. Forrest, C.	400	130	1300	475		2500					Conf'd.
	Engagement	Corinth, Miss.				2nd N. J. Cavalry.												
	Morgan's Raid	Cynthiana, Ky.				168th Ohio Regiment (100 days men.)												
	Morgan's Raid	Keller's Bridge, Licking River, Ky.				171st Ohio Regiment		13		54				700				
	(10th-11th). Skirmishes	Old Church, Va.				3rd Division Cavalry Corps Army of the Potomac.												
June 11	Skirmish	Wilson's Landing, Va.				1st U. S. Colored Cavalry.												
	Thirteenth Army Corps temporarily discontinued, and Troops transferred.																	
	Morgan's Raid	Cynthiana, Ky.				Cavalry of the Division of Kentucky	Gen. Burbridge, F.; Gen. Morgan, C.	K&W 300	395		275	400	1200					Conf'd.
	Engagement	Ripley, Miss.				3rd and 4th Iowa, 2nd N. J. and 4th Mo., Cavalry.												
	(11th-12th). Engagement	Trevellian Station, Central Railroad, Va.				1st, 2nd Div. Cav. Corps, Army of the Potomac	Gen. Sheridan, F.	85	K. W. & M. 370	490		400		160				Federal.
June 12	Engagement	McAfee's Cross Roads, La.				Cavalry, Army of the Cumberland.												
	Skirmish	Kingsville, Mo.		Scts		1st Mo., Militia Cavalry.												
June 13	Engagement	White Oaks, Swamp Bridge, Charles City Cross Roads, Va. (Riddle's Shop)				3rd Div. Cav. Corps, and 2nd Div. 6th corps, Army of the Potomac	Gen. Sheridan, F.											Federal.
	Skirmish	White Post, W. Va.				6th West Virginia Cavalry.												
June 14	Action	Pine Mountain, Ga.		Art.	Art.	4th, 14th and 20th Corps, Army of the Cumberland, 15th, 16th and 17th Corps, Army of the Tenn., 23rd Corps Army of Ohio	Gen. Sherman, F.; Gen. Thomas, F.; Gen. Johnston, C.; Gen. Polk, C.; Gen. Loring, C.											Federal.
	Skirmish	Lexington, Lafayette County, Mo.				Detachment, 1st Mo. Militia Cavalry.												
	Engagement	Buchanan near Lexington, Va.				Advance of Army of West Virginia.												
June 15	Engagement	Samaria Church, Malvern Hill, Va.				3rd Division, Cav. Corps, Army of the Potomac.												
	Skirmish	Moscow, Tenn.				55th U. S. Colored Troops (1st Alabama.)												
	Engagement	Baylor's Farm, Va.				3rd Division, 18th Corps Army of the James.												
	Siege of Petersburg, Va. (June 15th–April 2d, 1865).																	

CHRONOLOGICAL LIST OF EVENTS (1860-1865).—Continued.

Date	Event	Location	Duration	Force F.	Force C.	Composition of Force	Commanders	Killed F.	Killed C.	Wounded F.	Wounded C.	Prisoners taken by F.	Prisoners taken by C.	Missing F.	Missing C.	Guns taken	Stands of arms taken	Advantage
1864																		
June 15	(15th–18th) Battle (includes Baylor's Farm, Walthal, and Weir Bottom Church)	Petersburg, Va.				10th and 18th Corps, Army of the James, 2nd, 5th, 6th and 9th Corps, Army of the Potomac	Gens. Grant and Meade, F.; Gen. Lee, C.	1188	3500 (k.w. & p.)	6853			1814			4		Federal.
June 16	Skirmish	West Point, Ark.				9th Iowa Cavalry.												
	Engagement	Otter Creek near Liberty, Va.				Advance of Army of West Virginia.												
	Engagement	Wierbottom Creek, Va.				2nd Division, 18th Corps, Army of the James.												
	Engagement	Golgotha, Ga.				20th Corps.												
	Action near	Walthal, Va.				1st Division, 10th Corps, Army of the James.												
	Skirmish	Pierson's Farm, Va.				30th U. S. Colored Troops.												
June 17	Skirmish	Nose's Creek, Ga.				(During Kenesaw Mountain.)												
	(10th–18th). Engagements and Battle near	Lynchburg, Va.				1st and 2nd Division Averill's and Duffie's Cavalry Army of West Virginia	Gens. Grant, Sheridan, and Hunter, F.; Gen. Lee, C.	460	230	1930	700	430	540					—
June 19	Engagement	Pine Knob, Ga.				(During Kenesaw Mountain.)												
	Action off	Cherbourg, France				The *Kearsarge* and the *Alabama*		1	40	3	10							
June 20	Engagement	White House, Va.				Brigade of Federal Troops.	Gen. Sheridan, F.; Brig.-Gen. Abercrombie, F.											Federal.
	Engagement	Liberty, Va.				2nd Division, Cavalry, Army of West Virginia.												
	Affair near	Powder Springs, Ga.				Cavalry, Army of the Cumberland.												
	Engagement	Lattamore's Mills, Noonday Creek, Ga.				Cavalry, Army of the Cumberland.												
	(20th–30th). Skirmishes	Trenches in front of Petersburg, Va.				5th and 9th Corps, Army of the Potomac, 10th and 18th Corps, Army of the James	Gen. Grant, F.; Gen. Lee, C.; Gen. Beauregard, C.	112		506				800				Conf'd.
June 21	Engagement	Salem, Va.				2nd Division, Cavalry, Army of West Virginia.												
	Skirmish	Pine Bluff, Ark.				27th Wisconsin Regiment.												
	Naval Engagement	James River near Dutch Gap				(Forces not specified).												
	Skirmishes	White House Landing, Va.				Portions of the 1st and 2nd Divisions Cav. Corps, Army of the Potomac												Federal.
June 22	Skirmish	Buford's Gap, Va.				23rd Ohio Volunteers.												
	Skirmish	White River, Ark.				3 Co's., 12th Iowa and Federal Steamer *Lexington*.												
	(22d–30th). Wilson's Raid	Weldon Railroad, Va.		8000		Cav., Army of James, 3rd Div. Cav. Army of Potomac	Gen. Wilson, F.; Gen. Kautz, C.	76	300 (k.w. & m.)	265				700				—
	Engagement	Culp's House, Ga.				(During Kenesaw Mountain.)												
	Destruction of Railway (Wilson's Raid)	Ream's Station, Va.				Kautz's Cavalry, Army of the James, and 3rd Division of Cavalry, Army of the Potomac	Gen. Wilson, F.											
	(22d–23d. Actions near	Weldon Railroad, Va. (Williams' Farm, Davis' Farm, Jerusalem Plank Road)				2nd and 6th Corps, and 1st Division, 5th Corps, of the Army of the Potomac	Gen. Meade, F.; Gen. Lee, C.	604	300 (k.&w.)	2494		200	2317					Conf'd.
June 23	Engagement (Wilson's Raid)	Nottoway Court House, Va.			Cav.	3rd Division Cavalry, Army of the Potomac	Gen. Wilson, F.											Federal.
	Attack on Troops	Collinsville, Miss				(Train on the Charlestown and Mississippi Railroad.)												
	Engagement	Jone's Bridge, Va.				1st and 2nd Division, Cavalry Corps Army of the Potomac, and 38th U. S. Colored troops												
June 24	Engagement	Samaria Church, Va.				1st and 2nd Div. Cavalry Corps, Army of the Potomac.												
	Action	White River, Ark				Federal Steamer, *Queen City*, and Gunboat.												
	Wilson's Raid	Stanton Bridge, Va.				3rd Division Cavalry Corps, Army of the Potomac, and Kautz's Cavalry, of the Army of the James	Gen. Wilson, F.											Federal.
	Skirmish	La Fayette, Macon County, Tenn.				(Troops not specified.)												
June 25	Skirmish	Point Pleasant, La				64th U. S. Colored Troops.												
	(25th–29th). Engagements	Clarendon, St. Charles River, Ark. (Pikesville, St. Charles)				11th Mo., 9th Iowa, 3rd Mich. Cavalry, 126th Ill. Volunteers and Battery D, 2nd Mo. Artillery												
June 27	General Assault	Kenesaw Mountain, Ga		80,000		4th, 14th and 20th Corps, Army of the Cumberland, 15th, 16th, and 17th Corps, Army of the Tennessee, 23rd Corps, Army of the Ohio	Gen. Sherman, F.; Gen. McPherson, F.; Gen. Thomas, F.; Gen. Johnson, C.	3000 (k.w. & m.)	600 (k.w. & m.)									Conf'd.
	Engagement	Charleston, W. Va.				1st Division, Army of West Virginia.												
June 28	Engagement. Wilson's Raid	Stony Creek, Va.				Federal Cavalry	Gen. Wilson, F.											—
June 29	Engagement. Wilson's Raid	Ream's Station, Va.				Federal Cavalry	Gen. Wilson, F.											Conf'd.
June 30	Affair near	La Fayette, Ga.				4th and 6th Kentucky Cavalry.												
	Engagement	Four Mile Creek, Va.			Batt.	Federal Steamer *Hunchback*, and Monitor *Saugus*	Com. Nichols, F.; Com. Calhoun, F.											
July 1	(1st–31st). Engagements	In front of Petersburg, Va.				2nd, 5th and 9th Corps, Army of the Potomac, and 10th and 18th Corps, Army of the James	Gen. Grant, F.; Gen. Lee, C.; Gen. Beauregard, C.	419		2076				1200				
July 2	Skirmish	Saulsbury, Miss				3rd Iowa Cavalry.												
	Skirmish	Pine Bluff, Ark.				64th U. S. Colored Troops.												
	Engagement	Fort Johnson, James Island, S. C.				Troops of the Department of the South.												
	(2d–5th). Action	Nickajack Creek, Va. (Smyrna or Vining Station)				Army of the Cumberland, Army of the Tennessee	Gen. McPherson, F.; Gen. Thomas, F.; Gen. Johnson, C.											Federal.
July 3	Skirmish	Platte City, Mo.				9th Missouri Militia Cavalry.												
	Attack on outposts	North Mountain, Va.		Outp.		135th Ohio National Guard.												
	(3d–9th). Expedition from	Vicksburg to Jackson, Miss				Troops of 1st Division, 17th Corps.												
	Skirmish	Leetown, Va				1st N. Y. Cavalry and 10th W. Virginia Volunteers.												
	Engagement	Hammack's Mills, North River, W. Va.				163rd Ohio National guard.												
July 4	Skirmish	Searcy, Ark.		53		Detachment 3rd Arkansas Cavalry.	Capt. Hamilton, F.		7		4	56					18	Federal.
	Skirmish	Vicksburg, Miss				49th U. S. Colored Troops., 10th Louisiana												

CHRONOLOGICAL LIST OF EVENTS (1860-1865).—Continued.

DATE.	EVENT.	LOCATION.	DURATION.	FORCE. F.	FORCE. C.	COMPOSITION OF FORCE.	COMMANDERS.	KILLED F.	KILLED C.	WOUNDED F.	WOUNDED C.	PRISONERS TAKEN AT F.	PRISONERS TAKEN AT C.	MISSING F.	MISSING C.	[illegible]	[illegible]	ADVANTAGE.
1864 July 4	Skirmish	Clay County, Mo.				6th Missouri Militia Cavalry.												
	Affair near	Clinton, Miss.				2nd Wisconsin Cavalry.												
	Engagement	Point of Rocks, Md				Maryland Potomac Home Brigade.												
	(4th–5th). Engagements	Coleman's Plantation near Port Gibson, Miss.				52nd U. S. Colored Troops (2nd Miss.) and Mississippi Marine Brigade.												
	(4th–7th). Attack on	Bolivar and Maryland Heights, Va.				Reserve Division of the Army of West Virginia.												
July 5	(5th–19th). Expedition from	La Grange, Tenn. to Tupelo, Miss.				1st and 3rd Divisions, 16th Corps, Cavalry Brigade and one Brigade U. S. Colored Troops.												
	(5th–7th). Occupation of	John's Island, S. C.				Troops of the Department of the South.												
	Occupation by Confederate Forces of	Hagerstown, Pleasant Valley, Md				1st Maryland Cavalry Potomac Home Brigade.												
	(5th–6th) Expedition to	Jackson, Miss.				2nd Wis., 5th and 11th Ill., and 3d U. S. Colored Cavalry, 46th, 76th and 79th Ill. Volunteers.	Brig.-Gen. Dennis, F.											Federal.
July 6	Skirmish	Little Blue, Mo.				2nd Colorado Cavalry.												
	Skirmish	Mount Zion Church, Va.				2nd Massachusetts Cavalry.												
	(9th–10th). Engagements	Chattahoochee River, Ga.				Armies of the Ohio, Tennessee and Cumberland.		60	k.w. & m. 600	450				200				
	Action	Hagar's Mountain and Middleton, Md.				8th Ill. Cavalry and Alexander's Baltimore Battery.												
July 7	Engagement	Clinton, Miss.				11th Ill., and 2nd Wis. Cavalry, and Battery of 2nd Ill. Artillery.												
	Engagement	Canton Road, Miss.	5 hours.	2800	3300	Troops with General Dennis.	Brig.-Gen. Dennis, F.											Conf'd.
	Action	Solomon's Gap, Frederick City, Md.				8th Ill. Cavalry, 3rd Maryland Potomac Home Brigade and Alexander's Baltimore Battery.												
	Skirmish	Ripley, Miss.				2nd Iowa Cavalry.												
July 9	Battle	Monocacy Bridge, Md.		9000	20,000	1st and 2nd Brigade, 3rd Division, 6th Corps and Detachment of the 8th Corps.	Gen. Wallace, F.; Gen. Early, C.	90	k.w. & m. 400	235				1282				Conf'd.
July 10	Scout	Little Rock, Ark.		20		10th Illinois Cavalry Volunteers.			k.w. & m. 4			1						Federal
July 11	(11th–22d). Rousseau's Raid in	Alabama and Georgia.				8th Ind., 5th Iowa, 9th O., 2nd Ky., and 4th Tennessee Cavalry, and Battery E, 1st Mich. Artillery.												
	Occupation of	Pontotoc, Miss.				8th Wisconsin, 5th Minnesota and 11th Missouri Volunteers, and 2nd Iowa Cavalry.	Gen. Mower, F.											Federal
	Maj.-Gen. Ord, U. S. A., assigned to command of 8th Army Corps and of all Troops in the Middle Department.																	
	Maj.-Gen. Gillmore, U. S. A., assigned to temporary command of that portion of 19th Army Corps serving in the Department of Washington.																	
July 12	Attack on	Fort Stevens, Washington, D. C.				1st and 2nd Divisions, 6th and 22nd Corps, Convalescents, Marines, Home Guard and Citizens.	Gen. Augur, F.; Gen. Early, C.	k.w. & m. 200	100									Federal
	Skirmish	Petit Jean, Arkansas River, Ark.		1 Co.		3rd Arkansas Cavalry	Capt. Gill, F.		3									Federal
	Engagement	Lee's Mills near Ream's Station, Va.				2nd Div., Cavalry Corps, Army of the Potomac.												
July 13	(13th–15th). Battle	Tupelo, Miss., includes Harrisburg, and Old Town Creek, Miss.				1st and 3rd Divisions, 16th Corps, Cavalry, and a Brigade of Colored Troops.	Gens. Smith and Slocum, F.; Gen. Forrest, C.	85	k.w. & m. 700	563								—
	Brig.-Gen. Emory placed in command of portion 19th Army Corps serving in the Department of Washington.																	
July 14	(14th–15th). Skirmish	Ozark, Mo.				14th Kansas Cavalry.												
	Rousseau's Raid. Skirmish	Ten Islands, Coosa River, Ala. (Jackson's Ford)				8th Indiana and 5th Iowa Cavalry	Gen. Rousseau, F.; Maj. Graham, F.; B.-Gen. Clanton, C.		16	1	40							Federal
	Engagement	Farr's Mills, Montgomery County, Ark.		20	100	Battalion 4th Arkansas Cavalry	Capt. Green, F.; —Crook and Crawford, C.		4		6							Federal.
July 15	Confederates routed	Old Town Creek, Miss.				1st and 3rd Division, 16th Corps, Cavalry, and a Brigade of Colored Troops.	Gen. Mower, F.											Federal.
	Engagement	Stones' Ferry, Ala.				8th Indiana and 5th Iowa Cavalry.												
July 16	(16th–17th.) Engagement	Grand Gulf, Port Gibson, Miss.				72nd and 76th Ill. Volunteers, 2nd Wisconsin Cav., and 53rd U. S. Colored Troops.												
July 17	Engagement	Fredericksburg, Mo				2nd Colorado Cavalry.												
	Engagement	Snicker's Gap, Va.				Army of West Virginia.												Conf'd.
	General Hood, C. S. A., assigned to Command of Confederate Army of the Tennessee, vice General Johnston relieved by order of Jefferson Davis.																	
July 18	Rousseau's Raid	Auburn, Ga.				8th Ohio and 4th Tennessee Cavalry.												
	Skirmish	Chewa Station, Montgomery and West Point Railroad, Ga.				8th Ind., 5th Iowa, and 4th Tennessee Cavalry	Maj. Baird, F.; B.-Gen. Clanton, C.	1	40	4								1 Con., 3 Fed.
	Action near	Snicker's Ferry, Island Ford, Shenandoah River, Va.				Army of West Virginia and portion of 6th Corps.	Gen. Wright, F.; Gen. Early, C.											Conf'd.
	Skirmish	Ashby's Gap, Va.				Cavalry of the Army of West Virginia.												Conf'd.
July 19	Engagement	Darkesville, Va.				Portion of the Army of West Virginia.	Gen. Averill, F.											
July 20	Battle	Winchester, Va. (Stevenson's Depot and Carter's Farm).	3 hours.			2nd Cavalry Division, Army of West Virginia.	Gen. Averill, F.; Gen. Early, C.	k.w. & m. 250	k.w. & m. 300			200				4		Federal.
	Battle	Peach Tree Creek, Ga.	3 hours.			Army of the Cumberland.	Gen. Sherman, F.; Gen. Hood, C.	300	k.w. & m. 4796	1430								Federal.

CHRONOLOGICAL LIST OF EVENTS (1860-1865).—Continued.

DATE.	EVENT.	LOCATION.	Duration.	Force F.	Force C.	COMPOSITION OF FORCE.	COMMANDERS.	Killed F.	Killed C.	Wounded F.	Wounded C.	Prisoners Taken by F.	Prisoners Taken by C.	Missing F.	Missing C.	Guns Capt'd.	Stands of Colors Capt'd.	Advantage.
1864 July 21	Engagement	Deep Bottom, Va.				1st Division, 10th Corps, Army of the James.												
	Skirmish	Henderson, Ky.				(Troops not specified.)												
July 22	(Hood's First Sortie)	Atlanta, Ga.	8 hours.			Army of the Tennessee	Gen. Sherman, F.; Gen. Hood, C.	500	K.W. & M. 8499	2141				1000		10		Federal.
	Action	Vidalia, La.				6th U. S. Colored Heavy Artillery, 2nd Mississippi.												
July 23	Engagement	Kernstown, Va.				Cavalry of the Army of West Virginia	Gen. Crook, F.; Gen. Early, C.	K.W. & M. 1200										Conf'd.
July 24	Battle	Winchester, Va.		10,000		Portion of the Army of West Virginia	Gen. Crook, F.; Gen. Early, C.	K.W. & M. 1200	K.W. & M. 600									Conf'd.
	Skirmish	Carrolton Landing, Carolina Bend, Miss.				6th Michigan Artillery.												
July 25	Skirmish	Courtland, Ala.				18th Michigan and 32nd Wisconsin Volunteers.												
July 26	Engagement	Wallace's Ferry, Big Creek, Ark.		600	1500	15th Ill. Cavalry Co. E, 2nd U.S. Colored Artillery, 60th (1st Iowa), and 56th (3rd Ark.), U. S. Colored Troops	Col. Brooks, F.; Mj. Carmichael, F.; Gen. Dobbins, C.	K.&W. 30	K.&W. 136									—
	Skirmish	Des Arc, Ark.				11th Missouri Cavalry.												
	(26th–31st). Stoneman's Raid to	Macon, Ga.				Stoneman and Garrard's Cavalry Division, Army of the Cumberland	Gen. Stoneman, F.	K.&W. 300		100			2500			18		Conf'd.
	(26th–31st). McCook's Raid. (Destruction of Railway)	Lovejoy Station, Ga.		4000		1st Wis., 5th and 8th Iowa, 2nd and 8th Ind., 1st and 4th Tenn., and 4th Kentucky Cavalry	Gen. McCook, F.			100				500				Federal.
	Skirmish	St. Mary's Trestle, Fla.				75th Ohio Mounted Infantry.												
July 27	Attack on Federal Outpost	Mazzard Prairie, Fort Smith, Ark.		200	1500	6th Kansas Cavalry	Capt. Mefford, F.; Gen. Gano, C.	10	12	15	30		82					Conf'd.
	(27th–28th). Engagements	Deep Bottom, New Market and Malvern Hill, Va.				1st Division, 10th Corps of Cavalry, Army of the James, 2nd Corps, and 1st and 2nd Divisions Cavalry Corps, Army of the Potomac	Gen. Grant, F.; Gen. Sheridan, F.											Federal.
	Skirmish	Whiteside, Black Creek, Fla.				25th U. S. Colored Troops (1st N. C.)												
	(27th–30th). (Engagements and Explosion of Mine)	Petersburg, Va.				Army of the Potomac	Gen. Grant, F.; Gen. Lee, C.	K.W. & M. 5000	K.W. & M. 1200									Conf'd.
July 28	Maj.-Gen. Wallace, U. S. A., resumes command of 8th Army Corps, and all other Troops in the Middle Department.																	
	Indian Fight	Tah-Kah-o-Kuty, Dakota Territory				8th Minn. Mounted Infantry, 6th and 7th Iowa and Dakota and Brackett's Minnesota Cavalry												
	Affair near the	Atchafalaya River, La.				Portion of the 19th Corps.												
	Skirmish	West Point, Ark.				11th Missouri Cavalry.												
	(2d Sortie)	Ezra Chapel, Atlanta, Ga.				Army of the Tennessee	Gen. Logan, F.; Gen. Hood, C.	100	K.W. & M. 4642	600								Federal.
	McCook's Raid	Campbelltown, Ga.				Portion of McCook's Cavalry	Gen. McCook, F.											
	Stoneman's Raid	Flatshoals, Ga.				Portion of Garrard's Cavalry.												
	(28th–Sept. 2d). Siege	Atlanta, Ga.				Armies of the Cumberland, Tennessee, and Ohio.												
July 29	(29th–31st). Skirmish	Fort Smith, Ark.				Troops not specified.												
	(29th–30th). McCook's Raid	Lovejoy Station, Ga.				Cavalry of the Army of the Cumberland.												
	Engagement	Clear Springs, Md.				12th and 14th Pennsylvania Cavalry.												
July 30	Explosion of Mine and Engagement	Petersburg, Va.				9th Corps, supported by 18th Corps, and 2nd and 5th Corps as Reserve	Gen. Burnside, F.; Gen. Meade, F.	419	K.W. & M. 1200	1079				1910				Conf'd.
	McCook's Raid	Newman, Ga.		4000		Cavalry of the Army of the Cumberland	Gen. McCook, F.					600						Conf'd.
	Maj.-Gen. O. O. Howard, U. S. A., placed in command of Army of the Tennessee, vice Maj.-Gen. McPherson, killed in action.																	
	Destruction by Confederate Troops of	Chambersburg, Pa.				Federal Troops (in Carlisle Barracks)												Conf'd.
	Stoneman's Raid	Macon, Ga.				Cavalry, Army of the Cumberland	Gen. Stoneman, F.											Conf'd.
	Engagement	Lee's Mills, Va.				Davis' Brig., 2nd Cav. Division Army of the Potomac.												
	Skirmish	Lebanon, Ky.		1 Co.		12th Ohio Cavalry.												
July 31	Stoneman's Raid	Hillsboro', Ga. (Sunshine Church)				Cavalry, Army of the Cumberland.												
Aug. 1	Skirmish	Rolla, Mo.				5th Missouri Militia Cavalry.												
	(1st–31st). Fights near the	Trenches before Petersburg, Va.				2nd, 5th and 9th Corps, Army of the Potomac, and 18th Corps, Army of the James	Gen. Grant, F.	87		484								—
	Engagement	Cumberland, Md. (Flock's Mills)	4 hours.			Command of Brigadier-General B. F. Kelly	Gen. Kelly, F.											Federal.
Aug. 2	Skirmish	Green Springs Depot, W. Va. near Old Town, Md.		500		153rd Ohio Volunteers	Col. Stough, F.											Conf'd.
	Engagement	Osceola, Ark.				2nd and 3rd Militia and 1st and 6th Missouri Cavalry.												
Aug. 3	Action near	Elkchute, Mo.				Federal Troops	Col. Borris, F.											
Aug. 4	Skirmish	New Creek, Va.				(Troops not specified.)												
Aug. 5	(5th–23d). Actions. (Surrender of Gaines, 8th)	Fort Gaines and Morgan, Mobile Harbor, Ala.				Federal Steamers *Brooklyn, Octorora, Hartford, Ossippee, Itasca, Oneida, Galena, Metacomet, Richmond, Port Royal, Lackawanna, Seminole, Monongahela, and Tecumseh*, and 13th Army Corps	Ad. Farragut, F.; Gen. Granger, F.; Ad. Buchanan, C.; Gen. Page, C.	120		88		1756				150		Federal
	(5th–6th). Engagements	Utoy Creek, Ga.				Armies of the Cumberland, Tennessee and Ohio.												
	(5th–7th). Skirmishes	Cowskin, Mo.				8th Missouri Militia Cavalry.												
	Engagement	Decatur, Ga.				2nd Cavalry Division, Army of the Cumberland.												
	Skirmish	Donaldsonville, La.				11th N. Y. Cavalry.												
	Skirmish	Cabin Point, Va.				1st U. S. Colored Cavalry.												

CHRONOLOGICAL LIST OF EVENTS (1860-1865).—Continued.

Date.	Event.	Location.	Duration.	Force.		Composition of Force.	Commanders.	Killed.		Wounded.		Prisoners Taken by		Missing.		[illegible]	[illegible]	Advantage.
				F.	C.			F.	C.	F.	C.	F.	C.	F.	C.			
1864																		
Aug. 6	Action	Plaquemine, La. (Indian City Village)				4th Wis. Cav., and 11th and 14th R. I. Heavy Artillery												
Aug. 7	(7th-9th). Skirmishes	Tallahatchie River, Miss.				Cavalry and Infantry, 16th Corps.												
	Maj.-Gen. Sheridan, U. S. A., assigned to command of Middle Military Division (Middle Department and Departments of Washington, the Susquehanna and West Virginia.)																	
Aug. 8	Engagement, and surrender of	Fort Gaines, Ala				Federal Fleet	Adm. Farragut, F.											Federal.
	Engagement	Two Hills, Bad Lands, Little Missouri River, Dakota Territory				8th Minn. Volunteers and 2nd Minn., 6th and 7th Iowa, Brackett's Battery, Minnesota and 1st Battalion of Dakota Cavalry												
Aug. 9	Explosion of Ammunition at	City Point, Va.						70		130								
Aug. 10	Attack	On the Mississippi				Federal Steamer *Empress*		6		12								
	Skirmish	Berryville Pike, Va.	½ hour			Reserve Brig. and 1st Cav. Div., Army of the Potomac.	Gen. Gibbs, F.			30								Federal.
	Occupation by Federal Troops under Colonel Cesnola of	Millwood, Va.																
Aug. 11	Attack on Confederate Wagon-Train and Skirmish	Sulphur Springs Bridge and White Post, Va.	3 hours			1st and 3rd Div. and Res. Brig., Cav. Army of Potomac.	Gen. Custer, F.	K.&W. 250										Conf'd.
	Skirmish	Van Buren, Ark.				2nd and 6th Kansas Cavalry.												
Aug. 12	Engagement	Abbeville and Oxford, Miss.				Cavalry and Infantry of the 16th Corps.												
	Skirmish	Little Blue, Dakota Territory				Detachment, 7th Iowa Cavalry.												
	Reconnoissance of Federal Troops to Fawcet Gap, North Mountain, Va.																	
Aug. 13	Attack on Supply-Train	Near Snicker's Gap, Va.				144th and 149th Ohio Volunteers.												
Aug. 14	Engagement	Gravel Hill, Va.				2nd Cavalry Division, Army of the Potomac.												
	(14th-18th). Engagements and Battle	Strawberry Plains, Deep Bottom Run, Va.				2nd Cavalry Division, and 2nd Corps, Army of the Potomac, and 10th Corps, Army of the James	Gen. Grant, F.; Gen. Lee, C.	400	K.W. & M. 1100	1755				1400				Federal.
	Skirmish	Hurricane Creek, Miss.				Cavalry and Infantry of the 16th Corps.												
	(14th-16th). Skirmishes	Dalton, Ga.				2nd Missouri Volunteers and 14th U. S. Colored Troops.												
Aug. 15	Engagement	Fisher's Hill, near Strasburg, Va.				1st Cav. Div. and 6th and 8th Corps, Army of Potomac												
Aug. 16	Skirmish	Smoky Hill Crossing, Kansas				Detachment 7th Iowa and U. S. Cavalry.												
	Engagement	Crooked Run, Front Royal, Va.				1st and 2nd Brig., 1st Cav. Div., Army of the Potomac.	Gen. Merrill, F.; Gen'ls Lomax and Wickham, C.	70	300			300						Federal.
Aug. 17	Skirmish	Gainesville, Fla.				75th Ohio Mounted Infantry.												
	Action near	Cleveland, Tenn.				6th Ohio Heavy Artillery.												
	Occupation by Confederate Forces of	Winchester, Va.				3rd Cavalry Division, Army of the Potomac, and the New Jersey Brigade, 6th Corps												Conf'd.
Aug. 18	(18th, 19th and 21st). Engagements	Six Mile House, Weldon Railroad, Va.				Kautz's Cavalry and 2nd Cavalry Division, 5th and 9th Corps, Army of the Potomac	Gen. Warren, F.; Gen. Pickett, C.	212	K.W. & M. 4000	1155				3176				Federal.
	Engagement	Fairburn, Ga.				Cavalry of the Army of the Cumberland.												
	Engagement	Decatur, Ala.				2nd Cavalry Division, Army of the Cumberland, and 1st U. S. Colored Artillery												
	(18th-22d). Kilpatrick's Raid	Atlanta Railroad		5000		Cavalry, Army of the Cumberland	Gen. Kilpatrick, F.	K.W. & M. 314				1000						Federal.
Aug. 19	(Encounter with Mosby's Guerillas)	Snicker's Gap Pike, Va.				Detachment, 5th Michigan Cavalry.												
	Skirmish	Blockhouse No. 4, N. & C. R.R. Tenn.		1 Co.		115th Ohio Volunteers.												
	Skirmish	Martinsburg, Va.		1 Co.		Cavalry of Averill's Command.												
	Kilpatrick's Raid	Red Oak, Ga.				Cavalry, Army of the Cumberland.												
	(19th-20th). Kilpatrick's Raid. Occupation and Destruction of	Jonesboro, Ga.				2nd Division Cavalry, Army of the Cumberland	Gen. Kilpatrick, F.; Col. Minty, F.; Gen. Ferguson, C.	K.&W. 314	K.W. & M. 1000									Federal.
	(Murder by Guerillas)	Pine Bluff, Ark.				Detachment Company B, 83rd Ill. Mounted Infantry												
Aug. 20	Kilpatrick's Raid	Lovejoy Station, Ga.				Cavalry, Army of the Cumberland	Col. Minty, F.									4		Federal.
Aug. 21	Affair near	Dalton, Ga.				Federal Cavalry	Col. Siebold, F.; Gen. Wheeler, C.	30	150									Federal.
	Engagements	Summit Point, Va. (including Berryville and Flowing Springs)				1st and 3rd Divisions Cavalry Corps, and 6th Corps	Gen. Sheridan, F.; Gen. Early, C.	K.W. & M. 600		K.W. & M. 400								
	Skirmish	Duvall's Bluff, Ark.				11th Missouri Cavalry.												
	Raid by Confederate Cavalry	Memphis, Tenn.				Detachment 8th Iowa, 109th and 113th Ill., 39th, 40th and 41st Wis. Vols., 61st (2nd Tenn.) U. S. Colored Troops, 3rd and 4th Iowa Cavalry, and Battery G, 1st Missouri Light Artillery	Gen. Forrest, C.		80		100	15						Federal.
	(21st-23d). Engagement	College Hill, Miss. (Oxford Hill and Hurricane Creek)				4th Iowa, 11th and 21st Miss. Volunteers, 3rd Iowa and 12th Missouri Cavalry, of the 16th Corps												
Aug. 22	Skirmish	Canton, Ky.				(Troops not specified.)												
	Skirmish	Rodgersville, Tenn.				(Troops not specified.)												
Aug. 23	Bombardment	Fort Morgan, Ala.				Federal Naval Forces (Mobile Harbor.)	Adm. Farragut, F.											Federal.
	Engagement	Abbeville, Miss.				10th Mo., 14th Iowa, 5th and 7th Minn., and 6th Wisconsin Volunteers												
Aug. 24	Engagement	Halltown, Va.				Portion of the 8th Corps, Army of the Shenandoah.												
	(24th-25th). Engagements	Bermuda Hundred, Va.				10th Corps, Army of the James.		K.&W. 30				65						Federal.
	Skirmish	Fort Smith, Ark.				16th U. S. Colored Troops.												

CHRONOLOGICAL LIST OF EVENTS (1860-1865).—Continued.

DATE.	EVENT.	LOCATION.	DURATION.	FORCE. F.	FORCE. C.	COMPOSITION OF FORCE.	COMMANDERS.	KILLED. F.	KILLED. C.	WOUNDED. F.	WOUNDED. C.	PRISONERS TAKEN BY F.	PRISONERS TAKEN BY C.	MISSING. F.	MISSING. C.	[illegible]	[illegible]	ADVANTAGE.
1864																		
Aug. 24	Skirmishes	Jones' Hay Station and Ashley Station, Long Prairie, Ark.				9th Iowa and 8th and 11th Missouri Cavalry.												
Aug. 25	Engagements	Smithfield and Shepherdstown, Va. (or Kearneysville)				1st and 3rd Divisions Cavalry, Army of the Potomac.												
	Engagement	Ream's Station, Va.				2nd Corps and 2nd Cav. Div., Army of the Potomac.	Gen. Grant, F.; Gen. Lee, C.	127	K. W. & M. 1500	540				1700		9		Conf'd
	Engagement	Coxes Creek, Clinton, La.				Portion of the Cavalry of Army of the Gulf.												
		Sacramento Mountain, New Mexico				1st New Mexico Cavalry.												
	Siege raised by General Sherman of	Atlanta, Ga.																
	Engagement	Kearneysville, Va.			Inf.	Federal Cavalry												Federal.
Aug. 26	Skirmish	Bull Bayou, Ark.				9th Kansas and 3rd Wisconsin Cavalry.												
	(26th–27th). Engagement	Halltown, Va.				1st and 2nd Div., 8th Corps, Army of West Virginia.												
Aug. 27	Skirmish	Owensboro', Ky.				108th U. S. Colored Troops.												
	(27th–28th). Engagement	Holly Springs, Miss.				14th Iowa Volunteers, 11th U. S. Colored Troops (1st Ala. Artillery,) and 10th Missouri Cavalry												
Aug. 28	Fight with Indians	Fort Cottonwood, Nevada Territory				7th Iowa Cavalry.												
	Skirmish	Howard County, Mo.				Company E, 4th Missouri Militia Cavalry.												
Aug. 29	Skirmish	Ghent, Ky.				117th U. S. Colored Troops.												
	Attack on Federal Forces	Smithfield, Va.			Inf. & Cav.	1st Division Cavalry Corps, and 3rd Division, 6th Corps, Army of the Potomac	Gen. Merritt, F.											1 Con. 2 Fed.
	Skirmish	Wormley's Gap, Va.				Detachment of Federal Troops.	Capt. Blazer, F.											
	(29th–30th). Engagements	Arthur's Swamp, Va.				2nd Cavalry Division, Army of the Potomac.												
Aug. 30	Maj.-Gen. Crook, U. S. A., assigned to command of the Department of West Virginia, vice Maj. Gen. Hunter, relieved.																	
Aug. 31	Skirmish	Blockhouse No. 5, N. & C. R. R., Tenn.				115th Ohio Volunteers.												
	(31st–Sept. 1st). Battle	Jonesboro, Ga.	2 hours			Cavalry and Davis' Division, 14th Corps, Army of the Cumberland, 15th, 16th and 17th Corps, Army of the Tennessee	Gen. Sherman, F.; Gen. Howard, F.; Gen. Hood, C.; Gen. Hardee, C.		K. W. & M. 2000	1149								Federal.
Sept. 1	(1st–6th. Rousseau's pursuit of Wheeler	Tennessee				1st and 4th Tenn., 2nd Mich., 1st Wis., 8th Iowa, 2nd and 8th Ind., and 6th Kentucky Cavalry	Gen. Rousseau, F.											
	(1st–Oct. 30th). Skirmishes	Trenches before Petersburg, Va.				Army of the Potomac	Gen. Grant, F.	170	K. W. & M. 1000	832				812				—
	(Rousseau in pursuit of Wheeler)	Lavergne, Tenn.				Federal Cavalry												
Sept. 2	Occupation of	Atlanta, Ga.				20th Corps, Army of the Cumberland	Gen. Sherman, F.; Gen. Slocum, F.; Gen. Hood, C.											Federal
	(Rousseau in pursuit of Wheeler)	Franklin, Tenn.				Federal Cavalry.												
	(2d–6th). Engagement	Lovejoy Station, Ga.				23rd Corps, Army of the Ohio, and 4th Corps, Army of the Cumberland												
	Affair near	Big Shanty, Ga.				9th Ohio Cavalry (on railroad.)												
	Reconnoissance of Federal Troops under General Gregg on the Boynton Plank Road.																	
Sept. 3	Skirmish	Murfreesboro', Tenn.				100th U. S. Colored Troops.												
	(3d–4th). Engagement	Berryville, Va.				1st Cavalry Division, Army of the Potomac, 8th Corps, Army of West Virginia, and 19th Corps	Gen. Averell, F.; Gen. McCausland, C.	300				70						Federal.
Sept. 4	Engagement	Darkesville, Va.			Cav.	3rd Cavalry Division, Army of the Potomac	Gen. Crook, F.; Gen. Kershaw, C.											Federal.
	Engagement (Morgan killed)	Greenville, Tenn.				9th and 13th Tennessee and 10th Michigan Cavalry	Gen. Gillem, F.; John Morgan, C.		100			75						Federal
Sept. 5	(Rousseau in pursuit of Wheeler)	Campbellsville, Tenn.				Federal Cavalry	Gen. Rousseau, F.; —— Wheeler, C.											
Sept. 6	Skirmish	Searcy, Ark.				Detachment 9th Iowa Cavalry.												
Sept. 7	Skirmish	Readyville, Tenn.				Detachment 9th Pennsylvania Cavalry.												
	Bombardment by Confederates of Signal Tower at	Dutch Gap, Va.	3 hours			4th U. S. Colored Troops.												
Sept. 10	Capture of	Fort Hell, Jerusalem Plank Road, Va.				99th Penn., 2nd U. S. Sharpshooters and 20th Ind Vols	Gen. De Trobriand, F.	K. & W. 20				90						Federal
Sept. 13	Capture of Confederate Regt. (8th S. C.)	Abram's Creek, Va.; Lock's Ford, Opequan, Va.				Cavalry, Major-General Sheridan's Army. 2nd Brigade, 3rd Division, Cavalry Corps, Army of Middle Military Division	Gen. McIntosh, F.											Federal
	Skirmish	Pine Bluff, Ark.		2 Cos.		1st Indiana Cavalry.												
	Reconnoissance of Federal Troops under General Getty (Sheridan's Army) to the Opequan.																	
Sept. 16	(16th–19th). Attacks on	Fort Gibson, Indian Territory				79th U. S. Colored Troops (1st Kan.,) and 2nd Kan. Cav.												
Sept. 17	Engagement	Sycamore Church, Va.				1st D. C., and 13th Pennsylvania Cavalry	Gens. Gregg and Kautz, F.; Gen. Hampton, C.	K. W. & M. 110	K. & W. 90									—
	Engagement	Fairfax Station, Va.				13th and 16th N. Y. Cavalry.												
	Engagement	Belcher's Mills, Va.				Kautz's Cavalry of the Army of the James, and 2nd Cavalry Division, Army of the Potomac												
	(17th–20th). Skirmishes	Doniphan and Black River, Mo.		1 Co.		3rd Missouri Militia Cavalry.												
Sept 18	Engagement	Martinsburg, Va.				2nd Cavalry Division, Army of West Virginia.												
	Skirmish	Fort Cottonwood, Nevada Territory				7th Iowa Cavalry.												
Sept. 19	Battle	Opequan, Winchester, Va. (Bello Grove)	9 hours		15,000	8th Corps and 2nd Cav. Div., Army of W. Va., 6th Corps and 1st and 3rd Cav. Div., Army of Potomac, 1st and 2nd Divisions, 19th Corps, Army of the Middle Military Division	Gen. Sheridan, F.; Gen. Early, C.	826	K. & W. 3500	2600		4500	140	618		5		Federal

CHRONOLOGICAL LIST OF EVENTS (1860-1865).—Continued.

DATE.	EVENT.	LOCATION.	DURATION.	FORCE. F.	FORCE. C.	COMPOSITION OF FORCE.	COMMANDERS.	KILLED. F.	KILLED. C.	WOUNDED. F.	WOUNDED. C.	PRISONERS TAKEN BY F.	PRISONERS TAKEN BY C.	MISSING. F.	MISSING. C.	Guns Capd.	[illegible]	ADVANTAGE.
1864																		
Sept. 19	Engagement	Cabin Creek, Indian Territory				2nd, 6th and 14th Kansas Cavalry and 1st and 2nd Kansas Indian Home Guards												
Sept. 21	Engagement	Front Royal Pike, Va				3rd Division Cavalry Corps, Army of the Potomac.												
Sept. 22	(20th–1). Battle	Fisher's Hill, Va. (Woodstock)	3 hours	45,000	30,000	6th Corps, 1st and 2nd Cav. Div., Army of Potomac, 8th Corps, Army of W. Va., and 1st and 2nd Div., 19th Corps	Gen. Sheridan, F; Gen. Early, C.	K&W 600	K&W 400			1100				10		Federal
Sept. 23	Attack on Federal Garrison	Athens, Ala				106th, 110th and 114th U. S. Colored Troops, 3rd Tenn., Cav., and 18th Mich., and 102nd Ohio Vols.	Gen. Forrest, C.	K.W. & M. 950	K.W. & M. 30									Conf'd.
	Skirmish	Rockport, Mo.				3rd Missouri Militia Cavalry.												
	Skirmish	Blackwater, Mo				1 Battalion, 1st Missouri Militia Cavalry.												
Sept. 24	Engagement	Luray, Va				1st Div. Cav. Corps, Army of the Potomac	Gen. Torbert, F.											Federal
	Skirmish	Fayette, Mo				9th Missouri Militia Cavalry.												
	Engagement	Bull's Gap, Tenn				Cavalry and Mounted Infantry.												
	(24th–Oct. 28th). Price's Invasion of	Missouri				Mo. Militia Cav. and Cav. of Gen. A. J. Smith's Command, and Kansas Militia and Cav. of the Army of the Border	Gen. A. J. Smith, F; Gen. Price, C.	170		290		1958						—
Sept. 25	Capture of Federal Garrison at	Sulphur Branch, Trestle, Ala				111th U. S. Colored Troops (3rd Tenn.) and 9th Ind Cav.	Gen. Forrest, C.											Conf'd.
	Skirmish	Johnsonville, Tenn				13th U. S. Colored Troops.												
	Skirmish	Henderson, Ky				118th U. S. Colored Troops.												
Sept. 26	Expedition of Federal Troops under General McLean, from	Prestonburg to Saltville, Ky.																
	Skirmish	Vache Grass, Ark				14th Kansas Cavalry.												
	(26th–27th). Price's Invasion of Missouri	Fort Davidson, Pilot Knob, Mo., (Ironton)	9 hours	1051		47th and 50th Mo., and 14th Iowa Vols., 2nd and 3rd Mo. Cav., and Battery H., 2nd Mo. Light Artillery	Gen. Ewing, F.; Gen. Price, C.	9	K&W 1500	60				100				Federal.
	Attack on Federal Cavalry	Brown's Gap, Va				1st Cavalry Division, Army of the Potomac, and 2nd Cavalry Division, Army of West Virginia	Gen. Averill, F.											Conf'd.
	Skirmishes	Richland, Tenn				111th U. S. Colored Troops (3rd Alabama.)												Federal.
Sept. 27	Engagement	Weyer's Cave, Va				2nd Division Cavalry, Army of West Virginia.												
	Attack on Federal Garrison	Pulaski, Tenn				Federal Cavalry	Gen. Rousseau, F; Gen. Forrest, C.											
	Massacre	North Missouri R.R.				Furloughed Federal Soldiers.												
	Massacre (Price's Invasion of Missouri)	Centralia, Mo.		3 Cos.		39th Missouri Volunteers.												
	Engagement	Carter's Station, Watauga River, Ark				Federal Cavalry and Mounted Infantry	Gen. Ammen, F.											
	Capture, by Federal Forces, of	Mariana, Fla.				82nd U. S. Colored Troops, 7th Vermont Volunteers, and 2nd Maine Cavalry	Brig.-Gen. Asboth, F.	K&W 83				61					95	Federal.
	Fight with Indians	Fort Rice, Dakota Territory				Detachment 6th Iowa Cavalry												
Sept. 28	Skirmish	Clarksville, Ark				3rd Wisconsin Cavalry.												
	Occupation by Federal Forces, of	Waynesboro', Va				3rd Division Cavalry Corps, Army of the Potomac	Gen. Torbert, F.											Federal.
	(28th–30th). Engagements	New Market Heights, Va. (Chapin's Farm, Laurel Hill, Forts Harrison and Gilmore)				10th and 18th Corps and Cavalry, Army of the James	Maj.-Gen. Ord, F.	181	K&W 2500	788		800	1736			15		
	Engagement	Fort Sedgwick, Jerusalem Plank Road, Va				3rd Division, 9th Corps												
Sept. 29	Skirmish	Centreville, Tenn				2nd Tennessee Mounted Infantry.												
	(29th–30th). Price's Invasion of Missouri	Leesburg and Harrison, Mo.				2nd Mo. Militia Cav., Battery H, 2nd Mo. Light Artillery, and 14th Iowa Volunteers	Gen. Ewing, F.; Gen. Price, C.	150										Federal
Sept. 30	(30th–Oct. 1st). Battle	Preble's Farm, Poplar Springs Church, Va				1st Division 5th Corps, and 2nd Division 9th Corps	Gen. Warren, F.	141	K.W. & M. 800	788				1756				—
	(30th–Oct. 1st). Engagements	Arthur's Swamp, Va				2nd Cavalry Division, Army of the Potomac.												
	(30th–Oct. 1st).	Richmond and Petersburg, Va				Federal Troops under General Grant	Gen. Grant, F.; Gen. Lee, C.	K.W. & M. 5000	2400									—
Oct. 1	Surrender demanded by Confederates, of	Huntsville, Ala				Detachment 12th and 13th Indiana Cavalry	Gen. Buford, C.											Federal
	(1st–2d). Attack on Federal Garrison	Athens, Ala				73rd Indiana Volunteers	Lt.-Col. Slade, F.; Gen. Forrest, C.											Federal.
	Engagement	Clinch Mountain, Ky				30th and 45th, and 3 Companies 40th Ky. Regiments	Gen. Hobson, F.; —— Giltner, C.	3		10								Federal.
	Engagement	Franklin, Mo				Enrolled Missouri Militia	Col. Wolfe, F.											Federal.
	Re-occupation by Federal Forces under General Merrill, of	Fort Republic, Va																
	Reconnoissance on	Charles' City Cross Roads, Va				Spear's Cavalry Brigade and Terry's Brigade, 10th Corps, Army of the James.												
	Engagement	Laurel Gap, Ky				40th and 13th Kentucky	Gen. Hobson, F.; Col. True, F.											Federal
	(1st–5th). Engagements	Yellow Tavern, Weldon R. R., Va				3rd Division, 2nd Corps, Army of the Potomac.												
	(1st–3d). Engagements	Sweetwater, Noses, and Powder Spring Creeks, Ga				Cavalry, Army of the Cumberland	Gen. Kilpatrick, F											
Oct. 2	Engagement	Waynesboro, Va				Portions of 1st Division, and 3rd Division Cavalry Corps, Army of the Potomac.												

CHRONOLOGICAL LIST OF EVENTS (1860-1865).—Continued.

DATE.	EVENT.	LOCATION.	DURATION.	FORCE. F.	FORCE. C.	COMPOSITION OF FORCE.	COMMANDERS.	KILLED. F.	KILLED. C.	WOUNDED. F.	WOUNDED. C.	PRISONERS TAKEN AS F.	PRISONERS TAKEN AS C.	MISSING. F.	MISSING. C.	Guns lost.	Stands of Arms lost.	ADVANTAGE.
1864																		
Oct. 3	Engagement	SALTVILLE, VA.	8 hours			11th and 13th Ky., 12th Ohio, 11th Mich., 5th and 6th U. S. Colored Cavalry, and 26th, 30th, 35th, 37th, 39th, 40th and 45th Ky. Mounted Infantry.	Gen. Burbridge, F.											Conf'd
	Skirmish	GLADESVILLE POUND GAP, VA.		200		1st Kentucky Cavalry and 3rd Ky. Mounted Infantry.	Maj. Keene, F.											Federal.
	Expedition from Rodney, Miss., and Capture of Confederate Troops at	FAYETTE, MISS.																
Oct. 4	Skirmish	NEAR MEMPHIS, TENN.		1 Co.		7th Indiana Cavalry.												
Oct. 5	Engagement	JACKSON, LA.				23rd Wis. Vols., 1st Texas and 1st La. Cavalry and 2nd and 4th Mass. Battery.												
	Attack on Federal Garrison	ALLATOONA, GA.	8 hours.	1700	7000	7th, 12th, 50th, 57th and 93rd Ill., 39th Iowa, 4th Minn., 18th Wis. Vols., and 12th Wis. Battery.	Gen. Corse, F. / Gen. French, C.	142	K.W. & M. 1143	352				212				Federal.
	Skirmish	FORT ADAMS, LA.				2nd Wis., and 3rd U. S. Colored Cavalry.												
	Occupation by Confederate Forces of	HERMAN, MO.																
Oct. 6	Engagement	FLORENCE, ALA.				60th Ill. Vols., and 3rd and 8th Tenn. Cavalry.												
	Expedition and Capture of Confederate Troops at	CLINTON, MISS.				Federal Cavalry.	Gen. Lee, F.					47						Federal.
	Skirmish	NORTH SHENANDOAH, VA.				8th Ohio Cavalry.												
	Price's Invasion of Missouri	PRICE'S PLACE, OSAGE RIVER, COLE COUNTY, MO.				1st, 7th and 9th Mo. Militia Cavalry.												
	Expedition and Capture of Confederate Troops at	WOODVILLE, MISS.				(Troops not specified.)	By order of Gen. Dana, F.		40			86				8		Federal.
Oct. 7	Engagement	NEW MARKET, VA.				3rd Cavalry Division, Army of the Potomac.												
	Engagement	DARBYTOWN ROADS near NEW MARKET HEIGHTS, VA.				10th Corps and Cavalry, Army of the James.	Gen. Butler, F. / Gen. Anderson, C.	K.W. & M. 506	K.W. & M. 1000									
	Price's Invasion of Missouri	MOREAU BOTTOM, near JEFFERSON CITY, MO.				Missouri, Militia, Cavalry, Artillery and Infantry.												
Oct. 8	Reconnoissance to the	BOYDTON PLANK ROAD, VA.				5th and 9th Corps, Army of the Potomac.	Gens. Crawford and Parke, F.	60										—
Oct. 9	Engagement	TOM'S BROOK, STRASBURG, WOODSTOCK, VA. (Fisher's Hill).				1st and 3rd Divisions Cavalry, Army of the Potomac.	Gen. Sheridan, F. / Gen. Rosser, C.	K.W. & M. 580	K.W. & M. 1960							11		Federal.
	(8th–11th). Engagements	CALIFORNIA, MO.				4th and 7th Mo. Militia Cavalry and Batteries H. and L. 2nd Missouri Artillery.												
	(9th–11th). Price's Invasion of Missouri	BOONEVILLE, MO.				1st, 4th, 5th, 6th and 7th Mo. Militia Cav., 15th Mo., 17th Ill. Cavalry and Battery H, 2nd Mo. Light Artillery.												
Oct. 10	Skirmish	SOUTH TUNNEL, TENN.				40th U. S. Colored Troops.												
	Skirmish	EAST POINT, MISS.				61st U. S. Colored Troops (2nd Tennessee.)												
	The Secretary of War informs Maj.-Gen Dix that reports have been received from Generals Butler, Sherman, Thomas, Sheridan and Burbridge, "showing the favorable condition of military affairs in their respective fields of operation."																	
	General Grant rejoins from Washington, "the purpose of his visit having been accomplished."																	
Oct. 11	Attack on Federal Troops	FORT HEIMAN, TENN.		90	200	Portion of 4th U. S. Colored Artillery.	Col. Weaver, F.	4	K&W 27	9								Federal.
	Reconnoissance	STONY CREEK STATION, VA.				13th Pennsylvania Cavalry.						14						Federal.
	Engagement	NARROWS, GA.				Garrard's Cav. Div., Army of the Cumberland.												
Oct. 12	Affair near	GREENVILLE, TENN.				(Troops not specified.)	Gen. Vaughan, C.											Conf'd.
	Attack on	RESACA, GA.				Federal Troops (Garrison.)	Col. Weaver, F. / Gen. Hood, C.											Federal.
Oct. 13	Reconnoissance and Engagement	STRASBURG, VA.	8 hours.			1st and 2nd Divisions, 19th Corps, and 1st and 2nd Divisions, Army of West Virginia.	Gen. Crook, F. / Gen. Thorburn, F.	K&W 200										—
	Skirmish	TILTON, GA.				(Troops not specified.)												
	Surrender of	DALTON, GA.				Federal Troops.	Col. Johnson, F.											Conf'd.
	Skirmish	BUZZARD'S ROOST BLOCKHOUSE, GA.		1 Co.		115th Illinois Volunteers.												
Oct. 14	Reconnoissance and Engagement	DARBYTOWN ROAD, VA.				1st and 3rd Divisions, 10th Corps and Cavalry, Army of the James.	Gen. Terry, F.	K&W 414	K&W 200									Conf'd.
Oct. 15	(15th–16th.) Raid of Federal Troops (20th N. Y. Cavalry) under Cap't Carroll, from Suffolk to South Quay, Va.																	
	Skirmish	BAYOU BIDDELL, LA.				32nd U. S. Colored Troops (2nd Miss.)												
	(Price's Invasion of Missouri) Surrender of Federal Troops at	GLASGOW, MO.	5 hours.			43rd Mo. Vols., Detachment 17th Ill., 9th Mo. Militia and 13th Mo. Cavalry, and 62nd U. S. Colored Troops (1st Mo.)												Conf'd.
	Pursuit of Hood by Sherman	SNAKE CREEK GAP, GA.				Portion of the Army of the Tennessee.	Gen. Sherman, F.											
	(Price's Invasion of Missouri) Attack by Confederate Forces on	SEDALIA, MO.				1st and 7th Missouri Militia Cavalry												Conf'd.
Oct. 16	Capture of Confederate Troops	SHIP'S GAP, TAYLOR'S RIDGE, GA.				1st Division, 15th Corps	Gen. Sherman, F. / Gen. Hood, C.											Federal.
	Scout of Federal Troops under Captain Mason, between the James and Blackwater, Va.																	
Oct. 17	Attack on Federal Troops and Skirmish	CEDAR RUN CHURCH, VA.		Pkt.		Detachment Connecticut Cavalry.												Federal.
	Occupation of Lexington, Missouri, by Confederate Forces under Price																	
Oct. 18	Engagement	PIERCE'S POINT, BLACKWATER, FLA.				19th Iowa Vols., and 2nd Maine, and 1st Florida Cavalry.												
Oct. 19	(Price's Invasion of Missouri). Occupation of	LEXINGTON, MO.				3rd Wis., and 5th, 11th, 15th and 16th Kansas Cavalry	Gen. Blunt, F. / Gen. Price, C.											Conf'd.
	Battle	CEDAR CREEK, VA. (Middletown.)	6 hours.		20,000	1st and 3rd Div. Cav., and 6th Corps, Army of the Potomac, 8th Corps and Cavalry, Army of W. Va., and 1st and 2nd Divisions, 19th Corps	Gen. Sheridan, F. / Gen. Early, C.	588	K.W. & M. 4200	3316		1606	1000			Fed loss, 20; Con. loss, 49		1 Con. 2 Fed.
Oct. 20	(20th–28th). Skirmish	FORT LEAVENWORTH, KAN.				(Troops not specified.)												
	Engagement	LITTLE RIVER, TENN.				Cavalry and portion of 15th Corps.												

CHRONOLOGICAL LIST OF EVENTS (1860-1865).—Continued.

Date	Event	Location	Duration	Force F.	Force C.	Composition of Force	Commanders	Killed F.	Killed C.	Wounded F.	Wounded C.	Prisoners Taken by F.	Prisoners Taken by C.	Missing F.	Missing C.	Guns Taken	Stands of Arms Taken	Advantage
1864 Oct. 21	Skirmish	Harrodsburg, Kentucky				5th U. S. Colored Cavalry.												
	Engagements (Price's Invasion of Missouri)	Little Blue, Mo	4 hours			2nd Colorado, 3rd Wis., 5th, 11th, 15th and 16th Kan. Cav., and 1 Brig. Kan. Militia, 2nd and 5th Mo. Militia, and 2 Battalions 2nd Mo. Artillery	Gen. Curtis, F.; Gen. Price, C.											—
Oct. 22	Engagements (Price's Invasion of Missouri)	Independence, Mo.				2nd Colorado, 5th, 7th, 11th, 15th and 16th Kan. Cav. and Kan. Militia, 1st, 2nd, 4th, 6th, 7th, 8th and 9th Mo. Militia Cav., 13th Mo., 3rd Iowa, and 17th Ill. Cavalry	Gen. Pleasanton, F.; Gen. Fagan, C.		40			100				9		Federal
	Skirmish	White River, Ark.				53rd U. S. Colored Troops.												
	Gunboat Attacks on Federal Batteries	James River, Va.				Federal Batteries	Com. Mitchell, C.				11							
Oct. 23	Engagement	Hurricane Creek, Miss.				1st Iowa and 9th Kansas Cavalry.												
	Skirmish	Princeton, Ark.				3rd Missouri Cavalry.												
	Engagements (Price's Invasion of Missouri)	Westport, Big Blue, Mo.	7 hours			Mo. Militia Cav., Cav. of Gen. A. J. Smith's Command, and Cav. and Kan. Militia, of the Army of the Border	Gen. Curtis, F.; Gen. Pleasanton, F.; Gen. Shelby, C.					1000					150	1 Con. 3 Fed.
Oct. 24	Engagement	Cold Water Grove, Osage, Mo.				Kansas Cavalry of the Army of the Border.												
Oct. 25	Reconnoissance of Federal Troops under Major Gilson, in the	Luray Valley Va.																—
	Reconnoissance of Federal Troops under Colonel Caphart in the	Luray Valley Va.																
Oct. 26	Affair near	Milton, Blackwater, Fla.				10th Iowa Volunteers and 2nd Maine Cavalry.												
	(26th-29th). Attack by Confederate Forces on	Decatur, Ala.				18th Mich., 102nd Ohio, 68th Ind. Vols., and 14th U. S. Colored Troops	Gen. Hood, C.											Federal
	Battle	Mine Creek, Mo.				Federal Forces under General Pleasonton	Gen. Pleasanton, F.; Gen. Price, C.	K.&W. 1000	900			1000	2000				1500	Federal
	Battle (Pursuit of Price's Forces)	Mine Creek, Marias des Cygnes and Little Osage River, Kansas	10 hours			Cavalry of Gen. Pleasanton's and Curtis' Army	Gen. Pleasanton, F.; Gen. Price, C.					1600						—
Oct. 27	Engagement	Hatcher's Run, South Side R. R., Va. (or Boydtown Road, Vaughn Road and Burgess Farm)				2nd Cav. Div., 2nd and 3rd Div. 2nd Corps, 5th and 9th Corps, Army of the Potomac	Gen. Grant, F.; Gen. Lee, C.	156	1000	1047				699				
	(27th-28th). Battle	Fair Oaks, Va., (near Richmond)				10th and 18th Corps and Cav., Army of the James		120	451	783				400				
Oct. 28	(28th-30th). Engagement (Pursuit of Price's Forces)	Newtonia, Mo.				Cavalry of the Army of the Border	Gens. Blunt and Sanborn, F.; Gen. Price, C.		K.W. & M. 250									Federal
	Action	Fort Heiman, Tenn.				Federal Gunboats.												
	Destruction of Confederate Ram *Albemarle*			18			Lieut. Cushing, F.											
	Attack on Confederate Rear-guard	Fayetteville, Ark.				1st Arkansas Cavalry												Federal
Oct. 29	Engagement	Morristown, Tenn.				Federal Cavalry	Gen. Gillem, F.; — Vaughn, C.	K.W. & M. 31	K.W. & P. 670			200				5		Federal
	Skirmish	Beverly, W. Va.				8th Ohio Cavalry.												
	(26th-29th). Attack by Confederate Forces on	Decatur, Ala.				Federal Garrison	Gen. Hood, C.											Federal
Oct. 30	Engagement	Muscle Shoals, Raccoon Ford, Ala.				1st Brig., 1st Cav. Div., Army of the Cumberland.												
	Skirmish	Brownsville, Ala.				7th Iowa, and 11th Mo. Cavalry.												
	Engagement	Ladiga, Terrapin Creek, Ala.				Garrard's Cav. Div., Army of the Cumberland.												
Oct. 31	Action	Plymouth, N. C.				Federal Steamers *Commodore Hull*, *Shamrock*, *Otsego*, *Wyalusing* and *Tacony*.												
Nov. 1	Engagement	Black River, La.				6th U. S. Colored Heavy Cavalry.												
	(1st-4th). Skirmishes	Union Station, Tenn.				10th Missouri Cavalry.												
Nov. 2	Scout of Federal Cavalry under Major Stevens, through	Charles City and Henrico Counties, Va.																Federal
Nov. 3	Skirmish	Vera Cruz, Ark.		3 Co.		46th Missouri Volunteers.												
Nov. 4	(4th-5th). Engagement	Johnsonville, Tenn.				11th Tenn. Cav., 43rd Wis. Vols., and 13th U. S. Colored Troops.												
Nov. 5	(5th-6th). Engagement	Big Pigeon River, Tenn.				3rd North Carolina Mounted Infantry.												
	Engagement	Fort Sedgwick, Va.				2nd Corps, Army of the Potomac	Gen. Mott, F.; Gen. Gibson, F.	K.&W. 70	K.&W. 120									Federal
Nov. 7	Corps Organization, 19th Army Corps, abolished (Re-organized 18th February, 1865.)																	
	Brevet Maj.-Gen. Emory, U. S. A., appointed to command of 19th Army Corps, Headquarters with Sheridan's Army in the Field.																	
	19th Corps, Military Division of West Mississippi abolished.																	
Nov. 8	Engagement. (11th?)	Atlanta, Ga.				2nd Div., 20th Corps, Army of the Cumberland		K.&W. 20				600						Federal
Nov. 9	Engagement	Shoal Creek, Ala.				5th Div. Cav., Army of the Cumberland.												
Nov. 12	Engagement	Newtown, Nineveh, and Cedar Springs, Va.				1st and 3rd Div. Cav., Army of the Potomac, and 2nd Cav. Division, Army of W. Va.	— Powell, F.; Gen. Lomax, C.	K.&W. 30				150				2		Federal
Nov. 13	Engagement	Bull's Gap, Morristown, Tenn.				8th, 9th and 13th Tenn. Cavalry and Artillery	Gen. Gillem, F.; Gen. Breckenridge, C.	K.W. & M. 220								6		Conf'd.
Nov. 14	(14th-28th).	Cow Creek, Ark.				54th U. S. Colored Troops (2nd Ark.) and 3rd Kan. Indian Home Guards.												
	Maj.-Gen. McClellan, U. S. A., resigns, (to take effect from 8th Nov.)																	
Nov. 15	Expedition to	Clinton and Liberty Creek, La.				Federal Troops	Gen. A. L. Lee, F.											
Nov. 16	Engagement	Lovejoy Station, Jonesboro, Ga.				1st Brig., 3rd Div. Cav., Army of the Cumberland.												
	Engagement	Bear Creek Station, Ga.				2nd Brig., 3rd Div. Cav., Army of the Cumberland	Gen. Howard, F.; Gen. Wheeler, C.											Federal

CHRONOLOGICAL LIST OF EVENTS (1860-1865).—Continued.

DATE.	EVENT.	LOCATION.	DURATION.	FORCE. F.	FORCE. C.	COMPOSITION OF FORCE.	COMMANDERS.	KILLED. F.	KILLED. C.	WOUNDED. F.	WOUNDED. C.	PRISONERS TAKEN BY F.	PRISONERS TAKEN BY C.	MISSING. F.	MISSING. C.	Guns taken.	Stands of arms.	ADVANTAGE.
1864																		
Nov. 17	Capture of Federal Troops	Chester Station, Bermuda Hundred, Va.		Pkts.		209th Pennsylvania Volunteers	Gen. Butler, F.; Gen. Hunton and Stewart, C.	K&W 19	K&W 16			118						Conf'd.
	Skirmishes	Aberdeen and Butler Creek, Ala.				3rd Iowa Cavalry.												
Nov. 18	Skirmish	Myerstown, Va.				Detachment 91st Ohio Volunteers.												
Nov. 19	Engagement	Bayou la Fourche, La., (Ash Bayou.)				11th Wis. Vols., and 93rd U. S. Colored Troops.												
	Destruction by Federal Troops under General Howard, of	Milledgeville, Ga.																
Nov. 20	Engagement	Macon, Ga.		800		10th Ohio and 9th Penn. Cav., 92nd Ill. Mounted Inf., and 10th Wis. Batt'y, Army of Cumberland.	Gen. Kilpatrick, F.											—
Nov. 21	Engagement	Liberty and Jackson, La.				4th Wis. Cav., and 1st Wisconsin Battery.												
	Engagement and Occupation by Federal Forces of	Gordon, Ga.				Federal Cavalry under General Howard.	Gen. Howard, F.; Gen. Wheeler, C.											Federal
Nov. 22	Skirmish	Rolling Fork, Miss.				3rd U. S. Colored Cavalry (1st Miss.)												
	Engagement	Griswoldville, Ga.			5000	Walcott's Brig., 1st Div., 15th Corps and 1st Brig. 3rd Cav. Division, Army of the Tennessee	Gen. Walcott, F.; Gen. Phillips, C.		300		K&P 2200							Federal.
	Skirmishes	Clinton, Ga.				Advance of the 15th Corps.												
	Engagement	Rood's Hill, Va.				1st and 3rd Div., Cav. Corps, Army of Potomac, and 2nd Cav. Division, Army of W. Va.	Gen. Custer, F.; Gen. Rosser, C.	K&W 70										Conf'd.
	Occupation by Confederate Forces of	Lawrenceburg, Tenn.				5th Cav. Div., Military Division of the Mississippi.	Gen. Hood, C.											Conf'd.
	Attack by Federal Cavalry on General Price's Wagon Train		4 hours			3rd Arkansas Cavalry.	Capt. White, F.	7		0								Federal.
	Reconnoissance of Federal Cavalry to	New Market, Va.																
Nov. 23	Occupation by Confederate Forces of	Pulaski, Tenn.				Federal Cavalry	Gen. Hatch, F.; Gen. Hood, C.											Conf'd.
Nov. 24	Skirmish	Bent's Old Fork, Texas.				1st California Cavalry.												
	Engagements	Campbellville and Lynnville, Tenn.				5th Cav. Division, Military Division of the Missouri.												
	(24th–28th.) Engagements, and occupation by Confederate Forces of	Columbia, Duck Run, Tenn.				Capron's Brig., 1st Cav. Div., and 4th and 23rd Corps, General Thomas' Army	Gen. Thomas, F.; Gen. Hood, C.	K.W. & M. 800	K.W. & M. 600									Conf'd.
	(24th–25th). Engagements	Ball's Ferry, Oconee River, Ga.				1st Ala. Cav., Advance of the Army of the Tenn.												
Nov. 25	Skirmish	Pawnee Forks, Kansas.		1 Co.		1st Colorado Cavalry.												
	Skirmish	St. Vrain's Old Fort, N. Mex.		1 Co.		1st New Mexico Cavalry.												
Nov. 26	Skirmish	Madison Station, Ala.				101st U. S. Colored Troops.												
	Engagement, and occupation of	Sandersville, Ga. (Buffalo Creek)			Cav.	3rd Brigade, 1st Division, 20th Corps	Gen. Slocum, F.											Federal.
	Skirmish	Sylvan Grove, Ga.				8th Ind., and 2nd Kentucky Cavalry.												
	Maj.-Gen. Humphreys, U. S. A., assumes command of the 2d Army Corps.																	
Nov. 27	Engagement, and destruction of	Big Black River Bridge, Mississippi Central R.R.				Federal Cavalry and Artillery	Gen. Dana, F.; Col. Osband, F.											Federal.
	(27th–29th). Engagements	Waynesboro, Thomas Station and Buck Head Creek, Ga. (Reynold's Plantation, Jones' Plantation and Brown's Cross Roads).				3rd Cav. Div., Army Military Div. of the Mississippi	Gen. Slocum, F.; Gen. Wheeler, C.											
Nov. 28	Surprise and Capture of	Fort Kelly, New Creek, W. Va.			Cav.	Federal Garrison	Gen. Rosser, C.		5					700		4		Conf'd.
	First Army Corps re-organized under command of Maj.-Gen. Hancock.																	
	Attack on and Capture by Confederate Cavalry of	Shelbyville, Tenn.				Federal Troops												Conf'd.
	Bombardment by Confederate Batteries of	Fort Brady and Dutch Gap, Va.																
Nov. 29	Attack on Federal Troops	Spring Hill, Tenn. (Mount Carmel.)				4th Corps and Cavalry	Gen. Wilson, F.; Gen. Wood, F.; Gen. Rhoddy, C.											
	Skirmish	Big Sandy, Colorado Territory				1st and 3rd Colorado Cavalry												
	Expedition of Federal Forces, under General Foster, to destroy portion of Charleston and Savannah Railroad			8300		Federal Troops	Gen. Foster, F.											Federal.
Nov. 30	Battle, and Occupation by Confederate Forces of	Franklin, Tenn.	1 hour	15,000		4th Corps, Army of the Cumberland, and 23rd Corps Army of the Ohio	Gen. Scofield, F.; Gen. Hood, C.	189	1750	1033	3800	702	1104					Federal.
	Battle	Honey Hill, Broad River, S. C. (Grahamsville)	6 hours	5000	1500	25th Ohio, 56th and 155th N. Y. Volunteers and 26th, 32nd, 35th and 102nd U. S. Colored Troops, 54th and 55th Mass. Colored Troops, Army of the South.	Gen. Foster, F.; Gen. G. W. Smith, C.	66		645								—
	(30th–Dec. 4th). Skirmishes	Bermuda Hundred, Va.				Pickets of the 20th Colored Troops.												
Dec. 1	Skirmishes	Stoney Creek Station and Duvall's Mills, Weldon R. R., Va.	½ hour		Cav.	2nd Cav. Div., Army of the Potomac	Gen. Gregg, F.	K&W 40				175						Federal.
	Engagement	Yazoo City, Miss.				Detachment 2nd Wisconsin Cavalry.												
	(1st–31st). Skirmishes	Trenches before Petersburg, Va.				Army of the Potomac.												
	(1st–14th). Skirmishes	In Front of Nashville, Tenn.				4th Corps, Army of the Cumberland, and 23rd Corps Army of the Ohio, 1st and 3rd Div., 16th Corps, Army of the Tennessee, and Cavalry	Gen. Thomas, F.; Gen. Hood, C.											—
	Engagement	Miller Grove, Ga.				5th Ky., and 8th Ind. Cav., of Sherman's Army.												
Dec. 2	Skirmish	Rocky Creek Church, Ga.				3rd Ky., and 8th O. Cav., Advance of Sherman's Army.												
	Skirmish	Yazoo City Road, Miss.				2nd N. Y. Cavalry							28					Conf'd.
	(2nd–3rd). Attack on Federal Troops	Block House No. 2, Mill Creek, Chattanooga, Tenn.	15 hours	832	Cav.	Detachment 115th Ohio Vols., 44th and 2 Companies of 14th U. S. Colored Troops	Col. Johnson, F.	K&W 115										Conf'd.
	Maj. Gen. Dodge, U. S. V., appointed to command of Department of Missouri, vice Maj.-Gen. Rosecrans, relieved.																	
Dec. 3	Engagement	Thomas' Station, Ga.				92nd Illinois Mounted Infantry.												
	Tenth Army Corps discontinued (re-organized March 27th, 1865.)																	
	Eighteenth Army Corps discontinued.																	

CHRONOLOGICAL LIST OF EVENTS (1860-1865).—Continued.

Date.	Event.	Location.	Duration.	Force. F.	Force. C.	Composition of Force.	Commanders.	Killed. F.	Killed. C.	Wounded. F.	Wounded. C.	Prisoners Taken by F.	Prisoners Taken by C.	Missing. F.	Missing. C.	Guns Capt.	[illegible]	Advantage.
1864. Dec. 5	Twenty-fourth Army Corps formed, consisting of White Infantry of Tenth and Eighteenth Corps, Army of the James, under Maj.-Gen. Orr.																	
	Twenty-fifth Army Corps formed, consisting of Colored Troops of the Department of Virginia and North Carolina, under Maj.-Gen Weitzel.																	
Dec 4	Attack on Pickets	Jerusalem Road, Va.		Picket		3rd Pennsylvania Cavalry												Conf'd.
	Affair on	Coosa River, S. C.		800		25th Ohio Volunteers	Gen. Foster, F.									3		Federal.
	Engagement	Block House, No. 7, Overall's Creek, Tenn				Federal Troops	Gen. Milroy, F.; Gen. Bate, C.	K.&W. 44										—
	Engagement	Waynesboro and Brier Creek, Ga.				3rd Cav. Div., Army Military Department of the Miss.	Gen. Kilpatrick, F.; Gen. Wheeler, C.											Federal.
	Skirmish	Statesboro, Ga.				Foragers of the 15th Corps.												
Dec. 5	(5th-8th). Skirmishes	Murfreesboro, (or Cedars) Tenn.				Federal Troops	Gen. Rousseau, F.; —Forrest, C.											
	Attack on Federal Garrison	Block Houses Nos. 6 and 7, near Murfreesboro				Federal Troops										6		Federal.
Dec. 6	(6th-9th). Engagement	Deveaux Neck, S.C. (Tillafinny River, Mason's Ridge and Gregory's Farm)				26th, 33rd, 34th and the 102nd U. S. Colored Troops, 54th and 55th Mass. Colored Troops, 56th and 155th N. Y., and 25th and 107th Ohio Vols., and 3rd R. I. Artillery and Naval Brigade	Gen. Potter, F.	89	400	800				200				Federal.
	Engagement	White Post, Va.		60	80	21st N. Y. Cavalry	—Baylor, C.						87					Conf'd.
Dec. 7	Occupation by Federal Forces of	Gregory's Plantation, and Mackay's Point, Ga.																
	Engagement. (Attack on Confederate Position)	Murfreesboro, Tenn. (Wilkinson Pike)				Federal Troops	Gen. Milroy, F.	K.&W. 203				200				2		—
	Engagement	Ebenezer Creek, Cypress Swamp, Ga.				9th Mich., and 9th Ohio Cavalry, Rear Guard of Left Wing of Sherman's Army												
	(7th-9th). Skirmishes	Ogeechee River, Ga. (Jenk's Bridge, Eden Station and Poole's Station)				15th and 17th Corps, Right Wing of the Army of the Military Division of the Mississippi	Gen. Potter, F.; Cap. Thompson, C.											Federal.
	(7th-11th). Expeditions	Weldon Railroad				2nd Division Cavalry Corps, 5th Corps and 3rd Div. 2nd Corps, Army of the Potomac	Gen. Warren, F.	K.W.&M. 100										Federal.
Dec. 8	(8th-9th). Reconnoissance of Federal Troops to	Hatcher's Run, Va.				3rd and 13th Penn., and 6th Ohio Cav., and 1st Div. 2nd Corps	Col. Kirwin, F.											
	(8th-28th). Raid of Federal Troops to	Gordonsville, Va.				1st and 3rd Div. Cav., Army of the Potomac.												
	Skirmishes	Bellefield and Hicksford, Va.			Vid.	2nd Division Cavalry Corps, Army of the Potomac	Gen. Warren, F.; Gen. Hampton, C.	K.&W. 25										1 Fed. 2 Con.
Dec. 9	(9th-Jan. 14th, 1865). Expedition into Western North Carolina					3rd N. C. Volunteers.												
	Massacre of Indians	Fort Lyons, Indian Ter. (Sand Creek.)				1st Colorado Cavalry	Col. Chivington, F.											
	Engagement	Cutler's Plantation, Monteith Swamp, Ga.	2 hours			14th Corps, of the Left Wing of the Army Military Division of the Mississippi	Gen. Hatch, F.; Gen. Gartrell, C.											Conf'd.
	(9th-12th). Expedition to	Hamilton, N. C.				27th Mass., and 9th N. J. Volunteers, N. C. Cavalry and 3rd N. Y. Artillery	Col. Frankle, F.											
Dec. 10	Skirmish	Foster's Bridge and Spring Green Church, N. C.				27th Mass., and 9th N. J. Volunteers, N.C. Cavalry and 3rd N. Y. Artillery	Col. Frankle, F.					85						Federal.
	(10th-21st). Siege, and Occupation (21st)	Savannah, Ga.			15,000	14th and 20th Corps, Left Wing, 15th and 17th Corps Right Wing, Army Military Div. of the Miss.	Gen. Sherman, F.; Gen. Hardee, C.					800				150		Federal.
	Maj.-Gen. Dana, U. S. V., in command of the Department of the Mississippi.																	
	Maj.-Gen. Reynolds, U. S. A., in command of Seventh Army Corps and Department of Arkansas, vice Maj.-Gen. Steele, relieved.																	
	Assault on Federal Position	Hatcher's Run, Va				1st Division, 2nd Corps, and 1st and 3rd Div., 9th Corps.	Gen. Miles F.	K.&W. 25										Federal.
Dec. 12	Capture by Confederate Forces under General Lyon, of	Hopkinsville, Ky.																
	Skirmish	Butler's Bridge, N. C				27th Mass., and 9th N. J. Volunteers, N. C. Cavalry and 3rd N. Y. Artillery.	Col. Frankle, F.											
	Skirmish	Elkton, Ky.			R'Gd.	1st Cavalry Division	B.-Gen. McCook, F.; Gen. Lyons, C.											—
	(12th-21st). Stoneman's Raid from Bean's Station, Tenn., to	Saltville, Va.				Cavalry of the Army of the Ohio.	Gen. Stoneman, F.; Genls. Burbridge and Gillem, F.	2000				800						—
Dec. 13	Stoneman's Raid	Kingsport, Tenn.			Cav.	8th, 9th and 13th Tennessee Cavalry	Gen. Burbridge, F.; —Basil Duke, C.	K.W.&P. 150	K.&W. 34			100						Federal.
	Federal Assault on	Fort McAllister, Ga.	½ hour			2nd Division, 15th Corps, Sherman's Army	Gen. Hazen, F.	23	14	83	21	211						Federal.
Dec. 14	Engagement (Stoneman's Raid)	Bristol, Tenn. (Mount Airy.)				Federal Cavalry	Gen. Burbridge, F.; Gen. Gillem, F.					300				7		Federal.
	Skirmish	Memphis, Tenn.				4th Iowa Cavalry.												
Dec. 15	(15th-21st). Engagements	Savannah, Ga.				Federal Forces	Gen. Sherman, F.; Gen. Hardee, C.	400	K.&W. 600			1000				150		Federal.
	(Stoneman's Raid) Capture by Federal Troops of	Abingdon, Va.				Federal Cavalry	Gen. Burbridge, F.					20				1		Federal.
	Engagement	Murfreesboro, Tenn.				Federal Troops	Gen. Rousseau, F.; —Forrest, C.		K.W.&M. 1500									Federal
	Stoneman's Raid	Glade Springs, Va.				12th Kentucky Cavalry	Gen. Stoneman, F.; —Vaughn, C.											Federal.

CHRONOLOGICAL LIST OF EVENTS (1860-1865).—Continued.

DATE.	EVENT.	LOCATION.	DURATION.	FORCE. F.	FORCE. C.	COMPOSITION OF FORCE.	COMMANDERS.	KILLED. F	KILLED. C	WOUNDED. F	WOUNDED. C	PRISONERS TAKEN BY F.	PRISONERS TAKEN BY C.	MISSING. F	MISSING. C	Guns taken.	Stands of Arms taken.	ADVANTAGE.
1864																		
Dec. 15	(15th–16th). Battle	Nashville, Overton's Hills, Tenn. (Princeton)	Actual 9 hours.	50,000	40,000	4th Corps, Army of the Cumberland, 23rd Corps Army of the Ohio, 1st and 3rd Div., 16th Corps, Army of the Tennessee. Detachment of Colored Troops, Convalescents, Recruits, &c., and Cavalry Corps	Gen. Thomas, F. / Gen. Hood, C.	400	k. w. & m. 15,000	1740		5000				47	3000	Federal.
Dec. 16	Engagement	Hopkinsville, Ky.				2nd and 3rd Brigades, McCook's 1st Cavalry Division.												
	Stoneman's Raid	Marion and Wytheville, Va.				8th, 9th and 13th Tennessee Cavalry	Gen. Gillem, F.		20		30	809				4		Federal.
Dec. 17	Skirmish	Ashbyville, Ky				Federal Troops	Gen. McCook, F. / Gen. Lyon, C.									1		Federal.
	Attack on Scouts by Confederate Cavalry	Millwood, Va.		100		Detachment 14th Pennsylvania Cav., (Scouting Party.)	Capt. Miles, F. / Col. Mosby, C.	12		23				40				Conf'd.
	Engagement	Hollow Tree Gap, Tenn.				5th and 7th Div., Cavalry, General Thomas' Army.												
	Engagement	Franklin, Tenn.				6th Division Cavalry, Thomas' Army	Gen. Hatch, F. / Gen. Stevenson, C.					1750				8		Federal.
	Expedition of Federal Troops to	Blue Ridge, Va.				12th and 10th N. Y., and 6th Illinois Cavalry.												
	Skirmish	Mitchell's Creek, Fla.				82nd U. S. Colored Troops.												
	(17th–19th)	Pine Barren Creek, Ala.				82nd and 97th U. S. Colored Troops.												
Dec. 18	Stoneman's Raid	Marion, Va.				Cavalry of the Army of the Ohio.	Gen. Gillem, F. / Gen. Stoneman, F.					200						Federal.
	Engagement	Franklin Creek, Miss.				Troops of the 3rd Corps	Gen. Granger, F.											Federal.
	Expedition from	Winchester, Va				1st and 2nd Cavalry Divisions	Gens. Merritt and Powell, F.	k.&w. 50										
Dec. 19	Skirmish	Rutherford Creek, Tenn.				Cavalry of General Thomas' Army.												
	Call for 300,000 Federal Troops by President Lincoln.																	
Dec. 20	Engagement and Capture of	Saltville, Va			700	Gillem's and Burbridge's Cavalry	Gen. Burbridge, F. / Gen. Stoneman, F.									8		Federal.
	Skirmish	Madison Court House, Va.			Pkts.	Mich. Cav. Brig., 1st Cav. Div., Army of the Potomac.	Gen. Stagg, F.		k.&w. 13									Federal.
	(20th–21st)	Poplar Point, Roanoke River, N. C.	3 hours.			Federal Gunboats	Col. Frankle, F. / Gen. Leventhorpe, C.											Conf'd.
Dec. 21	Occupation by Federal Forces of	Savannah, Ga.			10,000	Federal Troops	Gen. Sherman, F.									150		Federal.
	Engagement	Stannardsville, Va.				Federal Brigade of Cavalry	Gen. Tibbett, F. / ——Lomax, C.											Federal.
	Attack on Federal Camp and Engagement	Lacey's Springs, Va.				Federal Cavalry	Gen. Custer, F. / Gen. Rosser, C.	3		22			40					Conf'd.
Dec. 23	Engagement	Jack's Shop near Gordonsville, Va.				1st Cavalry Division, Army of the Potomac, and 2nd Cavalry Divisions, Army of West Virginia.												
	Skirmish	Lynnville, Tenn.				Cavalry of General Thomas' Army.												
	Skirmish	Buford's Station, Tenn.				Cavalry of General Thomas' Army.												
Dec. 24	Skirmish	Elizabethtown, Ky.				1st Wisconsin Cavalry.												
	Stoneman's Raid	Moccasin Gap, Va				8th Tennessee Cavalry.												
	Skirmish	Murfreesboro, Tenn				12th U. S. Colored Troops.												
Dec. 25	Capture by Federal Sailors from the *Santiago* of	Pond Hill Battery, N. C										65						Federal.
	(24d–25th). Engagement	Fort Fisher, N. C.	12 hours.	6500	1087	North Atlantic Squadron and Troops of the 10th Corps, Army of the James	Gen. Butler, F. / R.-Adm. Porter, F. / Gen. Whiting, C.	107	k.&w. 1061			280						Conf'd.
	Engagements	Pulaski, Lamb's Ferry, Anthony's Hill and Sugar Creek, Tenn.				Cavalry of General Thomas' Army												
	Skirmish	Verona, Miss.				7th Indiana Cavalry.												
Dec. 27	(27th–28th). Engagement	Decatur, Ala.				Major-General Steadman's Provisional Division	Gen. Steadman, F.											
Dec. 28	Engagement	Egypt Station, Miss.				7th Ind., 4th and 11th Ill., 4th and 10th Mo., 2nd Wis., 2nd N. J., 1st Miss., and 3rd U. S. Colored Cavalry.												
Dec. 29	Engagement	Pond Spring, Ala.				15th Penn., and Detachment 2nd Tenn., and 10th, 12th and 13th Indiana Cavalry.												
Dec. 31	Attack on Federal Troops	Forts Wadsworth and Howard, Va		Pkts.	800	Federal Troops		3		8			85					Conf'd.
1865																		
Jan. 1	Wreck of the Steam Sloop-of-war *San Jacinto* on the Bahama Banks.																	
Jan. 2	Bombardment by Confederates, at	Dutch Gap Canal, Ga.																
	Skirmish	Franklin, Miss.				4th and 11th Ill., and 3rd U. S. Colored Cavalry.												
	Capture and Destruction of Hood's Supply and Pontoon Train	Nauvoo, Ala.				15th Penn. and Detachment 2nd Tenn., and 10th, 12th and 13th Indiana Cavalry												
	Attack on Federal Pickets at	Hardeesville, Va.																
Jan. 3	Attack on Confederate Troops	Thorn Hill, Ala.				15th Penn. and Detachment 10th, 12th and 13th Ind. and 2nd Tennessee Cavalry	Col. Palmer, F. / Gen. Russell, C.											Federal.
	Engagement	Howlett Batteries, Va.			Bat.	Federal Artillery.												
Jan. 4	Shelling of Richmond and Petersburg Railroad, Va., by Federal Artillery.																	
Jan. 5	Skirmish	Smithfield, Ky.				6th U. S. Colored Troops.												
Jan. 7	Indian Fight	Julesburg, Indian Territory		1 Co.		7th Iowa Cavalry.												
Jan. 8	Skirmish	Ivy Ford, Ark.				29th U. S. Colored Troops.												
	Skirmish	Scottsboro, Ala.		54		101st U. S. Colored Troops.												
	Maj. Gen. Butler relinquishes command of the Department of Virginia and North Carolina to Maj. Gen. Ord.																	
Jan. 10	Scout of Federal Troops (1st N. Y. & 1st Va. Cavalry) along	Winchester Pike to Berry's Ferry, Va.																
	(7th–?). Engagement	Greensburgh, Ky.			Cav. 900	General Lagrange's Brigade	Gen. Lagrange, F. / Gen. Lyon, C.											Federal.
	Attack on Federal Garrison	Scottsboro, Ala.				Federal Troops	Gen. Lyon, C.											Federal.
Jan. 11	Capture by Confederate Troops of	Beverly, W. Va.				34th Ohio Volunteers and 8th Ohio Cavalry	Gen. Rosser, C.	5		30				583				Conf'd.

CHRONOLOGICAL LIST OF EVENTS (1860-1865).—Continued.

DATE.	EVENT.	LOCATION.	DURATION.	FORCE. F.	FORCE. C.	COMPOSITION OF FORCE.	COMMANDERS.	KILLED. F.	KILLED. C.	WOUNDED. F.	WOUNDED. C.	PRISONERS TAKEN BY F.	PRISONERS TAKEN BY C.	MISSING. F.	MISSING. C.	GUNS TAKEN.	STANDS OF ARMS TAKEN.	ADVANTAGE.
1865																		
Jan. 13	(13th–15th). Bombardment and Assault	Fort Fisher, N. C.	6½ hours	3500	2300	2nd Div. and 2nd Brig. 1st Div. 24th Corps, and 3rd Div. 25th Corps, Army of the James, Sailors and Marines of the Atlantic Blockading Squadron	Gen. Terry, F.; Adm. Porter, F.; Gen. Hope, C.	184	K.W. & M. 2483	749				22				Federal.
Jan. 14	Maj.-Gen. Gibbon assigned to command of 24th Corps, Army of the James.																	
	Capture of Confederate Cavalry	Red Hill, Ala.			Cav. 600	15th Pennsylvania Cavalry	Col. Palmer, F.; Gen. Lyon, C.					100				1		Federal.
	(14th–16th). Engagement	Pocotaligo, S. C.				17th Corps, Army of the Tennessee	Gen. Blair, F.; Gen. Hatch, F.; Gen. McLaw, C.	K.W. 50										Federal.
	Engagement	Dardanelle, Ark.				2nd Kansas Cavalry and Iowa Cavalry.												
Jan. 16	Reconnoissance from	Eastport towards Corinth, Miss.				Div. of 16th Corps and 1st Brigade, 1st Division Cavalry.	Gen. Croxton, F.					35						Federal.
	Explosion of Magazine	Fort Fisher, N. C.				Troops of the Army of the James	Gen. Terry, F.	110	K.W. 440	536		2500				72		Federal
	Destruction by Confederate Forces of	Forts Caswell and Campbell, Va.																
	Abandonment, by Confederate Forces, of Works at	Smithville and Reeve's Point, Va.																
Jan. 17	Department of the Ohio merged into the Department of the Cumberland.																	
	Destruction of Federal Monitor *Patapsco* off Charleston by torpedo																	
Jan. 18	Skirmish	Columbia, Ky.	½ hour	1 Co.		Tennessee Cavalry			8									Federal.
	(18th–19th). Reconnoissance of Federal Troops, in force, under Gen. Paine, towards	Wilmington, Va.																
Jan. 19	Engagement	Half Moon Battery, Sugar Loaf Hill, N. C.				Portion of the 24th and 25th Corps, Army of the James.												
	Attack on Federal Dispatch Boat at	Fort St. Philip, Va.																
Jan. 24	Engagement with Confederate Flotilla	Fort Brady, Va. (Fort Burnham or Bogg's Mills)				U. S. Colored Troops and Heavy Art., Army of the James	Lieu. Dunnington, C. S. N.		6		14							—
Jan. 25	Skirmishes	Combahee River, S. C.				15th and 17th Corps, Army of the Tennessee	Gen. Sherman, F.											Federal.
	Skirmish	Powhattan, Va.				1st U. S. Colored Cavalry.												
	Skirmish	Simpsonville, Ky.				6th U. S. Colored Cavalry.												
Jan. 27	Skirmish	Chunky River, Va.				(Troops not specified.)												
Jan. 29	(29th–Feb. 11th). Expedition into	Western N. C.				3rd North Carolina Regiment.												
Jan. 30	Engagement	White's Point, S. C.				Federal Troops under General Howard.	Gen. Howard, F.											—
Jan. 31	Gen. R. E. Lee, C. S. A., appointed Commander-in-Chief of Confederate Forces by Jefferson Davis.																	
Feb. 3	(3d–9th). Engagement	Rivers' Bridge, Salkahatchie, S. C. (including Hickory Hill, Owen Cross Roads, Lawtonville, Duck Creek, and Whippy Swamp)				17th and 15th Corps, Army of the Tennessee	Gen. Sherman, F.; Gens. Mower and Smith, F.	K.&W. 88										Federal.
Feb. 4	Engagement	Rivers' Bridge, S. C.			Cav.	Federal Troops	Gen. Wheeler, C.											Federal.
	Failure of Peace Negotiations with Confederate Commissioners.																	
Feb. 5	(5th–7th). Engagement	Dabney's Mills, Hatcher's Run, Va. (Rowanty Creek and Vaughn Road)				2nd Cav. Div., 2nd and 5th Corps and 1st Div. 6th Corps, Army of the Potomac	Gens. Grant and Meade, F.; Gen. Lee, C.	147	K.W. & M. 12[illegible]	1062				186				Federal.
	Skirmish	Dunn's Lake, Volusia Co., Fla.				Detachment 17th Connecticut Volunteers.												
	Destruction by Federal Forces of	Barnwell, S. C.																
Feb. 7	Attack on Confederate Pickets	Blackville, S. C.		Cav.	Pkts.	Federal Cavalry	Gen. Wheeler, C.											Federal.
Feb. 8	Indian Fight	Mud Springs, Indian Territory				11th Ohio and 7th Iowa Cavalry.												
	(8th–9th). Skirmish	Williston, S. C.				Federal Cavalry	Gen. Kilpatrick, F.; Gen. Wheeler, C.											Federal.
Feb. 9	Engagement	Binnaker's Bridge, South Edisto River, S. C.				17th Corps Army of the Tennessee.												
	Indian Fight	Rush Creek, Indian Territory				11th Ohio and 7th Iowa Cavalry.												
	Maj.-Gen. Gillmore, U. S. A., assumes command of the Department of the South.																	
Feb. 10	Skirmish	James' Island, S. C.			Pkts.	Schimmelfennig's Division, Department of the South	Gen. Schimmelfennig, F.; Gen. Hartwell, F.	80				20						Federal.
	Maj.-Gen. Pope, U. S. A., in command of the Military Division of the Missouri (embracing Departments of Missouri, Arkansas and Kansas)																	
	Maj.-Gen. Curtis, U. S. A., in command of the Department of the Northwest, vice Maj.-Gen. Pope.																	
	Reconnoissance by Naval Forces under Lieut.-Commander Cushing, U. S. N., up Cape Fear River.																	
Feb. 11	Engagement	Blackville, S. C.				3rd Cav. Div., Army Military Div. of the Mississippi	Gen. Kilpatrick, F.											Federal.
	Engagement	Sugar Loaf Battery, Federal Point, N. C.				2nd Div. and 1st Brig. 1st Div., 24th Corps and 3rd Div. 25th Corps, Army of the James	Gen. Terry, F.	6[illegible]	100			65						Federal.
	Engagement	Aiken, S. C.				3rd Cavalry, Sherman's Army.	Gen. Kilpatrick, F.											Federal.
	Evacuation by Confederate Forces of	Branchville, S. C.																
Feb. 12	Occupation of	Orangeburg, North Edisto River, S. C.				17th Corps, Army of the Tennessee	Gen. Blair, F.											Federal.
Feb. 14	Skirmish	Gunter's Bridge, S. C.				3rd Cavalry Division, Sherman's Army.												
Feb. 15	Engagement	Congaree Creek, S. C.				15th Corps, Army of the Tennessee	Gen. Logan, F.											Federal.
	Expedition of Federal Troops under Colonel Maxwell from	Kernstown to Edinburgh, Va.																
Feb. 16	Skirmish	Cedar Keys, Fla.				2nd U. S. Colored Troops.												
	(16th–17th). Occupation by Federal Forces of	Columbia, S. C.				15th Corps, Army of the Tennessee	Gen. Sherman, F.; Gen. Logan, F.; Gen. Beauregard, C.	K.&W. 20								43		Federal.

CHRONOLOGICAL LIST OF EVENTS (1860-1865).—Continued.

DATE.	EVENT.	LOCATION.	DURATION.	FORCE. F.	FORCE. C.	COMPOSITION OF FORCE.	COMMANDERS.	KILLED. F.	KILLED. C.	WOUNDED. F.	WOUNDED. C.	PRISONERS TAKEN BY F.	PRISONERS TAKEN BY C.	MISSING. F.	MISSING. C.	GUNS TAKEN.	STANDS OF ARMS TAKEN.	ADVANTAGE.
1865:																		
Feb. 17	Attack on Federal Troops	Bermuda Hundred, Va.		Pkts.	Pkts.	Federal Troops												Federal.
Feb. 18	Thirteenth Army Corps re-organized, and Maj.-Gen. Gordon Granger placed in command.																	
	Sixteenth Army Corps re-organized, and Maj.-Gen. A. J. Smith, placed in command.																	
	Skirmish	Fort Jones, Ky.				12th U. S. Colored Heavy Artillery.												
	Skirmish	Ashby Gap, Va.				Detachment 14th Pennsylvania Cavalry.												
	Occupation by Federal Forces of	Charleston, S. C.				Troops of the Department of the South	Gen. Sherman, F.; Mayor Macbeth, C.									430		Federal.
	(17th–19th) Capture of	Fort Anderson, N. C.			3000	Federal Navy, Troops of the 24th Corps, Army of the James, and 23rd Corps, Army of the Ohio	Gen. Scofield, F.; R.-Adm. Porter, F.; Gen. Hope, C.	100				60						Federal.
	Surrender by Confederate Forces, of	Forts Sumter, and Moultrie and Castle Pinckney				Federal Forces												Federal.
Feb. 19	Evacuation, by Confederate Forces, of	Fort Anderson, N. C.																
	Charleston, S. C., placed under Martial Law by Lieut.-Colonel Bennett U. S. A., commanding.																	
Feb. 20	Skirmish	Fort Myers, Fla.				(Troops not specified.)												
	Skirmish and Engagements near	Town Creek, N. C.				3rd Div., 23rd Corps, Army of the Ohio	Gen. Terry, F.; Gens. Paine and Ames, F.; Gen. Cox, F.; Gen. Hope, C.	200				361				2		Federal.
Feb. 21	Raid of Confederate Cavalry into Cumberland, Va., and Capture of Federal Pickets and Maj.-Gens. Crook and Kelly	Cumberland, Va.																Conf'd.
Feb. 22	(20th–22d.) Capture by Federal Forces of	Wilmington, N. C.				2nd and 3rd Div., 23rd Corps, Army of the Ohio and a portion of the 24th Corps, Army of the James	Gen. Schofield, F.; R.Adm. Porter, F.; Gen. Bragg, C.	200				1072				80	500	Federal.
	Skirmish	Douglass Landing, Pine Bluffs, Ark.				13th Illinois Cavalry.												
Feb. 23	Capture of Federal Garrisons, by Confederate Cav. under Vaughan, at	Sweet Water and Athens, N. C.																
Feb. 26	Skirmish	Mount Clio, S. C.			Cav.	Detachment Mounted Troops	Capt. Duncan, F.; Gen. Butler, C.											Conf'd.
	Engagement	Leach Creek, S. C.				Advance of the 15th Corps.												
	Skirmish	Chattanooga, Tenn.				18th U. S. Colored Troops.												
Feb. 27	(27th–March 28th). Sheridan's Raid in	Virginia		8883	Cav.	1st and 3rd Div. Cav. Corps, Army of the Potomac	Gen. Sheridan, F.; Gen. Early, C.	60	6			1622				11		Federal
Feb. 29	(Sheridan's Raid). Engagement	Mount Crawford, Va.				3rd Brigade, 3rd Division Cavalry, Army of the Potomac	Gen. Capehart, F.; Gen. Rosser, C.											
Mar. 1	Skirmish, and Occupation by Federal Forces (Sheridan's Raid), of	Staunton, Va.				Federal Cavalry	Gen. Devin, F.											Federal.
Mar. 2	Engagement	Clinton, La.				4th Wisconsin Cavalry.												
	Battle (Sheridan's Raid)	Waynesboro, Va.				3rd Division Cavalry, Army of the Potomac	Gen. Sheridan, F.; Gen. Early, C.					1600				8		Federal.
	Skirmish, and Occupation of	Chesterfield, S. C.				Advance of the 20th Corps												
	(2–3d). Capture by Federal Forces of	Cheraw, S. C.				Advance of the 17th Corps	Gen. Sherman, F.									17		Federal.
Mar. 3	Skirmish	Florence, S. C.				Detachment of Mounted Infantry from Sherman's Army.												
Mar. 4	Inauguration of President Lincoln at Washington (Second Term).																	
Mar. 6	Skirmish	Olive Branch, La.				4th Wisconsin Cavalry.												
	Engagement	Natural Bridge, Fla.			2300	2nd and 99th U. S. Colored Troops and other Troops	Gen. Newton, F.; Gen. Jones, C.											Conf'd.
	Attack on Federal Troops	North Fork Shenandoah, Va.			Cav.	Portion of Sheridan's Cavalry	Col. Thompson, F.; Gen. Rosser, C.					27						Federal.
Mar. 7	Engagement	Rockingham, N. C.				Kilpatrick's Cavalry Division, Sherman's Army.												
Mar. 8	(8th–10th). Skirmishes and Engagement	Wilcox's Bridge, Wise's Fork, N. C.				1st and 2nd Div. of Dist. of Beaufort, and 1st Div., 23rd Corps, Army of the Ohio	Gen. Cox, F.; Col. Upham, F.	80	K. W. & M. 1500	421				600				Conf'd.
Mar. 10	Engagement	Monroe's Cross Roads, N. C. (Kingston)				Kilpatrick's Cavalry Division	Gen. Schofield, F.; Gen. Bragg, C.	K. W. & M. 1000	K. & W. 1200			400						Federal.
	Engagement, and Occupation by Federal Forces of	Fayetteville, N. C.				Kilpatrick's Cavalry Division	Gen. Kilpatrick, F.											Federal.
Mar. 11	Skirmish	Clear Lake, Ark.				3rd Wisconsin Cavalry.												
	Disfranchisement of Non-reporting Deserters ordered by President Lincoln.																	
	Engagement	Kingston, N. C.				Federal Troops	Gens. Cox and Couch, F.; Gens. Hill and Hoke, C.	K. & W. 610	K. W. & P. 2400				1500			3		Federal.
Mar. 14	Engagement	Silver Run, Fayetteville, N. C.				Advance of the 14th and 17th Corps.												
	Destruction of the Confederate Ram *Neuse* by Confederates.																	
Mar. 14	(13th–?). Occupation of	Kingston, N. C.				Federal Troops under General Schofield	Gen. Schofield, F.											Federal.
Mar. 15	Engagement	Taylor's Hole Creek, N. C.			R. Gd.	Kilpatrick's Cavalry	Gen. Kilpatrick, F.											Federal.
	Engagement and Destruction by Federal Forces of Bridge at	South Anna River, Va.				5th U. S. Cavalry	Gen. Devin, F.									8		Federal.
	Sheridan's Raid	Ashland, Va.				2nd Brigade, 3rd Division, Army of the Potomac.												
Mar. 16	Battle	Averasboro, N. C. (Smith's Farm)				20th Corps, and Kilpatrick's Cavalry Division, Sherman's Army	Gen. Sherman, F.; Gen. Hardee, C.	77	337	477		373						Federal.
Mar. 17	Wilson's Raid from Nashville to Selma, Montgomery and Mobile	Nashville, Tenn.		16,000		Federal Cavalry	Gen. Wilson, F.											
Mar. 18	Skirmish	Boyd's Station, Ala.				109th U. S. Colored Troops.												
Mar. 19	(19th–21st). Battle	Bentonville, N. C.			20,000	14th and 20th Corps, Left Wing, 15th and 17th Corps, Right Wing, and Cav. Div., Sherman's Army	Gen. Sherman, F.; Gen. Johnson, F.	191	167	1168		1625		287				Federal

CHRONOLOGICAL LIST OF EVENTS (1860-1865).—Continued.

DATE.	EVENT.	LOCATION.	DURATION.	FORCE. F.	FORCE. C.	COMPOSITION OF FORCE.	COMMANDERS.	KILLED. F.	KILLED. C.	WOUNDED. F.	WOUNDED. C.	PRISONERS TAKEN BY F.	PRISONERS TAKEN BY C.	MISSING. F.	MISSING. C.	GUNS TAKEN.	STANDS OF ARMS TAKEN.	ADVANTAGE.
1865 Mar. 20	(20th–April 6th). Stoneman's Raid	SOUTHWESTERN VA. and N. C.				Palmer's, Brown's and Miller's Brigades of Cavalry	Gen. Stoneman, F.		K.&W. 300			3000				14		Federal.
	Nineteenth Army Corps discontinued.																	
Mar. 21	Skirmish and Occupation of	GOLDSBORO, N. C.				Federal Troops under General Schofield	Gen. Schofield, F.											Federal.
	Skirmish	HAMILTON, VA.				12th Pennsylvania Cavalry.												
Mar. 22	(22d–April 24th). Wilson's Raid	CHICKASAW, ALA., to MACON, GA.				1st and 2nd Brig. 1st Div., 1st and 2nd Brig. 2nd Div., 1st and 2nd Brig. 4th Div. Cavalry Corps, Military Division of the Mississippi	Gen. Wilson, F.	99	K.&W. 1200	598		6820		28		288		Federal.
Mar. 23	Skirmish	SUMTERVILLE, S. C.				(Troops not specified.)												
Mar. 24	Engagement	REDROCK, ARIZONA TERRITORY				1st New Mexico Cavalry.												
	Skirmish	COX'S BRIDGE, N. C.				Terry's Provisional Corps.												
Mar. 25	Capture by Confederate and Re-capture by Federal Forces of	FORT STEADMAN, VA.				1st and 3rd Div. 9th Corps, Army of the Potomac	Gens. Meade and Parke, F.; Gen. Gordon, C.	68	K.W. & M. 2681	337				506				Federal.
	(25th–27th). Battle	PETERSBURG, VA.				2nd and 6th Corps, Army of the Potomac	Gens. Grant and Meade, F.; Gen. Lee, C.	103	K.W. & M. 834	864		2800		209				Federal.
	Engagement	PINE BARREN CREEK, ALA. (Bluff Spring.)			800	Cavalry advance of Gen Steele's Column	Gen. Steele, F.; Gen. Clanton, C.					203						Federal.
Mar. 26	(26th–April 9th). Siege and Occupation by Federal Forces of	MOBILE, ALA.		18,200	9000	Army of the Military Division of the West Mississippi	Maj.-Gen. Canby, F.; Gen. Maury, C.	K.&W. 2390	K.&W. [illegible]			4000				250		Federal.
	(26th–April 8th).	SPANISH FORT, ALA.		33,000	3000	13th and 16th Corps, Army of the Military Division of the West Mississippi, and Navy	Gens. Canby, A.J. Smith and Granger, F.; Gen. Gibson, C.	100	K.W. & M. 552	695						60		Federal.
Mar. 27	Maj.-Gen. Terry, U. S. A., in command of Tenth Army Corps, Re-organized of all Troops in North Carolina not belonging to 2nd, 9th and 23d Corps, and General Sherman's Army.																	
Mar. 29	Battle	QUAKER ROAD, GRAVELLY RUN, VA.				1st Division and 5th Corps, Army of the Potomac	Gen Sheridan, F.; Gen. Griffin, F.; Bushrod Johnson, C.	K.W. & M. 500	K.W. & M. 600									Federal.
	Engagement near	NEAR DINWIDDIE, VA.			80	21st Pennsylvania Cavalry												Federal.
Mar. 31	Engagements	BOYDTON and WHITE OAK ROADS, VA.				5th and 2nd Corps, Army of the Potomac	Gen. Sheridan, F.; Gen Lee, C.	177	K.W. & M. 1235	1134				556				Conf'd.
	Engagement	DINWIDDIE COURT HOUSE, VA.				1st, 2nd. and 3rd Div. Cav. Corps, Army of the Potomac.												
	Wilson's Raid	MONTEVALLO and SIX MILE CREEK, ALA.				4th Division Cavalry	Gen. Wilson, F.					50						Federal.
Apl. 1	Stoneman's Raid	BOONE, N. C.				Federal Cavalry.												
	Battle	FIVE FORKS, VA.	4½ hours.	20,000	10,000	Divs. of Cav., Army of the James, 1st, 2nd and 3rd Divs. Cav. Corps, 5th Corps, Army of the Potomac.	Gens. Sheridan and Warren, F.; Gen. Lee, C.	124	K.W. & M. 8500	700				54				Federal.
	(Wilson' Raid.) Engagement	TRION, ALA.				1st Brigade, 1st Division Cavalry Corps, Military Division of the Mississippi	Gen. McCook, F.											Federal.
	Skirmish	MOUNT PLEASANT, ALA				Cavalry of General Canby's Force.												
	Wilson's Raid	CENTREVILLE, ALA.				2nd Brig., 1st Division Cavalry Corps, Military Division of the Mississippi	Gen. McCook, F.											Federal.
	(Wilson's Raid). Engagement	BOGLER'S CREEK and PLANTERSVILLE, ALA. (Ebenezer Church and Maplesville.)			5000	2nd and 4th Divisions, Cavalry, Military Division of the Mississippi	Gen. Wilson, F.; Gen. Forrest, C.					300				3		Federal.
Apl. 2	(Wilson's Raid) Capture of	SELMA, ALA.			7000	2nd Cavalry Division, Military Div. of the Mississippi	Gen. Wilson, F.; Gen. Forrest, C.					3000				32		Federal.
	Wilson's Raid	SCOTTSVILLE, ALA.				2nd Brigade, 1st Division, Cavalry, Military Div. of the Mississippi												
	Assault, and Fall of	PETERSBURG, VA.	3½ hours.	18,000	10,000	2nd, 6th and 9th Corps, Army of the Potomac, 24th Corps, Army of the James	Gen. Grant, F.; Gen. Lee, C.	296	K.W. & M. 3000	2565		5000		500				Federal.
Apl. 3	Engagement	NAMOZINE CHURCH, WILLICOMACK, VA.				2nd, 6th and 9th Corps, Army of the Potomac, 24th Corps, Army of the James	Gens. Custer and Wells, F.											Federal.
	Occupation and Evacuation by Confederate Forces of	RICHMOND, VA.				Federal Troops under Gen. Weitzel	Gen. Weitzel, F.											Federal.
	(Stoneman's Raid). Capture of	SALEM, N. C.				Federal Cavalry	Col. Palmer, F.											Federal.
	(Stoneman's Raid). Capture of	WYTHEVILLE, VA.				15th Pennsylvania Cavalry.												
	Wilson's Raid	NORTHPORT, ALA.				1st Brigade, 1st Division, Cavalry, Military Div. of the Mississippi												
Apl. 4	Stoneman's Raid	DEEP RIVER BRIDGE, N. C.				Federal Cavalry												Federal.
	Wilson's Raid	TUSCALOOSA, ALA.				1st Brigade, 1st Division, Cavalry, Military Division of the Mississippi	Gen. Croxton, F.											Federal.
Apl. 5	Capture of Confederate Troops	AMELIA SPRINGS, VA. (Jetersville)				2nd Division Cavalry Corps, Army of the Potomac	Gen. Davis, F.									5		Federal.
	Skirmish	FAME'S CROSS ROADS, VA.				Federal Troops	Gen. Davis, F.											1 Fed. 2 Con.
Apl. 6	Battle	SAILOR'S CREEK, VA. (Harpers Farm, Deatonsville)				Cavalry Corps, 2nd and 6th Corps, Army of the Potomac	Gen. Sheridan, F.; Gen. Lee, C.	166	K.&W. [illegible]	1014		6000				10		Federal.

CHRONOLOGICAL LIST OF EVENTS (1860-1865).—Continued.

DATE.	EVENT.	LOCATION.	DURATION.	FORCE		COMPOSITION OF FORCE.	COMMANDERS.	KILLED		WOUNDED		PRISONERS TAKEN BY		MISSING		GUNS CAPT'D	STANDS OF COLORS	ADVANTAGE
				F	C.			F.	C.	F	C.	F.	C.	F.	C.			
1865 Apl. 6	Wilson's Raid	LITSEY SWAMP, ALA.				1st Brigade Cavalry, 1st Division, Military Division of the Mississippi												
	Engagement	HIGH BRIDGE, APPOMATTOX RIVER, VA.				Portion of the 24th Corps	Gen. Lee, C.	10		81			2 Rg					Conf'd
Apl 7	Battle	FARMVILLE, VA.				2nd Corps, Army of the Potomac	Gen. Ord, F.	K. W. & M. 855										Conf'd.
Apl 8	(8th–9th). Engagement	APPOMATTOX COURT HOUSE, VA. (Clover Hill)				Cavalry, Army of the Potomac, 24th Corps, and 1 Division 25th Corps	Gen. Sheridan, F. Gen. Lee, C.		K.&W. 200							25		Federal.
Apl. 9	(2nd–9th.) Siege of Mobile. Assault and Capture of	FORT BLAKELEY, ALA.			3500	13th and 16th Corps, Military Div. of W. Mississippi	Gen. Crosby, F. Gen. St. John Liddell, C.	K. W. & M. 115	2300	516		4000				32		Federal.
	Lee's Surrender	APPOMATTOX COURT HOUSE, VA.				Armies of the Potomac and James. Army of Northern Virginia (Confederate)	Gen. Grant, F. Gen. Lee, C.					[illegible]				170		Federal.
Apl. 10	Engagement	SUMTERVILLE, S. C.				Troops of the Department of the South.												
	Engagement	NEUSE RIVER, N. C.				Advance of Sherman's Army.												
	Engagement	LOWNDESVILLE, ALA.				2nd Brigade, 1st Division Cavalry, Military Division of the Mississippi												
Apl. 12	(12th–13th) Wilson's Raid and Surrender to Federal Forces of	MONTGOMERY, ALA.				2nd Brigade, 1st Division Cavalry, Military Division of the Mississippi	Gen. Wilson, F. Gen. Forrest, C.					1700				100		Federal.
	(Stoneman's Raid). Engagement, and Capture of	SALISBURY (Grant's Creek), N. C.				Federal Cavalry	Gen. Stoneman, F. —Gardner, C.					1800				14		Federal
Apl. 13	Engagement	WHISTLER'S STATION, ALA.				3rd Div., 13th Corps Army of the West Mississippi.												
	Memorandum or "basis of agreement" arranging capitulation of Confederate Forces prepared and signed by Maj.-Gen. Sherman, U. S. A., and Gen. J. E. Johnston, C. S. A.																	
Apl. 14	President Lincoln assassinated	WASHINGTON, D. C.																
	Destruction of the Federal Vessels *Ida*, *Laura*, *Itasca* and *Rose* by torpedoes, etc., near Mobile, Alabama.																	
Apl. 16	Skirmish	SOUTH FORK, JOHN DAY'S RIVER, OREGON		1 Co.		1st Oregon Cavalry.												
	Wilson's Raid	FORT TAYLOR, WEST POINT, GA.				2nd Brig. 1st Div. Cav. Military Div. of the Mississippi	Gen. LaGrange, F.					300				3		Federal.
	(Wilson's Raid) Capture of	COLUMBUS, GA.		400		4th Div. Cav., Military Division of the Mississippi	Gen. Upton, F.					1200				62		Federal.
Apl. 17	Surrender of Mosby's command	BERRYVILLE, VA.				Federal Troops under General Hancock	Gen. Hancock, F. —Mosby, C.											
Apl. 18	Engagement	BOYKIN'S MILLS, S. C. (Bradford's Springs)				Troops of the Department of the South.												
Apl. 19	Destruction of the Transport Steamer *Mary* by torpedo near Mobile, Ala.																	
	Engagement	SWIFT CREEK, S. C.				Troops of the Department of the South.												
	Stoneman's Raid	DALLAS, N. C.				Federal Cavalry												Federal.
	Stoneman's Raid	CATAWBA RIVER, N. C.				Federal Cavalry												Federal.
	Expedition of Federal Troops under Brig.-Gen. Osborne, from Randolph, Hatchie River and Fulton to Brownsville, Tenn.																	
Apl. 20	Wilson's Raid	TOBESOFKEE, GA.				17th Indiana Mounted Infantry.												
	(Wilson's Raid) Capture of	MACON, GA.				2nd Division, Wilson's Cavalry Corps	Gen. Wilson, F.											Federal.
Apl. 21	Rejection of Maj.-Gen. Sherman's Memorandum or "basis of agreement" by President Johnson.																	
Apl. 22	Wilson's Raid	TALLADEGA, ALA.				1st Brigade, 1st Division Cavalry, Military Division of the Mississippi												Federal
	Maj.-Gen. Halleck, U. S. A., assumes command of the Military Division of the James.																	
	Maj.-Gen. Banks, U. S. A., re-assumes command of the Department of the Gulf.																	
Apl. 23	(Wilson's Raid). Engagement	MUNFORD'S STATION, BLUE MOUNT, ALA.				1st Brigade, 1st Division Cavalry, Military Division of the Mississippi												Federal.
	Engagement	SOWANO GAP, N. C.				Gillem's Cavalry Command.												
	Affair between the Federal Vessels *Manhattan* and *Lafayette* and the Confederate Ram *Webb*.																	
Apl. 26	Gen. J. E. Johnston's Surrender	BENNETT'S HOUSE, near DURHAM'S STATION, N. C.				Armies of the Tennessee, Georgia and Ohio	Gen. Sherman, F. Gen. J. E. Johnston, C.					[illegible]				108		Federal
Apl. 29	Proclamation issued by President Johnson directing that "all restrictions upon internal, domestic and coastwise commercial intercourse be discontinued in such part of the States of Tennessee, Virginia, North Carolina, South Carolina, Georgia, Florida, Alabama, Mississippi, and so much of Louisiana as lies East of the Mississippi River, as shall be embraced within the lines of the National Military occupation, excepting only such restrictions as are imposed by the Acts of Congress * * * * * and excepting also * * * * the following articles, contraband of war, to wit: arms, ammunition, and all articles from which ammunition is manufactured; gray uniforms and cloth, locomotives, cars, railroad iron and machinery for operating railroads, telegraph wires, insulators and instruments for operating telegraph lines."																	
May 1	Surrender of Morgan's old command to General Hobson, at Mount Sterling, Ky.	MT. STERLING, KY.				Federal Troops	Gen. Hobson, F.					1200						Federal
	Strength of the Federal Forces (all ranks) 1,000,516.																	
	Maj.-Gen. Warren, U. S. V., assigned to command of the Department of the Mississippi, vice Maj.-Gen. Dana, relieved.																	
May 4	Surrender of Gen. R. Taylor with forces of W. Mississippi, to Gen. Canby, at Citronelle, Alabama	CITRONELLE, ALA.				Federal Troops	Gen. Canby, F. Gen. Taylor, C.					[illegible]						Federal.

CHRONOLOGICAL LIST OF EVENTS (1860-1865).—Continued.

DATE.	EVENT.	LOCATION.	DURATION.	FORCE. F.	FORCE. C.	COMPOSITION OF FORCE.	COMMANDERS.	KILLED. F.	KILLED. C.	WOUNDED. F.	WOUNDED. C.	PRISONERS TAKEN BY F.	PRISONERS TAKEN BY C.	MISSING. F.	MISSING. C.	[illegible]	[illegible]	ADVANTAGE.
1865																		
May 4	Surrender of Confederate Naval Forces under Commodore Farrand to Rear-Admiral Thatcher, U. S. N., at Citronelle, Alabama	Citronelle, Ala.																
May 6	General Molineux (General Gillmore's Force) assumes command at Augusta, Georgia.																	
May 8	Peace Proclamation issued by President Johnson.																	
May 10	Capture of Jefferson Davis	Irwinsville, Ga.				1st Wisconsin and 4th Michigan Cavalry	Lt.-Col. Pritchard, F.					20						Federal.
	Surrender of Gen. Sam Jones, C. S. A.	Tallahassee, Fla.				Detachment of Wilson's Cavalry	Gen. McCook, F.; Gen. Sam Jones, C					8000				40		Federal.
May 11	Surrender of Jeff. Thompson	Chalk Bluff, Ark.				Federal Forces under General Dodge	Gen. Dodge, F.; Jeff. Thompson, C					7454						Federal.
May 13	Engagement	Palmetto Ranch, Texas		800		62nd U. S. Colored Troops, 34th Indiana Volunteers and 2nd Texas Cavalry	Col. Barrett, F.; Gen. Slaughter, C	K.W. & P. 79										Conf'd.
May 17	The Military Division of West Mississippi and the Department of Key West abolished.																	
	Maj.-Gen. Canby, U. S. A., assigned to command of the Department of the Gulf (States of Louisiana, Mississippi, Alabama, Florida and Key West).																	
	Maj.-Gen. Banks, U. S. A., relieved from command of the Department of the Gulf.																	
	Maj.-Gen. Sheridan, U. S. A., assigned to command West of the Mississippi River (relieved from Middle Military Division).																	
May 19	Maj.-Gen. John A. Logan, assigned to succeed Maj.-Gen. Howard in command of the Army of the Tennessee.																	
May 22	(23-28). Review of the Army of the Potomac, and the Army under General Sherman, at Washington.																	
May 23	Maj.-Gen. W. B. Hazen, U. S. V., assigned to command of 15th Army Corps, vice Maj.-Gen. Logan.																	
May 26	Surrender of General Kirby Smith, C. S. A.	New Orleans, La.				Federal Troops under Major-General Canby	Gen. Canby, F.; Gn. Kirby Smith, C.					[illegible]				150		Federal.
	Total of Confederate Troops surrendered 174,223.																	
June 1	Twentieth Army Corps discontinued.																	
June 8	Maj.-Gen. Custer, U. S. A., to command the Department of Missouri (States of Missouri and Kansas).																	
June 28	Second, Fifth and Sixth Army Corps discontinued.																	
July 20	Thirteenth and Sixteenth Army Corps discontinued.																	
July 27	Ninth Army Corps discontinued.																	
Aug. 1	Fourth, Seventh, Eighth, Tenth, Fourteenth, Fifteenth Seventeenth, Twenty-third and Twenty-fourth Army Corps discontinued. (Twenty-fifth Army Corps discontinued on 8th January, 1866)																	
Nov. 15	Total of Federal Troops mustered out (April 29th–Nov. 15th) 800,963.																	
	The Federal Army organized in 5 Grand Divisions, under Maj.-Gens. Meade, Sherman, Sheridan, Thomas and Halleck, sub-divided into 19 Departments under Maj.-Gens. Hooker, Hancock, Augur, Ord, Stoneman, Palmer, Pope, Terry, Schofield, Sickles, Steadman, Foster, T. J. Wood, C. R. Wood, Canby, Wright, Reynolds, Steele, and McDowell.																	

ARMY CORPS FORMED DURING CIVIL WAR.

Organized under Section 9, of Act approved July 17th, 1862, authorizing the President to Establish and Organize Army Corps.

CORPS.	COMMANDERS. NAME.	DATE OF APPOINTMENT.	COMPOSITION.	DATE WHEN DISCONTINUED.	REMARKS.
First Army Corps	Maj.-Gen'l Fremont	12th August, 1862	Troops of the Mountain Department	23rd March, 1864.	Troops transferred, March, 23d, 1864. Reorganized 28th November, 1864.*
	" " Jno. F. Reynolds	15th April, 1863			
	" " Hancock	26th Nov., 1864			
Second Army Corps	General Banks	12th August, 1862	Troops of the Shenandoah Department	28th June, 1865	Became Eleventh Army Corps, 12th Sept. 1862, giving place to Corps arranged in G. O. No. 101 of March 13, 1862.
Third Army Corps	General McDowell	12th August, 1862	All troops under Gen'l McDowell, except those within the City and Fortifications of Washington	23rd March, 1864	Became Twelfth Army Corps, 12th Sept., 1862, giving place to Corps arranged G. O. No. 101, of March 13th, 1862.
			Corps arranged in G. O. 101, of March 13th, 1862	1st Aug., 1863	Transferred to other Corps.
Fourth Army Corps	Maj.-Gen'l Gordon Granger	28th September, 1863	From September 28th, 1863: Twentieth and Twenty-first Corps consolidated	1st Aug., 1865.	
Fifth Army Corps	Brig.-Gen'l Porter	22d July, 1862	Corps arranged in G. O. 125, of 1862	28th June, 1865.	
Sixth Army Corps	Brig.-Gen'l Franklin	22d July, 1862	Corps arranged in G. O. 125, of 1862	28th June, 1865.	
Seventh Army Corps	Maj.-Gen'l Dix	22d July, 1862	Forces under Maj.-Gen'l Dix	1st Aug., 1863	Transferred to Eighteenth Corps.
	" " Steele	6th January, 1864	Troops in the Department of Arkansas	1st Aug., 1865.	
Eighth Army Corps	Maj.-Gen'l Wool	22d July, 1862	Forces under Maj.-Gen'l Wool.		
	" " Lewis Wallace	12th March, 1863.			
	" " E. O. C. Ord	11th July, 1864.			
	" " Lewis Wallace	28th July, 1864		1st August, 1865	
Ninth Army Corps	Maj.-Gen'l Burnside	22d July, 1862	Troops under Maj.-Gen'l Burnside, and belonging to Dep't of North Carolina.	27th July, 1865.	
Tenth Army Corps	Maj.-Gen'l O. M. Mitchell	3d September, 1862.	Troops in the Department of the South	3d December, 1864	Reorganized.
	" " A. H. Terry	27th March, 1865	All troops in North Carolina not belonging to the Second, Ninth and Twenty-third Corps and Gen'l Sherman's Army	1st Aug., 1865.	
Eleventh Army Corps	Maj.-Gen'l Banks	12th September, 1862	Troops of the Shenandoah Department		Consolidated with Twelfth and constituted Twentieth Corps, 4th April, 1864.
Twelfth Army Corps	General McDowell	12th September, 1862	Troops under General McDowell (with some exceptions)		Consolidated with Eleventh and constituted Twentieth Corps, 4th April, 1864.
Thirteenth Army Corps	Maj.-Gen'l Grant	24th October, 1862	Troops of Department of the Tennessee.		
	" " J. A. McClernand	18th Dec., 1862		11th June, 1864.	Troops transferred.
	" " Gordon Granger	18th February, 1865	Reorganized	20th July, 1865.	
Fourteenth Army Corps	Maj.-Gen'l Rosecrans	24th October, 1862.	Troops of Department of the Cumberland.		Divided into three Corps (Fourteenth Twentieth and Twenty-first) 9th January, 1863.
	" " G. H. Thomas	9th January, 1863.		1st August, 1865	
Fifteenth Army Corps	Maj.-Gen'l W. T. Sherman	18th December, 1862	From troops of General Grant's command	1st August, 1865	
Sixteenth Army Corps	Maj.-Gen'l S. A. Hurlbut	18th December, 1862	From troops of General Grant's command		Corps organization abolished, Nov. 7, 1864.
	" " A. J. Smith	18th February, 1865	Reorganized	20th July, 1865.	
Seventeenth Army Corps	Maj.-Gen'l J. B. McPherson	18th December, 1862	From troops of General Grant's command	1st August, 1865.	
Eighteenth Army Corps	Maj.-Gen'l J. G. Foster	24th December, 1862	Troops in North Carolina		Seventh Army Corps transferred to the Corps.
	" " W. F. Smith	17th July, 1864	Troops of Department of North Carolina and Virginia serving with the Army of the Potomac in the field	3rd December, 1864.	
Nineteenth Army Corps	Maj.-Gen'l N. P. Banks	5th January, 1863	Troops in the Department of the Gulf.		Military Division of West Mississippi known as Nineteenth Corps, abolished 7th November, 1864.
	Brev't Maj.-Gen'l Emory	7th Nov., 1864		20th March, 1865.	
Twentieth Army Corps	Maj.-Gen'l A. McD. McCook	9th January, 1863.	Part of the Army of the Cumberland.		Consolidated with Twenty-first, and constituted Fourth Corps, Sept. 28th, 1863
	General J. Hooker	4th April, 1864	Re-formed of Eleventh and Twelfth Corps.	1st June, 1865	
Twenty-first Army Corps	Maj.-Gen'l T. L. Crittenden	9th January, 1863.	Part of the Army of the Cumberland		Consolidated with Twentieth and constituted Fourth Corps, 28th Sept., 1863
Twenty second Army Corps	Maj.-Gen'l Heintzelman	2d February, 1863	Troops in the Department of Washington.		
Twenty-third Army Corps	Maj.-Gen'l G. L. Hartsuff	27th April, 1863	First Formation: Troops in Kentucky not belonging to the Ninth Corps. Second Formation: Troops within the Department of the Ohio not belonging to the Ninth Corps (June 8, 1863)	1st August, 1865.	
	" " Stoneman	28th January, 1864			
	" " Schofield	4th April, 1864			
	" " J. D. Cox	27th March, 1865.			
Twenty-fourth Army Corps	Maj.-Gen'l E. O. C. Ord	3d December, 1864	White infantry of the Tenth and Eighteenth Corps, with Army of the James	1st August, 1865.	
Twenty fifth Army Corps	Maj.-Gen'l G. Weitzel	3d December, 1864	Colored Troops of the Department of Virginia and North Carolina	8th January, 1866.	
Cavalry Corps, Army of the Potomac	Maj.-Gen'l G. Stoneman	15th April 1863	Cavalry of the Army of the Potomac.		
	" " P. H. Sheridan	4th April, 1864			

* G. O.'s referred to were issued from the Headquarters of the Army of the Potomac.

Engagements During the Civil War.

STATES AND TERRITORIES.	1861	1862	1863	1864	1865	TOTAL.
New York	....	...	1	...	....	1
Pennsylvania	....	....	8	1	....	9
Maryland	3	9	10	8	....	30
District of Columbia	....	....	...	1	....	1
West Virginia	29	114	17	19	1	80
Virginia	30	40	116	265	38	519
North Carolina	2	27	18	10	28	85
South Carolina	9	10	17	9	21	60
Georgia	....	2	6	92	0	108
Florida	8	3	4	17	5	32
Alabama	....	10	12	23	24	79
Mississippi	...	42	70	67	1	180
Louisiana	1	11	34	50	2	118
Texas	1	2	8	1	2	14
Arkansas	1	42	40	78	0	167
Tennessee	2	82	124	80	1	298
Kentucky	11	66	30	31	4	138
Ohio	....	...	3	....	....	3
Indiana	....	....	4	....	....	4
Illinois	....	....	....	1	....	1
Missouri	65	95	48	41	....	244
Minnesota	....	5	1	....	...	6
California	....	1	4	1	...	6
Kansas	....	....	2	5	....	7
Oregon	....	....	..	3	1	4
Nevada	....	....	..	2	....	2
Washington Territory	....	....	1	....	...	1
Utah	....	....	1	....	....	1
New Mexico	3	5	7	4	....	19
Nebraska	....	....	2	....	....	2
Colorado	....	...	...	4	....	4
Indian Territory	....	2	9	3	3	17
Dakota	....	2	6	4	....	11
Arizona	....	1	1	1	1	4
Idaho	....	....	1	...	....	1
Totals	156	564	627	779	155	2,261

Number Enlisted for Federal Army During Civil War, by Periods of Service.

PERIODS.	NUMBER.	PERIODS.	NUMBER.
For 60 days	2,045	For 1 year	393,706
" 3 months	108,416	" 2 years	44,400
" 100 days	85,507	" 3 "	2,028,630
" 4 months	42	" 4 "	1,040
" 6 "	26,118		
" 8 "	373	AGGREGATE ENLISTMENTS	2,766,478
" 9 "	80,890		

Number of Soldiers who served in various Wars in United States prior to the Civil War.

Soldiers of the War of the Revolution, 1775-1783		309,716
Indian War, (General Wayne), 1794		2,843
" 1811		656
War with Great Britain, 1812-1815:		
Number of Soldiers, Sailors and Marines serving twelve months or more	63,179	
" Militia serving six months or more	66,325	
" " " three " "	125,643	
" " " one " "	125,307	
" " " less than one month	147,200	527,654
" Soldiers serving in the Seminole War, 1817-1818		5,911
" " " " Black Hawk War, 1831-1832		6,031
" " " " South Western Disturbances, 1836		2,803
" " " " Cherokee Country Disturbances, 1836-1837		9,926
" " " " Creek Disturbances, 1836-1837		13,418
" " " " Florida War, 1836-1842		41,122
" " and Sailors serving in Mexican War, 1846-1847		105,454
" " serving in New York Frontier Disturbances, 1838-1839		1,128
" " " Aroostook Disturbances, 1838-1839		1,480

STRENGTH OF THE FEDERAL ARMY AT VARIOUS DATES DURING CIVIL WAR.

DATE.	PRESENT.			ABSENT.			AGGREGATE.		GRAND TOTAL.
	REGULARS.	VOLUNTEERS.	TOTAL.	REGULARS.	VOLUNTEERS.	TOTAL.	REGULARS.	VOLUNTEERS.	
January 1st, 1861	14,663		14,663	1,704		1,704	16,367		16,367
July 1st, 1861	14,108	169,480	183,588	2,314	849	3,163	16,422	170,329	186,751
January 1st, 1862	19,871	507,333	527,204	2,554	46,159	48,713	22,425	553,492	575,917
March 31st, 1862	19,585	514,309	533,984	3,723	99,419	103,142	23,308	613,818	637,126
January 1st, 1863	19,169	676,633	698,802	6,294	213,095	219,389	25,463	893,728	918,191
January 1st, 1864	17,237	594,013	611,250	7,869	242,083	249,487	24,636	836,101	860,737
January 1st, 1865	14,661	606,263	620,924	7,358	331,178	338,536	22,019	937,441	959,460
March 31st, 1865	13,880	643,867	657,747	7,789	314,550	322,339	21,669	958,417	980,086
May 1st, 1865			797,807			202,709			1,000,516

AVERAGE MEAN STRENGTH OF THE FEDERAL ARMY DURING CIVIL WAR.

CHARACTER OF TROOPS.	PERIOD OF SERVICE.	PRESENT.	ABSENT.	AGGREGATE.
Regulars	January 1st, 1861 to January 1st, 1865	17,735	6,194	23,929
Volunteers	July 1st, 1861 to March 31st, 1865	544,704	196,803	741,507
White Troops		562,439	204,997	764,436
Colored Troops	September, 1862 to December 1867	33,640	6,690	42,330
Mixed Troops		585,679	211,606	808,775

AGGREGATE OF TROOPS FURNISHED, 1861-1865, WITH BOUNTIES PAID BY EACH STATE.

STATES AND TERRITORIES.	Troops furnished 1861-1865.	Colored Troops furnished, 1861-1865.	NUMBER OF MEN DRAFTED.					BOUNTIES PAID.
			Number Drawn.	Failed to Report.	Exempted.	Furnished Substitute or Paid Commutation.	Held for Service.	
Maine	73,114	104	27,324	3,760	12,997	4,046	1,091	$7,837,044
New Hampshire	34,629	125	10,606	464	5,478	3,654	210	9,636,313
Vermont	35,262	120	7,743	420	4,096	3,016	487	4,528,775
Massachusetts	152,048	3,966	41,882	5,107	27,070	8,383	919	22,965,550
Rhode Island	23,699	1,837	4,331	240	2,800	1,149	117	820,760
Connecticut	57,379	1,764	12,031	1,014	6,864	3,843	203	6,887,554
New York	467,047	4,125	151,488	31,745	66,006	81,539	3,316	86,620,228
New Jersey	81,010	1,185	23,295	6,265	8,234	9,050	951	23,868,967
Pennsylvania	366,107	8,612	178,873	31,300	70,913	40,607	8,015	43,154,087
Delaware	13,670	954	6,035	1,443	4,170	2,534	425	1,180,500
Maryland	50,316	8,718	29,319	9,207	11,011	6,134	1,426	6,871,098
West Virginia	32,068	196	3,180	1,014	589	219	349	864,737
District of Columbia	16,872	3,260	14,398	5,254	3,603	1,751	306	134,010
Ohio	310,659	5,022	50,400	9,388	19,751	10,988	4,241	23,557,373
Indiana	197,147	1,687	41,158	6,983	15,478	5,966	7,597	9,182,854
Illinois	259,147	1,811	30,085	9,519	9,533	5,450	3,538	17,296,205
Michigan	82,873	1,387	22,193	4,294	7,190	3,778	1,800	9,864,855
Wisconsin	96,424	165	38,395	11,742	14,732	6,718	3,722	5,855,856
Minnesota	25,053	104	10,796	3,058	4,449	1,281	983	2,090,464
Iowa	76,340	440	7,546	702	2,446	1,364	1,803	1,615,171
Missouri	109,111	8,344	21,619	9,444	5,781	1,888	1,031	1,282,140
Kentucky	79,025	23,703	29,421	9,603	8,086	5,787	1,960	632,077
Kansas	20,151	2,080	1,420	410	287	210	110	67,407
Tennessee	31,092	20,133	...	...	...	...	...	...
Arkansas	8,383	5,526	...	...	...	...	...	...
North Carolina	3,156	5,035	...	...	...	...	...	...
South Carolina	...	5,462	...	...	...	...	...	...
California	15,725	...	...	...	...	...	...	...
Nevada	1,080	...	...	...	...	...	...	...
Oregon	1,810	...	...	...	...	...	...	...
Washington Territory	964	...	...	...	...	...	...	...
Nebraska Territory	3,157	...	...	...	...	...	...	...
Colorado Territory	4,903	95	...	...	...	...	...	...
Dakota Territory	206	...	...	...	...	...	...	...
New Mexico Territory	6,561	...	...	...	...	...	...	...
Alabama	2,576	4,969	...	...	...	...	...	...
Florida	1,290	1,044	...	...	...	...	...	...
Louisiana	5,224	24,052	...	...	...	...	...	...
Mississippi	545	17,869	...	...	...	...	...	...
Texas	1,965	47	...	...	...	...	...	...
Indian Nation	3,530	...	...	...	...	...	...	...
Colored Troops*	93,441	...	...	...	...	...	...	...
Totals	2,859,132	178,975	776,829	161,244	315,509	73,607	46,347	$285,941,036
At large		733						
Not accounted for		5,083						
Officers		7,122						
	Total	186,017						

* Colored troops enlisted in seceded States.

TROOPS IN THE FEDERAL SERVICE, DURING THE CIVIL WAR—BY STATES.

States and Territories.	Cavalry.		Artillery.			Infantry.		Total.		
	Regiments.	Companies.	Regiments.	Companies.	Batteries.	Regiments.	Companies.	Regiments.	Companies.	Batteries.
Maine	2	..	1	3	7	30	22	33	25	7
New Hampshire	1	..	1	..	1	17	4	19	4	1
Vermont	1	..	1	1	3	17	..	19	1	3
Massachusetts	5	4	4	8	16	68	47	77	59	16
Rhode Island	3	2	3	..	1	8	1	14	3	1
Connecticut	1	..	2	..	3	24	..	30	..	3
New York	27	10	15	..	35	252	15	291	25	35
New Jersey	3	..	..	..	5	38	4	41	4	5
Pennsylvania	23	28	4	5	19	227	62	254	95	19
Delaware	..	8	..	1	1	9	4	9	13	1
Maryland	4	4	..	..	6	20	1	24	5	6
District of Columbia	1	1	..	..	..	2	33	3	34	..
West Virginia	7	2	..	..	6	17	2	24	4	6
Virginia	..	..	..	..	..	..	1	..	1	..
North Carolina	2	..	..	..	..	2	..	4	..	..
Georgia	..	..	..	..	..	..	2	..	2	..
Florida	2	..	..	..	..	..	..	2	..	..
Alabama	1	5	..	..	..	..	..	1	5	..
Mississippi	..	2	..	..	..	..	..	..	2	..
Louisiana	2	..	..	..	..	3	..	5	..	..
Texas	1	9	..	..	..	..	..	1	9	..
Arkansas	4	..	..	..	1	3	2	7	2	1
Tennessee	21	7	..	..	5	9	..	30	7	5

States and Territories.	Cavalry.		Artillery.			Infantry.		Total.		
	Regiments.	Companies.	Regiments.	Companies.	Batteries.	Regiments.	Companies.	Regiments.	Companies.	Batteries.
Kentucky	16	10	..	..	7	45	1	61	11	7
Ohio	13	18	3	..	27	218	11	234	29	27
Michigan	12	2	2	..	11	36	7	50	9	11
Indiana	13	1	1	..	26	123	16	137	17	26
Illinois	17	..	2	..	6	157	9	176	9	8
Missouri	30	26	..	..	8	61	20	94	46	8
Wisconsin	4	..	1	..	12	53	..	58	..	12
Iowa	9	..	..	..	4	40	..	55	..	4
Minnesota	2	10	1	..	3	11	..	14	10	3
California	2	4	..	..	..	9	..	11	4	..
Kansas	9	..	..	..	3	10	5	19	5	3
Oregon	1	..	..	..	..	1	..	2	9	..
Nevada	..	6	..	..	..	..	3	..	..	..
Washington Territory	..	..	..	..	..	1	..	1	..	..
New Mexico Territory	2	5	..	..	..	6	11	8	16	..
Nebraska Territory	3	4	..	..	..	..	2	3	6	..
Colorado Territory	3	..	..	..	1	..	2	3	2	1
Dakota Territory	..	2	..	..	..	..	..	..	2	..
U. S. Vet. Volunteer Infantry	..	..	..	..	..	10	..	10	..	..
U. S. Volunteer Infantry	..	..	..	..	..	6	1	6	1	..
United States Colored Troops	6	..	11	4	10	102	18	119	22	10
U. S. Army, Regulars	6	..	5	..	..	19	..	30	..	..
Total	258	170	57	22	222	1,666	306	1,981	498	232

UNITED STATES ARMY PAY TABLE.

Officers of Regulars and Volunteers. (During the Civil War.)

RANK AND CLASSIFICATION.	PAY PER MONTH	SUBSISTENCE.		SERVANTS.		TOTAL MONTHLY PAY.	FORAGE FURNISHED FOR HORSES	
		No. of Rations per day.	Monthly Commutation Value.	No. of servants allowed.	Monthly Commutation Value.		In time of War	In time of Peace
GENERAL OFFICERS:								
Lieutenant-General	$270 00	40	$360 00	4	$90 00	$720 00	And for Forage	$50 00
Aides-de-Camp and Military Secretary to Lieutenant-General, each	80 00	5	45 00	3	45 00	170 00	$9 00	9 00
Major General	220 00	15	135 00	4	90 00	445 00	7 00	5 00
Senior Aide-de-Camp to General-in-Chief	80 00	4	30 00	2	47 00	158 00	4 00	3 00
Aide-de-Camp, in addition to pay, etc. of Lieutenant	24 00					24 00	2 00	2 00
Brigadier-General	124 00	12	108 00	3	67 50	299 50	5 00	4 00
Aide-de-Camp, in addition to pay, etc., of Lieutenant	20 00					20 00	3 00	2 00
ADJUTANT-GENERAL'S DEPARTMENT:								
Adjutant-General—Brigadier-General	124 00	12	108 00	3	67 50	299 50	5 00	4 00
Assistant Adjutant-General—Colonel	110 00	6	54 00	2	47 00	211 00	5 00	3 00
Assistant Adjutant-General—Lieutenant-Colonel	95 00	5	45 00	2	47 00	187 00	4 00	3 00
Assistant Adjutant-General—Major	80 00	4	36 00	2	47 00	163 00	4 00	2 00
Judge-Advocate-General—Colonel	110 00	6	54 00	2	47 00	211 00	5 00	3 00
Judge-Advocate—Major	80 00	4	36 00	2	47 00	163 00	4 00	2 00
Judge-Advocate of Division—Major	80 00	4	36 00	2	47 00	163 00	4 00	2 00
INSPECTOR GENERAL'S DEPARTMENT:								
Inspector-General—Colonel	110 00	6	54 00	2	47 00	211 00	5 00	3 00
Assistant Inspector-General—Major	80 00	4	36 00	2	47 00	163 00	4 00	2 00
SIGNAL DEPARTMENT:								
Signal Officer—Major	80 00	4	36 00	2	47 00	163 00	4 00	3 00
QUARTERMASTER'S DEPARTMENT:								
Quartermaster-General—Brigadier-General	124 00	12	108 00	3	67 00	299 50	5 00	4 00
Assistant Quartermaster-General—Colonel	110 00	6	54 00	2	47 00	211 00	5 00	3 00
Deputy Quartermaster-General—Lieutenant-Colonel	95 00	5	45 00	2	47 00	187 00	4 00	3 00
Quartermaster—Major	80 00	4	36 00	2	47 00	163 00	4 00	3 00
Assistant Quartermaster—Captain	70 00	4	36 00	1	23 50	129 50	3 00	3 00
SUBSISTENCE DEPARTMENT:								
Commissary-General of Subsistence—Colonel	110 00	6	54 00	2	47 00	211 00	5 00	2 00
Assistant Commissary-General of Subsistence—Lieutenant-Colonel	95 00	5	45 00	2	47 00	187 00	4 00	3 00
Commissary of Subsistence—Major	80 00	4	36 00	2	47 00	163 00	4 00	2 00
Commissary of Subsistence—Captain	70 00	4	36 00	1	23 50	129 50	3 00	2 00
Assistant Commissary of Subsistence, in addition to pay, etc., as Lieutenant	20 00					20 00		
MEDICAL DEPARTMENT:								
Surgeon-General—Brigadier-General	124 00	12	108 00	3	67 50	299 50	5 00	4 00
Surgeons of ten years' service	80 00	8	72 00	2	47 00	199 00	4 00	2 00
Surgeons of less than ten years' service	80 00	4	36 00	2	47 00	163 00	4 00	2 00
Assistant Surgeons of ten years' service	70 00	8	72 00	1	23 50	165 50	3 00	2 00
Assistant Surgeons of five years' service	70 00	4	36 00	1	23 50	129 50	3 00	2 00
Assistant Surgeons of less than five years' service	53 33	4	36 00	1	23 50	112 83	2 00	2 00
PAY DEPARTMENT:								
Paymaster-General. $2,740 per annum	228 33					228 33		
Deputy Paymaster-General	95 00	5	45 00	2	47 00	187 00	4 00	2 00
Paymaster	80 00	4	36 00	2	47 00	163 00	4 00	2 00
CORPS OF ENGINEERS, TOPOGRAPHICAL ENGINEERS AND ORDNANCE:								
Chief of Ordnance—Brigadier-General	124 00	12	108 00	3	67 50	299 50	5 00	4 00
Colonel	110 00	6	54 00	2	47 00	211 00	5 00	3 00
Lieutenant-Colonel	95 00	5	45 00	2	47 00	187 00	4 00	3 00
Major	80 00	4	36 00	2	47 00	163 00	4 00	3 00
Captain	70 00	4	36 00	2	23 50	129 50	3 00	2 00
First Lieutenant	53 33	4	36 00	1	23 50	112 83	2 00	2 00
Second Lieutenant	53 33	4	36 00	1	23 50	112 83	2 00	2 00
Brevet Second Lieutenant	53 33	4	36 00	1	23 50	112 83	2 00	2 00
MOUNTED: DRAGOONS, CAVALRY, RIFLES, AND LIGHT ARTILLERY:								
Colonel	110 00	6	54 00	2	47 00	211 00	5 00	3 00
Lieutenant-Colonel	95 00	5	45 00	2	47 00	187 00	4 00	3 00
Major	80 00	4	36 00	2	47 00	163 00	4 00	2 00
Captain	70 00	4	36 00	1	23 50	129 50	3 00	2 00
First Lieutenant	53 33	4	36 00	1	23 50	112 83	2 00	2 00
Second Lieutenant	53 33	4	36 00	1	23 50	112 83	2 00	2 00
Brevet Second Lieutenant	53 33	4	36 00	1	23 50	112 83	2 00	2 00
Adjutant, in addition to pay of Lieutenant	10 00					10 00		
Regimental Quartermaster, in addition to pay of Lieutenant	10 00					10 00		
ARTILLERY AND INFANTRY:								
Colonel	95 00	6	54 00	2	45 00	194 00	4 00	3 00
Lieutenant-Colonel	80 00	5	45 00	2	45 00	170 00	3 00	3 00
Major	70 00	4	36 00	2	45 00	151 00	3 00	2 00
Captain	60 00	4	36 00	1	22 50	118 50		
First Lieutenant	50 00	4	36 00	1	22 50	108 50		
Second Lieutenant	45 00	4	36 00	1	22 50	103 50		
Brevet Second Lieutenant	45 00	4	36 00	1	22 50	103 50		
Adjutant, in addition to pay, etc., of Lieutenant	10 00					10 00	3 00	3 00
Regimental Quartermaster, in addition to pay, etc., of Lieutenant	10 00					10 00	2 00	2 00
Chaplains	100 00	2	18 00			118 00	1 00	1 00

Every Commissioned Officer below the rank of Brigadier-General received one additional ration per day for every five years' service.

UNITED STATES ARMY PAY TABLE.

Non-Commissioned Officers, Privates, etc., of Regulars and Volunteers. (During the Civil War.)

CAVALRY.

Sergeant-Major	$21 00	Corporal	$14 00
Quartermaster-Sergeant	21 00	Bugler	13 00
Chief Bugler	21 00	Farrier and Blacksmith	15 00
First Sergeant	20 00	Private	13 00
Sergeant	17 00		

ORDNANCE.

Sergeant	$34 00	Private, first class	$17 00
Corporal	20 00	Private, second class	13 00

ARTILLERY AND INFANTRY.

Sergeant-Major	$21 00	Artificer, Artillery	$15 00
Quartermaster-Sergeant	17 00	Private	13 00
First Sergeant	20 00	Principal Musician	21 00
Sergeant	17 00	Musician	12 00
Corporal	13 00		

SAPPERS, MINERS AND PONTONIERS.

Sergeant	$34 00	Private, second class	$13 00
Corporal	20 00	Musician	13 00
Private, first class	17 00		

BRIGADE BANDS.

Leader	$45 00	Drum Major	$17 00
Four of the Band at	34 00	Four of the Band at	20 00
Eight of the Band at	17 00		

MISCELLANEOUS.

Medical Cadets (and 1 ration per day)	$30 00	Matrons	$6 00
Hospital Stewards	30 00	Female Nurses, per day (and 1 ration)	40
Master Wagoners (3d Aug., '61)	17 00	Wagoners (3d Aug., '61)	14 00

NOTE.—(a) $2 per month allowed for re-enlistment, and $1 per month additional for each subsequent period of five years' service, provided the enlistment was made within one month after the expiration of each term.

(b) 12½ cents per month retained from the pay of each enlisted man of the army for the support of the "Soldier's Home."

UNITED STATES ARMY. PAY TABLE—OFFICERS (1885.)

GRADE OR RANK.	Officers on Active Service. Yearly Pay. First 5 Years' Service.	After 5 Years' Service.	After 10 Years' Service.	After 15 Years' Service.	After 20 Years' Service.	Retired Officers. Yearly Pay. First 5 Years' Service.	After 5 Years' Service.	After 10 Years' Service.	After 15 Years' Service.	After 20 Years' Service.
		10%	20%	30%	40%					
General	$13,500	.....	.....	.....	.....	.....	.....	.....	.....	.....
Lieutenant-General	11,000	.....	.....	.....	.....	.....	.....	.....	.....	.....
Major-General	7,500	.....	.....	.....	.....	$5,625	.....	.....	.....	.....
Brigadier-General	5,500	.....	.....	.....	.....	4,125	.....	.....	.....	.....
Colonel	3,500	3,850	4,200	*4,500	*4,500	2,625	2,887	3,150	3,375	3,375
Lieutenant-Colonel	3,000	3,300	3,600	4,000	*4,000	2,250	2,475	2,700	3,000	3,000
Major	2,500	2,750	3,000	3,250	3,500	1,875	2,062	2,250	2,437	2,625
Captain, mounted	2,000	2,200	2,400	2,600	2,800	1,500	1,650	1,800	1,950	2,100
Captain, not mounted	1,800	1,980	2,160	2,340	2,520	1,350	1,485	1,620	1,755	1,890
Regimental Adjutant	1,800	1,980	2,100	2,340	2,520	.....	.....	.....	.....	.....
Regimental Quartermaster	1,800	1,980	2,100	2,340	2,520	.....	.....	.....	.....	.....
First Lieutenant, mounted	1,600	1,760	1,920	2,080	2,240	1,200	1,320	1,440	1,560	1,680
First Lieutenant, not mounted	1,500	1,650	1,800	1,950	2,100	1,125	1,237	1,350	1,462	1,575
Second Lieutenant, mounted	1,500	1,650	1,800	1,950	2,100	1,125	1,237	1,350	1,462	1,575
Second Lieutenant, not mounted	1,400	1,540	1,680	1,820	1,960	1,050	1,155	1,260	1,365	1,470
Chaplain	1,500	1,650	1,800	1,950	2,100	1,350	1,485	1,620	1,755	1,890
Cadets, West Point $500										

* Maximum Pay of Colonels is limited to $4500, and of Lieutenant-Colonels to $4,000.

United States Army. Pay Table—Non-Commissioned Officers and Men (1885.)

GRADE.	Pay per Month.*	Pay per Year.	Pay for Five Years.
Sergeant Major, Cavalry, Artillery and Infantry	$23	$276	$1,380
Regimental Quartermaster Serg't, Cavalry, Artillery and Inf.	23	276	1,380
Principal Musician, Artillery and Infantry	22	264	1,320
Chief Trumpeter of Cavalry	22	264	1,320
Saddler Sergeant, Cavalry	22	264	1,320
1st Sergeant of a Company, Cavalry, Artillery and Infantry	22	264	1,320
Ordnance Sergeants of Posts	34	408	2,040
Commissary Sergeants of Posts	34	408	2,040
Hospital Steward, 1st Class	30	360	1,800
Hospital Steward, 2d Class	22	264	1,320
Hospital Steward, 3d Class	20	240	1,200
Sergeants, Cavalry, Artillery and Infantry	17	204	1,020
Corporals, Cavalry, Artillery and Infantry	15	180	900
Trumpeters, Cavalry	13	156	780
Musicians, Artillery and Infantry	13	15_6	780
Farriers and Blacksmiths, Cavalry	15	10^8	900
Saddlers, Cavalry	15	180	900
Private, Cavalry, Artillery and Infantry	13	15^6	780

*In addition to above rates, the following sums are allowed upon discharge after faithful and honest service: $1 per month for third year, $2 for fourth year and $3 for fifth year of enlistment.

For soldiers who have become infirm during twenty years' service, or who have been discharged for wounds received or sickness brought on in service, a Home is maintained in Washington. Twelve and a half cents per month is deducted from each soldier's pay, toward support of this institution.

Actual Strength of United States Regular Army, from 1789 to 1884.*

DATE.	OFFICERS.	MEN.	TOTAL.	DATE.	OFFICERS.	MEN.	TOTAL.
1789-90	60	672	732	1864	1,813	19,791	21,604
1795	212	3,228	3,440	1865	1,605	20,705	22,310
1800	248	3,803	4,051	1866	2,020	31,470	33,490
1805	166	2,564	2,730	1867	2,853	53,962	56,815
1810	486	5,468	5,954	1868	2,835	48,081	50,916
July, 1812	301	6,385	6,686	1869	2,700	34,074	36,774
Feby., 1813	1,476	17,560	19,036	1870	2,541	34,534	37,075
Sept., 1814	2,395	35,791	38,186	1871	3,105	26,848	29,953
Feby., 1815	2,386	31,038	33,424	1872	2,104	26,071	28,175
Dec., 1820	712	8,230	8,942	1873	2,076	26,576	28,652
1825	532	5,187	5,719	1874	2,080	26,364	28,444
1830	627	5,324	5,951	1875	2,068	23,250	25,318
1835	680	6,471	7,151	1876	2,151	26,129	28,280
1840	733	9,937	10,670	1877	2,178	21,707	23,885
1845	824	7,525	8,349	1878	2,153	23,665	25,818
1850	948	9,815	10,763	1879	2,127	24,262	26,389
1855	1,042	14,710	15,752	1880	2,152	24,259	26,411
1860	1,108	15,259	16,367	1881	2,181	22,994	25,175
1861	1,004	15,418	16,422	1882	2,162	23,024	25,186
1862	1,720	21,450	23,170	1883	2,143	23,335	25,478
1863	1,844	22,915	24,759	1884	2,143	23,357	25,500

* Retired officers not included.

Amount Expended for Pensions, 1856-1884.

YEAR.	AMOUNT.	YEAR.	AMOUNT.
1856	$1,296,229 65	1871	$34,443,894 88
1857	1,310,380 58	1872	28,533,402 76
1858	1,219,768 30	1873	29,359,426 86
1859	1,222,222 71	1874	29,038,414 66
1860	1,100,802 32	1875	29,456,216 22
1861	1,034,599 73	1876	28,257,395 69
1862	852,170 47	1877	27,963,752 27
1863	1,078,513 36	1878	27,137,019 08
1864	4,985,473 90	1879	35,121,482 39
1865	16,347,621 34	1880	56,777,174 44
1866	15,605,549 88	1881	50,059,279 62
1867	20,936,551 71	1882	61,345,193 95
1868	23,782,386 78	1883	66,012,573 64
1869	28,476,621 78	1884	60,875,100 00
1870	28,340,202 17		

UNITED STATES NAVY. PAY TABLE—OFFICERS, Etc.

RANK OR GRADE.	At Sea.	On Shore Duty.	On Leave, or Waiting Orders.
Admiral	$13,000	$13,000	$13,000
Vice Admiral	9,000	8,000	6,000
Rear Admiral	6,000	5,000	4,000
Commodores	5,000	4,000	3,000
Captains	4,500	3,500	2,800
Commanders	3,500	3,000	2,300
Lieutenant Commanders:			
First four years after date of commission	2,800	2,400	2,000
After four years from date of commission	3,000	2,600	2,200
Lieutenant:			
First five years	2,400	2,000	1,600
After five years	2,600	2,200	1,800
Lieutenants, Junior Grade:			
First five years	1,800	1,500	1,200
After five years	2,000	1,700	1,400
Ensigns:			
First five years	1,200	1,000	800
After five years	1,400	1,200	1,000
Ensigns, Junior Grade	1,000	800	600
Naval Cadets	950	800	600
Mates	900	700	500
Medical and Pay Directors, and Medical and Pay Inspectors and Chief Engineers, having the same rank at sea	4,400		
Fleet Surgeons, Fleet Paymasters and Fleet Engineers	4,400		
Surgeons, Paymasters and Chief Engineers:			
First five years after date of commission	2,800	2,400	2,000
Second five years	3,200	2,800	2,400
Third five years	3,500	3,200	2,600
Fourth five years	3,700	3,600	2,800
After twenty years	4,200	4,000	3,000
Passed Assistant Surgeons, Passed Assistant Paymasters and Passed Assistant Engineers:			
First five years after date of appointment	2,000	1,800	1,500
After five years	2,200	2,000	1,700
Assistant Surgeons, Assistant Paymasters and Assistant Engineers:			
First five years after date of appointment	1,700	1,400	1,000
After five years	1,900	1,600	1,200
Chaplains:			
First five years	2,500	2,000	1,600
After five years	2,800	2,300	1,900
Boatswains, Gunners, Carpenters and Sailmakers:			
First three years	1,200	900	700
Second three years	1,300	1,000	800
Third three years	1,400	1,300	900
Fourth three years	1,600	1,600	1,000
After twelve years	1,800	1,600	1,200
Cadet Engineers (after examination)	1,000	800	600
Naval Constructors:			
First five years	.....	3,200	2,200
Second five years	.....	3,400	2,400
Third five years	.....	3,700	2,700
Fourth five years	.....	4,000	3,000
After twenty years	.....	4,200	3,200
Assistant Naval Constructors:			
First four years	.....	2,000	1,500
Second four years	.....	2,200	1,700
After eight years	.....	2,600	1,900
Secretary to Admiral and Vice Admiral $2,500	.....	.....	.....
Secretaries to Commanders of Squadrons 2,000	.....	.....	.....
Secretary to Naval Academy 1,800	.....	.....	.....
Clerks to Commanders of Squadrons and Vessels 750	.....	.....	.....
First Clerks to Commandants of Navy Yards 1,500	.....	.....	.....
Second Clerks to Commandants of Navy Yards 1,200	.....	.....	.....
Clerk, Mare Island Navy Yard 1,800	.....	.....	.....
Clerk to Commandants, Naval Stations 1,500	.....	.....	.....
Clerks to Paymasters at Navy Yards:			
(a) Boston, New York, Philadelphia and Washington 1,800	.....	.....	.....
(b) Mare Island 1,800	.....	.....	.....
(c) Kittery, Norfolk, Pensacola 1,400	.....	.....	.....
(d) At other Stations 1,300	.....	.....	.....
Seamen 288	.....	.....	.....
Ordinary Seamen 240	.....	.....	.....

CORPS BADGES
OF THE
UNITED STATES ARMY
—1865.—

The form of the Badge designates the Corps. The Divisions of the respective Corps were distinguished by the *color* of the Badge worn. If the Badge was *Red*, the wearer belonged to the *First Division*; if *White*, to the *Second Division*; if *Blue*, to the *Third Division*; if *Green*, to the *Fourth Division*; if *Orange*, to the *Fifth Division*.

Sheridan's Cavalry Corps wore a *White* Badge with *Blue* Centre, on which were Cross-swords in *Gold*.

Wilson's Cavalry Corps Badge was a *Red* Banner, on which were *Gold* Cross-swords, the Banner suspended from a *Gold* Rifle.

THANKS OF CONGRESS.

LIST OF OFFICERS AND OTHERS WHO HAVE BY NAME RECEIVED THE THANKS OF CONGRESS.

Approved December 24, 1861.
Joint Resolution expressive of the recognition by Congress of the gallant and patriotic services of the late Brigadier-General Nathaniel Lyon, and the officers and soldiers under his command at the battle of Springfield, Missouri.

Approved February 22, 1862.
Joint Resolution giving the thanks of Congress to the officers, soldiers, and seamen of the Army and Navy of the United States, for the heroic gallantry that . . . has won the recent series of brilliant victories over the enemies of the Union and Constitution.

Approved July 12, 1862.
Joint Resolution to provide for the presentation of "Medals of Honor," in the name of Congress, to the enlisted men of the army and volunteer forces, who have distinguished or may distinguish themselves in battle during the present rebellion.

Approved March 3, 1863.
Joint Resolution giving the thanks of Congress to Major-General William S. Rosecrans, and the officers and men under his command, for their gallantry and good conduct in the battle of Murfreesboro, Tennessee.

Approved December 17, 1863.
Joint Resolution of thanks to Major-General Ulysses S. Grant, and the officers and soldiers who have fought under his command during this Rebellion; and providing that the President shall cause a medal to be struck, to be presented to Major-General Grant in the name of the People of the United States of America.

Approved January 28, 1864.
Joint Resolution of thanks to Major-General Nathaniel P. Banks, and the officers and soldiers under his command at Port Hudson.

Approved January 28, 1864.
Joint Resolution of thanks to Major-General Ambrose E. Burnside, and the officers and men who have fought under his command, for their gallantry, good conduct, and soldier-like endurance.

Approved January 28, 1864.
Joint Resolution, expressive of the thanks of Congress to Major-General Joseph Hooker, Major-General Geo. G. Meade, Major-General Oliver O. Howard, and the officers and soldiers of the Army of the Potomac, for the skill, energy, and endurance in covering Washington and Baltimore, and for the skill and heroic valor displayed at Gettysburg, Pa.

Approved February 19, 1864.
Joint Resolution of thanks to Major-General W. T. Sherman, and the officers and soldiers who served under him, for their gallant and arduous services in marching to the relief of the Army of the Cumberland and at the battle of Chattanooga.

Approved March 3, 1864.
Joint Resolution of thanks of Congress to the Volunteer Soldiers who have re-enlisted in the army.

Approved June 11, 1864.
Joint Resolution of thanks of Congress to Lieutenant-Colonel Joseph Bailey, Fourth Wisconsin Volunteers, for distinguished services in the recent campaign on the Red River, by which the gunboat flotilla under Rear-Admiral David D. Porter was rescued from imminent peril.

Approved January 10, 1865.
Joint Resolution tendering the thanks of the people and of Congress to Major-General William T. Sherman, and the officers and soldiers of his command, for their gallant conduct in their late brilliant movement through Georgia.

Approved January 24, 1865.
Joint Resolution to present the thanks of Congress to Brevet Major-General Alfred H. Terry, and to the officers and men under his command, for the unsurpassed gallantry and skill exhibited by them in the attack upon Fort Fisher, and for their long and faithful services and unwavering devotion to the cause of the country.

Approved March 3, 1865.
Joint Resolution of thanks to Major-General Geo. H. Thomas, and the army under his command, for the signal defeat of the rebel army under General Hood.

Approved April 21, 1866.
Joint Resolution of thanks to Major-General Winfield S. Hancock for his services with the Army of the Potomac in 1863.

Approved May 30, 1866.
Joint Resolution expressive of the gratitude of the Nation to the officers, soldiers, and seamen of the United States, by whose valor and endurance, on land and on sea, the rebellion has been crushed.

TOTAL INTERMENTS IN NATIONAL CEMETERIES.

Cemetery	Interments: Known.	Unknown.	Total.
Annapolis, Maryland	2,285	204	2,489
Alexandria, Louisiana	534	772	1,306
Alexandria, Virginia	3,402	120	3,522
Andersonville, Georgia	12,793	921	13,714
Antietam, Maryland	2,853	1,818	4,671
Arlington, Virginia	11,915	4,349	16,264
Ball's Bluff, Virginia	1	24	25
Barrancas, Florida	798	657	1,455
Baton Rouge, Louisiana	2,469	495	2,964
Battle Ground, District of Columbia	43	....	43
Beaufort, South Carolina	4,748	4,493	9,241
Beverly, New Jersey	145	7	152
Brownsville, Texas	1,417	1,379	2,796
Camp Butler, Illinois	1,007	355	1,362
Camp Nelson, Kentucky	2,477	1,165	3,642
Cave Hill, Kentucky	3,344	583	3,927
Chalmette, Louisiana	6,837	5,674	12,511
Chattanooga, Tennessee	7,999	4,963	12,962
City Point, Virginia	3,778	1,374	5,152
Cold Harbor, Virginia	673	1,281	1,954
Corinth, Mississippi	1,789	3,927	5,716
Crown Hill, Indiana	681	32	713
Culpeper, Virginia	456	911	1,367
Custer Battle Field, Montana	263	....	263

TOTAL INTERMENTS IN NATIONAL CEMETERIES.—Continued.

Cemetery.	Interments: Known.	Unknown.	Total.
Cypress Hills, New York	3,710	76	3,786
Danville, Kentucky	335	8	343
Danville, Virginia	1,172	155	1,327
Fayetteville, Arkansas	431	781	1,212
Finn's Point, New Jersey	....	2,644	2,644
Florence, South Carolina	199	2,799	2,998
Fort Donelson, Tennessee	158	511	669
Fort Gibson, Indian Territory	215	2,212	2,427
Fort Harrison, Virginia	239	575	814
Fort Leavenworth, Kansas	835	928	1,763
Fort McPherson, Nebraska	159	291	448
Fort Smith, Arkansas	711	1,152	1,863
Fort Scott, Kansas	390	161	551
Fredericksburg, Virginia	2,487	12,770	15,257
Gettysburg, Pennsylvania	1,967	1,608	3,575
Glendale, Virginia	234	961	1,195
Grafton, West Virginia	634	620	1,254
Hampton, Virginia	4,930	494	5,424
Jefferson Barracks, Missouri	8,584	2,906	11,490
Jefferson City, Missouri	349	412	761
Keokuk, Iowa	613	35	648
Knoxville, Tennessee	2,090	1,046	3,136
Laurel, Maryland	232	6	238
Lebanon, Kentucky	591	277	868
Lexington, Kentucky	805	108	913
Little Rock, Arkansas	3,265	2,337	5,602
Logan's Cross Roads, Kentucky	345	366	711
Loudon Park, Maryland	1,037	160	1,203
Marietta, Georgia	7,188	2,962	10,150
Memphis, Tennessee	5,160	8,817	13,977
Mexico City	284	750	1,034
Mobile, Alabama	750	118	868
Mound City, Illinois	2,505	2,721	5,226
Nashville, Tennessee	11,825	4,701	16,526
Natchez, Mississippi	308	2,766	3,068
New Albany, Indiana	2,159	676	2,818
New Berne, North Carolina	2,177	1,077	3,254
Philadelphia, Pennsylvania	1,881	28	1,909
Pittsburg Landing, Tennessee	1,229	2,361	3,590
Poplar Grove, Virginia	2,199	4,001	6,190
Port Hudson, Louisiana	596	3,223	3,819
Raleigh, North Carolina	619	562	1,181
Richmond, Virginia	842	5,700	6,542
Rock Island, Illinois	277	19	296
Salisbury, North Carolina	94	12,032	12,126
San Antonio, Texas	324	167	491
Seven Pines, Virginia	150	1,208	1,358
Soldier's Home, District of Columbia	5,314	288	5,602
Staunton, Virginia	233	520	753
Stone River, Tennessee	3,821	2,324	6,145
Vicksburg, Mississippi	3,896	12,704	16,600
Wilmington, North Carolina	710	1,398	2,108
Winchester, Virginia	2,094	2,365	4,459
Woodlawn, Elmira, New York	3,074	16	3,090
Yorktown, Virginia	748	1,434	2,182
Totals	171,302	147,568	*318,870

* Including about 6,000 known and 1,500 unknown civilians, and 1,700 known and 2,300 unknown confederates.

MILITIA FORCE OF THE UNITED STATES.

ABSTRACT OF THE MILITIA FORCE OF THE UNITED STATES (ORGANIZED AND UNORGANIZED) ACCORDING TO THE LATEST RETURNS RECEIVED AT THE OFFICE OF THE ADJUTANT GENERAL.

States.	Organized Strength: Year.	General Officers.	General Staff Officers.	Regimental, Field, and Staff Officers.	Company Officers.	Total commissioned.	Total non-commissioned Officers, Musicians, Privates, etc.	Aggregate.	Number of Men Available for Military Duty (unorganized).
Maine	1883	3	11	15	81	110	1,260	1,370	97,510
New Hampshire	1883	1	8	27	78	114	1,218	1,332	33,469
Vermont	1883	1	12	11	41	65	624	689	44,388
Massachusetts	1883	2	18	91	200	311	3,555	3,866	355,749
Rhode Island	1883	1	23	56	77	157	1,036	1,193	47,040
Connecticut	1883	1	9	44	119	176	2,218	2,401	75,748
New York	1883	15	100	149	408	788	10,779	11,567	492,628
New Jersey	1883	4	40	70	144	267	3,020	3,287	223,014
Pennsylvania	1883	4	42	108	378	552	7,454	8,006	491,489
Delaware	1883	....	....	6	15	21	234	255	*30,500
Maryland	1870	1	8	6	60	81	1,243	1,330	50,344
Virginia	1883	1	5	53	183	243	2,757	3,000	*220,000
West Virginia	1883	....	....	7	34	41	442	483	*110,000
North Carolina	1882	2	14	24	63	103	733	836	*220,000
South Carolina	1882	9	66	66	300	507	4,610	5,110	*100,000
Georgia	....	....	....	....	....	....	....	....	*180,000
Florida	1880	7	52	100	287	455	6,261	6,710	25,003
Alabama	1883	8	17	....	99	123	1,411	1,531	*170,000
Mississippi	1882	....	....	....	166	100	1,900	1,800	*140,000
Louisiana	1883	9	28	65	97	199	1,770	1,969	138,486
Texas	1883	3	23	43	114	183	1,462	1,645	*100,000
Arkansas	....	....	....	....	....	....	....	....	*100,000
Kentucky	1883	....	....	16	74	90	975	1,065	260,000
Tennessee	1868	....	....	....	....	....	....	....	*243,000
Ohio	1882	....	18	92	252	860	5,515	5,875	*500,000
Indiana	1883	....	....	80	138	168	2,352	2,520	369,048
Michigan	1883	1	8	30	86	126	1,664	1,040	*300,000
Illinois	1882	6	85	75	350	367	4,478	4,847	*400,000
Missouri	1883	1	7	35	118	156	1,142	1,298	*310,000
Wisconsin	1883	1	13	24	101	138	2,315	2,453	*300,000
Minnesota	1880	1	8	18	63	90	1,250	1,340	*125,000
Iowa	1883	2	16	42	138	198	2,102	2,300	216,040
Nebraska	1883	....	7	5	30	42	450	492	*50,000
Kansas	....	....	....	....	....	....	....	....	*130,000
Nevada	1882	3	27	4	42	76	615	691	12,779
Oregon	....	....	....	....	....	....	....	....	*20,000
California	1883	7	76	41	185	357	3,670	3,927	104,981
Colorado	1883	5	24	35	79	140	1,250	1,895	*40,000
Grand aggregate	....	80	707	1,429	4,330	6,602	81,208	87,810	6,687,921

* Estimated in Adjutant General's office.

NATION'S DEBT.

YEAR.	AMOUNT.	YEAR.	AMOUNT.	YEAR.	AMOUNT.	YEAR.	AMOUNT.
1791	$75,463,476 52	1815	$99,833,660 15	1839	$3,573,343 82	1863	$1,119,772,138 63
1792	77,227,924 66	1816	127,334,933 74	1840	5,250,875 54	1864	1,815,784,370 57
1793	80,352,634 04	1817	123,491,965 16	1841	13,594,480 73	1865	2,680,647,869 74
1794	78,427,404 77	1818	103,466,633 83	1842	20,601,226 28	1866	2,773,236,173 69
1795	80,747,587 39	1819	95,529,648 28	1843	32,742,922 00	1867	2,678,126,103 87
1796	83,762,172 07	1820	91,015,566 15	1844	23,461,652 50	1868	2,611,687,851 19
1797	82,064,479 33	1821	89,987,427 66	1845	15,925,303 01	1869	2,588,452,213 94
1798	79,228,529 12	1822	93,546,676 98	1846	15,550,202 97	1870	2,480,672,427 81
1799	78,408,669 77	1823	90,875,877 28	1847	38,826,534 77	1871	2,353,211,332 32
1800	82,976,294 35	1824	90,269,777 77	1848	47,044,862 23	1872	2,253,251,328 78
1801	83,038,050 80	1825	83,788,432 71	1849	63,061,858 69	1873	2,234,482,993 20
1802	86,712,632 25	1826	81,054,059 99	1850	63,452,773 55	1874	2,251,690,468 43
1803	77,054,686 30	1827	73,987,357 20	1851	68,304,796 02	1875	2,232,284,531 95
1804	86,427,120 88	1828	67,475,043 87	1852	66,199,341 71	1876	2,180,395,067 15
1805	82,312,150 50	1829	58,421,413 67	1853	59,803,117 70	1877	2,205,301,392 10
1806	75,723,270 66	1830	48,565,406 50	1854	42,242,222 42	1878	2,256,205,892 53
1807	69,218,398 64	1831	39,123,191 68	1855	35,586,858 56	1879	2,245,495,072 04
1808	65,196,317 97	1832	24,322,235 18	1856	31,972,537 90	1880	2,120,415,370 63
1809	57,023,192 09	1833	7,001,698 83	1857	28,699,831 85	1881	2,069,013,569 58
1810	53,173,217 52	1834	4,760,082 08	1858	44,911,881 03	1882	1,918,312,994 03
1811	48,005,587 76	1835	37,513 05	1859	58,496,837 88	1883	1,884,171,728 07
1812	45,209,737 90	1836	336,957 83	1860	64,842,287 88		
1813	55,962,827 57	1837	3,308,124 07	1861	90,580,873 72		
1814	81,487,846 24	1838	10,434,221 14	1862	524,176,412 13		

RATES OF PENSION

And Number Pensioned to each Rate of the Army and Navy Invalids on the Roll, June 30, 1884.

RATES.	ARMY.	NAVY.	TOTAL.	RATES.	ARMY.	NAVY.	TOTAL.
$1 00	1,445	20	1,465	$9 75	4	4	8
1 87	1	......	1	10 00	7,107	101	7,208
2 00	25,707	187	25,894	10 20	1	......	1
2 13	1	......	1	10 25	5	......	5
2 25	10	......	10	10 50	7	9	16
2 50	16	11	27	10 62	5	......	5
2 60	510	4	514	10 75	1	16	17
3 00	3,237	44	3,281	11 00	18	12	30
3 00	......	1	1	11 25	847	17	864
3 20	1	......	1	11 33	84	......	84
3 33	......	1	1	11 50	21	3	24
3 40	1	......	1	11 60	1	......	1
3 50	......	1	1	11 75	6	5	11
3 75	866	4	870	12 00	11,660	140	11,800
4 00	58,299	551	58,850	12 25	19	......	19
4 25	405	......	405	12 33	1	......	1
5 00	1,702	78	1,780	12 50	214	22	236
5 25	2	......	2	12 75	578	1	579
5 33	471	3	474	13 00	169	10	179
5 50	1	1	2	13 25	5	23	28
5 62	4	......	4	13 33	26	......	26
5 66	75	......	75	13 50	16	2	18
5 70	13	......	13	13 75	8	1	9
6 00	62,761	815	63,006	14 00	2,003	52	2,055
6 25	80	......	80	14 25	12	4	16
6 37	7	......	7	14 50	5	1	6
6 50	4	2	6	14 75	6	......	6
6 66	88	1	89	15 00	1,658	41	1,699
6 75	1	......	1	15 25	1	1	2
7 00	283	8	291	15 50	1	3	4
7 23	1	......	1	15 62	1	......	1
7 50	1,026	24	1,050	15 75	......	12	12
7 60	1	......	1	16 00	2,249	18	2,267
7 75	11	2	13	16 25	7	2	9
8 00	35,126	480	35,606	16 50	9	......	9
8 25	15	......	15	16 66	10	......	10
8 33	1	......	1	16 75	9	......	9
8 50	1,286	1	1,287	17 00	1,410	5	1,415
8 75	10	2	12	17 25	1	2	3
9 00	103	5	108	17 50	13	2	15
9 25	28	......	28	17 75	10	......	10
9 37	1	......	1	18 00	2,183	89	2,272
9 50	18	5	23	18 25	......	5	5

RATES OF PENSION—*Continued.*

RATES.	ARMY.	NAVY.	TOTAL.	RATES.	ARMY.	NAVY.	TOTAL.
$18 50	11	......	11	$27 50	5	......	5
18 75	111	2	113	28 50	1	......	1
19 00	6	1	7	30 00	7,436	105	7,541
19 25	8	......	8	30 75	......	1	1
19 50	......	3	3	31 25	175	2	177
20 00	1,061	18	1,079	31 75	......	1	1
20 75	1	2	3	36 00	33	......	34
21 00	8	......	8	37 50	7	......	7
21 25	3	......	3	38 25	......	1	1
21 75	1	......	1	38 50	......	1	1
22 00	1	......	1	40 00	6	......	6
22 50	98	2	100	40 25	......	1	1
23 75	3	......	3	45 00	1	......	1
24 00	18,101	151	18,252	47 00	1	......	1
24 50	2	......	2	48 00	1	......	1
25 00	297	1	298	50 00	534	14	548
25 75	......	3	3	72 00	842	23	865
26 25	1	......	1	100 00	1	......	1
26 00	1	......	1				
28 75	1	1	2	Total	218,956	2,916	221,872

Chief Commanders of the United States Army, 1789-1885.

NAMES.	TERM OF SERVICE. FROM	TO	RANK.
JOSIAH HARMAR	Sept., 1789	March, 1791	Lieut.-Col. of Inf'ry.
ARTHUR ST. CLAIR	Mar. 4, 1791	Mar. 5, 1792	Major-General.
ANTHONY WAYNE	Mar. 5, 1792	Dec. 15, 1796	Major-General.
JAMES WILKINSON	Dec. 15, 1796	July 5, 1798	Brigadier-General.
GEORGE WASHINGTON	July 5, 1798	Dec. 14, 1799	Lieut.-Gen. & Gen.
JAMES WILKINSON	June 15, 1800	Jan. 27, 1812	Brigadier-General.
HENRY DEARBORN	Jan. 27, 1812	June 15, 1815	Major-General.
JACOB BROWN	June 15, 1815	Feb. 24, 1828	Major-General.
ALEXANDER MACOMB	May 24, 1828	June 25, 1841	Major-General.
WINFIELD SCOTT	June 25, 1841	Nov. 1, 1861	Major-General.
GEORGE B. MCCLELLAN	Nov. 1, 1861	Mar. 11, 1862	Major-General.
HENRY W. HALLECK	July 11, 1862	Mar. 12, 1864	Major-General.
ULYSSES S. GRANT	Mar. 12, 1864	Mar. 4, 1869	Lieut.-Gen. & Gen.
WILLIAM T. SHERMAN	Mar. 4, 1869	Feb. 8, 1884	General.
PHILIP H. SHERIDAN	Feb. 8, 1884		Lieut.-General.

LIST OF PENSION AGENCIES,

With Location, Geographical Limits, and Names of Pension Agents, Showing the Balance of Funds in the Hands of each Agent, June 30, 1884.

LOCATION. CITY.	STATE.	NAME OF AGENT.	AMOUNT.	GEOGRAPHICAL LIMITS.
Augusta	Maine	Selden Connor	$1,124,622 28	The State of Maine: Navy pensioners in this district paid at Boston, Mass.
Boston	Massachusetts	Daniel W. Gooch	968,439 86	The States of Massachusetts, Connecticut, and Rhode Island; and all Navy pensioners residing in this and the Augusta and Concord districts.
Chicago	Illinois	Ada C. Sweet	724,636 85	The State of Illinois, and all Navy pensioners residing in this and the Columbus, Des Moines, Detroit Indianapolis, Louisville, Milwaukee, and Topeka districts.
Columbus	Ohio	Allen T. Wikoff	699,806 97	The State of Ohio: Navy pensioners in this district paid at Chicago.
Concord	New Hampshire	E. L. Whitford	630,218 50	The States of New Hampshire and Vermont: Navy pensioners in this district are paid at Boston.
Des Moines	Iowa	Jacob Rich	450,200 18	The States of Iowa and Nebraska: Navy pensioners in this district are paid at Chicago.
Detroit	Michigan	Samuel Post	481,812 44	The State of Michigan: Navy pensioners in this district are paid at Chicago.
Indianapolis	Indiana	Frederick Knefler	665,132 52	The State of Indiana: Navy pensioners in this district are paid at Chicago.
Knoxville	Tennessee	Henry R. Gibson	435,655 34	The States of Virginia, West Virginia, North Carolina, Tennessee, South Carolina, Georgia, Florida Alabama, Mississippi, Louisiana, Texas, and Arkansas: Navy pensioners in this district are paid at Washington, D. C.
Louisville	Kentucky	Robert M. Kelly	120,405 40	The State of Kentucky: Navy pensioners in this district are paid at Chicago.
Milwaukee	Wisconsin	Edward Ferguson	378,107 48	The States of Wisconsin and Minnesota, and the Territories of Dakota, Montana, and Wyoming: Navy pensioners in this district are paid at Chicago.
New York	New York	Charles R. Coster	1,226,883 52	The counties in the State of New York, of Albany, Clinton, Columbia, Delaware, Dutchess, Essex Greene, Kings, Queens, New York, Orange, Putnam, Richmond, Rensselaer, Rockland, Saratoga Schenectady, Sullivan, Suffolk, Ulster, Warren, Washington, and Westchester, and all Navy pensioners in the State of New York.
Philadelphia	Pennsylvania	H. G. Sickel	818,065 26	The counties in the State of Pennsylvania of Berks, Bradford, Bucks, Carbon, Chester, Columbia, Dauphin, Delaware, Lackawanna, Lancaster, Lebanon, Lehigh, Luzerne, Monroe, Montgomery, Montour, Northampton, Northumberland, Philadelphia, Pike, Schuylkill, Sullivan, Susquehanna, Wayne, Wyoming, York, and all Navy pensioners in the State of Pennsylvania.
Pittsburgh	.....do	Russell Errett	408,325 66	The counties in the State of Pennsylvania not in the Philadelphia district: All navy pensioners in the State are paid at Philadelphia.
San Francisco	California	Henry Cox	328,745 12	The States of California, Nevada, and Oregon; the Territories of Alaska, Idaho, Utah, and Washington, including the Navy pensioners.
Syracuse	New York	Theodore L. Poole	676,973 01	The counties in the State of New York not in the New York City district: All Navy pensioners in the State are paid at New York City.
Topeka	Kansas	Nathaniel A. Adams	349,190 84	The States of Missouri, Kansas, and Colorado; the Territory of New Mexico and the Indian Territory: Navy pensioners in this district are paid at Chicago.
Washington	District of Columbia	Theophilus Gaines	632,644 04	The States of New Jersey, Delaware, and Maryland, the District of Columbia, the inmates of the branches of the National Soldiers' Home, and pensioners residing in foreign countries, and all Navy pensioners in this and the Knoxville district.
Total			11,124,316 15	

AMOUNTS CONTRIBUTED TO THE NATION'S DEFENDERS BY PATRIOTIC CITIZENS OF THE VARIOUS STATES.

(Public Bodies.)

(From April 15 to May 21, 1861.)

Abington, Mass	$5,000	Edgerton, Wis	1,000	Mansfield, Mass	$5,000	Sag Harbor, New York	3,000
Acton, Mass	3,000	Elizabeth, New Jersey	11,000	Marblehead, Mass	6,000	Salem, Mass	17,000
Albany, New York	46,000	Elkhart, Indiana	5,000	Marlboro, Mass	10,000	Salisbury, Mass	5,000
Amesbury, Mass	5,000	Erie, Penn	25,000	Marshfield, Mass	5,000	Saratoga Springs, New York	2,000
Andover, Mass	17,000	Evansville, Indiana	15,000	Massachusetts, State	3,000,000	Schenectady, New York	8,000
Attica, New York	10,000	Fair Haven, Mass	5,000	" " advanced to		Schuylkill County, Penn	30,000
Auburn, New York	4,000	Fall River, Mass	10,000	United States	7,000,000	Seneca Falls, New York	3,000
Barre, Mass	2,000	Flemington, New Jersey	5,000	Melrose, Mass	3,000	Shopiere, Wis	1,000
Batavia, New York	5,000	Fond du Lac, Wis	4,000	Michigan, State	1,000,000	Shelburne, Vt	1,000
Bath, Maine	10,000	Framingham, Mass	10,000	Michigan, (various places)	60,000	Shrewsbury, Mass	2,000
Beaver Dam, Wis	3,000	Franklin, Mass	3,000	Middleboro, Mass	7,000	Shushan, New York	2,000
Bethel, Mass	2,000	Galena, Ill	1,000	Millbury, Mass	2,000	Somerset, Mass	3,000
Bedford, Mass	2,000	Georgetown, Mass	5,000	Milwaukee, Wis	32,000	Southboro, Mass	2,000
Bedford, New York	1,000	Glen Falls, New York	10,000	Monroe, Wis	1,000	Southbridge, Mass	8,000
Bennington, Vt	10,000	Gloucester, Mass	10,000	Morristown, New Jersey	3,000	Sparta, Wis	1,000
Berlin, Wis	2,000	Great Falls, New Hampshire	10,000	Mount Holly, New Jersey	3,000	St. Albans, Vt	10,000
Binghampton, New York	10,000	Green Bay, Wis	1,000	Mystic, Conn	7,000	Stockbridge, Mass	3,000
Bordentown, New Jersey	8,000	Greensburg, Indiana	2,000	N. Andover, Mass	3,000	Stockholm, New York	3,000
Boston, Mass	200,000	Hamilton, Ohio	1,000	Needham, Mass	3,000	Stowe, Mass	2,000
Bradford, Vt	2,000	Harrisburg, Penn	5,000	New Brunswick, New Jersey	2,000	Sutton, Mass	6,000
Braintree, Mass	2,000	Hartford, Conn	64,000	New Haven, Conn	30,000	Sycamore, Ill	4,000
Bridgeport, Conn	31,000	Hatfield, Mass	3,000	New Jersey, State	2,000,000	Syracuse, New York	84,000
Bridgeton, New Jersey	1,000	Hebron, Wis	2,000	New London, Conn	10,000	Taunton, Mass	40,000
Brooklyn, New York	75,000	Hempstead, New York	2,000	New York City	2,178,000	Toledo, Ohio	5,000
Brunswick, Maine	1,000	Hoboken, New Jersey	2,000	New York State	3,000,000	Troy, New York	48,000
Buffalo, New York	110,000	Hornellsville, New York	1,000	Newark, New Jersey	130,000	Upper Sandusky, Ohio	5,000
Burlington, New Jersey	4,000	Hudson, New York	4,000	Newbury, Mass	3,000	Utica, New York	14,000
Burlington, Vt	3,000	Illinois, State	3,500,000	Newburyport, Mass	4,000	Valatie, New York	4,000
Camden and Am. R. R. Co	10,000	Indiana, State	1,000,000	Newton, Mass	3,000	Vermont, State	1,000,000
Cambridge, New York	8,000	Indianapolis, Ind	5,000	Noblesville, Ind	10,000	Waltham, Mass	5,000
Canandaigua, New York	7,000	Iowa, State	100,000	North Andover, Mass	3,000	Warsaw, New York	6,000
Canton, Mass	5,000	Ipswich, Mass	4,000	Norwich, Conn	13,000	Washington County, Wis	30,000
Cass County, Indiana	6,000	Ithaca, New York	10,000	Ohio, State	3,000,000	Waterford, New York	8,000
Charlestown, Mass	10,000	Janesville, Wis	6,000	Omro, Wis	1,000	Watertown, Mass	2,000
Chicago, Ill	25,000	Jefferson, Wis	4,000	Oswego, New York	38,000	Watertown, New York	8,000
Cincinnati, Ohio	280,000	Jersey City, New Jersey	32,000	Ottawa, Ill	18,000	Waynesville, Ohio	2,000
Circleville, Ohio	2,000	Keene, New Hampshire	10,000	Ozaukee, Wis	1,000	Webster, Mass	4,000
Cleveland, Ohio	30,000	Kenosha, Wis	4,000	Palmyra, New York	5,000	West Cambridge, Mass	10,000
Clinton, Ill	5,000	Kenton, Ohio	2,000	Paterson, New Jersey	10,000	West Troy, New York	7,000
Clinton, New York	1,000	La Crosse, Wis	4,000	Pennsylvania, State	3,500,000	Westboro', Mass	8,000
Clinton, Wis	3,000	Lancaster, Penn	5,000	Peterboro, New York	10,000	Weymouth, Mass	5,000
Cohasset, Mass	1,000	Lawrence, Mass	5,000	Philadelphia, Penn	330,000	Whatley, Mass	2,000
Coleraine, Mass	2,000	Lebanon County, Penn	10,000	Piqua, Ohio	20,000	Whitewater, Wis	8,000
Concord, Mass	4,000	Lexington, Mass	4,000	Plymouth, Mass	2,000	Williamsburg Mass	2,000
Concord, New Hampshire	10,000	Lockport, New York	3,000	Portland, Maine	31,000	Wilmington, Ohio	3,000
Connecticut, State	2,000,000	London, Ohio	1,000	Poughkeepsie, New York	10,000	Wisconsin, State	225,000
Conway, Mass	2,000	Lowell, Mass	6,000	Prescott, Wis	1,000	Woburn, Mass	5,000
Damariscotta, Maine	3,000	Ludlow, Mass	2,000	Princeton, New Jersey	3,000	Woodbury, Conn	5,000
Dedham, Mass	10,000	Lynn, Mass	10,000	Quincy, Mass	10,000	Woodstock, Vt	1,000
Deerfield, Mass	5,000	Madison, Ind	8,000	Racine, Wis	8,000	Worcester, Mass	12,000
Detroit, Mich	50,000	Madison, Wis	10,000	Randolph, Wis	3,000	Wrentham, Mass	10,000
Dorchester, Mass	20,000	Madrid, New York	5,000	Richmond, Wis	1,000	Xenia, Ohio	14,000
Douglas, Mass	4,000	Maine, State	1,300,000	Rhode Island, State	500,000	Zanesville, Ohio	8,000
Dover, New Hampshire	10,000	Malden, Mass	12,000	Rochester, New York	60,000		
Dunkirk, New York	20,000	Manitowoc, Wis	2,000	Rockland, Maine	10,000	Total	$77,125,000

MILITARY COMMANDS AND POSTS, 1885, WITH POST OFFICES, TELEGRAPH STATIONS, AND NEAREST RAILROAD STATIONS OR BOAT LANDINGS.

ARMY OF THE UNITED STATES.—Headquarters, Washington, D. C.

DIVISION OF THE ATLANTIC.

Headquarters Governor's Island, New York Harbor. Embraces the Department of the East.

DEPARTMENT OF THE EAST.

Headquarters Governor's Island, New York Harbor.

Geographical limits.

The New England States, States of New York, New Jersey, Pennsylvania, Delaware, Maryland, Virginia, West Virginia, North Carolina, South Carolina, Georgia, Florida, Louisiana, Arkansas, Mississippi, Alabama, Kentucky, Tennessee, Ohio, Michigan, Wisconsin, Indiana, and the District of Columbia.

DIVISION OF THE MISSOURI.

Headquarters Chicago, Ill. Embraces the Departments of the Platte, Dakota, Missouri and Texas.

DEPARTMENT OF THE PLATTE.

Headquarters, Omaha, Nebraska.

Geographical limits.

States of Iowa and Nebraska; Territories of Utah and Wyoming, and as much of the Territory of Idaho as lies east of a line formed by the extension of the western boundary of Utah to the northeastern boundary of Idaho.

DEPARTMENT OF DAKOTA.

Headquarters, Fort Snelling, Minnesota.

Geographical limits.

State of Minnesota, and the Territories of Dakota and Montana.

DEPARTMENT OF THE MISSOURI.

Headquarters, Fort Leavenworth, Kansas.

Geographical limits.

States of Missouri, Kansas, Illinois, and Colorado; Territory of New Mexico, Indian Territory, and the posts of Fort Elliott, and Fort Bliss, Texas, including the town of San Elizario on the Rio Grande, and that portion of El Paso County lying north of an east and west line passing immediately south of San Elizario.

DEPARTMENT OF TEXAS.

Headquarters, San Antonio, Texas.

Geographical limits.

State of Texas, excepting the posts of Fort Elliott and Fort Bliss, Texas, and that portion of El Paso County embraced in the Department of the Missouri.

DIVISION OF THE PACIFIC.

Headquarters, Presidio of San Francisco, Cal. Embraces the Departments of California, Arizona, and the Columbia.

DEPARTMENT OF CALIFORNIA.

Headquarters, Presidio of San Francisco, Cal.

Geographical limits.

States of California and Nevada.

DEPARTMENT OF ARIZONA.

Headquarters, Whipple Barracks, Prescott, Arizona.

Geographical limits.

Territory of Arizona.

DEPARTMENT OF THE COLUMBIA.

Headquarters, Vancouver Barracks, Washington Territory.

Geographical limits.

State of Oregon, and the Territories of Washington, Idaho, and Alaska, excepting so much of Idaho as is embraced in the Department of the Platte.

PUBLIC LANDS.

HOMESTEADS FOR VETERAN SOLDIERS WITH LAWS RELATING TO, AND HOW THEY CAN BE OBTAINED.

ANY officer, soldier, seaman, or marine who served for not less than ninety days in the Army or Navy of the United States during the rebellion, and who was honorably discharged, and has remained loyal to the Government, is entitled to enter, under the provisions of the homestead law, one hundred and sixty acres of land, "including the alternate reserved sections along the line of *any* railroad or other public work." (Rev. Stat., 2304; Appendix No. 1.)

The time of service, or, if the party was discharged from service on account of wounds or disabilities incurred in the line of duty, the whole term of enlistment, shall be deducted from the period of five years during which an ordinary claimant, must, to perfect title, reside upon and cultivate the entered tract; but the party must, in every case, reside upon, improve, and cultivate his homestead for a period of at least one *year* after he shall have commenced his improvements. (Rev. Stat., 2305; Appendix No. 1.)

A party applying for the benefit of this provision of the law must file with the register and receiver a certified copy of certificate of discharge, showing when he enlisted and when he was discharged; or the affidavit of two respectable, disinterested witnesses corroborative of the allegations contained in the prescribed affidavit (Form 4–067) on these points, or, if neither can be procured, his own affidavit to that effect.

The filing must be accompanied by the oath of the soldier, stating his residence and post-office address, and setting forth that the claim is made for his exclusive use and benefit, for the purpose of actual settlement and cultivation, and not either directly or indirectly for the use or benefit of any other person; and that he has not theretofore either made a homestead entry or filed a declaratory statement under the homestead law. (Form 4–546.)

As implied by the requirement of the oath, a soldier will be held to have exhausted his homestead right by the filing of his declaratory statement; it being manifest that the right to file is a privilege granted to soldiers in addition to the ordinary privilege only in the matter of giving them power to hold their claims for six months after selection *before* entry; but is not a license to abandon such selection with the right thereafter to make a regular homestead entry independently of such filing. This is clear from the statutory language. Section 2304 provides that "the settler shall be allowed six months after locating his homestead and filing his declaratory statement, within which to make his entry and commence his settlement and improvement;" and section 2309 requires him "in person" to "make his actual entry, commence settlement and improvement on *the same*, and thereafter fulfill all the requirements of law." These must be done on "the same" land selected and located by the filing.

Following the accepted practice in pre-emption cases, the filing of a declaratory statement will not be held to bar the admission of filings and entries by others; but any person making entry or claim during the period allowed by law for entry of the soldier will do so subject to his right; and the soldier's application when offered within such time will be allowed as a matter of right and operate to exclude the intervening claim.

SOLDIERS' WIDOWS, OR MINOR ORPHAN CHILDREN.

THE widow, if unmarried—or in case of her death or marriage, the minor orphan children—of any such officer, soldier, sailor, or marine may enter land under the same conditions as might her husband if living; and if he died during his term of enlistment, the widow or minor children shall have the benefit of the whole term of enlistment to be deducted from the time heretofore required to perfect title to the land. (Rev. Stat., 2307; Appendix No. 1.)

Minor orphan children can act only by their duly appointed guardians, who must file certified copies of the powers of guardianship, which must be transmitted to the General Land Office by the registers and receivers with their abstracts of soldiers' declaratory statements.

In case of widows, the prescribed evidence of military service of the husband must be furnished, with affidavit of widowhood, giving date of the husband's death.

In case of minor orphan children, in addition to the prescribed evidence of military service of the father, proof of death or re-marriage of the mother must be furnished. Evidence of death may be the testimony of two witnesses or a physician's certificate duly attested. Evidences of marriage may be certified by copy of marriage certificate, or of the record of same, or testimony of two witnesses to the marriage ceremony.

The ruling relative to the widow or minor children of a deceased homestead party as to actual residence (page 15 Annual Report of the Commissioner of Pensions, 1884), is equally applicable to the widow or minor children of a deceased sailor or soldier; if the land is cultivated in good faith the law will be regarded as substantially complied with, although the widow or the children may not actually reside upon the land.

A SOLDIER'S CLAIM MAY BE FILED BY AN AGENT.

ANY such officer, soldier, sailor, or marine may file his claim for a tract of land through an agent, and may have six months thereafter within which to make his actual entry, and commence his settlement and improvements upon the land. (Rev. Stat., 2309; Appendix No. 1.)

An *entry* cannot be made for a soldier by an agent or attorney.

In addition to the oath heretofore prescribed, the oath, in case of filing by an agent, must further declare the name and authority of the agent and the date of the power of attorney or other instrument creating the agency—adding that the name of the agent was inserted therein before its execution. It should also state in terms that the agent has no right or interest, direct or indirect, in the filing of such declaratory statement. (Form 4–543.)

The agent must file (in addition to his power of attorney) his own oath to the effect that he has no interest either present or prospective, direct or indirect, in the claim; that the same is filed for the sole benefit of the soldier, and that no arrangement has been made whereby said agent has been empowered at any future time to sell or relinquish such claim, either as agent or by filing an original relinquishment of the claimant. (Form 4–545.)

The foregoing rule, however, will not be construed to require the rejection of an application to enter the tract filed upon after the lapse of six months, when climatic reasons are shown, which in case of an actual entry would, under the act of March 3, 1881 (21 Stat., 511; Appendix No. 11), justify an allowance of one *year* for establishing residence; nor in cases where the failure results from sickness, misfortune, or any insurmountable cause, which shall be properly alleged and satisfactorily shown, and where no adverse right has intervened.

Where such cause has prevented entry and an adverse right has been admitted, it will be held proper within the discretion of the General Land Office to allow an entry upon another tract: *Provided*, That it shall be shown to the full satisfaction of the Commissioner that the default was practically beyond the power of the claimant to avoid.

In case any register and receiver have cause to believe that any filing offered for record is not presented in good faith they will note such cause upon the same, and if it be sufficient to warrant rejection—such as a want of proper authentication or other palpable defect—they will reject the same, allowing an appeal from their ruling according to the regular practice. Where such cause is not sufficient to warrant an authoritative ruling, they will admit the filing, subject to investigation, and immediately proceed to make proper inquiry into the matter, reporting their action at once to the Commissioner of the General Land Office.

For the filing of a declaratory statement the register and receiver will be allowed to charge, each a fee of one dollar. This fee the receiver will account for in the usual manner, indicating the same in his account as fees for "homestead declarations," which will be charged against the maximum of $3,000 now allowed by law. In the States and Territories for which fifty per centum additional is allowed (see page 13 Annual Report of the Commissioner of Pensions, 1884), the additional allowance will apply to the fee herein named.

SOLDIER'S ADDITIONAL HOMESTEAD ENTRY.

ANY officer, soldier, seaman or marine who served for not less than ninety days in the Army or Navy of the United States during the rebellion, who had, prior to June 22, 1874, made a homestead entry of less than one hundred and sixty acres, may enter an additional quantity of land, adjacent to his former entry or elsewhere, sufficient to make, with the previous entry, one hundred and sixty acres. (Rev. Stat., 2306; Appendix No. 1.)

This right (extended by Sec. 2307, Rev. Stat., to the widow, if unmarried, otherwise to the minor orphan children by proper guardian) is a *personal* one, and is not transferable; it is not subject to assignment or lien, nor can it be exercised by another.

The practice which formerly prevailed of certifying the additional right as information from the records of the General Land Office and permitting the entry to be made by an agent or attorney has been discontinued.

The party desiring to make an additional entry, and being entitled thereto, must present himself at the land office of the district in which the land he wishes to enter is situated, and make his application in the same manner as in case of an original entry. (Form No. 4–068.)

In addition to the usual homestead affidavit the claimant must make a special affidavit showing—

First—His identity as the soldier he represents himself to be, reciting his military service, and stating his present residence and post-office address.

Second—The facts in detail, setting forth his right to make the additional entry, and that he has fully complied with the provisions of the homestead laws in the matter of residence upon, and cultivation and improvement of, his original entry, and stating whether or not he has proved up his claim and received a patent for the land. Proper reference must be made to the original homestead entry, giving the name of the district office wherein it was made, the date and number of the entry, and the description of the land.

Third—That he has not in any manner previously exercised his additional right either by entry or application, or by sale, transfer, or power of attorney, but that the same remains in him unimpaired.

The foregoing affidavits must be sworn to *and subscribed* in the presence of the register or receiver. This rule must be strictly adhered to in order to avoid false personation; and applications and affidavits presented to the register and receiver with signature attached *will not be received.*

The foregoing rules will not be deemed to apply to cases where the additional entry has heretofore been certified by the General Land Office, nor to cases pending which were filed therein prior to March 16, 1883.

Where the party's first entry has been consummated, the register and receiver will require him to pay the same fee and commissions as in cases of original entry; the receiver will issue his receipt for the money paid, and these papers will receive the current date and the proper numbers in their homestead series. Then, to complete the transaction—it being an object, for the convenience of business, that the additional entry papers and the final papers therefor, in such cases, shall be kept separate and distinct—the party will make payment of the usual final commissions on the entered tract, for which the receiver will issue his receipt; the register will thereupon issue his final certificate for the additional tract (Form 4–197) the receipt and certificate to bear their proper numbers in the final homestead series, likewise a reference to the original entry and to the final certificate thereon by their numbers, and also by their district where the party's first entry shall have been made in a different district.

In case the party has not made proof on his original homestead entry when he applies for additional land, he will be allowed to make the additional entry on proper application, as above stated, and paying the usual fee and commissions, for which the receiver will issue his receipt, the papers to receive their proper numbers in the homestead series, with a reference thereon to the original entry. Thereafter, when the party shall make final proof on the original entry, he will be required to pay the final commissions on both entries, when a final receipt will be issued for the money, and thereupon a final certificate issued to call both for the tract in the original entry and the additional tract. On these papers the register and receiver will make a reference to the original and the additional entry, and on them one patent will issue for both. But where it happens that the original entry and the additional entry are made in different land districts, this rule must be departed from so far as regards the issuing of one final certificate and receipt for both.

WARRANT LOCATIONS.

Warrants issued to soldiers of the United States as a bounty for Military services may be located upon any public land subject to private entry at the time of such location, application being made the same as if cash were to be paid as the consideration for the land. The warrant must be duly assigned. The amount of land called for by the warrant must be located in a compact body. (Rev. Stat., 2414, 2415.)

(Bounty warrants were not issued to soldiers and sailors for military services in the late civil war. The only privileges granted them in connection with the public lands, will be found set forth hereafter, under the head "Homestead Entries," page 31. The bounties for military services in the last war were not given in *land*, but in *money*.)

Military bounty warrants are not locatable upon any public lands except such as are at the time of location subject to sale at the minimum price, or one dollar and a quarter per acre (section 5 of act of March 3, 1855; 10 Stats., 702). Therefore, where the holder of a warrant wishes to obtain land subject to double minimum price he must furnish a warrant of such denomination as will, at the value of $1.25 per acre, cover the rated price of the land, or he must pay one dollar and a quarter per acre in addition to the surrendered warrant. For example, a tract of forty acres of land held at $2.50 per acre can be paid for with an eighty acre warrant, or with a forty-acre warrant and fifty dollars in cash.

If there is a small excess in the area of the tract over the quantity called for on the face of the warrant in any case, such excess may be paid for in money. If the tract contains a less number of acres, rated at $1.25 per acre, the warrant must be surrendered in full satisfaction. (Rev. Stat., Sec. 2415, Appendix, No. 1.)

The following fees are chargeable by the land officers, under section 2238 of the Revised Statutes, for their services in the location of land warrants, and the several amounts must be *paid at the time of location:*

For a 40-acre warrant, 50 cents each to the register and receiver; total	$1 00
For a 60-acre warrant, 75 cents each to the register and receiver, total	1 50
For an 80-acre warrant, $1 each to the register and receiver, total	2 00
For a 120-acre warrant, $1 50 each to the register and receiver; total	3 00
For a 160-acre warrant, $2 each to the register and receiver; total	4 00

INDEX

TO

ILLUSTRATIONS.

VOL. II.

G.

H.

I.

J.

K.

L.

M.

N.

O.

P.

PORTRAITS.

R.

S.

T.

U.

V.

W.

Y.

INDEX

TO

HISTORICAL MATTER.

VOL. II.

A.

B.

E.

F.

G.

H.

N.

O.

P.

Q

R.

S.

Y.

Z.

www.ingramcontent.com/pod-product-compliance
Lightning Source LLC
Chambersburg PA
CBHW032007300426
44117CB00008B/928
* 9 7 8 3 3 3 7 1 3 5 5 8 4 *